Guano and the Opening of the Pacific World
A Global Ecological History

For centuries, guano and the birds that produce it have played a pivotal role in the cultural activities of indigenous peoples in Latin America and Oceania. As the populations of North American and European powers ballooned during the Industrial Revolution, they came to depend on this unique resource as well. They did so to help meet their ever-increasing farming needs and imperial aspirations, until the Pacific's fertilizer supplies were appropriated by developmentalists in Peru, Japan, Australia, and other postcolonial states. This book explores how the production, commodification, and cultural impact of guano, nitrates, phosphates, coconuts, and fishmeal have shaped the modern Pacific Basin and the world's relationship to the region. Marrying traditional methods of historical analysis with a broad interdisciplinary approach, Gregory T. Cushman casts these once little-known commodities as engines of Western industrialization, offering new insight into uniquely modern developments such as the growth of environmental consciousness; conservation and cleanliness movements; the ascendance of science, technology, and expertise; international geopolitics; colonialism; and world war.

Gregory T. Cushman is an Associate Professor of History at the University of Kansas, where he teaches courses on Latin America and international environmental history. He works closely with environmental scientists in interdisciplinary research and teaching, and has published a number of articles on climate history and the history of climate science.

Studies in Environment and History

Editors
J. R. McNeill, Georgetown University
Edmund P. Russell, University of Virginia

Editors Emeriti
Alfred W. Crosby, University of Texas at Austin
Donald Worster, University of Kansas

(continued after Index)

Guano and the Opening of the Pacific World

A Global Ecological History

GREGORY T. CUSHMAN

University of Kansas

CAMBRIDGE
UNIVERSITY PRESS

CAMBRIDGE
UNIVERSITY PRESS

32 Avenue of the Americas, New York NY 10013-2473, USA

Cambridge University Press is part of the University of Cambridge.

It furthers the University's mission by disseminating knowledge in the pursuit of
education, learning and research at the highest international levels of excellence.

www.cambridge.org
Information on this title: www.cambridge.org/9781107655966

First published 2013
Reprinted 2013
First paperback edition 2014

A catalogue record for this publication is available from the British Library

Library of Congress Cataloguing in Publication data
Cushman, Gregory T., 1971–
Guano and the opening of the Pacific world : a global ecological history / Gregory T.
Cushman.
   p.   cm. – (Studies in environment and history)
Includes bibliographical references and index.
ISBN 978-1-107-00413-9 (hbk.)
1. Guano – Peru – History. 2. Peru – Environmental conditions. 3. Guano
industry – Pacific Area – History. 4. Pacific Area – Commerce – History. 5. Pacific
Area – Environmental conditions. 6. Guano – Social aspects – History. 7. Guano –
Environmental aspects – History. 8. Phosphate industry – History. 9. Human
ecology – History. I. Title.
S649.C85   2012
631.8′660985–dc23   2012010866

ISBN 978-1-107-00413-9 Hardback
ISBN 978-1-107-65596-6 Paperback

For my family
past, present, & future

With minute and amateurish interest, I found atop a scoop in the base of a big, drifted, scorched tree trunk five little piles of fox dung, a big owl's puke ball full of hair and rat skulls, and three fresher piles of what had to be coon droppings, brown and small, shaped like a dog's or a human's.

Why intrigued ignorance asked, did wild things so often choose to stool on rocks, stumps, and other elevations? Common sense replied: Maybe for the view....

The trouble was, I *was* ignorant. Even in that country where I belonged, my ken of natural things didn't include a little bird that went *heap-heap....* Or a million other matters worth the kenning....

With a box gushing refrigerated air (or warmed, seasonally depending) into a sealed house and another box flashing loud bright images into our jaded heads,... why should we sweat ourselves where the Eskimo curlew went?

— John Graves, *Goodbye to a River* (1960)

Contents

Illustrations and Tables

Illustrations

Tables

Preface

This project started with birds. Historians have long recognized the significance of guano to modern Peru. The fact that English speakers today use a Peruvian term to refer to bird and bat excrement is testimony to the former importance of international trade of this malodorous commodity. But what did the guano industry mean for the marine birds that produced it? I expected the answer to this would be a short, sad tale, in which greedy merchants and miners pushed the guano birds aside to get rich quick. I did not expect to discover that the Peruvian government organized one of history's most elaborate and successful bird conservation programs to maximize fertilizer production and drive Peruvian progress. I never dreamed that I would find guano and guano birds at the heart of Aldo Leopold's famous essay on our moral relationship to the earth, at the base of New Zealand and Australia's rise to First World status, or at the core of the identity of several Pacific peoples. This book demonstrates that marine bird excrement is at the root of modern existence and fundamental to the incorporation of the Pacific Ocean into global history – to the opening of the Pacific World.

I made these discoveries because I had the fortitude (or foolhardiness) to follow guano birds, their poop, and the people who cared about them around the world, no matter where they went. Many of the phenomena in this book have little respect for the borders we typically use to delineate ecosystems, regions, nation-states, or continents, much less for the boundaries that delimit the archives, academic disciplines, and languages we use to study them. I recently learned that there is a name for the "following" methodology. I used to produce this book.[1] I cannot recommend it enthusiastically to those concerned with establishing an academic career, raising a family, retaining their self-esteem, or doing things the easy way. However, I can highly recommend it if you want to learn how individual actions and

[1] Ian Cook et al., "Geographies of Food 1: Following," *Progress in Human Geography* 30 (2006): 655–66.

local histories were involved in building the modern world. This methodology provides a useful way to make sense of how the ocean and soil have been integral to the history of our species. Curiously, these two environments are little studied by historians, even though they cover most of the earth's surface. As this book shows, the earth's hydrosphere and pedosphere are connected to urban existence in unexpected ways, down to the "chicken from the sea" many of us eat.

At its root, this book is about interconnections, one of the central preoccupations of the fields of environmental and global history. A wide variety of readers will therefore find subjects of interest in this book, including many that are dear to American, British, and social history. Many readers will find some of my excursions to be disconcerting. Few of us, for example, think of Peru as part of the Pacific World. For that matter, most of us give little thought to the Pacific's place in history. Whole libraries have been written about the Atlantic World, but readers will be hard pressed to find a single historical monograph with "Pacific World" in its title – a truth that speaks volumes about my profession's tunnel vision.[2]

Others will find the sheer bulk of this book to be daunting. This book demonstrates how a host of remote territories, obscure peoples, and little-known organisms influenced some of the most powerful currents of modern history. No one needs to be convinced that the Black Death, African slave trade, or Second World War fundamentally altered the course of human development. It is quite another thing to convince you that guano is of comparable importance. Big claims of this sort require lots of evidence. A few years back, Richard White argued that one of environmental history's greatest shortcomings was its failure to establish causal connections between its locally based arguments and its global claims.[3] It is much easier to make such links when we make an effort to study places other than our own backyards.

Some conventions in this book require a bit of explanation. I have reported all monetary amounts in their original currencies, but whenever possible, I have converted them into 2007 US dollars. Historical conversions and calculations of real value over time for British, Australian, and U.S. currencies use the gross domestic product deflator, a conservative estimation applicable to a range of consumer goods, services, and financial products. These are derived from Lawrence Officer and Samuel Williamson's Institute of Measuring Worth, http://www.measuringworth.com. Calculations of real

---

[2] See "Special Issue: Oceans Connect," *Geographical Review* 89, no. 2 (1999); "AHR Forum: Oceans of History," *American Historical Review* 111, no. 3; "Forum: Beyond the Atlantic," *William & Mary Quarterly* 63, no. 4 (2006). Ashgate has published a series of compilations titled "The Pacific World: Lands, Peoples and History of the Pacific, 1500–1900."

[3] White, "Environmental History, Ecology, and Meaning," *Journal of American History* 76 (1990): 1111–16.

value for Peruvian soles (S/.) are based on Felipe Portocarrero et al.'s *Compendio estadístico del Perú*. These conversions are meant to provide a rough but meaningful standard for comparison of values across time and place understandable to a diverse international audience. For similar reasons, all other units have been converted to the metric system. To eliminate confusion in identifying species – which often take on different names when they move to new places – I always provide the most widely accepted scientific name, and in most instances common names as well.

As a direct result of some of the events described in this book, scientists have come to the realization that the El Niño–Southern Oscillation (ENSO), a climate phenomenon centered in the equatorial Pacific and Indian Oceans, is the single most important determinant of year-to-year variation in the earth's climate. It had a profound impact on the history traced here. Nonetheless, connecting specific environmental phenomena to the incidence of anomalously warm El Niño and cool La Niña events is a tricky business, and it becomes trickier the farther back we move in time. I have preferentially used a new monthly chronology called the Coupled ENSO Index (CEI) for defining events, because it combines consideration of oceanic and atmospheric features of this phenomenon, is based partly on instrumental records, and is most similar to the definitions used by scientists to define more recent ENSO events.[4] Secondarily, I have used a new chronology based on proxy records (or paleoarchives) such as coral reef cores, historical records of droughts and floods in certain regions, and tropical ice cores.[5] It goes back much farther in history but does not always line up neatly with the instrumental chronology. I give much less credence to older proxy chronologies developed by William Quinn and his associates, which are overly biased toward Peru.[6] All ascriptions of environmental phenomena to El Niño or La Niña in this book are somewhat tentative. The footnotes clarify whether CEI or paleoarchives provided the main basis for these determinations. The citation of more traditional archival sources follows the convention: archive-collection, box/folder. Frequently used archival collections and periodicals are abbreviated in accordance with a list following this preface. Full publication information will be provided at first citation in the footnotes for sources not in the select bibliography.

I want to thank a number of people and institutions that took a risk on me, believed in me, or at least tolerated my foibles, failings, and fascination with bird shit. My parents and grandparents taught me to be a naturalist. To them, this not only meant learning the names and habits of birds, bees, stars, and trees, but also the places you could find them and the people who cared about or threatened these treasures. To them, Nature provided

[4] Gergis and Fowler, "Classification of Synchronous Oceanic and Atmospheric ENSO Events."
[5] Gergis and Fowler, "A History of ENSO Events since A.D. 1525."
[6] Quinn and Neal, "The Historical Record of El Niño Events."

a revelation of the wisdom of the Creator, and its degradation prophesied the soon coming of the time "for judging the dead, and for rewarding your servants . . . and for destroying those who destroy the earth."[7] (If only I could still believe this were true.) As you will learn in this book, great evil and destruction sometimes resulted from my own forefathers' and foremothers' moral quest to improve the earth at the expense of others. This was probably my most enlightening and humbling discovery.

In Peru, Magnolia and Amanda Velásquez Jara opened their home to me – and made it feel like home; my cousin Chris Finch and his family did the same in San Diego; Beatriz Benítez did so in London. Several teachers provided me with the guidance and tools I needed to embark on this project. These include Gary Bradley, Karl Butzer, Marjorie Coon, Al Crosby, Joe Galusha, Mauricio Tenorio and especially Richard Graham, Bruce Hunt, and Rennie Schoepflin. I criticize some of Crosby's ideas here but see this book as a direct extension of the research program he laid out and credit to his inspiration. Participation in the Pacific Centuries conference series organized by Dennis Flynn and Arturo Giráldez and an NEH Institute on the Environment and World History organized by Terry Burke had a formative influence on the conceptualization of this project that is still growing. In Peru, Scarlett O'Phelan, Marcos Cueto, and several scientists connected to IMARPE provided encouragement and insight. On Easter Island, Pau Hito, Alberto Hotus, and Oscar provided invaluable help in familiarizing me with the people and environment of Rapa Nui. The American Meteorological Society History of Science Dissertation Fellowship provided vital support at an early stage in this project that, unlike many grants, enabled me to do multinational research. Ever since, Jim Fleming, the mastermind behind the creation of this program, has continued to serve as an advocate, mentor, and now a close friend. The University of Kansas has provided an extraordinary climate for the sort of interdisciplinary engagement needed for projects like this; I especially want to thank Chris Brown, Byron Caminero-Santangelo, Johan Feddema, Sara Gregg, Joane Nagel, Bill Tsutsui, Joy Ward, Bill Woods, and especially Don Worster for their interest and support. The KU Center for Research provided a series of summer research grants that enabled me to follow my research subjects to new places. The Hall Center for the Humanities Nature and Culture Seminar generated many other opportunities, including the ability to gain relevant insights from Deborah Fitzgerald, Susan Flader, Brett Walker, Kären Wigen, and Verena Winiwarter. A Fulbright Scholarship to Hungary presented the opportunity to work further with Winiwarter, Zoltán Alföldi, and Wenqi Ma on soil and ethical issues. Henning Krause provided admirable research assistance in Germany. An award from the Friends of the Hall Center helped support publication of the book. Santa

---

[7] Revelation 11:18, New International Version.

Arias accompanied me to the ends of the earth in seeing this book through to its finale.

Many research libraries, archives, institutions, and people who experienced these events opened their doors to me; most are cited in the bibliography. However, I want to express special gratitude to Deborah Day at SIO, the staff at IMARPE and PROABONOS, and to Basilia Díaz, the widow of Enrique Ávila. Her husband was "mostly Indian" and grew up close to Lake Titicaca; he became Peru's first native-born professional marine scientist. She tearfully gave me the few remaining papers of his that remained from the El Niño flood of 1982. This disaster destroyed boxes of personal archives and photographs from the guano islands, along with most of her possessions. Her husband died cursed with the knowledge that the birds and fish he had dedicated his life to studying and conserving had been wiped out by human overdevelopment. He personally experienced Rachel Carson's nightmare of a silent spring on Peru's guano islands.

I hope you appreciate the new perspective of the world that can come from contemplating heaps of bird manure. Perhaps this book will also make you "sweat where the Eskimo curlew went."

Abbreviations and Acronyms

ACAG	Archivos de la Compañía Administradora del Guano
ACL	Auckland City Libraries
AMFom	Archivo del Ministerio de Fomento y Obras Públicas
ATA	American Tunaboat Association
BCAG	*Boletín de la Compañía Administradora del Guano*
BCCAG	*Boletín científico de la Compañía Administradora del Guano*
BCIM	*Boletín del Cuerpo de Ingenieros de Minas*
BCNPN	*Boletín del Comité Nacional de Protección a la Naturaleza*
BCONAFER	*Boletín de la Corporación Nacional de Fertilizantes*
BMFom	*Boletín del Ministerio de Fomento*
Bol.Inst.Mar	*Boletín del Instituto del Mar del Perú*
BPC	British Phosphate Commission
CAG	Compañía Administradora del Guano
CEPAL	Comisión Económica para América Latina
DPL	Denver Public Library
ENSO	El Niño–Southern Oscillation
FAO	Food and Agricultural Organization of the United Nations
G&EI	Gilbert and Ellice Islands
IMARPE	Instituto del Mar del Perú
Inf.Inst.Mar	*Informe del Instituto del Mar del Perú*
IREMAR	Instituto de Investigaciones de los Recursos Marinos
IUCN	International Union for Conservation of Nature and Natural Resources
JLAS	*Journal of Latin American Studies*
MCAG	*Memoria del Directorio de la Compañía Administradora del Guano*
MCONAFER	*Memoria de la Corporación Nacional de Fertilizantes*

Mem.Inst.Mar	*Memoria anual del Instituto del Mar del Perú*
MMFom	*Memoria del Ministerio de Fomento*
NAUK-BFO	National Archives, UK–British Foreign Office
PMB	Pacific Manuscripts Bureau
PPC	Pacific Phosphates Company
PROABONOS	Proyecto Especial de Promoción del Aprovechamiento de Abonos Provenientes de Aves Marinas
S/.	Peruvian soles
SIO	Scripps Institution of Oceanography
SNP	Sociedad Nacional de Pesquería
UWDC-ALA	University of Wisconsin Digital Collections, Aldo Leopold Archives
WHOI	Woods Hole Oceanographic Institution

Prologue

Once there was a female *huaca* named Cauillaca, the woman of the ocean depths. Cauillaca had always remained a virgin. Because she was very beautiful, everyone longed for her. "I've got to sleep with her!" they thought, but she never consented. One day, this woman was weaving beneath a *lúcuma* tree. The wandering trickster Cuniraya Viracocha – provider of flowing water – turned himself into a bird and flew into the lúcuma tree. He put his white semen into a ripened fruit and plopped it next to Cauillaca. She swallowed its yellow flesh delightedly. Thus, she got pregnant even though she remained untouched by a man.

One year after this child's birth, she called everyone together on the bleak *altiplano* to find out who was the child's father. The local male huacas were overjoyed, and they all came dressed in their best clothes, each saying to himself, "It's me she'll love" – all, that is, except Cuniraya Viracocha. He often walked about as a miserably poor and kinless orphan (*guaccha*), dressed in rags, and covered with lice.

Cauillaca addressed the child: "Go, find your father." The child began at one end of the group and crawled along on all fours until it reached the other end where its father sat. On reaching him, the baby instantly brightened and climbed onto its father's knee. When its mother saw this, she became indignant, "*Atatay*, magical child, what a disgrace! How could I have given birth to the child of a beggar like that?" And taking her child in disgust, she headed down the river valley, straight for the deep sea below the painted temple of He Who Gives Motion to the World, Pachacamac. When she and her child reached her dwelling in the sea, they turned to stone where, today, two white guano islands that look like people still stand.

And then, while all the local huacas stood in awe, Cuniraya Viracocha changed into his golden garment and called after her: "Sister Cauillaca! Here, look at me now! I'm actually beautiful," as his raiment shimmered like sunlight on a pool of water.

He ran after her down the valley, shouting out to her from a distance, but soon lost sight of her. First, he met up with a condor and asked, "Brother, did you run into that woman?"

"Yes, right near here. You'll soon find her," replied the condor.

Cuniraya Viracocha answered back: "You will live a long life. You alone will feast on the dead guanacos and vicuñas of the wild mountain slopes. And if anybody should kill you, he also will die."

In similar fashion, Cuniraya Viracocha met up with a skunk, a puma, a fox, a falcon, and finally some parakeets. "She's already gone far away. You'll never find her now! You'll never find her now!" the parakeets told him.

"As for you," replied Cuniraya Viracocha, "although you may scream 'We'll spoil your crops! We'll spoil your crops!' when people hear you, they'll chase you away at once. You'll live in great misery as a pest amidst the hatred of humans." And so he traveled on. Whenever he met anyone who gave him good news, he conferred a good fortune, but he viciously cursed those who gave him bad news.

Finally, he reached the seashore at the place where Pachacamac's wife and two daughters lived guarded by a snake. Their mother had just gone into the deep sea to visit Cauillaca. In those days, there was not a single fish in the ocean. Only the girls' mother bred them, in a small, coastal lagoon. In anger, Cuniraya Viracocha came down like a flood and threw the fish into the sea. Ever since, fish have filled the ocean. He raped the older daughter, but her sister turned into a bird and flew away. That is why her mother's name, Urpi Huachac, means "she who gives birth to birds."

When Urpi Huachac heard of this from her daughters, she flew after him in fury down the seashore. She called out to him, again and again, and eventually he turned and waited for her. "Yes?" he answered.

"Oh Cuni, I just want to remove your lice." But while she preened him, feasting on this emblem of the great multitudes his hidden fertilizing powers could feed, she opened a huge abyss next to him. Cuniraya Viracocha recognized his danger and said, *"Hold on a minute, Sister. I really need to take a shit."* And with that, he made his getaway into the fields of a nearby village. He escaped death in the sea, and tricked many more huacas and people, too.[1]

In this way, life- and death-giving torrents flow from mountain to coast, birds took to the air and fish to the sea, and guano attained its place in fertilizing the world.

---

[1] Based on a Quechua text from circa 1608, *The Huarochirí Manuscript*, ch. 2.

Introduction

L'odeur de l'ordure dure òu l'or dort. / The stench of shit lingers where gold sleeps.

   – Dominique Laporte, *Histoire de la merde* (1978)

The Lord of Guano

In 1847, on a barren windswept island off the desert coast of central Peru, a guano miner unearthed a curious stone tablet buried under five and a half meters of accumulated bird excrement (fig. 1.1). During the nineteenth-century guano export boom – an event that utterly transformed the modern world's relationship with the Pacific Ocean, agricultural soils, and marine birds – miners discovered hundreds of ancient indigenous artifacts on Peru's guano islands. These included gold and silver objects, wooden sculptures, pottery, richly woven textiles, decapitated bodies, even a mummified penguin under as much as twenty meters of the world's richest naturally occurring fertilizer. No one ever discovered another artifact like this one, however.[1]

South American explorer William Bollaert got wind of this discovery and published a short article in a popular magazine accompanied by a detailed drawing of this "curious stone" with "quaint armorial bearings." He speculated that it "may have been brought from old Spain, and may have been intended for insertion over the doorway of a building belonging to the former owner of the island."[2] Inspired by the growing interest of North American ecologists in Peru's guano birds – a fascination that powerfully influenced the beginnings of the environmental movement of the late twentieth

---

[1] George Kubler, "Towards Absolute Time: Guano Archaeology," in *A Reappraisal of Peruvian Archaeology*, Memoirs of the Society for American Archaeology, no. 4 (Menasha, WI, 1948).

[2] Bollaert, "Carved Stone Found on the Chincha or Guano Islands," *Illustrated Times* (London) 5 Mar. 1859: 157.

FIGURE 1.1. The coat of arms of an indigenous Peruvian guano lord, circa 1560. This object was unearthed on Isla Chincha Norte in 1847 and donated to the British Museum by Henry Hucks Gibbs in 1859. The cross still bears traces of red pigment. It is unknown what occupied the niche at the center of the carving. *Source:* Prehistory & Europe section, object 1859,0322.1; reproduced courtesy of The Trustees of the British Museum.

century – Yale art historian George Kubler tried unsuccessfully to relocate the artifact during the mid-1940s. Because it clearly dated from the era soon after the Spanish Conquest, he hoped to use it as a benchmark for producing an absolute chronology of pre-Hispanic art styles found buried at deeper levels on the guano islands. The artifact was nowhere to be found, however. In 2006, with the aid of computer cataloging, staff at the British

Museum relocated and photographed the slab, which had been hidden away like Indiana Jones's legendary lost Ark of the Covenant in its complex of warehouses.

Until this time, no one had tried very hard to read the inscription, much less suspected the insights it could provide into the deep history of humanity's relationship with the sea and bird excrement. It reads:

don pedro guanneque prinsipal del valle de [c]hincha

From the form and content of its gothic script, we can conclude that this coat of arms belonged to an indigenous noble who lived during the sixteenth century.

Who was this mysterious man? From the first part of his name, we know that Don Pedro Guaneque (or Guañeque) was a baptized Christian of high social standing. The prefix of the second part may refer to *huanu* (alternatively *yzmay* or "shit"), the Quechua word for any form of manure used as an agricultural fertilizer. This is the origin of our modern word for the excrement of wild birds and bats, which was first introduced to the English language by José de Acosta's *Natural and Moral History of the Indies* in 1604. (This word is well known to today's youth thanks to the popular 1995 film *Ace Ventura: When Nature Calls*, in which actor Jim Carrey's nemesis plots to dispossess a group of African tribes of the fortune they possess in bat guano.) *Prinsipal* was a title of nobility indicating his status as paramount lord over an ethnic group living in the lowland valleys along the south-central coast of Peru. His subordinates owed him labor and allegiance as kin. In reciprocity, it was his sacred duty to please the ancestors, to keep their living children fed, and to protect them from the hazards of flood, drought, earthquake, famine, pestilence, and invasion so that they could multiply as a people. Relationships of this sort provided a basis for social power among peoples in many parts of the world before the disruptions of the modern age.[3] By the end of this book, readers will have learned how new configurations of ethnic difference separating races, nations, and species caused some of the worst social and environmental catastrophes in history, including the demise of Peru's guano birds.

According to court records from the late 1560s, an indigenous lord with this exact name rented a coastal lagoon at the mouth of the Mala River to a local Spaniard to pay part of the annual tribute his kin group owed to the new colonial regime. ("Mala" can also be read in the curious lettering at the base of Don Pedro Guaneque's coat of arms.) Lagoon environments were far more extensive back then, before they were drained by modern

3 *Oxford English Dictionary*, s.v. "guano"; Domingo de Santo Tomás, *Lexicon, o vocabulario de la lengua general del Perú* (1560; Lima, 1951), 58, 121, 134; Susan Ramírez, *To Feed and Be Fed: The Cosmological Bases of Authority and Identity in the Andes* (Stanford, CA, 2005), 96–97, 114, 142, 214.

irrigation technocrats. When properly cared for, these brackish pools can be used to corral large numbers of *lisa* or mullet (*Mugil cephalus*), one of the world's most common estuary fish. These lagoons also produce totora reeds (*Schoenoplectus californicus*), a valuable source of fiber and building material. According to the creation myth related in the prologue, the female deity Urpi Huachac was the inventor of this rudimentary form of aquaculture, which, thanks to a violent flood brought by the trickster Cuniraya Viracocha, gave birth to all the fish of the sea. Don Pedro's arrangement ended up in litigation because the lagoon failed to bear fish in abundance after his death and his kin were forced to repay in gold all rent they had received.[4]

This was a harsh, demeaning blow to Don Pedro's kin that threatened them with extinction as a people. Archaeologists and historians are beginning to recognize that coastal indigenous peoples not only viciously opposed their conquest by the Inca during the late fifteenth century but also aided the Spanish so that they could throw off the yoke of highland imperialism.[5] A number of indigenous nobles in the Americas adopted coats of arms with heraldic symbols of their own design during the sixteenth century to take credit for allying with the Spanish in their victory and to express a long-standing obsession with genealogical descent.[6] To a Spaniard, the bell tower and red cross in this coat of arms would appear to assert Don Pedro's loyalty to Christianity and the new colonial order. The image in the lower left quadrant displays Don Pedro's wooden *vara* or staff of authority. It appears to be crowned with feathers, a common feature of indigenous regalia symbolizing creative power – and altogether appropriate for a guano lord.[7]

Other elements in this design possessed deeper, hidden meanings. The image in the upper right quadrant is probably a guanay cormorant (*Phalacrocorax bougainvillei*), the most abundant and important of Peru's guano-producing birds. Guanays adopt this reclined neck posture and flash their wings when preparing to mate. It can also be interpreted as the literal image of Don Pedro's foremother Urpi Huachac, who was viewed as the mythic founder of a number of indigenous lineages along Peru's central coast. The most important religious site in the lower Mala valley before the Spanish Conquest was a sacred stone hill known as Sulcavilca. This *huaca* (any sacred being or object with power over death and procreation) was understood to

4 "Expediente de la causa seguida por Juan Sánchez de Aguirre en nombre de Diego Díaz contra los indios de Mala," 1566–69, Biblioteca Nacional del Perú, doc. A199, fol. 120^{r-v}, 180^r–181^r, 194^r–195^v, 208^v–209^r; Rostworowski, *Recursos naturales renovables*, ch. 1.
5 Noble David Cook, *Demographic Collapse, Indian Peru, 1520–1620* (Cambridge and New York, 1981), 157–58; "The Great Inca Rebellion," *Nova*, PBS, 26 June 2007.
6 Jaime Cuadriello, *Las glorias de la República de Tlaxcala* (Mexico City, 2004), 325–84; Carolyn Dean, *Inka Bodies and the Body of Christ: Corpus Christi in Colonial Cuzco* (Durham, NC, 1999), 142–54.
7 Ramírez, *To Feed and Be Fed*, 191–211; José Luis Martínez Cereceda, *Autoridades en los Andes: Los atributos del señor* (Lima, 1995), 79–84, 189–90.

be the embodiment of one of the four sons of the creator deity Pachacamac and his wife Urpi Huachac.[8] It is no coincidence that the highland area where the story in the prologue was recorded, Huarochirí, is located at the headwaters of the Mala River. Similar myths were widespread along Peru's central coast during the colonial era and are replete with symbols associated with guano, birds, fertility, and kinship.[9] In the prologue to this volume, Cuniraya Viracocha turned into a bird and plopped his white semen next to Cauillaca to impregnate her. The name Viracocha means "sea of fatness" or "sea of abundance," further indicating his links to fertility and the sea. Cauillaca and her child eventually turned into guano islands, known today as the islands of Pachacamac. One of Urpi Huachac's daughters turned into a bird to escape being raped and flew out to sea to find her mother, who was off visiting these islands. Urpi Huachac convinced Cuniraya to come within her reach so she could preen him – a common bond-forming practice among cormorant mate pairs. In the story's climax, he escaped death in the sea by running off "to take a shit" in a field. Unfortunately, the translator of this text ruined its punch line by prudishly favoring the phrase "I've got to go off for a moment to relieve myself" because "the plain translation 'to shit' sounds jarringly obscene."[10] This decision obscured the basic moral of this folktale: that which is repulsive can possess profound creative power. This mistranslation is symbolic of our larger failure to recognize the importance of shit to history.

The image in the lower right quadrant appears to portray the place in which this tablet was discovered: the three Chincha Islands (fig. 1.2). Indigenes from the coastal valleys of Chincha and Pisco directly associated these islands with the *huaca* Urpi Huachac and her two daughters. The people of Pisco – a word that itself means "bird" – also associated these islands with the term *quillairaca*, which means "silver vagina" or "the moon's vagina." To anyone who has ever set foot on one of Peru's guano islands, the semicircle on the central island in this image obviously portrays the raised, circular nest of a guanay. Until recently, millions of guanays flocked to these islands each spring to mate. Their nests are made from pure excrement and shine white in the sun; but in the light of the full moon, they glow silver. Conscious of this point, the makers of this coat of arms appear to have intentionally placed the north-coast word for the fisherman's most important celestial guide, the goddess of the moon "Si," apart from the rest of the text above the three islands. These vaginas of the moon serve as the birthplace for

---

[8] Cristóbal de Albornoz, "La instrucción para descubrir todas las guacas del Pirú" (ca. 1568–71) *Journal de la Société des Américanistes* 56 (1967): 34; Henry Tantaleón and Omar Pinedo, "Entre los Andes y el mar: El valle bajo del Mala antes y durante la ocupación Inca," *Revista de arqueología* (Madrid) 283 (2004): 54–63.

[9] Peter Eeckhout, "Relatos míticos y prácticas rituales en Pachacamac," *Bulletin de l'Institut français d'études andines* 33 (2004): 1–54.

[10] *Huarochirí Manuscript*, ch. 2, §28; Santo Tomás, *Lexicon*, 144; Ramírez, *To Feed and Be Fed*, 66.

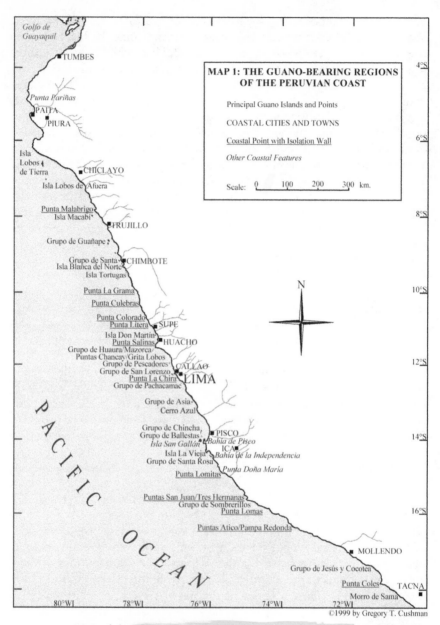

FIGURE I.2. Map of the guano-producing regions and irrigated valleys of the Peruvian coast. Map by author, used by permission.

every guanay ever born. They also provide an exceptionally rich source of agricultural fertilizer that enables the prosperity and reproduction of the humans who collect them, grind them up, and add them to fields of crops. Every image in this carefully composed coat of arms appears to assert Don Pedro's genealogical ties to age-old sources of reproductive power along the Peruvian coast, beliefs that were probably shared by a widespread descent group from this region who called themselves the *Lunaguaná* or *Runaguanay*, "guano birds of the people." Here we have a real-life *Da Vinci Code* asserting the shared feminine and masculine basis of human reproduction and prosperity.[11]

We know from a host of written records, oral traditions, and physical remnants that ancient Andean peoples were greatly concerned with maintaining the fertility of the land and sea. According to the best-known chronicler of the colonial era, indigenous Peruvians

fertilized the soil by manuring it, and in the valley of Cuzco and almost all the highland area they treated their maize fields with human manure [*runap huanu*], which they regarded as the best. They go to great trouble to obtain it, and dry it and pulverize it in time for the sowing season. In the [higher Sierra], . . . the climate is too cold for growing maize, and they sow potatoes and other vegetables: for this they use the manure of the Peruvian sheep [llamas and alpacas, *huanacup huanu*], which they regard as more beneficial than any other.

On the seacoast, from below Arequipa to Tarapacá, . . . they use no other manure but the dung of sea birds [*piscup huanu*], of which large and small varieties occur on the coast of Peru in such enormous flocks that they seem incredible to anyone who has not seen them. They breed on some uninhabited islands off the coast, where they deposit such an amount of dung that is no less incredible. From a distance the heaps of it look like the snowy crests of a range of mountains. . . . The dung of the sea birds produces great fertility. In other parts of the same coast, such as the basins of . . . Malla, and Chillca, and other valleys, they manure with the heads of sardines [*challuap huanu*].[12]

Fertilization represented only one of a host of techniques used by Andean land managers to maximize production from the soil while guarding against total crop failure caused by environmental extremes.[13]

---

[11] Santo Tomás, *Lexicon*, 161, 164–65, 169; Alonso Osorio, "Testimonio y extirpación de idolatrías," (1620), in Rostworowski, "Pescadores Artesanos y Mercaderes en el Perú prehispánico," *Revista del Museo Nacional* (Lima) 41 (1975): 344–45; Rostworowski, "Islas del litoral," 94–95; Rostworowski, "Guarco y Lunaguaná: Dos señoríos prehispánicos de la costa sur central," *Revista del Museo Nacional* 44 (1978–80): 166–67, 181–82; Ramírez, *To Feed and Be Fed*, 96–97, 114, 142, 214.

[12] Garcilaso de la Vega, *Royal Commentaries of the Incas* (1609; Austin, TX, 1966), 1:246–47; for Quechua terms, see *Markham in Peru: The Travels of Clements R. Markham, 1852–1853* (Austin, TX, 1991), 41, 143.

[13] William Denevan, *Cultivated Landscapes of Native Amazonia and the Andes* (New York, 2001), 34–48.

Never one to miss an opportunity to promote the accomplishments of the Inca emperors from whom he descended, Garcilaso de la Vega recalled that

in the times of the Inca kings these birds were so carefully watched that no one was allowed to land on the islands during the breeding season under pain of death, so that they should not be disturbed or driven from their nests. It was also illegal to kill them at any season either on the islands or elsewhere, under pain of the same penalty.

Each island was assigned, on the Inca's instructions, to a certain province, or if it was a large island, to two or three provinces ... in which each village had its piece and each householder in the village his part, according to the quantity of manure he was reckoned to need.[14]

As we see later in this book, twentieth-century conservationists loved citing this law to legitimate government regulation of Peru's marine environment, oblivious to their original imperialist intent to dispossess the coast's existing guano lords.

These episodes only begin to recount the importance of guano and the sea to the indigenous peoples of Peru. These relationships may extend back to the emergence of settled life along the Pacific coast of South America more than 5,000 years ago.[15] The history of guano deserves our attention, at the very least, for its significance to ancient Andean societies. However, the main purpose of this book is to demonstrate that guano, guano islands, and guano birds have been profoundly important to other peoples as well. This includes the ecological, cultural, and geopolitical history of the modern world – *our world*. This realization first requires us to abandon our intense prejudice toward excrement and recognize its basic importance to all living things.

Nitrogen, Phosphorus, and Shit in History

Excrement is not considered a topic of polite conversation, yet it is a fundamental and unavoidable feature of biological existence. City folk tend to view this foul substance with disdain, as a source of comedy or even fear. Such attitudes have ancient roots in taboos governing religious purity. The Mosaic law commanded:

Designate a place outside the camp where you can go to relieve yourself. As part of your equipment have something to dig with, and when you relieve yourself, dig

---

[14] De la Vega, *Royal Commentaries*, 1:246–47.

[15] Michael Moseley, *Maritime Foundations of Andean Civilization* (Menlo Park, CA, 1975); Charles Mann, "Oldest Civilization in the Americas Revealed," *Science* 7 (Jan. 2005): 34–35; Daniel Sandweiss et al., "Environmental Change and Economic Development in Coastal Peru between 5,800 and 3,600 Years Ago," *Proceedings of the National Academy of Sciences* 106 (2009): 1359–63.

a hole and cover up your excrement. For the LORD your God moves about in your camp to protect you and to deliver your enemies to you. Your camp must be holy, so that he will not see among you anything indecent and turn away from you.[16]

In our secular age, however, these attitudes are more a reflection of how divorced urban, industrial existence has become from natural cycles and civilization's agrarian roots. Thus, the ecologically enlightened in our disposable society now have to read special books to learn "how to shit in the woods" to protect the wilderness from harm and to teach our children that "everyone poops."[17]

An important source of this separation stems from the success that the modern state and experts in its employ have attained at manipulating natural processes for the rest of us. One major task they have been asked to perform is to hide, wash away, and otherwise protect us from our own excreta. In *Civilization and Its Discontents* (1930), Sigmund Freud postulated that our differentiation from the beasts of the field began when our species began to walk upright and we began to lose the olfactory sense. In Freud's view, gaining control over the anal constituent of life was indispensable to attaining the three essential characteristics of civilization: cleanliness, order, and beauty. Thus, the open sewer, manure heap, and public fart have become our most potent (and pungent) symbols of barbarity and backwardness. Thus, in colonizing efforts around the globe, "marines and latrines" had an inseparable affinity. Vanished excrement is as much a part of our mythology of modern existence as the moon's vagina was for Don Pedro's Peru. Yet our often unspoken obsession with excretory functions in everyday discourse reveals that our pretension of living in a civilization unconstrained by ecological limitations is "eternally, hopelessly soiled." The role that failed septic tanks played in the U.S. environmental movement testifies to this.[18]

Excretion is as basic to existence as eating, and in nonindustrial ecosystems it is fundamental to the cycling of nutrients and renewal of life, but industrial civilization has a very different set of values. Instead of deifying semen, soil, and excrement, we place emphasis on the dead building blocks of life. Thanks to the findings of molecular biology, we now know that all organisms need a variety of basic substances to function and grow.

---

[16] Deuteronomy 23:12–14, New International Version.

[17] Kathleen Meyer, *How to Shit in the Woods: An Environmentally Sound Approach to a Lost Art* (Berkeley, CA, 1989); Taro Gomi, *Everyone Poops* (Brooklyn, NY, 1993).

[18] Freud, *Civilization and Its Discontents* (New York, 2005), 79, 83–84, 87–88, 96–97; Laporte, *History of Shit*, x, 35; Corbin, *The Foul and the Fragrant*; Melosi, *The Sanitary City*; Chalhoub, *Cidade febril*; Merle Curti and Kendall Birr, *Prelude to Point Four: American Technical Missions Overseas, 1838–1938* (Madison, WI, 1954), ch. 6; Anderson, "Excremental Colonialism"; Adam Rome, *The Bulldozer in the Countryside: Suburban Sprawl and the Rise of American Environmentalism* (Cambridge and New York, 2001), ch. 3.

This book focuses on two of the most important of these, nitrogen (N) and phosphorus (P), and their role in transforming the metabolism of the modern world.[19]

Nitrogen is vital to a host of biochemical processes. It forms the chemical bonds between amino acids used to construct enzymes and other proteins, it constitutes part of the nucleic acid chains that code for reproduction and protein synthesis, and it is an important building block of chlorophyll, which creates nearly all of the biological energy that drives life on earth. Dietary experts recommend that for good health, adult men and women consume 0.75 grams of protein for every kilogram of body weight each day, but fast-growing infants need more than twice as much. As a consequence, protein deficiency (kwashiorkor) is one of the most significant nutritional problems facing the world's poorest children, with the conspicuous exception of those with access to marine sources of protein.

Nitrogen is one of the most abundant elements on earth – 78 percent of the atmosphere at sea level is nitrogen. Yet practically all of it is locked up in an unreactive form (N_2) that must first be converted to nitrogen oxides (NO_x) or ammonia (NH_3) to be used in biological systems. There are only two basic ways for this to occur: through the tremendous expenditure of energy or by the intervention of nitrogen-fixing organisms. Reactive nitrogen is also tremendously mobile and can be quickly removed from an environment by leaching, physical erosion, volatilization, combustion, or bacterial denitrification. For these reasons, reactive nitrogen is often in such limited supply compared with other nutrients that it places basic restrictions on the rate at which an organism can grow. (This is known as the "Law of the Minimum.") Its availability can even limit the productivity of an ecosystem as a whole.

Compared with nitrogen, phosphorus makes up a tiny proportion of the world's biomass and has received almost no attention from historians, but it is no less dispensable to life. Phosphorus, usually in the form of phosphate (PO_4^{3-}), is a critical constituent of the structural tissue of plants and the bones and teeth of animals. At a far more basic level, phosphate bonds in adenosine triphosphate (ATP) provide the main source of energy for cell metabolism. Phosphorus cycling in the environment is much slower and simpler than nitrogen cycling. It begins with the erosion of upland rocks by wind and water and ends with the deposition of phosphate-rich sediments in the ocean. Leaching is the principal way that phosphorus is removed from an environment. Humans have to consume substantial quantities because we wastefully excrete 98 percent of our intake each day. Thus, for

---

[19] The following is based in part on Vaclav Smil, "Nitrogen and Phosphorus," in *The Earth as Transformed by Human Action* (Cambridge and New York, 1990); Smil, *Enriching the Earth*; G. J. Leigh, *The World's Greatest Fix: A History of Nitrogen and Agriculture* (New York, 2004).

archaeologists, increased soil phosphate levels provide one of the most distinctive signs that a site was once populated by humans.

There are five basic ways that farmers can manage the availability of nitrogen, phosphorus, and other nutrients in agricultural soils:

1. By converting natural plant communities into cultivated fields. The North American Great Plains, South American Pampas, and Eurasian steppes are famous for their value as agricultural lands. Their relative aridity inhibits the leaching of soils by rainfall and enables the gradual concentration of nutrients. "Sodbusting" opened these virgin soils to cultivation, which produced a series of bumper crops as long as rainfall was sufficient. Swidden or "slash-and-burn" agriculture takes advantage of the ability of wild vegetation to reconcentrate nutrients during fallow periods. However, intensive farming will eventually deplete even the richest soils, which cannot be replenished except on very long timescales. Thus, this method is often referred to as soil mining.[20]

2. By manipulating the chemistry, texture, and biota of soils. The acidity of a soil and relative quantity of clay, sand, organic particles, and other chemicals it contains greatly affect the availability of nutrients. Soils that have too much clay may bind nutrients so tightly that plants cannot access them, whereas soils with too much sand may allow nutrients to wash away. In England and the antebellum United States, experimental farmers discovered that they could improve the productivity of some farms by adding lime or marl. These substances do not act as fertilizers; they help reduce the acidity of soils and make other nutrients available to crops. In Amazonia and along the North Atlantic shore, ancient farmers altered soils and increased their fertility to such a radical extent that they are known among experts as "anthrosols."[21] Soil organisms also greatly influence these characteristics. Late in life, Charles Darwin became obsessed with the capacity of earthworms (*Annelida*) to cycle through the soil and wondered "if there are any other animals which have played such an important part in the history of the world as these lowly organized creatures."[22]

3. By planting crops or trees that live in symbiosis with nitrogen-fixing microorganisms. Most of us are familiar with the use of leguminous plants such as clover (*Trifolium* spp.) and soybeans (*Glycine max*)

---

[20] Craven, *Soil Exhaustion.*

[21] Johannes Lehmann et al., eds., *Amazonian Dark Earths: Origin, Properties, Management* (Dordrecht, Netherlands, 2003); Hans-Peter Blume and Peter Leinweber, "Plaggen Soils: Landscape History, Properties, and Classification," *Journal of Plant Nutrition and Soil Science* 167 (2004): 319–27.

[22] Christian Feller et al., "Charles Darwin, Earthworms, and the Natural Sciences," *Agriculture, Ecosystems & Environment* 99 (2003): 29–49.

for this purpose. Wet paddy cultivation of rice (*Oryza sativa*), like-wise, promotes the growth of nitrogen-fixing cyanobacteria. Peruvian and New Guinean farmers discovered centuries ago that the planting of *Prosopis* and *Casuarina* trees influenced soil fertility, besides providing a valuable source of wood, nutrient-rich leaf compost, and seedpods.[23]

4. By recycling organic waste back to the soil. The recycling of vegetable compost, animal manures, decomposing bodies, and human excrement has been crucial to the maintenance of soil fertility in traditional forms of intensive agriculture. After harvest, many Old World peasant societies set out their livestock to convert crop waste and weeds into nutrient-rich animal waste. Animal and manure shortages were capable of holding back the development of entire regions.[24] The old Japanese practice of using "honey pots" to receive urban household excrement often attracted favorable interest from outsiders.[25] However, recycling can never fully close the circle and replace all nutrients removed by agricultural activities, particularly when products are exported from the farm and consumed far away.

5. By importing nutrients from other environments. Water and wind erosion can rapidly destroy the fertility of soils locally but may provide a windfall for farmers living downstream or downwind. The steady erosion of upland areas of northeast Africa and the Andean highlands has enabled the floodplains of the lower Nile and coastal Peru, respectively, to be cultivated intensely for thousands of years. In early modern Japan, intensive agriculture depended heavily on the importation of dried fish and soybean cake from elsewhere in the islands and provided an important motivation for the colonization of Ainu lands in Hokkaido.[26] This book focuses on the central importance of nutrient extraction from upwelling regions in the Pacific Ocean to modern livelihoods.

Historically, the most productive and sustainable agricultural systems tended to combine these methods. In the Valley of Mexico, indigenous cultivators of raised wetland gardens known as *chinampas* used lake sediments, decayed vegetation, recycled human excrement, and, later, livestock manure to augment the fertility of their fields. Like ancient Peru, central Mexico

[23] Dietrich Werner and William Newton, *Nitrogen Fixation in Agriculture, Forestry, Ecology, and the Environment* (Berlin, 2005).

[24] Christian Pfister, *Bevölkerung, Klima und Agrarmodernisierung, 1525–1860* (Bern, 1984); Krausmann, "Milk, Manure, and Muscular Power."

[25] H. Maron, "Extract from the Report to the Minister of Agriculture at Berlin on Japanese Husbandry," in Justus von Liebig, *The Natural Laws of Husbandry* (London, 1859), 390–92, 396.

[26] Howell, *Capitalism from Within*; Walker, *Conquest of Ainu Lands*.

possessed a rich excremental folklore.[27] In recent centuries, no one surpassed the farmers of southern China in these matters. In the Zhujiang (Pearl River) delta, crop and excrement recycling, silt produced by upland erosion, and aquaculture enabled preindustrial farmers to support an estimated seventeen to twenty-five people per cultivated hectare, while producing huge surpluses for export.[28]

Today's industrial agricultural systems operate on very different principles from those of the ecological old regime. Rather than seeking to minimize the expenditure of labor and maximize the efficiency of nutrient cycling, modern farms are fixated on *throughput*: they seek to maximize the production of food and fiber for consumption off the farm through massive, often wasteful expenditures of fossil fuel energy, nutrient inputs, fuel-hungry technologies, and scientific expertise. Throughput systems only move in one direction, from the extraction of raw materials, through lengthy commodity chains, to the consumption of finished products and dumping of useless waste.[29] The spectacular increase of nitrogen fertilizer and phosphate rock production worldwide during the course of the twentieth century provides a useful measure of the growth of input-intensive, throughput-oriented farming practices. The global human population increased spectacularly from 1.65 billion to 6.06 billion during the past century. However, annual rock phosphate production increased from 3.2 million to 132 million metric tons (a factor of 42), and nitrogen production increased from 340 thousand to 86 million tons of nitrogen per year – a whopping 252 times![30] The latter is valuable not only as fertilizer but also for producing high explosives, the energy of which can be used to mine rock and alter the landscape, or to destroy human accomplishments through warfare. Much of humanity's growing prosperity, power, and destructiveness as a species in recent times can be credited to our expanding capacity to produce nitrogen and phosphorus compounds. This book demonstrates that these practices came into being in direct response to the opening of huge new natural supplies of these substances in the Pacific World during the nineteenth and early twentieth centuries.

Human intervention in the cycling of nitrogen and phosphorus represents one of the central manifestations of human domination of the earth's ecosystems in recent times. In the soil, excess nitrogen fertilizer feeds denitrifying bacteria, which produce huge quantities of gaseous nitrous oxide (N_2O) – the

[27] Ross Hassig, *Trade, Tribute, and Transportation: The Sixteenth-Century Political Economy of the Valley of Mexico* (Norman, OK, 1985), 47–53; Alfredo López Austin, *Una vieja historia de la mierda* (Mexico City, 1988).
[28] Marks, *Tigers, Rice, Silk, and Silt*, 66–83, 282–88.
[29] Boserup, *The Conditions of Agricultural Growth*; Fitzgerald, *Every Farm a Factory*; Fischer-Kowalski and Haberl, eds., *Socioecological Transitions*.
[30] Smil, *Enriching the Earth*, app. F, L; "Phosphate Rock Statistics," U.S. Geological Survey Data Series 140, http://minerals.usgs.gov/ds/2005/140/phosphate.pdf.

third most important human contributor to global warming. Atmospheric NO_x is also responsible for ozone-depletion, acid rain, and photochemical smog, and the intake of nitrates is known to cause cancer. Phosphate, to a far greater extent than nitrogen, is responsible for fertilizing the growth of algae in the world's lakes, rivers, and estuaries. This process, known as eutrophication, can radically alter the availability of oxygen, penetration of sunlight, and diversity of life in affected waters. Among environmentalists, phosphate detergents have received an inordinate share of the blame for this phenomenon, considering that runoff from farms and our own excretion dwarfs the amount of phosphate pollution from detergents. On the bright side, we can dramatically decrease these ill effects and radically increase the efficiency of input-intensive farming by more carefully managing our wasteful use of fertilizers.[31] We will probably have to because much of the world's easily accessible, high-grade phosphate has already been exhausted. Global phosphate production peaked in 1988 at 166 million tons – a fact that has led some commentators to worry that we have already passed "peak phosphorus" and begun to live in a world of increasing nutrient scarcity. Someday soon, excrement may again be equated with silver.[32]

How did excrement change from an object of veneration in some quarters into something to be thrown away? How did nitrogen and phosphate fertilizers change from treasured commodities into something used so wastefully that they are fundamentally changing the environment of the entire earth? How did humans become cognizant of these spectacular ecological changes and the dangers they pose? The answer to these three questions hinges on the place that guano came to occupy in the modern world.

Overview

This global history explores the ecological, geopolitical, and cultural significance of guano, guano islands, and guano-producing birds since 1800, and guano's ensuing influence on the commodification of nitrates, phosphates, coconuts, and fishmeal. It is an ecological history in the sense that it examines the relationships among humans, other organisms, and the physical environment and explicitly applies theoretical insights from ecology, climatology, and other environmental sciences. Natural phenomena as vast as El Niño, as small as plankton, and as humble as excrement play significant roles in this account. It is a geopolitical history in that it focuses on the power and authority that individuals, classes, states, and empires have exercised over

[31] Galloway and Cowling, "Reactive Nitrogen and the World"; Ma et al., "Nitrogen Flows and Nitrogen Use Efficiency."

[32] Natasha Gilbert, "The Disappearing Nutrient," *Nature* 8 Oct. 2009: 716–18; Patrick Déry and Bart Anderson, "Peak Phosphorus," *Energy Bulletin* (13 Aug. 2007), http://www.energybulletin.net/node/33164.

the land, oceans, and resources they possess. Indigenous peoples, scientific experts, entrepreneurs, corporations, and nation-states are the main agents that compete for power and influence in this story. These may be as large and influential as the United States, Japan, and Australia or as seemingly inconsequential as Nauru, Niue, and Kiribati.[33] It is a cultural history in the sense that the perceived meanings of ecological change, geopolitical conflict, and guano to various actors form a critical part of the story. Above all, this history seeks to answer how several dozen tiny specks of land stretching across the equatorial belt of the world's largest ocean inspired such deep interest and far-reaching struggle.

This book has a seven-fold argument. Its first argument explores the geographical parameters of the Pacific World. The Pacific Ocean is the world's most important topographical feature. It covers a third of the earth's surface, an area so vast that all the world's land could fit within its boundaries. It contains a quarter of the world's water, with a capacity to absorb heat so large that modest alterations in sea surface temperature can drive weather anomalies on the other side of the planet. These facts are widely known, even to a generation infamous for its geographical ignorance.[34] Nevertheless, we tend to think of this world as a "Sea of Islands." In some respects, the tens of thousands of islands that dot this expanse each exists as a world apart. Many create their own weather. Some of the creatures that evolved on them are so odd that they inspired Charles Darwin to discard his belief in the fixity of species. Much the same can be said for the waters that surround them. A single coral reef in the Solomon Islands may possess greater biodiversity than the Caribbean Sea. Isolation has also influenced the indigenous societies that populate them, and it has left an indelible mark on the way outsiders tend to view them. Pacific Islanders still have a reputation for living a few steps closer to the Dreamtime and to Paradise – or for rapidly destroying the tranquility of these fragile environments.[35]

The Pacific World is equally defined by the continents that surround it, and by the travelers that have long traversed it.[36] This book will demonstrate the centrality of this vast region to the modern history of Australia, Japan, and the Americas. Latin America usually escapes mention in works of Pacific history, even though twelve of its twenty continental states have touched on

---

33 Pronounced NEE-oo-way and kee-REE-bas.
34 National Geographic Education Foundation and RoperASW, 2002 *Global Geographic Literacy Survey* (Washington, DC, Nov. 2002); National Geographic Education Foundation and Roper Public Affairs, *Final Report: 2006 Geographic Literacy Study* (Washington, DC, May 2006).
35 Matt Matsuda, "The Pacific," *American Historical Review* 111 (2006): 758–80; *Wild Pacific*, DVD (BBC Earth, 2009).
36 Martin Lewis and Kären Wigen, "A Maritime Response to the Crisis in Area Studies," *Geographical Review* 89 (1999): 161–68; Jerry Bentley, "Sea and Ocean Basins as Frameworks of Historical Analysis," in ibid., 215–24.

the Pacific Ocean for at least part of their history. The Pacific is also glaringly absent from Latin American area studies. Yet for some Latin American societies, this relation is ancient and profound. So-called Andean civilization had its origin on the Pacific coast 6,000 years ago, and its traditional cosmology continues to teach that the dwelling of the ancestors can be reached on the Pacific's far shore.[37] The presence of Polynesian watercraft, fishing gear, and borrow words among the California Chumash, and the spectacular diversification of a Mesoamerican domesticate, the sweet potato (*Ipomoea batatas*), among Pacific Islanders provide the clearest indications of the ancient impact of transoceanic voyagers moving in both directions, while the presence of seaweed and butchered cormorant remains at the Western Hemisphere's oldest confirmed settlements suggests that the ocean has provided a highway and home for human colonists from the Pacific World's earliest beginnings.[38] Migratory birds were the greatest of these travelers, and they provided reliable guides to new lands and fishing grounds across enormous distances. Many controversial ideas of this sort turn into revelations once we tear off the blinders bestowed on us by terracentric perspectives on world history.

The second argument explains how the modern Pacific World first came into being. Northerners' quest for whales and other marine resources played a decisive role in opening vast stretches of this oceanic realm to exploitation by outsiders after 1800. The independence of Latin America helped clear the way for these endeavors. However, it was the ensuing search for guano, then nitrates, phosphate, and workers to exploit them, that drove the creation of terrestrial empires incorporating some of the remotest parts of the Pacific Basin. The largest international war of the nineteenth century in this region was fought over possession of these deposits. This imperial expansion, moreover, often depended on the expropriation of land, labor, resources, and environmental knowledge belonging to peoples indigenous to the Pacific. In the process, routine, round-trip voyages of exchange supplanted the down-the-line networks that had given unity to the Pacific World

---

[37] Moseley, *Maritime Foundations*; Mann, "Oldest Civilization"; Sandweiss et al., "Environmental Change"; Gary Urton, *At the Crossroads of the Earth and the Sky: An Andean Cosmology* (Austin, TX, 1981), 38; Tristan Platt, "The Sound of Light: Emergent Communication through Quechua Shamanic Dialogue," in *Creating Context in Andean Cultures* (New York, 1997), 212.

[38] Terry Jones, ed. Polynesians in America: Pre-Columbian Contacts with the New World (Lanham, MD, 2011); Dapeng Zhang et al., "AFLP Assessment of Diversity in Sweetpotato from Latin America and the Pacific Region: Its Implications on the Dispersal of the Crop," *Genetic Resources and Crop Evolution* 51 (2004): 115–20; Mark Horrocks and Marshall Wisler, "Analysis of Plant Microfossils in Archaeological Deposits from Two Remote Archipelagos: The Marshall Islands, Eastern Micronesia, and the Pitcairn Group, Southeast Polynesia," *Pacific Science* 60 (2006): 261–80; Tom Dillehay et al. "Monte Verde: Seaweed, Food, Medicine, and the Peopling of South America," *Science* 320 (2008): 784–86; Jon Erlandson et al. "Paleoindian Seafaring, Maritime Technologies, and Coastal Foraging on California's Channel Islands," *Science* 331 (2011): 1181–85.

in earlier centuries, which magnified ecological and social inequalities that resulted from the opening of this region. During the twentieth century, aviation, the search for marine fish, and nuclear arms gave new geopolitical value to the region's guano islands.

The book's third argument highlights the agency of nature in the creation of the Pacific World. This four-dimensional process involved phenomena high up in the atmosphere and deep within the ocean and soil. This history cannot be understood without considering the habits of marine birds, the fish that they eat, and other associated organisms. The occurrence of El Niño and La Niña events and tropical cyclones profoundly influenced the timing and outcomes of imperial expansion in the region. Conquerors' alliance with winds, microbes, and other portmanteau biota sometimes aided and sometimes opposed these colonizing efforts, but did not rigidly determine their long-term outcomes.[39]

The fourth argument links the Pacific World to the Industrial Revolution. Experimentation with guano and related substances established the ecological basis for input-intensive agriculture in many parts of the earth. These innovations were an important prerequisite for the spectacular growth of human populations and industrial economies during the late-nineteenth and twentieth centuries, and they utterly transformed modern society's relationship with nitrogen and phosphorus. The sheer scale of these endeavors was significant, but their main importance stemmed from their ability to eliminate bottlenecks that limited production. This was especially true of the chemical industry, which used nitrates as a catalyst for the production of sulfuric acid, which was used in a host of other processes. From this perspective, the opening of the Pacific World had a historical impact comparable to the opening of the Carboniferous and its wealth of fossil energy.

The conquest of the Pacific's guano islands and nitrate deposits also contributed to industrialization in other ways. The mining of nutrients benefited not only the industrial North but also the postcolonial nations of Australia, New Zealand, and Peru. In fact, these three countries would never have attained the levels of productivity and prosperity that they did without making concerted efforts to maximize their use of phosphate, guano, and fish from the tropical Pacific. Australia and New Zealand would never have been able to maintain their superficial appearance as neo-Europes without exploiting their own overseas empires. Meanwhile, guano islands and Pacific indigenes played a small role in helping the industrialized world to clean up its act by producing coconut oil, the key ingredient of several leading brands of soap. It took decades, however, for benefits of this cleanliness industry to trickle down to the Pacific. These developmental efforts culminated after World War II in the Green and Blue Revolutions, which sought to feed the world's burgeoning population through the deployment of new technologies

[39] Crosby, *Ecological Imperialism*; Garden, *Droughts, Floods, and Cyclones*.

and the industrial production of crops, fertilizer, fish, and meat. Peru's efforts to become an industrial power ran aground because it overdeveloped its capacity to exploit the sea – mainly to serve the industrial North's appetites.

The fifth argument examines the cultural influence of these transformations. Guano became a cultural icon in a manner similar to tobacco, coffee, and bananas. Intellectual engagement with this uniquely powerful fertilizer, the birds that produce it, and the highly variable environments that surround the guano islands played a profound role in the development of modern ecological consciousness. The discovery of the El Niño-Southern Oscillation (ENSO) and repeated revival of Malthusian ideas on overpopulation owes much to the guano islands of the Pacific. Two key environmental thinkers, Aldo Leopold and William Vogt, have profound connections to the guano islands and wild birds of Latin America. Once again, modern environmental thought has important roots on tropical islands.[40]

The book's sixth argument identifies the social group that orchestrated much of these proceedings. Beginning with Prussian naturalist Alexander von Humboldt's visit to the coast of Peru in 1802, the history of guano and the Pacific World has been intimately tied to the rise of professional scientists, engineers, physicians, economists, and other experts to positions of political authority. This is one of the hallmarks of modern governance, and it represents one of the most significant engagements between science, technology, and society. As time passed, experts gradually usurped much of the authority over the Pacific's marine resources once possessed by entrepreneurs, politicos, and traditional guano lords. However, they eventually overreached the bounds of prudent authority and must bear a heavy measure of responsibility for the downfall of the world's largest fishing industry, for turning the Pacific's largest bird island into a laboratory for nuclear testing, and for the demise of "the greatest of all industries based upon the conservation of wild animals" the world has ever seen.[41]

The seventh argument evaluates the ethical ramifications of these actions. Humanity's modern relationship with guano has often been driven by a laudable moral quality: the desire to accomplish environmental improvement. This imperative sometimes accomplished wonderful things: the restoration of degraded soils; the construction of clean, livable cities; even the protection of the guano birds. The history of guano has sometimes been associated with some remarkable stories of successful environmental management, and there is much we can learn from these. Yet the fact that environmental degradation and social exploitation so often resulted anyway – despite the best of intensions – provides potent testimony of the exploitative nature of modern

---

[40] Grove, *Green Imperialism*.
[41] Robert Cushman Murphy, "Inter-American Conservation," *Bird-Lore* May–June 1940: 226.

civilization's imperial relationship to the ocean and the earth. It is difficult to argue that these efforts were really worth all the trouble they caused.

Each chapter possesses its own set of themes and arguments. Chapter 2 establishes the importance of marine bird excrement, mineral nitrates, and the opening of the Pacific World during a period Peruvians know as the "guano age." It begins with Humboldt's first, sneeze-inducing encounter with Peruvian guano then follows the history of international experimentation with this curious substance from the laboratories of Napoleonic Europe to the degraded soils of the remote Atlantic outpost of St. Helena. The Pacific whaling industry, Humboldt's handpicked disciples, and the experimentalism of northern farmers all played significant roles in the opening of the guano and nitrate trades. This chapter hinges on the argument that Peruvian guano and nitrates – the two richest natural sources of nitrogen compounds ever discovered – mainly fed the industrial North's appetite for plantation crops, meat, sulfuric acid, high explosives, and imperial power during an era notorious for famines. A global economic depression, Chile's own imperial pretensions, and the worst El Niño event of the nineteenth century together sparked the War of the Pacific (1879–84). This was the first major international conflict of the industrial age fought almost entirely over a coveted natural resource, and it brought an abrupt end to Peru's participation in the guano age.

Chapters 3 and 4 focus on a phenomenon I call neo-ecological imperialism. Alfred Crosby's path-breaking work identified some important characteristics of the initial, conquest stage of ecological imperialism. However, it has difficulty explaining how settled regions of Australia, New Zealand, Chile, and the United States consolidated and sustained their prosperity and status as neo-Europes after exhausting the windfall of frontier colonialism. This typically required a second stage of ecological imperialism involving the massive importation of soil nutrients and other natural resources from overseas empires in the Pacific Basin. Chile, in contrast, used its sea power to conquer its neighbors and then export nitrates on a massive scale. Chapter 3 examines two case studies. The first examines the extension of ecological empires in the Pacific Basin by Peru, Ecuador, Chile, and the United States. The rulers of these new, postcolonial nation-states all viewed overseas colonialism as a means to assert their power in the world. In the process, they brought older, conquest forms of ecological imperialism to a host of new territories – with devastating consequences for the guano bird–worshipping First People of Easter Island. The second case follows John Arundel and other Anglo adventurers with close ties to Australia and New Zealand who rushed to exploit bird islands in the Central Pacific after the United States' partial withdrawal from the region during its Civil War. They came, at first, to exploit guano and other wild commodities but eventually switched over to copra, the raw material used to produce coconut oil. In this instance, the history of Pacific guano islands intersected with the environmental movement against dirt, microbes, and human excrement, and even funded the Garden City movement. Chapter 4 explores the pre- and early colonial history of Banaba (Ocean Island), an isolated equatorial atoll that, like its neighbor Nauru to the west, happened to be blessed with some of the world's largest and most accessible concentrations of high-grade phosphate. The indigenous peoples of Easter Island, Banaba, Niue, and other islands all had their own reasons for participating in this new, exploitative ecological regime. Serving as contract laborers provided a risky, but valuable means for Pacific Islanders to extend their resource base beyond local limitations. In many cases, this enabled them to ensure their intergenerational survival, but at the cost of becoming vulnerable to invasive organisms and subjugated to parasitic forms of colonial trade and governance.

Chapter 5 examines the transformation of environmental governance at the turn of the twentieth century in comparative perspective. The enormous costs of uncontrolled environmental exploitation during the guano age inspired a reaction around the globe in which governments empowered a new class of trained professionals to manage key natural resources on a more sustainable basis. This chapter centers on the reappropriation of Peru's supply of guano and coastal irrigation water for local use in accord with the technocratic ideal. Scientists and engineers, both foreign and local, orchestrated these efforts in close alliance with the capitalists and agroexporters that dominated Peru's Aristocratic Republic (1895–1919) and the eleven-year dictatorship of Augusto Leguía (1919–30). They pushed forward the idea that Peruvian business, consumers, and guano birds required government help and expert supervision to survive the predatory tendencies of global capitalism and the international crisis of World War I.

The focus on Peru carries over to Chapter 6, which explores the new ecological and sociopolitical relationships that developed from these technocratic efforts. Beginning in 1909, a new kind of company, the Compañía Administradora del Guano (CAG), gradually consolidated its control over an agroecological system linking the enormous productivity of Peru's marine environment to the export of irrigated crops from the adjacent coast. Scientific conservation achieved one of its greatest triumphs as a global movement shepherding three species of guano-producing birds native to the Peruvian coast. CAG's managers used the latest scientific understanding not only to manipulate the wide variety of organisms affecting the welfare of the guano birds but also to manage the behavior of human beings who extracted and used guano. This chapter employs an agroecological perspective on history to show how input-intensive agriculture became conventional practice in coastal Peru but also identifies basic limitations that El Niño, the Great Depression, and populist politics posed toward technocratic aspirations.

Chapter 7 returns to the subject of Pacific geopolitics. It roots the international revival of Malthusian concerns regarding population growth, the food supply, and differential standards of living in the period linking the

First and Second World Wars. Some of the same historical currents that drove Peru's revival of the guano industry inspired these concerns, but they centered on the rise of densely populated Japan as a Great Power within the Pacific World. Malthusian ideas helped a small cadre of experts on human population dynamics to assert unprecedented influence over state-sponsored population movements during this era: from the exclusion of Asian immigrants from California, to the Japanese occupation of Manchuria, to the colonization of uninhabited guano islands by Gilbert Islanders, to the resettlement of the entire indigenous population of Banaba to a hurricane-prone island in the Fiji archipelago. The ideas and actions of these ethnocrats must bear substantial blame for World War II's battles for *Lebensraum* and genocidal atrocities, and they provide essential background for understanding why the worldwide environmental movement of the late twentieth century became so preoccupied with human population growth. Warren Thompson's discovery of the demographic transition even inspired the idea of dividing up the earth between First, Second, and Third Worlds.

Chapter 8 explains how Malthusian thinking came to be applied to the problem of environmental degradation, first in Latin America, then to the world as a whole. During the 1930s and 1940s, a host of scientists, engineers, and conservationists migrated north and south within the Western Hemisphere – some as instruments of U.S. geopolitical strategy, others to help Latin American nation-states fulfill developmental goals. Aldo Leopold, William Vogt, and a handful of others also journeyed south to witness the abundance of wild nature that their homelands had lost. This chapter follows Vogt from his employment as an ornithologist in Peru, to his work as a conservation organizer for the Pan American Union, to his publication of *Road to Survival* – the best-selling book on conservation, worldwide, before Rachel Carson's *Silent Spring*. Vogt's outspoken promotion of Malthusian ideas and international influence as a conservation organizer stemmed directly from his experience on Peru's guano islands.

The golden age of developmentalism that followed World War II was neither an "age of ecological innocence," nor a dark age preceding the environmental movement.[42] Ecological thinking drove many of the signature movements of the postwar era – most notably the Green Revolution in agriculture and Blue Revolution in pelagic fishing and aquaculture – as besieged governments struggled to keep up with the demands of their rapidly growing populations and navigate Cold War tensions. Chapter 9 examines the far-reaching influence of Malthusian ideas on development projects in Mexico, Peru, and other Third World countries. Mexico aborted its tentative attempt to establish a guano industry of its own, modeled after Peru, to devote itself to the industrial production of chemical fertilizers and promotion of input-intensive agricultural practices. In these ways, Mexico was a

---

[42] Guha, *Environmentalism*, 63–68.

model country for the Green Revolution. Peru, meanwhile, was *the* model country for the Blue Revolution, at first as a producer of canned fish for the wartime cause, then as the world's largest producer of fishmeal – most of it destined for chicken and hog farms in the industrial North. Following Peru's example, a number of Third World states sought to develop their own industrial fisheries and declared 200-mile territorial seas, ostensibly to provide their own citizens with protein and to prevent the open ocean's overexploitation by outsiders. Pursuing an industrial relationship with the sea presented difficult dilemmas. On the basis of ecological considerations, government technocrats consciously allowed Peru's guano birds to pass into oblivion to exploit their main food fish and to eliminate competition for Peru's floundering chemical industry. As a part of the bargain, fishing executives agreed to empower marine scientists to force the fishing industry to leave fish in the sea each season. However, the industry collapsed anyway during the strong El Niño of 1972 and contributed tangibly to the sense of environmental crisis that pervaded the world during the 1970s. This tragedy occurred not because of lack of state supervision over the ocean environment, as suggested by Garrett Hardin's influential essay "The Tragedy of the Commons," but because Peru's ecocrats possessed overconfidence in their ability to respond to abrupt variations in the ocean's productivity and determine what constitutes a sustainable relationship with the marine environment.

The concluding chapter investigates the collision between the guano age and the atomic age. It focuses on the transformation of Kiritimati (Christmas Island), the largest marine bird colony in the Central Pacific, into a testing ground for thermonuclear weapons. The fate of the Pacific's guano islands, their birds, and the humans who worked them would appear to confirm Rachel Carson's insight that authoritarians, temporarily vested with power to save their own nation and species from nuclear bombs and the population bomb, gratuitously turned too much of the planet into "a sterile world ungraced by the curving wing of a bird in flight." Guano has made us aware of daunting challenges that we face in continuing our species' ability to flourish on earth, but it is not too late to abide by the lessons that excrement can teach.

2

The Guano Age

God's gift Guano spread; the poorest soil / With smiling crops Free-Traders'
aim will spoil. / Well fed, well clothed, well housed, we need not fear, / Should
Praties fail or Cholera appear.
                    – George Burges, *Native Guano* (1848)

On 18 September 1802, under the watchful eyes of several Andean condors,
Alexander von Humboldt (1769–1859) and his traveling companions began
their final descent from the highlands of Peru to the Pacific Ocean. Humboldt
had long dreamed of visiting the South Seas, but his emotional state gradually
changed from joy to disdain as he left behind the sublime heights of the
Andes. He was amazed by the barrenness of these slopes and deepness of
the valleys that cut into them. Great torrents of water had obviously flowed
through these dry canyons, perhaps he noted in his journal, "at a time when
the abundance of water was much greater around the globe." Humboldt was
particularly interested in what appeared to be newer valleys. They were too
remote from the highlands to have been caused by seasonal runoff. Perhaps a
massive earthquake had thrown great quantities of dust into the atmosphere
and caused an enormous rainstorm? Humboldt never discussed this subject
with local scientists, however, and was therefore oblivious to the fact that
recurrent El Niño floods had created this deeply eroded landscape.

Suddenly, in the midst of the desert, Humboldt and company came upon
a massive wall defending the coast from ancient highland invaders, and
below that the "sad remains" of canals and aqueducts. It gradually dawned
on Humboldt that he might have seen something analogous to this situation in the coastal highlands of Venezuela, two years before. According
to Venezuelan locals, the level of Lake Valencia had fallen dramatically
in recent decades. In line with desiccationist ideas of the day, Humboldt
reasoned that systematic deforestation and the construction of irrigation
systems for colonial export agriculture had opened the soil to the sun and

eliminated local sources of humidity in Lake Valencia's enclosed, island-like lake basin. This caused local springs and streams to dry up – except during occasional cloudbursts that briefly turned local streams into erosive torrents. Humboldt applied these insights to Peru's coastal desert and concluded that its desolation had taken place during the recent epoch of man – and that Incan and European colonialists were to blame. "A bad government destroys everything," he recorded in his journal. "Away from their own lands, Europeans are as barbarous as Turks, or more, since they are more fanatical." From that day forward, the desert coast of Peru became the ultimate degraded landscape to Humboldt.[1]

On 26 September 1804, near the indigenous village of Huaman ("bird of prey"), Humboldt finally made it to the seashore. Unbeknownst to him, in the days of Don Pedro Guaneque, indios from this small town had sailed each year to collect guano from nearby Guañape Island to fertilize their own crops, to barter for other goods, and to pay tribute.[2] Humboldt carefully measured the barometric pressure at sea level – an act crucial for calculating the altitudes of the sites he had recently visited. He also measured the air and sea-surface temperature and was impressed by the coolness of the ocean at this latitude. Humboldt later speculated (incorrectly) that the coldness of Peru's coastal waters originated in Antarctica and was analogous to the warming effect of the Gulf Stream on the North Atlantic. For this reason, the cool, northward current along the Pacific Coast of South America is often referred to as the Humboldt Current.[3]

Humboldt soon turned his attention away from the sea to the labyrinthine ruins and mud-brick pyramids of the city of Chan Chan, the ancient capital of the Chimor empire. He even arranged to meet Chayhuac ("Lord of Fish"), the latest of a long line of indigenous nobles descended from the last Chimu king. The Inca conquered the Chimu at the end of the fifteenth century, followed soon after by the Spanish in the 1530s. Like generations of his lineage before him, Chayhuac used gold and silver looted from the tombs of his ancient ancestors to pay his kin's tribute to the Spanish.[4] For Humboldt, this provided yet another sign that abusive, colonial governance was responsible for the degradation of the Peruvian coast and the decay of its indigenous civilization. He wondered how green the coast must have been before the invading Inca, then the Spanish, disrupted the Chimu's aqueduct networks and cut off the thick, silt-laden water that once fertilized the

[1] Humboldt, "Diario de viaje," (1802) in *Humboldt en el Perú*, ed. Núñez and Petersen, 71–73; Humboldt, *Viaje a las regiones equinocciales* (1816–31; Caracas, 1991), 3:96–112; Cushman, "Humboldtian Science."

[2] Rostworowski, "Islas del litoral," 82.

[3] Federico Schwab, "Memoria sobre la corriente fría del mar en el litoral peruano," in *Humboldt en el Perú*," 223–38.

[4] Miguel Feijóo de Sosa, *Relación descriptiva de la ciudad, y provincia del Truxillo* (1763; Lima, 1984), 25, 85.

Peruvian coast "like the mud of the Nile." Otherwise, he was unimpressed by Peru's coastal environment. During the two weeks it took to journey south from Trujillo to Lima, he walked mile after mile along the barren seashore, depressed by the springtime gloom and monotony of sand dunes, granite rocks, and biting wind. There were "innumerable birds" but none of the riotous tropical plant life he had come to expect at these latitudes. Only the occasional sight of a coastal oasis, British whalers at work offshore, and the "picturesque" form of Guañape Island proved capable of waking him from a trancelike state.[5]

By this time, Humboldt had refocused his mind on the celestial realm. He was eager to attend to important business in Lima, the capital of the Viceroyalty of Peru. He had planned his entire five-year journey to the Americas to observe the transit of Mercury across the disk of the sun on 9 November 1802 with the hope of determining the longitudinal position of this "City of Kings" more precisely than ever before. He stationed his instruments a couple of days early on the tower of the great fort of Callao, the foremost symbol of Spanish imperial prowess in South America, right next to the Pacific. While waiting for this celestial event, Humboldt passed the time by recording the arrival of low and high tides, measuring the altitude of nearby islands, and even took the time to sketch a dead female fur seal (*Arctocephalus australis*) brought to the docks of Callao.[6]

One phenomenon impressed itself on Humboldt's senses more powerfully than any other during his time on the Peruvian coast. While prowling the docks of Callao, he could not help but notice several barges filled with a yellowish-brown substance known among locals by the Quechua word *wanu*. It smelled so powerfully of ammonia that he erupted in fits of sneezing whenever he got close. He had first seen piles of this manure north of Lima ready to be laid on coastal agricultural fields. From conversations with locals, Humboldt found out that as many as 100 barges, mostly piloted by sailors from the port of Chancay, sailed regularly to the Chincha Islands where they were filled with guano mined from deposits thought to be at least fifteen meters thick. Indigenous informants swore that these great mounds had been laid down by enormous colonies of marine birds, but Peruvian-born Creoles and previous scientific travelers thought that birds were incapable of producing such prodigious quantities. Everyone agreed, however, that guano was an extremely powerful fertilizer and supported a lucrative coastal trade. Humboldt possessed enormous skill as a scientist but was a poor ornithologist. After passing Huaura Island on Christmas Day, 1802, during the first leg of his long voyage home, he speculated that herons, flamingos,

5 Humboldt, "Diario de viaje," 74–81.
6 Humboldt to Johann Jakob von Tschudi, ca. 1844, Humboldt Forschungsstelle, Berlin-Brandenburgische Akademie der Wissenschaften; Humboldt, "Diario de viaje," 84; Schwab, "Memoria sobre la corriente fría," 225–26.

and cormorants he had seen congregated around salt marshes on his way down the coast must be responsible for the "thin white crust" of fresh guano he observed capping this island from afar. This led Humboldt to "completely doubt" indigenous opinion as to the avian origin of these deposits and to conjecture that they might have formed as a result of some primordial catastrophe, similar to the coal beds of Europe. Humboldt also thought he now understood the secret to the former glory of Peru's coastal indigenous civilizations: they had used massive quantities of guano to make this desert landscape bloom.[7]

Humboldt returned to France in August 1804 after five years traveling in the New World. He wasted no time arranging for Europe's foremost chemists to analyze the samples of guano he brought back from Callao. This became an immediate and lasting source of his scientific prestige. Following the old rules of scientific patronage, Humboldt favored those who had played an important role in mentoring him when divvying out specimens for analysis. He gave first access to his close friend, analytical chemist Louis Nicolas Vauquelin. On 26 November 1804, Vauquelin and Antoine François Fourcroy presented their results before the leading scientific institution of Napoleonic France. Their analysis concluded that uric acid made up a quarter of guano's contents – an extraordinarily high concentration of this nitrogen-rich compound for an old organic substance. Humboldt followed this up with a report in which he credited Peru's indigenous peoples for guano's discovery and posited that Peru's guano reserves had formed over eons of geological time. The latter supposition prevented generations from recognizing that vast quantities of guano can be produced on a sustainable basis each year from Peru's living population of marine birds. Prussia's leading analytical chemist, Martin Heinrich Klaproth, published an extended report of his own analysis of guano's contents in his widely read mineralogy series.[8]

These acts certified the discovery of guano by Western science and marked the beginning of the world's guano age (1802–84). As we have already seen, guano was not unknown within European intellectual circles. A long list of writers had praised its merits as a fertilizer but always treated it as a local curiosity.[9] These experiments changed everything. Did other deposits

---

[7] Humboldt, "El guano," (1806) in *Humboldt en el Perú*, 170–72; Núñez and Petersen, *Humboldt en el Perú*, 22, 25; Tschudi, *Travels in Peru* (New York, 1854), 156.

[8] Fourcroy and Vauquelin, "Guano, ou sur l'engrais naturel del îlots de la mer du Sud," *Memoires de l'Institut des Sciences, Lettres et Arts: Sciences Mathématiques et Physiques* 6 (1806): 369–85; Institut de France, Académie des Sciences, *Procès Verbaux des Séances de L'Academie* (Paris, 1804–07), 3:159; Klaproth, "Chemische Untersuchung des Guano aus den Inseln der Peruanischen Küste," in *Beitrage zur chemischen Kenntnis der Mineralkörper* (Berlin, 1807), 4:299–313; Wolfgang-Hagen Hein, *Alexander von Humboldt: Life and Work* (Ingelheim am Rhein, 1987), 155–59, 164–65.

[9] For example, Jorge Juan and Antonio de Ulloa, *Voyage to South America* (London, 1772), 2:99–100.

exist elsewhere? If guano could make Peru's coastal desert bloom, could it reverse the exhaustion of soils in other regions? Did any of its chemical constituents contain the secret of soil fertility? These questions captured the fascination of laboratory chemists, experimental farmers, globe-trotting explorers – even an occasional poet. They saw in guano the possibility of discovering enormous, untapped sources of wealth and power in the unexplored recesses of the planet. In their quest to understand this curious substance, they not only discovered the indispensable role that nitrogen plays in biological systems but also profoundly changed our understanding of the relationships that connect ecological producers, consumers, and recyclers.

The application of scientific discoveries requires concerted human effort and favorable circumstances, all of which operate within ecological limitations. Handpicked disciples of Humboldt with an interest in promoting his accomplishments played a significant role in stimulating the international guano trade. However, they were far more successful at implanting the technocratic ideal in Latin America: the belief that experts should govern society and our relationship with the natural world. The guano trade finally took off in the 1840s as an extension of the vast hunting industry that was emptying the world's oceans of whales and fur-bearing mammals. This trade also benefited greatly from preexisting interest in manures and soil fertility among improving farmers. Peruvian guano proved so powerful and profitable as a fertilizer that it inspired a global rush to locate other similar resources and substitutes – including the vast nitrate deposits of southern Peru. These concentrated fertilizers from the far ends of the earth played a critical role in popularizing input-intensive agricultural practices, and in synergy with coal and increased use of animal power, in replacing the ecological old regime that constrained humanity's domination of the earth with the consumption-oriented regime of the industrial age.

The international guano trade has long been viewed as an exemplar of the "fictitious prosperity" that sprouts up around enclave economies, only to melt away when boom turns to bust, while Humboldt's discovery has been portrayed as an archetype of the expropriation of indigenous knowledge of the natural world for the benefit of outsiders.[10] The founding fathers of postcolonial Peru did not see things this way, however. To them, this incredible geographic advantage provided a means to engineer a modern nation. Peru's rulers only belatedly recognized the problems associated with relying on a nonrenewable resource for their prosperity, but they made far greater mistakes in overestimating the stability of the global capitalist system and Pacific climate and underestimating the greed of jealous outsiders.

---

[10] Mary Louise Pratt, *Imperial Eyes: Travel Writing and Transculturation* (London and New York, 1992), 135–36; Jonathan Levin, *The Export Economies: Their Pattern of Development in Historical Perspective* (Cambridge, MA, 1960), pt. 1; Bonilla, *Guano y burguesía*.

In Humboldt's Footsteps

In 1805, English chemist Humphry Davy (1778–1829) also gained access to a sample of guano, even though he was outside Humboldt's social circle. While Humboldt had been away in South America, Davy achieved international fame for his experiments with nitrous oxide (N_2O), also known as laughing gas. He shared Humboldt's Romantic affinity for nature and passion to uncover its occult powers – desires that led him and his companion Samuel Taylor Coleridge to toy with the idea of establishing a laboratory together to explore the mind-expanding possibilities of chemistry, then to consider running away to live as poets in England's Lake District. Instead, at the behest of England's Board for the Encouragement of Agriculture and Internal Improvement, Davy redirected his chemical talents toward the practical study of manures and increasing the bounty of the land.[11]

The great improving landlords who backed the Board of Agriculture had ideological reasons for seeking Davy's expertise. They hoped to respond to the challenges laid out by Thomas Robert Malthus's incendiary *Essay on the Principle of Population* (1798). Malthus intended to upset the cornucopian dreams of the Enlightenment and the age of revolution. In his view, humanity's enormous fertility and innate laziness meant a "perpetual tendency in the race of man to increase beyond the means of subsistence." As a consequence, hunger for food and land, self-destructive vice, infanticide, war, pestilence, natural disaster, and famine guaranteed misery and premature death for the majority of humankind. In this first edition, Malthus actually expressed a measure of ecological consciousness and social conscience: "Where is the fresh land to turn up? Where is the dressing to improve that which is in cultivation?" And he blamed "increased demand for butcher's meat of the best quality" and the keeping of horses for pleasure among the upper classes for diminishing "the quantity of human subsistence in the country, in proportion to the general fertility of the land."[12] As we shall see in later chapters, no work in the history of modern thought has done more to influence discussion of overpopulation and nature's limitations.[13] Inspired by Malthus, historians today refer to a "biological old regime" that governed human numbers during early modern times.

For Davy, nitrogenous manures seemed to provide an answer to these problems. In a celebrated series of public lectures, he reported on his experiments into the chemical basis of agriculture. These presentations were aimed

---

[11] David Knight, *Humphry Davy: Science and Power* (Oxford, 1992), 28–39, 47–49; Molly Lefebure, "Humphry Davy: Philosophic Alchemist," in *The Coleridge Companion* (Humanities-Ebooks, 2007).

[12] Malthus, *Essay on the Principle of Population* (London, 1798), 9, 35, 44, 59, 99–100, 108, 111–12.

[13] Glacken, *Traces on the Rhodian Shore*, 632–49; Worster, *Nature's Economy*, 149–59.

at the growing class of gentlemen farmers "who have endeavored to improve agriculture, and to apply scientific principles to this most important of arts." They popularized the notion that farmers could treat the soil itself as a laboratory. Davy gave particular attention to the "noxious" constituents of manure and produced a chemical explanation for what farmers' noses had been telling them for years: that manures with high contents of ammonia make excellent fertilizers. By this criterion, Peruvian guano merited special notice. Its high concentrations of ammonia-rich uric acid, as well as phosphoric acid, lime, potassium salts, and other constituents, all pointed to "its fertilizing properties," as did its reputation for enabling "the sterile plains of Peru" to bear fruit. Davy had no clear idea what role ammonia played in plant nutrition, although he speculated that putrefaction of the soil must somehow be involved. To Davy, these realizations provided an antidote to the Malthusian vice of laziness: it was as if the Creator had placed "the modification of the soil, and the application of manures... within the power of man, as if for the purpose of awakening his industry, and of calling forth his powers."[14]

In 1813, Davy collected these lectures into a book. It was an immediate best-seller and was quickly translated into other European languages and republished in a variety of contexts. Ferenc Pethe translated the text into Hungarian. He belonged to a group of progressive aristocrats who looked to England and science for leadership in their quest to turn their seigneurial domains into major exporters of grain and improved livestock. To this end, his patron György Festetics established the Georgikon Faculty of Agriculture in 1797, Europe's first advanced school for agricultural studies. Félix Varela translated Davy's book into Spanish for the first time in 1826 in New York City. He was a Cuban priest and philosopher whose advocacy for the autonomy of his homeland from Spanish rule eventually forced him to live out his life in the United States, where Davy's works were popular. By these routes, knowledge of Peruvian guano spread quickly to many parts of the world, often in loose association with other liberal causes.[15]

Unfortunately, the guano samples Humboldt brought back were far too small for field trials. Davy analyzed some fresh cormorant dung collected near his parents' home in Cornwall in the hope of finding a substitute, but British marine guanos, leached by rainfall and high humidity, proved

[14] Davy, *Elements of Agricultural Chemistry: In a Course of Lectures for the Board of Agriculture Delivered between 1802 and 1812* (London, 1839), v, 16, 279–80.
[15] Other early editions appeared in London (1813), Paris (1813), Berlin (1814), Milan (1814), and New York and Philadelphia (1815). Davy, *A' Földmivelési Kímia gyökere Egymásból Letzkékben*, trans. Pethe (Vienna, 1815); Davy, *Elementos de quimica, applicada a la agricultura*, trans. Varela (New York, 1826); Margaret Rossiter, *The Emergence of Agricultural Science: Justus Liebig and the Americans, 1840–1880* (New Haven, 1975), 11–19; Cohen, *Notes from the Ground*, ch. 3.

disappointing as fertilizers. The first successful field trials with guano outside South America took place at a remote locale that nonetheless provided a spectacular stage for demonstrating its agricultural potential. In
July 1808, Scottish military engineer Alexander Beatson (1759–1830) took
command as governor of St. Helena for the East India Company. This
isolated volcanic island on the mid–Atlantic Ridge had a reputation for
being one of the most degraded environments in the world. Like other
"Fortunate Isles" used by European colonizers as stepping stones across
the Atlantic, invasive biota had wrecked havoc on St. Helena's unique tree
fern, gumwood, and ebony woodlands and decimated its endemic fauna –
including three now-extinct species of marine birds. Loss of tree cover had
destroyed much of the island's mist-catching potential and made it far more
vulnerable to extended droughts like those of the El Niño–plagued 1720s
and 1790s. These disasters, in turn, had inspired repeated campaigns by
colonists to reverse the island's environmental deterioration.[16] After serving
in British military campaigns in India and Mauritius, Beatson had spent
several years in recuperative retirement as a gentleman farmer in Sussex
and become an avid participant in the British movement for agricultural
improvement. From the moment of his arrival on St. Helena, he set out to
prove that this isolated colony could be disciplined to "the English practice of
husbandry."[17]

   Beatson's appointment presented a timely opportunity to another of the
era's great organizers of global scientific research, Joseph Banks. The botan-
ical garden on St. Helena (established in 1787) was central to his budding
plans to transplant tropical plants and cochineal insects between the Americas, East Indies, and the Royal Botanic Garden at Kew. Humboldt had
made a point of emphasizing the latitude at which Peruvian guano could be
found. Banks wondered: What if this strategic locale at the same latitude
also possessed manure of Peru's "infinitely superior" caliber?[18] At Banks's
behest, Beatson sent a local naturalist to collect dung from Egg Island only
four days after his disembarkation. Today, this site hosts colonies of black

---

[16] *A Description of the Island of St. Helena* (London, 1805), ch. 3–4; T. H. Brooke, *A History
of the Island of St. Helena from Its Discovery* (London, 1808), ch. 5–6, 8; H. R. Janisch,
Extracts from the St. Helena Records (St. Helena, 1885): 3 May 1694, 19 May, 19, 31
July 1709, 7 Mar. 1710, 16 Oct. 1716, 21 Mar. 1718, 31 Oct. 1727, 30 Jan. 1730, 17
Jan. 1733; Q. C. B. Cronk, "The Past and Present Vegetation of St. Helena," *Journal of
Biogeography* 16 (1989): 47–64; Beau Rowlands et al., *The Birds of St. Helena*, British
Ornithologists' Union Checklist no. 16 (1998); Grove, *Green Imperialism*, 95–104, 345;
Crosby, *Ecological Imperialism*, ch. 4.

[17] Andrew Grout, "Beatson, Alexander," in *ODNB*; Beatson, *Tracts Relative to the Island of
St. Helena: Written during a Residence of Five Years* (London, 1816), pt. 1, §27.

[18] Banks, quoted in Beatson, *Tracts*, pt. 1, §2, n. 1; Janisch, *Extracts*, 24 Jan. 1814; William
Roxburgh to Banks, 25 Apr. 1795 and 17, 19 June 1813, State Library of New South
Wales, Banks papers; Grove, *Green Imperialism*, 340–45; Drayton, *Nature's Government*,
120.

FIGURE 2.1. Plantation House, St. Helena. This idealized landscape vividly illustrates Alexander Beatson's aesthetic and social goals for this drought-prone colonized realm. Beatson hoped to create a gentrified neo-Europe in the tropics by making use of an array of local and exotic species imported from the four corners of the earth: cattle, ornamental peacocks, grass and fodder crops, as well as "oriental plants and shrubs...intermixed with those of the more northern regions" including bamboo, magnolia, aloe, and fir. Beatson hoped guano from Egg Island would jump-start the conversion of St. Helena into a more productive agrarian environment. *Source:* George Hutchins Bellasis, *Views of St. Helena* (London, 1815); reproduced courtesy of the British Library Board.

and brown noddies (*Annous minutus* and *A. stolidus*), two circumequatorial species of tern. However, in the seventeenth and eighteenth centuries, Egg Island was a major seasonal source of fresh eggs laid by the "egg bird" or sooty tern (*Sterna fuscata*), which East India Company officials had long sought to protect from depletion.[19]

Beatson sent a guano sample back to England for analysis and began experiments on the lawn of Plantation House (fig. 2.1). Thanks to timely rain showers, these experimental plots were soon "covered with the most exuberant grass that can be imagined." In 1809, he initiated systematic comparisons of the effects of Egg Island guano, horse dung, and pig dung applied to plots of mangel wurzel and potatoes planted in the "black stiffish soil" of his upland manor. Guano significantly outperformed these

[19] Rowlands et al., *Birds of St. Helena*; J. C. Meliss, *St. Helena: A Physical, Historical, and Topographical Description* (London, 1875), pt. 3; Janisch, *Extracts*, 8 Oct. 1707, 17 Aug. 1714, 10 Sept. 1716, 10 July 1718.

other manures and unfertilized control plots. These experiments confirmed Beatson's prejudice, acquired during long service in India, that local ignorance of enlightened agricultural techniques – and above all, lack of ambition – were mostly responsible for St. Helena's environmental problems. Beatson submitted these findings to the *St. Helena Register* and Board of Agriculture in London, and later republished them in a widely read book. For years, these experiments were widely cited as evidence of guano's superior fertilizing power, even after he became an advocate for intensive farming without manure. Beatson was actually far more interested in agricultural production than soil and forest conservation, and following his lead, St. Helena colonists more than doubled the amount of land under cultivation during his domineering regime as governor. They were still collecting guano and eggs for local use in the 1840s and briefly engaged in an export trade.[20]

Meanwhile, tectonic shifts in the geopolitical realm prevented anyone from repeating these experiments using the genuine Peruvian article. In 1807, the self-crowned emperor of France, Napoleon Bonaparte, invaded Spain and Portugal. This sparked two decades of global warfare that culminated in the independence of most of Spanish and Portuguese America, as well as to Napoleon's own exile to St. Helena. Humboldt played a significant role in these movements. He helped stir things up by openly criticizing Spanish colonialism in his widely read *Political Essay on the Kingdom of New Spain* (1808–11). He explicitly targeted poor treatment of the soil as a factor legitimating the overthrow of Spanish rule and looked like a prophet when Central Mexico's drought-stricken peasantry joined in the massive Hidalgo Revolt (1810–11).[21] A wealthy Venezuelan and confidant of Humboldt, Simón Bolívar, led the independence struggle in northern South America. In 1820, his second-in-command, Medellín-born botanist Francisco Antonio Zea, hired two young disciples of Humboldt to help organize the mega-state Gran Colombia, which included what became Venezuela, Colombia, and Ecuador. Mariano de Rivero (1798–1857) exemplified the Creole intellectuals who looked to Humboldt and Europe for legitimation as they sought to open their homelands' emporium of natural resources to the world and to build modern nation-states founded on white dominance. He came from one of the leading families of Arequipa, Peru, and spent much of the war

[20] Contra Grove, *Green Imperialism*; Beatson to Banks, 17 May 1811, 18 Sept. 1812, Banks papers; Beatson, *Tracts*, pt. 1, §2, 10, 24, 26–27; Beatson, *A Supplement to a New System of Cultivation without Lime or Dung, or Summer Fallows* (London, 1821); T. E. Eden, *The Search for Nitre and the True Nature of Guano, Being an Account of a Voyage to the South-West Coast of Africa* (London, 1846), 121.

[21] Humboldt, *Political Essay on the Kingdom of New Spain* (London, 1811), 2:405–6, 469, 507–8, 529–30; Nicolaas Rupke, "A Geography of Enlightenment: The Critical Reception of Alexander von Humboldt's Mexico Work," in *Geography and Enlightenment* (Chicago, 1999).

years studying to become a mining engineer at the prestigious École Polytechnique and École des Mines in Paris. He had long aspired to become a technocrat.[22] Jean-Baptiste Boussingault (1802–87) exemplified the European travelers and traders who descended in droves on the liberated territories of Latin America and the North American West in the hope of converting the hemisphere into a scene of industry and efficiency. He was born in a poor, polluted, parchment-making district of Paris, and after completing a degree in mining engineering, he obtained a comfortable administrative post at a mine that was rapidly consuming the forests and landscape of mineral-rich Alsace. Boussingault had already been approached by recruiters seeking mining expertise for Egypt, Chile, and Guatemala but jumped at the opportunity to follow directly in Humboldt's footsteps. Humboldt, for his part, hoped these engineers would establish a lasting center for scientific excellence in the northern Andes where "educated youth" from all over South America would come for training then fan out across the continent to establish regional centers dedicated to opening the continent's unknown interior to scientific understanding, rational exploitation, and technocratic governance. He even fantasized about traveling together with Boussingault to the American tropics or South Seas, "wherever I can be closest to you."[23] These plans reveal the personal and imperial nature of Humboldt's designs for the planet.[24]

Bolívar's world-changing campaign to liberate South America finally ended, symbolically, at the surrender of the great fort of Callao in January 1826. Following an established pattern, he invited Rivero to take charge of Peru's postcolonial reconstruction as the director general of mines and public education. Rivero faced enormous expectations and responsibilities in this position but still made time to answer a number of questions regarding the nature of Peruvian guano. He probably learned about guano for the first time not in Peru but during his attendance at Davy's lectures while studying as a youth in London. In 1826, he and Irish-born scientist Joseph Barclay Pentland made a pilgrimage to the guano islands as part of an expedition to extend the Humboldtian scientific program to Peru's far southern coast and the southern Andes.[25] Rivero did not hesitate to criticize his mentor's

[22] F. Urbani, "Mariano Eduardo de Rivero y Ustáriz," *Boletín histórico de geociencias* (Caracas) 46 (1992): 18–38; Jean-Baptiste Boussingault, *Memorias* (1892; Bogotá, 1985), 1:100–3; Pratt, *Imperial Eyes*, ch. 7; Safford, *Ideal of the Practical*.

[23] Humboldt to Boussingault, 5, 22 Aug. 1822, in Boussingault, *Memorias*, 1:21, 39–42, 69–85, 100–03, 149–51, 164–67, 175–77; Pratt, *Imperial Eyes*, ch. 8; Goetzman, *Exploration and Empire*.

[24] Contra Sachs, *The Humboldt Current*.

[25] Rivero to Humboldt, 21 Apr. 1825, 21 June 1826, in *Mariano Eduardo de Rivero en algunas de sus cartas al Barón Alexander von Humboldt* (Arequipa, 1999), 68–70; Urbani, "Rivero"; William Sarjeant, "An Irish Naturalist in Cuvier's Laboratory," *Bulletin of the British Museum of Natural History, Historical Series* 6 (1979): 245–319.

findings, however. His investigations all pointed to guano's relatively recent animal origin: the chemical constituents of older red and brown guanos proved to be almost identical to fresh white guano. So did the discovery of bird remains and indigenous artifacts deep within deposits and the fact that deposits were only found in places frequented by modern birds. Rivero also recognized that huge quantities of fresh excrement could be harvested after a season of heavy nesting. As a zoologist, Pentland was eager to correct Humboldt's misidentification of Peru's main guano birds after seeing the Pescadores and Hormigas islands "black from the quantity of cormorants" during peak nesting season.[26] Yet another disciple of Humboldt, Swiss naturalist Johann Jakob von Tschudi, mostly confirmed these views during six weeks of exploration around the port of Huacho in 1841, but he self-servingly proclaimed the *piquero* or Peruvian booby (*Sula variegata*) – a bird he is credited with making known to modern science – as the most important guano producer.[27]

In typical Humboldtian fashion, Rivero also tried to quantify the extent of the coastal guano trade. He reported that farmers in the Chancay valley, the largest consumers of guano during this era, applied 1,900 metric tons of guano to their fields in 1828. According to Rivero, ports along the southern coast harvested around 2,000 metric tons a year for trade to farmers living in Arequipa and other upland valleys. Purchases of guano and other fertilizers represented the largest single cost of maize cultivation in this region – a telltale sign of an input-intensive agroecosystem. Peruvian farmers also preferentially consumed fresh guanos known to have the strongest fertilizing qualities and are solely responsible for exhausting the ancient deposits at Iquique. This regional trade continued through the guano age.[28]

Rivero did not express much interest in the social relations that governed guano production. These had become seriously disrupted since the days of Don Pedro Guaneque, thanks to civil wars, depopulation, forced migration, and the abolition of inherited rights to marine resources.[29] For example, in 1797, José Rudecindo Alvarardo, a Muchik Indian from Lambayeque, was expelled from Huacho for trespassing on the legal monopoly of local indigenes to exploit the vast salt marshes of this district. He belonged to a group of Mochica who had been relocated from the north coast by colonial authorities to take up fishing and harvest guano in the area but who

[26] Rivero, *Memorias*, 1:159–71.

[27] Tschudi, *Travels in Peru* 146–48, 156, 167–69; Tschudi, *Untersuchungen über die Fauna peruana* (St. Gallen, Switzerland, 1844–46), 3:312–15.

[28] Rivero, *Memorias*, 1:170–71, 2:224–27; Nicolás de Piérola, "Informe sobre el estado del carguío de guano en las islas de Chincha," (1853) in *BCAG* 4 (1928): 169; Bollaert, "Observations on the Geography of Southern Peru," *Journal of the Royal Geographical Society* 21 (1851): 105.

[29] Rostworowski, "Islas del litoral," 83, 98–101.

instead took advantage of the new, open-access legal regime to hunt guano birds. He and his kin killed up to 6,000 birds a week, which were used to produce a stew called *lagua*, and gathered innumerable eggs, which were consumed directly or used to produce mortar. These actions no doubt had a detrimental impact on the local bird population and infuriated more ancient indigenous lineages from the vicinity. According to seventeenth-century lore, the founding ancestor of the fishing village of Végueta had been turned into the guano island known as Don Martín in retribution for the murder of the woman who gave birth to maize, *yuca* root, and squash. Others were known for paddling out "to the islands for guano, near the headlands of Huaura" where they "worshipped a *huaca* named Huamancantac as lord of guano and made offerings to him so that he would let them take guano."[30] A significant share of the coastal guano trade still remained under the control of indigenous lords at the turn of the nineteenth century. For example, the Pukina and other highland peoples retained rights to guano islands off the southern coast of Peru. In this region, guano was but one part of a trade system organized by migratory llama herders, who came down to the desert coast each year during the season of mists (*garua*) to graze their animals and to obtain guano, dried fish, salt, shellfish, and red algae to take back with them to the highlands. This system lasted in modified form all the way until the 1950s when a lasting La Niña drought decimated their herds and shifted marine trade over to the bus system.[31]

Rivero did express concern, however, regarding the marked decline of the guano bird population along the far southern coast during the early nineteenth century. He ascribed this "to the excessive heat of recent summers," lack of fish to eat, and human disturbance during the independence wars. The owners of Jesús Island even sent an 1812 request to Spain to ban ship traffic near the southern guano islands in order to protect the birds. This inspired Rivero to make a public call for the new "Government to take measures in favor of the reproduction of this fertilizer, by severely punishing those who frighten the birds away from the islands." He published these views in the inaugural issue of a Peruvian scientific journal he founded in 1827, which Pentland passed on to Humboldt for republication in Europe. The dissemination of Rivero's article helped reenergize foreign interest in Peruvian guano, although few outsiders seem to have digested its conclusions.[32]

[30] Arriaga, *Extirpation of Idolatry*, 52, 64; Rostworowski, *Recursos naturales renovables*, 76, 84–86; Rostworowski, *Señoríos indígenas de Lima y Canta* (Lima, 1981), ch. 4.

[31] Julien, "Guano and Resource Control," 189, 192, 210–12; Shozo Masuda, "Algae Collectors and *Lomas*," in *Andean Ecology and Civilization* (Tokyo, 1985).

[32] Rivero, *Memorias*, 167; Humboldt, "Sobre los trabajos geográficos y geognósticos del señor Pentland en el Perú meridional," in *Humboldt en el Perú*, 154–70, originally published in German (1829), then French (1829) and English (1834); J. C. Poggendorff, "Über den Guano," *Annalen der Physik und Chemie* 21 (1831): 604–7.

Simón Bolívar hoped to install Jean-Baptiste Boussingault in a similar governmental position in Gran Colombia, but Boussingault turned him down, eager to return home after a decade in South America. There were still two last things he wanted to do, however. Following in the footsteps of Humboldt and Bolívar, Boussingault climbed the great Ecuadorian volcano Chimborazo and reached a record altitude of 6,004 meters above sea level on its icy peak. He then immediately set sail for the booming whaling port of Paita on the desert coast of Peru in January 1832. After a decade living in the humid tropics, Boussingault was astounded by what he saw: "The surroundings are as arid as a person could imagine; not a plant, nor a stream, sand is everywhere." According to locals, Paita had not experienced a substantial rainstorm since 1814–15. Boussingault blamed the barrenness and desiccation of this locale on deforestation and overgrazing by goats. He also asked around about the existence of seabird colonies. Could guano provide salvation for this unproductive landscape?[33]

Boussingault later credited this brief pilgrimage to Peru's desert coast for changing the course of his life. Back in Paris, he became a close associate of Jean-Baptiste Dumas, France's leading organic chemist and an outspoken promoter of technocratic governance. Circa 1834, Dumas taught Boussingault a powerful new laboratory technique for quantifying the nitrogen content of organic substances. Boussingault also married into a wealthy, landed family that enabled him to engage in large-scale field trials on the family estate in Alsace. He dedicated the remainder of his career to studying the role that guano's most distinctive constituent, nitrogen, plays in agricultural systems. He began by studying the value of fertilizers in forming nitrogen-rich plant gluten, as well as the connection between the nitrogen content of forage and the production of milk and manure. During the late 1830s, Boussingault also puzzled over the fact that certain crops deplete nitrogen from the soil, whereas clover and other legumes seem to increase it. He spent the next three decades studying the ability of plants to fix atmospheric nitrogen, the role of rain water in providing nitrogen compounds to plants, and the relationship between nitrates and ammonia salts in the soil. When he got the chance, he studied Peruvian guano and nitrates directly. No scientist accomplished more in delineating what ecologists now call the "nitrogen cycle."[34]

Boussingault also sought to identify other basic ecological relationships that link the animal, vegetable, and mineral kingdoms. Working in close collaboration with Dumas and his disciples, Boussingault summarized his

[33] Boussingault, *Memorias*, 3:97–100, 5:131–49; Boussingault, *Rural Economy in Its Relations with Chemistry, Physics, and Meteorology* (London, 1845), 333.

[34] Richard Aulie, "Boussingault and the Nitrogen Cycle," *Proceedings of the American Philosophical Society* 114 (1970): 435–79; Dana Simmons, "Waste Not, Want Not: Excrement and Economy in Nineteenth-Century France," *Representations* 96 (2006): 77–79; Leo Klosterman, "A Research School of Chemistry in the Nineteenth Century: Jean Baptiste Dumas and His Research Students," *Annals of Science* 42 (1985): 33.

initial findings in two wildly popular works: a long, practical book titled *Rural Economy* (1843–44) and a short, theoretical book, the *Balance of Organic Nature* (1844). The former, based on a decade of lab and farm experience, ratified Davy's view "that the most powerful manures are derived from animal substances, . . . precisely those that contain the largest proportion of azotized principles," or nitrogen. Boussingault left no doubt regarding the origin of this line of thinking:

Along a great extent of the coast of Peru, the soil, which . . . is perfectly barren of itself is rendered fertile, and is made to yield abundant crops, by the application of guano; and this manure, which effects a change so prompt and so remarkable, consists almost exclusively of ammoniacal salts. It is with this fact before me that in 1832, when I was on the coasts of the Southern Ocean, I adopted the opinion which I now proclaim in regard to ammonia in the phenomenon of vegetation.[35]

The latter book divided organic nature into two kingdoms: (1) a kingdom of *producers* (plants), which use chemical reduction to create complex organic compounds from the air and the earth, and (2) a kingdom of *consumers* (animals), which use chemical oxidation to recreate inorganic substances and restore them to the air and earth, where the cycle of organic life begins again. By this eco-logic, bird excrement was akin to gold and silver, and of greater intrinsic value.[36]

Boussingault's wide experience with environmental degradation in the forests, mines, and deserts of South America and his obsession with manure shaped his philosophical stance on the nature of wealth. Rather than glorifying industrial throughput, Boussingault emphasized the merits of conservation, efficiency, recovery, and reuse. He became an outspoken advocate of forest conservation and the recovery of human excrement for use in agriculture and eventually distilled his ecological philosophy into a classroom mantra: "to conserve is to produce."[37] These ideas acquired a large following, especially in France and British India, because they represented scientific confirmation of what many already considered to be common wisdom.[38] Boussingault realized that this schema oversimplified the chemical relationships involved in soil fertility, plant growth, and animal nutrition – a point his critics were quick to point out.[39] Scientists today nonetheless use a modification of his definition of producers and consumers to describe energy and

[35] Boussingault, *Rural Economy*, 333–34.
[36] Dumas and Boussingault, *The Chemical and Physiological Balance of Organic Nature* (New York, 1844); Aulie, "Boussingault and the Nitrogen Cycle," 451–52.
[37] Boussingault, *Rural Economy*, 673–89; Simmons, "Waste Not, Want Not," 79.
[38] George Perkins Marsh, *Man and Nature* (1864; Cambridge, MA, 1965), 173–78; Grove, *Green Imperialism*, 375–79, 427–30; Caroline Ford, "Nature, Culture and Conservation in France and Her Colonies, 1840–1940," *Past & Present* 183 (2004): 173–98.
[39] Aulie, "Boussingault and the Nitrogen Cycle," 452–55; Klosterman, "A Research School," 67–71; F.W.J. McCosh, "Boussingault versus Ville: The Social, Political and Scientific Aspects of Their Disputes," *Annals of Science* 32 (1975): 475–90.

nutrient flow within ecosystems. One of the founding concepts of modern ecology is rooted in guano.

The End of the Ecological Old Regime

The decolonization of most of Latin America by 1826 accomplished one of Alexander von Humboldt's overriding aspirations for the hemisphere. He and his many followers held out great hopes that this movement would liberate the region's subjugated peoples from the shackles of colonialism and slavery and open its emporium of natural wealth for the benefit of all humankind. This opening possessed profound implications for the ecological relationships that governed human societies around the globe.

Following Malthus, *Annales* historian Fernand Braudel first deployed the concept of a "biological old regime" to describe the environmental factors that determined the ebb and flow of human population and economic production in early modern times. Key factors in this regime included climate, the food supply, disease, and other natural hazards. Drought, damp, unseasonable frost, flood, locusts, and the like periodically placed severe limits on agricultural production, which in turn exercised a powerful check on human numbers. In 1815, for example, the eruption of the Indonesian volcano Tambora spewed so much sulphate dust into the upper atmosphere that it veiled the sun and abruptly cooled the whole earth. In Europe, harvest failures in 1816, "the year without a summer," caused food prices to skyrocket and in some districts brought famines. These difficulties proved so severe that they nearly forced two figures central to the story of guano, Boussingault and Justus von Liebig, to drop out of school and give up the pursuit of scientific careers.[40] Hunger kills in a variety of ways. During periods of dearth, some die of starvation outright, but malnutrition also weakens the body's defenses against takeover by viruses, bacteria, and other parasitic organisms. Smallpox and plague may have been the most dramatic killers of humankind historically, but diarrheal illnesses were far more likely to cause premature death among the malnourished and immunocompromised living under this biological old regime. Epidemic dysentery (or "bloody flux") actually caused more deaths than starvation in western Europe during the cold, wet years of the early 1740s, the mid-1810s, and the potato famine of the mid-1840s. This is a critical point to remember when we explore the impact of European colonialism on the Central Pacific.[41]

---

[40] Boussingault, *Memorias*, 1:41, 46, 56; William Brock, *Justus von Liebig: The Chemical Gatekeeper* (Cambridge and New York, 1997), 7.

[41] Fernand Braudel, *The Structures of Everyday Life: The Limits of the Possible* (New York, 1981), 70–92; Robert Marks, *The Origins of the Modern World: A Global and Ecological Narrative* (Lanham, MD, 2002), 22–39, 101–7; Post, *Last Great Subsistence Crisis*, 120–31; Creighton, *A History of Epidemics in Britain*, vol. 2, ch. 3, 8.

Other ecological factors also constrained the growth and prosperity of premodern societies. The muscles of humans and domesticated animals provided the main source of useful energy to this world, supplemented by wind, flowing water, and the burning of wood and other biomass. All of these sources of energy ultimately derived from the power of the sun, which in agricultural societies depended on the total amount of land allocated to food and fodder crops, pasture, woodland, or wetland. This is why land and labor were the two primary sources of wealth and prestige within premodern societies.[42]

There were two basic ways to increase the productivity of agricultural societies living under what is more accurately termed the "ecological old regime":

1. To intensify production from the land. This required the removal of barriers to rapid cycling of energy and nutrients through an agroecosystem, which usually required substantial human or animal effort. As Boussingault discovered, the availability of nitrogen was a critical bottleneck, in part because it was a key constituent of the muscle tissue that provided the main source of useful work to this regime.[43]

2. To extract materials from another environment. There were a variety of ways to accomplish this, through transhumance, conquest, trade, or turning to the sea. Indigenous Andean lords, for example, often sought to control resources and peoples at different altitudes.[44] All of these strategies, however, required the expenditure of energy for transportation and involved ecological exploitation, because the exact materials exchanged were never returned to their original context. Rapid economic growth in preindustrial contexts typically involved sudden human entry into lightly exploited environments and their rapid despoliation.[45]

Since 1750, the mining of ancient deposits of coal, then petroleum, natural gas, and uranium, has provided our industrial civilization with vast sources of energy, which in turn, has allowed our species to escape a major limitation imposed by the ecological old regime. Similarly, the mining of ancient accumulations of guano, then coprolites, nitrates, rock phosphate,

[42] Rolf Peter Sieferle, *The Subterranean Forest: Energy Systems and the Industrial Revolution* (Cambridge, 2001), ch. 1; Fischer-Kowalski and Haberl, eds., *Socioecological Transitions.*

[43] Boserup, *Conditions of Agricultural Growth*; Kraussman, "Milk, Manure, and Muscular Power."

[44] John Murra, "'El Archipiélago Vertical' Revisited," in *Andean Ecology and Civilization,* 3–13; Mary Van Buren, "Rethinking the Vertical Archipelago: Ethnicity, Exchange, and History in the South Central Andes," *American Anthropologist* 98 (1996): 338–51.

[45] John Richards, *The Unending Frontier: An Environmental History of the Early Modern World* (Berkeley and Los Angeles, 2003).

potassium-rich kainite, and other strata, has allowed our industrial civilization to escape the limitations imposed by nutrient recycling. Until the advent of the internal-combustion engine, intensive farming continued providing huge amounts of energy to the industrial world, in the form of food fed to draft animals and human workers. Nitrogen-based explosives also provided an additional source of energy used to mine the earth of its accumulated wealth. By jump-starting these revolutionary trends, the exploitation of Peruvian guano and nitrates during the guano age played a supremely important role in bringing an end to the ecological old regime and its replacement by a new industrial order based on throughput.

However, the new and significant in history, as Karl Marx and David Ricardo realized, must grow out of existing relationships, "the dung of the contradictions."[46] The Peruvian guano trade emerged out of two tendencies of the ecological old regime: (1) growing trade with the Pacific Basin, led by North Americans, focused initially on the hunt for whales and other marine organisms, and (2) growing interest among farmers in accelerating the cycling of nutrients through their lands, led by the British, focused especially on animal manures and ground bone. Members of Peru's Europeanized elite, for the most part, were happy to mine their new nation's patrimony, as long as it returned a nice cut of the profits produced by industrial capitalism that could be used to purchase further progress.[47]

When Boussingault visited Paita in 1832, he paid little attention to the reason this bustling port existed in the first place: to exploit the region's bountiful marine environment and export its biological riches to the industrializing North. Hunters of sperm whales (*Physeter macrocephalus*) began trickling around Cape Horn from the heavily exploited Atlantic around 1788. This brought the World Hunt that drove early modern economic growth to the heart of the Pacific Basin.[48] The opening of Spanish American ports to free trade during the independence wars threw open the floodgates. During the 1820s, ships from New Bedford and Nantucket, Massachusetts – the two behemoths of industrial whaling during this era – offloaded 100 million liters of sperm whale oil per year from the tropical Pacific. During the 1830s, when pelagic whaling reached its peak in the region, the industry as a whole killed approximately 5,000 sperm whales per year. Hunters targeted these animals because their enormous heads are filled with oil and waxy spermaceti, substances valuable as sources of light, as lubricants, and for an array of industrial uses. These huge carnivores use their heads to amplify loud clicks to echolocate squid and other cephalopods in the ocean's murky

---

[46] Marx, *Theorien über den Mehrwert* (Stuttgart, 1910), 3:94.

[47] Paul Gootenberg, *Imagining Development: Economic Ideas in Peru's "Fictitious Prosperity" of Guano, 1840–1880* (Berkeley and Los Angeles, 1993); Brooke Larson, *The Trials of Nation Making: Liberalism, Race, and Ethnicity in the Andes, 1810–1910* (Cambridge and New York, 2004), ch. 4.

[48] Richards, *Unending Frontier*, pt. 4.

depths. Their prey lives on detritus filtering down from the surface – another form of marine guano. Sperm whales were especially abundant and easy to kill in the vicinity of the so-called Humboldt Current: a narrow band of intense upwelling that stretches in a discontinuous arc from the coast of northern Chile, past Paita and the Galápagos, out toward the Line Islands in the central equatorial Pacific.[49] Before the arrival of harpoon-wielding humans, these nutrient-rich waters provided a safe nursery for clans of nursing females and their vulnerable calves. Intense hunting placed steady downward pressure on sperm whale numbers and, according to new research, probably encouraged these large-brained mammals to impart their own cultural knowledge about how to avoid – or even to attack – their pursuers. As a consequence, the industry soon moved on to naïve populations in the western equatorial Pacific in the 1830s, the Indian Ocean in the 1840s, then the western Arctic in the 1850s.[50]

This extractive industry established a new ecological relationship between northerners and Peru's coastal environment that was eventually filled by the guano industry. The ecological footprint of whaling was much greater than its impact on cetaceans. Andean condors and other scavengers, for example, prospered on the offal left by whalers. Whaling was also an essential component of neo-ecological imperialism as described in the next chapter: in New England, it produced jobs, a far-reaching demand for natural resources such as wood and copper, and a financial windfall for a region that had little new land to clear, depleted soils, and grim prospects as a producer of agricultural wealth. At Paita, firewood, charcoal, soap, and meat loaded by whalers for their long Pacific voyages all came from nearby *algarrobo* (*Prosopis*) woodlands, which were replaced little by little by sandy wastes. Paita had no water resources of its own but could provide tar in great abundance from local petroleum deposits. As an ancillary industry, locals harvested slow-growing lichens (*Roccella* spp.), which northern chemists used to make orchil dyes. This product drove the systematic exploitation of coastal fog forests, worldwide, until the invention of "Perkin's mauve" the first of the coal tar dyes, which cut the legs from under natural dyestuff producers except for specialized uses such as orchil-tinted litmus paper.[51]

---

[49] The Line Islands include Caroline, Christmas (Kiritimati), Fanning (Tabuaeran), Flint, Jarvis, Kingman Reef, Malden, Palmyra, Starbuck, Vostok, and Washington (Teraina) Islands. Jarvis, Kingman Reef, and Palmyra are territories of the United States. The other eight are now part of Kiribati.

[50] William Lofstrom, *Paita, Outpost of Empire: The Impact of the New England Whaling Fleet on the Socioeconomic Development of Northern Peru, 1832–1865* (Mystic, CT, 1996), 19, 65–71; Hal Whitehead, *Sperm Whales: Social Evolution in the Ocean* (Chicago, 2003), passim; Lance Davis et al., *In Pursuit of Leviathan: Technology, Institutions, Productivity, and Profits in American Whaling, 1816–1906* (Chicago, 1997), ch. 4, 9, table 8A.2.

[51] Lofstrom, *Paita*, 26–32, 74–75, 104–06; P. Perkins, "Ecology, Beauty, Profits: Trade in Lichen-based Dyestuffs through Western History," *Journal of the Society of Dyers and Colourists* 102 (1986): 221–27; Philip W. Rundel, "Ecological Relationships of Desert

Whaling ships always carried trade goods to pay for these items and in the process established round-trip networks of exchange in many new corners of the Pacific World. Yankee traders following in their wake brought a world of consumer goods to postcolonial Peru. To the chagrin of Peruvian producers, they brought huge quantities of cotton and woolen cloth woven on industrial looms lubricated with whale oil, as well as cheap flour, cured meat and cod, butter, and lard harvested from the oceans, prairies, and forests of North America. In response, Peruvian conservatives erected a series of protectionist trade barriers but had to fight constant battles with free-trade liberals for control of the Peruvian state during the country's first decades of independence. Regardless of which political faction was in charge, this North-South trade was unequal. Many ships returned home half-empty, and northerners were always looking for something bulky and profitable to fill them.[52]

Foreshadowing things to come, foreign warships were also never far beyond the horizon. In 1821, the U.S. Navy sent a 74-gun ship-of-the-line under the command of Charles Stewart to protect its growing interest in the "Pacific Station." In the tradition of the ship's namesake, Benjamin Franklin, Stewart saw himself as an extension of the country's growing scientific capabilities. He outfitted the ship with a 1,500-volume library managed by Charles Wilkes, the future commander of the U.S. South Seas Exploring Expedition. Stewart also collected a number of "curious articles and valuable seeds" for study back home.[53] This included a sample of guano from Mollendo that he forwarded to the editor of *The American Farmer* – the most prominent voice for agricultural improvement in the United States. Echoing Davy's findings, this paper not only celebrated guano's "astonishing fertilizing properties" and the "very profitable business" that already surrounded its exploitation but also the agricultural potential that it suggested for western soils lying beneath the vast forest roosts of the passenger pigeon.[54] As we see in the next chapter, for the small but vocal class of agricultural improvers in the United States, manures of this virtue presented a possible remedy to soil exhaustion, rural emigration, and the erosion of political power from the eastern seaboard to the western frontier.

Like many of Peru's founding fathers, these North American patricians tended to look to the Old World for leadership on these matters. At the

Fog Zone Lichens," *The Bryologist* 81 (1979): 277–93; Anthony Travis, "Perkin's Mauve: Ancestor of the Organic Chemical Industry," *Technology and Culture* 31 (1990): 51–82.

[52] Lofstrom, *Paita*, 100–3; Gootenberg, *Between Silver and Guano: Commercial Policy and the State in Postindependence Peru* (Princeton, NJ, 1989), ch. 3–5.

[53] Claude Berube and John Rodgaard, *A Call to the Sea: Captain Charles Stewart of the USS* Constitution (Dulles, VA, 2005), ch. 8–9; U.S. Naval Historical Center, *Dictionary of American Naval Fighting Ships*, s.v. "Franklin III."

[54] "Guano – A Celebrated Manure Used in South America," *The American Farmer* (Baltimore) 24 Dec. 1824: 316–17.

outset of the guano age, there was "nothing like muck" for experimental farmers in England who wanted to maximize the productivity and profitability of their land. Historians continue to debate exactly when, where, and why an agricultural revolution transformed rural production in the British Isles and opened the way for the region's industrialization and urbanization, but they virtually all agree that the widespread embrace of fertilizers and soil conditioners and their incorporation into complex patterns of field rotation were critical to this revolution. Decades, even centuries before the guano age, English farmers already possessed a vast array of options for manipulating the fertility of their soils. Depending on location, soil type, and labor availability, they could apply vegetable composts, plant green manure crops, burn turf, apply farm and fishing waste, purchase urban and industrial wastes, apply mineral fertilizers and soil conditioners, or recycle animal or human manure. Together these techniques enabled farmers with sufficient cattle and labor to gradually increase the productivity of their fields during the early modern period, and they provided an ecological foundation for Great Britain's early industrialization.[55] These "land-saving" practices nevertheless caused their own forms of environmental destruction: the removal of medieval hedgerows, the conversion of heathlands and fenlands to farms, and the unsightly pitting of many landscapes to supply coal-fired lime kilns with calcareous stone.[56]

Maritime industries and manure experimentalism made the international guano trade possible, but they did not make it an instant success. Political instability during the late 1820s and 1830s greatly complicated efforts to start the guano trade and resulted in Mariano de Rivero's exile from Peru. In November 1840, an old collaborator in his highland mining schemes, Francisco Quirós y Ampurdia (1798–1862), orchestrated an exclusive deal between a group of French businessmen in Lima, a Liverpool merchant house, and the conservative government of Agustín Gamarra to commercialize the export of guano. This agreement aggressively abolished all traditional claims to this resource belonging to Peru's old guano lords and classified guano as a "property without owner" subject to state control.

[55] Rowland Prothero, *The Pioneers and Progress of English Farming* (London, 1888), 99–100; J. D. Chambers and G. E. Mingay, *The Agricultural Revolution, 1750–1880* (New York, 1966), 4, 13, 54–59; Eric Kerridge, *The Agricultural Revolution* (London, 1967), 243–49; F. M. L. Thompson, "The Second Agricultural Revolution, 1815–1880," *Economic History Review* 21 (1968): 66; G. P. H. Chorley, "The Agricultural Revolution in Northern Europe, 1750–1880: Nitrogen, Legumes, and Crop Productivity," *Economic History Review* 34 (1981): 92; M. E. Turner et al., *Farm Production in England, 1700–1914* (Oxford, 2001), 81–88; Tom Williamson, *The Transformation of Rural England: Farming and the Landscape, 1700–1870* (Exeter, England, 2002), 6, 20–21, 27; Liam Brunt, "'Where There's Muck There's Brass': The Market for Manure in the Industrial Revolution," *Economic History Review* 60 (2007): 333–72.

[56] Williamson, *Transformation of Rural England*, 6, 13, 21–22, 26, 67–70, 91–97.

Quirós and his partners paid a stiff price for this privilege: 40,000 pesos and a wardrobe of military dress uniforms. The biggest barrier to this venture's success was Britain, however. Cultivators were well aware that a farming practice that worked for one crop, microclimate, and soil might fail miserably for another. Quirós almost went bankrupt because British farmers had taken to heart Davy's dictum to treat the soil as a laboratory and only purchased small experimental allotments.[57]

Fortunately for Quirós, Britain's agricultural press responded with a vigorous campaign in favor of Peruvian guano. One of the country's most trusted writers on the subject of manures, Cuthbert Johnson (1799–1878), provided a major boost with his digest of the existing literature on guano, including Beatson's experiments. Interestingly, Johnson portrayed guano as a means to recover nutrients lost to the ocean by soil erosion and flushed sewage – a signal of the recycling mentality that shaped this era's obsession with manures.[58] British "agents of the genuine guano" also got into the act by publishing their own compilations of field experiments. These testimonials reveal how widely and rapidly interest in Peruvian guano and nitrate of soda spread during the early 1840s. They reported results from hundreds of locales in the British Isles, several islands in the British West Indies, even Prince Edward Island in Canada. Agricultural societies also provided an important venue for investigating guano's attributes. Outside the British Isles, societies based in Hamburg, Munich, Prague, Massachusetts, New York, Maryland, Virginia, and Mauritius all took part in this experimental movement. These reports reveal that quantitative measures of harvested crop per acre and profit margin served as important indicators of what constituted a "successful crop," but farmers also gave guano high marks for the green, vigorous appearance it gave to growing plants. This was a practical indication of a plant's ability to resist pests and moisture extremes and an important quality that local agricultural societies looked for when granting awards for the "best field of turnips" or some other crop. Unlike most techniques for manipulating soil fertility, guano produced almost instantaneous effects, akin to the application of Miracle-Gro to today's gardens. Agricultural science from below proved just as important as discoveries by great men of science to the beginnings of the guano age.[59]

[57] *Exposición que Don Francisco Quirós y Don Aquiles Allier elevan al Soberano Congreso* (Lima, 1845), 3–4, 10–13, 22; Cristina Mazzeo, "Un proyecto económico en el siglo XIX. Un estudio de caso: Francisco Quirós," in *La experiencia burguesa en el Perú* (Madrid and Frankfurt, 2004); Mathew, *House of Gibbs*, 25–28, 39; Gootenberg, *Between Silver and Guano*, 80–83, 119–20.

[58] Johnson, *On Guano as a Fertilizer* (London, 1843), 8, 24–26, 33–38; Nicholas Goddard, "Johnson, Cuthbert William" in *ODNB*.

[59] *An Account of the Manure Guano* (Liverpool, 1843); Antony Gibbs & Sons, *Guano: Its Analysis and Effects* (London, 1843), 26–28, 34–35; Joshua Trimmer, *Science with Practice; or Guano, the Farmer's Friend* (London, 1843); Antony Gibbs & Sons, *Peruvian & Bolivian*

To Quirós's chagrin, however, the supply side of the guano trade quickly went global – again following routes laid down by whalers and sealers (fig. 2.2). In October 1828, a New York–based sealing ship under the command of Benjamin Morrell landed at Ichabo Island on a remote stretch of the Namib Desert coast in southwestern Africa. Like many hunters, Morrell had a keen eye for nature. He noticed in the course of clubbing to death 1,000 seals destined to become fur coats that this island was covered with a thick cap of bird manure produced by nesting colonies of shags, gannets, and penguins. Fourteen years later, a Liverpool merchant happened across Morrell's description and organized a secret expedition to relocate these deposits with the help of American whalers. Word of this discovery got out, and by 1846, mariners had swept clean every islet in the region. By official count, they exported a whopping 462,057 metric tons of nitrogenous guano to Great Britain. British guano pirates headed next to Patagonia, then to the Khurīyā Murīyā Islands off the southeastern Arabian Peninsula. They even took 5,000 tons of guano from St. Helena back to England. The flood of guano from these territories depressed prices in the short term and inspired merchants of Peruvian guano to divert part of their supply to the United States. However, lower prices and broader distribution convinced many new consumers to give guano a try, which expanded the market for "genuine guano" and all other "foreign manures."[60]

All told, from 1840 to 1879, Peru exported an estimated 12.7 million metric tons of guano from its islands with a sale value in the range of £100 to 150 million (fig. 2.3).[61] This quantity of guano contained approximately 1.6 million tons of elemental nitrogen, similar quantities of phosphate and lime (CaO), 300,000 tons of potash (K_2O), and smaller amounts of manganese, iron, and other trace elements necessary for plant growth. Even though its nutrients were not balanced to true agricultural needs, Peruvian guano was the most complete, most concentrated fertilizer available on the world market for many years. British farmers purchased the lion's share of this production, followed by farmers in the Low Countries, Germany, the

Guano (London, 1844), 19–20, 65–66, 80–82, 85–91; *Hints to Farmers on the Nature, Purchase, and Application of Peruvian, Bolivian, and African Guano* (Liverpool, 1845); Prothero, *Pioneers and Progress*, 86–88; Mathew, *House of Gibbs*, 51–56, 95–96; Wines, *Fertilizer in America*, 35–36; Skaggs, *Great Guano Rush*, 6; William Storey, *Science and Power in Colonial Mauritius* (Rochester, NY, 1997), 35.

[60] Morrell, *A Narrative of Four Voyages* (New York, 1832), 253, 293–94; Eden, *Search for Nitre*, 79–91; Arthur Watson, "The Guano Islands of Southwestern Africa," *The Geographical Review* 20 (1930): 631–41; Hutchinson, "Biogeochemistry of Vertebrate Excretion," 134–57; Mathew, *House of Gibbs*, 57–61, 99–115; Wines, *Fertilizer in America*, 54–55.

[61] Roughly equal to US$13 to 20 billion in 2007. Value estimates are based on wholesale prices reported by Mathew, "Peru and the British Guano Market, 1840–1870," *Economic History Review* 23 (1970): 117, 120; Robert Greenhill and Rory Miller, "The Peruvian Government and the Nitrate Trade, 1873–1879," *JLAS* 5 (1973): 110–11; Wines, *Fertilizer in America*, 49–51.

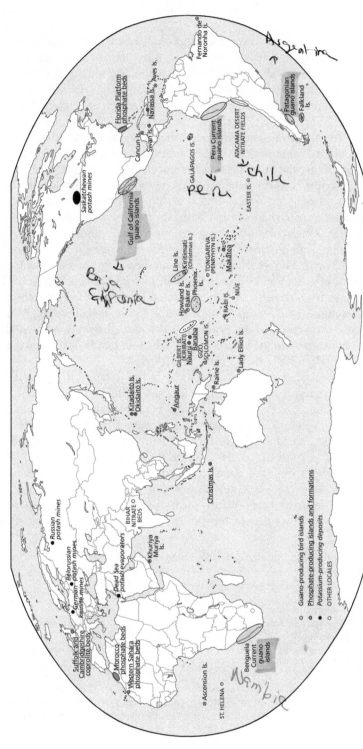

FIGURE 2.2. World map of historical fertilizer-producing regions, including guano-producing bird islands, phosphate-producing islands, formations of potassium-producing deposits, and other locales.

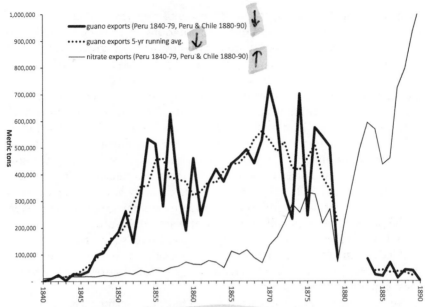

FIGURE 2.3. Guano and nitrate exports from Peru and Chile, 1840–90. *Source:* Hunt, "Price and Quantum Estimates of Peruvian Exports," table 21; Carmen Cariola and Osvaldo Sunkel, "The Growth of the Nitrate Industry and Socioeconomic Change in Chile, 1880–1930," in *The Latin American Economies: Growth and the Export Sector, 1880–1930,* ed. Roberto Cortés Conde and Shane Hunt (New York, 1985), table 8.

United States, and other European countries. By the 1870s, the Peruvian guano trade had become truly global. Plantations in Cuba, Puerto Rico, and other Caribbean colonies, Mauritius, Réunion, and China together bought 134,000 metric tons during the last decade of Peru's guano boom. A handful ended up in Brazil, Central America, and Australia, although the industry always favored northwestern Europe.[62]

In Great Britain, the consumption of guano and other concentrated fertilizers was a hallmark of what Victorians called "high farming": a high-input, high-output, capital-intensive system of agriculture that experienced its heyday from 1840 to 1879. Guano worked wonders with a variety of crops, soil types, and moisture conditions, but its use was concentrated among certain crops and soils. A huge share went to fertilize turnips (*Brassia rapa*), swedes (*B. napobrassica*), mangel wurzel (*Beta vulgaris*), and other root crops – all sources of cattle feed. By this time, many English farmers had stopped fallowing their fields in favor of producing root and legume crops

---

[62] Cushman, "Lords of Guano," app. 1; Hunt, "Price and Quantum Estimates," 42–49, table 21; Mathew, *House of Gibbs*, 99–115, 130; Hutchinson, "Biogeochemistry of Vertebrate Excretion," 82–86.

to be consumed by cows, sheep, horses, and pigs. By adding guano and other concentrated inputs to their crop rotations, improving farmers were able to shift production even more heavily toward root crops and livestock and away from nitrogen-fixing legumes and traditional fodder crops such as oats and rye. Cereal farmers initially disliked the tendency of nitrogenous fertilizers to produce more straw than grain, but many eventually came to value this effect because it increased the bulk and nitrogen content of their crops, which made them more valuable as animal feed. The cultivators of light, nutrient-hungry soils in the south and east of England were the most enthusiastic consumers of Peruvian guano, but cultivators of heavy clay soils in the Midlands and even a few upland farmers also consumed it. The latter preferentially applied it to hay grasses to be eaten by horses and pit ponies. Guano and other new fertilizers that rode its coattails preferentially went to the production of animal energy, meat, wool, dairy products, and barnyard dung. In these ways, guano helped drive Britain's industrialization and enabled the affluent to eat higher on the food chain and feel more prosperous but did little to increase the production of agricultural staples for the British Isles' exploding population.[63]

New genetic research suggests that high farming's openness to innovation left the door ajar to ecological catastrophe. During the early modern period, the cultivation of potatoes (*Solanum tuberosum*), a gift to the world from the Andes, rapidly spread among poor subsistence farmers in Europe. Potatoes produce far more calories per cultivated hectare than grain, and their cultivation relaxed one limitation on population growth under the ecological old regime.[64] In 1842, an unfamiliar blight appeared almost simultaneously in crops of potatoes in the vicinity of Philadelphia and New York City, Belgium, Holland, Germany, Denmark, England, Scotland, and Ireland. The disease spread rapidly from there, culminating in the devastating famine of 1845–47 that killed more than a million people in British-ruled Ireland. This disaster inspired an unprecedented wave of immigration from rural Europe to industrial cities and neo-Europes elsewhere in the world. What caused this epidemic? Some blamed guano for causing late blight in potatoes – although just as many credited it with saving their crops. The Belgians and

---

[63] J. C. Nesbit, *On Peruvian Guano* (London, 1852), 4, 16–23; Chambers and Mingay, *Agricultural Revolution*, ch. 7; Mathew, "Peru and the British Guano Market," 112–16, 122–25; C. S. Orwin and E. H. Whetham, *History of British Agriculture, 1846–1914* (Newton Abbot, England, 1971), 10–11; Mathew, *House of Gibbs*, 93, 136, 177, 182; Turner et al., *Farm Production in England*, 81–88, 95–107, fig. 3.6–3.9b; Williamson, *Transformation of Rural England*, 139, 153, 163–67; Krausmann, "Milk, Manure, and Muscular Power."

[64] Alfred Crosby, *The Columbian Exchange: Biological and Cultural Consequences of 1492* (Westport, CT, 1972), ch. 5; Redcliffe Salaman, *The History and Social Influence of the Potato* (Cambridge and New York, 1985).

Dutch noted that Lima, Cordillieres, and Peruvienes varieties newly introduced from South America were hit early and hard by this new disease, whereas Jean-Baptiste Boussingault reported the blight's resemblance to a disease endemic to damp areas in the Andes. Europe's founding generation of plant pathologists eventually identified the culprit as *Phytophtora infestans*, a fungus-like organism. Recent sequencing of DNA from *P. infestans* strains found in museum specimens strongly supports the hypothesis that late blight arrived with new potato varieties imported from Peru in the early 1840s. Thus, the same cultural movement that brought Peruvian guano also contributed to one of the worst disasters ever to strike Western Europe.[65]

Potato blight, in turn, strongly affected cultivation patterns and guano consumption, especially on the Continent. Farmers in damp, blight-stricken coastal regions of the Netherlands rapidly switched over to other high-yielding vegetable crops, whereas farmers in well-drained, unaffected areas of the eastern Netherlands increased their reliance on potatoes but combined it with the cultivation of fertilized pastures. Both groups became heavy guano purchasers and livestock producers. Farming in Belgium followed similar trends but used far greater amounts of recycled urban excrement, which became known as the "Flemish system of agriculture."[66] The rapid expansion of sugar beet cultivation in the Low Countries and Germany beginning in the 1850s also demanded prodigious amounts of Peruvian guano and nitrates, which in turn stimulated the production of cattle fed on beet tops and the leftovers of sugar pressing. These transformations helped these countries to experience their own agricultural and industrial revolutions during the second half of the nineteenth century.[67] Some sugar cane planters did their best to keep up with this new competition. Despite their reputation for soil mining, which is not entirely deserved, planters on more intensively cultivated islands in the West Indies and Indian Ocean

[65] Mathew, *House of Gibbs*, 94; Gloria Abad and Jorge Abad, "Another Look at the Origin of Late Blight of Potatoes, Tomatoes, and Pear Melon in the Andes of South America," *Plant Disease* 81 (1997): 682–88; K. B. May and J. B. Ristaino, "Identity of the mtDNA haplotype(s) of *Phytophthora infestans* in Historical Specimens from the Irish Potato Famine," *Mycological Research* 108 (2004): 471–79; Luis Gómez-Alpizar et al., "An Andean Origin of *Phytophthora infestans* Inferred from Mitochondrial and Nuclear Gene Genealogies," *Proceedings of the National Academy of Science* 104 (2007): 3306–11.

[66] J. L. van Zanden, *The Transformation of European Agriculture in the 19th Century: The Case of the Netherlands* (Amsterdam, 1994), 46, 54, 59–62, 81, 87, 107, 113–19; van Zanden, "The First Green Revolution: The Growth of Production and Productivity in European Agriculture, 1870–1914," *Economic History Review* 44 (1991): 231–32.

[67] J. A. Perkins, "The Agricultural Revolution in Germany, 1850–1914," *Journal of European Economic History* 10 (1981): 71–118; Noel Deerr, *The History of Sugar* (London, 1950), ch. 29.

purchased substantial quantities of Peruvian guano from the beginning of the trade.[68]

Guano's popularity and profitability also drove the search for substitutes. Humboldt's belief that Peru's deposits were an ancient geological formation conditioned the discovery of other sources of "guano" beneath the earth. In 1842, German chemist Justus von Liebig (1803–73) made a tour of the English countryside to promote his new ideas on agricultural chemistry. Paleontologist William Buckland, Britain's undisputed expert on antediluvian feces, took Liebig to see a brown sedimentary formation "densely loaded with dislocated bones and teeth and scales of extinct reptiles and fishes, interspersed abundantly with coprolites... the cloaca maxima of ancient Gloucestershire." Liebig promptly proclaimed this local source of phosphate-rich "fossil guano" to be the solution to Great Britain's search for fertilizer supplies and to "poverty and misery" caused by Malthusian population pressure.[69] However, Liebig's rival, John Bennet Lawes (1814–1900), beat him in the race to develop these resources commercially. Well before the global guano rush, ground bone had emerged as a popular field dressing in Britain. Consumption soon outpaced local supplies, so merchants began importing cattle bones in massive quantities from Russia and the Pampas of South America. During the late 1830s, Lawes developed a technique to improve the fertilizing power of bone by treating it with sulfuric acid. In 1842, he patented this process and built a factory for manufacturing "superphosphate of lime" strategically located to make use of bone charcoal thrown away by factories refining Caribbean sugar, but soon expanded his reach to include coprolites. Over the next three decades, the coprolite mining industry overturned large stretches of countryside in eastern England to unearth phosphate nodules. Lawes made a fortune off the inaccurate perception that superphosphates were made from fossilized animal feces similar to guano.[70] Other entrepreneurs with a chemical bent tried to produce imitations that incorporated industrial by-products. These early name-brand fertilizers, including Liebig's own patent field dressing, proved

---

[68] R. S. Fisher, "Statistics of Guano," *Journal of the American Geographical and Statistical Society* 1 (1859): 181–89; David Watts, *The West Indies: Patterns of Development, Culture and Environmental Change since 1492* (Cambridge and New York, 1987), 395–405, 425–28, 435–36, 444–46, 497, 551 n. 44; Storey, *Science and Power in Colonial Mauritius*, 35.

[69] Buckland, "Fossil Faeces of Icthyosaurus" *Proceedings of the Geological Society* 3 (1829): 97; Buckland, "On the Causes of the General Presence of Phosphates in the Strata of the Earth," *Journal of the Royal Agricultural Society* (1849): 520; Liebig, *Familiar Letters*, 524–25; Brock, *Justus von Liebig*, 120–21, 163.

[70] F. M. L. Thompson, "Lawes, Sir John Bennet, First Baronet," in *ODNB*; Thompson, "Second Agricultural Revolution," 68–70; Turner et al., *Farm Production in England*, 81–88, fig. 3.6; Mathew, *House of Gibbs*, 180–85; Williamson, *Transformation of Rural England*, 140; Richard Grove, *The Cambridgeshire Coprolite Mining Rush* (Cambridge, 1976).

expensive to produce, however, and often did not work. The first generation of professional agricultural chemists had a far easier time establishing their reputations as detectors of fraudulent guano.[71]

We must be careful not to exaggerate the quantitative importance of Peruvian guano to farming during this period. According to systematic surveys of farm account books, only a quarter of English farms used guano during the period 1840–79.[72] Guano was mainly consumed by large, prosperous landowners who loudly trumpeted their accomplishments to demonstrate their dedication to the new religion of progress.

Their pretensions immediately became a subject of parody. Guano played a starring role in the fictional tale of John Jorrocks, a rich Cockney Londoner. Jorrocks set out to establish a rural manor where he would "try all the new experiments on a liberal scale – guano, nitrate o' soder, bone manure, hashes and manure mixed, soot, salt, everything in fact." Whenever he got the chance, Jarrocks dropped references to "Guano! nitrate o' sober! gipsey manure!" into conversations with his social betters in a ridiculous attempt to wash off the taint of his low-class upbringing. The author explicitly hoped this commentary would "repress the wild schemes of theoretical men, who attend farmers' meetings for the pleasure of hearing themselves talk, and do more harm than good by the promulgation of their visionary views."[73] The novel *Yeast: A Problem* harshly criticized the secular tendency of British cultural life, in which a person's moral state could be "developed by wearing guano in his shoes and training himself against a south wall."[74] Guano quickly achieved the status of cultural icon in other countries as well. Circa 1845, the German humorist Joseph Viktor von Scheffel wrote a comic poem sung to the tune of "Lorelei" that addressed the linkage between guano and destiny; he viewed "this most perfect manure" as refuting the Enlightenment belief that nature was inferior in the New World.[75]

Guano's historical significance was as much cultural as it was ecological and economic. By itself, guano did not represent a radical departure from applying manure, bone meal, and other local inputs to increase crop output, and it fit with the prevailing recycling mentality that governed their

---

[71] Mathew, *House of Gibbs*, 95–96; Brock, *Justus von Liebig*, 123–24, 128–29; Wines, *Fertilizer in America*, 98, 128–35.

[72] Turner et al., *Farm Production in England*, fig. 6.8; contra Brett Clark and John Bellamy Foster, "Ecological Imperialism and the Global Metabolic Rift: Unequal Exchange and the Guano/Nitrates Trade," *International Journal of Comparative Sociology* 50 (2009): 311–34.

[73] Robert Smith Surtees, *Hillingdon Hall: Or, the Cockney Squire* (London, 1888), 29, 92, 98, 109, 116, 121, 154, 285–89, 453, 472; originally serialized in *New Sporting Magazine* in 1845.

[74] Charles Kingsley, *Yeast: A Problem* (London, 1851), 2.

[75] Antonello Gerbi, *The Dispute of the New World: The History of a Polemic, 1750–1900* (Pittsburgh, PA, 1973), 450–51.

use. However, it marked a spectacular expansion in the geographic reach of these farms and smoothed the way for the purchase of other inputs. Together, these practices gradually displaced the old system of farm self-sufficiency and waste recycling and opened the way for the eventual triumph of input-intensive farming practices based on one-way patterns of production, consumption, and waste.[76]

High farming and guano use were not without their critics. Cambridge classicist George Burges harshly criticized the "impious simpletons" who "go thousands of miles to fetch a manure, inferior to what is found in every town, and at almost every door," and beseeched his countrymen to make proper use of the abundant "human guano" that had been "put into our hands by an all-wise and beneficent Creator."[77] Some disapproved of these practices in terms familiar to today's environmentalists. French rural economist Léonce de Lavergne recognized the value of this "immense revolution" for "putting the land into good condition" but was repulsed by England's abusive treatment of cows and pigs and the impact of high farming on the landscape:

Agriculture changes from a natural, and becomes more and more a manufacturing process; each field will henceforth be a kind of machine.... The peculiar charm of the English fields threatens to disappear with the green fields and hedges; the feudal character is weakened by the destruction of the game; parks themselves are attacked as depriving the plough too much space.

Like Malthus, Lavergne saw no way around this: "The great value of necessity speaks out. Every energy must be used to feed that population which unceasingly multiplies.... The cost of meat must be lowered as much as possible.... Adieu, then, to the pastoral scenes of which England was so proud."[78]

The most forceful criticism of the international guano trade from an ecological point of view, ironically, came from a figure often credited with inspiring the chemical revolution in agriculture. Historians have been wrong to credit Liebig's textbook *Chemistry in Its Application to Agriculture and Physiology* (1st ed., 1840) with inspiring the global guano rush. In early editions of the book, Liebig was of the opinion that "experiments upon the efficacy of this manure in England have not yet been sufficiently multiplied to enable us to judge whether or not its virtues have been overrated." In stark contrast to Boussingault, he adamantly believed that "nature, by means of the atmosphere, furnishes nitrogen to a plant in quantity sufficient for its normal growth" and for many years discounted the value of nitrogen-rich

---

[76] Thompson, "Second Agricultural Revolution," 64, 67, 70–71.

[77] Burges, *Native Guano: The Best Antidote against the Future Fatal Effects of a Free Trade in Corn* (London, 1848), 1, 3–4, 30, 33.

[78] Lavergne, *The Rural Economy of England, Scotland, and Ireland* (Edinburgh, 1855), 182, 187, 196.

manures.[79] By the late 1850s, Peruvian guano had become emblematic to Liebig for all that was wrong with the "European system of cultivation called high farming." In *Letters on Modern Agriculture*, he praised guano as "one of the infallible means of raising the produce of corn and flesh." Nevertheless, Liebig lambasted England's "nitrogen champions" and "worshippers of manure" for advocating its use on false pretenses. Although British farmers were not guilty of "the open system of robbery of the American farmer" where soil mining was concerned, they instead practiced a "more refined system of spoliation." "Good fortune kindly sent guano to rescue them in their utmost need, . . . but in their fatal hands, this blessing is actually turned into an instrument for impoverishing the land in the course of time more completely."[80] In *The Natural Laws of Husbandry* (1863), Liebig explained why. Even though guano was "a very remarkable mixture," it did not contain all the nutrients that were needed by plants and removed from the field at harvest. Liebig accurately understood that fields fertilized with guano would lose their fertility over the years, because guano is an unbalanced fertilizer and has a relative lack of potassium salts and other minerals. The Law of the Minimum dictated that "the average crop of an unmanured field is always regulated by that element of food which is present in *minimum* quantity" and that "the effect of a manure when beneficial is merely to increase the relative proportion of this *minimum* element."[81]

Liebig reserved his harshest criticism in these later works for Britain's vampire-like ecological imperialism. "Guano will ultimately come to an end, and then what is to be done? . . . It is almost to be feared that guano will play a momentous part in history. . . . Bloody wars have sometimes sprung from causes of less importance."[82] Little did he know that Spain had just sent out an armada to seize Peru's Chincha Islands under the guise of a scientific expedition to the Pacific – the opening battle of South America's Nitrogen Wars.

Peru in the Guano Age

The massive international trade in bird excrement during the mid-nineteenth century had a profound impact on coastal and highland Peru. Both Peruvians and outsiders, alike, have long found it convenient to blame many of Peru's shortcomings as a nation on the mistakes of the guano age. It is a fallacy, however, to assert that Peru was bled dry by foreign exploitation.

---

[79] Liebig, *Chemistry in Its Application to Agriculture and Physiology* (London, 1842), 165–66, 177, 189–92.

[80] Liebig, *Letters on Modern Agriculture* (London, 1859), 159–65, 183, 198, 200–2, 231, 265–67.

[81] Liebig's emphasis, *Natural Laws of Husbandry*, iii–iv, 256–65.

[82] Ibid., 231, 269–70; Brock, *Justus von Liebig*, 177–78.

Historians figure that the Peruvian state received 60 percent of the total income produced from the guano trade.[83] This enabled Peru's postcolonial rulers to expend vast sums of money to purchase political order, economic progress, social aggrandizement, and protection from invasion and disease. In the modern history of export industries this was an astounding accomplishment, comparable to some of today's oil-exporting countries. But was this money well spent?

When the Peruvian government promulgated its original contract with Francisco Quirós, it nationalized ownership of this valuable resource to charge royalties on its extraction. These royalties soon became Peru's largest source of revenue. General Ramón Castilla's first government (1845–51) devoted most of this income to stabilizing and expanding the functions of the Peruvian state. This gave Mariano de Rivero a free hand to accomplish many of his developmental dreams. As prefect of the Departments of Junín and Moquegua under Castilla, Rivero opened new schools, accelerated the construction of highways and bridges, oversaw the continued mechanization of highland mineral extraction, established a College of Mines at Huánuco, and even raised a monument to Bolívar's battlefield victory at Junín. Rivero also aggressively promoted the colonization of the Amazonian lowlands, which reopened the indigenous Asháninka to kidnapping and enslavement, and their lands to violent seizure by outsiders. All told, government expenditure on public works and services of this sort consumed 29 percent of total state income from the guano trade.[84]

The threat of international invasion was ever present. In 1845, the French and British navies blockaded Buenos Aires to secure free navigation for themselves in the region. In 1847, U.S. marines stormed the "Halls of Montezuma" in Mexico City on their way to taking half of Mexico's territory, and Ecuador's former president Juan José Flores hatched a well-financed plot to reestablish monarchical rule in northwestern South America. Castilla took these threats seriously and organized a Pan-American meeting in Lima that resulted in a collective defense agreement between Peru, Ecuador, and Chile. To back up these gestures, Castilla's government signed an 1849 agreement with Antony Gibbs & Sons that provided a new loan in return for monopoly control over guano exports to Great Britain. It paid off many of Peru's creditors and funded a military build-up. Actions of this sort actually fueled internal rivalry and warfare over who in Peru would control and benefit from the trade, however. All told, military spending and payoffs to foreign and Peruvian debt holders consumed 24.5 percent, 8 percent, and 11.5 percent of total state income from the guano trade, respectively.[85]

---

[83] Hunt, "Growth and Guano," 270, table 3.

[84] Rivero, *Memorias*, 2:186–211; Urbani, "Rivero"; Stefano Varese, *Salt of the Mountain: Campa Asháninka History and Resistance in the Peruvian Jungle* (Norman, OK, 2002), 113–23; Hunt, "Growth and Guano," 275, table 7.

[85] Mathew, *House of Gibbs*, 80–85, 195–97; Heraclio Bonilla, "Peru and Bolivia from Independence to the War of the Pacific," in *The Cambridge History of Latin America*

Castilla's eventual victory in the resulting civil wars brought a long peace, the Pax Castilla (1854–62). After spending the first decade of the guano trade courting the favor of European capitalists and buying the loyalty of Peru's Creole elite, Peruvian nation builders made two dramatic gestures toward Peru's poorest people. In 1854–55, Quirós personally supervised the payout of 9.1 million pesos to slaveholders to free all 25,505 of Peru's black slaves. Peru also abolished the head tax paid by indigenous peoples, which made the national government all the more dependent on guano revenues. All told, 7 percent of total state income from the guano trade went to the abolition of these abusive institutions.[86]

The end of slavery and indigenous tribute eliminated two major sources of coerced labor. In response, like counterparts elsewhere in the world, Peruvian entrepreneurs looked to China to augment the coastal labor supply. From 1847 to 1874, Peruvians contracted more than 92,000 coolie laborers, most coming from regions of South China suffering severe environmental degradation and political unrest. About 10 percent died on the long voyage across the Pacific. Most survivors went to coastal plantations, but thousands ended up working as virtual slaves alongside convicts and debt peons on the guano islands. Labor unrest was frequent. Floggings were routine. Dozens committed suicide. British humanitarians expressed outrage against this new form of "yellow slavery" but never succeeded at interrupting the importation of guano. As late as the 1920s, a grisly relic of the guano age was visible on almost "every island – the Chinese graveyard – where garments, detached bones, and twisted corpses of poor coolies have for many years been exposed to the merciless sun."[87]

Life on the guano islands possessed other hazards as well. Strong winds from the Paracas Peninsula periodically blew up great clouds of recently mined guano dust. The most dangerous job, loading ships through long fabric chutes, fell to well-paid workers who wore makeshift masks made of steel wool to protect their lungs. They ran a constant risk of falling into the sea or being buried alive under tons of excrement. At the peak of the guano industry in the 1860s, the waterless Chincha Islands possessed a population of more than 3,000 and gained a notorious reputation for fights, robbery, murder, gambling, prostitution, alcohol, and opium abuse. Of course, this made them little different from frontier boomtowns in Australia, Siberia, or the American West.[88]

(Cambridge and New York, 1985), 3:557–59; Ronn Pineo, *Ecuador and the United States: Useful Strangers* (Athens, GA, 2007), 32–37; Hunt, "Growth and Guano," 275, table 7.

[86] Mc Evoy, *La utopia republicana*, ch. 1; Bonilla, "Peru and Bolivia," 3:552, 554; Hunt, "Growth and Guano," 263, 273–75, table 7.

[87] Murphy, *Bird Islands*, 314; Cecilia Méndez, *Los trabajadores guaneros del Perú, 1840–1879* (Lima, 1987), 43, 46–47, 50–51, 62–65, 77–78; Gonzales, *Plantation Agriculture*, ch. 5; Stewart, *Chinese Bondage in Peru*, passim; Marks, *Tigers, Rice, Silk, and Silt*, 333–45.

[88] BCAG 4 (1928): 158–59, 163, 174; Méndez, *Los trabajadores guaneros*, 15–18, 22–24, 27, 57, 61.

In 1862, Castilla's successor transferred control over the guano trade from Gibbs & Sons back to Peruvians. Five to ten percent of total income resulting from the guano trade beyond what entered state coffers ended up in the hands of Peruvian guano contractors. These contracts created the fortunes of several of Peru's key ruling families. For others, fortune proved more fleeting. Domingo Elías (1805–67), a native of Ica, used his income from the guano trade to build a vast agricultural empire along the south-central Peruvian coast. During the 1830s, Elías purchased the right to extract guano from the Chincha Islands for use on his nearby estates and sent off some experimental allotments in the hope of starting an export trade. During the guano boom, he made a fortune selling food to workers and ships at the Chincha Islands and from 1849 to 1853 possessed lucrative monopolies on guano loading and the importation of Chinese contract workers. He also brought the first cotton gin to Peru and played a major role in establishing the cultivation of short-staple cotton (*Gossypium hirsutum*) along the Peruvian coast; these acts prove important later in the book. Elías even briefly aspired to the presidency. These endeavors depended heavily on loans, coerced labor, and influence peddling, however, and Elías left his heirs saddled with debts.[89]

The prosperity of Peru's guano plutocrats paid for a flood of imports to Peru. These included British cottons, French silks, and woolens produced on the looms of these two great industrial nations. Peru's guano age elite eagerly bought the latest fashions from Paris and London and consumed the best French wines, brandies, and Havana cigars. Industrially produced metal implements such as plows, pumps, cotton gins, sugar boilers, steam tractors, and railroad stock proved vital to the reestablishment of Peru's coastal valleys as producers of export crops, but coastal Peru also became heavily dependent on far more basic goods, including coal, pine boards, lard, candles, paper, iron, and whale oil to lubricate these machines. The guano trade broke the back of Peruvian protectionists.[90]

In 1864, an act of aggression by Spain threatened to bring these developments to a crashing halt. With the United States preoccupied by its own Civil War, Spain tried to reassert its status as a Great Power in the Western Hemisphere. It recolonized Santo Domingo, helped France place an Austrian noble on the throne of Mexico, and outfitted three frigates to explore the Pacific in the style of Captain Cook's voyages for Great Britain. This naval expedition illustrates the overt ties that linked science, technology, and

---

[89] Peter Blanchard, "The 'Transitional Man' in Nineteenth-Century Latin America: The Case of Domingo Elías of Peru," *Bulletin of Latin American Research* 15 (1996): 157–76; Bonilla, *Guano y burguesía*, 30–33; Mathew, *House of Gibbs*, 186, 189, 191; Méndez, *Los trabajadores guaneros*, 12, 52; Hunt, "Growth and Guano," 275, table 7.

[90] Hunt, "Growth and Guano," 258–59, 266–68, 275, 282–88, tables 1, 7; Gootenberg, *Between Silver and Guano*, 121–37.

imperial prowess during this era.[91] By a prearranged plan, these ships abruptly abandoned their scientific contingent on the coast of Chile and sailed north to seize the Chincha Islands. They were quickly joined by a Spanish naval blockade, which tried to force Peru to cede all of its coastal islands. Spain foolishly underestimated the military strength that guano had purchased for Peru, however. During a climactic battle on 2 May 1866, land-based artillery and a fleet of steam-powered, ironclad gunboats repelled Spain's bombardment of Callao, severely damaged five of its best warships, and sank Spain's geopolitical pretensions in the Americas.[92]

Excrement of a different sort soon seized the attention of the lords of Peru's guano age. On 12 February 1868, health officials reported a case of yellow fever in the port of Callao that exploded into the worst epidemic of this sort in Peru's history. Yellow fever infected more than a tenth of the population of Callao and Lima and officially killed 4,445. To make matters worse, a blight similar to the one that struck Ireland devastated crops of potato, tomato, and pear melon (*Solanum muricatum*) in the vicinity. The cause of epidemics of this sort was a subject of open debate. According to one theory, yellow fever was a contagion passed from person to person, and the best way to stop an epidemic was to isolate its victims. Thus, in 1849, General Castilla's government used its guano income to establish a corps of health inspectors to quarantine incoming ships with signs of smallpox. Regional prefects also gained the power to quarantine whole municipalities. According to another theory, foul-smelling miasmas emanating from excrement, corpses, and other putrefying waste were thought to generate diseases, and the best way to rid a place of illness was to open it up to clean air and eliminate its filth. At least one Peruvian physician blamed exceptionally hot summers for exacerbating this risk.[93]

Manuel Pardo (1834-78), a French-educated businessman who had gotten rich in the guano trade, took command of relief efforts during the 1868 epidemic. He vividly remembered his childhood experience with this illness and made daily visits to hospitals and organized a service to clean the streets and remove corpses. Soldiers fired artillery in an attempt to cleanse the air of miasmas. City notables rewarded these efforts by electing him mayor of

---

[91] Leoncio López-Ocón and Miguel Ángel Puig-Samper "Los condicionantes políticos de la Comisión Científica del Pacífico," *Revista de Indias* 47 (1987): 667-84; Gregory T. Cushman, "The Imperial Politics of Hurricane Prediction: From Calcutta and Havana to Manila and Galveston, 1839-1900," in *The Nation-State and the Transnational Environment* (New York, 2013); Drayton, *Nature's Government*.

[92] Edmundo Heredia, *El imperio del guano: América Latina ante la guerra de España en el Pacífico* (Córdoba, Argentina, 1998), passim; Danuta Bartkowiak, *Ernesto Malinowski: Constructor del ferrocarril transandino, 1818-1899* (Lima, 1998), ch. 9.

[93] Jorge Lossio, *Acequias y gallinazos: Salud ambiental en Lima del siglo XIX* (Lima, 2002), 58-62, 66-9, 75; Bustíos, *Cuatrocientos años de la salud pública*, 267-70, 330-33; Abad and Abad, "Origin of Late Blight."

Lima. In those days, like in many cities around the world, excrement left by mules, horses, and other livestock littered the streets. Lima's residents dumped their household waste into corrals, vacant lots, waterways, or open ditches in the middle of the street (where it nourished black vultures, feral dogs, and pigs). Sometimes this foul-smelling refuse was eventually picked up by trash collectors, who took it to the outskirts where it was fed to herds of pigs, composted, and recycled into food by local farmers and the meat industry. As mayor, Pardo inaugurated a massive tree-planting campaign and required property owners to pay for the deepening of these channels so they could be flushed seasonally by water diverted from the Rímac River, but in this rainless environment, a more comprehensive solution required help from the central government.[94]

To attack problems of this sort, the newly elected government of Colonel José Balta (president, 1868–72) eliminated the private system of guano concessions that had enriched men like Pardo and reallocated nearly all of Peru's guano income to a single cause: the construction of public works. "For us, these signify salvation: the triumph of order and prosperity," Balta explained. Most of this money went to railroads – including the two highest railways ever built anywhere in the world. All told, 20 percent of the Peruvian states' total guano income went to these wonders of modern engineering.[95] Guano also paid for a network of underground sewers in Lima and a network of storage dams in the highlands to increase flow during the dry season. The transformation of Lima's urban environment did not stop there. Guano paid for the removal of the old defensive wall enclosing the colonial center of Lima and its replacement by a broad avenue reminiscent of Vienna's Ringstrasse. In July 1872, vast crowds attended the opening of the centerpiece of this project, a Great Exposition modeled after European world's fairs. It left behind a vast, leafy park containing a zoo, an artificial lake, a formal French garden, and a permanent museum to art, science, and industry. A steam railway headed south from the park to the burgeoning beach resorts and cleansing water of Miraflores, Barranco, and Chorrillos. In 1875, a monumental, 600-bed public hospital opened on the upper end of this ring avenue. Medical professionals took the lead in organizing these projects. Together they marked the decisive beginning of the conversion of Lima's rich agricultural hinterland into suburban developments and the exodus of Lima's ruling class from its center.[96] These actions clearly marked the arrival of the cleanliness movement to Peru, an early manifestation of a

[94] Lossio, *Acequias y gallinazos*, 63–6, 73–6, 88–9; Bustíos, *Cuatrocientos años de salud pública*, 271, 285–87, 595, 600; Gootenberg, *Imagining Development*, 71–89.

[95] Bonilla, *Guano y burguesía*, 56, 62, 69, 75; Bartkowiak, *Ernesto Malinowski*, ch. 8, 10–11; Hunt, "Growth and Guano," 273, 275, 287, table 7.

[96] James Higgins, *Lima: A Cultural History* (New York, 2005), 11–12, 111–12, 158–62; Mc Evoy, *La utopía republicana*, 79–83; Lossio, *Acequias y gallinazos*, 70–1, 76–89; Bustíos, *Cuatrocientos años de salud pública*, 286–87, 322–23.

global environmental movement. Severe yellow fever epidemics during the 1870s and 1890s inspired similar urban renewal projects in Buenos Aires, Memphis, Rio de Janeiro, and New Orleans – all of which had an obsession with excrement.[97]

These new temples to science, reason, and progress did not work as talismans against further disaster. Only days after the inauguration of Exposition Park, violence related to the election of Manuel Pardo as Peru's new president resulted in Balta's assassination. A mob hung the mutilated bodies of the instigators of this plot from the towers of the main cathedral, then decapitated and burned them.[98]

The incoming president had much bigger problems on his hands – Peru was running out of guano. To many this came as a shock. Over the years, Peru's rulers had made a valiant attempt to estimate how long the guano bonanza would last, so they could plan for the future. Early guesses of the size of Peru's guano reserves ranged as high as 117 million tons for the Chincha Islands alone. In 1853, Domingo Elías caused an enormous stir when he reported that only six million tons remained on the Chincha Islands. Within a week, the Peruvian executive hired a commission to study the deposits and working conditions on the islands. These experts estimated that 11.4 million metric tons of guano remained on these three islands, making "this precious fertilizer inexhaustible for many years to come." An 1863 survey of the islands north of Lima identified 6.8 million metric tons of phosphatic guano on Isla Lobos de Tierra alone. All of these proved to be gross overestimates.[99] Some foreigners believed that new guano reserves would continue to be discovered in "the solitudes of the earth" where it "is daily being accumulated, and will ever be on the increase, so long as the sea-bird finds a home on the coasts and promontories, or on the islands of the ocean. The demands of commerce and agriculture, be they ever so vast, cannot, therefore, exhaust the rich store of nature."[100]

As it turned out, Elías had good reason to be alarmist. It became undeniable in the late 1860s that the Chincha Islands were nearing exhaustion. Guano mining relocated to a number of islands to the north and south with lower-quality guano. This not only placed greater stress on Peru's living guano birds but also removed a transportation bottleneck that had limited guano loading to only a couple ships at a time. This enabled Peruvian

---

[97] Scobie, *Buenos Aires*, 122–26, 153–54, 193; Melosi, *The Sanitary City*, ch. 8; Chalhoub, *Cidade febril*, ch. 1–2.

[98] Mc Evoy, *La utopia repúblicana*, 103–4; Pike, *Modern History of Peru*, 130–32.

[99] Antonio Raimondi, *Informes y polémicas sobre el guano y salitre (Perú, 1854–1877)* (Lima, 2003), 81–110; Raimondi, "Islas, islotes y rocas del Perú" *Boletín de la Sociedad Geográfica de Lima* 63 (1946): 12–21; Hutchinson, "Biogeochemistry of Vertebrate Excretion," 40–42; Mathew, *House of Gibbs*, 146–47; Bartkowiak, *Ernesto Malinowski*, 107; Pike, *Modern History of Peru*, 99–103.

[100] Fisher, "Statistics of Guano," 189.

guano exports to reach an all-time high in 1870 of more than 700,000 tons. Arriving at "peak guano" perpetuated the illusion of abundance, with tragic consequences.[101]

The Nitrogen Wars of the Atacama

The rulers of guano age Peru were not too worried by the exhaustion of their country's ancient guano reserves because of the discovery of another nitrogen source in the southern province of Tarapacá. Vast deposits of salitre, also known as nitrate of soda or sodium nitrate ($NaNO_3$), lay close beneath the surface crust of Peru's Atacama Desert (fig. 2.4). "Nitrate of soda," one booster predicted in 1861, "is one day going to be called to replace guano in the markets of Europe when these become exhausted; salitre is going to last for centuries and Europe is going to be obligated to buy it to feed its impoverished soils."[102] During the nineteenth century, the history of guano and nitrates were intimately intertwined, but they had an essential difference. Nitrates not only provide the ability to grow things, they also gave industrial civilization unprecedented power to synthesize chemicals, to destroy, and to kill.

The origin of Peru's nitrate deposits has long been a subject of geologic controversy. The discovery of fossilized birds, eggs, and guano in the central Atacama led some to suggest that they were nitrified guano deposits of great antiquity, but recent isotopic studies indicate that they formed from the gradual deposition of ions from the atmosphere. Ore-grade deposits of this sort occur naturally in many parts of the world where extreme aridity prevents their consumption by bacteria and plants.[103] The sodium nitrate beds of the Atacama are so large for a simple reason: they formed in the oldest desert in the world. They have been slowly accumulating for at least 15 million years, and perhaps much longer.[104]

The Atacama is also the driest desert in the world, but it is not totally devoid of life. The richest concentrations of nitrates in the region formed on the western edge of the Pampa de Tamarugal, a vast inland valley named

---

[101] Raimondi, *Informes y polémicas*, 111–16, 151–52, 238, 251–56; A. J. Duffield, *Peru in the Guano Age* (London, 1877), ch. 3.

[102] Quoted in Bermúdez, *Historia del salitre*, 154.

[103] George Erickson, *Geology and Origin of the Chilean Nitrate Deposits*, Geological Survey Professional Paper 1188 (Washington, DC, 1981), 1–3, 21–23, 25–26; J. K. Böhlke et al., "Stable Isotope Evidence for an Atmospheric Origin of Desert Nitrate Deposits in Northern Chile and Southern California," *Chemical Geology* 136 (1997): 135–52; Greg Michalski et al., "Long term Atmospheric Deposition as the Source of Nitrate and Other Salts in the Atacama Desert," *Geochimica et Cosmochimica Acta* 68 (2004): 4023–38.

[104] Tibor Dunai et al., "Oligocene-Miocene Age of Aridity in the Atacama Desert Revealed by Exposure Dating of Erosion-Sensitive Landforms," *Geology* 33 (2005): 321–24; Adrian Hartley et al., "150 Million Years of Climatic Stability: Evidence from the Atacama Desert," *Journal of the Geological Society* 162 (2005): 421–24.

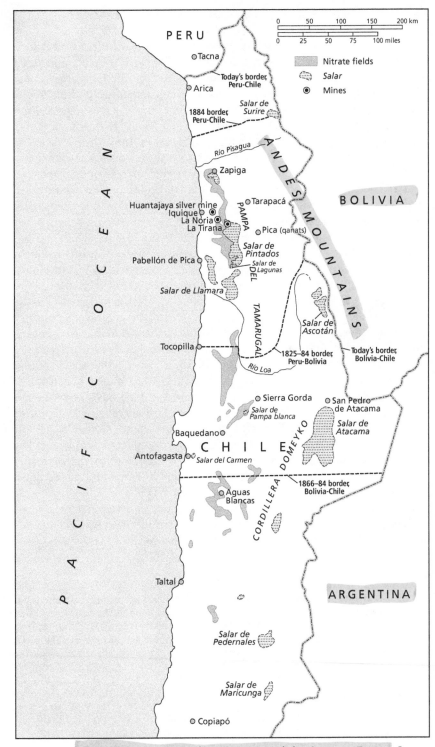

FIGURE 2.4. Map of the nitrate-producing regions of the Atacama Desert. *Source:* Based on Erickson, "Geology and Origin of Chilean Nitrate Deposits," fig. 1.

after the tamarugo tree. Great floods occasionally descend from the Andes, turning the valley bottom into a network of lakes. Flamingos and other waterfowl flock down from the highlands to feed on the temporary abundance of water life. In favored locations, young tamarugo and algarrobo trees (*Prosopis tamarugo* and *P. juliflora*), relatives of the mesquite, use this opportunity to sprout. If they are fortunate, they will lay down roots that reach all the way down to the permanent water table. The northern Atacama and its surrounding mountains were quite a bit wetter during the late Pleistocene, when a woodland formed along the eastern margin of the Pampa de Tamarugal. This ancient forest still stood at the beginning of the nineteenth century, in some places down to the smallest twig, even though most of it had been dead for millennia.[105]

Human life in this extreme environment required special adaptations under the ecological old regime. People have lived in the Atacama for more than 10,000 years. The Chinchorro culture (9000–2500 BP) lived almost exclusively on marine resources and artificially mummified its dead – the first people in the world known to have done so. Studies of ancient human excrement show that early settlers first came inland mainly to consume algarrobo seeds. During the colonial period, males belonging to a coastal indigenous group known as Changos used inflated sealskin rafts to hunt for conger eels and to extract guano for local trade, while their spouses and children herded livestock in desert pastures fed by the ocean mists. The Changos lived in symbiosis with Aymara-speaking oasis communities along the eastern margin of the desert. Aymara farmers religiously manured their crops with guano and in some locales dug tunnels, similar to Middle Eastern *qanats*, over two kilometers deep to access underground water. The livelihoods of these peoples began to change rapidly with the discovery of rich silver deposits in the coastal mountains just inland from Iquique. In 1767, miners established an ore processing facility on the Pampa de Tamarugal that began consuming huge quantities of desert trees and grass for fuel and fodder. These same miners also surreptitiously produced a crude black blasting powder from local nitrates for use in the mines.[106]

[105] John Blake, "Geological and Miscellaneous Notice of the Province of Tarapaca," *American Journal of Science* 45 (1843): 3; William Bollaert, *Antiquarian, Ethnological and Other Researches* (London, 1860), 263; Isaiah Bowman, *Desert Trails of Atacama* (New York, 1924), 16, 42, 68; Erickson, "Geology and Origin of Chilean Nitrate Deposits," 10; Peter Nester et al., "Perennial Stream Discharge in the Hyperarid Atacama Desert of Northern Chile during the Latest Pleistocene," *Proceedings of the National Academy of Sciences* 104 (2007): 19724–29.

[106] Calogero Santoro et al., "People of the Coastal Atacama Desert," in *Desert Peoples: Archaeological Perspectives* (Malden, MA, 2005); L. R. Williams, "Analysis of Coprolites Recovered from Six Sites in Northern Chile," in *Prehistoric Trails of the Atacama: Archaeology in Northern Chile* (Los Angeles, 1980); Blake, "Notice of the Province of Tarapaca," 11–12; William Bollaert, "Observations on the Geography of Southern Peru," *Journal of*

To put the revolutionary impact of the nineteenth-century nitrate trade in perspective, we first need to trace the global history of nitrates under the ecological old regime. Nitrogen compounds are not only valuable as fertilizers, they are also capable of burning at an explosive rate. Within the Hispanic world, this knowledge dates back to Muslim alchemists of the Middle Ages, but it acquired unprecedented importance during the early modern period when technological advances in metal forging enabled firearms to become devastating weapons. Many governments worldwide tried to control the manufacture and sale of gunpowder. Some even passed laws regulating the collection of excrement to encourage production of gunpowder's key ingredient – known variously as saltpeter, nitrate of potash, or potassium nitrate (KNO_3). So-called niter farms consumed large quantities of nitrogenous manure that otherwise might have been returned to the field and also placed heavy pressure on alder (*Alnus* spp.) and other broad-leafed tree species burned to produce potash.[107]

This method placed exorbitant demands on farm, forest, and labor, but one region of the world took on the main costs of early modern nitrate production. In 1638, the Mughal ruler of Bengal first allowed the Dutch East India Company to legally export saltpeter from Bihar. This prosperous region where the Gandak and Ghaghra rivers flow into the Ganges was uniquely suited for high-quality saltpeter production. In most years, the annual monsoon dumps prodigious amounts of rain and snow over the general region. Water flow in the Gandak may change by a factor of 50 during the course of a year. This erosive runoff carries huge quantities of silt packed with potassium salts, which form rich alluvial soils when they reach the lowlands. These soils supported a dense agrarian population of humans and livestock, which in turn, produced lots of nitrogen-rich manure and muscle power. In November and December each year, low-caste workers carried excrement to recently flooded wastelands and used cattle to work it into the potassium-rich soil. Unbeknownst to them, nitrifying bacteria converted ammonia in this waste into nitrates, which crystallized as potassium salts on the soil surface in the intense sun of the dry season. This product was collected, filtered, and refined for sale before the next monsoon opened the rivers for downstream transport. The indigenous merchants of Patna and other trading centers in Bihar grew fabulously wealthy by selling

the *Royal Geographical Society* 21 (1851): 104–6, 113; Bowman, *Desert Trails*, 20–21; Bermúdez, *Historia del salitre*, 19–25, 47–48.

[107] Wayne Crocroft, *Dangerous Energy: The Archaeology of Gunpowder and Military Explosives Manufacture* (Swindon, England, 2000), 4–28, 38–39; Stephen Bown, *A Most Damnable Invention: Dynamite, Nitrates, and the Making of the Modern World* (New York, 2005), ch. 2; William McNeill, *The Pursuit of Power: Technology, Armed Force, and Society since A.D. 1000* (Chicago, 1984), 79–102; Jan Kunnas, "Potash, Saltpeter and Tar: Production, Exports and Use of Wood in Finland in the 19th Century," *Scandinavian Journal of History* 32 (2007): 281–311.

saltpeter and other products to European traders in return for silver and gold – much of it mined in colonial Peru. The Dutch East India Company dominated the first century of the Bihar saltpeter trade. During times of war, it made profits as high as 1,000 percent. During times of peace, it produced enough blasting powder to power a revolution in hard rock mining and canal construction in Europe – key factors in the region's economic development. The saltpeter trade also inspired constant political intrigues and an occasional nitrogen war. In 1757, during the earth's first true world war, the British East India Company orchestrated the overthrow of the nawab of Bengal and installed a native ruler who gave the company a near-monopoly over South Asian saltpeter exports. This action not only opened the way to British colonialism in India and gunboat imperialism elsewhere, it also enabled the British to starve its rivals of gunpowder and tighten its dominance over the trans-Atlantic slave trade through sales of guns and gunpowder. These extremely profitable articles, in turn, fueled slaving wars between African lords. Even though the bulk of the global nitrate trade was rather small, its geopolitical impact was huge. Take Bihar nitrates out of this equation, and suddenly the "European Miracle" and "Rise of the West" become far more improbable.[108]

Colonial officials in Spanish America, meanwhile, worked hard to establish independent sources of saltpeter supply. The Viceroyalty of Peru opened its first gunpowder works in Lima in 1589. Peruvian niter farmers preferred to use ancient indigenous graveyards as a nitrogen source – including a site at the mouth of the Mala River where the decomposing kin of Don Pedro Guaneque were converted into a tool of empire. The sodium nitrate deposits of Tarapacá were of limited use for explosives, however, because they quickly absorb humidity from the air and fail to burn. The Napoleonic wars changed this. In 1808, the Peruvian viceroy sent an expedition to Tarapacá to see if these deposits could be used to bolster colonial defenses. For years, regional chemists had been trying to develop a viable technique to convert "cubic niter" (sodium nitrate) to "prismatic niter" (potassium nitrate). Enter the scientific expert. A Lima entrepreneur traveled all the way to Cochabamba in Upper Peru to consult Bohemian naturalist Tadeáš Haenke (1761–1817). Haenke revealed the chemical process for synthesizing potassium nitrate from sodium nitrate using burnt cactus as the source

---

[108] *Report of the Committee of Warehouses on a Memorial from the Manufactures of Gunpowder* (London, 1793), app. 1–2; Om Prakash, *The Dutch East India Company and the Economy of Bengal, 1630–1720* (Princeton, NJ, 1985), 7, 38, 43, 58–60, 185–86, 200–1; Kumkum Chatterjee, *Merchants, Politics and Society in Early Modern India: Bihar, 1730–1820* (Leiden, 1996), 28, 79–98, 102–17; Bowrn, *A Most Damnable Invention*, ch. 2, 4; H. W. Wild, "Black Powder in Mining: Its Introduction, Early Use, and Diffusion over Europe," in *Gunpowder: The History of an International Technology* (Bath, England, 1996); W. A. Richards, "The Import of Firearms into West Africa in the Eighteenth Century," *Journal of African History* 21 (1980): 43–59.

of potash. Gunpowder produced from Tarapacá nitrates contributed significantly to the death toll of the independence wars in South America, and some even made it to Europe. In 1821, a Tarapacá industrialist happened to meet up in Madrid with Mariano de Rivero, who was touring Spain at Humboldt's behest. Rivero passed on a sample for crystallographic analysis in Paris and published an article in the *Annales de Mines* pointing to the existence of large processed quantities sitting in Iquique waiting for a buyer. This disciple of Humboldt is thus often credited with the scientific discovery of Peruvian nitrates. However, the end of the Napoleonic wars in Europe and independence wars in the Americas caused global demand for gunpowder to fall sharply. Repeated attempts by the new Republic of Peru to export salitre to Europe failed because of the market glut and trade preferences enjoyed by the British East India Company.[109]

In 1830, Peru finally located buyers in Britain and France, but not for gunpowder production. Until now, historians of the nitrate trade have failed to recognize the main reason for the rapid growth of Peruvian exports to Europe – their immense value to the production of sulfuric acid (H_2SO_4) "the workhorse chemical of the industrial world." Most sulfuric acid during this era was produced in lead-lined containers using a process developed by Birmingham industrialist John Roebuck in 1746. The burning of elemental sulfur and nitrates over a pool of water in these corrosion-resistant chambers produced a liquor containing 35 to 45 percent sulfuric acid, which could be further concentrated by boiling. The large-scale use of sulfuric acid in the Leblanc process to synthesize soda ash $(NaCO_3)$ enabled industrialists to wean themselves of reliance on limited supplies of burnt kelp (*Fucus* spp.) from the Scottish seacoast and saltwort (*Salsola soda*) from Spanish salt marshes. This innovation, in turn, allowed dramatic increases in the manufacture of glass, soap, pottery glaze, paper, dyes, and bleach. Industrialists used sulfuric acid for a host of other applications, including the production of nitric acid, a powerful oxidizing agent easily derived from Peruvian nitrates. In 1846, an Italian chemist created yet another demand for these chemicals by using nitric acid, sulfuric acid, and glycerol (a waste product of the soap and candle industries) to synthesize nitroglycerin. This explosive possessed five to seven times as much power as black powder but had the dangerous tendency to explode spontaneously. Cheap sulfuric acid was also vital to the production of superphosphates and ammonium sulfate (a by-product of coal gas generation), two other major contributors to the fertilizer revolution of the mid-nineteenth century. Unfortunately, the production of these acids also generated nitrogen oxides (NO_x), which were gassed off as a waste product and caused caustic air pollution. In the early days, nitrate

[109] Bermúdez, *Historia del salitre*, 22–25, 30–41, 44–61, 65–67, 87, 98–103; Rivero, *Memorias*, 1:5–6; Bollaert, "Observations on the Geography of Southern Peru," 113; Bollaert, *Antiquarian Researches*, 266–67; Crocroft, *Dangerous Energy*, 61–62.

consumption was the most expensive part of the lead-chamber process and inspired Humboldt's companion Joseph Louis Gay-Lussac to develop a technique for recovering this strategic substance from waste gas in 1827. However, the growing availability of cheap Peruvian nitrates, which worked just as well as Bihar saltpeter in these processes, made chemical manufacturers reluctant to invest in this technology for many years, to the detriment of plants, animals, and people living downwind. From these vantage points, Peruvian nitrates were as important to the revolutionary development of the chemical industry during the mid-nineteenth century as guano was to the fertilizer industry.[110]

When the Dutch East India Company dominated the South Asian nitrate trade, it imported less than 100 tons per year to Europe. In the late eighteenth century, the British East India Company annually imported around ten times this amount. Peruvian nitrate imports immediately dwarfed these numbers, rising from an average of 2,500 tons per year in the 1830s, to 17,000 tons in the 1840s, to 42,000 tons in the 1850s.[111] British farmers also experimented with Peruvian nitrates, and found them to be especially valuable for fertilizing grass and barley on the light soils of southeastern England to be used as cattle feed. These experiments helped in a small way to open the guano trade.[112] Peruvian nitrates also served a growing South American market for mine explosives, which enabled the completion of two great drainage tunnels designed by Mariano de Rivero at Cerro de Pasco that for a quarter century allowed Peru to become the world's number-two producer of silver. The availability of explosives also enabled the large-scale exploitation and export of copper pyrite ($CuFeS_2$) from Peru, which formerly had been discarded as a waste product of silver mining, but now possessed triple value as a source of copper, iron, and sulfur to northern industrialists. The economic boom of Peru's guano age was not built just on guano, but more broadly on a number of raw chemicals that allowed the Industrial Revolution to move into its second phase.[113]

The Peruvian state organized a series of scientific surveys of Tarapacá to help advance mineral production in the region. The first of these was undertaken in 1827–28 by George Smith (1802–70) and William Bollaert

---

[110] David Kiever, "Sulfuric Acid: Pumping up the Volume," *Today's Chemist at Work* Sept. 2001: 57–58; Gracia, ed., *Estado y fertilizantes*, 133–34; Joaquín Fernández, "La elaboración de la sosa en España," *Antilia* 4 (1998), http://www.ucm.es/info/antilia/revista; Margaret Ferguson, "Riches from the Sea," *Chemistry Review* 10 (Sept. 2000): 2–6; Maurice Crosland, *Gay-Lussac: Scientist and Bourgeois* (Cambridge and New York, 1978), 199–204; Crocroft, *Dangerous Energy*, 148–50.

[111] Hunt, "Price and Quantum Estimates," table 21.

[112] Cuthbert Johnson, *Saltpetre and Nitrate of Soda as Fertilizers* (London, 1840), 17, 38–46.

[113] José Deustua, *The Bewitchment of Silver: The Social Economy of Mining in Nineteenth-Century Peru* (Athens, OH, 2000), ch. 2; Eric Hobsbawm, *Industry and Empire: The Birth of the Industrial Revolution* (New York, 1999), ch. 6.

(1807–76). Bollaert had worked as an assistant of Humphry Davy and Michael Faraday since age thirteen but decided to give up a promising career in the laboratory for more lucrative work as a Humboldtian scientific explorer. Bollaert attained his greatest fame as an ethnographer and first made the existence of Don Pedro Guaneque's coat of arms known to the world. Smith was an English entrepreneur who settled down permanently in Tarapacá to devote his life to nitrate mining after this trip. Together they bore witness to the steadily growing ecological footprint of the nitrate industry. The Pampa de Tamarugal already bore deep scars from a half-century of colonial mining when they first arrived. In the early days, nitrate production relied on fuel and human labor provided by local trees and Aymara-speaking Indians. During Smith and Bollaert's first survey, they saw a number of new saplings that had taken root during the great flood of 1819. By 1852, the next time these floods recurred, the living woodlands that had given this inland valley its name were virtually extinct, and indigenous woodcutters had turned their attention to Pleistocene wood buried close to the surface. Before the construction of steam-powered cableways and railroads to the nitrate fields, the transport of conglomerate ore, processed nitrate, food, and fuel required enormous numbers of draft animals. Smith and Bollaert estimated that as many as 8,000 mules, horses, and donkeys a year marched over the Andes from the Pampas of northern Argentina to work in the northern Atacama during the 1850s. Locally produced alfalfa and desert grasses only provided a part of the fodder they consumed – mainly barley imported from central Chile. Drivers often worked these animals to collapse, then left them to die where they fell – to the benefit of massive proliferations of green flies and Andean condors. This resulted in the accumulation of thousands of mummified corpses and millions of bones. The nitrate industry is responsible for turning the northern Atacama into a dead desert waste.[114]

The introduction of steam machinery during the early 1850s and a spike in nitrate prices during the Crimean War (1853–55) set off a race to develop new technological systems capable of maximizing the efficiency, scale, and profitability of nitrate manufacture in Tarapacá. This attracted an influx of foreign investment and expertise, which in turn, led to the discovery of additional deposits in coastal Bolivia, and the parallel exploitation of borax and iodine salts. Increasingly, coal imported from Chile and Great Britain fueled the industry, but the high cost of technological innovation, steadily falling nitrate prices, progressive exhaustion of high-grade deposits, and

[114] William Brock, "William Bollaert, Faraday and the Royal Institution," *Proceedings of the Royal Institution* 42 (1968): 75–86; Blake, "Notice of the Province of Tarapaca," 7–8, 10; Bollaert, "Observations on the Geography of Southern Peru," 103, 112, 127–29; Bollaert, *Antiquarian Researches*, 263–67; Bollaert, "Additional Notes on the Geography of Southern Peru," *Proceedings of the Royal Geographical Society* 12 (1867–68): 154–57, 163; Bermúdez, *Historia del salitre*, 111, 113–15, 128–32.

increasing dependence on imported goods gradually forced the industry's founders out of business, both local and foreign. In 1865, George Smith had to sell out to his main creditor, Antony Gibbs & Sons, which was reinvesting its guano wealth in a global array of stocks, railways, and extractive industries, and eagerly bought into nitrate mining. The megathrust earthquake of 13 August 1868 off Arica, Peru, accelerated the shakeout of the nitrate industry. This magnitude 9.0 quake caused a tsunami comparable to the 2004 Indian Ocean event and obliterated a number of ports along the southern coast of Peru; it caused major damage as far away as New Zealand. Johann Gildemeister (1823–98), a Bremen-born merchant living in Lima, sent a subordinate by the quickest route to Hamburg with instructions to buy up nitrate before news of the disaster reached Europe and prices shot up. He used this windfall to buy a huge nitrate mine and factory that went into foreclosure because of the earthquake, which he and his kin later converted into massive landholdings on the northern coast of Peru.[115]

The post-earthquake spike in nitrate prices inspired President Balta's government to impose a small duty on nitrate exports from Peru. To further leverage the country's financial position and pay for the aforementioned public works, Balta's economic mastermind Nicolás de Piérola made a deal with French financier Auguste Dreyfus and U.S. railroad magnate Henry Meiggs in 1869 to consolidate all of Peru's outstanding debt and float £64 million worth of loans.[116] These would be paid off by future guano proceeds. Loans of this magnitude – the largest ever for a Latin American government – required pooling the assets of a number of French, Genoese, German, and Peruvian banks. Balta's successor, Manuel Pardo (president, 1872–76), allowed the last of the Dreyfus bond issues to go through, but Peru only received £8.3 million from a loan expected to raise four times that amount, most of which went to refinancing old loans and pay off Dreyfus. Then a worse catastrophe struck. A financial panic took hold in central Europe's overstretched banks in June 1873, and eventually spread to New York, London, Paris, and Latin America. Germany began dumping silver on the open market on its way to converting to a gold standard, which steadily eroded the ability of Peru, Bolivia, and other silver-producing nations to pay their bills.[117]

[115] Bermúdez, *Historia de salitre*, 132–50, 163–68, 185–207, 253–58, 264–68, 312–16; Mathew, *House of Gibbs*, 223–25, 244–45; Thomas O'Brien, *The Nitrate Industry and Chile's Crucial Transition, 1870–1891* (New York, 1982), 15–16; Diana Comte and Mario Pardo, "Reappraisal of Great Historical Earthquakes in the Northern Chile and Southern Peru Seismic Gaps," *Natural Hazards* 4 (1991): 23–44.

[116] Equal to US$6.3 billion in 2007.

[117] Bonilla, *Guano y burguesía*, 69, 77–81, 99–101, 129–35; Greenhill and Miller, "The Nitrate Trade," 108–9; Carlos Marichal, *A Century of Debt Crises in Latin America: From Independence to the Great Depression, 1820–1930* (Princeton, NJ, 1989), 99;

Despite these severe dislocations, long-term prospects for the nitrate industry could hardly have been better, thanks to several new technological innovations in the industrial North. In 1857 in Delaware, Lamont du Pont patented a method using graphite to reduce the moisture-absorbing tendency of black powder produced directly from Peruvian nitrates. Brisk sales of "blasting powder B" to anthracite coal miners in Pennsylvania brought about a rapid improvement in the Du Pont Corporation's fortunes and energized the industrialization of the United States. In 1861, the German town of Stassfurt began large-scale excavation of potassium-rich salt deposits from deep underground. This industry was premised on the availability of cheap explosives but also made it economical to use Peruvian nitrates as a raw material for gunpowder production – to the chagrin of Swedes, Finns, and South Asians who produced potash and saltpeter. More significantly, industrial-scale potassium mining enabled its use as a fertilizer and drove increases in production from 2,293 metric tons in 1861 to more than eleven million tons a year on the eve of World War I. But Swedish entrepreneur Alfred Nobel accomplished the most important innovation of all. From 1862 to 1867, he developed a relatively safe means for transporting and detonating nitroglycerin, which he marketed as "dynamite." Nobel and other chemists also developed military applications of nitroglycerin explosives that soon made gunpowder obsolete. Germany's dramatic victory during the Franco-Prussian War (1870–71) sparked an international arms race involving heavy artillery that continued until the end of First World War. These events inspired another investment boom in the nitrate fields of Tarapacá and the expansion of the industry into coastal Bolivia and northern Chile.[118]

President Pardo took aggressive steps to use nitrates to shore up Peru's economic situation but only succeeded in propelling the region toward a nitrogen war. In 1873, he proposed creating a parastatal corporation, the Compañía Administradora del Estanco del Salitre, that would have possessed monopoly control over Peruvian exports and the majority of the world's nitrate supply. Foreign nitrate producers vociferously opposed the creation of a Peruvian-controlled cartel and ramped up production to force down prices and undermine the government's position. This had the effect of underselling Peruvian guano, which was already in trouble because of declining quality, competition from other fertilizers, and the financial panic. In retribution, Pardo raised export duties on nitrates. All of this caused

Antonio Mitre, *Los patriarcas de la plata: Estructura socioeconómica de la minería boliviana en el siglo XIX* (Lima, 1981).

[118] Jack Kelly, *Gunpowder: The History of the Explosive That Changed the World* (New York, 2004), 219–23; Fred Mohme, "The Potash Industry of Europe," *Economic Geography* 5 (1929): 141–48; Kunnas, "Potash, Saltpeter and Tar"; Bown, *Most Damnable Invention*, 51–69, 114–32, 156; Crocroft, *Dangerous Energy*, 67–69, 94–95, 121–29; Bermudez, *Historia del salitre*, 205–38, 283–307.

enormous volatility in the international market for nitrogen compounds. In 1875, Pardo's government nationalized the entire Tarapacá nitrate industry, to be paid for by £7 million in loans based on future nitrate exports. Pardo placed expropriation under the control of two expert commissions, a policy that fit well with his administration's overarching goal to create a "Practical Republic" managed by highly trained public servants. Time and fiscal constraints prevented government engineers from individually surveying each nitrate plant, however, and forced them to rely heavily on inflated valuations provided by owners. Peru's economic situation deteriorated even more when the Turkish bond market collapsed and forced the Ottoman Empire to stop servicing £100 million owed to European creditors. This pushed the world's entire capitalist system into the worst depression it had ever experienced and compelled Peru to bring in the New Year 1876 by defaulting on its £33 million debt. Pardo moved forward with nationalizing the nitrate industry, anyway, with financing from Peruvian banks. Two-thirds of nitrate manufacturers accepted the government's offer of interest payments and IOUs, and holdouts were allowed to keep producing in return for a fixed commission. The old guano magnate Gibbs & Co. acted as the sole international marketing agent for this cartel.[119]

Then nature intervened in a manner so far-reaching that it propelled agricultural systems into crisis all over the world. In 1877–78, intense rains pummeled the northern coast of Peru and southern Ecuador. This created a "year of abundance" for coastal peasants who pastured cattle and knew to plant rain-fed crops during these periodic events, but floods severely damaged the steam pumps, railroads, and irrigation canals that served the region's cotton and sugar industries. Even the Pampa de Tamarugal experienced a rare flood in 1878, just one year after a second earthquake and tsunami on the scale of 1868 devastated Atacama nitrate producers and caused drownings as far away as Japan. In stark contrast, most of the highlands of southern Peru and Bolivia endured two consecutive years of severe drought. Cochabamba, Bolivia's breadbasket, exported starving peasants instead of food. Regional grain prices skyrocketed, and as so often happens during times of dearth, epidemic disease spread rapidly. The processing of silver at Potosí and Oruro also ground to a halt because of lack of water and the influx of famine refugees. These upsets exacerbated a deep crisis in Bolivia's economy, which had already forced the country to default on its foreign debt. Chile usually had plenty of grain to export to its northern neighbors, but it also experienced strange weather in 1877–78. Winter floods devastated the southern half of Chile's central valley, along with the wheat crop, which had just suffered three terribly dry years. Central

[119] Bermúdez, *Historia del salitre*, 330–49; Greenhill and Miller, "The Nitrate Trade," 112–19; O'Brien, *The Nitrate Industry*, 21–24, 26, 29, 31, 35; Mc Evoy, *La utopía republicana*, ch. 3; Marichal, *A Century of Debt Crises*, 102–3, 108–10.

California and the Argentine Pampas also received extreme rains in 1877–78 but in quantities that allowed them to produce bumper crops of wheat. This confirmed their takeover of the trans-Pacific and South Atlantic grain trades from Chile, the original provider of California's wheat cultivars. This fact further dampened the spirits of progress-minded Chileans.[120]

The eastern shore of the Pacific Basin got off easy in 1876–78 compared with regions far to the west. Australia mostly escaped severe problems, and the country produced a decent wheat crop. New Zealand, on the other hand, experienced extreme rainfall, snow, drought, and flood. Hawaii, New Caledonia, the Philippines, the Dutch East Indies, southern Africa, northeastern Africa, and many other regions endured major droughts, and French Polynesia felt the rare fury of three tropical cyclones. These problems paled, however, before the apocalypse that struck British-ruled India, northern China, and northeastern Brazil. We now know that this global climate catastrophe, in many locales, was driven by the strongest El Niño event of the nineteenth century – made worse by the fact that it was preceded and followed by strong La Niña conditions.[121]

For reasons unrelated to ENSO, farmers in the British Isles also experienced major difficulties during these years. Rinderpest virus struck the cattle industry in 1872–73 and again in 1877. Cool, wet weather disrupted the growing season from 1875–77. The year 1879 was simply disastrous – the third coldest year and second wettest summer since instrumental records began in the seventeenth century. The ballooning costs of input-intensive practices and financial panic made these environmental shocks all the more difficult to bear. Many farmers could no longer afford to buy guano, nitrates, or other fertilizers. Tenant farmers left the land in hoards. Food production plummeted, and Great Britain had to rely all the more heavily on grain purchased abroad – to the point that it drained food from famine-stricken

---

[120] Patricio Aceituno et al., "The 1877–1878 El Niño Episode: Associated Impacts in South America," *Climatic Change* 92 (2009): 396, 400–5, 408–10; Luc Ortlieb, "Eventos El Niño y episodios lluviosos en el desierto de Atacama," *Bulletin de l'Institut Français d'Etudes Andines* 24 (1995): 519–37; Comte and Pardo, "Reappraisal of Great Historical Earthquakes"; Roberto Querejazu Calvo, *Guano, salitre, sangre: Historia de la Guerra del Pacífico* (La Paz, Bolivia, 1979), ch. 12; Michela Pentimalli and Gustavo Rodríguez, "Las razones de la multitud (hambruna, motines y subsistencia: 1878–79)," *Estado y sociedad: Revista boliviana de ciencias sociales* 5 (1988): 15–33; Mitre, *Los patriarcas de plata*, 68–77, 122–23, 127–28; Benjamín Vicuña MacKenna, *El clima de Chile: Ensayo histórico* (1877; Buenos Aires, 1970), ch. 16–17; Luis Ortega, "Nitrates, Chilean Entrepreneurs and the Origins of the War of the Pacific," *JLAS* 16 (1984): 339–46; Scobie, *Revolution on the Pampas*, 39, 117–18; Donald Pisani, *From Family Farm to Agribusiness: The Irrigation Crusade in California and the West, 1850–1931* (Berkeley and Los Angeles, 1984), 3–11, 286–89; Edward Melillo, "Strangers on Familiar Soil: Chile and the Making of California, 1848–1930," (Ph.D. diss., Yale Univ. 2006), ch. 2.

[121] CEI and paleoarchives; Garden, *Droughts, Floods, and Cyclones*, ch. 5–6; Davis, *Late Victorian Holocausts*, pt. 1.

regions such as India. Rural life in England never recovered. The "age of high farming" was over.[122]

The lords of the guano age had hoped that the globalization of the fertilizer trade would help liberate humanity from the vagaries of nature and increase the world's food security, but the combined tragedies of the 1870s suggest that they actually made the world dangerously vulnerable to ecological and economic disruptions. Industrial capitalism and the new imperialism did not accomplish this on their own: this was the death rattle of the world's ecological old regime.

The end of the ecological old regime involved many kinds of violence, including violence against nature. It also inspired a great war over nitrogen. From 1878 onward, Peruvian guano sold at its lowest price in a quarter century. Northern nitrate purchasers held back orders, expecting prices inflated by the 1877 earthquake to come back down to earth. The government of Pardo's successor tried to take advantage of this situation by buying up beleaguered nitrate companies in Bolivia's sector of the Pampa de Tamarugal. Many sold out, but by far the largest concern, the Antofagasta Nitrate & Railway Company, refused. This British- and Chilean-owned company soon got into trouble with the Bolivian government. At the end of 1877, congressmen representing the coast proposed a tax on nitrate exports to pay for the repair and improvement of ports damaged by the 1877 quake. Desperate for funds, the Bolivian Congress imposed a modest export tax of 100 cents per metric ton. The Antofagasta Company refused to pay, however, on the grounds that this violated an 1874 treaty that exonerated Chilean companies from paying Bolivian taxes for 25 years to encourage coastal investment during the Great Panic. In January 1879, with a worsening crisis in the highlands on its hands, the Bolivian government began seizing company assets to cover unpaid taxes.[123]

Chile's rulers, with British acquiescence, brought Liebig's prophecy to fruition. For years, Chile had aggressively asserted territorial rights in the Atacama region. Bolivia and Chile might have gone to war over the Mejillones guano islands in the 1860s if Spain had not tried to seize the Chincha Islands. This danger convinced these two neighbors to settle their differences over guano and set the contested Chile-Bolivia border at 24 degrees south, but no one was in a mood for compromise this time. A vocal group of Chilean capitalists, led by those owning interests along the Bolivian coast,

[122] Greenhill and Miller, "The Nitrate Trade," 123; T. W. Fletcher, "The Great Depression of English Agriculture 1873–1896," *Economic History Review* 13 (1961): 417–32; Prothero, *Pioneers and Progress* ch. 11; Orwin and Whetham, *History of British Agriculture*, 9–11, 138, 148, 357–62; Turner et al., *Farm Production in England*, fig. 3.8, 3.9b; Michael Hulme and Elaine Barrow, eds., *Climates of the British Isles: Present, Past, and Future* (London and New York, 1999), 272, 278, tables D.1–2.

[123] Greenhill and Miller, "The Nitrate Trade," 123–24, 128; Bermúdez, *Historia del salitre*, ch. 8; Querejazu, *Guano, salitre, sangre*, ch. 9–10.

had already begun promoting war as salvation from these difficult times months before Bolivia took action against the Antofagasta Company. Even though most Chilean-owned nitrate firms had gone bankrupt and come under Peruvian government control by this date, jingoists argued that Chile possessed a natural right to the Atacama because Chilean entrepreneurs and workers had invested so much in the region.[124] Historians have buried the events that followed under a heap of nationalist posturing and legalist rhetoric, but no one denies that Chilean marines invaded coastal Bolivia on 14 February 1879 to protect the interests of the Antofagasta Company. Chile knew that Peru and Bolivia had signed a mutual defense pact in 1873 for just this sort of situation, so it also made a preemptive strike to the north that soon resulted in the occupation of Tarapacá, Peru's guano islands, even Lima itself. Peru and Bolivia nevertheless fought a long, bloody war of attrition. By the Treaty of Ancón signed in 1884, Chile took Bolivia's entire coastline and Peru's province of Tarapacá, which gave Chile sole control over the world's most valuable source of nitrogen compounds. Chile also took half of Peru's guano proceeds during the 1880s. This brought an abrupt end to Peru's guano age.[125]

The War of the Pacific (1879–84) was one of the largest armed conflicts ever fought in the Americas and provided a preview of the massive wars fought over phosphate, petroleum, *Lebensraum*, and other resources during the twentieth century. It violently confirmed the significance of nitrogen compounds to global history during the nineteenth century. As expected, global demand for Atacama nitrates continued to grow – to more than one million tons a year by 1890 – and continued to feed the North's industrialization. Meanwhile, European demand for traditional forms of manure and gunpowder fell into precipitous decline and brought ruin to Bihar, which was further devastated by the abrupt relocation of the Gandak and Ghaghra rivers and two horrific droughts. Chile, too, proved unable to escape the curse of dependence on nitrate exports and experienced another debt crisis and its own civil war over nitrogen before the century was done.[126]

Alexander von Humboldt and his followers had high hopes for this revolutionary age, which opened Pacific South America to the world like never before. Peruvian guano and nitrates fascinated chemists and agricultural improvers of the nineteenth century, who in turn revealed the significance of nitrogen to life and its ability to power technologies of death. Guano and nitrates enabled Peru to make a name for itself as an independent nation and

---

[124] Ortega, "Origins of the War of the Pacific"; William Sater, "Chile and the World Depression of the 1870s," *JLAS* 11 (1979): 67–99; Querejazu, *Guano, salitre, sangre*, 44–57, 60–67, 241–50; O'Brien, *The Nitrate Industry*, 45–49.

[125] Sater, *Andean Tragedy: Fighting the War of the Pacific, 1879–1884* (Lincoln, NE, 2007).

[126] Anand Yang, *Bazaar India: Markets, Society and the Colonial State in Gangetic Bihar* (Berkeley and Los Angeles, 1999), 28, 47, 50, 52, 74–78, 175–78; Harold Blakemore, *British Nitrates and Chilean Politics, 1886–1896* (Ann Arbor, MI, 1999).

propelled the Industrial Revolution forward to a new phase. Nitrate-derived explosives even endowed the Nobel Prizes. How many things have played such a transformative role in history?

In other ways, however, the guano age truly deserves its reputation as an "age of shit." Rather than improving the world's food supply during an era of profound environmental instability, Peruvian guano mainly served northern consumers of meat and sugar. Rather than inaugurating an epoch of peace and prosperity, guano and nitrates inspired wars and fueled the growth of inequalities between classes and nations. Although guano and sewage disposal helped improve the soil and urban environments, nitrate mining deeply scarred the most ancient arid landscape on earth. Most significantly, Peruvian guano opened the gateway to modern farming's addiction to inputs. This does not even begin to consider the relationship between guano and imperialism in the Central Pacific, the subject of the next two chapters.

3

Neo-Ecological Imperialism

Anno. 1621. Then the sickness begane to fall sore amongst [us], and the weather so bad as they could not make much sooner any despatch. . . . Afterwards (as many as were able) began to plant there corne, in which servise Squanto stood them in great stead . . . And he tould them excepte they gott fish and set with it (in these old grounds) it would come to nothing, and he showed them . . . wher to get other provisions necessary for them . . . Which made many afterwards write so largely of their plenty hear to the freinds in England.

    – William Bradford, "Of Plimmoth Plantation" (ca. 1630)

In 1621, before embarking for New England to join the original colonists of Plymouth Plantation, Robert Cushman gave what is now considered a notorious sermon on the environmental ethics of colonialism. "What right have I to go live in the heathen's country?" he asked. In his view, he had a moral duty to go forth and *improve* this foreign land: "Their land is spacious and void, and there are few, and do but run over the grass, as do also the foxes and wild beasts. They are not industrious, neither have art, science, skill or faculty to use either the land or the commodities of it; but all spoils, rots, and is marred for want of manuring, gathering, ordering, &c."[1]

Once he arrived, Cushman discovered a situation different from what he expected. The New England coast had not always been unsettled or unimproved: "By reason of a great mortality that fell amongst [the Indians] three years since, . . . hath so wasted them, as I think the twentieth person is scarce alive." Because this pestilence had vacated the land of most of its indigenous inhabitants, "They offer us to dwell where we will. We found the place where we live empty, the people being all dead and gone away,

[1] Robert Cushman, "Reasons and Considerations Touching the Lawfulness of Removing Out of England into the Parts of America," in *A Historical and Biographical Genealogy of the Cushmans: The Descendants of Robert Cushman, the Puritan, from the Year 1617 to 1855*, by Henry Wyles Cushman (Boston, 1855), 31, 34.

75

and none living near by 8 or 10 miles." He also found out that if not for the teaching of a formerly enslaved Patuxet Indian named Tisquantum and a cache of maize found during the previous winter, the original *Mayflower* Pilgrims all might have perished from scurvy and starvation and never would have enjoyed an abundant harvest at the end of their first year. In light of these discoveries, Robert Cushman thought the Plymouth settlers had a reciprocal moral duty toward the local Indians to "have them in our houses eating and drinking, and warming themselves,... because they should see and take knowledge of our labors, order and diligence, both for this life and a better."[2]

The full moral significance of these actions was not revealed for several generations. Cushman's descendants increased in number and subdued the bounteous garden and ocean that Tisquantum revealed to them in New England, but they also cursed the ground in many places, causing it to produce thorns and thistles.[3]

A number of ecological factors helped the Cushman race accomplish these deeds. These included microbial epidemics, new crop plants, Old World livestock and weeds, and other portmanteau biota that prosper alongside human disturbance. The Cushmans' never-ending connection by wind and wave to a storehouse of people back in the mother country was also vital. These forces of "ecological imperialism," as historian Alfred Crosby called them, played a pivotal role in the initial conquest of the Americas and Pacific Basin by European-derived peoples. These forces not only powered "the Caucasian tsunami" that swept many parts of the world during the modern era, but also at some level helped the First Peoples who settled Australasia, the Americas, and the Pacific Islands during ancient times. This has led some to wonder if *Homo sapiens* evolved a unique tendency to act as an "exterminator species."[4]

The ecological bounty produced by colonizing lifestyles is bound to be short-lived, however. Invasive farmers and herders – even hunters and gatherers – will eventually use up the abundance they find in newly conquered lands. The forces of conquest ecological imperialism do not adequately explain how settler colonies continued to prosper, much less how they developed into prosperous postcolonial nations.[5] Colonizing societies that hope

---

[2] Robert Cushman, "To His Loving Friends and Adventurers for New-England" (12 Dec. 1621) in *Genealogy of the Cushmans*, 43–44; these documents have been republished frequently.

[3] Genesis 1:28, 3:17–19; William Cronon, *Changes in the Land: Indians, Colonists, and the Ecology of New England* (New York, 1983), esp. 56–57.

[4] Crosby, *Ecological Imperialism*, esp. 300; Tim Flannery, *The Future Eaters: An Ecological History of the Australasian Lands and People* (Chatswood, Australia, 1994), ch. 8.

[5] Timothy Weiskel, "Agents of Empire: Steps Toward an Ecology of Imperialism," *Environmental Review* 11 (1987): 275–88.

to endure have three basic options: (1) they can leave and colonize new environments, (2) they can learn to live within the ecological limits imposed by local environments, or (3) they can import goods, services, and energy from other ecosystems and search for the "ultimate sink" where unwanted waste can be exported. Several chapters in this book trace the historical consequences of pursuing this third option. I call the more exploitative forms of this pursuit "neo-ecological imperialism."

There are many reasons for referring to these trends as neo-ecological imperialism. First and foremost, it is distinct ecologically and follows in succession from the forms described by Crosby. Rather than enabling the conquest of new environments and their settlement by invasive organisms and ethnicities, neo-ecological imperialism primarily focused on the maintenance and improvement of environments already inhabited by European-derived peoples. In the Pacific World, neo-ecological imperialism at first focused on the search for whales, manure, and minerals, which were used to provide light, replenish soils, and produce meat in locales close to imperial centers of population and power. Later, it shifted to the production of soap and marine fish, which were used to improve health, beauty, and living standards in these locales. To a major extent, neo-European societies in the United States, Australia, New Zealand, Peru, and Chile propelled the conquests described in the next two chapters, not the Great Powers of Europe. These postcolonial nations turned imperial powers did so, in large part, to remedy the depopulation and degradation of lands conquered during earlier phases of ecological imperialism. They sometimes did so without formally colonizing the overseas territories and peoples they were exploiting, a phenomenon known variously as neocolonialism, informal imperialism, or even the "American form of colonialism." These trends were also integrally linked to the insatiable appetite of northerners for tropical commodities and the search for overseas markets to sell industrially produced consumer goods. Scholars often refer to these tendencies as the "New Imperialism." The period from 1850 to 1945 was the heyday of these new forms of imperialism, a century that witnessed the complete integration of the islands, continents, and waters of the Pacific World into the main currents of modern global history.[6]

Neo-ecological imperialism has many similarities with its conquest form and sometimes worked in concert with it. Disease-causing microbes and

---

[6] To avoid adding an additional level of complexity to this study, it will not make a formal distinction between "colonialism" and "imperialism." Robert Young, *Postcolonialism: A Historical Introduction* (Malden, MA, 2001), ch. 3–4; Tulio Halperín, *The Contemporary History of Latin America* (1969; Durham, NC, 1993), ch. 4–5; Tucker, *Insatiable Appetite: The United States and the Ecological Degradation of the Tropical World* (Berkeley and Los Angeles, 2000).

other portmanteau biota often prospered in the disturbed environments created by neo-ecological imperialism. However, dysentery and tuberculosis, two diseases that thrive on people with beaten-down immunological defenses who are poorly fed and overworked, did more killing than so-called virgin soil epidemics under this regime. Colonized regions and peoples also bore the brunt of the environmental degradation and human suffering generated by neo-ecological imperialism. It is nevertheless vital to recognize that non-European peoples who provided labor and know-how to these imperial projects often did so in an attempt to circumvent ecological limitations imposed by their own home environments. This was especially true of Pacific Islanders. Unlike many studies of the relationship between ecology and empire, this account will give sustained attention to the agency of indigenous peoples in these transformations.

During the late nineteenth and early twentieth centuries, God, glory, gold, and guano motivated outsiders to seek to dominate the indigenous environments and societies of the Central Pacific. This chapter examines two case studies, both intimately tied to the expansion of the guano industry, in which the forces of neo-ecological imperialism subordinated some of the earth's most isolated territories and peoples to improve the lives of neo-European societies elsewhere. The first case focuses on the aspirations of American nation-states in the Island Pacific. U.S. overseas imperialism got its start by claiming dozens of uninhabited atolls with guano deposits in the Pacific and Caribbean Basins, starting with an aborted attempt to seize islands already claimed by Peru. The U.S. Civil War severely disrupted the United States' relationship with the rest of the world and inspired guano age traders in Peru and Chile to look west for labor and land to colonize. This unleashed one of the most destructive episodes of conquest ecological imperialism the world has ever seen, particularly on isolated Easter Island. The second case follows Anglos with close ties to Australia and New Zealand who also took advantage of the Civil War to move into the Central Pacific. They later converted the bird islands of the region into producers of coconut oil, a key ingredient in several popular brands of soap. In one of the tragic ironies of history, their activities greatly improved their home environments, to the point of driving the Garden City movement. However, they also spread deadly diarrheal illnesses in the Pacific, a class of disease that soap and good hygiene were supposed to prevent. This second case also examines the participation of the First Peoples of Niue and other drought-prone coral atolls in this new ecological regime. Paid work harvesting guano or planting coconut palms (*Cocos nucifera*) provided a valuable means to extend their families' resource base beyond local constraints, particularly during extreme phases of the El Niño-Southern Oscillation. It also provided them with access to a world of improvements from the other side of the sea, but at the cost of subjugating themselves to parasitic forms of governance and trade and increasing their vulnerability to invasive organisms.

Guano and American Expansionism

Polycarpus and Henry Cushman (1778–1855, 1805–63) did not agree on politics: in 1844, the elder Whig patriarch beat his Democratic son in a race for the State Senate of Massachusetts. However, they agreed enthusiastically on the value of agricultural and civic improvements. Both men hoped to create community cohesion for a cattle-raising region in agrarian decline and agonizingly close to environmental exhaustion. During the 1850s, they were instrumental in the establishment of the Franklin County Agricultural Society and County Fair "to show what can be done by the application of science in the improvement of the soil" and "to furnish a rational, well-conducted and improving holiday for the whole people."[7] Father and son took this improving spirit to Boston. As a freshman state representative, Henry successfully introduced a bill in 1837 directing the State Geological Survey to focus its attention on the Commonwealth's soils. As lieutenant governor, he pushed through the establishment of a State Board of Agriculture in 1852. Like so many other rich, ambitious, socially prominent farmers of the day on the eastern seaboard, Henry wanted to deepen both the agricultural and social roots of his state's citizenry. Thus, he played a leading role in antebellum movements to promote scientific agriculture, build monuments to the Pilgrims of Plymouth Colony, and celebrate family reunions such as Thanksgiving.[8]

Polycarpus and Henry Cushman also took to heart their forefather's dictum to use every "art, science, skill or faculty" at their disposal for manuring their land. Henry even endorsed an indigenous technology from South America for this purpose. In his first experiment with guano, he staked off a piece of poor, worn-out property that had not been manured for three or four years. "On the 16th of May, a damp day, I sowed on this piece at the rate of 215 lbs. of Peruvian guano to the acre.... The result was a very visible and immediate effect on the growth of grass.... The quantity of grass produced, so near as I could judge without weighing, was almost *double* that on the adjoining land." He got even better results with buckwheat. Improved cattle feed entailed more meat and milk production on his farm, more animal manure to invest on his fields, and greater profits in years to come. Perhaps it meant salvation for New England's declining cattle economy.[9]

---

7 Henry Cushman quoted in Mark Mastromarino, " 'Cattle Aplenty and Other Things in Proportion': The Agricultural Society and Fair in Franklin County, Massachusetts, 1810–1860," *UCLA Historical Journal* 5 (1984): 65; Ritchie Garrison, *Landscape and Material Life in Franklin County, Massachusetts, 1770–1860* (Knoxville, TN, 1991).

8 Cushman, *Genealogy of the Cushmans*, 245–47, 439–48; James O'Gorman, "The Colossus of Plymouth: Mammatt Billings's National Monument to the Forefathers," *Journal of the Society of Architectural Historians* 54 (1995): 288; Elizabeth Pleck, "The Making of the Domestic Occasion: The History of Thanksgiving in the United States," *Journal of Social History* 32 (1999): 773–89.

9 Cushman's emphasis, quoted in Charles Bartlett, *Guano: A Treatise* (Boston, 1860), 16–17.

Henry was not alone in these sentiments. His neighbors to the south who grew tobacco were just as enthusiastic because guano helped young plants outgrow weeds and reputedly caused tobacco worm to "turn sick." With the help of guano, they converted the Connecticut valley into a lasting exporter of some of the world's finest tobacco. They also sold off lower-grade leaf for trade on the other side of the earth where addicted Pacific Islanders eagerly enslaved themselves to this "new god."[10] On light, easily leached soils surrounding Chesapeake Bay, Peruvian guano and other new inputs enabled grain farmers to resume cultivation of abandoned pine scrublands that had been worn out by tobacco cultivation during the early colonial period. Some plantation owners close to major ports in the Deep South also used guano in great quantities. Even slaves who grew market crops were known to pool their own capital so they could purchase guano.[11]

For the small but vocal class of agricultural improvers in the antebellum United States, manures of this virtue presented a possible remedy to soil exhaustion, rural emigration, and the erosion of political power from the eastern seaboard to the western frontier. Many hoped that careful steward-ship of the land would reduce the temptation to move and, in the process, create a better, more lasting world. From his tireless genealogical research, Henry realized how many of his farming kin had uprooted themselves from the lands of their birth to "seek bread for his family in a wilderness." For many in this colonizing society, the temptation to move on to enjoy the ecological bounty of new lands was great. To take but one example known to him, Henry's distant cousins Barnabas and Silas Cushman (1787–1861, 1837–1927) – the author's direct ancestors – migrated west from the forested wilderness of the Green Mountains of Vermont, to the shores of Lake Eire, to the Lead Rush district of Wisconsin. Silas and his son Elmer (1868–1958) then continued on to a sod house in the heavily indigenous Dakota Terri-tory, to a chicken ranch on the California-Mexico border, and finally to a suburban home in smoggy Los Angeles – all in the course of three lives.[12] They migrated west with swarms of Anglo colonists, causing drastic envi-ronmental changes wherever they tarried. Stories of "improvers" such as Polycarpus and Henry and "emigrants" like Barnabas, Silas, and Elmer are

[10] Bartlett, *Guano*, 16–17, 32–33; James O'Gorman, *Connecticut Valley Vernacular: The Vanishing Landscape and Architecture of the New England Tobacco Fields* (Philadelphia, 2002); Macdonald, *Cinderellas of Empire*, 18–19, 24, 39.

[11] Wines, *Fertilizer in America*, 36–42, 47–53; Weymouth Jordan, "The Peruvian Guano Gospel in the Old South," *Agricultural History* 24 (1950): 211–21; Ira Berlin and Philip Morgan, *Cultivation and Culture: Labor and the Shaping of Slave Life in the Americas* (Charlottesville, VA, 1993), 272.

[12] Cushman, *Genealogy of the Cushmans*, v, 145, 182, 447–48, 541; *Commemorative Bio-graphical Record of the Counties of Rock, Green, Grant, Iowa, and Lafayette, Wisconsin* (Chicago, 1901), 685–86; family documents, photographs, and oral tradition from Arthur Cushman (Elmer's grandson and the author's father).

not special to the author's family. They are central to the ecological history of North America.[13]

Yet was Henry Cushman's decision to use every "art, science, skill or faculty" available to him to improve his lands *morally* superior to the emigrant path taken by my direct ancestors during their destructive march to the Pacific? With guano added to the accounting, it becomes clear that both emigrant and improving lines of the Cushman race in America achieved better lives for themselves and their progeny at great ecological cost – and at the direct expense of people like Tisquantum.

This was an era of unbridled territorial expansionism by the United States. U.S. historians tend to obscure the fact that Latin American events played a fundamental role in almost every major conquest by the United States from 1800 to 1850: from the purchase of the Louisiana Territory in 1803 after France's defeat by Haitian revolutionaries, to the occupation of Florida during the 1810s during the Spanish American independence wars, to the seizure of half of Mexico during the war of 1846–48. This does not begin to account for the number of U.S. "filibusters" who intervened in Latin American affairs. To the chagrin of Northeasterners like Polycarpus and Henry Cushman, these new possessions nurtured hosts of agricultural competitors and enabled the expansion of chattel slavery to new lands.[14]

But some forms of territorial expansion directly served the interests of improving farmers. During the 1850s, American entrepreneurs began combing the earth's oceans for guano islands so they could bypass the Peruvian monopoly. They received indispensable support from the U.S. federal government. Alfred Benson (1804–78), a Brooklyn merchant, took the lead in these efforts as a way to fill his ships' holds on their way back from Gold Rush California. In 1852, he hatched a plan with Secretary of State Daniel Webster – an improving farmer and enthusiastic guano consumer in his own right – to use navy gunboats to lay claim to the Lobos Islands off the northern coast of Peru. Great Britain and Peru vociferously objected, and the United States backed off, but the Lobos affair nonetheless set off an international race to claim small oceanic islands. The British Navy instructed its ships to look carefully for unclaimed territories and formally annexed the Khurīyā Murīyā Islands off what is now Oman, even though their ancient deposits had already been removed. José Villamil (1788–1866), the founder of a cattle-ranching and penal colony on the Galápagos, returned from the gold fields of California to look for guano to help secure Ecuador's claim to

[13] Steven Stoll, *Larding the Lean Earth: Soil and Society in Nineteenth-Century America* (New York, 2002), 49–68, 187–94; Cohen, *Notes from the Ground*, 54–5, 79–80, 133–34.

[14] James Loewen, *Lies My Teacher Told Me: Everything Your American History Textbooks Got Wrong* (New York, 1996), 150–52; Anders Stephanson, *Manifest Destiny: American Expansionism and the Empire of Right* (New York, 1995), ch. 2; Robert May, *Manifest Destiny's Underworld: Filibustering in Antebellum America* (Chapel Hill, NC, 2002).

these islands. He found none of significance, however, and Ecuador's efforts at overseas imperialism on the Galápagos continued to languish until the lichen-harvesting boom of the 1860s to produce orchil dyes. Meanwhile, Benson redirected his sights to equatorial atolls in the Central Pacific. Other Americans targeted tiny bird islands in the Caribbean, leading to protests from the governments of Mexico, Venezuela, and Haiti against unauthorized guano mining on islands they claimed. In 1858, President James Buchanan sent the USS *Saratoga* to Navassa Island off the southwestern tip of Haiti to fend off two Haitian warships trying to stop the removal of "rock guano" by Baltimore fertilizer merchants. Two years earlier, the U.S. Congress had passed the Guano Island Act to legitimate these actions. This law empowered U.S. citizens to lay temporary territorial claim to uninhabited guano islands based on the class of laws that enabled hunting of wild animals on public commons and the open seas. All told, the United States laid claim to 66 islands around the world under the Guano Act, nine of which are still official possessions.[15]

U.S. claims under the 1856 Guano Islands Act represent an important landmark not only in the history of U.S. imperialism but also for the place of remote islands in global geopolitical history. Not to be outdone, the United Kingdom claimed Kiritimati (Christmas) and Malden Islands in the Central Pacific and belatedly annexed the Namibian guano islands. Claiming a guano island became a favored way for a country to assert itself as a colonizing power: France, the Kingdom of Hawaii, Japan, Mexico, Germany, and Australia, among others, all joined the scramble in the Pacific. Ecuador and Chile colonized remote islands with other resources. In later years, these islands took on new geopolitical importance as coaling stations, relay points for undersea telegraph cables, and eventually as air bases. By World War I, nearly every insular territory in the Pacific Basin except on its far southern rim was theoretically subject to some distant government.[16]

The global guano rush had a discernible environmental impact on these islands. This was not the first time that humans had visited many of these

[15] Skaggs, *Great Guano Rush*, ch. 2–4, 6, 11; Mathew, *House of Gibbs*, 147–65; Dan O'Donnell, "The Lobos Islands: American Imperialism in Peruvian Waters in 1852," *Australian Journal of Politics and History* 39 (1993): 37–55; Christina Duffy Burnett, "The Edges of Empire and the Limits of Sovereignty: American Guano Islands," *American Quarterly* 57 (2005): 779–803; Rexford Sherman, "Daniel Webster, Gentleman Farmer," *Agricultural History* 53 (1979): 475–88; Octavio Latorre, *El hombre en las Islas Encantadas: La historia humana de Galápagos* (Quito, 1999).

[16] Skaggs, *Great Guano Rush*, ch. 5, 7; Dan O'Donnell, "The Pacific Guano Islands: The Stirring of American Empire in the Pacific Ocean," *Pacific Studies* 16 (1993): 43–66; Wines, *Fertilizer in America*, ch. 4; Hutchinson, "Biogeochemistry of Vertebrate Excretion," figs. 45, 61, 67, 69; Gerard Ward, ed., *American Activities in the Central Pacific, 1790–1870* (Ridgewood, NJ, 1967), 3:421–22, 5:467–69; Ben Daley and Peter Griggs, "Mining the Reefs and Cays: Coral, Guano and Rock Phosphate Extraction in the Great Barrier Reef, Australia, 1844-1940," *Environment and History* 12 (2006): 395–433.

remote locales. On the Line and Phoenix Islands, basalt artifacts originating from Samoa and the Marquesas indicate that Polynesian mariners began frequenting these low atolls during the twelfth century.[17] Like the coast of Peru, these arid islands are also subject to long droughts, especially when La Niña conditions prevail. Their terrestrial biodiversity is extremely low, freshwater scarce, and agriculture difficult. Polynesians came mainly to harvest birds, eggs, green turtles (*Chelonia mydas*), and other marine organisms nourished by intense upwelling along the equator. As with other "mystery islands" of Remote Oceania, however, Polynesians abandoned the Line and Phoenix Islands during the calamitous fourteenth century, perhaps because of human-induced resource depletion.[18]

In 1855, Alfred Benson formed the American Guano Company to harvest guano from the Line and Phoenix Islands. New England whalers provided intelligence vital to locating these specks of land, and two major figures in the American colonization of Hawaii, missionary physician Gerrit Judd and his son Charles, supplied logistical support. The Judds recruited indigenous Hawaiians to work the guano deposits and released rabbits to diversify the local meat supply. A chemical analysis of fresh guano that they arranged also started the rumor that the Central Pacific possessed vast deposits equivalent to the genuine Peruvian article. Following in the footsteps of the South Seas Exploring Expedition commanded by Charles Wilkes, the U.S. Navy sent a ship to Baker and Jarvis Islands to investigate the situation. Joseph Henry, the most celebrated figure of the time in American science, orchestrated the analysis of seventeen guano samples at the Smithsonian Institution's chemical laboratory. The Smithsonian concluded that these deposits were indeed avian guano and subject to claims under the Guano Act but were "almost entirely deficient in nitrogenous matter" thanks to periodic heavy rainfall and about "as valuable as bone dust." This did not stop New England newspapers from heavily promoting this new source of fertilizer, a strategy that backfired badly when the American Guano Company returned home with its first cargoes in 1858 and discovered they were mixed with worthless gypsum. To prevent such expensive errors, the company hired a virtual clone of Mariano de Rivero, mining engineer James D. Hague, to survey the

---

[17] The Phoenix Islands include Birnie, Canton (Abariringa), Enderbury, Gardner (Nikumaroro), Hull (Orona), McKean, Phoenix (Rawaki), and Sydney (Manra) Islands. They are now part of Kiribati. Two U.S. territories, Baker and Howland Islands, are nearby.

[18] Anne Di Piazza and Erik Pearthree, "Voyaging and Basalt Exchange in the Phoenix and Line Archipelagoes," *Archaeology in Oceania* 36 (2001): 146–52; idem, "An Island for Gardens, an Island for Birds and Voyaging: A Settlement Pattern for Kiritimati and Tabuaeran," *Journal of the Polynesian Society* 110 (2001): 149–70; Atholl Anderson et al., "Towards a First Prehistory of Kiritimati," *Journal of the Polynesian Society* 109 (2000): 273–93; Patrick Nunn and James Britton, "Human-Environment Relationships in the Pacific Islands around A.D. 1300," *Environment and History* 7 (2001): 3–22.

region systematically. Hague was greatly impressed by the geological diversity of deposits on these islands and noted that nesting bird populations, just recently "very numerous... have since been perceptibly decreasing." Other changes to the islands appeared quite old, however. The ancient inhabitants of Howland Island had apparently planted groves of *kou* trees (*Cordia subcordata*) – of great value for wood carving – and left behind a population of tiny Pacific rats (*Rattus exulans*). These rodents had since become "almost as numerous as the birds" and long since destroyed the breeding populations of several ground-nesting species.[19] Hague went on to play a key role in the extension of mining in the North American West, again demonstrating the overt linkage between Humboldtian science, ecological imperialism, and U.S. expansionism.[20]

As we learned in Chapter 2, whaling, Humboldtian exploration, and Pacific trade all helped start the global guano rush. These trends, in turn, fed the growth of merchant and industrial cities in the eastern United States, which enabled well-situated farmers like Henry Cushman to make a killing supplying them with agricultural products. However, the election of a frontier farmer turned free-soil politician named Abraham Lincoln to the U.S. presidency in 1860 severely disrupted these expansionist tendencies. Intense rivalry over the extension of slavery to newly conquered lands in the U.S. West exploded into one of the most destructive armed conflicts the world had ever seen. This five-year Civil War not only disrupted the U.S. South's ability to consume guano and supply the industrial North with raw cotton produced by slave labor, its influence extended to the farthest reaches of the earth. Ethically minded men and women were hopeful that the destruction of the South's "peculiar institution" would create a better, more prosperous world. Henry Cushman believed "that all sorts of slavery – moral, political, conventional, as well as physical – are to be ameliorated and abolished by the diffusion of knowledge, Christianity, and republicanism; and that such an advance in civilization is to come through the great democratic ideas and the democratic organizations of our country."[21] In the short term, however, the U.S. Civil War dramatically accelerated the enslavement and destruction of indigenous peoples and environments around the world, especially in the Central Pacific. These far-reaching impacts were not part of the moral calculus of people like Henry Cushman.

[19] Isaac Toucey to Henry, 8, 24 Mar. 1858; Henry to Toucey, 28 May 1858; Henry, Desk Diary, 25 Mar., 29 May 1858, Smithsonian Institution Archives, Henry papers 6/18, 14/1. Hague, "On Phosphatic Guano Islands of the Pacific Ocean," *American Journal of Science* 34 (1862): 224–43; Skaggs, *Great Guano Rush*, 68–69, 72–73, 77–78, 144.

[20] Contra Sachs, *The Humboldt Current*. Cf. Goetzmann, *Exploration and Empire*, 433–34; John Harrison, "Science and Politics: Origins and Objectives of Mid-Nineteenth Century Government Expeditions to Latin America," *Hispanic American Historical Review* 35 (1955): 175–202.

[21] Cushman, *Genealogy of the Cushmans*, 447.

With the U.S. South preoccupied, farmers, traders, and industrialists from Brazil and Peru to Angola and India scrambled to establish new sources of cotton supply, often using coerced forms of labor. Peru's ability to grab a quick share of this trade was a result of earlier efforts by guano age improvers like Domingo Elías. Unlike plantation owners in Brazil and Angola, Peruvian planters could not use enslaved blacks for labor, thanks to the abolition decree of 1854 funded by Peru's guano receipts. Instead, many hired indentured laborers from South China.[22]

At this opportune moment, an Irish-born swindler named Joseph Byrne brought the idea of importing Pacific Islanders to Peru. He was one of the most notorious "emigration vultures" of the age, and a tireless agent of the sort of ecological imperialism described by Crosby. From 1847 to 1852, he convinced more than a thousand British colonists to establish cotton farms in Natal, southern Africa, claiming that their resettlement would reduce industrial Britain's Malthusian overpopulation and its immoral dependence on cotton produced by American slaves. Cotton failed miserably on the cool, arid scrublands he sold to most settlers, compelling Byrne to slink off to the gold rush district of Australia where he had earlier worked as a sheepherder. He later obtained a huge land grant to settle European colonists in New Caledonia and even tried to convince Belgium to colonize the New Hebrides. Most of his schemes ended up in bankruptcy court.[23]

Byrne showed up in Lima at the height of the wartime boom and soon obtained an official permit to recruit "natives of the South Western Islands of the Pacific" to work in Peru. By this date, the Pacific Island labor trade had become well established in some regions. During the late 1840s, one of Australia's most famous early cattle barons, Benjamin Boyd, recruited a few hundred Melanesians to drive sheep across the interior of New South Wales. Pacific Islanders, however, preferred the more familiar work provided by coconut plantations springing up around the region, such as those on Fanning Island (Tabuaeran), one of the wettest of the Line Islands. In July 1862, Byrne's first and last Peruvian recruiting voyage laid anchor at Tongareva, a large atoll on the southern margin of settlement in the Central Pacific dry zone, 8,800 kilometers due west of Callao. By luck, he arrived in the midst of a prolonged La Niña drought when most of the island's coconut palms had died or stopped bearing, food and water were scarce, and many families were eager to escape famine. Some Tongarevans had experience working on Fanning Island, and a number had already left for plantations

---

[22] Stewart, *Chinese Bondage*, ch. 2, 4; Anne Pitcher, "Sowing the Seeds of Failure: Early Portuguese Cotton Cultivation in Angola and Mozambique, 1820–1926," *Journal of Southern African Studies* 17 (1991): 43–70.

[23] Matthew Schnurr, "Lowveld Cotton: A Political Ecology of Agricultural Failure in Natal and Zululand, 1844–1948," (Ph.D. thesis, Univ. of British Columbia, 2008), 52–74; Shelagh O'Byrne Spencer, "Joseph Byrne," in *British Settlers in Natal, 1824–1857*, http://shelaghspencer.tripod.com/id9.html.

in Tahiti. With the encouragement of local missionaries, eighty-three families accepted Byrne's offer to go to Peru for several years as indentured workers. None ever saw their homes again. Byrne died on the return voyage, but his partners earned a profit on the sale of their labor contracts surpassing 300 percent.[24]

This rather unexceptional episode in the history of the Pacific labor trade grew into one of history's monstrous catastrophes when another thirty South American vessels hurriedly rushed west to see whether they could find workers for Peru's booming cotton plantations. Peruvian labor merchants have a reputation for coercive behavior in this saga that is not entirely deserved. We know from climatic reconstructions that the entire Pacific Basin experienced an exceptionally long and intense La Niña event from 1860 to 1863, which brought severe drought not only to the Central Pacific but also to the midwestern United States.[25] As a consequence, Peruvian labor merchants found many willing recruits on drought-stricken islands in a triangle stretching north and west from Tongareva and the Marquesas to the southern Gilbert Islands (now Kiribati), but they had little success in parts of southern Polynesia typically blessed by abundant rains during La Niña events. Rather than sailing away empty-handed, however, Peruvians often resorted to deceit or kidnapping to fill their holds. One ship captain, for example, told recruits they were headed for Kiritimati to harvest sea cucumber and pearl shell. A few captured islanders fought their way off these thinly disguised slaving ships, but many others died in the attempt.[26]

Peruvian labor recruiting had its most devastating effect on Easter Island (Rapa Nui), a place famous for its enormous stone statues and scale of its environmental degradation. At one time, it possessed the richest assemblage of seabirds of any single island in Polynesia – at least twenty-five species. The arrival of humans at least 800 years ago resulted in a holocaust for Easter Island's avian inhabitants and disappearance of its native palm woodlands by the end of the seventeenth century.[27]

The First People of Easter Island, the Rapanui, learned to adapt – even flourish – in these degraded conditions. In stark contrast to Henry Cushman and his kin, they had to rely on local resources to do so. They learned to burn grass and ferns instead of wood for fuel. They decreased their

[24] H. E. Maude, *Slavers in Paradise: The Peruvian Labour Trade in Polynesia, 1862–1864* (Canberra, 1981), 4–11; Kerry Ross Howe, "Tourists, Sailors and Labourers: A Survey of Early Labour Recruiting in Southern Melanesia," *Journal of Pacific History* 13 (1978): 22–35.
[25] Paleoarchives; Herweijer et al., "North American Droughts."
[26] Maude, *Slaving in Paradise*, 21, 51, 55–59, 90–91, tables 1, 8.
[27] David Steadman, "Prehistoric Extinctions of Pacific Island Birds," *Science* 24 Feb. 1995: 1123–31; Terry Hunt and Carl Lipo, "Late Colonization of Easter Island," *Science* 17 Mar. 2006: 1603–6; Hunt and Lipo, "Revisiting Rapa Nui (Easter Island) 'Ecocide,'" *Pacific Science* 63 (2009): 601–16; V. Rull et al., "Paleoecology of Easter Island: Evidence and Uncertainties," *Earth-Science Reviews* 99 (2010): 50–60.

consumption of deep-sea fish and drought-sensitive crops and increased their reliance on drought-resistant sweet potatoes (*Ipomoea batatas*) and chicken husbandry. They built sunken gardens with stone-lined walls to protect sensitive crops from the wind, and they mulched their fields with stones and grass. Archaeologists have detected increased levels of soil phosphorus in these cultivated soils. This strongly suggests the use of fertilizers, which also increase crops' drought resistance.[28] Oral tradition from the 1910s states that the Miru clan possessed the exclusive right to fertilize prestige crops with small fish. They also possessed major responsibilities when drought struck the island. When rain was needed, clan elders would dress in leaves and place wreaths decorated with the tail feathers of male chickens on their heads. They would then climb together to the top of the island's highest volcanic peak where they built a circle of white coral rocks (*punga*). The leader of this ceremony, the island's paramount lord (*'ariki mau*), painted half of his body black with charcoal, the other half of his body red with the juice of the *pua nako nako* berry (*Lycium carolinianum*), leaving a bright white stripe running down the middle. Whiteness was a Rapanui symbol for creative power (*mana*). He waved a bird back and forth while the others sang, danced, and chanted inside the circle asking the sky to alleviate their sorrow by weeping on them. Afterward, the group would journey down to the island's sweet potato fields and bury five to ten white *karakoma* stones in each mound. These buoyant, sponge-like pumice stones float to the island from distant volcanic eruptions. They have excellent water absorption qualities, and the Rapanui used them to add moisture to the ground and retain soil moisture thereafter. (Today they are used in hydroponics.) The Rapanui built elaborate stone chicken enclosures and used white chicken-feather pennants (*maro*) in these soil fertility rituals, but no traditions remain regarding the possible use of chicken guano (*tuta'e*) as a fertilizer. Clan elders also inherited many other forms of creative power described in songs, chants, and genealogies that were written down in an enigmatic script (*rongorongo*)– the only indigenous writing system to develop in Oceania.[29]

The preconquest Rapanui learned to express their respect for birds in other ways. Each year, they eagerly anticipated the return of *manutara* or sooty terns (*Sterna fuscata*), the Central Pacific's most important guano

---

[28] Steadman et al., "Stratigraphy, Chronology, and Cultural Context of an Early Faunal Assemblage from Easter Island," *Asian Perspectives* 33 (1994): 79–96; Cristophe Stevenson et al., "Prehistoric and Early Historic Agriculture at Maunga Orito, Easter Island," *Antiquity* 80 (2006): 919–36; Geertrui Louwagie et al., "The Impact of Moderate to Marginal Land Suitability on Prehistoric Agricultural Production and Models of Adaptive Strategies for Easter Island," *Journal of Anthropological Archaeology* 25 (2006): 290–317.

[29] Pau Hito, personal communication, 19 June 2012; RGS-WSR 4/3/1, p. 19, 4/8, vol. 1, pp. 52–53, 62–63; Katherine Scoresby Routledge, *The Mystery of Easter Island: The Story of an Expedition* (London, 1919), 241–54; Fischer, *Island at the End of the World*, 63–64, 82–83.

bird. A flock returns each spring soon after the constellation of the birdman twins Haua and Makemake – which we know as Gemini – reappears out of the rising sun's glare on the eastern horizon. The arrival of these birds and bird stars announced the end of the southern winter and a change in the dominant winds from west to east, which heralded the reappearance of tuna and other deep-sea fish in abundance. Oceanographic research has shown that abrupt changes in the predominant wind field can cause intense bursts of upwelling and blooms of phytoplankton on the leeward side of seamounts, which attract birds and fish in large numbers.[30]

This combination of events possessed enormous significance for the pre-conquest Rapanui. Men selected from each clan gathered on two small islets to search for the first egg of the season. The fortunate individual who found the first egg gave it to his clan sponsor, who became the year's birdman (*tangata manu*). Possession of this powerful fertility symbol transformed the birdman and his retainers into personifications of the *makohe* or great frigatebird (*Fregata minor*). For the next twelve cycles of the moon, he and his victorious clan lived out the year by taking food and other items from the rest of the island's populace – by violence if necessary. These actions mimicked frigatebirds, which are well known for kleptoparasitism, the practice of harassing other marine birds to drop their catch. In reciprocity, the birdman and the egg together bestowed fertility to the land and sea. As the *manutara*'s breeding season progressed, a party from the birdman's clan swam out to these islets to collect eggs and chicks. No eggs could be gathered or consumed until this time, which gave most the chance to hatch and prevented the species' destruction. Some birds were eaten, a few others were raised until they could fly, when they were banded with a small strip of red cloth and sent off with the words, "*Ka oho ki Hiva*. Go forth to the World Outside."[31]

Peruvian labor traders came crashing into the world of Easter Island's birdmen in October 1862. The Rapanui were not naïve to the dangers of dealing with outsiders. Many men and women had experience working as deck hands or in the sex trade with visiting whalers. In 1805, a U.S. seal-hunting vessel kidnapped twenty-two Rapanui to work on the Juan

---

[30] The author identified the relationship between these natural phenomena, heretofore unrecognized by scholars, with help from the star-mapping utility Your Sky (http://www.fourmilab.ch/yoursky) using skies dated for 1862; RGS-WSR 4/3/1, pp. 5, 9, 4/8, vol. 1, p. 103, 108; Veronica du Feu, *Rapanui* (London and New York, 1996), 202; P. F. Coutis and J. H. Middleton, "The Physical and Biological Impact of a Small Island Wake in the Deep Ocean," *Deep Sea Research Part 1* 49 (2002): 1341–61; Jamison Gove et al., "Temporal Variability of Current-Driven Upwelling at Jarvis Island," *Journal of Geophysical Research* 111 (2006): C12011.

[31] RGS-WSR 4/3/1, p. 10, 44–45, 47, 51, 4/3/2, p. 4, 18–19,24, 4/8, vol. 1, p. 6, 11, 56, 95–99; Routledge, *The Mystery of Easter Island*, 254–66; Fischer, *Island at the End of the World*, 57–60; Weinerskirch et al., "Foraging Strategies."

Fernández Islands, which were later colonized by Chile. They might have come back for more if the endemic Fernández Island fur seal (*Arctocephalus philippii*) had not already been driven to the brink of extinction, forcing the sealers to move elsewhere for prey. There are indications that many Rapanui willingly accepted indentures to work in Peru in 1862. One Rapanui elder who witnessed these events as a small boy even claimed that the *'ariki mau* left voluntarily for Peru, never to return. Perhaps Easter Island was also stricken with drought. There is no doubt, however, that labor traders made huge profits back in Callao from the first labor shipments, leading to a much larger return expedition in December. This time, few Rapanui were willing to leave for the outer world, and the Peruvians instead resorted to trickery and force. Sailors placed cotton trade goods within an enclosure, ostensibly as gifts, then waited for locals to begin grabbing for them. On a prearranged signal, kidnappers fired weapons into the air, rushed the natives, and "tied them like sheep." The first slavers captured around 350 before warriors repelled these invaders with a huge brush fire; subsequent slave raids captured hundreds more. In all, Peruvian labor traders took away more than 1,300 people – as much as half of the indigenous population of Easter Island. No biological allies were required to accomplish this cruel deed.[32]

This was only the first wave of tragedy that struck the Rapanui. A second tragedy began on the voyage to Peru. Dysentery, a classic disease of crowded conditions and poor nutrition, killed hundreds of Pacific Islanders in transit or soon after their arrival – just as it did to Chinese contract laborers, Africans on the Middle Passage, and islanders involved in later phases of the Pacific labor trade. There is no hard evidence that any Pacific Islanders ended up on Peru's guano islands, but a few contributed to the guano industry in a small way – by shitting their lives away from dysentery on the manure heap of coastal cotton plantations.[33]

A third tragedy awaited them on the coast of Peru. Most historians have explained the high death rates of Polynesian workers in Peru – and indigenous depopulation more generally – as the inevitable consequence of exposure to unfamiliar microbes. But 1863 was a bad year for disease in Peru no matter who you were. A measles epidemic broke out in February, and the strain of influenza that year was so malignant that locals named it *"mala fe"* (bad faith). Tuberculosis, a respiratory disease that also thrives on poorly

---

[32] RGS-WSR 4/8, v. 1, pp. 68, 80, loose sheet between 84–85, 109; Grant McCall, "European Impact on Easter Island: Response, Recruitment and the Polynesian Experience in Peru," *Journal of Pacific History* 11 (1976): 90–93, 96–97; Maude, *Slavers in Paradise*, 12–20, 188, 192; Fischer, *Island at the End of the World*, 72–80, 87–90; Busch, *War against the Seals*, 11–18, 194–95.

[33] Maude, *Slavers in Paradise*, 57, 65–66, 73, 116–21, 129–38; Stewart, *Chinese Bondage*, ch. 3; Schlomowitz, "Epidemiology and the Pacific Labor Trade"; Kenneth Kiple, *The Caribbean Slave: A Biological History* (Cambridge and New York, 1984), ch. 4.

nourished individuals living in enclosed environments, was actually the lead-ing cause of mortality among islanders whose cause of death was recorded, slightly outnumbering those killed by diarrheal illness. A far more frightful epidemic took hold during the southern winter. In late May 1863, Callao authorities placed a U.S. whaling vessel, the *Helen Snow*, under quarantine for smallpox. This ship had left New Bedford, Massachusetts, in October 1862. After leaving Peru, it headed to the far North Pacific, picking up a crew of sixteen native Hawaiians on the way. It eventually sent 112,000 liters of whale oil and 6,940 kilograms of whalebone back to the United States to be converted into light and fertilizer. The 1863 smallpox epidemic that followed this ship to Peru was by far the worst that struck the coun-try during the course of the nineteenth century, killing a quarter of those infected.[34]

Misplaced humanitarianism brought a fourth wave of tragedy. By the time these epidemics took hold, liberal-minded Peruvians and outsiders had long since denounced the importation of Polynesian laborers as "a true slave trade." Under intense diplomatic pressure, the Peruvian government banned the Pacific Island labor trade in March 1863. At first, customs officials simply herded new arrivals into a warehouse-prison on the docks of Callao, but the outbreak of smallpox led the government to try to wash its hands of the whole affair by deporting all surviving Pacific Islanders from the country. On 18 August 1863, a Peruvian ship embarked for Easter Island and points west. Of the 470 repatriates crammed on board, 162 died before the ship even left Callao, and only 15 of the 100 Rapanui on this disease-ridden deathtrap lived to see Easter Island again. No one knows how many died from the smallpox epidemic they brought back home. Other ships of repatriation took sick islanders to the French-ruled Marquesas and uninhabited Cocos Island, an overseas possession of Costa Rica, sowing epidemics there as well. One ship abruptly repopulated Tongareva with 111 Gilbert Islanders – some of whom found their way home again years later by taking up work mining guano in the Central Pacific.[35]

Colonizers originating from Chile and France used these tragedies to begin turning Easter Island into an overseas possession. Eugène Eyraud (1820–68), a French-born mechanic who made a small fortune working in the southern Atacama, decided to give his life to the Catholic Church and lead a small mission to the island. He arrived with seven Rapanui repatriates from Tahiti in January 1864. Contrary to the way the story is usually told, smallpox, slaving, and self-induced "ecocide" had come nowhere close to sweeping

34 McCall, "European Impact," table 3; Bustíos, *Cuatrocientos años de la salud pública*, 274–78; Alexander Starbuck, *History of the American Whale Fishery from Its Earliest Inception to the Year 1876* (1878; New York, 1964), 586–87; "Hawaiian Seamen on Whaling Ships," http://www2.bishopmuseum.org/whaling/mainscreen.asp.
35 Maude, *Slavers in Paradise*, ch. 18–21; Eugenio Eyraud, "Carta al Superior General," (1866) in *El apostol de la Isla de Pascua* (Santiago de Chile, 1918), 24; McCall, "European Impact," 97–99.

away the Old Ways on Easter Island. The Rapanui roasted and ate the five goats he brought along with him, trampled his small garden of Eurasian cultivars, and stripped him of his clothes after the birdman festival. After nine months, he left on a Chilean rescue ship but returned as part of a full-fledged missionary expedition in 1866. This turned the scales completely against the Old Ways on the island. Tuberculosis killed dozens – including Eyraud and the last '*ariki mau*. In 1870–71, neo-European settlers imported 658 sheep from Chile and Australia to start a wool industry. Not all of the Rapanui gave in to these outside influences, however. A violent competition broke out between pro- and anti-missionary factions, fueled by old interethnic rivalries. This proved to be the worst tragedy of all. The first mission census of 1868 counted 930 Rapanui. In 1871, the missionaries evacuated the island and took 275 indigenes with them, including all but 30 women, ostensibly to protect them from violence and a return to paganism as they harvested pearl shell and coconuts in Mangareva and Tahiti. Easter Island's remnant revived the birdman ceremony after they left, but skilled readers of the *rongorongo* script were long gone. In 1888, when Chile formally annexed the Isla de Pascua as part of its policy of territorial expansion, 5,600 sheep, 269 cows and horses, and a mere 178 Rapanui lived on Easter Island. No one had bothered to celebrate the birdman cult for a decade. Easter Island's birdmen were extinct, victims of ecocide committed by outsiders.[36]

Thanks to colonizing forces unleashed by Peru's guano age and the U.S. Civil War, Easter Island went on to become a mirror image of neo-European ranching districts elsewhere in the Pacific, populated by introduced grasses, eucalyptus trees, and up to 70,000 sheep at a time. In many ways, this is a classic story of conquest ecological imperialism – with enslavement also playing a key role.[37] Easter Island was so isolated and forlorn from the point of view of outsiders, however, that it always maintained an indigenous majority. As a consequence, the Rapanui lived on as a people, maintained remnants of their old traditions and language, and eventually recovered their old numbers under Chilean colonial rule. This continuing story is one of history's great cases of indigenous survival.[38]

"The Cecil Rhodes of the Pacific" and Workers of Niue

Henry Cushman and other improving farmers in North America also exploited the ocean close to home in their quest for soil nutrients. Back

[36] Eyraud, "Carta," 31–33, 38, 45–48; *El apostol*, 13–15, 50–53; Fischer, *Island at the End of the World*, 92–116, 119, 123, 140–41.
[37] Paul Kelton, *Epidemics and Enslavement: Biological Catastrophe in the Native Southeast, 1492–1715* (Lincoln, NE, 2007).
[38] Fischer, *Island at the End of the World*, ch. 4–5; Grant McCall, *Rapanui: Tradition and Survival on Easter Island* (Honolulu, 1994).

in 1621, Tisquantum taught the New England Pilgrims the importance of fertilizing maize planted on old, worn-out lands with a species of small fish. Algonquian speakers called these once abundant fish *munnawhatteaûg*, or "he enriches the land," whereas the Abenaki called them *pauhagen* or "fertilizer." Anglo settlers shortened these indigenous names to menhaden or pogy (*Brevoortia tyrannus*). This agricultural technique regained popularity during the early nineteenth century along the Atlantic seaboard. With the help of menhaden, kelp, and a little Peruvian guano, Massachusetts statesman Daniel Webster converted a stretch of coastline that had been degraded by Plymouth Colony into a prize-winning showcase of modern cattle husbandry. His estate even featured Peruvian llamas grazed on fish-enriched pastures. During the 1850s, with sperm whale populations on the decline, New England oil producers turned their attention toward nearby schools of menhaden, "the miniature whale," to keep local homes and industry well lit and lubricated. Fertilizer manufacturers soon developed techniques to convert the smelly leftovers of menhaden oil extraction into nitrogen-rich fishmeal. This innovation made it far more worthwhile to mine nitrogen-poor phosphatic guano from distant islands in the Caribbean and Central Pacific. For several years, the Pacific Guano Company of Woods Hole mixed menhaden fishmeal with guano from Howland Island to produce a "soluble Pacific guano" similar in potency to the Peruvian variety.[39]

These innovations ultimately proved unsustainable, just like the whaling industry on which they were built. Strong El Niño events half a world away helped initiate the search for alternative nutrient supplies. Severe squalls wrecked several ships full of guano at Howland and Baker Islands in 1864–65 and 1868. Torrential rains and tidal surge soaked the remaining deposits. Similar "bad seasons" even washed invasive rats out of their holes and out to sea.[40] In response, the Pacific Guano Company bought the Swan Islands in the Caribbean and started substituting phosphate nodules from lands it had recently snapped up near war-devastated Charleston, South Carolina. The latter decision propelled domestic phosphate rock production past guano imports in 1869, which increased demand for Peruvian nitrates and sulfuric acid to treat the rock and accelerated the scarring of southeastern landscapes by phosphate quarries. Meanwhile, town folk frequently objected to the vile fumes emitted by fishmeal factories and forced many of them to close. This led a few crafty entrepreneurs to build floating plants offshore beyond the reach of regulatory authorities. American inventors also developed a new technology for menhaden fishing, the steam-powered purse

[39] Bruce Franklin, *The Most Important Fish in the Sea: Menhaden and America* (Washington, DC, 2007), 13–15, 50–72; Sherman, "Daniel Webster, Gentleman Farmer," 481, 484; Wines, *Fertilizer in America*, ch. 6; Skaggs, *Great Guano Rush*, 145.

[40] Paleoarchives; Ward, ed., *American Activities in the Central Pacific*, 3:252–320; "Sundry Data," Jan. 1877, PMB 494; Anne Ellis to Cousin John, 17 Feb. 1888, PMB 1227-JTA, 7/2.

FIGURE 3.1. An Anglo guano lord and his Niuean servant. This portrait of John T. Arundel (1841–1919, left) was taken in Australia, circa 1870, at the beginning of his long career as a guano prospector, trader, coconut planter, and phosphate miner in the South Pacific. Mouga (ca. 1865–1902, right) sat for this portrait in London in 1886. Mouga means "mountain" in Niuean – a natural feature his home island entirely lacks. Like many of his countrymen, he adopted a surname during the 1890s: "Faka.Satauro." *Source:* Arundel family archive, PMB 1227-JTA; reproduced courtesy of Anthony Aris.

seine net. This dramatically increased the efficiency with which industrial fisheries could attack schooling fish, and it caused depletion of Atlantic menhaden stocks to become a serious problem by 1880. A few menhaden fishermen returned to whaling and marketed rendered whale remains as fertilizer. These innovations had profound implications for the eventual development of Peru's fishmeal industry, as we see in Chapter 9.[41]

Anglo adventurers with close ties to Australia and New Zealand took over the initiative in the Central Pacific at this juncture. Their tireless search for guano and phosphate deposits in the region helped convert these aspiring neo-Europes into rulers of vast Pacific empires. John T. Arundel (fig. 3.1) emerged as the world's most important guano producer of the late nineteenth century. By family lineage and training, he was deeply implicated in British imperialism in the Pacific Basin. His grandfather served for twenty-six years

[41] Wines, *Fertilizer in* America, 79–82, 87–95, 112–24; Skaggs, *Great Guano Rush,* 134–35, 145–53; Franklin, *The Most Important Fish,* 55–72.

as home secretary of the London Missionary Society (LMS). From a young age, Arundel worked for the emigration department of Houlder Bros. & Co. of London. Similar to other "emigration vultures" of this time, his main job was to convince British farming families "who had been hit by the industrial revolution and bad seasons" to take passage to New Zealand and Australia. Circa 1860, Arundel became ill, reputedly because of religious overdedication to work, and took a life-changing trip to the South Seas to relax and recuperate. He briefly visited Peru's Chincha Islands and later met a whaler involved in land colonization schemes in New Zealand who assured him of the existence of similar, unexploited bird islands in the Central Pacific. Arundel had to bide his time until U.S. guano companies began losing interest and other Anglo-Australian companies proved the profitability of exploiting guano in this remote region. In 1870, he received the Houlder brothers' blessing to set up a similar business for them on isolated Starbuck Island.[42]

First, however, Arundel had to locate willing laborers. He called initially at Rarotonga, site of an important LMS mission station. Guano islands had a hideous reputation thanks to the recent activity of Peruvian slavers in the region, but Arundel's name got him help from local LMS missionaries in convincing twenty-one Rarotongans to accompany him north for a year. They stopped briefly at Makatea Island en route. Unbeknownst to Arundel, he walked across geologic deposits that contained more phosphate than all of the Central Pacific bird islands put together, but Makatea lacked any *living* sign of the mineral wealth it possessed, in stark contrast to Starbuck Island's screaming colonies of "wideawakes, boobies, frigatebirds, mockingbirds, and seagulls." Arundel considered life on the guano islands to be a form of evangelism that acculturated Pacific Islanders to pious lives of hard work. One of the numerous religious tracts he distributed read: "*His* work must be completed,/ His lessons set;/ *He* is the higher workman; Do not forget!" The difficult conditions on the guano islands often brought out the worst in human nature, however. By Arundel's own admission, his tyrannical lordship over Starbuck Island brought his Rarotongan subordinates close to revolt and forced him to look elsewhere for workers in future seasons.[43]

In 1873, Arundel made his first of many stops to recruit laborers at Niue. None of the things he accomplished on the guano islands of the Central Pacific would have been possible without a hearty contribution from the indigenous people of this remote island. Niue is a huge, uplifted coral atoll

[42] "Memoir of the Late Rev. John Arundel," PMB 1227-JA, 1/2/2; Sydney Arundel Aris, "Notes on the Life of John T. Arundel," PMB 1227-JTA, 1/1, 1/2; "Sundry Data," July 1870, PMB 494; Robert Langdon, "Arundel, the Shy Cecil Rhodes of the Pacific Islands," *Pacific Islands Monthly* Apr. 1974: 59–61.

[43] Arundel's emphasis; "Sundry Data," Nov. 1870; "Lecture to Geographical Society of the Pacific," 3 Mar. 1885, both PMB 494. I. M. Fletcher, "Material Gathered Concerning John Thomas Arundel," pp. iv, 47, 67, PMB 1227-JTA, 2; Tracts distributed in the South Pacific, PMB 1227-JTA, 7/3.

located 430 kilometers east of the Tonga group. Recent archaeological investigations show that humans initially settled this forested limestone island approximately 2,000 years ago. As on Easter Island, Niue's first colonists caused significant environmental changes. They hunted two endemic species of flightless bird to extinction and may have been responsible for creating the sterile Fonuakula soils of southern Niue. Yet there is no compelling evidence that Niuean society ever experienced a major ecological collapse, even though the island is often subject to severe droughts and tropical cyclones, is blessed with infertile soils laced with high levels of mercury and radioactive isotopes, and by many measures would seem to be "near the limits of long-term settlement viability." Indigenous Niueans long ago established a sustainable subsistence system well adapted to this difficult environment based on slash-and-burn agriculture, reef fishing, and chicken husbandry.[44]

Niue was an unlikely candidate to become a key contributor to the Pacific Island labor trade. It acquired a reputation for extreme xenophobia after a visit by the second Cook expedition in 1774. Both ritual and ecological fear of foreign contamination strongly motivated this xenophobia. In 1830, the LMS kidnapped a boy named Uea from Niue for religious indoctrination. A couple years later, it took him back home to work as an evangelist. This strategy had resulted in the rapid conversion of Rarotonga and other islands in the general vicinity, but Uea reputedly brought back fever (*kafukula*) along with Christianity on his return home. Rivals killed him, his father, and sick members of his village to destroy this polluting influence. Niueans had other reasons to distrust outsiders. In 1862–63, three Peruvian ships kidnapped more than 100 Niue islanders. Only Taole made it home again from Peru. He escaped from the docks of Callao with the help of indigenous Hawaiian whalers and, years later, used a contract to mine guano for Arundel on Starbuck Island to make his way from Hawaii back to Niue. By this time, Niuean attitudes toward the outside world had abruptly reversed course, helped along by the establishment of an LMS mission in 1861 and conversion of most islanders to Christianity. To sustain agriculture on the island's infertile soils, Niuean males periodically expended enormous amounts of labor clearing regrown brush and forest to plant new fields, which they left to Niuean females to till for a few years, before moving on to new plots and repeating the process. Pacific labor contractors learned to exploit the willingness of male Niueans to leave home for extended periods and perform rigorous, physical "bush" work. Periodic hurricanes, El Niño droughts,

---

[44] Richard Walter and Atholl Anderson, *The Archaeology of Niue Island* (Honolulu, 2002) 1, 7, 11, 13, 93–94, 103, 107, 115–19, 130–32; Anderson and Walter, "Landscape and Culture Change on Niue Island," in *Pacific Landscapes: Archaeological Approaches* (Los Osos, CA, 2002); T. H. Worthy et al., "Fossil and Archaeological Avifauna of Niue Island," *Notornis* 45 (1998): 177–90; N. E. Whitehead et al., "The Elemental Content of Niue Island Soils," *New Zealand Journal of Geology and Geophysics* 36 (1993): 243–54.

Malthusian population pressure, social competition for land, and a desire for trade goods also played a role in the adoption of these new migrant lifestyles.[45]

During the 1870s, Arundel and crews of workers from Niue and other remote islands shuttled from atoll to atoll in the Line and Phoenix Islands harvesting guano. On Baker, Howland, and Jarvis Islands, they took advantage of new excrement that had accumulated since their initial exploitation by U.S. companies, as well as hard "rock guano." Unlike other guano prospectors, Arundel tried to make a long-term profit from these territories by converting them into plantations. Beginning on the two southernmost of the Line Islands, Flint and Caroline, he directed workers to plant coconut palms. Thanks to timely El Niño rains, these groves prospered, and Arundel went on to plant experimental groves throughout the Line and Phoenix Islands, even on dry atolls devoid of trees.[46]

During Arundel's first recruiting visit to Niue, a boy named Mouga (fig. 3.1) begged to come along to the guano islands. Mouga was too young for hard labor, even by the low standards of that era, but Arundel took him on as his personal servant. For thirteen years, he loyally accompanied Arundel to at least a dozen guano islands. Under his influence, Mouga became a devout Christian and learned to read and write. In classic Victorian style, he kept a devotional journal and wrote frequent, deeply personal letters in the lingua franca of guano workers from this era: a mix of Tahitian, English, and Niuean. These materials provide us with a unique glimpse into life on the guano islands from the perspective of an indigenous worker.[47]

Working on the guano islands sometimes brought extreme hardships, particularly during the grim time in 1874 when "severe sickness" swept the guano camp on Caroline Island and the company ran out of food. It also brought incredible opportunities. In 1885–86, the Arundel family made Mouga a primary caregiver to its two daughters, and he traveled with them from the remote guano island where the youngest was born, across the United States, eventually to London. But Mouga's troublesome tendency after employment disputes to disappear for hours with his wards on the streets of London eventually convinced the Arundels to send this "responsibility" back to the Pacific.[48]

45 Sue McLachlan, "Savage Island or Savage History?: An Interpretation of Early European Contact with Niue," *Pacific Studies* 6 (1982): 26–51; Basil Thompson, *Savage Island: An Account of a Sojourn in Niue and Tonga* (1902; Papakura, NZ, 1984), 3, 71–77; Edwin Lowe, *History and Traditions of Niue* (Honolulu, 1926), 31–33; Walter and Anderson, *Archaeology of Niue Island*, 18–21; Maude, *Slavers in Paradise*, 55–59, 137, 180–81, 204–05.

46 "Sundry Data," passim, PMB 494; Langdon, "Arundel"; Maude, *Of Islands and Men*, 326–27.

47 Notes by Sydney Arundel Aris on "Monga," PMB 1227-JTA, 11/1; notes by H. E. Maude on the diary of H. I. N. Moouga, PMB 14.

48 "Sundry Data," Mar.-Apr. 1874, 3 Nov. 1886, PMB 494; Mouga, "to my parent" J. T. Arundel, 1 May 1887; Notes on "Monga," PMB 1227-JTA, 11/1.

Homecoming was a melancholy affair after spending so many years abroad with little to show for it. Mouga aspired to open a small trade store on his home island but had failed to save up any money during his career as a domestic. Therefore, he decided to return to the guano islands in 1887, this time as foreman of a crew of Niuean and Atiuan laborers. The situation Mouga encountered on Canton Island was a rude awakening from his relatively privileged life as a household servant. "Contrary winds" related to La Niña seriously disrupted the 1887 expedition, and eight members of the party – including Mouga's brother – drowned when their boat sank. Mouga insisted on returning to Niue at the earliest chance, and Arundel's cousin, George Ellis, severely cut his pay.[49]

Without money or family to pay for the requisite feasts, Mouga had no way to attract a good marriage partner. So in 1889, he again accepted Arundel's offer to serve as foreman on Flint Island. When Arundel first visited Flint Island in 1873, it was covered by a mixed forest dominated by *buka* or grand devil's-claw trees (*Pisonia grandis*) in desiccated senescence, thanks to the severe La Niña drought of the early 1870s. After extracting 30,000 tons of guano for export to places such as Australia and Massachusetts, Arundel and his men planted coconut trees in some of the area they had cleared. Now it was Mouga's job to direct a team of eight Niuean workers to harvest the fruit of these labors and convert the rest of the island into one large coconut plantation. They razed approximately half the native forest and, in the process, destroyed the arboreal nesting sites of the guano birds that had made this island valuable to outsiders in the first place. Mouga and his men also had to deal with nests of introduced ants that had tagged along with the first coconut seedlings. Sparse, contaminated food made work all the more unpleasant. Mouga's hardest job, as on Canton Island, involved acting as an intercessor between workers and management. In January 1891, after a year and a half, Mouga was deeply depressed and more than eager to leave this islet. "Poor me," he wrote on the last page of his journal.[50]

Replete with cash and trade goods, Mouga soon found a wife upon his return home, but he did not adjust well to the limited opportunities available on Niue. He expressed open shame in his letters to the Arundel daughters that his wife was illiterate, dressed poorly, and cultivated taro, bananas, and sugar cane for their subsistence. His ambitions also got him into trouble with Niue's elected *patuiki* (paramount chief), Tataaki. In many ways, Tataaki shared Mouga's desire for improvement. During the eighteenth century, the *patuiki* had been mainly responsible for performing rituals to protect

[49] Paleoarchives and CEI; Mouga to J. T. Arundel, 7 Apr., 1 May, 5 May 1887, PMB 1227-JTA, 11/1.
[50] Paleoarchives and CEI; Mouga to J. T. Arundel, 10 June 1887, 1 Mar., 24 Mar., 4 Oct. 1890, PMB 1227-JTA, 11/1; Diary of H. I. N. Moouga, pp. 1, 2, 126, PMB 14; Lowe, *History and Traditions of Niue*, 72–75; "Sundry Data," Sept. 1873, PMB 494; Mueller-Dombois and Fosberg, *Vegetation of the Tropical Pacific Islands*, 314, 317, 328, 330.

the island from natural disasters; failure could result in his ritual slaying. Tataaki expanded this office to include promotion and control of Niue's participation in the regional labor economy, took the title "king of Niue," and advocated for the establishment of a British protectorate. Both Mouga and Tataaki followed the fashion of the time and adopted surnames, but Mouga failed to convince his "father" Arundel to provide him with "a good name[,] an English name" to further increase his prestige on Niue.[51]

Mouga's tribulations on the guano islands were actually quite tame. In 1883, Arundel sent three Niueans to Jarvis Island to plant coconuts under the supervision of Squire Flockton, a highborn Englishman desperate to escape alcoholism. A violent illness (probably dysentery) convinced Flockton to go back to the bottle as a curative. The solitude eventually caused him to lose his mind to the point that he forced his subordinates into a drunken reenactment of the Last Supper that devolved into a wild shooting spree and Flockton's suicide. In 1901, Arundel's company left a Niuean couple to fend for themselves as overseers on Hull Island for 13 straight months without replenishing their supplies. For the last six months, they lived on nothing but coconuts, crabs, and rainwater.[52] Tales of this sort influenced the literary realm. In Joseph Conrad's novel *Lord Jim*, a bloodthirsty seal hunter suspected of cannibalism seemed a bit too eager to take work as a foreman on an isolated Pacific guano island, "as good as a gold mine, . . . stuff that would send the sugar-cane shooting sky-high. The making of Queensland!"[53] Mouga's case helps us to understand why Niuean workers kept accepting contracts to the guano islands, despite such awful stories, until the exploitative nature of this new ecological regime fully revealed itself at the turn of the century.

John Arundel slowly built an empire of trade that stretched over 12,000 kilometers across the Pacific Ocean. By the end of the nineteenth century, it encompassed small islands from Australia's Great Barrier Reef in the west to Porfirian Mexico's Clipperton Island in the east. But Arundel's wealth was not built solely on supplying guano to Australian and U.S. superphosphate producers. It was also based on exploiting wild creatures – things such as shark fin, sea cucumber, and Niuean fungus used in Chinese cuisine and medicine; tortoise and pearl shell to adorn the world's fashion conscious; and wood from the *kanawa* or *kou* tree (*Cordia subcordata*) coveted by

[51] Mouga to S. A. Arundel, 3 Sept. 1893; Mouga to J. T. Arundel, 3 Sept. 1893, 1 May 1900; Frank Lawes to J. T. Arundel, 14 Jan. 1901, PMB 1227-JTA, 11/1, 11/5. Walter and Anderson, *Archaeology of Niue*, 11; Anderson and Walter, "Landscape and Cultural Change on Niue," 159; Thomson, *Savage Island*, 36–37; Katherine Luomala, "Symbolic Slaying in Niue: Post-European Changes in a Dramatic Ritual Complex," in *The Changing Pacific* (Melbourne, 1978), 155–56.

[52] Statement by Agatoa, Lio, and Fană to Frank Lawes, 31 Mar. 1883, PMB 1227-JTA, 11/8; Fulton and Greenhalgh, "Notes on Hull Island," Dec. 1902, PMB 1139-reel 2.

[53] Conrad, *Lord Jim* (London, 1900), ch. 14.

indigenous Pacific Island carvers. The main source of Arundel's profit actually derived from trading manufactured goods produced by the industrial world and its agricultural colonies –...things such as rice and preserved meat, printed cloth and cotton clothing, steel knives and church bells, addictive tobacco and soap. The indigenous inhabitants of Niue, Tokelau, and the Ellice Islands (now Tuvalu) bought these trade goods by bartering the foregoing natural articles, locally produced coconut, and their own muscle power. These transactions brought profit margins approaching 100 percent. Arundel's status as an empire builder ultimately depended on advantageous terms of trade with Pacific Islanders like Mouga, and these activities foisted these island societies straight onto the path to underdevelopment.[54]

The Age of Soap and Water

J. T. Arundel & Co. and other guano miners accomplished major ecological transformations on the bird islands of the Pacific. They cut down the grove of ancient *kou* trees on Howland Island, for example. Like colonizers elsewhere, guano miners intentionally introduced rabbits, pigs, and goats to diversify the local meat supply and unintentionally introduced the Norway rat (*Rattus norvegicus*). On some islands, this large rat species extirpated the small Pacific rat introduced by Polynesian voyagers. To control these invasive vermin, Anglo colonists also introduced terriers and domestic cats. In 1901, one of Arundel's employees transplanted 27 cats from Australia to Sydney Island. Most died on the voyage, but those that made it rapidly proliferated, noticeably reduced the rat population, and produced kittens for transfer to other islands. Cats were also highly regarded by Arundel's native employees, who smuggled a few back home, but these introductions wrecked havoc on the islands' indigenous creatures. Conservation biologists blame cats and rats for eradicating wedge-tailed shearwaters (*Puffinus pacificus*) and petrels (*Pterodroma* spp.) from their nesting burrows on many Pacific guano islands. Arundel's daughter Sydney played her own role in this history of ecological invasion. She brought a pregnant cat along for companionship on the family's last voyage to the guano islands and gave the kittens away during the course of the trip. When they were shipwrecked on Makatea Island, she gave this pet to a French colonial physician. He named its newest kitten Microbe, a name pregnant with ecological symbolism for this era.[55]

---

54 "Sundry Data," esp. May–July 1891, PMB 494; Fulton and Greenhalgh, "Reports on Island Properties and Trading Stations," 6 Dec. 1902, PMB 1139-reel 2; Langdon, "Arundel"; Williams and Macdonald, *The Phosphateers*, 8–9; Daley and Griggs, "Mining the Reefs and Cays."
55 Fulton and Greenhalgh, "Notes on Sydney Island," 6 Sept. 1902, PMB 1139-reel 2; "Notes by Sydney Aris on the Fate of her Cat Johnnie," PMB 1227-JTA, 12/12; Skaggs, *Great Guano Rush*, 72–73; Ian Atkinson and Toni Atkinson, "Land Vertebrates as Invasive Species

John Arundel recognized that unfettered environmental exploitation would eventually destroy his livelihood: native populations were decreasing. Wild nature was disappearing. On many Pacific islands, even the climate seemed to be "altering for the worse." Arundel was not content to play the role of frontiersman forever. He hoped that planting coconut plantations on these islands would attract more rainfall to the region and create a more lasting source of profit.[56]

His project to improve the bird islands of the Central Pacific brought these remote specks of land into new forms of engagement with the industrial world. During the second half of the nineteenth century, exploding demand for meat and other animal by-products helped propel the conquest of frontier grasslands and forests by cattlemen in western North America, the Río de la Plata, Siberia, Europe's Carpathian Basin, Australia and New Zealand, even Hawaii. This frontier industry also provided valuable inputs to improving farmers. As we learned in Chapter 2, bone meal was already wildly popular as a fertilizer when Peruvian guano first appeared on the northern market. Guano's popularity, in turn, inspired the invention of nitrogen-rich substitutes produced from slaughterhouse waste. Ironically, consumption of these new fertilizers undermined the ability of improving farmers to profitably raise livestock. Chicago's goliath meatpackers used economic advantages in the large-scale production of slaughterhouse by-products to underwrite their takeover of the North American meat industry during the late nineteenth century. This created a vicious circle in which many farmers could not compete as meat producers and were forced to get rid of manure-producing livestock. These trends only increased the pressure to consume fertilizers manufactured off the farm and brought an end to the era of "high farming" for many Northeasterners.[57]

In the process, the guano age gave way to the age of soap and water. The cleanliness movement of the late nineteenth century is the world's first instance of a global movement aimed at improving urban life. The importance of fresh water supplies and sewage disposal to the development of modern cities, industrial centers, and governments is well known, but we have only begun to recognize the role that soap played in these trends. Our association of soap with personal cleanliness, good health, and civilization was still a brand-new concept at the end of the nineteenth century. The

on the Islands of the South Pacific Regional Environment Programme," in *Invasive Species in the Pacific* (Apia, Samoa, 2000) 23–27, 31–33, 47–49; Warren King, "Conservation Status of Birds of Central Pacific Islands," *Wilson Bulletin* 85 (1973): 89–103.

[56] J. T. Arundel to Secretary of the Pacific Islands Co., 2 Dec. 1897; Fulton and Greenhalgh, "Report on Christmas Island," 6 Nov. 1902, PMB 1139-reel 2.

[57] Wines, *Fertilizer in America*, 83–87, 133–34; William Cronon, *Nature's Metropolis: Chicago and the Great West* (New York, 1991), ch. 5; Rudolf Clemen, *By-Products in the Packing Industry* (Chicago, 1927), ch. 1, 11, 14.

same goes for our linkage of feces with contagion, disorder, and backward-ness.[58]

Both sets of bourgeois attitudes were premised on massive slaughterhouse production of soap, fertilizer, and other by-products. Circa 1885, tallow produced from the killing of cows and sheep provided the world's number-one source of fatty acids used in factory production of soap. The spectacular growth of this notoriously dirty industry produced far-reaching ecological effects. All the way back in the 1790s, New York City's first public health officers blamed "noxious effluvia" emitted by local soap and candle manufacturers for causing deadly yellow fever epidemics that struck the city. The target of this early environmental activism later proved to be misdirected but gave birth to an influential set of zoning regulations aimed at "unhealthy, dangerous, and annoying industries" worldwide. North American passenger pigeons (*Ectopistes migratorius*) also could have done without the droves of pigs that roamed the beech forests of the U.S. Midwest, fattening-up on the pigeons' main source of food, only to be turned into Proctor & Gamble soap, candles, and other pork products. The growing availability of cheap tallow and lard, meanwhile, put downward pressure on the price and profitability of other oils and fats. This was good from the sperm whale's point of view but proved devastating for artisanal processors of oil palm fruit in the rainforests of West Africa.[59]

These trends also depressed the price of coconut oil, but coconut oil possessed valuable properties these other fats lacked. Industrial chemists recognized that no other source of fatty acid combined so readily with caustic soda, modern soap's other major active ingredient, or produced such a high yield of soap. (The production of caustic soda was itself premised on abundant supplies of Atacama nitrates, sulfuric acid, and soda ash.) Consumers liked the fact that coconut oil soaps were hard, long lasting, and produced a quick, abundant lather – even in cold seawater. They nearly monopolized the market for marine soaps used on ships and port side, which were indispensable for maintaining the whiteness of official uniforms worn by colonizers of the era. Unlike tallow, lard oil, and palm oil soaps, coconut oil

[58] Richard Bushman and Claudia Bushman, "The Early History of Cleanliness in America," *Journal of American History* 74 (1988): 1213–38; Laporte, *History of Shit*, 11, 32, 57; Corbin, *Foul and the Fragrant*, 129–30, 159–60, 176–81; Juliann Sivulka, *Stronger than Dirt: A Cultural History of Advertising Personal Hygiene in America, 1875 to 1940* (Amherst, NY, 2001), ch. 2–3; Mariana Valverde, *The Age of Light, Soap, and Water: Moral Reform in English Canada, 1885–1925* (Toronto, 1991).

[59] W. L. Carpenter, *A Treatise on the Manufacture of Soap, Candles, Lubricants and Glycerin* (London, 1885), 14–15, 32–36; Association of Tallow Chandlers and Soap Makers, *The Case of the Manufacturers of Soap and Candles in the City of New York* (New York, 1797), ch. 1; Scobie, *Buenos Aires*, 198–99; Clemen, *By-Products in the Packing Industry*, ch. 6; Oscar Schisgall, *Eyes on Tomorrow: The Evolution of Proctor & Gamble* (Chicago, 1981), 1–11; A. W. Schorger, *The Passenger Pigeon: Its Natural History and Extinction* (Madison, WI, 1955), 36–38, 125–26, 131, 206–7, 212, 257.

soaps were naturally white, a semiotic sign for purity and cleanliness, and required no bleaching. Coconut oil also contains an unsurpassed percentage of glycerol – a crucial ingredient of nitroglycerine, dynamite, and a whole range of munitions incorporating nitrates. Circa 1885, the recently cleared coastal lowlands of British-ruled Ceylon produced the world's largest quantities of coconut oil. Pacific Islanders eager to participate in the world of trade also produced a growing supply of coconut oil and dried copra, the albuminous pulp from which coconut oil is produced.[60]

Two companies were mainly responsible for turning coconut oil into a key contributor to the age of soap and water. William Lever (1851–1925) got his start as a businessman specializing in the importation of butter and eggs to Britain's industrial Midlands from colonial Ireland. Inspired by low vegetable oil prices and the exploding market for cleanliness, Lever began experimenting with soap manufacture during the late 1880s. With the assistance of an experienced soap boiler and a university-trained chemist, Lever created a blended household soap formulated from 41.9 percent coconut or palm kernel oil and smaller measures of cottonseed oil, tallow, and American pine rosin. Following advertising strategies developed by U.S. manufacturers, Lever aggressively marketed Sunlight-brand household soap first in Great Britain, then "all over the civilized world." Early campaigns targeted women of modest means who worried they would "look old sooner than a man" from slavery to housework and harsh rosin soaps. Advertisements also targeted those who aspired to improve their social status by associating themselves with the color white: the color of cleanliness, white-collar livelihoods, racial purity, and coconut-based soap. Australian gold miners embraced Sunlight soap just as readily for use in the brackish waters of the Outback, and it soon became the British Empire's best-selling soap brand. In the United States, Cincinnati-based Proctor & Gamble developed its own coconut oil-based soap during the 1880s to help make up for declining prospects for lard-based candles. Millions of consumers still use this brand today: Ivory, "the soap that floats."[61]

William Lever's model industrial town, Port Sunlight (est. 1888), provided the very best amenities that the age of soap and water had to offer. This "shrine for the worship of cleanliness" built on a tidal marsh near Liverpool is widely recognized as a birthplace for the Garden City movement.

---

[60] Anderson, *Treatise on the Manufacture of Soap*, 23–26, 32–44, 173, 199, 207–14, 294–308; Geoffrey Martin, *The Modern Soap and Detergent Industry, Including Glycerol Manufacture* (London, 1924), vol. 1, §1, pp. 39–40, 45–46, 50–52, §2, pp. 7–8, 21–22, §7, pp. 4, 6, 9, 41–42, vol. 3, §1, p. 5; Sivulka, *Stronger than Dirt*, 103–4; "Cultivation of Coconut Palm in Ceylon," PMB 1139-reel 2.

[61] Joseph Meek to Lord Leverhulme, 26 Apr. 1926, PMB 1139-reel 2; Charles Wilson, *The History of Unilever: A Study in Economic Growth and Social Change* (London, 1954), 1:22–23, 27, 29, 31, 37–41, 52, 57–58, 67, 94; Sivulka, *Stronger than Dirt*, 50–54, 70–91; The Advertising Archive, images 30521551, 30527531, 30527545, 30550930.

Similar to Henry Cushman, Lever hoped to "get back again...that close family brotherhood that existed in the good old days." Lever believed an open, airy, aesthetically pleasing environment would breed healthy, loyal, productive workers for generations to come. Port Sunlight's detached worker cottages, company-manicured front yards, "Old English" architecture, wide roadways and walks, and open parkland would be immediately familiar to residents of planned suburban communities today. Circa 1909, every worker cottage had running water, a bathtub, and flush toilet. Port Sunlight workers even shared in company profits, and like residents of all Garden Cities, experienced lower death rates and had larger families than residents of polluted industrial centers. This model industrial town paid for itself many times over as an advertisement for Lever Bros.' products and the cleanliness movement.[62]

With big players like Lever on the scene, John Arundel acted aggressively during the late 1890s to expand his investment in coconut plantations. Intense climate variability in the Pacific provided a key motivation for this decision – and ultimately helped bring Arundel and Lever together as partners in the largest guano island development project in history. During the prolonged La Niña drought of 1892–94, Arundel's plantations failed on most of the Line and Phoenix Islands. This led him to buy up groves in Fiji damaged by the great hurricane of January 1895 and to approach Tataaki's successor King Togia to lease 200 overgrown acres in the center of Niue. Togia refused. In Niuean legal tradition, planting fruit-bearing trees was the one act that conferred *permanent* private ownership over land. Arundel also went into partnership with Arthur Hamilton-Gordon, the Lord Stanmore, one of the most experienced and controversial colonial administrators of the age. Arundel hoped Lord Stanmore's political connections would enable their company to attract investors and obtain lucrative land grants in newly colonized territories. As governor of Fiji, Gordon witnessed a horrific measles epidemic that killed a quarter of the indigenous Fijian population. This convinced him that Pacific Islanders were doomed by lack of evolutionary fitness to racial extinction.[63]

Lord Stanmore's prediction seemed to be well on its way toward coming true on Niue, a locale that starkly illustrates the inequalities that opened up

[62] Wilson, *History of Unilever*, 1:34–36, 144–51; Standish Meacham, *Regaining Paradise: Englishness and the Early Garden City Movement* (New Haven, 1999), ch. 2; Jeremy Rowan, "Imagining Corporate Culture: William Hesketh Lever at Port Sunlight, 1888–1925," (Ph.D. diss., Louisiana State University, 2003), 110, 112, 114, 123, 132; Ewar Culpin, *The Garden City Movement Up-to-Date* (London, 1913), 11, 41.

[63] Paleoarchives and CEI; Arundel to Secretary of Pacific Islands Co., 2 Dec. 1897, PMB 1139-reel 2; Garden, *Droughts, Floods & Cyclones*, 325–32; Langdon, "Arundel"; Williams and Macdonald, *The Phosphateers*, 8–9; Thomson, *Savage Island*, 137–38; Mark Francis, "Gordon, Arthur Charles Hamilton, First Baron Stanmore (1829–1912)," in *ODB*; Roberts, *Population Problems in the Pacific*, 78.

between those living in cleaned-up parts of the industrial world and man-
ual laborers in colonized realms who produced key industrial commodities.
In some ways, Niue looked like it was experiencing the latest chapter in
the history of conquest ecological imperialism. A closer look at the situation suggests that the Pacific labor trade itself was largely responsible for
demographic decline on the island. Niueans certainly interpreted things this
way and took aggressive action to ensure their survival as a people. In
1899, a measles epidemic brought home by returning plantation workers
killed 100 before a strict quarantine brought it to a halt. In 1900, thirteen members of a crew harvesting guano on Baker Island also died from
an epidemic, probably a manifestation of the global flu and pneumonia
pandemic that spread like wildfire around the Pacific that year. Surviving
guano workers flat-out refused to accept transfer to newly discovered phosphate deposits on Banaba Island and demanded to return home to protect
their health. By this date, Niue's resident population had fallen to 3,544,
almost a third less than it had been back when LMS missionaries first settled on the island and began advocating participation in the Pacific labor
trade (table 3.1). Missionary Frank Lawes greatly regretted his role in this
but blamed greedy indigenous chieftains for the worst abuses. "Niue in
so far as guano fields are concerned is worked out," he sadly reported to
Arundel. With Lawes's encouragement, Niue's assembly of elders raised
monthly wage requirements to £2 per month for plantation work and a
hefty £5 per month for work on guano islands (two to five times the previous rate). Great Britain used this opportunity to formally colonize Niue,
ostensibly to protect its native inhabitants from further harm. Against the
expressed wishes of the island's indigenous leaders, it handed over administration to New Zealand, an aspiring imperial power in its own right. New
Zealand's first resident commissioner promptly established a land court to
regularize the takeover of native lands by settlers and effectively banned
the off-island labor trade to maintain the local labor supply. Mouga's fate
appeared to confirm the expectation that Niue was destined to become a
neo-Europe like New Zealand. In 1901, he caught a case of the flu, fell into
a moribund state lasting another year, and died without ever fathering a
child.[64]

Niue was hardly alone in this experience. Soap sales benefited enormously
from the deadly wave of bubonic plague, influenza, dysentery, and other
epidemics that swept the world at this exact time. These diseases not only
struck indigenous peoples, they also killed millions stricken by drought,
famine, and the New Imperialism in India, China, Southeast Asia, East

---

[64] Lawes to Arundel, 14 Jan. 1901, 14 Nov. 1902, PMB 1227-JTA, 11/5; Fulton and Greenhalgh, "Notes on Trading Stations: Niue or Savage Island," 12 Dec. 1902, PMB 1139-reel
2; Thomson, *Savage Island*, 4, 44, 133–34; Robert Craig, *Historical Dictionary of Polynesia*
(Lanham, MD, 2002), 149; Howe et al., *Tides of History*, 71–74.

TABLE 3.1. *Indigenous Population of Niue Island, Pacific Ocean, 1862–2006*

	Population	Niueans Abroad
1862	5,021	–
1875	5,076	378
1884	5,070	503
1887	4,726	363
1891	4,482	369
1895	4,433	421
1900	4,105	561
1902	4,015	–
1906	4,074	–
1911	3,943	–
1921	3,719	~200[a]
1931	3,797[b]	–
1945	4,253[b]	–
1966	5,194[b]	–
1981	3,281[b]	–
2001	1,788[b]	20,642[c]
2006	1,625[b]	24,700[c]

[a] Estimate; not included in total population.
[b] Total population, regardless of ethnicity or place of permanent residence.
[c] Population of Niuean birth or ancestry living in New Zealand and Australia.
Sources: Maude, *Slavers in Paradise*, 8; Frank Lawes, "The Population of Niue, 1875–1900," PMB 1227-JTA, 11/5; Loeb, *History and Traditions of Niue*, 6–7; Government of Niue, "Total Population of Niue, 1900–2004," http://www.spc.int/prism/country/nu/stats/Social/Population/Popstats.htm; Niue, National Planning and Development Office, *Niue Population Profile Based on 2006 Census of Population and Housing: A Guide for Planners and Policy-makers* (Noumea, New Caledonia, 2008); Charles Stahl and Reginald Appleyard. *Migration and Development in the Pacific Islands: Lessons from the New Zealand Experience* (Canberra, 2007), table 1.2; Australian Bureau of Statistics, "Population Characteristics: Ancestry of Australia's Population," *Social Trends* no. 4102.0 (2003).

Africa, and the Pacific World.[65] Lever Bros. deliberately sought to capitalize on this situation by aggressively marketing Lifebuoy Royal Disinfectant Soap. This was one of the first household soaps to contain carbolic acid (phenol), a strong-smelling antiseptic. Advertising campaigns promised to

[65] David Patterson, *Pandemic Influenza, 1700–1900: A Study in Historical Epidemiology* (Totowa, NJ, 1986), 77–82, 91; Bruno Lisa, "History of Influenza Pandemics," in *Paleomicrobiology: Past Human Infections* (Berlin, 2008), 203; Robert Wolfe, "Alaska's Great

"save life" by providing "safe, sure, and simple Protection from Infection." The ubiquitous life preserver and other images of steamship travel in ads preyed on fear of disease overseas. Most of its washing power still came from coconut oil derivatives, however.[66]

Industrialists were not immune to the environmental disturbances of the turn of the century. A catastrophic, seven-year drought in Australia (1896–1903) compelled cattlemen to slaughter their sheep and cows in huge numbers and leave the degraded inland range to be taken over by dust storms, rabbits, and prickly pear cactus. In the short term, this disaster flooded the tallow market, to the preferential benefit of Lever's competitors. Climate extremes and environmental degradation had fearful long-term ramifications for the supply of other raw materials as well. For wheat growers and foresters, colonial officials and peasant farmers alike, "famine" was the operative word of the late 1890s in many parts of the world. In 1898, the president of the British Association for the Advancement of Science even predicted an impending nitrogen famine, leading to a frantic search for new resources. What would Lever Bros. do in the case of a coconut famine in the Indo-Pacific? Its British factories might be able to survive on West African palm oil, but its new Australian operations and planned conquest of emerging Pacific markets would be doomed.[67]

In November 1901, at the height of Australia's Long Drought, Lever journeyed to Sydney to celebrate the opening of his first soap factory in the Southern Hemisphere. This integrated facility crushed copra, produced oil-cake for use as cattle feed, and boiled soap using coal from deep beneath Sydney harbor. Unlike Port Sunlight, however, it conspicuously lacked worker housing, profit sharing, or even a single tree. Lever never reached a point where he thought providing these kind of amenities to his southern workforce created enough "capital value" in public goodwill to be worth the bother: "There is no goodwill in a business that is not making money." One Port Sunlight was enough.[68]

Sickness, 1900: An Epidemic of Measles and Influenza in a Virgin Soil Population," *Proceedings of the American Philosophical Society* 126 (1982): 91–121; Mohr, *Plague and Fire*; Cueto, *Return of the Epidemics*, ch. 1; Davis, *Late Victorian Holocausts*, pt 2.

[66] The Advertising Archive, images 30515656, 30527299, 30530168, 30542602, 30549112, 30536237, 30642698; Sivulka, *Stronger than Dirt*, 100–6; Timothy Burke, *Lifebuoy Men, Lux Women: Commodification, Consumption, and Cleanliness in Modern Zimbabwe* (Durham, NC, 1996), 17–23, 150–56.

[67] "Address by Sir William Crookes"; Garden, *Droughts, Floods & Cyclones*, ch. 7; Michael Williams, *Deforesting the Earth: From Prehistory to Global Crisis* (Chicago, 2002), 384–95; Wilson, *History of Unilever*, 1:51–52, 63.

[68] Joseph Meek to Lever, 6 Aug. 1913; Meek to Lord Leverhulme (son), 27 Apr. 1926, both PMB 1139-reel 2. Views of Sunlight Works, Balmain, 1900, 1921, PMB 1139-reel 4; Fieldhouse, *Unilever Overseas*, 64–66; Wilson, *History of Unilever*, 1:90; "Balmain's Own Coal Mine," *Primefact* 556 (Feb. 2007).

By a world-changing coincidence, Lever shared his long steamship journey home from Sydney to San Francisco with John Arundel. With Lord Stanmore's help, Arundel was frantically looking for investors to fund two colossal new ventures: (1) a huge land concession in the British Solomon Islands for coconut plantations and (2) a new company, in partnership with Jaluit Gesellschaft of Hamburg, to exploit high-grade phosphate just discovered on Nauru and Banaba Islands. Lever rightly thought he had stumbled on "a gold brick." He invested £25,000 in each cause.[69]

These events mark the beginning of Lever Brothers' conversion into a vertically integrated business that soon encompassed vast areas of the Solomon Islands and the Belgian Congo, where it became a major agent of tropical deforestation. When Lever Bros. merged with the Margarine Union in 1929, the company since known as Unilever instantly became one of the earth's most far-reaching multinational corporations. During the 1930s, Unilever alerted the world to the microbial menace of "B.O." and "undie odor" and went on to develop or absorb a number of the world's most-valuable consumer brands: Lux soap and Dove cleansing bar, Rinso and Persil washing powder, Sunsilk and Seda shampoo, Signal and Pepsodent toothpaste, Rama and I Can't Believe It's Not Butter! margarine, Birds Eye and Nordsee frozen foods, Lipton tea, Axe deodorants, and an icon of socially conscious business, Ben and Jerry's ice cream. From Alaska to Zimbabwe, Unilever products make it easier for the world's consumers to make use of distant ecosystems and rinse away unwanted waste – to participate in the benefits of neo-ecological imperialism. All of this got its start with soap factories and the purchase of Arundel's vast network of trading depots and guano islands in the Central Pacific.[70]

These global conquests were not preordained. Lever Brothers' first foray into tropical agriculture was a miserable failure. Lever and his associates had no interest in guano or island trade – the real generators of profit for Arundel – except as a temporary means to pay for the conversion of eight guano islands into 20,000 hectares of coconut monoculture. Everyone concerned knew it would take years to transplant 2.3 million coconut seedlings to these remote islands and then another decade for them to reach full production. Profuse El Niño rains in 1902 made the project even more daunting than expected. Invasive vines and vermin overtook scrublands and plantations on Flint, Caroline, Sydney, Hull, and Kiritimati islands. With Niue closed off from recruitment, hiring enough workers to clear this growth

[69] Equal to US$2.7 million in 2007; Meek to Lever, 23 Feb. 1923, PMB 1139-reel 1; "Solomon Islands Concession: Certificate of Occupation," 28 Apr. 1903, PMB 1139-reel 2; Williams and Macdonald, *The Phosphateers*, 15, 53, 56; Fieldhouse, *Unilever Overseas*, 449–57.

[70] Fieldhouse, *Unilver Overseas*, esp. 448–51; Burke, *Lifebuoy Men, Lux Women*; Geoffrey Jones, *Renewing Unilever: Transformation and Tradition* (New York, 2005).

posed a major difficulty.[71] What really raised the eyebrows of Port Sunlight managers was the exorbitant cost of completing a 15,712-kilometer roundtrip to service these far-flung islands. From 1903 to 1905, Lever Bros. Pacific Plantations hemorrhaged £24,209, mostly to pay for transportation, which led the company to refocus its investments to Guadalcanal and the Solomon Islands. By 1914, Lever Brothers had completely dismantled Arundel's Pacific empire with the exception of one outlying property, Rabi Island.[72] The enormous size of the Pacific World doomed this endeavor to turn guano islands into gardens. In stark contrast, phosphate mining turned out to be as lucrative as gold for Arundel and Lever and brought the full benefits of neo-ecological imperialism to neo-European farmers and herders living in Australia and New Zealand, as we see in the next chapter.

In this chapter, we have learned how the quest for guano, coconut oil, and human labor in the Central Pacific opened the region to parasitic forms of exploitation and colonial governance and made it vulnerable to several forms of ecological imperialism, old and new. This happened despite the lofty moral intentions of Henry Cushman and Peruvian abolitionists to rid the world of "all sorts of slavery – moral, political, conventional, as well as physical." Arundel and Lever's attempts to convert the Line and Phoenix Islands into productive croplands did little better. Indigenous islanders like Mouga, for their part, hoped that engagement with the outside world would ensure their intergenerational survival and improvement – but all too often ended up paying with their own lives. Guano and soap may have made the industrial North greener and cleaner, but they did so at the direct expense of the native birds, forests, and peoples of the Pacific Islands. Both cases prove an overarching point of this chapter: that we cannot fully decide whether an individual's subjective ethical decisions lead to just results without taking account of larger systemic forces operating over vast geographic and temporal distances.[73] The fact that so many colonizers were conscious of these impacts and still moved forward only makes these stories more troubling.

[71] CEI and paleoarchives. "General Instructions," 24 June 1902; "Data of Cocoa Nut Properties," 25 Jan. 1902; "Approximate Acreage Available," 22 Jan. 1902; Fulton and Greenhalgh, "Report on Christmas Island," 6 Nov. 1902; idem, "Report on Caroline Island," 2 Dec. 1902; idem, "Notes on Flint Island," 3 Dec. 1902; idem, "Report on Island Properties and Trading Stations," 6 Dec. 1902, all PMB 1139-reel 2.

[72] Meek to directors of Lever Brothers' Pacific Plantations Ltd., 30 Jan. 1906; Meek to Lever, 30 Jan. 1906; Meek to Lord Leverhulme (son), 27 Apr. 1926; "Statistical Records, 1902–1925," 4–5, PMB 1139-reels 1–3. Fieldhouse, *Unilever Overseas*, 462–64.

[73] Kohák, *The Green Halo*, pt. 3, §B.

4

Where Is Banaba?

Where is Banaba?...Banaba's all over Australia, New Zealand and every-
where else in the world. Been used as phosphate. So where is my country?
Where is my island?
— Raobeia "Ken" Sigrah (1997)

In 1956, Raobeia Sigrah was born on Rabi Island,[1] a verdant volcanic
isle in the Fiji archipelago. None of us can control where we are born,
who our parents are, or our upbringing, but these facts did not prevent
Sigrah from deeply resenting his origin. His parents, like generation upon
generation before them, had been born on a small equatorial atoll they called
Banaba, short for *ubanabannang* or "land of rock."[2] In 1900, as a direct
extension of the imperialist ventures described in the last chapter, outsiders
suddenly became aware that Banaba possessed enormous reserves of high-
grade phosphate. This discovery sparked an epic struggle between the First
People of Banaba and neo-European colonizers that eventually resulted in
the Banabans' resettlement to Rabi 2,075 kilometers to the southeast.

"Ken," as Sigrah is often known, obtained a satisfactory education from
Fijian schools and eventually obtained employment with the Rabi Island
government. During the 1970s, he became a traditional dancer and activist
with the Banaban nationalist movement and traveled widely – always with
"a great chip on my shoulder." He is deeply pained by the historical fate
of his people and the environmental catastrophe that beset his ancestral
homeland: "At the moment,... Banaba's just like a moonscape. It's all pinnacles, 60 foot high, 80 foot high." It is impossible to walk across Banaba.
Ken hopes that someday the world will find a way to heal this sun-baked
rock: "If we can reserve land for birds and animals (it costs millions and

---

[1] Pronounced RAHM-bee.
[2] Sigrah and King, *Te Rii ni Banaba*, 92. For a 1936 map of the island showing settlements
and mined areas, see http://en.wikipedia.org/wiki/File:Banaba_Island.svg.

billions of dollars) why can't we do it for Banaba?" He no longer feels sorry for himself as a powerless victim of circumstance, however. In recent years, he has seized on the value of historic research to preserve the memory of this lost island and the people who once made it their home. As a spokesman for the te Aka clan, he convinced his elders to break their ancient vow of secrecy and reveal their traditions and memories to the world. He also obtained invaluable help in these efforts from Stacey King, an Anglo-Australian whose great-grandfather helped colonize Banaba for the benefit of neo-Europeans living in the Antipodes.[3] Thanks to their work, it is now possible to reconstruct the history of this island, both from the point of view of those who benefited from its systematic erosion and those who were forced to give up their lands and livelihoods to serve the modern world's appetite for concentrated fertilizer. The central goal of this chapter is to make this important little island known to a much wider world.

Banaba's struggles also tell us something important about the ecological constitution of the modern world. Australia and New Zealand never would have sustained their skin-deep appearance as neo-Europes without a concerted, second stage of neo-ecological imperialism. As in North America, early Anglo settlers caused enormous changes in the land they colonized with the help of biological allies. Contrary to the way Alfred Crosby has portrayed this process, however, ecological forces such as invasive weeds, and ENSO winds often worked against colonizing efforts in the Antipodes.[4] These southern lands also could not have sustained their status as huge exporters of wool, meat, wheat, and other produce without the massive importation of soil nutrients from overseas empires within the Pacific World. These postcolonial nations might never have attained First World status during the course of the twentieth century if not for Banaba, Nauru, and other overseas colonies.

The People of the Rock

Banaba Island is a raised coral atoll, similar to Niue, Makatea, and Nauru in the Pacific; Christmas Island in the Indian Ocean; and Navassa Island in the Caribbean. In fact, Banaba, Niue, and Makatea all mean "rock" in local parlance.[5] The origin of Banaba Island is a contentious issue, even among Banaba's original human inhabitants. According to the Auriaria clan, Banaba is the navel of the world, the first of all places. It came into being

---

3 Ibid., 11–19, 364–67. Sigrah quoted in "The Pacific," *Encounter*, Radio National, Australian Broadcasting Corp., 5 Dec. 1999, http://www.abc.net.au/rn/relig/enc/stories/s70850.htm; Sigrah, "A Research Trip to Canberra," Dec. 1997, http://www.banaban.com/ken1.htm.
4 Crosby, *Ecological Imperialism*, esp. ch. 10; Garden, *Droughts, Floods, and Cyclones*.
5 Sigrah and King, *Te Rii ni Banaba*, 92; Hutchinson, "Biogeochemistry of Vertebrate Excretion," 160–61, 208–52, 285–87, 322–25.

during the Time of Black Darkness when Heaven rooted itself in the ocean depths against the Earth. The copulation of Heaven and Earth gave birth to the first ancestors. With a wooden staff given to him by his father the sea turtle, Auriaria pierced the rock of Heaven, raised it to a great height, then shattered it to pieces with a powerful blow. Great chunks fell into the sea, forming a multitude of islands. Banaba was special because it landed upside down on top of Auriaria's father with its stone roots high in the air.[6] According to the te Aka clan, who see themselves as the islands' first settlers, Banaba was uninhabited and thickly forested when they arrived from the west at least sixteen generations back. This "people of the first hamlet" set up their first settlement between two tall *itai* trees (*Calophyllum inophyllum*) at the center of the island. According to the te Aka clan, Auriaria ("the fiery one who appeared on the horizon") and his people arrived second, as invaders, followed a long while later by Nei Anginimaeao ("she of the great multitudes") who sought refuge for a group of castaways fleeing the Gilbert Islands to the east.[7] The clans of Banaba have since developed an elaborate system of ownership, rights, and duties toward the land and ocean founded on precise knowledge of genealogical relationships. Knowledge of clan genealogy and history – "the backbone of Banaba" (*te rii ni Banaba*) – defines an individual's relationship to nature and society.[8]

Recent geologic research indicates that Banaba and its neighbor Nauru were indeed born in the blackness of the ocean depths approximately 120 million years ago when a superplume of magma erupted from deep inside the earth, perhaps after an asteroid shaken loose from the heavens punctured the ancient Pacific. One hundred million years later during the Miocene – the same geological epoch when Peru's guano birds and Atacama nitrate deposits began to evolve – two extinct volcanic seamounts of the Nauru Igneous Province became homes to a reef ecosystem enriched by intense equatorial upwelling. Deep-sea uplift eventually raised these two atolls to their present height sixty-five to eighty meters above the waves. Like Nauru, Banaba is surrounded by a flat coral shelf and living reef, but unlike Nauru, this shelf is uninhabitable at today's sea level. All of Banaba's terrestrial inhabitants live on "topside."[9]

[6] Arthur Grimble, *Migrations, Myth and Magic from the Gilbert Islands: Early Writings of Sir Arthur Grimble* (London, 1972), 46–51.
[7] Sigrah and King, *Te Rii ni Banaba*, 26–29, 91–94, 117–120; Stephen Trussel and Gordon Groves, eds., *A Combined English-Kiribati Dictionary* (2003), http://www.trussel.com/f_kir.htm#Gil.
[8] Sigrah and King, *Te Rii ni Banaba*, 61, 103, 145; Silverman, *Disconcerting Issue*, 4, 17.
[9] Patrick Nunn, *Environmental Change in the Pacific Basin* (Chichester, UK, 1999), 77, 105, 112–13; Kimihiro Mochizuki et al., "Massive Early Cretaceous Volcanic Activity in the Nauru Basin Related to Emplacement of the Ontong Java Plateau," *G3: Geochemistry, Geophysics, Geosystems* 6 (2005): 1–19; Stephanie Ingle and Millard Coffin, "Impact Origin

Like the first settlers of other Pacific islands, Banabans caused significant ecological changes to their new home. By the late nineteenth century, only one wild bird species, the *kunei* or common noddy (*Anous stolidus*), nested in significant numbers. Banaban men went to great lengths to keep one kind of marine bird on the island, however: the frigatebird. These supreme fliers of the tropical ocean breed 1,500 to 4,000 kilometers away in trees or shrubs on the guano islands of the Central Pacific between March and July. As we learned in Chapter 3, breeding frigatebirds often prey on other nesting bird species or practice kleptoparasitism, but when other nesting birds become scarce, frigatebirds scatter to the open sea where they obtain most of their sustenance. They never alight on the water and, when foraging, continually search for dolphins and tuna capable of bringing scarce schools of food fish within reach from below. A few make it each year all the way to Easter Island. Male and female frigatebirds differ so much in size that Banabans gave them separate names. Females are larger, have white breasts, and are known as *eitei*; males are smaller, mostly black, have a red gular pouch, and are known as *tarakura*. Only experts can distinguish between great and lesser frigatebirds (*Fregata minor* and *F. ariel*), the two species that frequent the island.[10]

As on Easter Island, frigatebirds are harbingers of seasonal change on Banaba. For nine or ten months of the year, relatively arid easterly trade winds and a strong, westward current predominate in the equatorial Pacific. The Banaban New Year begins in late November when the Pleiades (Nei Auti) appear in the eastern sky just after sunset. This typically marks the time when the prevailing winds turn to the west, bringing monsoonal rains. In El Niño years, the equatorial current may reverse itself entirely, bringing abundant showers and valuable driftwood from the distant rainforests of the Solomon Islands. At that time of year, Banabans eagerly watched for the appearance of *tarakura*, which foretell the arrival of small black rain clouds. The journey of frigatebirds back to the east during this season was thought to bring them eventually to the land of the rising sun – an event of such symbolic importance that it is now emblazoned on the Kiribati national flag.[11]

for the Greater Ontong Java Plateau?" *Earth and Planetary Science Letters* 218 (2004): 123–34.
[10] John Webster, *Last Cruise of "The Wanderer"* (Sydney, n.d.), 45, 56–57; Lillian Arundel, "Six Months on a South Sea Island," (1905), p. 33, PMB 1227-JTA, 12/1; Peter Child, *Birds of the Gilbert and Ellice Islands Colony*, Atoll Research Bulletin No. 74 (1960), 2–3, 14–16; Schreiber and Ashmole, "Sea-bird Breeding Seasons," 376–77; Weinerskirch et al., "Foraging Strategies."
[11] Ellis, *Ocean Island and Nauru*, 44–45; Grimble, *Migrations, Myth and Magic*, 223–25; Eugene Rasmusson and Thomas Carpenter, "Variations in Tropical Sea Surface Temperature and Surface Wind Fields Associated with the Southern Oscillation/El Niño," *Monthly Weather Review* 110 (1982): 354–84; Child, *Birds of the Gilbert and Ellice Islands*, 15; Trussel and Groves, *Kiribati-English Dictionary*.

In the old days, Banabans believed this special relationship with the rising sun imbued frigatebirds with tremendous power. Several forms of traditional dance are based on their flight. In the old days, male Banabans competed to see who could snare and tame the most frigatebirds. Young boys developed these skills using a toy bird made from feathers. Their fathers maintained roosts, especially on the eastern, windward side of the island next to cliff-side terraces built for the performance of sunrise ceremonies (*kauti*). Snaring frigatebirds was thought to capture the power of the rising sun. *Kauti* magic involved the ability to control the wind, to make rain, and to ensure that the sun did not scorch fruit-bearing trees. It also provided protection from illness and the skill to find *ati* or bonito (*Sarda chilensis*). Torchlight, an embodiment of the sun's fire, helped lure flying fish (*Exoceoetidae*), the frigatebirds' favorite food, into reach on moonless nights. The indigenous inhabitants of Nauru and the Gilbert Islands also kept roosts of frigatebirds and reputedly used them to exchange small gifts and messages with each other over great distances, similar to the Rapanui.[12]

In the old days, the ocean and atmosphere were the exclusive extractive domain of Banaban men. Foraging frigatebirds not only served as local guides to offshore fish, their appearance from afar also foretold the arrival of fish in abundance. When the westward equatorial current slackens, it creates abrupt bursts of upwelling that concentrate plankton in Banaba's leeward wake and bring other pelagic creatures in abundance. Systems of genealogical descent strictly regulated who could participate in these extractive activities. The descendants of Auriaria were forbidden to kill and eat their cousin the sea turtle. Nei Anginimaeao's progeny, on the other hand, possessed an exclusive right to butcher turtles and beached porpoises and to collect driftwood – all gifts from the sea to the land.[13]

Banaba's first settlers also caused significant changes to the plant life on this isolated atoll – by dramatically *increasing* its biodiversity. According to plant ecologists, *Calophyllum* trees dominated the primeval vegetation of Banaba and its neighbor Nauru, in line with te Aka clan tradition. Large stands of these valuable trees still remained when neo-European miners colonized the island. They were interspersed with carefully tended, fruit-bearing groves of *kaina* (screw-pine, *Pandanus tectorius*), *ni* (coconut), *kunikun* (wild almond, *Terminalia catappa*), and an occasional mango (*Mangifera indica*) introduced by the Banabans. According to tradition, women, the caretakers of the earth, had been responsible for turning the island into a

---

[12] Webster, *Last Cruise of "The Wanderer,"* 31, 44, 47; [Arthur Mahaffy], "Ocean Island," *Blackwood's Edinburgh Magazine* Nov. 1910: 576, 578–81; Silverman, *Disconcerting Issue*, 38–39; Sigrah and King, *Te Rii ni Banaba*, 80–83, 108–12; Ernest Sabatier, *Astride the Equator: An Account of the Gilbert Islands* (Melbourne, 1977), 30–31; Grimble, *Migrations, Myth and Magic*, 133–36, 197–98, 282–83; Grimble, *Tunguru Traditions: Writings on the Atoll Culture of the Gilbert Islands* (Honolulu, 1989), 10–14, 37–39.

[13] Silverman, *Disconcerting Issue*, 77; Sigrah and King, *Te Rii ni Banaba*, 101, 108–12, 135–37; Ellis, *Ocean Island and Banaba*, 76.

fertile garden and possessed the all-important right to enter the earth's damp interior. They performed the laborious task of pressing oil from coconuts, plaiting pandanus leaves, and pounding fibrous pandanus pulp into *kabubu*, a sun-dried powder that could dependably sustain life two years after it was stored. In favorable locations, women also kept gardens of pumpkin (*Cucurbita pepo*) and other useful plants. No female would climb a tree to gather fruit or coconut sap, however; that was the job of males. Like the Rapanui, Banaban women cooked in earth ovens to minimize consumption of biomass energy. On an island this isolated and small – only 5.9 square kilometers – a population of a few hundred could rapidly exhaust the earth's capacity to reproduce.[14]

This was particularly true during La Niña years. Banaba lies close to the margin of the Pacific Ocean's equatorial dry zone. During strong La Niña events, the western monsoon may never arrive, reducing the abundance of fish and causing severe drought. According to Banaban tradition, crabs saved the island's first settlers from certain death during one of these episodes by revealing the existence of limestone caverns containing permanent pools of water (*bangabanga*). Small *manai* (land crabs, *Cardisoma carnifex*) revealed the entrance to these wet caves, but a spirit in the form of a giant *ai* (coconut crab, *Birgus latro*) blocked the way. It would only allow passage by women bearing tokens of its favorite food plant, the coconut tree. In recognition of this sacred gift, indigenous Banabans would never kill a coconut crab – in stark contrast to outsiders who hunted these tasty creatures to local extinction on the island during the twentieth century. Water rights were held in common by entire lineages, "the kindred of the well." During extended droughts, community regulations precisely prescribed how much water could be removed by "drinkers at the stone" to ensure supplies would last.[15]

Life on Banaba changed yet again during the nineteenth century when the equatorial Pacific became integrated into the world's new industrial economy. Sperm whalers first landed on Banaba in 1801 and rechristened it Ocean Island. During fruitful years, visiting ships traded for fish, firewood, vegetables, freshwater, able-bodied crew members, and sexual favors in return for addictive tobacco, metal implements, exotic foods, and a chance to see the world.[16] Na Itinaumaere, for example, left Banaba to take part in the California Gold Rush. He fell overboard on the trip back and would

---

[14] Harley Manner et al., "Phosphate Mining Induced Vegetation Change on Nauru Island," *Ecology* 65 (1984): 1454–65; Webster, *Last Cruise of "The Wanderer,"* 46, 49; Silverman, *Disconcerting Issue*, 77; Sigrah and King, *Te Rii ni Banaba*, 103, 238; Grimble, *Migrations, Myth and Magic*, 121–23, 311–13.

[15] Sigrah and King, *Te Rii ni Banaba*, 47, 73; Silverman, *Disconcerting Issue*, 46, 64; Trussel and Groves, *Kiribati-English Dictionary*.

[16] Macdonald, *Cinderellas of Empire*, 17–18, 94; Sigrah and King, *Te Rii ni Banaba*, 168, 176, 179–80; Ellis, *Ocean Island and Nauru*, 9, 15; Silverman, *Disconcerting Issue*, 85–88.

FIGURE 4.1. The precolonial landscape of Banaba Island, 1851. Scotland native John Webster (1818–1912) was the only neo-European naturalist to produce detailed portrayals of precolonial Banaba. Na Itinaumaere served as his guide – and only narrowly prevented him from gunning down a sacred flock of frigatebirds. To the uneducated eye, this composition presents a typical atoll from the tropical Pacific. However, several features speak to Banaba's unique environmental and cultural situation: the sparse spacing of coconut palms, the prominence of rock walls and a rock terrace, a woman carrying a coconut water vessel, children learning to snare a toy frigatebird, and a small ancestral shrine at the base of a palm. Years later, Webster regretted that he had shot so promiscuously at the wild animals and "wild men" of the Pacific, and he eventually gave up cattle driving and logging to become a model farmer in New Zealand's far North. Webster's means of improving his adopted land, however, eventually brought total environmental destruction to Banaba. *Source:* Webster, *The Last Cruise of "The Wanderer."*

have died if not for the near miraculous intervention of an animal messenger (known as *man*). A seagull following in the ship's wake landed on his head, filling him with strength and showing his shipmates where he was swimming. This enabled him to return home safely with a chest full of trade goods, eager to marry and take up his family inheritance. Na Itinaumaere also provided one of New Zealand's most famous colonizers with the opportunity to visit Banaba and sketch its landscape and inhabitants (fig. 4.1).[17]

---

[17] John Webster journal, Aug. 1851, APL-NZMS 118; Webster sketchbook, 1851, APL-NZMS 113; Webster, *Last Cruise of "The Wanderer,"* 23, 41–44, 46, 49–50; John Webster, *Reminiscences of an Old Settler in Australia and New Zealand* (Chirstchurch, NZ, 1908).

Na Itinaumaere left to seek his fortune, but many other Banabans fled the island simply to survive. An unforgettable La Niña drought struck Banaba during the early 1870s. No rain of consequence fell on the island for almost three years. Its fruiting trees all died or went into senescence; even deep-rooted *Calophyllum* trees lost their leaves. To save water, a council of elders decided that "drinkers at the stone" could only remove a single coconut shell of freshwater per day to serve their entire household. Adventurous women scratched their way deeper into the island's caves and discovered new wells, and adventurous men paddled far out to sea in search of rain showers, but these finds only delayed catastrophe. The experiences of a teenage boy named Eri illustrate the heartbreak that came with such dark times. He was betrothed to a girl named Marawa and expected to marry when the drought broke and it was possible to feast again. During the third year of drought, Eri received word that Marawa's parents had died of "the drought sickness." Banaban tradition had ways to deal with this situation. During famines, the destitute could move in with families that possessed food and water; in return, adoptees willed "lands of life-giving" to their new family. Eri's mother sent him across the island to ask Marawa to join their family. He found her on the edge of death, covered by sores caused by scurvy, at the feet of her decomposing parents. She died in his arms. Rain clouds eventually returned, but not in time to save Eri's mother. In a desperate battle to stay hydrated and avoid scurvy, Eri's family sucked seaweed and lay in tide pools covered by mats during the day. His mother drowned while soaking in a tide pool, too weak to swim against the returning sea. The deaths of these two women cut off Eri and his father from the water of life and forced them to leave the island altogether to survive.[18]

Banaba was not the only place that experienced catastrophe during these years. Strong La Niña conditions lasted almost continuously from 1870 to 1876 and killed hundreds on the Gilbert Islands to the east. On the faraway Great Plains, a locust plague long credited by the *Guinness Book of World Records* as the greatest concentration of animals in history descended on drought-stricken Kansas and Nebraska. By this date, however, the Great Plains and Central Pacific had come to occupy very different niches within the world's new ecological regime. Kansas received free trainloads of grain on the transcontinental railroad and soon resumed exporting food mined from its deep prairie soils. Banaba, on the other hand, received swarms of ships eager to mine the island for desperate humans. A New Zealand ship took Eri and his father to work on Oahu. Thousands more from the region accepted temporary work on plantations or as domestic servants in

---

[18] Arthur Grimble, *Return to the Islands: Life and Legend in the Gilberts* (New York, 1957), 34–43; Sigrah and King, *Te Rii ni Banaba*, 155, 176, 188–90; Silverman, *Disconcerting Issue*, 44, 86–87; Albert Ellis diary, 5 May 1900, PMB 497.

Queensland, Fiji, Samoa, Tahiti, and Kusaie Island. A La Niña during the early 1890s generated another wave of recruitment that took workers as far away as the coffee plantations of Guatemala. It also inspired migratory movements on the Great Plains, where the author's great-grandparents abandoned a desiccated homestead in the new state of South Dakota to become health reformers in Chicago. About half of the voyagers who left Banaba and similar islands never returned. Those who did exposed their homes to measles, Christianity, and other dangers. The "late Victorian holocausts" of the nineteenth century, thus, had already brought the Banaban people into partial subjugation to outsiders when neo-European phosphate miners appeared on the scene at the start of a disastrous new century.[19]

The Ecology of Invasion

In 1899, an Anglo colonizer made a discovery that forever changed Banaba's place in the world. Albert Ellis (1869–1951) was born in the heart of Queensland's cattle-raising district. His father, George Ellis, soon gave up trying to make it as a frontier farmer in Australia to work for his first cousin, John Arundel, in the Central Pacific. In 1888, George was severely injured on Howland Island while dynamite fishing, and he left the difficult work of lording over the guano islands to Albert and his brothers. In July 1899, Albert again took over for his father as Arundel's main chemical assayer and island prospector.[20]

Chemistry had long since supplanted marine birds as the best guide to valuable guano deposits, and Arundel employees made a regular practice of collecting samples from islands they visited. News had recently gotten out of a spectacular discovery on Christmas Island, a limestone-capped seamount in the Indian Ocean south of Java. While writing up the geologic publications of the 1872–76 *Challenger* expedition, Canadian-born naturalist John Murray realized its raised central plateau had deposits of high-grade phosphate

[19] CEI and paleoarchives; Herweijer et al., "North American Droughts"; Jeffrey Lockwood, *Locust: The Devastating Rise and Mysterious Disappearance of the Insect That Shaped the American Frontier* (New York, 2004); Lilian Arundel, "Six Months on a South Sea Island," (1905), p. 27, PMB 1227-JTA, 12/1; Sigrah and King, *Te Rii ni Banaba*, 186–87, 190–91; Silverman, *Disconcerting Issue*, 91; Macdonald, *Cinderellas of Empire*, 32–35, 54, 58, 60; Richard Bedford et al., "Population Estimates for Kiribati and Tuvalu, 1850–1900," *Journal of the Polynesian Society* 89 (1980): 206, 209–10, 236, 239 n. 1, 240 n. 9; David McCreery and Doug Munro, "The Cargo of Montserrat: Gilbertese Labor in Guatemalan Coffee, 1890–1908," *The Americas* 49 (1993): 272–73, 285–86; Davis, *Late Victorian Holocausts*, ch. 4.
[20] *Encyclopedia of New Zealand* (1966), s.v. "Ellis, Sir Albert Fuller"; I. M. Fletcher, "The Izods," (1960), PMB 1227-JTA, 2; Ellis, *Ocean Island and Nauru*, 50, 164.

rock – the first discovery of its kind. Murray initiated commercial mining in 1899 and was soon supplying large quantities to the nascent chemical industry of Japan.[21] Albert Ellis was always on the lookout for promising specimens and noticed the resemblance between a stone used to prop open his laboratory door and a small deposit of "rock guano" he and his father had discovered back in 1887 on Baker Island. He was nonetheless surprised by its extremely high content of tricalcium phosphate, as well as its place of origin: the German colony of Nauru. Arundel arranged for a trusted employee to bring back samples from both Nauru and Banaba, which were geologically similar. To their delight, Banaba turned out to have even higher-grade deposits.[22]

Arundel and Ellis realized they had to act fast or risk losing these discoveries to a competitor, but a number of factors complicated the situation. Banaba and Nauru were the first major fertilizer-producing islands anyone had dealt with that had significant indigenous populations. Nauru was governed by Germany, and Banaba was one of the few islands in the Pacific that had not yet been claimed by an imperial power. Epidemic disease also caused delays. Arundel fell sick from the same flu pandemic that struck down Mouga on Niue, and an outbreak of plague in Sydney precluded anyone from visiting Fiji to discuss formal colonization with British officials. However, no quarantine prevented Ellis's embarkation for Baker Island to arrange the transfer of guano-mining operations to Banaba. This normally arid atoll was in the throes of a full-blown El Niño. Heavy surf had wrecked the most recent supply ship, and torrential rains had ruined most of the island's provisions. Everyone was hungry and wet; half of the island's Niuean crew was sick; some had died; most of the rest refused to work and demanded repatriation. This brought an abrupt end to Niue's participation in the guano age.[23]

After this detour, Ellis arrived at Banaba in the midst of an El Niño squall on 3 May 1900. His shipboard encounter with Temate, the supposed "King of Ocean Island," has been one of the most scrutinized events in the history of colonialism in the Pacific. Temate had inherited the Auriaria clan's exclusive right to board a foreign vessel. After trading for some shark fin and curios, Ellis signed a contract with this "fine example of nature's gentlemen," ostensibly "on behalf of the entire population of Ocean Island." It granted Arundel's company "the sole right to raise and ship all the Rock *and* Alluvial

[21] Ellis to Sydney Arundel Aris, 2 May 1949, PMB 497; Harold Burstyn, "Science Pays Off: Sir John Murray and the Christmas Island Phosphate Industry, 1886–1914," *Social Studies of Science* 5 (1975): 5–34; Williams and Macdonald, *The Phosphateers*, 27–28, 44–48.

[22] Ellis, *Ocean Island and Nauru*, 50; Ellis, *Mid-Pacific Outposts*, 254; Williams and Macdonald, *The Phosphateers*, 9–10, 15, 18, 24.

[23] CEI and paleoarchives; Williams and Macdonald, *The Phosphateers*, 12, 15, 18, 22–25, 42.

Phosphate on Ocean Island" in return for £50 per annum "or trade to that value" over a term lasting 999 years.[24]

This contract has come to symbolize a century of unjust Banaban treatment under colonial and postcolonial rule, but it was actually quite ordinary in most of its features. It was similar to lease agreements that Arundel had made over the years for guano islands and coconut lands, both in payment and duration. On Niue and elsewhere, Arundel's employees had grown accustomed to recruiting laborers through a local "king" or chieftain in return for a payoff in trade goods. "Kingmaking" was a tried-and-true strategy of British colonialism among indigenous peoples around the world. As we have already seen, Banabans were hardly new to the exploitative ways of the capitalist world. In fact, Na Itinaumaere was still imparting his memories of the California Gold Rush at the time of Ellis's visit. Many Banabans were eager for the trading opportunities this turn of events represented. Eri, a drought survivor and Protestant convert eager for progress on the island, lent his signature to a number of contracts on behalf of Uma district, including the infamous one first signed by Temate. However, some expressed open skepticism about Ellis's proposals, particularly the prospect of sharing water. Even though Banaba was greener than it had been in years, the droughts of the 1870s and 1890s were still a vivid memory. Ellis promised to build cisterns and share water from a desalination plant – if natives helped with construction and provided fuel.[25]

One feature of this original contract was particularly open to abuse. In company parlance, "alluvial phosphate" meant fairly recent surface deposits of bird dung. "Rock guano" was quite different in composition and uncommon on most guano islands. Banabans expressed grave concern, from the beginning, about the environmental impact of island mining. To obtain their marks on the original contract, Ellis promised "not to remove any Alluvial Phosphate from where cocoanut and other Fruit Trees or Plants cultivated by the said Natives are growing." Ellis knew this would be a hard promise to keep. During his initial survey, Ellis realized that most of Banaba's 451 inhabitants lived on top of vast deposits of "rock phosphate" and their

[24] Emphasis added; contract signed by Albert Ellis of Pacific Islands Co. and marked by Temati and Kariatabewa, 3 May 1900, cosigned by Eri and marked by Kumeraia and Pulalang, 18 Sept. 1900, facsimile in Williams and Macdonald, *The Phosphateers*; Ellis diary, 3, 12 May 1900, PMB 497; Ellis, *Ocean Island and Nauru*, 70; Sigrah and King, *Te Rii ni Banaba*, 170–71.

[25] Ellis diary, 7–8, 12, 14, 17 May 1900, PMB 497; "Deed of Partnership for the Working of Guano Islands," 28 Oct. 1882, PMB 1227-JTA, 9; Contract between J. T. Arundel & Co. and 54 natives, Niue, 29 May 1884, PMB 1227-JTA, 11/4; Lawes to Arundel, 14 Jan. 1901, PMB 1227-JTA, 11/5; Williams and Macdonald, *The Phosphateers*, 27–28, 34, 51; Donald Denoon, "New Economic Orders: Land, Labour and Dependency," in *The Cambridge History of Pacific Islanders* (Cambridge and New York, 1997), 228; Jane Samson, *Imperial Benevolence: Making British Authority in the Pacific Islands* (Honolulu, 1998), ch. 4; Ellis, *Ocean Island and Nauru*, 64, 66–67; Ellis, *Mid-Pacific Outposts*, 235.

groves grew directly out of "alluvial guano." Nauru, likewise, was "one huge mass of Rock Guano." From the beginning, he and his partners recognized that large-scale mining would result in massive environmental change. This misrepresentation lay at the root of a century of conflict.[26]

Ellis immediately realized that Banaba was "not a *guano* island" like any he had ever seen. In 1902, Arundel consulted U.S. coral reef expert Alexander Agassiz to figure out the origin of its huge phosphate deposits. Agassiz hatched the idea that Banaba, Nauru, Navassa, and other raised atolls might be guano islands of enormous age, an insight that led directly to Arundel's discovery of deposits on Makatea.[27] Several features of these raised atolls contradicted Agassiz's hypothesis, however – most notably, their lack of bird fossils, heavy impregnation with reef organisms, and dangerous enrichment by heavy metals. After decades of debate, geologists have concluded that several distinct processes were involved in creating the world's phosphorus formations. Banaba and other raised atoll deposits were probably formed in ancient atoll lagoons fed by organic matter from the surrounding marine environment. Mats of cyanobacteria likely played a critical role in creating them. The phosphate formations of the Florida Platform and North Africa and so-called coprolite beds of England, on the other hand, were created by phytoplankton and sea-floor bacteria in ancient regions of marine upwelling. Today, this process of phosphate deposition is most active on the ocean floor far beneath the guano islands of coastal Peru and Namibia. The persistent but mistaken popular belief that these deposits originated from the feces of ancient birds is a lasting legacy of the guano age. In reality, they are the waste of microorganisms.[28]

In May 1901, Arundel personally supervised a thorough survey of Banaba and Nauru by an Australian engineering firm. This survey conservatively estimated Banaban phosphate reserves at 13.1 million tons – an amount slightly larger in gross weight than all of the guano taken from Peru during the guano age. Nauru had perhaps 41 million tons of phosphate. Both turned out to be marked underestimates. After seeing these numbers, soap-magnate William Lever jumped at the chance to invest heavily in the new Pacific Phosphates Company (PPC) formed by Arundel, Lord Stanmore, and Jaluit Gesellschaft. The Royal Navy, in contrast, only consented to a formal flag-raising ceremony over Banaba in September 1901 under intense political

---

[26] Ellis diary, 8, 10, 25 May 1900, PMB 494; Ellis contract, 3 May, 18 Sept. 1900, facsimile in Williams and Macdonald, *The Phosphateers*, also pp. 11–12, 35; Macdonald, *Cinderellas of Empire*, 97.

[27] Ellis's emphasis; quoted in Williams and Macdonald, *The Phosphateers*, 58, 79–80.

[28] Sabatier, *Astride the Equator*, 296; Craig Glenn et al., eds., *Marine Authigenesis: From Global to Microbial* (Tulsa, OK, 2000), ix–xi, 21–33, 185–99, 481–98; Jörg Trappe, *Phanerozoic Phosphate Depositional Systems* (Berlin, 1998), 63, 71–76, 98–100; Julia Diaz et al., "Marine Polyphosphate: A Key Player in Geologic Phosphorus Sequestration," *Science* 2 May 2008: 652–55.

pressure from Lord Stanmore, which made it an official part of the United Kingdom's Gilbert and Ellice Islands (G&EI) Protectorate.[29]

Climate variability and disease presented much greater barriers than capitalist finance and colonial politics to phosphate mining during these early years. In October 1900, a familiar fever from the guano islands – probably flu – laid up Ellis and a crew of Ellice Islanders brought to work Banaban deposits. In 1902 and 1905, heavy El Niño rains disrupted the sun-drying of phosphate ore to such an extent that the PPC decided to install an expensive set of coal-powered rock crushers and dryers. This created a new environmental problem: coal smoke and "enormous clouds" of phosphate dust. By the 1920s, this facility was coating the land and lungs of island residents with 80 tons of dust per day, leading efficiency-minded managers to install electrostatic precipitators to reduce this waste. Banaba's aural environment, meanwhile, became dominated "day and night" by "the mighty crash and whir of machinery, the clamor and din of many workshops, the shrill shrieks of locomotives, the deafening rattle of phosphate laden trucks," and periodic blasts of dynamite.[30]

Banaba's new rulers liked to think their activities improved the lives of their native subjects by providing "free medical attention" and other benefits of modern civilization. Ellis provided ointment therapy for the debilitating skin disease yaws during his first visit, both to gain the Banabans' favor and bolster the island's able-bodied workforce. The introduction of neo-salvarsan therapy from German-ruled Jaluit Atoll during the 1910s dramatically reduced its incidence on Banaba and other nearby islands.[31] Nevertheless, PPC activities actually made these islands far more vulnerable to microbial epidemics. Company ships brought hundreds of new Gilbertese, Ellice Islander, Japanese, Chinese, and Anglo workers every year – each a potential vector of disease. Their sheer numbers severely overtaxed Banaba and Nauru's capacity to dilute and wash away human waste. This created ideal ecological conditions for a dysentery epidemic. In 1907, hundreds fell ill on Nauru during the first season of large-scale mining; between 5 and 10 percent of the indigenous Nauruan population died. But this was no virgin soil epidemic: 179 of 624 Chinese recruits on the island died from dysentery or beriberi, a situation that was exacerbated by withholding rations from laborers who protested against poor working conditions. Things were not quite so bad on Banaba, but dysentery soon spread to the island despite

---

[29] Williams and Macdonald, *The Phosphateers*, 53, 56, 91; Macdonald, *Cinderellas of Empire*, 99.

[30] Ellis, *Ocean Island and Nauru*, 98, 111, 150–51, 188; "The 'Let's-All-Be-Thankful Island," *Penny Pictorial* 20 Sept. 1919: 131; Grimble, *We Chose the Islands: A Six-year Adventure in the Gilberts* (New York, 1952), 23, 38–39; Williams and Macdonald, *The Phosphateers*, 26–27, 51, 57, 62, 64.

[31] Ellis diary, 13, 16 May 1900; Ellis, *Ocean Island and Nauru*, 66, 138; Sigrah and King, *Te Rii ni Banaba*, 180–81; Simmons, *Global Epidemiology*, 1:264–65.

efforts to keep it quarantined. Dysentery and other diarrheal illnesses tended to flare up each year when water became scarce during the dry season and were the leading cause of hospitalization and death among Banaban and white residents, the second leading cause for Japanese workers, and third leading cause for Pacific Islanders recruited from elsewhere, according to the island's first official health report in 1910. Dysentery was the leading cause of death among Pacific migrant workers during this era, and Banaba and Nauru were no exception.[32]

The prevalence of dysentery in this region again illustrates the widening environmental inequalities that developed during this age of soap and water. All forms of dysentery involve severe inflammation of the intestines marked by profuse, bloody diarrhea and intense abdominal pain. A number of organisms are capable of causing dysentery, most of them transmitted by fecal-contaminated water, food, hands, and clothing. The most dangerous form of dysentery is caused by the bacterial genus *Shigella*, which is highly contagious and can cause death in as little as a week from dehydration or bacterial toxins. A protozoan, *Entamoeba hisolytica*, also causes acute and chronic forms of the disease; it forms cysts that remain latent within a host or soil for years, waiting for appropriate ecological conditions to proliferate. Under the ecological old regime, dysentery was one of the world's biggest killers, regardless of climate. Abundant clean water supplies, cheap soap, and improved nutrition all contributed to the dramatic decline of this classic starvation sickness in the industrialized world during the second half of the nineteenth century. In the Pacific World, on the other hand, the rapid movement of poorly nourished working peoples involved in fertilizer and coconut oil extraction dramatically increased the prevalence of dysentery during the late nineteenth and early twentieth centuries. Perversely, tens of thousands shit their lives away to produce the exact commodities that made Lever and Arundel fantastically wealthy, and growing swarms of ethnic Europeans around the world well fed and squeaky clean.[33]

When colonial officials first took command of Banaba, they issued a series of rules to discipline native behavior and improve public hygiene, well before the outbreak of these epidemics. They required the burying of ancestral remains in cemeteries; prohibited "obscene games," "sorcery," and alcoholic beverages; punished families who allowed their children to go naked or kept dirty houses; and banned nighttime activities and dancing

---

[32] Dr. Wigmore to Arthur Mahaffy, 28 Oct. 1911, NAUK-CO, 881/12, no. 192, pp. 179–84; Sigrah and King, *Te Rii ni Banaba*, 182–83; Williams and Macdonald, *The Phosphateers*, 72; Schlomowitz, "Epidemiology and the Pacific Labor Trade"; Bedford et al., "Kiribati and Tuvalu Populations," 209–10, 240 n. 9; Stewart Firth, "German Labour Policy in Nauru and Angaur, 1906–1914," *Journal of Pacific History* 13 (1978): 39–43; Roberts, *Population Problems in the Pacific*, 77.

[33] "Dysentery," *Encyclopedia Britannica*, 1911 ed., 2008 ed.; Creighton, *A History of Epidemics in Britain*, vol. 2, ch. 3, 8; Post, *The Last Great Subsistence Crisis*, 120–31.

except on public holidays. They also punished parents who failed to report a sick child and forbade natives to use the island hospital.[34] When dysentery became a problem, Banaba's colonizers engineered the wholesale environmental transformation of the island. For indigenous residents of clan-based hamlets scattered among Banaba's coconut and pandanus groves, this meant forced congregation into four villages focused on Protestant churches. These were laid out with stick-straight streets in accord with regulations first developed by the 1893 Commission on Fijian Depopulation. Like other colonized peoples in the G&EI Protectorate, each Banaban household had to rebuild its dwellings with raised wooden floors to improve ventilation, rigorously isolate sleeping quarters from food preparation, remove the sacred remains of ancestors to an underground cemetery, and dig its own pit latrine according to approved designs. For individuals suffering from dysentery, these reeking outhouses might serve as prisons until the disease took its course. Every Saturday, Banabans were required to participate in "village clean-up-day" and had to submit their dwellings to inspection. By 1910, the PPC had built an elaborate system of salt-water flush toilets for its employees. Cash-strapped government staff had to make do with Kaustine chemical toilets.[35] Excrement was an obsession of Banaba's "guano" miners – just as it was for empire builders in Fiji, the Philippines, and wilderness camps in the United States.[36]

Banaba's colonizers vaguely understood that poor hygiene causes dysentery, but their tactics owed far more to racial prejudice and aesthetic preference than to the new bacteriology. Anglos also wore white clothing in an attempt to protect themselves from filth and the tropical climate. PPC laundry facilities supplied with Lever Bros. soap kept these outfits scrupulously clean. Some sought to protect themselves further by washing with strong-smelling Lifebuoy Disinfectant Soap – yet another reason that PPC officials "stank in the nostrils of the landowners" on Banaba. John Arundel's family made sure to bring numerous cases of French champagne when they visited to prevent stomach ailments. These precautions failed to prevent many colonizers from suffering premature death, however. Albert Ellis's young family fared particularly poorly. His infant son died in 1908. His wife Florence

[34] Charles Major to Sec. of State, 25 July 1904, NAUK-CO 881/12, no. 100–1, pp. 68–72.
[35] Wigmore to Mahaffy, 28 Oct. 1911; Simmons et al., *Global Epidemiology*, 258; [Mahaffy], "Ocean Island," 583–84; Ellis, *Ocean Island and Nauru*, 135; Silverman, *Disconcerting Issue*, 104–5, 144, 340–41; Sigrah and King, *Te Rii ni Banaba*, 218–22, 300; Macdonald, *Cinderellas of Empire*, 80, 86–87, 102, 115, 117–18; Williams and Macdonald, *The Phosphateers*, 72, 84, 86–87.
[36] Anderson, "Excremental Colonialism"; Roberts, *Population Problems in the Pacific*, 84, 254–55, 389–90; Philip Curtin, *Death by Migration: Europe's Encounter with the Tropical World in the Nineteenth Century* (Cambridge and New York, 1989), 147–50; Abigail Ayres Van Slyck, *A Manufactured Wilderness: Summer Camps and the Shaping of American Youth, 1890–1960* (Minneapolis, 2006).

rededicated her life to caring for sick indigenes at the island's first hospital for natives but died in June 1909.[37]

Other epidemics also struck the islands. Tuberculosis and whooping cough were deadly dangers for the Banabans. Influenza, bronchitis, and pneumonia were periodic problems for everyone. All these illnesses were made worse by breathing ubiquitous phosphate dust. In 1910, one of the worst incidents of poliomyelitis the world has ever seen struck German-ruled Nauru. It infected at least one-third of Nauru's inhabitants, including 470 indigenes, 220 Caroline Islanders, two Europeans, but no East Asians, killing 38 and leaving 50 paralyzed. This classic virgin-soil epidemic spared Banaba. So, too, did the 1918–20 influenza pandemic – unlike Nauru, Tonga, Fiji, Samoa, and the faraway California household of Elmer, Mary, and Lester Cushman. But in 1935, a severe outbreak of flu and pneumonia on Banaba killed 41 Pacific Islanders. Polio broke out again and killed several on Nauru and Banaba in 1952 – the same year it struck the Cushman household and tens of thousands of families in the United States and Denmark. These epidemics illustrate the deadly danger that faces *any* population when it becomes part of a much larger world.[38]

It would be wrong to portray Banaba as an archetype of the diseased Pacific, however.[39] Compared with many regions of the world – including industrial tenements – it was actually quite healthy, and for some residents more closely resembled a tropical paradise. For the Arundel daughters, both avid naturalists, "Everything seemed to sparkle in the sunshine, the thick shiny leaves of trees and bushes, and the luxuriant trumpet-shaped hibiscus flowers... with the silvery brown lizards darting over the grey coral pinnacles." They spent many days on the island observing "the mermaid's beautiful garden" beneath the sea and sketching Banaba's native flora and inhabitants. Just before their departure, they each planted coconut trees at their favorite picnic sites – still listed on maps as Lilian and Sydney Points. Their father led them to believe that the PPC would eventually replant the whole island "with coconut trees, so that the natives should not lose by the transaction."[40]

---

[37] E. C. Eliot, *Broken Atoms* (London, 1938), 139; Williams and McDonald, *The Phosphateers*, 31, 84, 86–88, 188, plates; Assorted photographs, 1905, PMB 1227-JTA, 12; Lever to Meek, 12 Apr. 1912, PMB 1139-reel 1.

[38] Wigmore to Mahaffy, 28 Oct. 1911; A. Müller, "Eine epidemisch auftretende Erkrankung des Nervensystems auf Nauru," *Archiv für Schiffs und Tropen-Hygiene* 14 (1910): 535–43; M. Smallman-Raynor and A. D. Cliff, *Poliomyelitis: A World Geography: Emergence to Eradication* (New York, 2006), 180, 268, 362; Simmons et al., *Global Epidemiology*, 1:263–64; Williams and Macdonald, *The Phosphateers*, 72, 86, 183, 275, 405; Denoon, "New Economic Orders," 243–49.

[39] Rod Edmonds, *Representing the South Pacific: Colonial Discourse from Cook to Gauguin* (Cambridge and New York, 1997), ch. 7.

[40] Lilian Arundel, "Six Months," pp. 3–4, 35, 38, 40, PMB 1227-JTA, 12/1.

Phosphate and the Grasslands Revolution

For indigenous Banabans, their island was neither Heaven nor Hell – it was simply Home. But as time passed, phosphate miners converted more and more of it into a stony wasteland to "make the desert blossom like a rose" in faraway regions of neo-European settlement. Segments of Banaban society fought from the outset to prevent this outcome, ultimately without success.

The first thing to disappear from Banaba's precolonial landscape was its vast network of low stone walls. These fences helped delineate complex patterns of inherited, private ownership that made up "the backbone of Banaba." Ellis paid eight shillings per ton in trade goods for these stones and managed to export 1,575 metric tons by the end of 1900. PPC ore production on Banaba grew to 13,564 metric tons the next year, then to 213,527 metric tons in 1908, by which time Banaban production represented 5 percent of annual phosphate output, worldwide. During the first decade of production, the PPC only paid out a grand total of £3,737 to Banaban landowners for this privilege – £6 8s for every Banaban man, woman, and child alive on the island in 1909, mostly in the form of store goods sold at a steep markup.[41] Some Banaban property owners refused to allow their walls and lands to be touched. In most cases, miners simply worked around them, leaving high, inaccessible, drought-prone "eyes of the land" surrounded by mined-out devastation. In 1903, Albert Ellis and John Arundel asked the colonial administration to force one reluctant woman to lease her lands for exploitation. The G&EI resident commissioner strongly criticized the environmental damage they were causing but allowed them to proceed – in the woman's case, without her consent – as long as the PPC paid extra for cutting down coconut trees and replanted them at a later date.[42]

Indigenous women were far more likely than men to oppose mining. In Banaban society, sons and daughters inherited land equally via a complex system of bilateral descent. Women, however, controlled most of the things that gave land its economic and spiritual value. In the old days, an ideal Banaban family had one boy to fish, but two girls to collect water, the island's most precious resource. Under the PPC's new ecological regime, outsiders eagerly purchased fish and coconut toddy and gave jobs to men but expressed little interest in the fruits of the land produced by women. Destruction of the earth, trees, and hidden waters and the proliferation of imported food, water, clothing, and building materials further eroded women's

---

41 Equal to US$405,500 and US$697 in 2007, respectively, if paid in cash. Ellis, *Ocean Island and Nauru*, 106; Ellis diary, 5, 7, 9, 12 May 1900, PMB 494; PPC memorandum to Colonial Office, 5 Apr. 1909, NAUK-CO, 881/12; [Mahaffy], "Ocean Island," 570; Williams and Macdonald, *The Phosphateers*, 41, 51, 60–61, 99.

42 Macdonald, *Cinderellas of Empire*, 99; Williams and Macdonald, *The Phosphateers*, 60; Silverman, *Disconcerting Issue*, 99–100.

economic status. Colonial officials ruthlessly punished mothers who practiced infanticide, abortion, or allowed their children to get diarrhea – implicitly blaming them for the Banabans' failure to multiply.[43]

Female elders also had political reasons to resent colonial rule. Anglo
invaders routinely dismissed them as "old hags" rather than respected,
authoritative figures within the island's traditional gerontocracy. It took
Albert Ellis seventeen days during his first visit to figure out that one elder,
Nei Teinemakin, might "be higher rank than the king." She was "particularly friendly" toward Ellis, nonetheless, and sold some of her lands to him.
Five years later, she consented to sit for a portrait, adorned with frigatebird
feathers and a long cotton dress. Her attitude had changed: "I am the King,
the only King of the island," she told the Arundel sisters with undisguised
anger.[44] Banaba's colonial patriarchy long operated on the false assumption
that native society "was patrilineal and usually patrilocal" – then wondered
why women so "arbitrarily and blindly opposed" their plans, with such
"formidable... feminine influence."[45] This situation was hardly unique to
British-ruled Banaba. Four thousand kilometers to the northwest, on Palau's
Angaur Island, native women unanimously refused to validate a 1908 agreement to exploit the island's vast phosphate deposits negotiated between their
husbands and the Deutsche Südsee-Phosphate-Aktien Gesellschaft. The company responded by restricting the entire indigenous population to a tiny,
forty-hectare reserve and took the other 95 percent of the island for its own.
Like many colonized peoples, Banaba had a far more gender-balanced society before the imposition of colonial rule, and indigenous women fought
resolutely to keep this balance from tipping against them.[46]

In 1908, the Western Pacific High Commission in Fiji moved G&EI Protectorate headquarters to Banaba. This subjected Banabans to far more
invasive supervision but also gave them a modicum of legal protection
from the PPC. The prevalence of dysentery and sheer scale of environmental destruction on the island horrified Banaba's newest official residents. It
was painfully obvious that in just a matter of decades, "the island would
become perfectly uninhabitable for men – and a mere desert of pointed

[43] Macdonald, *Cinderellas of Empire*, 9–10, 73, 107–8; Silverman, *Disconcerting Issue*, 99;
Sigrah and King, *Te Rii ni Banaba*, 155.

[44] Lilian Arundel, "Six Months," pp. 19, 26–27, 35, PMB 1227-JTA, 12/1; photograph of
"the Queen" (1905), PMB 1227-JTA, 12/13; Ellis diary, 20 May 1900, PMB 494; Sigrah
and King, *Te Rii ni Banaba*, 170, 222.

[45] Language used by H. E. Maude, A. F. Grimble, and H. R. McClure; quoted in Silverman,
Disconcerting Issue, 28; Macdonald, *Cinderellas of Empire*, 107.

[46] Firth, "German Labour Policy"; Hutchinson, *Biogeochemistry*, 230–31; Howe et al., *Tides
of History*, 104, 237–42; Claudia Lauterbach, "'Bitang mi Bitang': Geschlecterbalance und
Modernisierung in Palau," in *Gender and Power in the Pacific* (Berlin, 2003); Lynn Wilson,
Speaking to Power: Gender and Politics in the Western Pacific (London and New York,
2003).

coral rocks."[47] A succession of resident commissioners tried to convince the PPC to regularize the process it used to obtain land rights and to restrict their activities to contiguous plots, avoid native settlements, and rehabilitate mined-out areas. Activities on Banaba began attracting negative publicity all the way in Britain. Led by women, native Banabans became more unified than ever against the PPC. This sparked a vigorous debate within the company. It was raking in profits that would make an oilman jealous: over £1.75 million during its first 13 years of existence, less than 0.1 percent of which made it into the hands of Banaban landowners.[48] This fact did not make the PPC's devout Christian ownership any more charitable. Albert Ellis felt that Banabans were "born tired" and too lazy to properly exploit existing fruit trees, much less replanted groves; to give them anything more would violate the Protestant work ethic. Lord Stanmore urged inaction. He thought Banabans, were doomed to extinction by the end of the century – overlooking the fact that Banaba's indigenous population had grown to 582 in 1909, thanks to the return of many emigrants. William Lever opposed profit sharing in the Pacific, either among white Australians or brown Banabans. He instead proposed "a final solution to the problem" on Banaba: native resettlement elsewhere in the Pacific. This would not require "the slightest surrender of the smallest term of our rights on the island.[49]

In 1913, the Colonial Office brought in Edward Carlyon Eliot (1870–1940) as resident commissioner "to bring the Ocean Islanders to reason." Eliot had more experience with old and new forms of ecological imperialism than he could stomach. As a young cowboy on the South American Pampas, he watched cattle tick fever slowly decimate his herd. This was the same protozoal disease that brought an end to the great Texas cattle drives and made "Queensland dip" a requirement for raising cattle in many aspirant neo-Europes.[50] In 1912, two years after amebic dysentery forced him to abandon a West African post to preserve his health, Eliot faced a severe epidemic of bacillary dysentery as Magistrate of Tobago that caused 500 deaths in ten weeks. His wife eventually died of complications blamed on

[47] Mahaffy to High Commissioner for the Western Pacific, 14 Apr. 1909, NAUK-CO, 881/12; Macdonald, *Cinderellas of Empire*, 100; Howe et al., *Tides of History*, 79.
[48] Equal to US$184 million in 2007.
[49] J. Q. Dickson to High Commissioner for the Western Pacific, 14 Dec. 1909, NAUK-CO, 881/12, no. 134, pp. 97–99; F. H. May to Secretary of State, 9 Oct. 1911, NAUK-CO 881/12, no. 187, pp. 163–65; Meek to Lever, 6 Aug. 1913, PMB 1139-reel 1; Eliot, *Broken Atoms*, 175; [Mahaffy], "Ocean Island," 570; Williams and Macdonald, *The Phosphateers*, 87–90, 95–96, 98, 100–1; Macdonald, *Cinderellas of Empire*, 98–101; Silverman, *Disconcerting Issue*, 109–10.
[50] Eliot, *Broken Atoms*, 13, 15; Tamara Haygood, "Cows, Ticks, and Disease: A Medical Interpretation of the Southern Cattle Industry," *Journal of Southern History* 52 (1986): 551–64; Beverley Angus, "The History of the Cattle Tick *Boophilus microplus* in Australia and Achievements in its Control," *International Journal of Parasitology* 26 (1996): 1341–55.

"tropical dysentery." Microbial stowaways in their intestines might have been responsible for the deadly outbreak that struck government staff on Banaba soon after their arrival. Eliot convinced 185 Banaban landowners to sign off on a deal that dramatically increased the payments they received and compelled the PPC to begin replanting worked-out lands. Much of this money stayed in a trust fund under government control, however, and the PPC refused to pay for destroyed pandanus and wild almond trees, arguing that the Banabans had come to favor imported foods and cloth over these traditional staples.[51]

Global events conspired to accelerate destruction on Banaba. In 1916–17, a severe La Niña drought killed all of the replanted trees and provided a convenient excuse for abandoning the whole rehabilitation program. World War I fundamentally changed the ecological context in which these mines operated. Before the war, the Japanese, Australian, and German chemical industries consumed most of the phosphate rock mined from Banaba, Nauru, and Angaur. As part of the spoils of war, Japan gained control of German Micronesia, including Angaur and other small phosphate islands to go along with Kita- and Oki-Daitō Islands near Okinawa, two phosphate-rich atolls it had long since colonized. Australia occupied the big prize, Nauru, and only reluctantly agreed to share its postwar administration with New Zealand and the United Kingdom. The Nauru Island Agreement of 1919 preserved Banaba as a British colony but established a new, tripartite organization, the British Phosphate Commission (BPC) to mine both islands. It had the legal mandate to supply low-priced phosphate to these three nations, "so far as those requirements extend." PPC stockholders received £3.5 million as part of the bargain. Banabans and Nauruans got virtually nothing. New Zealand made Albert Ellis its first Phosphate Commissioner – a position he held for the next 31 years.[52]

This agreement stayed in effect until the exhaustion of Banaba's high-grade reserves. All told, the BPC distributed 116.3 million metric tons of phosphate ore from 1920 through 1981: 17.7 million mined from Banaba under colonial auspices, 41.0 million mined from colonial Nauru, 16.5 million purchased from postcolonial Nauru, 28.3 million mined or purchased from Christmas Island, and 12.8 million bought from Makatea and other suppliers. Australia and New Zealand directly consumed 76.8 and 32.5 million metric tons of BPC phosphate, respectively. Great Britain, Japan, and plantations of Southeast Asia divided up the remainder. These overseas possessions enabled Australia and New Zealand to develop their own chemical

[51] Eliot, *Broken Atoms*, 9, 124, 128–29, 139; Grimble, *We Chose the Islands*, 37; Macdonald, *Cinderellas of Empire*, 101–2; Silverman, *Disconcerting Issue*, 109–11; Sigrah and King, *Te Rii ni Banaba*, 235.

[52] Equal to US$170 million in 2007; Williams and Macdonald, *The Phosphateers*, 135–50, 559; Macdonald, *Cinderellas of Empire*, 116; Hutchinson, *Biogeochemistry*, 236–47.

industries and their white citizens to come to see themselves as confident masters of self-governing, postcolonial states.[53]

These phosphate colonies also enabled parts of the Antipodes to become far more like their mother country in biological terms – if only skin deep. Before the widespread introduction of phosphate fertilizers, Eurasian plants nutritious to livestock failed to take over Australia or New Zealand with anything like the vigor that "Kentucky" bluegrass (*Poa pratensis*) and other portmanteau biota took over the North American Midwest. Australia's ancient, weathered soils are typically very low in nutrients. Native plants possess a marked competitive advantage over most foreign weeds in these nutrient-poor conditions, even under heavy grazing. Those foreign weeds that did prosper were not particularly nutritious. For example, purslane (*Portulaca oleracea*) causes greenish diarrhea if consumed in quantity by small livestock.[54] Eurasian plants fared better in New Zealand but converting indigenous fern brakes and tussock grassland into productive sheep pasture required great effort and frequent use of the firestick. "A turf of English grass" did not come into existence spontaneously in New Zealand – it had to be sown. After a brief boom of productivity, most blocks of improved pasture then steadily declined in feeding value and filled with undesirable weeds, as their nutrients were exported from the land in the form of wool, meat, and tallow. Even the honeybee (*Apis mellifera*), Alfred Crosby's vaunted symbol of neo-European conquest, failed to hold out as soil fertility declined and neo-European plants disappeared. On sheep stations such as Tutira, "The exuberant prosperity of the bee . . . passed away with the disappearance of the white clover and the thistle" at the beginning of the twentieth century.[55] This situation was not much different from the one that faced Henry Cushman in Massachusetts before he discovered Peruvian guano.

The colonization of Banaba and Nauru was a godsend to the rural economies of Anglo Australia and New Zealand. In Australia's southeast and New Zealand's North Island, stock raisers achieved remarkable gains after the turn of the century when they applied superphosphate to pastures

[53] Williams and Macdonald, *The Phosphateers*, 3–4, 157, 172–73, 190, 384, 428, 564–65; Deborah Gare, "Britishness in Recent Australian Historiography," *The Historical Journal* 43 (2000): 1145–55.

[54] CSIRO, *The Australian Environment* (Melbourne, 1960), 39–40, 85–86; Greg McKeon et al., eds., *Pasture Degradation and Recovery in Australia's Rangelands* (Queensland, 2004), 89–99; W. Obied et al., *"Portulaca oleracea* (Purslane): Nutritive Composition and Clinico-Pathological Effects on Nubian Goats," *Small Ruminant Research* 48 (2003): 31–36; cf. Crosby, *Ecological Imperialism*, 157–58, 168–69.

[55] H. Guthrie-Smith, *Tutira: The Story of a New Zealand Sheep Station* (Edinburgh, 1953), ch. 18–19, 21, 25, esp. pp. 310–11, 340–41; Peter Holland et al., "Remaking the Grasslands of the Open Country," in *Environmental Histories of New Zealand* (Melbourne, 2002); cf. Crosby, *Ecological Imperialism*, 95–96, 187–90, 240, 268.

sown with introduced rye grass (*Lolium perenne*), cocksfoot (*Dactylis glom-erata*), and nitrogen-fixing white clover (*Trifolium repens*). This practice helped establish these two regions as important dairy centers but required plowing, substantial labor, suitable rains, and high commodity prices to maintain. Wheat farmers noticed that Eurasian weeds nutritious to cattle could establish themselves in fields left to go fallow after phosphorus appli-cations. Stock raisers in both countries hired sharecroppers to plow the land and grow a couple crops of wheat and oats with superphosphate as a range improvement strategy. On Tutira station, Herbert Guthrie-Smith welcomed the return of bees "owing to ploughing and use of artificial manures." During the 1920s, sheepherders discovered the value of sowing annual subterranean clover (*T. subterraneum*) with phosphate-treated pastures of native wallaby grass (*Austrodanthonia* spp.) and Eurasian rye grass in regions of southern Australia subject to winter rainfall.[56]

Phosphate was no magic bullet for Australia and New Zealand's rural ills, however. Cheap fertilizer enabled wheat growers and livestock raisers to push the land that much harder, which eventually turned the gnawing can-cer of soil erosion into a runaway catastrophe. During the late 1920s and early 1940s, dust bowl conditions enveloped large swaths of southern Aus-tralia, particularly in plowed, wheat-growing areas. The former event helped tumble Australia into the Great Depression, whereas the latter produced a November 1944 dust storm so large that it "tinged the snow of the mountain peaks of New Zealand with the red of Australia's heartland."[57] In 1916–17 and 1938 on the eastern slopes of New Zealand's North Island, La Niña–fueled storms washed away slopes, turned small under-runners into deep gulches, filled valleys and estuaries with silt, even caused entire lakes to dis-appear. Settlers in the Tutira hills begged one meteorological observer to stop forwarding his returns, "Science may be right enough, perhaps, in its proper place . . ., but he was ruining the district and hampering settlement with his blessed rainfalls."[58]

In the wake of these disasters, southern scientists led the way in produc-ing a cavalcade of soil conservation legislation for New Zealand and the Australian states. Like their peers in the United States, they sought "salva-tion through technique."[59] However, local innovation, not foreign influence,

---

[56] Ellis, *Nauru and Ocean Island*, 288–290; Guthrie-Smith, *Tutira*, 341; Tom Brooking et al., "The Grasslands Revolution Reconsidered," in *Environmental Histories of New Zealand*, 170; CSIRO, *Australian Environment*, 87, 112–13; Williams and Macdonald, *The Phos-phateers*, 172–73, 239–40.

[57] Quoted in McKeon et al., eds., *Pasture Degradation*, 100–10, 118–28.

[58] Guthrie-Smith, *Tutira*, 5, 7, 15, 36–41, 57–58, 177, 196–99, 276–77; L. W. McCaskill, *Hold This Land: A History of Soil Conservation in New Zealand* (Wellington, 1973), ch 1.

[59] Donald Worster, *Dust Bowl: The Southern Plains in the 1930s* (New York, 1979), 212.

produced the most distinctive strategy aimed at forestalling "the decline and fall" of this neo-European "empire of grass."[60] In New Zealand, Doug Campbell (1906–69) took charge of the 1940s war against erosion. He personally witnessed the devastating floods of 1938 while teaching agronomy courses at Hawkes Bay, a mere 30 kilometers from Tutira station, and dedicated the next decade of his life to rallying the nation "against the great 'fifth column' menace of all time – soil erosion." In 1946, the Ministry of Works appointed him as its senior soil conservator. Campbell used this position to promote a homegrown, high-tech solution to highland erosion. Local experimenters had already demonstrated the feasibility of using aircraft to sow clover seed and soil micronutrients in areas where the plow could not reach. In 1948–49, Campbell oversaw highly publicized trials with aerial spreading of superphosphate. He hoped to use this technique on a large-scale to build up plant cover on erosion-prone slopes. As an added benefit, it provided skilled work to veterans and made use of surplus aircraft leftover from World War II. Australian agronomists soon took notice and began advocating the aerial spread of subterranean clover and superphosphate as a means to increase the stocking capacity of Australia's temperate rangelands without plowing. This led Campbell to take off around the world advocating the use of aircraft in large-scale land management.[61]

The broad popularity of aerial topdressing triggered the soil conservation movement in these two countries to become much more narrowly focused on the fertility of pastureland. The scale of the resulting environmental engineering project was colossal: in 1963–64, New Zealand fliers dropped 757,970 metric tons of superphosphate and lime on 2.7 million hectares of grassland, in addition to huge quantities of seed, fencing materials, and pesticides. By this date, the area of sown pasture in Australia surpassed nine million hectares. With the help of cheap petroleum and large government subsidies, these techniques enabled the extension of input-intensive range management to vast areas of Australia's arid interior and New Zealand's South Island during the 1960s and 1970s. By the mid-1980s, when this agroecological regime reached its apogee, these two countries were applying millions of tons of agrochemicals to rural areas each year. Agricultural production increased by leaps and bounds – particularly for meat, much of it for export to the United Kingdom, the United States, and oil-rich Middle East. This "Grasslands Revolution" allowed Australians and New Zealanders to

[60] Doug Campbell, quoted in Brooking et al., "Grasslands Revolution," 173.
[61] Michael Roche, "Campbell, Douglas Archibald," in *Dictionary of New Zealand Biography* (Wellington, 2000); Roche, "'The Land We Have We Must Hold': Soil Erosion and Soil Conservation in Late Nineteenth- and Twentieth-Century New Zealand." *Journal of Historical Geography* 23 (1997): esp. 451; Roche, "The State as Conservationist, 1920–60: 'Wise Use' of Forests, Lands, and Water," in *Environmental Histories of New Zealand*, 192–95; CSIRO, *Australian Environment*, 87–90, 110–13.

eat high on the food chain and enjoy some of the best living standards in the world.[62] This, in turn, inspired thousands of Niueans, Chileans, Peruvians, and hundreds of thousands of nonwhite immigrants from elsewhere in the Pacific Basin to flock to Australia and New Zealand so they, too, could enjoy First World livelihoods. Much of this was premised on cheap phosphate from Banaba and Nauru. Soil conservation in the southwestern Pacific, like ecology, was a science of empire.[63]

Toward a "Final Solution"

It was only a matter of time before the BPC sought to exploit more of the Banabans' land to meet this voracious demand. In 1923, the BPC approached the Colonial Office for permission to mine another tenth of the island – including the central plateau's "entire best food producing area." As expected, this proposal met with fierce opposition, particularly among Banaban women.[64]

The BPC and the Colonial Office left the task of ironing out this situation to newly promoted Resident Commissioner Arthur Grimble (1888–1956). He and his newlywed wife had first come to the island in 1914 in the midst of a deadly dysentery epidemic. This Cambridge-educated, sonnet-writing cadet had hoped to discover a piece of the world untouched by modern civilization. Instead, he found a "dreadful, corrugated-iron factory... from which enormous clouds of dust were being thrown sky high... loading all of the greenery of the island's flank with a grey pall." After his first five-year tour of duty, Grimble sent his amoeba-infected wife and four young daughters back to England so they could grow up with plenty of fresh milk, butter, and red meat. This decision came close to killing them: his children contracted whooping cough, measles, and impetigo, in turn, during the long voyage home, proving that virgin-soil epidemics show no racial bias. Grimble often longed to go "back to England once again, where lush things grow... to all the clean dear things." But he stayed on, alone, for another thirteen years. He did so in the belief that he was the man best suited to slowing down the erosion of traditional indigenous culture in the Gilbert and Ellice Islands.[65]

Grimble tried a variety of tactics to convince Banaban landowners to sign a new agreement with the BPC. He hoped that the long-time Native Magistrate, Eri, and other male elders could use their influence to bridge the

---

[62] Williams and Macdonald, *The Phosphateers*, 568–69; Brooking et al., "Grasslands Revolution"; Roche, "State as Conservationist," 196–97; CSIRO, *Australian Environment*, 88–89, 101; R. L. Heathcote, *Australia* (Burnt Mill, England, 1994), 99–106, 141–43.

[63] See table 3.1; Libby Robbin, "Ecology: A Science of Empire?" in *Ecology and Empire: Environmental History of Settler Societies* (Seattle, 1997).

[64] Quoted in Macdonald, *Cinderellas of Empire*, 103.

[65] Grimble, *We Chose the Islands*, 23, 28, 37, 92, 104–5, 113, 263, 312, 334–35, 338; Macdonald, "Grimble of the Gilbert Islands."

impasse. But Eri possessed no more authority over land issues than he had back in 1900, and he now had to face up to a new generation of Banabans, led by Rotan Tito (b. 1900), eager to obtain the best deal possible for their lands. The Australian and New Zealand governments grew impatient with Banaban intransigence and suggested their "immediate removal to another island."[66] Grimble, instead, proposed the gradual creation of a Provident Fund from mining proceeds that could be used to buy a new island for the Banabans. Eri reputedly liked the idea of purchasing "a happier home for our children's children to dwell in . . . not haunted by the ghosts of our unburied dead."[67] However, the rest of the population refused Grimble's request to send a delegation to depopulated Kuria Island in the southern Gilberts to investigate its possibilities for resettlement. This infuriated Grimble and led him to take coercive action. In 1928, the high commissioner of the Western Pacific approved new ordinances for the G&EI Colony that required natives to submit to vaccination and that divested them of all subsoil property rights. Grimble warned the residents of the central plateau in no uncertain terms: "If you do not sign the Agreement . . . *Your land will be compulsorily acquired for the Empire.* . . . What will happen to your children and your grandchildren if your lands are chopped up by mining and you have no money in the Bank? . . . If you choose suicide than I am sorry for you."[68] Grimble also enforced a new set of *Regulations for the Good Order and Cleanliness of the Gilbert and Ellice Islands* (1930) that filled the colony's prisons with men and women convicted of offenses against good hygiene. Even Grimble's superiors considered his actions "draconic in their severity," but deferred to his supposed expertise on "native ideas of right and wrong."[69]

The situation continued to fester until 1931 when an imperial arbitrator ruled emphatically against the Banabans, but holdouts still refused to mark out the boundary lines that had been taken away during the first year of mining on the island. Grimble gave the order to begin clearing trees anyway. This brought the controversy to the point of violence. Like the Chipko Movement of the 1970s in India, Banaban women threw their arms around their trees to try to halt their destruction – in this case, not only to protect their customary use by future generations but also their right to private property. According to Rotan Tito, "The Company started to cut down coconut trees and dig lands, and we saw, that two pieces of land whose boundaries

---

[66] Governor-General of Australia to Secretary of State for Dominion Affairs, 22 Oct. 1927, reproduced in Sigrah and King, *Te Rii ni Banaba*, 323–24.

[67] Quoted in Grimble, *Return to the Islands*, 43.

[68] Grimble's emphasis; Grimble to the People of Buakonikai, 5 Aug. 1928, reproduced in Christopher Weeremantry, *Nauru: Environmental Damage under International Trusteeship* (Melbourne, 1992), 217–18; P. A. McElwaine and W. K. Horne, "Western Pacific," *Journal of Comparative Legislation and International Law* 12 (1930): 139–40.

[69] Quoted in Macdonald, *Cinderellas of Empire*, 128.

had not been obtained by the BPC were nearly finished." A large group marched on BPC headquarters, but "Mr. Grimble released the prisoners to accompany his constables and with guns they resisted our approach; . . . he also accompanied his constables. We were willing to die for our lands at the time, but we respected our elders' word of advice under the Banaba Custom that to shed blood is prohibited on their island." At this juncture, Rotan and his allies reluctantly agreed to pace out their lands and turn them over to the BPC, "not because we had agreed to the amount of compensation or to their alienation, but simply because of love for [the land]. We could not bear the thought of losing them completely . . . without knowing their position and compensation value." By this final act of protest, Rotan refused to let Banaba's colonizers treat him as a faceless member of an indigenous people, possessed of nothing but community rights to land. For decades, his foes tried to turn the Banabans against Rotan as a greedy individualist, but without success. As recent criticism of Guatemala's Rigoberta Menchú makes clear, hypocritical First Worlders still have trouble conceding that an *individual*'s sense of entitlement against his or her peers can provide a powerful source of community cohesion and activism among indigenous peoples.[70]

Grimble believed the Banaban Nation would survive only if it could be isolated from modern, industrial life. Quite the opposite turned out to be true. This showdown inspired a revival of island traditions that played a critical role in ensuring Banaban cultural survival. In October 1931, a Lands Commission of fourteen male and two female representatives opened a six-month session to resolve all outstanding disputes between natives over land, water caves, sacred sites, and reef fishing. This gave Banabans a renewed sense of empowerment regarding their territory. Thanks to prolific El Niño rains, these were also years of exceptional abundance and a perfect occasion for feasting. In December 1931, the Banabans held a huge festival in the old style that revived a number of old dances and games, including *kabwane eitei*, a competition to snare wild frigatebirds. The Empire Census of 1931 revealed yet another cause to celebrate. The indigenous population of Banaba had grown to 550.[71]

Population growth here and elsewhere also meant growing demand for land, food, fertilizer, and other resources. Phosphate Commissioner Albert Ellis had no regrets about what had come to pass on Banaba, because elsewhere in the world, its phosphate "would 'make the desert blossom like

[70] Quoted in Silverman, *Disconcerting Issue*, 122–28, 139; Macdonald, *Cinderellas of Empire*, 103–10, 126–29; Williams and Macdonald, *The Phosphateers*, 205, 214, 226–30, 237–40, 248–50, 257. Cf. Guha, *The Unquiet Woods*, ch. 7; David Stoll, *Rigoberta Menchú and the Story of All Poor Guatemalans* (Boulder, CO, 1999), ch. 2.

[71] CEI; Silverman, *Disconcerting Issue*, 40–43, 47, 129–32; Sigrah and King, *Te Rii ni Banaba*, 75–88, 95, 136, 147–54, 183.

a rose,' would enable innumerable hard-working farmers to make a living, and would facilitate the production of wheat, butter and meat for hungry millions" for years to come.[72] He watched in great satisfaction as Australia and New Zealand used cheap phosphate to help claw their way out of the Great Depression, but others were less sanguine about these trends. As Chapter 7 shows, some began grumbling about the dangers of Malthusian overpopulation in the Pacific, and others expressed alarm at Japan's hunger for colonies and resources and Germany's demand for *Lebensraum*. In the meantime, each carload of phosphate removed from Banaba made the island less habitable and hastened the day when the BPC would seek to enact William Lever's "final solution" and force the Banabans to live elsewhere.

In this chapter, we have seen how ethnic Europeans took advantage of La Niña famines, crowd diseases, and other forms of ecological disturbance in their drive to colonize new regions of the planet. In the case of Banaba and Nauru, these conquests were accomplished not to create new regions for European settlement but to remedy the environmental destruction of lands they had recently colonized. The conversion of Australia and New Zealand into mirror images of the British Isles and Anglo North America did not happen naturally. It required the systematic destruction of several tropical islands to remake the soils and biota of these southern lands. This is the definitive case of neo-ecological imperialism. Indigenous Banabans fought valiantly to protect their human rights to subsistence and property. Their struggle starkly reveals, yet again, the failure of liberal-minded colonizers to maintain the environmental integrity of conquered territories and to protect the life, liberty, and property of subjugated populations. It remains to be seen whether Raobeia Sigrah's dream of making Banaba verdant again will ever be realized. Perhaps he can draw a small bit of inspiration from the spectacular restoration of Peru's mined-out guano islands, to which we now turn.

[72] Ellis, *Ocean Island and Nauru*, 89.

5

Conservation and the Technocratic Ideal

Laws... are eternal principles founded in the nature of things: principles that cannot be perceived with clarity except by experts accustomed to overcoming the difficulties of mental work and trained in scientific inquiry.... The right to decree laws pertains to the most intelligent – to the aristocracy of knowledge, created by nature.
  – Bartolomé Herrera, "Tercer respuesta" (1846)

In 1904, cotton farmers in the Pisco valley noticed the telltale signs of an emerging plague: young plants grew slowly, then developed yellow leaves edged in brown. In severe cases, their leaves wilted altogether, leading to crop failure. Most locals at first ascribed these changes to *hielo*. This age-old term referred not to frost but instead to seasonal bouts of bad health affecting plant, human, and beast when the weather turns cool and clammy. Farmers tried the usual remedy: they let affected fields go fallow hoping that a season or two of rest would recharge the land, but this wilting disease continued to spread. To make matters worse, the Pisco River abruptly changed course during the flood of April 1907, in part because locals had systematically removed trees and shrubs from the riverbank to expand their fields to the river's edge. This flood not only washed away farmland, it also disrupted this desert valley's all-important irrigation system and spread spore-infected soil and water. Pisco valley entrepreneurs had a history of getting rich off the fortunes and misfortunes of others, a world away. Cotton farming for export got its start in the valley when Domingo Elías purchased Urrutia estate during the early days of the guano boom. The U.S. Civil War, in turn, provided a boon to cotton growers and set in motion events that nearly destroyed the Rapanui. Later in the century, cottonseed oil and seedcake consumption by northern soap manufacturers and meat producers created an additional market. Peruvian growers profited mightily during the late 1890s when the boll weevil (*Anthonomus grandis*) crossed from northern Mexico to Texas and sent world cotton prices skyrocketing. Now, Peruvians faced similar disasters of their own.[1]

The pathogen that causes cotton wilt, *Fuserium oxysporum* formae speciales *vasinfectum*, belongs to a sophisticated genus of soil-based fungi known to cause dozens of diseases in a striking range of crops. This group includes *F. oxysporum* f. sp. *cubens*, the cause of Panama disease, a plague that spread rapidly between Caribbean banana plantations about this time. In the Pisco valley, *F. oxysporum* f. sp. *vasinfectum* invisibly thrived during the warm, summer season when cotton growers had plenty of water descending from the Andes to irrigate their fields. Unlike in Honduras, where banana growers could cut down virgin tracts of tropical forest and move to new fields to escape fungus infestations, Pisco valley farmers could not abandon their ancient irrigation networks. They either had to find a disease-resistant variety or stop growing their most lucrative cash crop.[2]

In accord with the technocratic ideal explored in this chapter, the Peruvian government looked abroad for help. U.S. Department of Agriculture scientists confirmed microscopically in 1910 that this disease was caused by the same organism that infected Alabama cotton fields. Peruvian government agronomists at first tried a ready-made technological fix: they imported disease-resistant strains of upland cotton from the United States but could not find one that could stand up to Peruvian insect pests and thrive in Peru's unique coastal climate. Recent genetic studies show that the importation of improved cotton varieties probably caused Peru's problem in the first place; spores likely tagged along in infected seeds imported from the U.S. South by enterprising Pisco valley planters.[3]

A Puerto Rican–born immigrant relying on local genetic resources eventually solved this problem. Fermín Tangüis (1851–1932) fled to Peru to escape Cuba's failed war for independence during the 1870s and eventually settled down as a tenant cotton farmer in the Pisco valley in 1890. Then, just at the moment when his enterprise had expanded to include Elías's old Urrutia estate, cotton wilt appeared and the "new river" of 1907 flooded straight across his fields. Tangüis decided to face these crises head-on. He had studied toward a medical degree in Cuba and, from reading foreign scientific literature, suspected a fungus was responsible for his withering

---

[1] Cueto and Lossio, *Inovación en la agricultura*, 28–29, 36–37, 71–73; Vincent Peloso, *Peasants on Plantations: Subaltern Strategies of Labor and Resistance in the Pisco Valley* (Durham, NC, 1999), 64, 81–82, 109; Gonzales, "Rise of Cotton Tenant Farming," 61–62; Thorp and Bertram, *Peru 1890–1977*, 51–54.

[2] W. C. Snyder, "Introduction," in *Fusarium: Diseases, Biology, and Taxonomy* (University Park, PA, 1981); S. N. Smith et al., "Fusarium Wilt of Cotton," in ibid.; Soluri, *Banana Cultures*, 52–55, 70–73.

[3] Cueto and Lossio, *Inovación en la agricultura*, 44, 85–86; Kerstin Skovgaard et al., "Evolution of *Fusarium oxysporum* f. sp. *vasinfectum* Races Inferred from Multigene Genealogies," *Phytopathology* 91 (2001): 1231–37.

crops. In 1905, he began collecting seed heads from plants around the valley that appeared to be resistant. He systematically replanted them in infected fields to see whether they were capable of producing high-yielding bolls. He was helped along in this quest by the fact that many farmers in the Pisco valley had resisted planting thirsty monocultures of imported upland cotton and continued to grow drought-resistant native varieties originally domesticated by the ancient peoples of the Peruvian coast. These "routinists" have often been accused of blocking agricultural progress in Latin America, but in this case, they provided material critical to Tangüis's triumph over cotton wilt.[4]

In 1908, Tangüis discovered an especially promising plant and began the painstaking task of deriving a variety that would breed true. In 1912, he arrived at a high-yielding, wilt-resistant strain based on these native stocks that thrived in Peru's cool, dry coastal climate. As an added bonus, it produced strong, white, ultra-long fibers ideal for high-speed textile machinery, and it responded spectacularly when fertilized with Peruvian guano. Tangüis elected not to profit selfishly from his invention (he was profiting handsomely from sharecroppers he subcontracted), and he distributed seed to whomever wanted it in the belief that the fruits of scientific progress should belong to everyone. Tangüis cotton became the darling of Liverpool cotton merchants during World War I, saved the Peruvian cotton industry, and turned Tangüis into a national hero.[5]

This brief environmental history of Tangüis cotton highlights both the promise and perils of living in such an interconnected world. This scientific triumph confirmed a widespread belief among Peru's ruling class at the turn of the twentieth century that men like Tangüis, the embodiment of an "aristocracy of knowledge," were best equipped to protect Peru from disaster and to engineer a modern nation. "Less politics, more administration" served as the organizing philosophy of the architects of Peru's so-called Aristocratic Republic (1895–1919) and the eleven-year authoritarian regime that succeeded it (1919–1930). This chapter explains why Peru's national rulers placed experts in positions of authority during this period and gave them unprecedented control over Peru's coastal environment. They institutionalized the idea that Peru's long-neglected guano birds required expert supervision and protection to survive the predatory tendencies of global capitalism.

These trends extended far beyond Peru. Today, for all the lip service we give to democracy, many of us desire some form of *technocracy*, or government ruled by experts. The administrative reordering of the state, society,

[4] *BCIM* 79 (1913): 12–13; Cueto and Lossio, *Inovación en la agricultura*, ch. 2; Peloso, *Peasants on Plantations*, 141. Cf. Scobie, *Revolution on the Pampas*, ch. 8; Stanley Stein, *Vassouras: A Brazilian Coffee County, 1850–1900* (1958; Princeton, NJ, 1985), ch. 9.
[5] Cueto and Lossio, *Inovación en la agricultura*, ch. 4; Gonzales, "Rise of Cotton Tenant Farming," 63–64.

and nature by experts is one of the defining phenomena of modern times.[6] In 1990 and 2001, Peruvians elected two successive U.S.-trained experts to the presidency, mathematician Alberto Fujimori and economist Alejandro Toledo. Taiwan and the People's Republic of China are extreme examples of countries where scientists, engineers, agronomists, and economists have risen to positions of political power in recent years. Even the United States, a country dominated by lawyers and businessmen, is not impervious to this trend. Why else did Hollywood fantasize for so long about a West Wing of the White House presided over by a Ph.D. who had won the Nobel Prize in Economics? Who among us disputes the merits of knowledge, efficiency, objectivity, practicality, cost-consciousness, incorruptibility, and competence – all values associated with the technocratic ideal?[7]

Today's environmentalists, on the other hand, have an ambivalent attitude toward expertise. Activists routinely deploy the findings of scientific research and ally themselves with technical experts holding positions of authority to exercise political influence.[8] Three of the world's best-known environmental writers and activists, Rachel Carson, Vandana Shiva, and Maathai Wangari, symbolize this ambivalence. All three started their careers as scientists but later developed a deep suspicion, even hostility, toward the accomplishments of modern science and technology. The image of technology run amok is deeply ingrained within the history of political thought, and it is so common in environmental histories that it is almost cliché.[9]

What are the historical origins of these attitudes? How did expertise become so indispensable to modern politics and environmental management, but an object of disdain for some? Who were the ideologues and architects of this great transformation? Environmental concerns provided powerful motivation for the rise of experts to prominence. A century ago, all over the world, governments empowered trained professionals to manage three overlapping environmental realms: (1) conservationists sought to manage forests, rivers, soils, and other rural environments to maximize the long-term production of natural resources desired by industrial society. Many of them were inspired by the perception that frontier imperialism and the

[6] Miguel Angel Centeno, "The New Leviathan: The Dynamics and Limits of Technocracy," *Theory and Society* 22 (1993): 307–35; Markoff and Montecinos, "The Ubiquitous Rise of Economists"; Jean Meynaud, *Technocracy* (New York, 1968).
[7] "The U.S. Poet Laureate," episode of *The West Wing*, first broadcast 27 Mar. 2002; NBC broadcast this television series from 1999 through 2006. Megan Greene, *The Origins of the Developmental State in Taiwan: Science Politics and the Quest for Modernization* (Cambridge, MA, 2008), ch. 5, concl.
[8] Sheila Jasanoff, *The Fifth Branch: Science Advisers as Policymakers* (Cambridge, MA, 1990); Samuel Hays, *Beauty, Health, and Permanence: Environmental Politics in the United States, 1955–1985* (Cambridge and New York, 1987), ch. 10–12.
[9] Langdon Winner, *Autonomous Technology: Technics-Out-of-Control as a Theme in Political Thought* (Cambridge, MA, 1977).

exploitative "robber economies" of the guano age were eroding the earth's
capacity to sustain civilization's progress.[10] (2) Hygienists of the age of soap
and water sought to manage urban streets, sewers, markets, and factories,
and often entered homes in order to stop the spread of disease. Many of them
were inspired by the perception that immigrant microbes, plants, animals,
and people caused epidemics, and that proper manipulation of soap, water,
and excrement would cure a host of societal problems.[11] (3) Agronomists
combined the concerns of both groups in managing rural production of
domesticated plants and animals. They also achieved remarkable success
at becoming career politicians in many countries.[12] In all three cases, these
experts moved around the globe with astounding speed – just like many of
the things they studied – and their activities can only be understood properly
in global perspective.

An engineering mind-set drove all three groups. Most of us are quite
familiar with engineers' reliance on technology to dominate and control the
environment, but we tend to forget that engineers have long been taught
to recognize limitations presented by nature. This concern for nature's limits helps explain why turn-of-the-century conservationists were so obsessed
with scarcity and waste. According to the doctrine of "nature's government," those who dedicated themselves to the study of nature's laws not
only possessed the best hope of learning how to maximize human prosperity
but were also most fit to govern. This doctrine provided a powerful ideological motivation for imperial expansion during the late nineteenth century. It
also helps explain why the rulers of postcolonial states converted so rapidly
to "the gospel of efficiency" and "scientific politics" soon after.[13]

Conservation experts helped legitimate the activities of an astonishing
range of governments during this age of empire, but they also served a disturbingly narrow range of interests. As we saw in Chapter 4, conservation
experts have been powerful agents of colonialism and ecological change in
their own right. As a consequence, they have rarely attracted the support of
traditional peoples who depend on the land and sea for their sustenance.[14]
But at times, popular defiance profoundly influenced conservation policy in

[10] Clarence Glacken, "Changing Ideas of the Habitable World," in *Man's Role in Changing
the Face of the Earth* (Chicago, 1956), 81–86; Guha, *Environmentalism*, ch. 3.

[11] Melosi, *The Sanitary City*; Chalhoub, *Cidade febril*; Cueto, *Return of the Epidemics*; Anderson, "Excremental Colonialism"; Jean-Pierre Goubert, *The Conquest of Water: The Advent
of Health in the Industrial Age* (Princeton, NJ, 1989); Manuel Perlo Cohen, *El paradigma
porfiriano: Historia del desagüe del Valle de México* (Mexico City, 1999).

[12] McCook, *States of Nature*.

[13] Samuel Hays, *Conservation and the Gospel of Efficiency: The Progressive Conservation
Movement, 1890–1920* (Cambridge, MA, 1959); Drayton, *Nature's Government*, ch. 7;
Charles Hale, "Political and Social Ideas in Latin America, 1870–1930," in *The Cambridge
History of Latin America* (Cambridge and New York, 1986), 4:387–89, 392.

[14] James Scott, *Seeing Like a State*, ch. 1; Guha, *Unquiet Woods*; Jacoby, *Crimes against
Nature*.

Peru and proved capable of pushing the world's technocrats to act aggressively in the interests of the masses. The tragic events of World War I brought these issues to a head on a global scale.

Order, Then Progress

The War of the Pacific described in Chapter 2 and protracted civil war that followed caused enormous devastation in Peru, but disasters of this sort always present opportunities for a few survivors and outsiders able to colonize new ground for themselves. Some argue that these upsets have been essential to the growth of modern capitalism.[15] An Irish immigrant with close ties to the United States, Michael Grace (1840–1920), jumped at this chance to expand his family's business empire in Peru. The powerful multinational corporation W. R. Grace & Co. got its start during the 1850s as an outfitter of ships loading guano at the Chincha Islands. During the war-torn 1880s, Michael sold arms to the Peruvian government and bought up properties that had been devastated by war, financial crisis, and El Niño floods. The violent passing of Peru's guano age contributed mightily to the fortunes of this firm and, in no small way, to the rise of New York City's economic elite to global prowess. His Irish-born brother's election as mayor of New York epitomized this trend. In January 1890, after five years of contentious negotiations, Michael convinced British bondholders and the Peruvian government to sign the so-called Grace Contract. This agreement canceled the gargantuan foreign debt Peru had accrued since the default of 1876.[16] In return, bondholders received shares in a new multinational firm, the Peruvian Corporation of London, which would rebuild and control Peru's railways for sixty-six years and export two to three million long tons of guano. The costs and benefits of this agreement have been hotly debated ever since.[17]

One of the Grace Contract's main opponents produced a political solution to Peru's postwar crisis. In 1895, the charismatic strongman Nicolás de

[15] Kevin Rozario, "What Goes Down Must Go Up: Why Disasters Have Been Good for American Capitalism," in *American Disasters* (New York, 2001); Seth Reice, *The Silver Lining: The Benefits of Natural Disasters* (Princeton, NJ, 2001), ch. 2; Davis, *Late Victorian Holocausts*.

[16] £51 million, equal to US$5.8 billion in 2007.

[17] William Bishel, "Business Ideology and U.S. Foreign Policy: Michael P. Grace and the Grace Contract in Peru, 1880–1890" (Ph.D. diss., Indiana Univ., 1991), 13–15, 18–20, 51–52; Alexander DeSecada, "Arms, Guano, and Shipping: The W.R. Grace Interests In Peru, 1865–1885," *Business History Review* 59 (1985): 597–621; Sven Beckert, *The Monied Metropolis: New York City and the Consolidation of the American Bourgeoisie, 1850–1896* (Cambridge and New York, 2001), 267, 310, 331; Rory Miller, "The Making of the Grace Contract: British Bondholders and the Peruvian Government, 1885–1890," *JLAS* 8 (1976): 73–100; Miller, "The Grace Contract, The Peruvian Corporation, and Peruvian History," *Ibero-Amerikanisches Archiv* 9 (1983): 319–48.

Piérola (president 1879–81, 1895–99) organized a "Civic Union" to push General Andrés Cáceres out of power. Piérola was the son of one of Peru's first generation of technocratic rulers. He deserves substantial blame for the catastrophe that brought an end to Peru's guano age. Following in his father's footsteps as minister of finance, Píerola was the mastermind of the disastrous guano loans of 1870–72. He and his followers also led frequent armed rebellions against the Civilist Party and Cáceres regime. But when Piérola assumed the presidency in 1895, he agreed to share power with many of his old enemies along the Coast and the landed aristocracy of the Sierra to put Peru back on the path to prosperity. Like their brethren in other parts of Latin America, this group tended to view science and technology, education, European immigration, foreign investment, public hygiene, "scientific politics" – and oligarchic rule – as essential to establishing Order and Progress on a national level. As we saw in Chapter 2, this elitist ruling ethos had a long genealogy in Peru, but it gained deep institutional roots during the period known as the Aristocratic Republic (1895–1919).[18]

New laws and bureaucracies created the opportunity for experts to gain unprecedented control over Peru's coastal environment. In January 1896, President Piérola established a full-fledged Ministry of Development and appointed a British-trained civil engineer from his hometown of Arequipa to lead it. In line with similar institutions elsewhere in the world, its primary mission was to develop the "moral" and "physical energies and natural riches of the country" and diffuse "all classes of useful knowledge." It institutionalized a principle dear to the conservative regimes he and his father had served during the guano age, that "the right to decree laws pertains . . . to the aristocracy of knowledge."[19] Ministry technocrats focused their initial efforts on building monuments to their own glory intended to improve the urban environment. They built a palatial School of Medicine to anchor the upper end of the grand ring boulevard that marked the beginning of Lima's burgeoning streetcar suburbs, and they paved over parts of Lima's Exposition Park to make room for the avenue, the Municipal Institute of Hygiene, and National Meteorological Observatory. Provincial cities also benefited. Several North Coast towns received running water and sewage networks, concrete-floored "hygienic" markets, and new cemeteries and bridges to replace those damaged by the El Niño floods of 1891.[20] In May 1896, another decree established the National Agricultural Society (SNA), which

---

[18] *Enciclopedia ilustrada del Perú*, s.v. "Piérola, Nicolás de"; Michael Gonzales, "Planters and Politics in Peru, 1895–1919," *JLAS* 23 (1991): 515–31; Miller, "The Coastal Elite and Peruvian Politics, 1895–1919," *JLAS* 14 (1982): 97–120; Manuel Burga and Alberto Flores Galindo, *Apogeo y crisis de la república aristocrática* (Lima, 1984).

[19] *MMFom* 1 (1896): 3, 7–8, 70; Bartolomé Herrera, *Escritos y discursos* (Lima, 1929), 1:131; Mc Evoy, *Utopía republicana*, ch. 1, 6–7.

[20] AMFom 32/1068, 32/1071, 32/1565, 32/5993 (1898), 34/1581–1611 (1899); 39/1589–45/1597 (1900); 2/1260, 16/1302 (1901); 52/2219, 53/2232 (1904); 72/169 (1905);

quickly became dominated by large sugar planters and a lasting bastion of oligarchic politics. Both the Ministry and SNA sponsored scientific expeditions and sent Peruvians as far away as Java and Australia to acquire field expertise and advanced degrees. In 1901, agricultural chemist George Vanderghem (1875–1932) led a team of Belgian agronomists on an agricultural survey of Peru. He stayed on as head of the new School for Agricultural and Veterinary Science. Meanwhile, the notorious Electoral Law of November 1896 provided a political framework for strengthening oligarchic control of the Peruvian state. It centralized jurisdiction over national elections in one, all-powerful Electoral Junta based in Lima. In one fell swoop, this law uprooted power over elections from its local base and restricted what had been a comparatively large, mobilized electorate to a miniscule class of literate males. On the bright side, these reforms put a lid on electoral violence lasting several years.[21]

Changes in the public administration of coastal irrigation water vividly illustrate how conflicts over natural resources contributed to the emergence of technocratic forms of governance and to the spread of conservation ideology under the Aristocratic Republic. Since time immemorial, water distribution in the Andes had been adjudicated by an elaborate set of traditions, rituals, and codified practices that were eminently local in nature. (In many places, this still is true.) Community governance, of course, does not necessarily entail social harmony. Battles over water rights have been a ubiquitous feature of Andean agricultural history that was intimately tied to local systems of social stratification. According to Hispanic law, private landowners possessed first priority (*derecho de cabecera*) to all the water that flowed across their property but, unlike under Anglo-American law, could not sell water as a commodity separate from the land. This meant that property owners at the head of a river or canal system possessed enormous advantages over their downstream neighbors, but that smallholders, indigenous communities, and wetland ecosystems could continue to prosper in the lower reaches of these irrigation networks. Those downstream took advantage of water that leaked through these patchwork earthen systems, and they also negotiated agreements – some dating from ancient times – that traded water for labor to maintain them. Over the years, many of these agreements became established legal rights. The logistical complexity of divvying up this precious resource also caused conflict. Timing the opening and closing of individual floodgates was critical to the success or failure of crops grown within the entire administrative system governing a watershed, but

41/2063, 54/1811 (1906); Higgins, *Lima*, 159–63; Bustíos, *Cuatrocientos años de la salud pública*, 492–94.

[21] *BMFom* 2 (May 1904): 105; 6 (June 1908): 87–88; 7 (Apr. 1909): 96–97; Jorge Basadre, *Historia de la República del Perú*, 6th ed. (Lima, 1968), 10:167–73, 301; *Enciclopedia ilustrada del Perú*, s.v. "Vanderghem, Jorge"; Mc Evoy, *Utopía republicana*, 353–56.

the flow of water in Peru's coastal valleys varies considerably from season-to-season and year-to-year. Therefore, conflict was inevitable – and violence an omnipresent threat – when the yearly flood arrived early or late, or in exceptionally large or small quantities, and disrupted a valley's irrigation schedule.[22]

In the Pisco valley, one such conflict overflowed its local context and directly influenced the formation of the Aristocratic Republic. In 1894, Vicente del Solar, a loyal *pierolista* and brother of the vice president, requested an extra allotment of water for his crop of upland cotton on San Jacinto estate. Antero Aspíllaga, the most prominent member of a family of coastal planters tied to the rival Civilist Party, refused to accommodate and give up part of his upstream water rights as owner of Palto estate. In response, del Solar's dependents built a dike in the riverbed that diverted water to his own property by weakening the flow of water into the valley's main irrigation canal. Aspíllaga ordered his dependents to destroy this dangerous threat to local order. The resulting water war not only mobilized the local peasantry but also possessed national ramifications. President Cáceres sent an army expedition to the Pisco valley to sack and burn del Solar's hacienda. In retaliation, del Solar and a band of *pierolista* guerrillas from a neighboring valley swooped down on Palto estate and stole its herd of pack and draft animals. Cáceres, however, was no friend of the Aspíllagas, and his cronies took money and horses from Palto for their own faction of this escalating civil war. The Del Solar and Aspíllaga families eventually sealed the fate of Cáceres when they put down their differences and joined Piérola's Civic Union but never forgot their rivalry as lords of the Pisco valley.[23]

Piérola's government initiated a long process intended to place water distribution in the country under rationalized supervision and control. The National Water Law of 1902 created a network of district water boards overseen by the Ministry of Development. The local vote for board members was apportioned to individual landowners in proportion to the amount of land they had in active cultivation. This nakedly discriminated against smallholders. The law also contained a potentially revolutionary innovation that further adjusted water rights in accord with crop needs, but like many attempts at centralized legal reform in Latin America, most coastal valleys continued to operate for years as if this law did not exist.[24]

[22] Juan Vicente Nicolini, *La policía de las aguas en el Perú* (Lima, 1919); Paul Gelles, *Water and Power in Highland Peru: The Cultural Politics of Irrigation and Development* (New Brunswick, NJ, 2000); Paul Trawick, *The Struggle for Water in Peru: Comedy and Tragedy in the Andean Commons* (Stanford, CA, 2003); María Teresa Oré, *Agua: Bien común y usos privados: Riego, Estado y conflictos en La Anchirana del Inca* (Lima, 2005), esp. 81–99.

[23] Peloso, *Peasants on Plantations*, 28–30; González, "Planters and Politics."

[24] BCIM 79 (1913): 54; 101 (1921): 24–26; Nicolini, *Policía de las aguas*, 30–31; Klarén, *Modernization*, 55–60; Oré, *Agua*, 99.

Engineers indoctrinated with "the gospel of efficiency" took on the task of forcing change in the countryside. In 1902, Peru's first engineer-president, Eduardo López de Romaña (president 1899–1903), established a national Corps of Mining Engineers to survey Peru's terrestrial resources. It hired a brigade of foreign geologists and engineers, predominantly from the U.S. Geological Survey (USGS), to organize these studies and develop local expertise. In July 1904, the Ministry of Development placed George Adams and Charles Sutton (1877–1949) in charge of surveying the water resources of Peru's coastal valleys. The latter was a graduate of the University of Washington, specializing in topographic mapping, who also played a role in colonizing the Philippines and converting the Lower Colorado and Yakima into great "Rivers of Empire." His study of the Pisco and Ica river valleys became a model for hydrographic basin development in Peru.[25] Sutton's quantitative, instrumentalist approach to resource conservation and globetrotting tendencies typified the "bright young men" who ran John Wesley Powell's Irrigation Survey of the early 1890s and the "engineer-administrators" who built the U.S. Bureau of Reclamation into "the largest bureaucracy ever assembled in irrigation history." Similarly, Argentina's most celebrated scientist from this era, paleontologist Florentino Ameghino, advocated a national system of integrated river basin management for his country run by state-employed engineers, foresters, and agronomists.[26]

Sutton was disgusted by the amount of Peruvian water lost to human use by canal leakage and free-running rivers. By his estimate, Ica valley farmers lost more than 60 percent of the water flowing into their canals, and the Pisco River lost 0.5 percent of its flow per kilometer to seepage and evaporation. Sutton, however, was no "innocent abroad" oblivious to the "despotic social organization" of Peru's coastal valleys.[27] He was equally upset by "the injustice and inexactitude" of water distribution under existing Peruvian law. He openly advocated using the 1902 Water Law to empower irrigation technocrats to dole out water within each hydrographic basin based on the measured volume available and objective requirements of crops being grown. Echoing the social philosophy of the United States' own Reclamation Act of 1902, he thought it was "indisputable that the establishment of the largest number of *efficient* colonists as owners of irrigated land" would result in "the highest land values, maximal production, greatest social and economic efficiency, . . . and *most commercial and political stability*."[28] In

[25] *BCIM* 1 (1902): 12; 28 (1905); 56 (1907): 7, 9–11; 79 (1913): 21–22, 104; 88 (1918): 12–13, 16–18, 24; USGS, *Needles Special Map* (1904); USGS, *Zillah* (1910); Víctor Pérez Santisteban, *Sutton y la irrigación de Olmos* (Lima, 1980), 7–8.

[26] Donald Worster, *Rivers of Empire: Water, Aridity, and the Growth of the American West* (New York, 1985), 131–42, 148, 170, 177; Antonio Elio Brailovsky and Dina Foguelman, *Memoria verde: Historia ecológica de la Argentina* (Buenos Aires, 1991), 176–79.

[27] Cf. Worster, *Rivers of Empire*, 150–51.

[28] Emphasis added; *BCIM* 79 (1913): 17, 24, 54, 62, 113; 101 (1921): 10–11, 26, 34–35.

1911, Sutton obtained the authority to begin making this vision a reality as head of the Ministry of Development's new Coastal Irrigation Service. He prioritized the installation of current meters and rain gauges and completed the topographical survey of all coastal river basins, but for the time being, budgetary limitations strictly circumscribed what he could accomplish in terms of reclamation projects. Nevertheless, Sutton achieved one critical goal: he helped build a cadre of Peruvian technicians eager to implement his technocratic vision of resource conservation. Some of them eventually attained positions of major influence – most notably pluviometrics expert Manuel Prado, who years later became president of the republic.[29]

The Guano Problem

Escalating conflict over coastal resources provided a beachhead for the infiltration of conservation ideology in other contexts. The rapid expansion of thirsty cotton, sugar cane, and rice estates at the turn of the century placed a major strain on the young, fertile, alluvial soils of Peru's coastal valleys. Even in the best soils, any crop grown intensively on the same plot of ground for several seasons will deplete the soil of nutrients and result in declining crop yields. Turn-of-the-century Peruvian farmers possessed an array of techniques for maintaining soil fertility. Traditionalists welcomed the summertime flood, both for its life-giving waters as well as for the nutrient-rich silt (*yapana*) it provided to their fields; even destructive floods bestowed the gift of future agricultural abundance. Particularly during drought years, farmers let their fields go fallow and allowed cattle to recharge the soil with manure, following ancient Mediterranean practice. Farmers also rotated cash crops with nitrogen-fixing legumes, such as lima beans and alfalfa, or spread barnyard excrement. Those living near sugar refineries had access to industrial waste products that could be recycled as fertilizer, but only the most prosperous could afford to import Chilean nitrates or manufactured fertilizers from the industrial North. Profit-minded estate managers almost universally preferred a locally produced fertilizer – guano – over all these techniques.[30]

Coastal farmers never stopped using this richest of natural fertilizers during the guano age. Significant ancient deposits of lower quality still remained on northern islands, but Peruvian farmers, officials, and foreign contractors were all aware that Peru's *living* colonies of guano birds produced the most valuable fertilizer. Thus, the original directive that created the

[29] BCIM 84 (1917): 2–13, 24–25, 70; 85 (1917): 11–16; 88 (1918): 20, 24–25, 29; Pérez, *Sutton*, 26; Oré, *Agua*, 100–1; Roberto Michelena, "Perdida de la capacidad técnica del Estado," *El ingeniero civil* (Lima) May–June 2004: 22–26.

[30] Oré, *Agua*, 94; BMFom 2 (Apr. 1904): 30–31; 4 (Mar. 1906): 13, 24–29, 76–77; Cushman, "Lords of Guano," table 1.

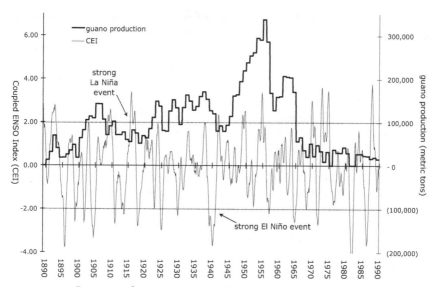

FIGURE 5.1. Guano production in Peru and ENSO, 1890–1990. *Source:* Cushman, "Lords of Guano," app. 2; Gergis and Fowler, "Classification of Synchronous Oceanic and Atmospheric ENSO Events."

Ministry of Development declared a ban on egg collecting, required the gathering of statistics on the industry, and mandated the search for new ways to encourage "the reproduction of fertilizer." However, the few million guano birds that had survived the abuses of the guano age could not keep up with the increase in demand that accompanied the signing of the Grace Contract and establishment of the Aristocratic Republic (fig. 5.1). The strong El Niño of 1905 made this situation look even worse by causing the birds to abandon their nests. Guano became so precious that contractors "swept the islands with brooms."[31] In 1906, an agronomic engineer involved with the Ministry of Development's coastal surveys, José Otero, forthrightly declared, "It is time for the Government to solve definitively the matter of providing guano... exclusively for the agriculture of this country, by prohibiting its exportation, properly regulating its extraction, and seeing that it arrives... to small farmers, in quantities related to need." He proposed the creation of a network of government offices that would sell a certified product and distribute scientific propaganda encouraging its efficient use. This homegrown conservation evangelist also railed against the wanton destruction of wood resources and proposed creating a government service to replant Peru's "extinguished coastal forests." In November 1906, the Ministry of Development responded to the country's escalating

[31] CEI; *MMFom* 1 (1896): 7–8; Walter von Ohlendorff, *Die Guano-Fundorte in Peru* (Hamburg, 1903); Cushman, "Lords of Guano," app. 1, 3.

"fertilizer crisis" by closing the Chincha Islands to human visitation during the summer nesting season to maximize the replenishment of fresh guano, but the Peruvian state delayed taking more radical action pending further study.[32]

Peru's coastal technocrats had already begun to envision the Pacific Ocean as the country's next great frontier for development. In June 1906, the Ministry of Development approached the U.S. Bureau of Fisheries to recommend a scientist who could "procure, with scientific principles as a guide, the conservation and reproduction of species of fish" in Peruvian territorial waters.[33] The bureau recommended Robert E. Coker (1875–1967), the son of a prominent cotton planter from South Carolina who had been educated at Johns Hopkins University, the country's most important breeding ground for zoological researchers. Coker also had practical experience in devising conservation policy. In 1905, he devised a spectacularly successful plan for the North Carolina Department of Conservation and Development to end competitive overexploitation of oysters.[34]

Coker arrived in Peru in November 1906, just when the guano controversy was gathering steam. He spent the next fourteen months systematically exploring the ports, islands, and peninsulas of the Peruvian coast in a specially appointed sailboat. He was explicitly instructed to pay attention, "not only to those species that have or could have commercial value, but also... to their enemies or competitors and those [species] that serve as their food;" his goal: to "propose adequate regulations for fishing, guano extraction, and the sea lion hunt."[35]

The richness of Peru's marine environment awed Coker: "Perhaps there are no other waters in the world that are more copiously stocked with small fish than those of Peru." He was also impressed both by the efficiency of indigenous fishing technologies he observed and the willingness of coastal fishermen to adopt new practices, such as the use of trammel nets. Coker was puzzled, however, by the lack of attention most Peruvian fishermen paid to the small anchoveta (*Engraulis ringens*), "the most valuable resource of the waters of Peru," and he was downright alarmed by the prevalence of dynamite fishing, an unintended consequence of Peru's booming mining economy. He proposed creating a fishing police to bring order to this anarchy, ideally in association with a scientific "office that has as its object the *permanent* study of fish and fisheries." Like Arthur Grimble, he was hesitant

---

[32] *BMFom* 4 (July 1906): 35–41; 4 (Aug. 1906): 60–78; 4 (Oct. 1906): 66–68; *MMFom* 12, pt. 2 (1908): 12–13, 18.

[33] *MMFom* 10 (1906): xxiv; *BMFom* 4 (July 1906): 93.

[34] Coker, *Oyster Culture in North Carolina* (Raleigh, 1905); Eugene Lehman, "Robert Ervin Coker," *Journal of the Elisha Mitchell Scientific Society* 84 (1968): 333–34; George Simpson, *The Cokers of Carolina: A Social Biography of a Family* (Chapel Hill, NC, 1956), 247–49; Jane Maienschein, *Transforming Traditions in American Biology* (Baltimore, 1991).

[35] *MMFom* 11 (1907): 293–95.

to propose radical changes to indigenous life: "Modernizing the fishery is not sought for itself, for many of the original Peruvian methods of capture are suited to the natural conditions and best adapted to the social nature, the abilities, and the wants of the people.... In attempting to introduce new and larger methods, it would be unnecessary and unjust to hamper or antagonize a kindly people, poor in wealth but rich in contentment, who are working out a peaceful and honorable life after the bent of their nature."[36]

Coker reserved his most forceful recommendations for Peru's guano islands. He thought the exhaustion of Peru's last remaining ancient deposits was imminent, and after watching Peruvian Corporation workers destroy a rookery of 80,000 pelicans on Isla Lobos de Afuera, he feared this important guano-producing species might lead the whole industry into extinction. Coker did find reasons for hope on the Chincha Islands, however. There, thanks to the government closure, the guano birds had a peaceful "home" in their "natural environment." This led Coker to the conclusion that Peru's guano birds could produce enough excrement to satisfy everyone, if Peruvians stopped acting "like beasts of prey" and began treating them as "domestic animals." "The problem for the Government, for national agriculture, and for the export company is this:... What system of exploitation will produce the largest guano deposit in twenty years?" In line with his recommendations for North Carolina oysters, he proposed a system of monopoly concessions for each island that would eliminate rapacious competition between private interests. To keep each island in a state of peace, Coker envisioned a system that rotated the guano harvest between the islands – the longer the closed period, the better. Coker shared Otero's belief that a government company was most likely to make this work. Coker argued convincingly that harvesting guano in this way on the basis of sustained yield would raise far more money than it cost. To clinch this argument, he "conservatively appraised" the lifetime value of each pair of guano birds at US$14.30. With a population numbering in the millions, this made Peru's "wealth producing-birds" the most valuable birds in the world.[37]

In accord with the technocratic ideal, the 1909 law that created the Compañía Administradora del Guano (CAG) closely followed Coker and Otero's recommendations for administering the guano islands and guano sales, but the fingerprints of Cuban-born financial wizard José Payán de Reyna (1844–1919) were all over this parastatal company's business plan.

---

[36] Coker's emphasis; *BMFom* 8 (Apr. 1910): 14; *MMFom* 12, app. 150 (1908): 412–25, 445, 465, 470–71, 558–63; Coker, "The Fisheries and the Guano Industry of Peru," *Bulletin of the Bureau of Fisheries* 28 (1908): 338, 355.

[37] Equal to US$118 in 2007; *MMFom* 12, app. 161 (1908): 11–13, 17–18, 30; Coker, "Regarding the Future of the Guano Industry," *Science* 10 July 1908: 59; Coker, "Peru's Wealth-Producing Birds," *National Geographic Magazine* June 1920: 540, 552–53.

Payán had taken the lead in forming two of the Aristocratic Republic's key financial institutions, the Bank of Peru and London and the Lima Commercial Exchange. Payán's rules for CAG sought to rally a range of interests behind it. A board of nine directors periodically formulated official company policy and regulations. The Peruvian state held a majority of shares in CAG, and its directorial board eventually included permanent representatives from the National Agricultural Society and government creditors. The majority of CAG's directors were elected by private stockholders, which tended to be large-scale producers of sugar cane and cotton for export. This lasting administrative structure embodied Payán's belief that a public-private consortium was the best way to raise capital, spread risk, and broaden the financial and political stake in new enterprises in Peru's unstable environment. Like many "reform Darwinists" of this era, Payán believed that local capitalists required some level of governmental protection if they were to survive the ruthless, natural laws of economic competition. It was a small step for him and for the agro-exporters who dominated the Aristocratic Republic to extend these protections to the guano birds, as well. This benevolent, managerial understanding of Darwinian selection was especially popular in Latin America and profoundly influenced the global spread of scientific conservation during this era. Under the right conditions, capitalism was a powerful friend of conservation.[38]

These protections almost were not enough. To fulfill the terms of the Grace Contract, the Peruvian Corporation of London still retained jurisdiction over most of Peru's main guano islands. To make matters worse, a "sinister ocean current" arrived at the beginning of the breeding season in 1911 and caused the guano birds to flee the islands en masse. Local demand skyrocketed as farmers hoarded whatever they could of a dwindling supply, making a mockery out of CAG's pretensions to distribute guano rationally. This business experiment survived this rough beginning because conservation technocrats rushed to its defense. "The guano problem is eminently a national problem," agronomist José Antonio de Lavalle unequivocally declared. He blamed the El Niño phenomenon and foreigners for draining the "vital forces and productive energy of the nation" and putting this progressive scientific program in jeopardy. He had an enticingly simple answer to the guano problem: Peru should enforce the clause of the Grace Contract that gave priority to "the government of Peru to consume the guano that is

[38] "Extracción y venta del guano," *La Prensa*, 3 Mar. 1909, morning ed.; "Compañía Administradora del Guano para la agricultura del país," *La Prensa*, 8 Mar. 1909, morning ed.; "Información comercial," *La Prensa*, 11 Apr. 1909, morning ed.; *Estatutos de la Compañía Administradora del Guano* (Lima, 1923), 6–12, 18–19; Macera, "Guano y la agricultura," 324, 327–30; Carlos Camprubí, *José Payán de Reyna* (Lima, 1967), esp. 24; Mike Hawkins, *Social Darwinism in European and American Thought, 1860–1945* (Cambridge and New York, 1997), ch. 7–8; Nancy Stepan, *"The Hour of Eugenics": Race, Gender, and Nation in Latin America* (Ithaca, NY, 1991), ch. 3.

necessary for its agriculture" and limit the Peruvian Corporation to "guano existing" at the time of its signing. To its credit, the Peruvian Corporation realized that the guano bird's "conservation and increase" was in its own long-term interest and agreed to debate this question on scientific terms. Its managers handpicked a highly regarded Scottish naturalist to study the issue.[39]

Henry Forbes (1851–1932) was the quintessential colonial scientist of the age of British imperial expansion. From 1885 to 1887, he led an official expedition to explore the Owen Stanley Range of New Guinea, the high spine of mountains lying between German claims to the north and Great Britain's newly established protectorate on the southern coast. Forbes named the highest peak he could find Huxley Pinnacle, after the famed Darwinian, only to see the peak rechristened Mt. Victoria by another competing explorer.[40] He had far greater success when he shifted his emphasis from geographic to biological exploration. During his tenure as a museum administrator in New Zealand and Liverpool, he led scientific expeditions to two of the world's hotspots of biodiversity: the Chatham Islands off the coast of New Zealand and Socotra Island off the coast of Somalia. He was the first scientist to describe a number of rare, endemic species on these isolated lands, including two close relatives of the Peruvian guanay: the critically endangered Chatham Island shag (*Phalacrocorax onslowi*) and Socotra cormorant (*P. nigrogularis*), an important guano bird on islands off the Arabian Peninsula.[41]

If Peruvian Corporation officials thought Forbes would automatically take his country's side in the guano controversy, they had not done their homework. Henry and his wife Anna – a significant ornithologist in her own right – had become outspoken advocates for a kind of conservation very different from that advocated by Sutton and Coker. During their travels around the world, they had personally witnessed an avian holocaust, in which a single ship departing the Moluccas, New Guinea, or Brazil might carry half a million wild bird skins bound for millinery shops in London and other fashion capitals. They dreamed of the day when "'ladies'... whose example is powerful in the social world refuse to wear feathers altogether, and express their abhorrence of this cruel destruction... going on all over the globe." They were also well aware that other forms of market hunting and "the very rapid advance of the plough" into British wetlands during the age

[39] MCAG 3 (1912): 3, 5, 44, 47, 49, 51–56; Basadre, *Historia de la República*, 15:151–52.

[40] *Who Was Who, 1929–1940* (London, 1941), s.v. "Forbes, Dr. Henry Ogg"; J. W. Lindt, *Picturesque New Guinea* (London, 1887), 8, 19–20, 55; Gavin Souter, *New Guinea: The Last Unknown* (Sydney, 1963), 59–69.

[41] Forbes, "The Chatham Islands: Their Relation to a Former Southern Continent," *Supplementary Papers of the Royal Geographical Society* 3 (1893): 605–37; Forbes, *Natural History of Sokotra and Abd-el-Kuri*, (Liverpool, 1903), 21, 49–50; Johnsgard, *Cormorants, Darters, and Pelicans*, 239–42, 275–77; 2008 IUCN Red List.

of high farming had caused the regional extinction of several British birds.[42] The Forbes were in the vanguard of a global movement, led by women, bird enthusiasts, and scientists, to protect the grandeur of the animal world from destruction.[43]

Henry Forbes arrived in Peru on Christmas Day 1911, just in time to witness the advent of a significant El Niño event. Vast numbers of dead guano birds could be observed floating in the ocean along a 200-kilometer band of the northern coast. Although he did not realize it, Forbes had personally witnessed the ravages wrought by the great El Niño drought of 1877–78 on the other side of the Pacific in Dutch-ruled Indonesia.[44] He spent most of his year in Peru watching marine birds interact with humans around Pisco Bay. In his final report of May 1913, he discounted the impact of El Niño and disease on the guano birds but considered predatory birds and coastal fishermen to be genuine threats. Therefore, he recommended arming a guardian force to keep the islands in "a perfect state of rest." Forbes also lambasted the Peruvian Corporation for allowing independent contractors to interfere with nesting on guano islands under their management. "This is without a doubt one of the principal causes of the decline of the birds" and led him to conclude that the entire coast, except Lobos de Afuera Island, should be placed under CAG's more capable administration.[45] Social circumstances entitled Forbes to make such a forthright pronouncement against his employer's interests. Like Coker, his career did not depend on his recommendations, and he did not have to stay in Peru and live with the consequences. These circumstances exemplify why foreign consultants remain so vital to the politics of expertise around the world: their authority depends on their social distance from the problem at hand.

The loose political consensus that governed the Aristocratic Republic came close to unraveling on a few occasions. This was particularly true during the short-lived government of Guillermo Billinghurst (president 1913–14), one of the old lords of the Tarapacá nitrate trade. His approach to politics contrasted starkly with the technocratic tendencies of the age. He acquired the nickname "Pan Grande" (Big Loaf of Bread) for his advocacy of

---

[42] *British Birds, with Their Nests and Eggs*, ed. Arthur Butler (London, 1896–98), 3:161, 175, 4:17, 30, 46–48, 6:59, 75, 90.

[43] Graham, *Audubon Ark*, ch. 2; Barrow, *Passion for Birds*, ch. 5; David Evans, *A History of Nature Conservation in Britain* (London and New York, 1997), ch. 3; Peter Boomgaard, "Oriental Nature, Its Friends and Its Enemies: Conservation of Nature in Late-Colonial Indonesia, 1889–1949," *Environment and History* 5 (1999): 257–92; Regina Horta Duarte, "Pássaros e cientistas no Brasil: Em busca de proteção," *Latin American Research Review* 41 (2006): 3–26.

[44] MCAG 3 (1912): 51–56; Forbes, *A Naturalist's Wanderings in the Eastern Archipelago* (London, 1885), 51–117.

[45] MCAG 5 (1914): 57–101.

government-controlled food prices and urban environmental improvements, and he encouraged the working people of Lima to flood the streets in his support. In February 1914, a military junta overthrew Billinghurst to put down this threat to public order. Soon after taking power, the military deployed the Forbes report against the Peruvian Corporation to rally agroexporters behind its new regime. It eventually reached a compromise: CAG would purchase guano from the Peruvian Corporation at the going international rate, then sell it at a government subsidized price to all Peruvian farmers who wanted it.[46]

This plan immediately expanded the national guano supply, but failed to address Forbes's conservation concerns or rationalize distribution. In 1914, CAG hired one of Peru's young scientific talents to formulate a definitive solution. José Antonio de Lavalle (fig. 5.2) was the outstanding graduate of 1909 at Peru's National School of Agriculture and a veteran of the search for wilt-resistant varieties at the national cotton experiment station. His family name carried even more weight than his résumé: his father and grandfathers had been major figures during the guano age and defined "the aristocratic center" of Peruvian society that governed the country.[47] Following chemical methods taught to him by Vanderghem, Lavalle completed an agricultural census of the northern and central coast. The fact that he was able to do this at all is testimony to the growing power of the Peruvian state and influence of the technocratic ideal. Local interests opposed to centralized taxation and government control had disrupted similar attempts to quantify Peru's agricultural production in 1875, 1896, 1903, and 1911. Lavalle discovered, to his surprise, that Peru's most intensively cultivated soils possessed high concentrations of key nutrients. Yet rather than praising coastal farmers for taking good care of the land, he concluded that indiscriminate overapplication of fertilizer was contributing to Peru's guano shortage – and therefore required forceful intervention by a conservation technocrat.[48] In 1915–16, CAG implemented a protocol for distributing guano based on Lavalle's calculations of local needs. With the aid of strong La Niña conditions and an increased bird population, Peru's "guano problem" quickly evaporated. The guano supply increased dramatically, and CAG even started producing a substantial profit. This policy worked so well that Lavalle's cousin, José Pardo (president 1904–8, 1915–18) began laying the administrative groundwork for rationing coastal irrigation water in a similar manner.[49]

[46] MCAG 5 (1914): 29–41, 44–48; 7 (1916): iv, 86–87; Peter Blanchard, "A Populist Precursor: Guillermo Billinghurst," *JLAS* 9 (1977): 251–73; Klarén, *Peru*, 222–25.

[47] *Diccionario biográfico de peruanos contemporáneos*, s.v. "Lavalle y García, José Antonio de" and "Lavalle y Pardo, José Antonio."

[48] MCAG 6 (1915): ix; Lavalle, *Las necesidades de guano de la agricultura nacional* (Lima, 1916); Macera, "Guano y la agricultura," 359–60, 388, 396–401.

[49] CEI; MCAG 7 (1916): iv, x; Cushman, "Lords of Guano," app. 2–4; Oré, *Agua*, 99–100.

FIGURE 5.2. Two guano bird scientists, North and South. José Antonio de Lavalle y García (1888–1957, left) was an outspoken leader of the Aristocratic Republic's new technocratic elite and a major defender of marine bird conservation. William Vogt (1902–68, right) became interested in population ecology while working on Peru's guano islands and went on to become a leading proponent of neo-Malthusian ideas as an international conservation activist. Both accomplished groundbreaking research on the ecological impact of El Niño events. *Source:* William Parker, *Peruvians of To-Day* (Lima, 1919), reproduced courtesy of the Benson Latin American Collection, University of Texas Libraries, The University of Texas at Austin; photograph of Vogt near Arequipa, 1939, DPL-VP 4/1, reproduced courtesy of the Denver Public Library, Western History Collection.

"A Practicable Soviet of Technicians"

During the 1910s, a horrific World War intensified the ongoing transformation of South America's relationship with the rest of the globe and vividly revealed the basic social injustice of these changes for working peoples all over the world. The revolutionary events of those years ultimately caused the collapse of oligarchic governments in Mexico, Russia, and Peru but left more people than ever aspiring for an orderly world run by technocrats.

To win, the Allies took full advantage of their ecological reach and consumed vast quantities of agricultural staples and minerals from South America. From 1914 through 1919, Chile sold more than 16 million tons of nitrates to keep Europe's guns firing. (This had a tangible, down-the-road impact on the "emigrant" strand of the Cushman family. For twelve years, the author attended school and played in a landscape dominated by smokestacks, lights, and emission plumes from a massive Du Pont chemical plant that had sprung up in the Tennessee bottomlands to produce nitrogen explosives from Chilean nitrates and Chicago glycerine for the war effort.) Meanwhile, brisk demand for long-staple cotton to produce tires, aircraft fabric, and other high-performance products and the collapse of European beet-sugar production caused Peruvian sales of these articles to skyrocket. From 1914 through 1919, Peru's cotton and sugar exports earned a combined US$87 million – 42 percent of Peru's foreign exchange. Many beneficiaries of the nineteenth-century guano and nitrate booms again benefited from wartime trade, especially Du Pont and W. R. Grace, which ascended to number 8 and 53 in *Fortune* magazine's ranking of U.S. industrial firms. Europe abandoned its importation of Peruvian guano, however, to the direct benefit of Peruvian farmers.[50]

World War I is also distinctive because it initiated a fundamental change in the world's ecological relationship with nitrogen. It is often referred to as "the chemist's war" because of the prevalence of poison gas warfare,[51] but it also deserves this name for its massive use of nitrogen compounds in munitions and explosives. In 1909 – the same year CAG was founded – German chemist Fritz Haber made a critical breakthrough in formulating a catalytic process for synthesizing ammonia from purified atmospheric nitrogen at high pressure. Industrial engineer Carl Bosch soon developed a cost-effective way to scale up this technique. In 1914, German industrial giant BASF manufactured 5,500 tons of reactive nitrogen during its first full year of production using the Haber-Bosch process. This was about the same amount produced by Peru's guano birds that year, but this new system was not reliant on the productivity of a distant marine environment and allowed Germany to continue fighting to the bitter end after it was cut off from the Chilean nitrate trade. Chemical engineers in other countries developed similar processes during the war. In an ecological sense, nitrogen production was now limited mainly by the availability of fossil fuels or hydroelectricity needed to power this extremely energy-intensive process. In 2000, variations of the Haber-Bosch process produced 85 *million* tons of reactive nitrogen. These supplies have freed millions of farmers and the populations they feed from natural constraints posed by the cycling of nitrogen under the ecological old regime, albeit at enormous financial and environmental cost. No technological change during the twentieth century – not even the internal

---

[50] Equal to US$820 million in 2007. Bill Albert, *South America and the First World War: The Impact of the War on Brazil, Argentina, Peru, and Chile* (Cambridge and New York, 1989), 96–100, 105–16, 165; Michael Monteón, *Chile in the Nitrate Era: The Evolution of Economic Dependence, 1880–1930* (Madison, WI, 1982), 111–22; Cushman, "Lords of Guano," app. 1, 5–6; Thomas Navin, "The 500 Largest American Industrials in 1917," *Business History Review* 44 (1970): 360–86; Du Pont, "Our Old Hickory Heritage: The Evolution of a Company & a Village," http://www.oldhickoryrecord.com/heritage.htm.

[51] Edmund Russell, *War and Nature: Fighting Humans and Insects with Chemicals from World War I to Silent Spring* (Cambridge and New York, 2001), ch. 2–3.

combustion engine – has done more to change humanity's impact on the earth.[52]

In the short term, almost all of these supplies were used to kill, rather than helping people live by replenishing the soil. Scarcity-minded scientists had long foreseen the importance of nitrogen to military conflict. In 1898, William Crookes caused an international furor by raising the specter of Malthus in his presidential address to the British Association for the Advancement of Science. "England and all civilised nations stand in deadly peril of not having enough to eat," Crookes warned. Their "wheat-producing soil" was "unequal to the strain put upon it." Peruvian guano and "uncultivated prairie land" were all but exhausted, and "Chili saltpetre" would eventually be gone. Even in the short term, Great Britain might starve if it were attacked by "a hostile combination of European nations" and cut off from its far-flung ecological empire. But Crookes had a technological fix in mind for the world's "wheat problem." He called on his "brilliant audience" of scientific experts to conserve "the treasure locked up in the sewage and draining of our towns" and to renew their efforts toward fixing nitrogen directly from the atmosphere: "It is through the laboratory that starvation may ultimately be turned to plenty." As we see in later chapters, Crookes anticipated the neo-Malthusian thinking that inspired World War II, the Green and Blue Revolutions, and the modern environmental movement.[53]

Crookes's prophecy of a global wheat famine came horribly true during World War I. An extreme oscillation between La Niña and El Niño played a role in this. In the central United States, a severe drought, stem rust epidemic, and frigid winter severely reduced the wheat harvest in 1916 and 1917. Canada also experienced a sharp decline in wheat yields, exacerbated by farmers' abandonment of moisture and nutrient-saving practices in the hope of reaping wartime profits. Things were downright grim in Argentina. From April to December 1916, the Pampas experienced one of its worst droughts in history, made all the more terrible by unseasonable frost, a locust plague, and rinderpest outbreak. These conditions made Germany's submarine attacks on trans-Atlantic shipping all the more devastating.[54]

---

[52] Smil, *Enriching the Earth*, 51–107, app. F, L; Arjan van Rooij, "Engineering Contractors in the Chemical Industry. The Development of Ammonia Processes, 1910–1940," *History and Technology* 21 (2005): 345–66; Galloway and Cowling, "Reactive Nitrogen and the World."

[53] Crookes, "Address by Sir William Crookes," 4, 7, 14–15, 18–19.

[54] Perkins, *Geopolitics and the Green Revolution*, 85–88, 93–98; Harold Berger and Hans Landsberg, *American Agriculture, 1899–1939* (New York, 1942), 42–43, 281, 332; Albert, *South America and the First World War*, 63–64; John Thompson, "'Permanently Wasteful but Immediately Profitable': Prairie Agriculture and the Great War," *Historical Papers* 11 (1976): 193–206; Gregory Marchildon et al., "Drought and Institutional Adaptation in the Great Plains of Alberta and Saskatchewan, 1914–1939," *Natural Hazards* 45 (2008): 391–411.

For related climatic reasons, India experienced two of its rainiest monsoon seasons of the past century in 1916–17 – with a third to half of the subcontinent receiving "exceptional" quantities of precipitation. This was followed in 1918 by the worst drought of the twentieth century. Their combined impact was significantly worse in intensity than the notorious El Niño event of 1877–78. Calamitous drought and winter cold also struck Central Asia and the Middle East and, as we saw in the last chapter, brought an abrupt end to plans to rehabilitate Banaba.[55]

Climate anomalies had a direct impact on agriculture in war-torn Europe, as well. Too much moisture can be just as devastating as too little to cereal harvests, especially in northern climes. For Europe as a whole, 1915 and 1916 were by far the wettest pair of years of the century, with as much as a third of the continent experiencing "severe" excesses of soil moisture and its soldiers a corresponding outbreak of trench foot. Total harvest and per hectare yields of wheat and rye fell drastically in Great Britain, France, Germany, and Austrian-ruled lands from 1914–15 to 1916–17 and dropped significantly in Hungary and Russia, two of the world's grain-producing powers of the prewar period. Until now, historians have overlooked the possible impact of this widespread climatic disturbance on the war.[56]

In combination with disruptions in transportation, trade, taxation patterns, and field labor, these wartime disasters pushed the world price of wheat, wheat flour, and many other foods into the stratosphere. Lack of bread played a fundamental role in the breakup of the Austro-Hungarian Empire, the Arab revolt in the Ottoman Empire, and, more famously, the Russian Revolution of 1917. At one point, Great Britain only had seven weeks' supply of wheat on hand. These regions were much better off, however, than large segments of Turkestan, Syria, Lebanon, Persia, and northwestern India. They had no bread at all, nor means to buy it, and succumbed to disastrous famines, epidemics, depopulation, and then to a new phase of domination by the Soviets, French, and British. Poor subsistence must also have contributed markedly to the enormous death toll of the 1918–20 influenza and pneumonia pandemic, which was concentrated in areas dependent on food imports and regions subject to rainfall extremes during ENSO events. This combined catastrophe therefore qualifies as the last and arguably the worst of the "late Victorian holocausts" generated by

[55] CEI; U. S. De et al., "Extreme Weather Events over India in the Last 100 Years," *Journal of the Indian Geophysical Union* 9 (2005): 173–87; Benjamin Giese et al., "The 1918/19 El Niño," *Bulletin of the American Meteorological Society* 91 (2010): 177–83.

[56] G. van der Schrier, "Summer Moisture Variability across Europe," *Journal of Climate* 19 (2006): 2818–34; Hermann Flohn and Roberto Fantechi, *The Climate of Europe: Past, Present and Future* (Dodrecht, 1984), 283–85; Dronin and Bellinger, *Climate Dependence and Food Problems in Russia*, 64–66; National Bureau of Economic Research, Macrohistory Database, http://www.nber.org/databases/macrohistory/contents.

the New Imperialism and globalization of food production at the end of the nineteenth century.[57]

Urban areas in many parts of Latin America also suffered greatly from the war's "wheat problem" and became vulnerable to influenza and unrest. For many years, rising demand for meat, grain, and cooking fat in Peru had far outpaced increases in local supply, resulting in rapid inflation. Prices for meat and cooking fat in Lima more than doubled again from 1914–20, and rice, maize, and wheat flour nearly did so. Meanwhile, exporters of Tangüis cotton snapped up surplus supplies of fallow land, irrigation water, and guano that might have gone to food production. Until President Pardo belatedly banned the practice, Peru exported significantly more food than it had before the war (especially rice), but because of exorbitant prices, imported much less. Employers raised their wages but failed to keep up with local price inflation.[58]

A different sort of expert rose to meet these challenges. Cambridge agricultural scientist Thomas Middleton took command of the U.K. Board of Agriculture and Fisheries' endeavors to increase the wartime food supply. He helped lay the basis for a lasting, technocratic program to make Britain more self-sufficient, with nitrogen and phosphate fertilizer at its center. When the United States entered the war in April 1917, President Wilson appointed Herbert Hoover to make sure the "oppressive price of food" did not defeat the Allies. Hoover was a veteran of the U.S. Geological Survey and had long experience managing the gold mines of the Australian Outback, coalfields of northern China, slag heaps of highland Burma, and boardrooms of London. He saw engineers as "the real brains of industrial progress" and encouraged them to take command of the world's "mining armies of millions." During the early years of the war, Hoover attained international celebrity for organizing a massive humanitarian campaign to supply Belgium with food. As U.S. Food Administrator, he appointed scientific experts to positions of authority and spoke out in favor of "food conservation" and "the gospel of the clean plate." Once the war was won, Hoover took charge of supplying hungry Europe with food, where "empty

---

57 Clifford Wargerlin, "The Economic Collapse of Austro-Hungarian Dualism, 1914–1918," *East European Quarterly* 34 (2000): 261–88; L. Schatkowski Schilcher, "The Famine of 1915–1918 in Greater Syria," in *Problems of the Modern Middle East in Historical Perspective* (Reading, UK, 1992); Marco Buttino, "Study of the Economic Crisis and Depopulation of Turkestan, 1917–1920," *Central Asian Survey* 9 (1990): 59–74; Mohammed Gholi Majd, *The Great Famine and Genocide in Persia, 1917–1919* (Lanham, MD, 2003); Niall Johnson and Juergen Mueller, "Updating the Accounts: Global Mortality of the 1918–1920 'Spanish' Influenza Pandemic," *Bulletin of the History of Medicine* 76 (2002): 105–15; cf. Davis, *Late Victorian Holocausts.*

58 Augusto Ruiz Zevallos, *La multitud, las subsistencias y el trabajo: Lima, 1890–1920* (Lima, 2001) 133–45, 207, 219–24, 229; Albert, *South America and the First World War*, 110–11, 297; Thorp and Bertram, *Peru 1890–1977*, 132–40.

stomachs mean Bolsheviks."[59] In 1919, an Anglo-American engineer coined a new term to describe the sort of government that Hoover implemented – *technocracy* – and intellectuals from across the political spectrum began to think experts would fulfill a greater historical destiny. In the United States, Thorstein Veblen called on "inventors, designers, chemists, mineralogists, soil experts, crop specialists, production managers and engineers" living in "advanced industrial countries" to form "a Practicable Soviet of Technicians" to overthrow "the Vested Interest." In Germany, Oswald Spengler pointed an accusing finger at "the quiet engineer . . . the machine's master" as the last hindrance preventing the fall of "the dictature of money and its political weapon, democracy."[60]

These men were all acutely aware of Russian events. It is a testimony to the political adaptability of the technocratic ideal that the victorious Bolsheviks organized a series of commissariats run by experts (*tekhnika*) to manage the Soviet Union's transition from an aristocratic to a socialist state. This enabled professional foresters and ecologists to quickly entrench themselves as the country's environmental managers, notwithstanding rampant peasant opposition.[61] Experts also played a starring role in the rise and fall of a major oligarchic regime in the Western Hemisphere. In Mexico, a group of trained professionals known collectively as the *científicos* (scientists) attained tremendous power during the long dictatorship of Porfirio Díaz (1876–1911). A junior member of this group, Miguel Ángel de Quevedo (1862–1946), served as supervising engineer of a vast project to drain Mexico's Central Valley of water and sewage. In 1906, he took charge of a program to plant trees to remedy the horrible dust storms that beset Mexico City after the drainage of its ancient saline wetlands, and he later proved instrumental in the establishment of the country's first national parks. Mexico's *científicos* fatally underestimated popular discontent with their vision of Order and Progress, however. In 1911, an agronomist belonging to a powerful family of cotton planters, Francisco Madero, organized a dissident movement to push Díaz and his cronies out of power. This revolt opened the floodgates to a massive revolution that took three decades to play

[59] Quoted in Nash, *The Life of Herbert Hoover*, 1:480–86, 2:362, 3:41–45, 152–60, 227–55, 478; Perkins, *Geopolitics and the Green Revolution*, 86–92.

[60] William Smyth, "Technocracy: National Industrial Management, Practical Suggestions for National Reconstruction," *Industrial Management* 57 (1919): 208–12; *Oxford English Dictionary*, s.v. "technocracy"; Veblen, *The Engineers and the Price System* (1921; New York, 1936), 60–61, 133, 138–69; Spengler, *The Decline of the West* (1918–22; New York, 1991), 413–14.

[61] Don Rowney, *Transition to Technocracy: The Structural Origins of the Soviet Administrative State* (Ithaca, NY, 1989); Douglas Weiner, *Models of Nature: Ecology, Conservation, and Cultural Revolution in Soviet Russia* (Bloomington, IN, 1988); Brian Bonhomme, *Forests, Peasants, and Revolutionaries: Forest Conservation and Organization in Soviet Russia, 1917–1929* (New York, 2005).

out. Tellingly, one of the Mexican Revolution's main centers of unrest took place in the cotton-growing Laguna District, a focus of efforts by Madero and the *científicos* to reform the administration of irrigation water on the basis of conservation principles in order to benefit export agriculture. In both Russia and Mexico, scientific conservation, technocratic rule, and peasant opposition were closely intertwined.[62]

High food prices and global political ferment also inspired organized protest in Peru that eventually resulted in the collapse of the Aristocratic Republic. Strikes broke out over the cost of living in the cotton fields of the Huaura valley in 1916 and at highland copper mines and North Coast sugar plantations the following year. In January 1919, in the face of a massive general strike, President Pardo decreed an eight-hour day for Peru's working class, and he appointed a technocratic commission, headed by CAG agronomist José Antonio de Lavalle, to develop strategies for increasing Peru's homegrown food supply. Emboldened by these decisions, labor activists scheduled a general strike for Lima to correspond with the presidential election in May 1919. More than 100 died in the ensuing violence – much of it targeted against symbols of foreign influence such as Asian shop owners and the offices of W. R. Grace & Co. These events mirrored the labor unrest and xenophobia that shook Chile, Argentina, Germany, Hungary, India, and a host of other countries at the end of the war.[63]

One of the Aristocratic Republic's many discontents, Augusto Leguía, turned this chaotic situation to his advantage. After winning the presidential election on a platform promising to lower the cost of living, only to see his enemies in the Supreme Court threaten to snatch it away, Leguía convinced the military to support a coup d'état to guarantee his victory and preserve social peace. This marked the abrupt end of Peru's Aristocratic Republic and the beginning of an eleven-year authoritarian regime known as the *oncenio* (1919–30). With the help of massive foreign loans, Leguía proceeded to build a New Fatherland (*Nueva Patria*) based on the principle that "the State is... the most efficacious agent for carrying out the beautiful work of human solidarity."[64]

[62] Simonian, *Defending the Land of the Jaguar*, ch. 4; Perlo, *El paradigma porfiriano*, 223–25; Alan Knight, *The Mexican Revolution* (Cambridge and New York, 1986), 1:21–24, 55–57, 62; Clifton Kroeber, *Man, Land, and Water: Mexico's Farmlands Irrigation Policies, 1885–1911* (Berkeley and Los Angeles, 1983), ch. 3, 8.

[63] David Parker, "Peruvian Politics and the Eight-Hour Day: Rethinking the 1919 General Strike," *Canadian Journal of History* 30 (1995): 417–38; Ruiz, *La multitud*, 153–63; Albert, *South America and the First World War*, 236, 295–302; Klarén, *Peru*, 236–38; David Arnold, "Looting, Grain Riots and Government Policy in South India 1918," *Past & Present* 84 (1979): 111–45.

[64] Quoted by Paul Drake, *The Money Doctor in the Andes: The Kemmerer Missions, 1923–1933* (Durham, NC, 1989), 220; Klarén, *Peru*, ch. 9.

Leguía frequently used technocratic means to conciliate his opponents and diffuse social unrest. He promptly created a General Subsistence Directorate to enforce price controls in September 1919. Two years later, he sent a crack team of experts, again including Lavalle, to resolve a tense situation among sugar industry workers in the Chicama Valley. Lauro Curletti (1876–1949), Leguía's new minister of development, headed this group. This chemistry professor turned physician had impeccable credentials as a friend of the workers' cause dating back to his days as Billinghurst's director of public health. Curletti's report recognized the right of labor unions to organize, but in accord with Taylorist theories of scientific management, also recommended the use of government inspectors to supervise sugar workers' "physical and moral" environment, both at work and at home, and payment based on quantitative measures of their productivity.[65] In 1920, President Leguía proudly announced the construction of "a model mining population" to serve a vast new copper smelter in the highland railroad town of La Oroya. This factory cemented Peru's position as one of the world's main suppliers of base metals to the industrial North but had horrific results for highland plants, animals, soils, and people poisoned by air and water pollution spewed out by this massive facility. In response, thirty-two indigenous communities and twenty-eight hacienda owners organized to seek recompense. Leguía sent José Bravo, one of the Aristocratic Republic's most prominent engineers, to forge a compromise. Bravo recommended a technological fix: the installation of Cottrell electrostatic scrubbers to reduce pollution and increase the efficiency of mineral production. The Cerro de Pasco Corporation also arranged to buy out thirteen haciendas comprising more than 2,000 square kilometers of polluted land and to pay eleven native communities yearly indemnities. Almost overnight, this U.S.-owned company became the largest landowner in Peru but never bothered to accomplish any significant environmental improvements. Today, La Oroya remains one of the world's most polluted places, with 99 percent of its children suffering from dangerously high lead levels.[66]

Peru's engineers had no interest in forming "a practicable Soviet of technicians" to fundamentally reorder Peruvian society, but many of them honestly believed their actions would remedy some of Peru's persistent inequalities. This is particularly true in the case of coastal irrigation and guano. In 1918, President Pardo pushed a controversial bill through Congress that charged a small water tax and gave government engineers unprecedented

---

[65] Curletti, *El problema industrial en el Valle de Chicama* (Lima, 1921), 5, 10–16, 20, 26–27, 30–33; *Diccionario histórico y biográfico*, s.v. "Curletti, Lauro Ángel"; Klarén, *Modernización*, 38–49.

[66] BCIM 108 (1926): 20, 69, 90–103; Florencia Mallon, *The Defense of Community in Peru's Central Highlands: Peasant Struggle and Capitalist Transition, 1860–1940* (Princeton, NJ, 1983), 222–29, app. 2; Blacksmith Institute, "World's Most Polluted Places 2006," http://www.blacksmithinstitute.org/ten.php.

authority over Peru's coastal water resources. Leguía's government enthusiastically enforced this law's provisions, in part, to punish political enemies
that owned large coastal estates. To this end, the engineer who took charge
of the Ica Valley Water District, Ezequiel Gagó, autocratically reserved all
water flowing at night through the Anchirana canal for use by indigenous
communities. At first, indigenous farmers welcomed him – until he required
them to pay a fee for a resource they felt already belonged to them. They
eventually organized a valley-wide protest movement against technocratic
control that incorporated indigenous farmers, sharecroppers, and plantation workers. Gagó appealed to Lima for help, and it eventually arrived
in 1924 in the form of a military crackdown that reinstituted local planter
dominance. Leguía also recalled Charles Sutton to Peru and gave him control over water reclamation in the country. Guano again proved central to
these plans. Leguía used the government's renewed control over guano sales
to underwrite the so-called London Contract of 1922, which provided the
country's first major foreign loan since the guano age.[67] Most of this money
went to expand the country's system of highways and irrigation canals. The
first major irrigation project opened in the Cañete valley in 1924. In accord
with Sutton's long-held belief that small family farms would "democratize"
property ownership and produce the "greatest social and economic efficiency," no one was allowed to purchase a plot larger than forty hectares.
The second project sought to divert a tributary of the Amazon underneath
the Andes to conquer 650 square kilometers of northern desert in Leguía's
home province. However, massive El Niño floods, cost overruns, local resistance, and the coming of the Great Depression all conspired against the
realization of this pharaonic plan.[68]

This was only one part of Leguía's grand strategy to put qualified experts
"in charge of every branch of our government's activities." Public health,
the postal service, telegraph communications, tax collection, the Ministry
of Education, secret service, national police, army, navy, air force, Lima
traffic service, and countless construction projects all came under the direct
supervision of foreign technicians during Leguía's *oncenio*. Outside interests also encouraged these technocratic interventions. As part of the bargain
that exchanged guano receipts and petroleum exports for foreign loans,
North Atlantic lenders compelled Leguía to appoint a disciple of Princeton
economics professor Edwin Kemmerer to supervise Peru's customs service.
Some of these schemes achieved dystopian levels of invasiveness. Leguía

---

[67] Equal to US$63 million in 2007.
[68] *Estatutos*, 76–83; Pardo, "Mensaje a la nación ante el Congreso el 28 de julio de 1918," 58–
59, http://www.congreso.gob.pe/museo/mensajes/Mensaje_1918.pdf; Oré, *Agua*, 99–109;
Pérez, *Sutton*, 26–39; Eduardo Zegarra et al., "El Proyecto Olmos en un territorio árido
de la costa norte peruana," ch. 20 of *Territorios rurales: Movimientos sociales y desarrollo
territorial rural en América Latina* (n.p., 2006); Pike, *Modern History of Peru*, 227–29.

hired U.S. physician Henry Hanson, a veteran of antimosquito campaigns in the Panama Canal Zone, to take command of a house-to-house campaign against yellow fever along the far northern coast. But Hanson had greater ambitions. He advised hiring a U.S. engineering firm to burn down and rebuild the entire plague-ridden port of Paita, but popular resistance enabled nine-tenths of the city to escape the calamitous fate of Honolulu's Chinatown, the historic centers of Rio and Lima, and other urban districts that were razed during this era to make the world safe from contagion.[69]

A public ceremony performed in the old colonial heart of Lima on the first day of spring, 1925, enunciated a concrete linkage between these technocratic trends, export agriculture, and scientific conservation in Peru. On that day, the Compañía Administradora del Guano opened a new office building befitting its growing prominence on Peru's modern landscape. It stood one block from Congress, two blocks from José Payán's Bank of Peru and London, and three blocks from the newly reconstructed presidential palace. In stark contrast to W. B. Lange's modernist design for the Gildemeister building, just around the corner, CAG's neoclassical façade was explicitly intended to be "reminiscent of Saxon banking institutions," its colonnaded central hall to convey the "sobriety" of its administrators, and its "elegant and severe English-style furniture" to create trust in their capabilities. Its hierarchically compartmentalized interior and well-equipped laboratory advertised this domain as a model of scientific order and cleanliness. A host of notables attended the opening ceremony for this new headquarters. The presence of Leguía and presidents of both chambers of Congress perpetuated the fiction that Peru was a parliamentary democracy. The managers of Lima's main banks stood for guano's renewed importance in attracting foreign loans and private investment. The director of Peru's meteorological service and president of the National Agrarian Society represented the marriage between environmental science and agribusiness. Finally, an Augustinian friar blessed this new Palace of Scientific Administration. The world's capital cities are littered with similar monuments to the technocratic ideal.[70]

Peru was hardly alone in embracing these technocratic trends. In Brazil, physicians and engineers heading the Oswaldo Cruz Institute and the Inspectorate for Works to Combat Drought implemented a host of sanitation, irrigation, and reforestation programs to attack problems facing "backlanders" living in the drought-prone Northeast, long before the technocratic programs of Getúlio Vargas's Estado Novo.[71] In Colombia, California-trained

---

[69] Drake, *Money Doctor*, 212–21, 267; Basadre, *Historia de la República*, 13:215–16; Cueto, *Return of the Epidemics*, ch. 2; Mohr, *Plague and Fire*.

[70] *BCAG* 1 (1925): 375–79; 4 (1928): July issue insert.

[71] Nancy Stepan, *Beginnings of Brazilian Science: Oswaldo Cruz, Medical Research and Policy, 1890–1920* (New York, 1976), ch. 5; Eve Buckley, "Drought and Development: Technocrats and the Politics of Modernization in Brazil's Semi-Arid Northeast, 1877–1964" (Ph.D. diss., Univ. of Pennsylvania, 2006), ch. 3–4; Barbara Weinstein, *For Social Peace in Brazil:*

mining engineer Pedro Nel Ospina campaigned for president in 1922 on the premise that he would introduce "probity and efficiency" to state administration. Once elected, he invited a commission of experts led by Kemmerer to tour the country and help Colombia attract foreign loans and investment. Two future giants of conservative politics then took turns distributing this largesse as Ospina's minister of public works: his son Mariano Ospina Pérez, a Louisiana-trained agronomist, and Laureano Gómez, a civil engineer with a penchant for red-baiting oratory. Teams of experts also worked on overhauling agricultural education, forestry, and water use in Colombia and Venezuela. Meanwhile, Kemmerer helped Mexico's new Revolutionary Government launch itself in 1917, and personally led financial missions to the Philippines, Guatemala, Chile, Ecuador, Bolivia, Weimar Germany, South Africa, Poland, China, Turkey, and eventually to Peru. His disciples helped form the financial institutions of U.S.-occupied Haiti, Brazil, Romania, Czechoslovakia, Yugoslavia, Austria, and Armenia.[72] As secretary of commerce and the United States' first engineer-president, Herbert Hoover campaigned to eliminate waste in industry, to restore depleted salmon stocks in Alaska, to build roads in national and state parks, and to convert the wild Colorado River into one vast water storage facility.[73]

A massive economic and political crisis soon threatened to undo these accomplishments. In retrospect, it is clear that these efforts made the world's capitalist economy far more integrated during the Roaring Twenties but also vulnerable to collapse. The all-out drive to increase staple crop and fertilizer production after the First World War played a significant role in destabilizing commodity prices and the agricultural underpinnings of the global economy. Chilean nitrate producers, for example, began to suffer intense competition from manufacturers using variations of the Haber-Bosch process. Colonel Carlos Ibáñez seized control of the Chilean state in 1927 and proceeded to install the most technocratic government Latin America had ever seen to stop the country's downward economic slide.[74]

The Great Depression resulted in similar political revolutions all over the world. Leguía asked Kemmerer to come advise Peru after the Great Crash

Industrialists and the Remaking of the Working Class in São Paulo, 1920–1964 (Chapel Hill, NC, 1996), ch. 1.

[72] Drake, *Money Doctor*, 1, 9–10, 26, 30–75, 215, 266–68; Safford, *Ideal of the Practical*, 152–56, 225, 238; James Henderson, *Modernization in Colombia: The Laureano Gómez Years, 1889–1965* (Gainesville, FL, 2001), ch. 5; Pamela Murray, *Dreams of Development: Colombia's National School of Mines and Its Engineers* (Tuscaloosa, AL, 1997), ch. 3; McCook, *States of Nature*, 111–26; Cushman, "Humboldtian Science."

[73] Kendrick Clements, *Hoover, Conservation, and Consumerism: Engineering the Good Life* (Lawrence, KS, 2000), ch. 5–6.

[74] Dietmar Rothermund, *The Global Impact of the Great Depression, 1929–1939* (London and New York, 1996); Patricio Silva, "State, Public Technocracy and Politics in Chile, 1927–1941," *Bulletin of Latin American Research* 13 (1994): 281–97.

of 1929, but he was busy in Colombia and arrived too late to save Leguía's regime. In August 1930, a military junta led by Luis Sánchez Cerro (president 1930–33) imprisoned Leguía and sacked a long list of officials with technocratic credentials, including Charles Sutton, who faced a show trial as scapegoat for the *oncenio*'s corruption. These events opened a brief window of opportunity for popular democracy in Peru. In 1931, Sánchez Cerro used a populist platform to defeat Raúl Haya de la Torre, the charismatic leader of the Alianza Popular Revolucionaria Americana (APRA), in the first mass election in Peruvian history. The ascendance of populist politics could have dealt a nasty blow to the technocratic ideal in Peru, but Sánchez Cerro dutifully welcomed a team of experts headed by Kemmerer to obtain international legitimation for his regime. Engineers also took over all the top positions at CAG after Leguía's cronies were deposed.[75]

The economic upheaval of the Great Depression attracted more people than ever to the technocratic ideal. Franklin D. Roosevelt installed his own "brain trust" after he replaced Hoover as U.S. president in 1933. Thanks to globetrotting evangelists of the technocracy movement, derivations of "technocracy" became part of German (*technokratie*), Japanese (*tekunokurashi*), Spanish and Portuguese (*tecnocracia*), and a host of other languages during the 1930s.[76] Even in the ultra-politicized Soviet Union, Stalinist productivity experts rose to positions of unprecedented influence, and scientists proved capable of using their credentials to protect a "little corner of freedom" for themselves and the nature protection movement.[77]

In this chapter we have seen how scientific conservation and the technocratic ideal became tied up with oligarchic politics in Peru and many other countries around the globe between 1890 and 1940. Technocrats achieved unprecedented authority and influence after the First World War based on the belief that they could prevent the sort of conflict and scarcity that rocked the planet during the 1910s. The scarcity and turmoil generated by the Great Depression provided technocrats with yet another opportunity to increase their influence – sometimes as instruments of populist politics. These activities might seem far removed from today's environmental values, but in those

---

[75] *New York Times* 31 Aug. 1930: 3; 9 Sept. 1930: 2; 10 Sept. 1930: 2; 2 Aug. 1931: E8; MCAG 22 (1931): xv–xvi; BCAG 10 (1934): 76–77; Drake, *Money Doctor*, 16–17, 63–75, 221–43; Steve Stein, *Populism in Peru: The Emergence of the Masses and the Politics of Social Control* (Madison, WI, 1980).

[76] Takeshi Haga, *Tekunokurashi kaisetsu* (Tokyo, 1933); Jorge Álvarez Lleras, *La technocracia y sus conclusiones* (Bogotá, 1933); William Akin, *Technocracy and the American Dream: The Technocrat Movement, 1900–1941* (Berkeley and Los Angeles, 1977); Stefan Willeke, *Die Technokratiebewegung in Nordamerika und Deutschland zwishen den Weltkriegen* (New York, 1995).

[77] Lewis Siegelbaum, *Stakhovanism and the Politics of Productivity in the USSR, 1935–1941* (Cambridge and New York, 1988); Douglas Weiner, *A Little Corner of Freedom: Russian Nature Protection from Stalin to Gorbachev* (Berkeley and Los Angeles, 1999).

days, some of the world's most powerful men viewed the conservation of natural resources and other environmental improvements as indispensable to the maintenance of social peace and the continuation of economic growth, no matter where they stood on the political spectrum.

In the process, Peru's guano birds became "the most valuable birds in the world" not as the objects of veneration they were for Peru's ancient indigenous peoples but as an instrumental means to a set of developmental ends. In the upshot, a small cadre of capitalists, scientists, engineers, and physicians achieved the power to convert Peru's guano islands into an ecological laboratory where they could test the efficacy of the technocratic ideal, both for controlling humanity and wild nature. What ecological changes did they accomplish? Did any of their schemes improve the human condition in Peru? It is to these questions that we now turn.

6

The Most Valuable Birds in the World

> The Peruvian Guano Administration... operates the greatest of all industries based upon the conservation of wild animals.
> – Robert Cushman Murphy, "Inter-American Conservation" (1940)

Imagine yourself on the crest of Isla Don Martín, a large, dry, rocky outcrop poking its head above the blue-green swells and white foam of the Pacific Ocean. It is the height of summer in 1950, and the island is bathed with warm afternoon sunlight. A wall of marine haze cordons off the island from the open sea to the west, but the brown hills and green valleys of the coastline are easily visible to the east. In ages past, the inhabitants of these lands believed a great chieftain was cursed and turned to stone to form the island on which you now stand. To the north, a turbulent patch of birds is visible, slowly pressing along the ocean surface looking for food "as the great flocks of passenger pigeons are said to have once rolled through open North American forests in which oak or beech mast lay thick upon the leafy floor." The dark forms of surfacing sea lions and jumping dolphins are scattered among them, as far as the eye can see. From the south, an endless river of black and white guanays is flooding the island. The ancients said that the first of these birds to build a nest here laid three eggs that gave birth to the three classes of human society: a gold egg for noble men, a silver egg for noble women, and a copper egg for commoners.[1]

As the light grows hazy and the day draws toward its end, other sensations begin to take precedence over the sense of sight. The sound grows deafening as a million hopeful baby birds call out to their returning mothers and fathers, eager to fill their bellies with the latest catch. Many stick their tails over the edge of their disklike nests and defecate in anticipation. A breeze picks up over this roiling colony, kicking up dust and causing the stench of

---

[1] Murphy, *Oceanic Birds*, 904; Rostworowski, *Señoríos indíginas*, 144–46.

ammonia to become downright oppressive. Try your best to appreciate it. It is the smell of money being made.

This sublime spectacle is by all appearances wild, but appearances can be deceiving. It is actually the combined result of the natural abundance of this upwelling ecosystem and decades of careful efforts by conservation technocrats to turn the management of Peru's living guano birds into a profitable enterprise, often in the face of concerted opposition from nature and society. This chapter traces the history of these struggles from the founding of the Compañía Administradora del Guano (CAG) in 1909 until the tragic El Niño event of 1957–58. During this half century, CAG gradually consolidated its control over a complex agroecological system linking the enormous productivity of Peru's marine environment to the export of staple crops from the adjacent coast. CAG technocrats used the latest principles of scientific management not only to manipulate the wide variety of organisms affecting the welfare of the guano birds but also to manage the behavior of human beings who extracted and used guano. In the process, they built what many considered "the greatest of all industries based upon the conservation of wild animals" the world has ever seen.

To understand how this management regime developed and functioned, it is useful to think of it as an *agroecological system*. An agroecosystem is a conceptual tool used to delineate the multiple ecological relationships that exist within a crop cultivation regime. They explicitly encompass both human manipulations and feedback relationships with the natural environment. Donald Worster has advocated the use of the agroecosystem concept to provide a theoretical framework for research in environmental history. He did so not in the hope of reducing human interaction with the environment to a set of material relationships (or more narrowly, to the study of agrarian life) but to provide an explicit method for investigating the interaction between the natural and cultural realms, and to resist the ongoing temptation to reduce environmental history to just another variety of social or cultural history.[2] The agroecosystem concept has also proven useful (1) for calculating the changing "social metabolism" or "ecological footprint" of entities as small as an individual or farm or as large as a city or nation-state, (2) for identifying key "socioecological transitions" when human society and the natural world rapidly coevolved to take on new organizational forms, (3) for delineating the reciprocity between changing systems of production and consumption, and (4) for developing strategies for maximizing the biodiversity of landscapes heavily affected by human activities. From the point of view of the originators of the concept, the agroecosystem provides a set of "guiding principles" for "the design and management of sustainable ecosystems" in today's world that will allow farmers to reverse the

[2] Worster, "Transformations of the Earth: Toward an Agroecological Perspective in History," *Journal of American History* 76 (1990): 1087–1106.

modern trend toward dependence on manufactured chemicals without sacrificing food security or modern gains in productivity.[3] This chapter uses an agroecological perspective to do the reverse: to show how input-intensive agriculture became conventional practice and impacted conservation policy and environmental understanding in twentieth-century Peru.

Protecting Peru's "Billion-Dollar Birds"

Peru's guano industry ultimately depended on the primary productivity of the eastern tropical Pacific Ocean, which by some measures is the most productive marine environment on earth. Large-scale geophysical forces cause prevailing southeast trade winds to blow along the Peruvian coast. These forces push the surface water toward the northwest to be replaced by cool, subsurface water enriched with nitrates and other nutrients welling up from below. This sustains enormous populations of microscopic phytoplankton feeding on sunlight from above, which in turn provision a complex web of grazing and predatory organisms including zooplankton, fish, seals, whales, and birds. Marine biomass becomes most accessible to surface-feeding organisms when coastal upwelling slows and becomes concentrated in pockets during the austral summer. This explains why guano birds nest at this time. Unfortunately for the creatures that depend on this abundance, the Peruvian littoral is periodically disturbed during El Niño events when the trade winds slacken and upwelling shuts down, allowing warm, nutrient-poor waters to invade from the north and west. The productivity of the Peru Current ecosystem also varies on decadal and secular timescales, periodically resulting in lasting "regime shifts" in fish abundance. Sediment studies indicate that regional upwelling has gradually become much greater since the guano age ended in the 1870s. Thus, a natural trend in Peru's marine environment contributed to the guano birds' emergence as "the most valuable birds in the world" during the early twentieth century.[4]

Three species of marine birds have been responsible for producing most of the excrement laid down on Peru's guano islands during recent millennia (figs. 6.1 and 6.2). They belong to the order Pelicaniformes, an ancient lineage that includes pelicans, cormorants, boobies, darters, tropicbirds, and the sacred frigatebirds of the Banabans and Rapanui. The Peruvian coast has had guano islands of some sort for at least eleven million years. During the middle Miocene, upwelling greatly intensified in the eastern tropical Pacific

---

[3] Stephen Gliessman, *Agroecology: Ecological Processes in Sustainable Agriculture* (Chelsea, MI, 1998), 13, 301–10; Fischer-Kowalski and Haberl, eds., *Socioecological Transitions*; Soluri, *Banana Cultures*; Ivette Perfecto, et al., *Nature's Matrix: Linking Agriculture, Conservation and Food Sovereignty* (London, 2009).

[4] Arnaud Bertrand, ed., "The Northern Humboldt Current System: Ocean Dynamics, Ecosystem Processes, and Fisheries," special issue of *Progress in Oceanography* 79 (2008): esp. 167–76, 190–97, 401–12.

FIGURE 6.1. Guanays, or Peruvian cormorants on Santa Rosa Island, Peru.

at the same time that hyperarid conditions took hold in the Atacama Desert and the whole earth became cooler. This provided penguins, cormorants, boobies, and other cold-water-adapted species the chance to proliferate in Peruvian waters. All Pelicaniformes have large wings and are excellent fliers, with the marked exception of the flightless Galápagos cormorant (*Phalacrocorax harrisi*). Pelicaniformes are unique among birds in using the warmth of their feet to incubate their young. Their chicks are born exceptionally small and helpless, which greatly prolongs their parental dependence and increases the amount of guano deposited by nestlings in comparison to other birds.[5]

Since Robert Coker, scientists have recognized the *guanay* or Peruvian cormorant (*Phalacrocorax bougainvillii*, Lesson 1837) as Peru's most important guano birds. During the austral spring, male guanays establish dense nesting colonies, preferably on the windward slope of islands. Females take the lead in courting and engage in elaborate allopreening to establish bonds with their new mate – much like the behavior of Urpi Huachac described at the climax of the prologue. As in the origin myth of Isla Don Martín, females

---

[5] Johnsgard, *Cormorants, Darters, and Pelicans*, 3–5, 26, 107–8, 111, 115; Nunn, *Environmental Change in the Pacific Basin*, 98–99, 105–6; Marcelo Stucchi, "Los piqueros (Aves: Sulidae) de la Formación Pisco, Perú," *Boletín de la Sociedad Geológica del Perú* 95 (2003): 75–91; Thomas DeVries, "Oligocene Deposition and Cenozoic Sequence Boundaries in the Pisco Basin (Peru)," *Journal of South American Earth Sciences* 11 (1998): 217–31.

FIGURE 6.2. Piqueros, or Peruvian boobies on Pescadores Island, Peru. Francis Lee Jaques (1887–1969) painted these landscapes of the Central Coast of Peru based on field sketches he made in 1925 and 1935 while collecting materials for dioramas in the Hall of Oceanic Birds at the American Museum of Natural History in New York. Jaques created a total of 80 dioramas in museums across the United States. These exhibits enable city-bound people to obtain a glimpse of the earth's wilderness areas and biodiversity, and often promote wildlife conservation. *Source:* Murphy, *Oceanic Birds of South America*; reproduced courtesy of the American Museum of Natural History Research Library.

typically lay three eggs but raise two young during a single annual reproductive cycle lasting four months. Hatchlings instinctively defecate outside of the nest once they are able to stand, which gradually forms the distinctive crater-shaped ring of guano known in ancient times as *quillairaca* ("the moon's vagina"). Both adults and young tend to defecate in the vicinity of the nest.[6]

Guanays are a classic boom-or-bust species. Both members of a mating pair make at least one trip per day away from the colony to feed, but will eventually abandon their nests if they have to spend more than half of

[6] Johnsgard, *Cormorants, Darters, and Pelicans*, 10–11, 47–48, 52–53, 250–52; Humberto Tovar and Demósthenes Cabrera, *Conservación y manejo de aves guaneras* (Callao, 2005), 85, 87.

the daylight hours searching for food. They feed cooperatively in enormous rafts, usually landing on the surface above a school of fish, then diving down as far as twelve meters in search of prey – typically in the company of bonito, sea lions, and dolphins attacking from below. Based on the study of regurgitated bones, we know that an adult guanay will consume around 430 grams of fish each day when food is abundant. Guanays eat small schooling fish of several kinds and can adapt their feeding depending on availability, but they prefer to eat anchoveta (*Engraulis ringens*) and pejerrey (*Odontestes regia*). These small fish subsist almost entirely on sixty species of diatom, a class of photosynthetic phytoplankton at the base of the marine food chain. Most marine food chains have far more trophic levels than terrestrial food chains – a critical factor in determining the extraordinary abundance of anchoveta, guanays, and guano that Peru's marine environment is capable of producing. Female anchoveta reach sexual maturity after about one year and rarely live more than a couple years – they are also a classic boom-bust species. Both anchoveta and guanays are extremely sensitive to environmental variation. Even mild El Niño conditions can make fish difficult to find and cause increased adult and chick mortality. Extreme El Niño events have been known to kill 85 percent of the adult guanay population, but guanays have also been known to abandon their nests en masse in years with La Niña conditions when upwelling is strong but dispersed. During seasons of abundant food, they concentrate along the coast of Peru and northern Chile, but during years of scarcity, they may migrate as far as Panama and Tierra del Fuego.[7]

The second-most important guano-producing bird, the *piquero* or Peruvian booby (*Sula variegata*, Tschudi 1845) has a much higher reproductive rate than other boobies and gannets, which allows it to take rapid advantage of food abundance when upwelling conditions predominate. The piquero has a similar range to the guanay and may compete with it for nesting space. Nesting colonies of piqueros tend to be more tolerant of windless areas and heat stress, however, and many breed in solitary cliff-side nests. Piqueros subsist on the same fish species as the guanay but tend to feed in small bands, sometimes with flocks of guanays. They have buoyant air sacks in their bodies and cannot swim down for their prey. Instead, they hover in the air, then dive down abruptly to catch surface fish. This distinctive behavior is widely depicted in the ancient art of coastal peoples and provided inspiration for their Spanish common name, which means "lancer."[8]

The third-most important guano bird is the *alcatraz* or Peruvian pelican (*Pelecanus occidentalis thagus*, Molina 1782). Most taxonomists consider it

---

[7] Tovar and Cabrera, *Conservación y manejo de aves guaneras*, 81–86; Johnsgard, *Cormorants, Darters, and Pelicans*, 61–61, 68, 125–26, 248–52; Enrique Ávila to Mary Sears, 25 Apr. 1956, WHOI-MC9; *Inf.Inst.Mar* 6 (1965): 8–17, 25, 37.

[8] Tovar and Cabrera, *Conservación y manejo de aves guaneras*, 88–92; Johnsgard, *Cormorants, Darters, and Pelicans*, 125–26; Murphy, *Oceanic Birds*, 2:838–46.

to be a geographically distinct subspecies of the American brown pelican (*P. occidentalis occidentalis*) which is smaller in size and a harbinger of El Niño events along Peru's central coast. Similar to frigatebirds, they are supremely adapted for soaring, and only occasionally flap their wings to gain lift. Like piqueros, they forage for anchoveta and other small fish in bands or as solitary individuals, but they can feed efficiently either by plunging from the air or by scooping for fish while swimming on the surface. Their range corresponds closely to the guanay and piquero, but they will only nest in flat areas, are extremely skittish, and produce guano heavily mixed with detritus.[9] A handful of other marine bird species also produced usable quantities of guano historically. These include the tropical *camanay* or blue-footed booby (*Sula nebouxii*), which nests in significant numbers on the Lobos Islands, as well as the *potoyunco* or Peruvian diving petrel (*Pelecanoides garnotii*) and *pájaro niño* or Humboldt penguin (*Spheniscus humboldti*), which once nested in large numbers in burrows on the guano islands.[10]

With the formation of CAG in 1909, Peruvians established the bare bones of a technocratic apparatus to manage the guano industry, but it remained to be seen whether Peru's guano birds could be managed as "domestic animals" as its founders hoped. The most significant action taken by CAG during its early years involved protecting the guano birds from the guano industry itself. This was the key to CAG's initial success at increasing guano production. According to local tradition, vast numbers of young birds had been "driven to slaughter by wanton guano contractors in the old time purely [to get] them out of the way of the diggers." Following Henry Forbes's recommendation, CAG permanently stopped contracting out the guano harvest in 1914. This gave CAG far more control over the behavior of island workers. CAG also set harvest times to come after the end of peak nesting on each island. Nesting guanays eventually became acclimated to the presence of workers – even tolerating Caterpillar bulldozers and colonizing island buildings. Island trespassers collecting guano, eggs, or chicks also posed a significant threat to the guano birds. In 1914–15, CAG established year-round guardians at nine islands and three coastal locales, and gradually extended this network to encompass almost every major bird colony along the Peruvian coast. Their existence inspired lasting antagonism between CAG and local fishermen over access to the waters surrounding the guano islands, however. This evolved into a hateful rivalry, ultimately with catastrophic political consequences for the guano industry.[11]

[9] Tovar and Cabrera, *Conservación y manejo de aves guaneras*, 92–95; Johnsgard, *Cormorants, Darters, and Pelicans*, 15–16, 56, 60, 139–40, 387–97; Murphy, *Oceanic Birds*, 2:819, 822–25.

[10] Murphy, *Oceanic Birds*, 1:452–65, 2:773–79, 829–38.

[11] Murphy, *Bird Islands*, 278; MCAG 4 (1913): 53; 6 (1915): vii; 12 (1921): 84; 27 (1936), 180; 33 (1942): xliii; Tovar et al., "Monthly Population Size," 213–14.

CAG's activities had a negative impact on some coastal species, however. Island guards routinely hunted three birds to provide fresh meat for their sparsely provisioned tables: the potoyunco, the Humboldt penguin, and *chuita* or red-legged cormorant (*Phalacrocorax gaimardi*). Guano extraction also greatly disturbed the breeding of potoyuncos and penguins by removing the material they need to dig nesting burrows. These birds remained vulnerable to hunting and egg collecting and, in the case of penguins, to capture by the pet and zoo trades. Despite legal protections, the chuita is today classified as "near threatened" and the Humboldt penguin as "vulnerable." As recently as 1938, more than 100,000 potoyunco pairs bred on Isla Chañaral in Chile, but introduced foxes have since destroyed this colony. Ornithologists blame guano extraction for the potoyunco's disappearance most everywhere else. Today, the potoyunco only breeds in four known locations and is in immanent danger of extinction. These marine birds were unintended victims of the guano industry's success.[12]

CAG intentionally tried to rid natural enemies of the guano birds from Peru's coastal islands. The *simeón* or band-tailed gull (*Larus belcheri*), the *cleo* or kelp gull (*L. dominicanus*), the *pájaro ladrón* or Chilean skua (*Catharacta chilensis*), the *gallinazo* or turkey vulture (*Cathartes aura*), and the *buitre* or Andean condor (*Vultur gryphus*) all preyed on eggs, chicks, and dead birds and stole fish from the guano bird colonies. The *halcón real* or peregrine falcon (*Falco peregrinus*) caught adult guano birds on the wing. In 1915, in line with Forbes's recommendation, CAG began systematic extermination of these predatory birds and, in 1918, armed its entire force of island guardians to shoot them on sight. This was not wanton killing from CAG's point of view. There is abundant evidence that condors were capable of destroying small nesting colonies at the beginning of the breeding season. Robert Cushman Murphy (1887–1973), a New York scientist who spent several years studying Peru's marine birds, at first thought it "seemed criminal that sharpshooters...should be employed for the express purpose of killing such magnificent creatures as condors.[13] But after witnessing the damage that these birds had done" to a colony of guano birds in matter of days in 1919, his "sympathies inclined more toward the victims and the practical attitude of the guano administration." Because CAG was raising "defenseless" guano birds in "a system of more or less artificial culture," Murphy's moral calculus allowed these "veritable harpies" to be executed with little remorse. CAG directly credited the systematic destruction of the large condor

---

[12] Murphy, *Bird Islands*, 266–68, 276–77; Murphy, *Oceanic Birds*, 1:292–93, 453–54, 2:774–75, 778, 877; David Duffy et al., "The Conservation Status of Peruvian Seabirds," in *Status and Conservation of the World's Seabirds* (Cambriddge, 1984), 246, 253; *2008 IUCN Red List*.

[13] Murphy's given name suggests that he was a descendant of the Pilgrim Robert Cushman, but he has no confirmed ties to "emigrants" or "improvers" in the Cushman family line.

population around the Bahía de Independencia for enabling guanays to colonize Isla La Vieja in unprecedented numbers during the early 1950s, turning the island into CAG's most significant guano-producing territory.[14] Such campaigns against predatory animals were typical of wildlife management programs aimed at agricultural improvement elsewhere in the world during this era and in some cases resulted in extinctions. Fortunately for lovers of these majestic creatures, these campaigns were never extensive enough to greatly reduce the populations of these birds along the coast as a whole.[15]

The same cannot be said for Peru's once vast population of *lobos del mar* or sea lions (*Otaria flavescens*). These animals had long figured prominently in the livelihoods of coastal Peruvians. The ancient Moche and Chimu hunted and consumed sea lions but also revered them. Indigenous shamans greatly valued the healing power of stones recovered from their stomachs and believed that sea lions carried the souls of the dead to the Otherworld across the Pacific. Significantly, the coastal words for sea lion and the famous crescent knives used in coastal indigenous ritual were one and the same (*tumi*). Sea lion hides, meat, and oil continued to serve as important articles of trade and indigenous tribute during the colonial era.[16]

During the nineteenth century, North American hunters came close to exterminating the South American fur seal (*Arctocephalus australis*) and several other related species during their destructive sweep through the Pacific World in search of skins and oil. In the 1870s, these hunters redirected their attention to sea lions living along the Pacific coast of the Americas. Many parts of the lobos del mar were potentially valuable. Modern hunters typically used rifles to kill aggressive males but used clubs or lassos to kill females and their young to protect their hides, which were used to produce purses, gloves, hats, and other leather products. They cooked down blubber using charcoal and wood from coastal forests to supply a regional market for oil and lubricants. By far the most valuable parts of a sea lion were testicles, gall bladders, canine teeth, and whiskers, which were used in Chinese traditional medicine and as opium pipe cleaners. On occasion, their ligaments were used as sinews, and their meat salted or roasted for local sale or ground

[14] Murphy, *Bird Islands*, 88–89, 122–23, 204–6, 282–83, 287–89; Murphy, *Oceanic Birds*, 2:1013–16, 1052–71; *MCAG* 5 (1914): 88–91; 6 (1915): vii; 8 (1917): ix, 43–46; 9 (1918): 9; 44 (1953): iii–vi; Vogt journal, 5 May 1939, DPL-CONS76; Tovar and Cabrera, *Conservación y manejo de aves guaneras*, 96–97.

[15] Worster, *Nature's Economy*, ch. 13; Lance Van Sittert, "'Keeping the Enemy at Bay': The Extermination of Wild Carnivora in the Cape Colony, 1889–1910," *Environmental History* 3 (1998): 333–56; Brett Walker, "Meiji Modernization, Scientific Agriculture, and the Destruction of Japan's Hokkaido Wolf," *Environmental History* 9 (2004): 248–74; *2008 IUCN Red List*.

[16] Arriaga, *Extirpation of Idolatry*, 64; Izumi Shimada, *Pampa Grande and the Mochica Culture* (Austin, TX, 1994), 26, 46, 184; Garth Bawden, *The Moche* (Cambridge, MA, 1996), 66, 128, 161–63; Rostworowski, *Recursos naturales renovables*, 112–14; Julien, "Guano and Resource Control," 191, 223.

up for dog food or cattle feed. Hunters typically discarded almost everything but their hides and blubber, however – to the great benefit of condors and other scavengers – and sometimes only took away their snout and organs for trade with Chinese populations scattered around the Pacific World. By the 1890s, the sea lion hunt had already taken a major toll on Pacific rookeries north and south. Artisanal fishermen in Peru complained that the decline of the lobos affected the availability of fish. Many believed that "a working understanding" operated between lobos and the guano birds in which sea lions attacked schools of fish from below and herded them to the surface where birds and men could pick them off at will. Ornithologists have since confirmed that many species of marine birds depend on large undersea predators to help them find and capture prey. This folk understanding had a direct impact on modern Peruvian conservation policy. In 1896, the government banned lobos hunting, ostensibly to help the country's struggling fishing and guano industries.[17]

The advent of a new breed of conservation technocrat adhering to the "gospel of efficiency" dramatically altered the fate of Peru's lobos del mar. Robert Coker estimated that a few thousand could be hunted sustainably each year "under important and specified restrictions" that protected the species' ability to reproduce, leading President Leguía to reopen lobos hunting in 1910. Guano harvesters participated enthusiastically in the legalized hunt. In 1911, CAG employees officially killed 6,800 lobos; the Peruvian Corporation killed many times that number. Later that year, the guano birds abandoned their colonies en masse, causing guano production to plummet. Some congressional partisans blamed the lobos hunt for this disaster. In response, guano industry representatives argued that sea lions sometimes hunted young, unwary birds and competed directly with them for food. Following this logic, they advocated culling a quarter of the sea lion population along the Peruvian coast, and the total destruction of all sea lions and cetaceans in the vicinity of the Chincha Islands. In accord with the technocratic ideal, the Peruvian government appointed a naval scientist to study the issue. He concluded – wrongly as it turned out – that sea lions and guano birds ate fish of completely different size, and rejected the idea that sea lions assisted the feeding of guano birds. In his view, the hunt could continue: "Experience will tell us the number of lobos that can be hunted annually without causing the extinction of the species."[18]

Conservation science failed to provide clear guidelines for how the sea lion population should be managed. Over the next three decades, the Peruvian state handed out the monopoly concession to hunt sea lions to a series

---

[17] BMFom 5 (Dec. 1907): 64–95; MCAG 7 (1916): 78; BCAG 20 (1944): 122, 127; Murphy, *Bird Islands*, 79; Busch, *War against the Seals*, 200–4; Raúl Palacios Rodríguez, *Historia marítima del Perú* (Lima, 1991), bk. 12, vol. 2, p. 346.

[18] BMFom 5 (July 1907): 96; 5 (Dec. 1907): 64–95; MCAG 3 (1912): 3, 11, 45–54, 57; 7 (1916): 75–79; 8 (1917): ix, 43–46.

of parties, including CAG, but exercised no control over the number of animals killed, which could number more than 75,000 a year. The scale of this slaughter eventually attracted harsh criticism from Peru's budding conservation movement. In a 1940s book titled *Privilegios naturales del Perú*, physician Alberto González Zúñiga upbraided Peru's lobos hunters for "sowing terror with garrote in hand," thereby transforming the sea lions' "homes" into "concentration camps" and creating "a happy world for the birds of prey . . . the worst enemy of the guano birds." CAG scientists implored the Peruvian state to implement a management plan for the sea lions based on "scientific precaution" because "nobody knows if the lobo has some ecological value in the natural equilibrium of the life of the sea." This cause garnered furious opposition from industrial fishermen, who had come to see these animals as destructive pests that ate fish from their lines and became tangled in their nets.[19]

In 1950, the Peruvian government introduced a closed season to protect breeding animals from destruction, but the continuation of hunting, the rapid growth of industrial fishing, and the strong 1957–58 El Niño caused sea lion numbers to plummet. In November 1958, President Manuel Prado finally banned sea lion hunting altogether. The cessation of legal hunting allowed the population to recover gradually from a nadir of 8,000 in the early 1960s to about 35,000 in 1984. Under similar protection, the fur seal population recovered from a low of 4,000 to about 16,000 in 1984. Their numbers have continued to grow, but neither species is anywhere near its former abundance today, thanks to intense competition for food from Peru's gargantuan fishing industry.[20] Because Peru's sea lions had no lord protectors with a strong interest in their long-term conservation, sustained-yield management was never seriously considered an option by anyone who mattered politically. This points out a major shortcoming of scientific conservation: instrumental valuation will *never* protect wild creatures that do not have substantial utilitarian value to humans.[21]

Disciplining Workers, Serving Agribusiness

Guano digging has always depended on human muscle power – and still does, even today. Under CAG, it first involved backbreaking labor with pickaxes and crowbars to break up recently deposited guano, which was shoveled and then swept into burlap sacks to make sure every possible gram was harvested (fig. 6.3). The use of jute sacks connected Peruvian

---

[19] Erwin Schweigger to William Vogt, 25 May 1942, DPL-CONS76; *MCAG* 14 (1923): 25–26; 15 (1924): xxi, 89–90; 22 (1931): xiv; 25 (1934), xi, 179–81; *BCAG* 12 (1936): 340; 15 (1939): 397–99; 16 (1940): 296–97; 18 (1942): 40, 80–81, 111; 20 (1944): 119–35.

[20] *Pesca y caza* 9 (1959): 1–29; Belaúnde, *Legislación pesquera*, 283, 290, 294–95; P. Muck and H. Fuentes, "Sea Lion and Fur Seal Predation on the Peruvian Anchoveta, 1953 to 1982," in *The Peruvian Anchoveta and Its Upwelling Ecosystem* (Callao, 1987).

[21] Kohák, *Green Halo*, pt. 1.

FIGURE 6.3. Sweeping the guano islands clean, Isla Santa Rosa, May 1939. Over the years, CAG published dozens of photographs to propagandize its efforts to improve the lives of indigenous highlanders it employed. Working with bare feet made guano workers especially vulnerable to *garrapata* bites (an ectoparasite that infected the guano birds) and to skin infections caused by scratching. Note the presence of guanays calmly nesting in the background. *Source: BCAG* 15 (1939).

agroecosystems to fields of jute (*Corchorus* spp.) in British-ruled Bengal and burlap weavers in Scotland until the early 1950s, when Peru developed its own import-substituting source of Congo jute (*Urena lobata*) grown on floodplain fields in Amazonia. Guano workers continued to rely on burros, small railway cars, and cable trolleys to move guano around the islands, although CAG gradually supplemented this infrastructure with docks, roads for motorized tractors, and dozens of service buildings.[22]

The guano industry no longer imported coolie workers from East Asia. Instead, CAG recruited seasonal laborers from the Sierra through the

[22] Simón Rivero, "Peru Guards Its Guano as Demand Soars," *New York Times* 30 May 2008, online ed.; Murphy, *Bird Islands*, 96; Coker, "Peru's Wealth-Producing Birds," 562–64; *BCAG* 30 (1954): 28–30; Javier Arce-Nazario, "Human Landscapes Have Complex Trajectories: Reconstructing Peruvian Amazon Landscape History from 1948 to 2005," *Landscape Ecology* 22 (2007): 89–101.

enganche system, a form of debt peonage particular to the Andean region. CAG paid an agent (*enganchador*) to journey to the highlands to recruit indigenous male peasants with a cash advance. They then worked off the advance (typically at an interest rate of 20 to 30 percent) over four to nine months, and ideally made some extra cash to take back home, where they spent the remainder of the year growing food and herding animals with their families. Compared with seasonal jobs elsewhere, employment on the guano islands offered good pay and benefits, and many individuals returned year after year. In 1919, the year the eight-hour day became national law, CAG workers typically received S/.7.20 plus rations for working a 48-hour week. CAG raised its wages steadily over the years, although periods of rapid inflation tended to consume these gains.[23]

Living and working conditions on the guano islands were difficult, although they were a marked improvement over the guano age. During CAG's early days, most workers slept on the ground in beds and crude tents made from broken jute sacks and ate a spartan diet of cheap, dried foods. Labor activists often spoke out against these conditions, including the "epidemic" of houseflies (*Musca domestica*) that bred in human excrement left scattered over the islands by guano diggers. In response, CAG commissioned a series of physicians to visit the islands, recommend improvements, and provide free medical care to its workers. During the 1920s, CAG implemented a standard ration of fresh beef, rice, beans, bread or crackers, pasta, sugar, lard, and tea that provided more than enough calories, protein, fat, and iron to sustain a worker of small to medium frame undergoing heavy exertion.[24] These rations tended to skimp on vegetables and other fresh foods, however. Fresh, clean water was often in short supply on these dusty waterless islands, particularly for washing. As a consequence, dysentery and other gastric troubles were prevalent and guano workers sometimes suffered from scurvy, beriberi, and other vitamin deficiencies. Influenza, chronic bronchitis, and *vivax* malaria were the most common infectious illnesses that beset guano workers. Intervention by experts eventually led to the construction of hospitals, "scientifically prepared, hygienic habitations," and sports facilities on the islands. The fact that CAG was publicly owned forced it to be far more receptive than privately owned businesses in the region to populist pressure to improve working conditions.[25]

---

[23] Equal to US$0.31 per hour in 2007. *MCAG* 11 (1920), ix; "Resumen de los gastos y promedios," Dec. 1945, Feb. 1950, Dec. 1956, Dec. 1960, Dec. 1965, ACAG-Zona Norte, detailed in Cushman, "Lords of Guano," table 3; Macera, "Guano y la agricultura," 410–14, 470; Peter Blanchard, "The Recruitment of Workers in the Peruvian Sierra at the Turn of the Century: The Enganche System," *Inter-American Economic Affairs* 33 (1979): 63–83.

[24] Based on CAG ration lists and U.K. Department of Agriculture nutrient data and dietary recommendations.

[25] Murphy, *Bird Islands*, 341–42; *MCAG* 9 (1918): 12; 14 (1923): xv-xvi; 23 (1932): xvii; *BCAG* 1 (1925): 435–40, 487–88; 2 (1926): 47–51; 18 (1942): 343–401; 30 (1954):

This attention was not all positive from the workers' point of view. It also exposed them to the disciplinary zeal of hygienic reformers. Alcohol was strictly forbidden on the islands, and this prohibition sometimes extended to coca leaf chewing. Physicians also acquired the authority to inspect the fitness of all new employees and force them to purchase prophylactic drugs. Besides obsessing about defecation habits, physicians complained that the lonely, prison-like conditions of the guano islands caused frequent fights and "a lamentable confusion of instincts" among highlanders. This supposedly resulted in masturbation, sodomy, and the homosexual corruption of young workers. (For similar reasons, the British Phosphate Commission encouraged wives to accompany Pacific Islanders contracted to work in the phosphate mines of Banaba and Nauru.) In line with Taylorist principles of scientific management, CAG gradually developed an elaborate, written set of work standards and, during the 1940s, hired a new class of overseers (*tarjadores*) charged with quantifying the efficiency of guano production on each island and paying workers by task. CAG experienced occasional bouts of organized resistance on the guano islands. In the mid-1930s, the military government sent detachments of the Guardia Civil to keep order on the islands and publicly accused the Yungay newspaper *Adelante* of stirring up discontent. In the main, however, CAG's paternalistic, ameliorative approach toward labor relations kept a lid on worker unrest.[26]

From this economic base on the guano islands, CAG gradually built an integrated industry with near-monopoly control over most levels of fertilizer production, transport, and sale in Peru. As we saw in Chapter 5, the rulers of Peru's Aristocratic Republic created CAG to serve Peruvian agribusiness, but this reality did not prevent CAG technocrats from extending their authority to the use of guano on fields of crops. Through this and other avenues, CAG contributed mightily to the dissemination of technological innovation, scientific knowledge, a rationalist spirit, and input-intensive practices within Peruvian agriculture in ways that paralleled or even anticipated industrializing trends in agriculture elsewhere in the Americas.[27]

CAG's most important innovation in the realm of distribution involved standardizing the price of each bag of guano. As we saw in Chapter 2, guano sales were highly susceptible to fraud. A port official approved by CAG and the National Agrarian Society removed samples from every sack of guano that reached the mainland and sent them to CAG's central laboratory for assay. Farmers purchased guano on credit and later paid a standard price

16–20; Vogt journal, 5 May 1939, DPL-CONS76 3/1; photograph by Vogt, Aug. 1939, DPL-CONS76 4/1.

[26] *BCAG* 2 (1926): 37, 39–41, 45, 48–49, 51–52; *MCAG* 26 (1935): v; Guido Razetto, "Rendimiento y costos de las areas," 22 Sept. 1969, and similar documents in ACAG-Zona Norte; Macera, "Guano y la agricultura," 418–20, 471.

[27] Cf. Fitzgerald, *Every Farm a Factory*.

set by Peru's central government based on the average nitrogen content of each allotment. An impersonal standard set by faraway technocrats thus supplanted the face-to-face negotiation of the marketplace that had once determined the sale value of guano. This anticipated the kind of state interventions in agricultural pricing that came to predominate Latin America during the mid-twentieth century, and contrasts with the privately owned futures markets and cartels typical of North American and international systems of agricultural trade.[28]

When they were not busy analyzing guano samples, José Antonio de Lavalle and other CAG technicians also performed free fertilizer, soil, water, plant disease, and pesticide analyses for farmers at three regional laboratories or during field expeditions. By law, CAG provided special discounts and loans to farmers for using guano and other agrichemicals, especially to food producers and smallholders. In 1925, Lavalle regularized CAG's publication of technical pamphlets by establishing an illustrated magazine to "instruct farmers in a simple manner on the principles of... soil types and the application of guano." Several hundred copies of this *Boletín* were circulated free-of-charge, each month, to Peruvian farmers, scientists, and engineers, as well as to agricultural schools and extension services throughout the Americas. It was published continuously until the late 1960s – a remarkable achievement for a technical periodical in Latin America. These publications provided a vital public outlet for agricultural and environmental research in Peru, and they constantly reminded farmers that much of their crop productivity derived from marine birds. This bucked the international trend toward the abstraction of commodities from their original ecological context that is so characteristic of modern systems of production, trade, and consumption.[29]

Large-scale agribusiness in Peru reaped enormous benefits from all this. During CAG's first decades, only a handful of companies consumed the overwhelming majority of guano produced by CAG. Tens of thousands of small farmers bought guano by the bag, but a mere 567 companies were responsible for nine-tenths of CAG's sales from 1909 to 1935. Of this number, the 25 largest purchasers consumed half of the excrement Peru's guano birds produced during those years. These purchasers constitute a who's-who list of influential families and multinational corporations in early-twentieth-century Peru, a pattern that reflects the concentration of coastal land

---

[28] *MCAG* 14 (1923): 55–57; Macera, "Guano y la agricultura," 420–26, 435–40. Cf. Steven Topik, *The Political Economy of the Brazilian State, 1889–1930* (Austin, 1987), ch. 3; William Cronon, *Nature's Metropolis: Chicago and the Great West* (New York, 1991), ch. 3.

[29] *MCAG* 3 (1912): 59; 12 (1921): 15; 13 (1922): 14; 14 (1923): xiii–xv, 11; 17 (1926): xvi–xviii; 20 (1929): xiv, xvi; 23 (1932): v, xiv; *BCAG* 1 (1925): 1–10; 2 (Nov. 1926): 592–606; Ávila to Vogt, 23 July 1945, DPL-CONS76 1/1; Macera, "Guano y la agricultura," 423–24.

TABLE 6.1. *Principal Guano Consumers in Peru, 1909–1935*

Plantation (Owner circa 1914, Region)	Consumption (rank/ metric tons/percentage)		
Casa Grande & Sausal (Gildemeister & Co., Chicama)	1.	141,352	8.4
Cartavio (W. R. Grace & Co., Chicama)	2.	72,490	4.3
Paramonga (Sociedad Agrícola Paramonga, Supe)[a]	3.	48,413	2.9
Pomalca y Collud (Gutiérrez brothers, Lambayeque)	4.	44,466	2.6
Tumán y Calupe (Pardo family, Lambayeque)	5.	43,148	2.6
Chiclín (Larco Herrera brothers, Chicama)	6.	41,687	2.5
Cayaltí (Aspíllaga brothers, Lambayeque)	7.	39,546	2.4
Laredo (José Ignacio Chopitea, Moche)[b]	8.	38,067	2.3
San Nicolás (Barreda y Laos family, Supe)[c]	9.	37,525	2.2
Infantas (Sociedad Agrícola Infantas, Lima)	10.	28,186	1.7
Humaya (Sociedad Agrícola Humaya, Huaura)	11.	26,920	1.6
San Benito (Nosiglia brothers, Cañete)	12.	26,387	1.6
Santa Bárbara (British Sugar Co., Cañete)	13.	25,968	1.5
San Jacinto (British Sugar Co., Chimbote)[c]	14.	25,923	1.5
Tambo Real (Peruvian Sugar Est., Chimbote)	15.	24,086	1.4
Chiquitoy (Larco Herrera brothers, Chicama)	16.	23,938	1.4
Esquivel y Retes (del Solar brothers, Chancay)	17.	22,504	1.3
Hualcará (Felipe Espantoso, Cañete)	18.	20,508	1.2
Unánue (Luis Larraburre, Cañete)	19.	20,090	1.2
Roma (Víctor Larco Herrera, Chicama)[b]	20.	19,058	1.1
Palpa (Empresa Agrícola Palpa, Chancay)	21.	16,820	1.0
Pátapo y Tulipe (Cía. Agrícola Chiclayo, Lambayeque)	22.	16,312	1.0
Herbay Alto (Sociedad Agrícola Herbay Alto, Cañete)	23.	14,801	0.9
Huando (Antonio Graña, Chancay)	24.	12,763	0.8
Montalván (Reynaldo Luza, Cañete)[c]	25.	12,654	0.8
Total guano *rico* consumption:		1,686,009	50.2

[a] Later purchased by W. R. Grace & Co.
[b] Later purchased by Gildemeister & Co.
[c] Later operated by Pedro and Felipe Beltrán Espantoso.
Source: "Anexos: Detalle de la distribución y venta del guano," *MCAG* 5, 26 (1914, 1935); Gonzales, *Plantation Agriculture*, 26–33, 45–51; Thorp and Bertram, *Peru 1890–1977*, 360 n. 10; Cushman, "Lords of Guano," app. 8.

ownership and political power in the hands of a few (table 6.1). The largest single guano purchasers were sugar plantations, although a few large estates cultivating Tangüis cotton also show up on this list. Taxes charged on each bag of guano went directly to a number of coastal development projects, and provided a major source of income for the National Agricultural Society, Peruvian agribusiness's main lobbying group. The Peruvian state further subsidized the expansion of input-intensive agriculture by building vast new irrigation and highway networks with loans underwritten by guano sales. Agribusinessmen owning shares of CAG also received dividends directly from the guano industry. All told, CAG produced a profit for its investors from 1909 to 1963 amounting to US$435 million in 2007 dollars. CAG was profitable even though it sold fertilizer at prices far below what the market would bear. From this perspective alone, Peru's guano birds more than lived up to their new reputation as "the most valuable birds in the world."[30]

Guano also helped Peruvian agribusinessmen recover quickly from the Great Depression. CAG slashed the prices it charged after the Great Crash and made arrangements to provide easy credit for fertilizer purchases. This paved the way for the establishment of the Banco Agrícola in 1936, an institution that dramatically improved the availability of rural credit in Peru. Growers of Tangüis cotton consumed the overwhelming majority of cheap fertilizer, irrigation water, and credit made available by the Peruvian state during the 1930s. This miracle strain represented only 8.1 percent of national cotton production in 1918, but increased to a peak of 92.9 percent in 1937. During the boom of the 1930s, cotton monoculture gobbled up thousands of coastal hectares that had once been devoted to food crops, forage, or natural desert and riparian vegetation; it provided a living to approximately half of Peru's coastal population; and it consumed more guano than all other Peruvian crops put together.[31] These far-reaching changes paralleled those brought about by the introduction of new sugar cane and banana varieties elsewhere in the Tropics and foreshadowed those associated with the Green Revolution after World War II. Plantation agriculture in places like Peru thus contributed mightily to the birth of what we now call "conventional" input-intensive agriculture.[32]

Coping with Resistance

An agroecological perspective on history warns us that a monoculture so dependent on one crop and a single source of fertilizer is highly vulnerable to disruption. In struggling against ecological and social resistance to the progress of the guano industry, CAG technocrats became acutely aware

---

[30] Cushman, "Lords of Guano," fig. 7, app. 4; *Estatutos de la Compañía Administradora del Guano* (Lima, 1923), 17, 32–33, 73, 76–83; *MCAG* 3 (1912): 18–19; 4 (1913): vii; 14 (1923): 55–57; 34 (1943): v–vi; 50 (1959): xiii; Macera, "Guano y la agricultura," 460–61.

[31] Cushman, "Lords of Guano," app. 1–7, fig. 3–6; *MCAG* 22 (1931): xiv; 23 (1932): v, ix, 207; 24 (1933): vii; 27 (1936): ix; *MCAG* 29 (1938): vii; Macera, "Guano y la agricultura," 433–34, 438; Thorp and Bertram, *Peru 1890–1977*, 54–59, 170–77; Cueto and Lossio, *Inovación en la agricultura*, ch. 5; Peloso, *Peasants on Plantations*, ch. 6.

[32] McCook, *States of Nature*; Soluri, *Banana Cultures*.

of the strength and complexity of the forces that govern the economy of nature. In the process, they taught the world of the existence of the El Niño phenomenon and demonstrated both the utility and limitations of the technocratic approach to ecosystem management.

We have already learned of several instances when El Niño and La Niña influenced historical events in the Pacific World. A quantitative reconstruction of El Niño and La Niña event intensities is reproduced in fig. 5.1. It shows an obvious tendency for guano production to rise when La Niña conditions prevailed and to decline after strong El Niño events. "El Niño" first became a scientific category during the 1890s when Peruvian scientists attached this name to a warm ocean current that occasionally runs counter to the cool, north-flowing Peru Current along the far northern coast of Peru. In 1891, torrential rains and catastrophic floods struck many parts of the country and captured the attention of a group of professionals belonging to the newly founded Geographical Society of Lima. As a result of this regional tradition of scientific research, CAG scientists were well aware that the "El Niño countercurrent" was a recurrent event that influenced a broad range of anomalous environmental phenomena.[33]

Peruvian scientists were never content to simply blame problems on El Niño, however. As we saw in Chapter 5, the appearance of "sinister ocean currents" off the Peruvian coast in 1911–12 gravely threatened CAG's early survival. A similar die-off took place in March 1917. These events inspired José Antonio de Lavalle to give systematic attention to the connection between changes in the coastal climate, the prevalence of disease, and the welfare of Peru's guano birds. His interest in the environmental determinants of bird sickness and health grew directly from another tradition of scientific excellence in Peru – biomedicine. Lavalle was a veteran of struggles against cotton wilt and foot-and-mouth disease in Peru, and he shared the widespread belief that tropical medicine would soon conquer the worst diseases of the region.[34] A third of the guanays that Lavalle dissected in 1917 had infections of *Aspergillus fumigatus* in their lungs, a genus of fungi that feeds on decaying organic matter. Aspergillosis had been widely studied by veterinary scientists during the nineteenth century as a disease of domestic and wild fowl, and was understood to be a classic environmental illness caused by poor hygiene. Lavalle concluded that heat and humidity associated with the El Niño countercurrent were responsible for causing a mass outbreak of disease affecting the guano birds. As a precautionary

---

[33] Cushman, "Enclave Vision: Foreign Networks in Peru and the Internationalization of El Niño Research during the 1920s," *History of Meteorology* 1 (2004): 65.

[34] *MCAG* 3 (1912): 51–56; Lavalle, "Fiebre aftosa ad portas," *La Prensa*, 28 Oct. 1910; Lavalle, "Medidas sanitarias contra la fiebre aftosa," *La Prensa*, 1 Dec. 1910; Cueto, *Return of the Epidemics*; Cueto, *Excelencia científica en la periferia: Actividades científicas e investigación biomédica en el Perú, 1890–1950* (Lima, 1989).

measure, he recommended burning all bird corpses, killing all sick birds, and sanitizing the islands with disinfectant soap and hot water after each harvest. (Scientists have since come to view aspergillosis as a disease caused by malnourishment or some other cause that depresses the immune system. Aspergillis is a prominent cause of illness among advanced AIDS sufferers and fan corals in the Caribbean stressed by global warming. The 1917 die-off actually took place during a powerful La Niña event.)[35]

Lavalle also made a careful study of bird nesting practices and learned that guanays tend to favor locations with few surface rocks that are exposed to prevailing winds. Rocks provided shelter for blood-sucking ticks or *garrapatas* (*Ornithidorus amblus*), which feasted on both guano birds and guano diggers. Lavalle suspected these arthropods served as vectors for some sort of infectious disease. Similar research elsewhere in Latin America had led to the discovery that insects spread yellow fever and malaria in humans and mosaic disease in sugar cane – microbial diseases that could be attacked by systematically altering the environmental conditions favoring their vectors. Lavalle's hypothesis gave CAG workers yet another reason to remove surface stones from the islands, a policy that appeared to result in spectacular increases in the size of nesting colonies in some locales.[36]

Peruvian researchers never discovered a vector that causes disease in guano birds, but they did make some groundbreaking discoveries regarding the guano islands' smallest inhabitants. During the autumn of 1923, another El Niño year, Peru's guano birds once again abandoned their nesting colonies en masse and died in large numbers. CAG officials gave several sick guanays to the Municipal Institute of Hygiene in Lima's Exposition Park for study. From these birds, Peruvian bacteriologist Julio Gastiaburú (1881–1960) isolated the first wild instance of the organism that causes avian cholera ever detected by the global scientific community. This "virulent, usually fatal and highly infectious disease" was greatly feared by poultry raisers and received abundant scientific attention during the nineteenth century – most famously from microbiologist Louis Pasteur. Gastiaburú's discovery had frightening implications. He and other Peruvian experts were acutely aware of the

[35] CEI; *MCAG* 8 (1917): 61–63, 82–88; Raymond Pearl et al., *Diseases of Poultry* (New York, 1915), 173–77; Gary Wobeser, *Diseases of Wild Waterfowl* (New York, 1981), 87–94; R. A. Kunkle, "Aspergillosis" in *Diseases of Poultry*, by Y. M. Saif et al. (Malden, MA, 2003), 883–95; Kiho Kim and Drew Harvell, "Rise and Fall of a Six-Year Coral-Fungal Epizootic," *American Naturalist* 164 (Nov. 2004): S52–63.

[36] *MCAG* 8 (1917): ix; 9 (1918): 207–13; 12 (1921): 11; *BCAG* 1 (1925): 77–89, 475–77; 2 (1926): 49–51; Vogt journal, 11 Feb. 1939, 5 May 1939, DPL-CONS76 3/1; Nancy Stepan, "The Interplay between Socio-Economic Factors and Medical Science: Yellow Fever Research, Cuba and the United States," *Social Studies of Science* 8 (1978): 397–423; Paul Sutter, "Nature's Agents or Agents of Empire?: Entomological Workers and Environmental Change during the Construction of the Panama Canal," *Isis* 98 (2007): 724–54; McCook, *States of Nature*, ch. 4.

devastation that plague, influenza, rinderpest, and hoof-and-mouth disease had wrought among human and livestock populations in recent decades. The discovery of a poultry disease this virulent among wild birds meant that the guano industry was similarly vulnerable to collapse. In response to this threat, CAG prohibited the keeping of poultry on the guano islands. As it turned out, they had good reason for concern: a fowl cholera epidemic killed an estimated two million birds along the northern coast of Chile in 1951.[37]

A far more destructive environmental upheaval struck Peru in 1925. In northern sugar-growing districts, torrential rains washed out cemeteries, caved in adobe buildings, undermined railways, clogged ports with silt, and turned vast areas into stagnant lakes, leading to malaria and dysentery outbreaks. Floods descending from the highlands caused similar damage to the cotton-growing districts of Ica and Piura, notwithstanding the existence of new flood-control structures designed by Charles Sutton. Lima also experienced rainstorms – an extreme rarity, even during El Niño events. Not just the coast was affected by this powerful El Niño event. On the northeastern slope of the Andes, the indigenous residents of Uchucmarca saw most of their village disappear beneath a massive landslide (*huaico*) and begged unsuccessfully for government permission to move their town to a safer location. Potable water was nearly impossible to come by in many areas, and a few towns experienced brief famines when their crops and stores were destroyed and they were cut off from the outside world. All told, disastrous weather affected at least a dozen of Peru's twenty-five departments, from Tumbes in the far north, to Tacna in the far south, to Madre de Dios in the Amazon Basin.[38]

This natural disaster severely affected the agroecological system that CAG managed on almost every level. The guano birds abandoned their nesting colonies and guano production plummeted. To make matters worse, rainfall caused direct damage to deposits on northern islands. Many agribusinessmen, already stressed by the volatility of export crop prices after World War I, could not afford to plant after the storms, much less to buy fertilizer. Like always, a few opportunists found ways to benefit. Gildemeister and W. R. Grace again used their advantageous access to international finance to buy out bankrupt neighbors, as they had at the end of the guano age – this time to become the undisputed kings of sugar production in Peru. Vultures and condors had a field day on drowned corpses. On the other hand, traditional

---

[37] *MCAG* 15 (1924): 94–108; *BCAG* 1 (1925): 93–108; 10 (1934): 271–74; 10 (1934): 43–44; Ávila to Sears, 2 Aug. 1951, WHOI-MC9; Bustíos, *Cuatrocientos años de la salud pública*, 492–94; Pearl et al., *Diseases of Poultry*, 102–10; John Glisson et al., "Fowl Cholera," in *Diseases of Poultry*, by Saif et al., 658–75; Wobeser, *Diseases of Wild Waterfowl*, 47–59.

[38] AMFom 294/5434 (1924–25); 5/1365, 196/3356–3360, 197/3403–3411, 217/3904, 218/3908–3923 (1925); 202/3580 (1925–26); *BCAG* 2 (1926): 171–72; 3 (1927): 371–72; 4 (1928): 585–601; Stephen Brush, *Mountain, Field, and Family: The Economy and Human Ecology of an Andean Valley* (Philadelphia, 1977), 33, 52.

farmers in the North Coast Department of Piura took advantage by harvesting rain-fed crops from desert sands, fattening cattle on wild vegetation, and hunting ducks that descended on ephemeral lakes – just like they always had during similar "years of abundance" along the far northern coast.[39]

Regional scientists put their heads together to try to delineate the causes of this far-reaching disaster. Foreign technicians working for Gildemeister and the International Petroleum Company set up marine observatories to track the event's development. Gastiaburú repeated his bacteriological investigations of 1923 and declared that avian cholera was responsible for the deaths of most adult guano birds in 1925. But others were not so sure. Robert Cushman Murphy also happened to be in the country doing research on marine birds when the warm "El Niño countercurrent" made its appearance. It dramatically affected the behavior of a broad range of organisms, including a rare flock of tropical sooty terns seen near the Bahía de Independencia. Murphy interpreted this as a signal that El Niño affected a vast region of the eastern tropical Pacific: "Within a few days after the sight record, indeed, temperatures of unparalleled warmth characterized this littoral. It is extremely interesting and suggestive that Sooty Terns should be among the organisms which serve as accompaniments, *or even precursors*, of such profound cyclic oceanographic phenomena."[40] Murphy transmitted all these observations to scientists in the United States who reported them, in turn, to meetings of the Pan-Pacific Science Congress in Japan and the Dutch East Indies. In this way, the international scientific community came to recognize that Peru's El Niño was part of a periodic ecological upheaval capable of affecting the entire Pacific World. The events of 1925 also led Lavalle to a new interpretation of volatility in guano production that modified his earlier emphasis on epidemics. He came to believe that the inflow of tropical waters during El Niño years made it difficult for Peru's guano birds to locate schools of anchoveta, their main source of food. With little to eat, they became highly vulnerable to heat exhaustion, parasites, disease, and outright starvation, leading many birds to abandon the Peruvian coast for greener waters to the south. Lavalle's hypothesis has endured years of scientific scrutiny, but few international scientists are aware of his contribution because Murphy neglected to credit him – or any native Peruvian, for that matter – in his foreign publications.[41]

---

[39] *MCAG* 16 (1925): xiii, 41; 17 (1926): vi, ix, xv–xvi; 18 (1927): ii; *BCAG* 1 (1925): 91; 2 (1926): 176; 3 (1927): 369, 371, 377–78; Klarén, *Modernization*, 16, 18–20; cf. Víctor Eguiguren, "Las lluvias en Piura," *Boletín de la Sociedad Geográfica de Lima* 4 (1894): 241–57.

[40] Emphasis added; Murphy, *Oceanic Birds*, 2:1132.

[41] *BCAG* 1 (1925): 91–93, 477; 2 (1926): 137–38; Murphy, "Oceanic and Climatic Phenomena along the West Coast of South America during 1925," *The Geographical Review* 17 (1926): 26, 32, 35 n. 9, 48, 53; Cushman, "Enclave Vision."

CAG officials acted aggressively on these findings to extend their technocratic authority over Peru's coastal environment. Lavalle's hypothesis
had profound implications for CAG's already troubled relationship with
Peruvian fishermen. The Peruvian state had long sought to regulate coastal
fishing. In 1822, the newly declared republic required fishermen to register
with the government, and in 1884, it banned dynamite fishing, known collo-
quially as the "American net" (*chinchorro americano*). Beginning in 1909,
the Peruvian government passed a series of laws limiting the activities of
fishing fleets in the vicinity of guano islands to protect nesting guano birds
from disturbance. During the mid-1920s, the Port Authority of Callao even
experimented with the use of closed seasons (*vedas*) and rotational fishing
zones in order to protect rare species of fish.[42]

Enforcing these regulations was a far more difficult matter. As we saw in
Chapter 5, the technocrats who ran Peru's Coastal Irrigation Service often
butted heads with local *sargentos de agua* who had different ideas about
what constituted just distribution of water. The same was true of fishing.
Local law enforcement in fishing communities during this era – where it
existed – depended on local deputies of Peru's Maritime Authority known
as *sargentos de playa*. Like *sargentos de agua*, they were appointed by local
communities and used their authority to distribute political patronage and to
protect traditional notions of human rights and responsibilities toward the
natural world. During the 1910s and early 1920s, Peru's Maritime Authority tended to give preference to traditional uses of the sea in the vicinity
of the guano islands, despite repeated protests that they were undermin-
ing the rule of law in the country. CAG's guardians were also hesitant to
denounce trespassers. Fishermen were the guardians' only source of goods
and companionship during much of the year, and some guardians derived
from fishing communities. Fishermen were also likely to win in the case of a
violent conflict at these lone outposts.[43] These issues underscore a perennial
problem with nature sanctuaries. Conservation programs only work effectively if local peoples benefit in some way from their existence. Otherwise,
these programs are bound to generate resentment, resistance, even revolt
among locals toward police enforcement.[44]

[42] Belaúnde, *Legislación pesquera*, 336–37; Palacios, *Historia marítima*, bk. 12, vol. 2, pp.
331, 340, 342; CAG, *Estatutos*, 47, 49–50, 55, 61–64; MCAG 14 (1923): 20–23; 15 (1924):
79–82.
[43] MCAG 11 (1920): 41–42; 12 (1921): 54–57; 13 (1922): 69–73; 14 (1923): 15–20; 15
(1924): 71–74; 17 (1926): xxii; BCAG 1 (1925): 340–41; Eugene Hammel and Ynez Haase,
A Survey of Peruvian Fishing Communities (Berkeley and Los Angeles, 1962), 212; John
Gillin, *Moche: A Peruvian Coastal Community* (Washington, DC, 1947), 28–37.
[44] Stephan Amend and Thora Amend, eds., *National Parks without People?: The South American Experience* (Quito, 1995); Guha, *Unquiet Woods*; Simonian, *Defending the Land of the
Jaguar*; Louis Warren, *The Hunter's Game: Poachers and Conservationists in Twentieth-
Century America* (New Haven, 1997); Jacoby, *Crimes against Nature*.

The great El Niño of 1925 dramatically changed the legal climate affecting marine fishing. CAG redoubled its attempts to obtain meaningful enforcement of laws designed to protect the sanctuary and subsistence of the guano birds. In October 1928, President Leguía gave CAG permission to organize its own Fishing Police. With the help of three high-speed motorboats custom-built in Europe, CAG's police force dramatically increased the rate at which fishermen were detained and prosecuted for breaking the law – and criminalized the traditional activities of a significant segment of Peru's coastal population in the process. CAG also endeavored to place fishery management under technocratic administration. To this end, CAG hired a German fishery scientist, Erwin Schweigger, to explore ways to improve fishing education, regulation, and practices in Peru. The overthrow of Leguía by populist military officers in 1930 brought an abrupt end to this despised experiment in maritime policing, and fishermen quickly returned to their old fishing grounds around the guano islands.[45]

Where parasites, El Niño, and fish were concerned, CAG technocrats reached abrupt limits to their totalitarian aspirations to control the agroecological system surrounding the production and consumption of guano in Peru. In the process, they created deep enmity between Peruvian fishermen and the guano industry that had tragic long-term consequences for the guano birds. Resistance, however, only made the guano industry's managers more dedicated to the idea that scientific research was capable of solving their administrative problems. This eventually led them to acquire the services of one of the most important conservation scientists of the twentieth century.

The Lord of the Guanays

After the brief upset caused by the 1925 El Niño, Peruvian guano production rebounded to its highest levels since the guano age. But guano's popularity among growers of Tangüis cotton during the 1930s turned out to be too much of a good thing. CAG technocrats worked desperately to maintain the agroecological system they had built, and campaigned tirelessly to promote efficient use of this scarce resource. By 1938, however, CAG could only fulfill half of total requests, a turn of events that forced some grumbling farmers to buy nitrates from Chile to make up for the fertilizer shortfall. CAG's existence had always been controversial, and it became a lightning rod for criticism under these conditions, even though by most measures it was flourishing.[46]

---

[45] CAG, *Estatutos*, 51–52; MCAG 16 (1925): xv, 30–38; 17 (1926): xv–xvi; 19 (1928): 248–53; 19 (1929): 248–62; 22 (1931): 227–34, 276–80; MCAG 23 (1932): 217–31; 25 (1934): xi, 172–76; 26 (1935): xiii, 269–70.

[46] MCAG 26 (1935): v, 237, 244–45, 339; 27 (1936): vii, ix, xvi, 183; 29 (1938): vii, ix, 240; 30 (1939): iv, vi–vii, 50–55; BCAG 11 (1935): 511; 17 (1941): 3–5.

The Peruvian state turned to a new generation of technocrats to fix these problems. In 1936, General Oscar Benavides (president 1914–15, 1933–39) hired Carlos Alayza y Roel to audit CAG's entire operations. Alayza was a mining engineer who had made a career as a mediator of labor conflicts at Peru's highland mines. He enthusiastically endorsed CAG's guano rationing policy and called for stepped-up enforcement of its conversation procedures, including the revival of the Fishing Police. At this juncture, CAG brought in two foreign scientists to study ways to manipulate the productivity of Peru's marine environment. It rehired Erwin Schweigger as its resident oceanographer and tried to convince Robert Cushman Murphy, the world's undisputed authority on the marine birds of South America, to resume his studies under CAG's auspices, but Murphy was busy serving as president of the National Association of Audubon Societies. In his stead, he recommended a fellow birder from New York City, his friend William Vogt (fig. 5.2). Few people in the world were better qualified to take on the tasks that CAG gave him.[47]

Vogt's three-year sojourn in Peru marked a turning point in the history of environmental management in Peru. His holistic study of the ecology of Peru's guano birds represents an astounding application of advances in ecological theory to practical problems, but the historical importance of this journey extended far beyond Peru's borders. It fundamentally changed the trajectory of Vogt's career as a conservation organizer and ecological thinker. As later chapters show, no single figure was more influential in framing Malthusian overpopulation of humans as an ecological problem – an idea that became one of the pillars of modern environmental thought. We can trace this tendency straight back to Vogt's experience watching Peru's guano birds die during the El Niño of 1939–41.

To understand the pivotal significance of Vogt's time in Peru, it is necessary to detail Vogt's little-known career as a bird enthusiast before he arrived. He was born in Mineola, New York, in the midst of the Hempstead Plains at a time when that part of Long Island was mostly open grassland and people still remembered seeing the now-extinct heath hen. It greatly pained him, later in life, to see this easternmost stronghold of the Great American Prairie paved over to build airports and suburban developments like Levittown. His family moved to Brooklyn in 1914, but family vacations in the wild Adirondacks provided him with opportunities to escape from the big city. He was permanently handicapped when he contracted polio on a Boy Scout field trip during the great epidemic of 1916, but Vogt never allowed his physical condition to prevent him from trekking through the rough in search of his life's passion – wild birds.[48]

---

[47] *BCAG* 11 (1935): 556–57; 12 (1936): 155–63; *MCAG* 29 (1938), xiv; 30 (1939), 64–65; *Diccionario histórico y biográfico*, s.v. "Alayza y Roel, Carlos."

[48] "Some Notes on WV," n.d., DPL-CONS76 5/1; Robert Askins and Julie Zickefoose, *Restoring North America's Birds: Lessons from Landscape Ecology* (New Haven, 2002), 6–7, 19–21.

Vogt was in the vanguard of North American ornithology during the 1930s. His activities exemplified the links between avocational bird watching, scientific research, and conservation activism that developed during this period. Vogt first got to know Roger Tory Peterson and other famous birders at the American Museum of Natural History and during excursions with the Bronx County Bird Club. In 1930, while counting ducks along the Hudson, Vogt offered to help Peterson compile his bird drawings into a book. This became *A Field Guide to the Birds* (1934), the first of the celebrated Peterson Field Guide series, which contributed enormously to U.S. interest in birding and to growing public concern about these creatures. Meanwhile, Vogt acquired his first experience in wildlife management as director of the Jones Beach State Bird Sanctuary on Long Island, a reserve attached to the rustic-styled state park built by New York City Parks Commissioner Robert Moses. Vogt never acquired formal scientific training. Instead, he nurtured his scientific credentials in apprenticeship to Ernst Mayr and other scientists employed by the American Museum of Natural History. In accord with Mayr's dictum that even amateur birders "should have a problem" to research, Vogt took to observing the behavior and ecological relationships of a Jones Beach shorebird, the eastern willet (*Catoptrophorus semipalmatus*) and won the 1938 Linnaean Prize for Ornithological Research for his work.[49] In 1934, the National Association of Audubon Societies purchased the journal *Bird-Lore* and made Vogt its editor. With Peterson's assistance as illustrator, Vogt gave the magazine a complete face lift and turned it into one of the era's most forward-thinking platforms for conservation advocacy. However, Vogt's zeal eventually brought him into open conflict with the executive director of the Audubon Societies, and he found himself jobless and in the hospital suffering from "nervous exhaustion" at the opportune moment when CAG was looking to hire an ornithologist. From a myopic Americanist point of view, Vogt's time in Peru was "his Elba," but it actually turned Vogt into a conservationist of global stature.[50]

On the last day of January 1939, a patrol launch from CAG's Fishing Police brought Vogt to the guano islands for the first time. He immediately began implementing a multiyear research program that was on the cutting edge of several scientific disciplines. To track nesting mortality and bird migration, he organized the first large-scale bird-banding program in Peruvian history. He and his assistants also established several island meteorological observatories and introduced the use of aerial photographs for counting nesting birds. Vogt hoped that these efforts would enable him to

[49] "Some Notes on WV"; *Who Was Who in American History* (Chicago, 1976), s.v. "Vogt, William"; John Devlin and Grace Naismith, *The World of Roger Tory Peterson* (New York, 1977), 62–66; Graham, *Audubon Ark*, 133–34; Mark Barrow, *A Passion for Birds: American Ornithology after Audubon* (Princeton, NJ, 1998), ch. 7–8.

[50] Margaret Morse Nice to Vogt, 9 Dec. 1937, DPL-CONS76 1/2; contra Graham, *Audubon Ark*, 117–18, 142–44.

estimate the future guano bird population using the latest mathematical laws of population growth.[51] Vogt was also deeply familiar with revolutionary work in the field of ethology – the study of animal behavior in the field. During the late 1930s, he worked closely with several of the discipline's founding figures including Mayr, G. K. Noble, Margaret Morse Nice, and Niko Tinbergen. Building on his work with willets, Vogt implemented the "phenomenological" method of field research pioneered by Nice and Tinbergen, and he gave sustained attention to bird territoriality and "releaser" mechanisms for specific behaviors.[52] Vogt was also influenced by plant ecologist Frederic Clements's insight that all ecological communities tend toward a "climax" state of maximum productivity determined by the climate of a region. Vogt was not a prisoner to the steady-state assumptions that lay behind Clementsian ecology and its technocratic prescriptions, however. He had collaborated with Robert Cushman Murphy on a study of the anomalous migration of little auks (*Alle alle*) in 1932 that built on Murphy's interest in El Niño. Vogt was also familiar with the work of animal ecologist Charles Elton and his collaborators, who sought to account for dramatic historical fluctuations in the numbers of fur-bearing animals in Canada. Vogt applied four Eltonian principles to his studies of Peru's guano birds: the food chain, appropriate food size, the pyramid of numbers, and the ecological niche – all of which were based on the fundamental supposition that food availability is the basic determinant of ecological relationships.[53]

Vogt's approach to Peru's guano birds owed the most to conservation scientist Aldo Leopold (1887–1948). He relied heavily on Leopold's *Game Management* (1933), "the bible of the wildlife profession," while designing his research. This textbook was a font of technocratic optimism. It explicitly sought "control over nature" through "co-ordination of science and use." The twin concepts of "carrying capacity" and "balance between species" provided the foundational doctrine of the book, in which the Malthusian "biotic potential" of an animal population worked in opposition to hunting, predation, malnutrition, starvation, disease, parasites, accidents, and other forms of "environmental resistance." At one stage of his career, Leopold

[51] Vogt journal, 31 Jan., 1 Feb., 25 Apr., 5, 18 May 1939, 18 Feb. 1940, DPL-CONS76 3/1; "Nest Densities," DPL-CONS76 3/3; Vogt to Aldo Leopold, 29 July 1939, 10 Jan. 1940, UWDC-ALA; *BCAG* 15 (1939): 287–88, 311–12; 16 (1940): 145, 160; 17 (1941): 161; 18 (1942): 26; Sharon Kingsland, *Modeling Nature: Episodes in the History of Population Ecology* (Chicago, 1995), ch. 3.

[52] Vogt journal, 6 Feb., 23 Mar. 1939, 6 Apr. 1941, DPL-CONS76 3/1; *BCAG* 18 (1942): 47–50; Devlin and Naismith, *The World of Roger Tory Peterson*, 83–84; Barrow, *A Passion for Birds*, 195–97; Richard Burkhardt, Jr., *Patterns of Behavior: Konrad Lorenz, Niko Tinbergen, and the Founding of Ethology* (Chicago, 2005), 1, 5–6, 10–11, 213–17, 529 n. 75.

[53] Murphy and Vogt, "The Dovekie Influx of 1932," *The Auk* 50 (1933): 325–49; *BCAG* 18 (1942): 25; Worster, *Nature's Economy*, 205–20, 271–74, 294–301; Anker, *Imperial Ecology*, ch. 3.

thought it would be possible for scientific game managers "to substitute a new and objective equilibrium for any natural one which civilization may have destroyed." By the late 1930s, he and animal ecologist Paul Errington had substituted this optimism for a pessimistic obsession with fluctuations and disruptions in the balance of nature. Vogt had become a close friend of Leopold and Errington during his time as editor of *Bird-Lore* and sought to apply their new insights to the "prodigality of problems" he faced as a student of the guano birds.[54]

"The Peruvians have done a really fine piece of work – better than most of our fish and game commissions," Vogt wrote in one of his numerous letters to Leopold from Peru. "It is because they have done most of the obvious things for the birds, with such great success, that I must work so hard."[55] Vogt gave his most focused attention to the conditions determining the initiation, expansion, and abandonment of nesting colonies. After three seasons of exacting observation from field blinds, Vogt felt he could describe the four-month life cycle of a typical colony of guanays: colonizing males struggled intensely among themselves to establish nesting territories in locations with a favorable microclimate. Males then sought to attract females to these sites through specific calls, gestures, and the construction of distinctive nest mounds made from guano. He postulated that a colony would grow outward from this nucleus of maximal desirability as the season progressed, with predatory birds helping to keep the colony together from the outside by picking off stragglers on the margins. From his interaction with Leopold, Vogt already doubted the ecological wisdom of culling predatory birds when he arrived in Peru, and the latter observation reinforced this holistic view of ecological relationships.[56]

Vogt made extensive observations of other organisms that inhabited the environs of the bird colonies. Unlike earlier scientists, Vogt was predisposed to believe that parasites might have a positive impact on the health of a colony as a whole by eliminating weak birds, thereby reducing the colony's vulnerability to a more virulent epidemic. Vogt ingeniously used his own body as a scientific subject to pursue this line of inquiry: he carefully counted the number of parasites that bit him while he sat in the blind and tried to correlate these attacks to local climatic conditions. This self-observation provided the basis for some of his conclusions regarding the microclimate of nesting colonies. Vogt also paid a great deal of attention to the predators of these parasites. He marked 300 *lagartija* and *saltojo* lizards (*Tropidurus*

[54] Leopold, *Game Management*, vii, 26, 50–58, 172; Vogt to Leopold, 29 July 1939, 11 Feb. 1940, UWDC-ALA; Newton, *Aldo Leopold's Odyssey*, 131–33, 200–7, 380 n. 61; Flader, *Thinking Like a Mountain*, 164–66.

[55] Vogt to Leopold, 11 Feb. 1940, UWDC-ALA.

[56] Vogt journal, 5 Feb., 10 Aug., 15, 23 Nov. 1939, 4 Apr., 12 Oct. 1941, DPL-CONS76 3/1; BCAG 15 (1939): 294–95; 18 (1942): 42–43, 47–50, 53–54, 81–82, 125.

peruvianus and *Phillodactylus* sp.) to track their behavior, and experimented with the construction of small shelters so lizards could regulate their body temperatures in areas that had been cleared of rocks by guano workers in their drive to eliminate parasites.[57]

Vogt's observations were profoundly influenced by the chance appearance of an "ecological depression on the Peruvian coast" that lasted almost continuously from 1939–41. This powerful El Niño severely disrupted his inquiry into baseline conditions but provided an unparalleled opportunity to study the circumstances that resulted in the failure of guano bird colonies. Vogt palpably shared the discomfort of nesting birds as temperatures rose far above normal on the guano islands. Many older chicks began a dangerous search for water to drink and cool off. This led thousands to plunge over cliffs to their deaths – the sort of image that led Vogt and lemming ecologists to believe that overpopulation naturally leads to higher rates of suicide among organisms.[58] It did not take long once El Niño conditions presented themselves for adult birds to begin "withdrawing like a window shade" from the guano islands, leaving their eggs and chicks to certain death. After a while, even adult birds began to perish by the millions. So many died at Iquique that this Chilean port had to hire trucks for their removal. Not all animals suffered from these changed conditions, however. Condors, vultures, skuas, and flies (*Sarcophaga* sp.) had a field day on the carrion. Blue-footed boobies appeared like "Cassandra's voices of death" as they expanded their nesting range a thousand kilometers farther south than usual. This event also provided Vogt with a chance to learn where the guano birds went during El Niño: helpful observers returned leg bands from as far away as Buenaventura, Colombia, and Chiloé Island in southern Chile.[59]

What, exactly, caused Peru's guano birds to abandon their young and fly such vast distances? Tropical heat could not be the only answer, because it would not explain how a handful of remaining birds successfully recruited young. CAG's guardians thought that the absence of anchoveta determined these behaviors. Vogt, at first, thought this belief was "overdone" and searched for alternatives. A team from Peru's National Institute of Hygiene again investigated the possibility that disease was involved but could find no conclusive evidence of an epizootic. As time passed, Vogt became more and more convinced that food supply was the key to the stability of bird colonies and guano production. Vogt observed abundant signs of starvation among moribund chicks and adults. Vogt's investigations of plankton in the

[57] Vogt journal, 5, 10, 13 Feb., 20, 31 Oct., 9, 11 Nov. 1939, DPL-CONS76 3/1; *BCAG* 15 (1939): 293–96, 346–48; 18 (1942): 112–16.

[58] Dennis Chitty, *Do Lemmings Commit Suicide?: Beautiful Hypotheses and Ugly Facts* (New York, 1996).

[59] Vogt journal, 20, 23 Nov. 1940, 1 Mar. 1941, 21 Jan. 1942, DPL-CONS76 3/1; Vogt to Leopold, 29 July 1939, UWDC-ALA; *BCAG* 16 (1940): 311, 316, 328–29; 17 (1941): 127–38, 143–44; 18 (1942): 5, 59, 93.

vicinity of the guano islands also provided crucial insight. These indicated a fundamental change in the community of marine organisms surrounding the guano islands, and catastrophe for animals like the guano birds living at the apex of Elton's "pyramid of numbers." These observations were largely confirmed by Mary Sears, a visiting planktonologist from Woods Hole Oceanographic Institution. With Vogt's help, she obtained a U.S. government grant to journey to Peru to investigate the relation between nutrient cycling and plankton production – the only time during this "dark age for women in the professions" that this prominent marine scientist was allowed to do shipboard oceanographic research.[60]

All of these observations had profound significance for the management of Peru's guano birds, as well as for the prospects of input-intensive agriculture and industrial fishing in Peru. Because guano birds could only travel a limited distance from their nests each day, breeding failure was inevitable whenever an El Niño struck and anchoveta were difficult to find. However, Vogt was adamant that these "ecological depressions" were not something to be feared by Peru's environmental managers. In Vogt's estimation, they provided a natural form of cyclic population control that maintained the guano bird population at a level close to the average carrying capacity of Peru's marine environment, thereby preventing catastrophic, boom-bust population "irruptions." This also meant that the guano industry had limited possibilities for growth and that *any* human exploitation of anchoveta put the guano birds at risk. Beyond a certain level, Peruvian farmers would have to look elsewhere for concentrated sources of agricultural nutrients. This reasoning clearly reflects the application of Aldo Leopold's ecological ideas, a subject we examine further in Chapter 8.[61]

Yet these considerations did not preclude humans from working with natural processes "to help conserve the balance between species continually sought by Nature."[62] Vogt reasoned that the guano islands had been substantially altered from their primordial state when their ancient deposits were removed during the nineteenth century, so there was no harm in further alterations, particularly if they were aimed at replicating the pristine

---

[60] Vogt journal, 13, 18 Mar., 2 Apr. 1939, 30 Dec. 1940, 5, 12, 21 Sept., 29 Oct. 1941, DPL-CONS76 3/1; Vogt to Francisco Ballén, 16 May 1941, DPL-CONS76 3/2; Vogt to Leopold, 29 July 1939, 15 Dec. 1940, UWDC-ALA. Sears, "Cruise Notes from Peru," 14, 18, 28–29 Oct., 8 Dec. 1941; Sears to Enrique Ávila, 3 Apr. 1951, WHOI-MC9. *BCAG* 16 (1940): 151–52; 17 (1941): 459–61; 18 (1942): 4, 22, 60–64, 66, 69–77, 79, 113–14; Rossiter, *Women Scientists in America*, xv, 7, 243, 247, 338, 500 n. 13; Kathleen Broome Williams, *Improbable Warriors: Women Scientists and the U.S. Navy in World War II* (Annapolis, MD, 2001), ch. 2.

[61] Vogt to Leopold, 11 June 1941 UWDC-ALA; *BCAG* 15 (1939): 296; 16 (1940): 324; 17 (1941): 127–38; 18 (1942): 22, 84–86, 88–89, 109, 111, 118–20; Leopold, *Game Management*, 50–58.

[62] *BCNPN* 1, no. 1 (1944): 10.

island conditions of centuries past. To create more desirable nesting conditions, Vogt proposed the use of explosives to flatten the topography on more crowded islands to open them up to the wind and recreate the "aerodynamic" quality they once possessed before they were mined to bedrock. Some CAG employees suggested exterminating the piquero and alcatraz populations to rid the guanays of competition for food and nesting space. Vogt strongly objected to this simplistic proposal and instead recommended techniques for taking advantage of the distinct ecological niches these bird species occupied. For example, Vogt experimented with the construction of cliffside nesting platforms for piqueros that could be safely raised to harvest accumulated guano. Vogt also proposed building safety ramps to help young birds reach the ocean. This would reduce the number of accidental deaths and help control parasites, especially during hot El Niño years.[63]

Vogt also thought CAG should rethink its approach to guano island hygiene. In some ways, CAG had made the islands *too* clean. By removing surface rocks, CAG had eliminated shelter needed by lizards so they could naturally control bird parasite numbers. Island cleaning also removed material needed to construct nests and perhaps increased the struggle between males for desirable nesting locales. Vogt admonished CAG to stop culling gulls and vultures, based on the argument that these predators helped maintain the dense structure of bird colonies and played a role in preventing population "irruptions." He shared the view that Andean condors posed a threat but thought they should be killed only after they had been observed preying on a colony – otherwise these "majestic" birds might suffer the fate of the endangered California condor. In other ways, Vogt thought the islands were not clean enough. He harshly criticized CAG for failing to keep predatory cats and disease-carrying chickens off the guano islands. Like other progeny of the age of soap and water, Vogt was disgusted by the open-air defecation practices of island employees (including his own university-educated scientific assistant). Human excrement created an unnatural food source for flies, dung beetles, and rats, which potentially distracted island lizards from preying on parasitic ticks and lice. Vogt implored his superiors to install clean, comfortable latrines near work sites and to provide artificial shelters for the lizards. He also recommended against the systematic use of chemical poisons to control pests because they often killed species besides their intended target and created the problem of acquired resistance. In their stead, he suggested the periodic use of male ferrets to eliminate invasive rats.[64]

Vogt clearly shared the technocratic optimism that drove northern ecologists to demand a role in managing the dust-choked Great Plains and other

---

[63] Vogt journal, 21 Mar., 14 Aug. 1939, DPL-CONS76 3/1; *BCAG* 16 (1940): 145–68; 18 (1942): 3–4, 35–41, 83, 90–91, 96, 98–99, 122–23, 125–26.

[64] Vogt to Leopold, 15 Dec. 1940, UWDC-ALA; *BCAG* 15 (1939): 346–48; 16 (1940): 150, 158–59; 17 (1941): 165, 167; 18 (1942): 40–41, 81–82, 112–13, 115–18, 121, 123, 125.

threatened environments during this era. The holistic scope of these proposals is nonetheless remarkable, even according to much later scientific
standards.[65] The fact that Vogt's Leopoldian insights powerfully influenced
human exploitation of this rich marine environment only bolsters the claim
that Peru had created the "greatest of all industries based upon the conservation of wild animals" the world had ever seen.

Opening New Horizons

Vogt was not the man to oversee the expansion of human vigilance over
Peru's marine environment. He expected to go to the University of Wisconsin
to complete a Ph.D. in avian ecology under Leopold after his three-year contract with CAG expired, but the chance intervention of El Niño enamored
Vogt with the idea of staying in South America for another five years to
continue his exploration of the linkage between climate variability and bird
population dynamics. CAG was eager to cooperate, but the United States'
entry into World War II made his continued employment untenable. Vogt
made an aborted attempt to publish his El Niño research in the journal
Ecology but soon became wrapped up in wartime diplomatic service and
abandoned the pursuit of a scientific career. As a consequence, few outside of Peru learned of his groundbreaking scientific discoveries.[66] On the
bright side, the war created the opportunity for Vogt's handpicked assistant Enrique Ávila to study at Woods Hole with Sears and Wisconsin with
Leopold. Ávila's English skills and uneven scientific education proved to be
great obstacles, and at one point Leopold advised him to go home. Ávila
would have none of this. Completing a foreign degree "would mean the
opening of new opportunities.... In a country like mine, a degree of any
kind has the magic power of a pass word." He coveted "the advantage"
such an accomplishment "would give me in dealing with some petty politics of my country." In 1945, Ávila returned triumphantly to Peru with a
master of science degree in hand and a five-year contract to work for CAG
as his country's first native-born professional ornithologist. The fact that
he grew up in a family of indigenous farmers near the shores of Lake Titicaca and often faced racial prejudice because of his heritage makes these
accomplishments all the more remarkable.[67]

[65] Worster, *Nature's Economy*, ch. 12, 17; Joel Hagen, *An Entangled Bank: The Origins of Ecosystem Ecology* (New Brunswick, NJ, 1992), 138–40.

[66] Vogt to Leopold, 10 Jan., 15 Dec. 1940, 11 Mar., 24 Aug., 31 Dec. 1941, 4 Feb., 16 May 1942, UWDC-ALA; Francisco Ballén to Vogt, 18 Dec. 1941, DPL-CONS76 1/1; David Duffy, "William Vogt: A Pilgrim on the Road to Survival," *American Birds* 43 (1989): 1256–57.

[67] Interview with Basilia Díaz viuda de Ávila, 13 June 2001. Vogt to Leopold, 15 Dec. 1940, 9 May, 11 June 1941; Leopold to Vogt, 29 Jan., 30 June, 11, 18 Oct. 1944, UWDC-ALA.

Meanwhile, under the onslaught of a three-year El Niño, the agroecological system linking guano production to the export of cotton and sugar fell
apart. Guano sales bottomed out at 67,537 metric tons in 1943, the lowest
figure since El Niño and avian cholera struck in 1922–23. This only met one-
fourth of national demand. The outbreak of World War II exacerbated these
problems. The civilian government of Manuel Prado (president, 1939–45,
1956–62) acted aggressively to control the price of food, provide scientific
extension services to food growers, and limit the amount of coastal property planted with export crops. In 1943, Prado's administration established
an independent Ministry of Agriculture to oversee these improvements and
compelled CAG to give absolute priority to food producers when rationing
guano. These policies strengthened Prado's alliance with the populist APRA
party, while strengthening the technocratic tendencies of the Peruvian state.
"Dr. Prado," as he liked to be known, enthusiastically adopted the persona
of engineer-president and made agronomic engineer Carlos Moreyra Paz
Soldán one of his closest aides. This again illustrates the historical com-
patibility of populist and technocratic politics. On the other hand, these
policies further eroded the power, privileges, and income of sugar and cotton exporters, along with their political support for CAG.[68]

Old guard agroexporters did not give in easily to these changes. They
still owned a large share of private stock in the guano industry and tried
to use this power to take control of CAG from within. Gerardo Klinge
(1887–1961) was elected company president at the annual shareholders'
meeting of 1945. His selection possessed potent political symbolism. Klinge
fit the technocratic mold: he was an agronomic engineer who had fought
against cotton wilt and headed the national agricultural research station at
La Molina. But Klinge was also a founder of the ultra-conservative Partido
Nacional Agrario, which vehemently opposed Prado's alliance with APRA
and took an unyielding stance against governmental intervention in the economy. The national election of June 1945 derailed Klinge's efforts to redirect
guano production back toward sugar and cotton. Prado's favored candidate, José Luis Bustamante, won the presidential vote, and APRA gained
control of Congress. Bustamante's government did "a total house cleaning"
at CAG and appointed loyal technocrats to top positions, including agronomic engineer Carlos Llosa Belaúnde as general manager. APRA made sure
a far greater portion of the nation's tax burden fell onto agroexporters and
forced through basic reforms in the sharecropping system. The rightwing
did not have to wait long to exact its revenge. The cost of food and other

Ávila to Vogt, 16 Oct. 1944, 26 Apr. 1948, DPL-CONS76, 1/1–2; Sears to Milner Schaefer,
  4 Feb. 1953, WHOI-MC9.
[68] Cushman, "Lords of Guano," app. 6, tables 4, 6; *MCAG* 36 (1945): iv; Thorp and Bertram,
  Peru 1890–1977, 173, 177–79, 199–200; Klarén, *Peru*, 279–85; Pike, *Modern History of
  Peru*, 276–81; *Diccionario histórico y biográfico*, s.v. "Moreyra Paz Soldán, Carlos."

necessities climbed steadily upward from 1945–48. Bustamante's government was forced to ration many basic goods. Things got so bad that Ávila sent his wife and daughter back to Lake Titicaca to live off the land with his family. There was actually little Bustamante's government could have done to alleviate this suffering. Severe food scarcities affected many parts of the world in 1946–47: some as an aftereffect of war, others as a result of climate extremes. These problems greatly exacerbated Cold War tensions and brought Herbert Hoover out of retirement to serve one last time as an antifamine technocrat. Few were surprised in this polarized environment when a military coup overthrew Bustamante's faltering government and installed a right-wing dictatorship headed by General Manuel Odría (president 1948–56).[69]

This administrative turnover injected new energy into CAG's bird conservation efforts. Carlos Llosa took a personal interest in seeing that CAG acted on Vogt's insights but brought an engineering mind-set to the job. Llosa assigned work crews to regularize the surface of several islands using explosives, who proceeded to build 31 kilometers of cliffside containment walls with leftover stone. Vogt had observed that adult birds tend to defecate on takeoff. These walls were intended to prevent chicks from falling to their deaths and to encourage adult birds to poop over the islands, rather than wasting their guano over the sea. These alterations had an immediate impact on Isla La Vieja, which became Peru's most important guano-producing territory once workers reconditioned its surface and eliminated its condor population. Llosa also came up with what he hoped would provide a technological fix for El Niño. He seized on Vogt's observation that many birds hung around coastal points in southern Peru during the 1939–41 crisis. Llosa reasoned that wild foxes (*Dusycyon sechurae*) and other terrestrial predators prevented the establishment of breeding colonies in these locales. He therefore directed company employees to build isolation walls around southern peninsulas frequented by guano birds and to eliminate predatory animals in order to turn them into artificial "island" sanctuaries. CAG completed the construction of isolation walls at three locales in 1948. Birds almost immediately colonized Punta Coles, even though it was not an El Niño year. This unexpected result inspired the extension of this policy to a stretch of the north-central coast without guano islands in order to promote "even exploitation of the sea surface" by feeding birds (fig. 1.2). This policy immediately proved its worth. By the mid-1950s, coastal points were

[69] Ávila to Vogt, 23 July, 17 Sept., 16 Oct., 12 Dec. 1945, 24 Apr. 1946, 17 Sept. 1947, DPL-CONS76 1/1; *MCAG* 37 (1946), x–xi; 40 (1949): lii–liii; *Diccionario histórico y biográfico*, s.v. "Klinge, Leonidas [sic]"; Klarén, *Peru*, 286–305; Barton Bernstein, "The Postwar Famine and Price Control, 1946," *Agricultural History* 38 (1964): 235–40; Nicholas Ganson, *The Soviet Famine of 1946–47 in Global and Historical Perspective* (New York, 2009).

producing 30 percent of total guano production in Peru.[70] In a remarkable case of synchronicity, the South African government implemented a similar strategy along the Namibian coast during the 1930s to expand the nesting area available to South Atlantic birds – also with great effect (fig. 6.4).

These policies worked so well that Llosa was (barely) able to keep hold of his job after the revolution of 1948. Bustamante's government had wisely arranged for cotton and sugar cane planters to obtain greater access to guano and imported fertilizers at state-subsidized prices. This policy continued under Odría, although his government required farmers to pay far more for the privilege. Both regimes stuck to the policy of using guano to encourage the adoption of input-intensive agricultural practices by food producers, however. Unprecedented population growth and the growing flood of rural migrants to Lima's shantytowns made this a political necessity. This policy was especially successful among coastal rice growers and highland wheat and potato cultivators in the Mantaro Valley above Lima. CAG came to administer a far more diversified agroecological system during the late 1940s and 1950s.[71]

The rapid expansion of the guano supply during these years helped enormously with these efforts. Peru's guano birds had the good fortune of enjoying a long succession of years with strong upwelling and abundant anchoveta. La Niña conditions were particularly strong from 1954 through 1956. During the last of those glorious years, CAG harvested an all-time record 332,223 metric tons of fresh guano containing 6,200 tons of potassium, 31,600 tons of phosphate, and 47,000 tons of nitrogen, at a profit of $48 million in 2007 US dollars. For a couple of seasons, Peru's living guano birds produced more fertilizer than was mined in an average year during the guano age! This enabled Peruvian farmers to consume fertilizer in proportions approaching those of industrialized countries. By this critical measure, Peru enjoyed one of the main benefits of the Green Revolution well before anyone in the Third World.[72]

CAG's new generation of managers hoped that these alterations to Peru's coastal environment would enable the guano birds to attain a stable

[70] Cushman, "Lords of Guano," app. 8; Ávila to Vogt, 25 Nov., 12 Dec. 1945, DPL-CONS76 1/1; *MCAG* 38 (1947): i–ii, v–vi; 39 (1948): vii; 40 (1949): v–viii; 41 (1950): xi–xii; 42 (1951): iii–iv; 44 (1953): iv–vi; 45 (1954): v; 46 (1955): vi; 47 (1956): vi, xvii; 48 (1957): vi; 49 (1958): xvii–xviii; 52 (1961): xi; 54 (1963): anexos; Robert Cushman Murphy, "Peru Profits from Sea Fowl," *National Geographic Magazine* Mar. 1959: 401, 404–5, 408–9.

[71] Cushman, "Lords of Guano," table 6, app. 7, Ávila to Sears, 4 Apr., 20 July 1949, WHOI-MC9; *MCAG* 37 (1946): iv–v; *MCAG* 38 (1947): vi, xix; 39 (1948): xiv–xv; 41 (1950): xvii–xviii, lxxxii; 42 (1951): xvii; David Collier, *Squatters and Oligarchs: Authoritarian Rule and Policy Change in Peru* (Baltimore, 1976), ch. 4–5.

[72] CEI; Cushman, "Lords of Guano," app. 3, 5; CEPAL, *Uso de fertilizantes en América Latina*, 6, 8, 14–15, 94.

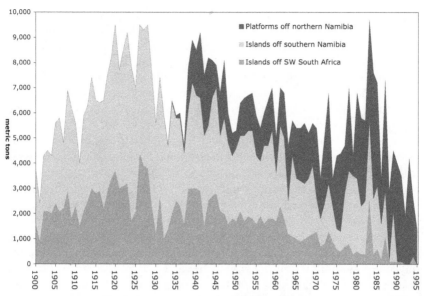

FIGURE 6.4. Guano production in southern Africa, 1900–95. During the late 1890s, the South African government began harvesting guano on a sustained-yield basis from island reserves. Three species of marine birds were responsible for most of this production: the Cape gannet (*Sula capensis*), Cape penguin (*Spheniscus demersus*), and Cape shag (*Phalacrocorax capensis*). In 1914–16 and 1929–34, unfavorable climatic conditions caused a notable decrease in fish numbers and collapse of the Cape shag population. In response, South Africa banned egg collecting and built a series of nesting platforms along the northern Namibian coast in the hope of expanding the area of the Benguela upwelling ecosystem accessible to breeding birds. The collapse of industrial exploitation of sardine (*Sardinops sagax*) during the 1960s and 1970s and anchovy (*Engraulis capensis*) during the 1980s and 1990s, eventually caused the near demise of the guano industry. Despite their similarities, there is no evidence that the guano industries of twentieth-century Peru and southern Africa were ever connected. *Source:* P. B. Best et al., "Top Predators in Southern Africa's Marine Ecosystems," *Transactions of the Royal Society of South Africa* 52 (1997): 188–91, fig. 2; Hutchinson, *Biogeochemistry of Vertebrate Excretion*, 134–57; Lance van Sittert, University of Cape Town, personal communication.

"climax" population much larger than before.[73] Enrique Ávila repeatedly cautioned his superiors that these ecological changes might have negative, unintended consequences. In a short 1954 essay titled "Ethics on the March," Ávila warned that the "material conquest" of nature would prove to be "ephemeral" or even "illusory" by "future societies." Taking a page out of Aldo Leopold's work, Ávila asserted the moral imperative to leave "an equally giving, equally productive, equally *healthy* earth" to the next

[73] BCCAG 2 (1955): 113, 117.

generation. He also took a jab at the white-skinned technocrats who ran CAG and Peru's national bureaucracy: "There will no true *Conservation* while this discipline is the patrimony of distinguished professors, outstanding academic circles, cultivated social nuclei, [and] calloused institutions."[74] But Ávila was easy to ignore. He was repeatedly passed over for raises and promotions because of his heritage and politics and at various points was forbidden from publishing studies that went against his superiors' position. In 1950, he was abruptly exiled to a field station on Isla Don Martín to give his mainland laboratory to the son of a senator. Ávila dreamed of working in a place where he "would feel free to put down my ideas in black and white without being punished for it," and he eventually fled Peru to study population dynamics at the Scripps Institution of Oceanography in California. "No prophet is accepted in his own country," Ávila's widow explained.[75]

Ávila also warned that small decreases in food availability could have major consequences for bird colonies that were pushing the upper limits of their carrying capacity.[76] In 1957, a strong El Niño again struck Peru and stayed around until the end of 1958. After a decade of fat years, the population of nesting guanays withered, from a whopping 33.5 million in August 1955, to a low of 3.1 million in January 1958 (usually prime nesting season). The population of nesting piqueros and pelicans fell even more precipitously. Guano production plummeted accordingly to 108,919 metric tons in 1959. CAG scientists scrambled to make sense of this irruptive collapse. They dissected hundreds of dead and moribund birds and restored several to health in a beautifully conceived feeding experiment that emphatically confirmed Vogt and Ávila's ecological ideas. Llosa's idea of building southern outposts for migrating guano birds did little to help the situation, but CAG, nonetheless, tried to find another quick technological fix for this catastrophe. Guardians intensified the killing of condors, gulls, and sea lions. CAG scientists also experimented with the use of aldrin, BHC, and other locally available pesticides to use against the guano birds' parasites, in case an unknown epidemic was underway. Fortunately, these wrong-headed experiments did not work, because these agrichemicals are now know to cause egg-thinning, breeding failure, and direct poisoning in the exact birds CAG was trying to protect. On the other hand, working with nature by gathering *lagartija* lizards on the mainland and releasing them in large numbers within nesting colonies worked wonders in reducing parasite numbers and

74 Ávila's emphasis; *BCAG* 30 (May 1954): 22–23; republished in *BCNPN* 12 (1955): 69–70.
75 Díaz interview; Ávila to Vogt, 25 Nov., 12 Dec. 1945, 24 Apr., 7 Oct., 19 Dec. 1946, 12, 26 Apr. 1948, 27 Apr. 1950; Robert Cushman Murphy to Vogt, 15 Nov. 1946, DPL-CONS76 1/1; Ávila to Mary Sears, 3 Apr. 1949, 9, 12, 24 May, 8 Dec. 1950, 20 Feb., 17 Apr., 7 July 1951, 15 Oct. 1954, 9 Feb. 1955, WHOI-MC9.
76 Ávila to Vogt, 6 Apr. 1949, DPL-CONS76 1/1; Ávila to Sears, 3 Apr. 1952, 23 May 1953, 2 Sept. 1953; Sears to Ávila, 10 June, 11 Aug. 1953, WHOI-MC9.

was put into operational use at a number of locales.[77] An oceanographer from Scripps Institution of Oceanography, Warren Wooster, happened to be on hand directing efforts to improve Peru's marine science capabilities when this strong El Niño struck Peru. He reported his observations to a special symposium in California held to investigate this "year of change" in the Pacific Basin, which inspired renewed scientific interest in El Niño in the United States.[78]

Peru's guano birds were not the only ones experiencing famine. The resulting decline in the fertilizer supply exacerbated a deep-seated crisis in Peruvian agriculture. The strong La Niña of the mid-1950s may have been a boon to Peru's marine productivity, but it was devastating to farmers living in the drought-stricken Sierra. In 1956, national potato production was 33 percent below levels two years previously; barley, wheat, and maize harvests fell off by 30, 25, and 11 percent, respectively. National food production barely improved in 1957, and inhabitants of the altiplano around Lake Titicaca came close to starvation. Food prices skyrocketed, and Manuel Prado's government had to import huge amounts. Cotton and sugar growers came under intense political scrutiny in these circumstances. High international prices, state-funded expansion of Peru's irrigation network, and other accommodations by Odría's regime had driven a boom in the production of these export crops that dwarfed the increases of the 1910s and late 1930s.[79] Good economic times tended to obscure the fact that many coastal growers were up to their necks in debt acquired to purchase fertilizers and pesticides, most of the latter imported. The conversion of entire coastal valleys into year-round monocultures created an insatiable hunger for nutrients and ideal conditions for an irruption of insect pests. Cañete valley cotton planters were among the first farmers in the world to use DDT and BHC on a large scale as insecticides – and also among the first to witness the rapid evolution of pest resistance to these synthetic chemicals and to experience debilitating secondary pest outbreaks. This reality convinced a number of growers to try German-Peruvian entomologist Johannes Wille's groundbreaking method of integrated pest management using crop rotation, predatory insects, and

---

77 Cushman, "Lords of Guano," fig. 8, app. 2; Tovar, et al., "Monthly Population Size," 208–18; *MCAG* 49 (1958): v–vi, xxiii, 18, 21; 50 (1959): v; *BCAG* 35 (Apr. 1959): 10–22; Rómulo Jordán to Luis Massa, "Informe sobre experimentos con garrapaticidas," 15 Apr. 1960, ACAG-Isla Don Martín; Johnsgard, *Cormorants, Darters, and Pelicans*, 139–40; Tovar and Cabrera, *Conservación y manejo de aves guaneras*, 96–97, 161.

78 Cushman, "Choosing between Centers of Action: Instrument Buoys, El Niño, and Scientific Internationalism in the Pacific, 1957–1982," in *The Machine in Neptune's Garden: Historical Perspectives on Technology and the Marine Environment* (Sagamore Beach, MA, 2004).

79 Cushman, "Lords of Guano," fig. 3–6, app. 5–6; Hopkins, *Desarrollo desigual y crisis*, 44, 62; Thorp and Bertram, *Peru 1890–1977*, 278–79.

occasional sprayings, but no one thought to question the wisdom of input-intensive agriculture.[80]

One thing was clear in all this: Peru's rapidly growing population could not feed itself, and never would, at least on the basis of agricultural nutrients provided by Peru's "billion dollar birds." From 1909–56, CAG technocrats engineered a remarkable revival of the guano industry based on the principle of sustained-yield conservation. But their aspirations did not stop there. They built an agroecological system that put the rich Pacific environment to work toward achieving a broad range of developmental goals. As we have seen in this chapter, large-scale producers of export crops benefited the most from this project. Predatory animals, burrowing marine birds, and coastal fishermen suffered the most, and in the last case, turned into potent rivals of the guano industry. Some compared this achievement to the Pan American Highway and Panama Canal, as the most successful animal conservation project of the modern world.[81]

Peru's guano birds had a troublesome tendency to boom and bust in sync with El Niño, however, and this made them potentially dangerous as a source of economic and political instability. Even during the most productive year of the century – 1956 – CAG only managed to supply a little over half of national requests. Now where would the country go to obtain the food, fertilizer, and foreign exchange it needed to feed its tired soils and exploding human population? What if human societies were subject to the same ecological laws affecting the guano birds?

By this date, a number of prominent thinkers had begun to ask these questions for the rest of the world – William Vogt among them. To an extent unrecognized by scholars, Malthusian concerns of this sort profoundly influenced public policy and geopolitical conflict during the mid-twentieth century. Phosphates and the Pacific World again provided flash points for these controversies to unfold, the focus of the next chapter.

[80] Wille, "Biological Control of Certain Cotton Insects and the Application of New Organic Insecticides in Peru," *Journal of Economic Entomology* 44 (1951): 13–18; Teodoro Boza, "Ecological Consequences of Pesticides Used for the Control of Cotton Insects in Cañete Valley, Peru," in *The Careless Technology: Ecology and International Development* (Garden City, NY, 1972); Douglas Murray, *Cultivating Crisis: The Human Cost of Pesticides in Latin America* (Austin, TX, 1994), 15, 37.

[81] Mae Galarza, *The Guano Islands of Peru* (Washington, DC, 1945), 3, 5, 14, 16, part of the Pan American Union Series for Young Readers.

7

When the Japanese Came to Dinner

From 1600 to 1867 the population of Japan was apparently stabilized at about 26,000,000. . . . Soon after the Americans opened the door the population of Japan began to grow at a rate of more than one per cent per year. . . . The Japanese were already living on a far lower material standard than the West. As the population pressure increased, they were faced with the choice of lowering the living standard still further or expanding the means of feeding the people. . . .

The culpability of Japan in seeking this way out of her Malthusian dilemma is a culpability shared by most of the nations that have been self-righteously preaching democracy. We grabbed enormous territories from Mexico, . . . [but] we did not have the very eminent excuse of such population pressure as confronted Japan. . . . Japan, then, with a population that had mounted to 76,000,000 with trade channels closed to her, and being unwilling or not wise enough to seek a sharp limitation of her population, was faced with the dilemma: starve or fight.

         – William Vogt, *Road to Survival* (1948)

"After more than a century of intermittent haunting, the ghost of a gloomy British clergyman, Thomas Robert Malthus, was on the rampage last week," warned the 8 November 1948 issue of *Time* newsmagazine. This unsigned article claimed to represent the outcry of "real agricultural scientists" against the scaremongering of William Vogt, a man who "seems to care as much for 'wildlife' as he does for the human species."

Malthus, who died in 1834, predicted that the world's population would soon outgrow its food supply. Then war, pestilence and famine, caused by overpopulation, would slap down presumptuous man. This did not happen. The world's population has doubled since Malthus' time, from one billion to two, but new lands were cultivated and old lands made more productive. Better transportation brought surplus food from afar to feed the hungry industrial cities. There were local famines, as there had always been, but the world never ran out of food. The gloomy Malthus, who had underestimated both nature's resources and man's resourcefulness, *had been wrong.*[1]

Time, Inc. had taken a similar stance before. In February 1941, Time/Life editor Henry Luce forcefully attacked the Malthusian idea that struggle over land and natural resources had led the world to war: "Our world of 2,000,000,000 human beings is for the first time in history one world, fundamentally indivisible," he enthused and "is capable of producing all the material needs of the entire human family." This was part of a now famous call to arms to the people of the United States to fulfill their historical destiny as architects of the American Century. "We must undertake now to be the Good Samaritan of the entire world. It is the manifest duty of the country to undertake to feed all the people of the world who as a result of this worldwide collapse of civilization are hungry and destitute," so that everyone could enjoy the "fundamentally... American promise" of "the more abundant life." For this Asia-obsessed son of American missionaries raised in the Japanese treaty port of Shandong, the belief in natural limitations was just as dangerous to his global vision of unbridled consumption as creeping socialism and the "virus of isolationist sterility."[2]

If Luce had bothered to read Malthus closely, he would have discovered not only that he was wrong about Malthus on certain points but also that he shared basic aspects of his worldview. In later editions of the *Essay on Population*, under the influence of Humphry Davy and other lords of manure science, Malthus expressed the newfound belief that the fertility of the soil could be endlessly manipulated. For advanced societies like England, he replaced his original emphasis on environmental limitations with a theory based on wages, rents, and other economic abstractions. Malthus also adopted a far more diversified perspective on the causes of variation in human numbers. For example, he used the term "irruption" to refer to the tendency of American Indians (and all primitive peoples) to go to war with neighboring tribes when they outgrew local resources. He portrayed the dense indigenous societies of Latin America as already verging on collapse when Spanish conquistadors arrived, but he also highlighted the preventative power of "promiscuous intercourse, infanticide, and war" in controlling Polynesian numbers in the Pacific. Toward the end of his life, Malthus even came to believe that his infamous principle of population would promote the progress of civilization. Malthus had professional reasons for taking

---

[1] Emphasis added; "Eat Hearty," *Time* 8 Nov. 1948: 27–28.

[2] Luce, "The American Century," *Diplomatic History* 23 (1999): 166, 168, 170, originally published in *Life* 17 Feb. 1941; cf. Michael Hunt, "East Asia in Henry Luce's 'American Century,'" in ibid., 321–53.

these perspectives: he was the British Isles' first chaired professor of political economy and trained a generation of bureaucrats at East India College for service as agents of empire.[3]

This chapter demonstrates that Vogt and Luce's preoccupation with the connection between population and prosperity derived from a quarter century of international research and debate regarding the linkages among population growth, food production, standard of living, and war. Historians have begun to recognize that the idea of a ticking population bomb ready to plunge the whole world into an era of scarcity and war is not principally a phenomenon of the late twentieth century.[4] This chapter shows that worries of this sort profoundly shaped intellectual discourse and public policy on agriculture and population movements during World War I and the 1920s. This was especially true among neo-European populations concerned by the rise of Japan as a Great Power within the Pacific World but also extended to Japan itself. This controversy went on to exercise a profound influence over geopolitical conflicts around the globe during the 1930s and 40s. A small cadre of population experts used these concerns to assert unprecedented power over state-sponsored population movements during this period – including an interwar project to settle Gilbert Islanders on the uninhabited guano islands of the Central Pacific and the less-than-voluntary resettlement of the entire indigenous population of Banaba to a hurricane-prone isle in the Fiji archipelago after the Second World War.

Perhaps no group of technocrats has influenced global history so profoundly yet attained so little recognition for their accomplishments. The ideas and actions of these ethnocrats must bear substantial blame for the ethnic chauvinism and genocidal atrocities of the interwar period and Second World War. As we see in the book's final chapters, ethnocratic discourse is also deeply responsible for the postwar world's obsession with the pace of development and improved standards of living – no matter what the environmental costs. It also explains why the worldwide environmental movement of the late twentieth century expressed so much concern over human population growth and the disappearance of wilderness. Some of this colonialist ethnocratic rhetoric even survives in recent histories of ecological imperialism.

---

[3] Malthus, *Essay on the Principle of Population*, 6th ed. (London, 1826), 1:29, 48–49, 66, 71–72, 74, 78, 85, 2:118, 129–30, 155, 441, 514, 540; Glacken, *Traces on the Rhodian Shore*, 640, 645; Patricia James, *Population Malthus: His Life and Times* (London, 2006).

[4] Linnér, *The Return of Malthus*; Robertson, "The Population Bomb"; Alison Bashford, "Nation, Empire, Globe: The Spaces of Population Debate in the Interwar Years," *Comparative Studies in Society and History* 49 (2007): 170–201; Connelly, *Fatal Misconception*.

"An Era of Diminishing Returns"

The specter of Reverend Malthus made another appearance at the end of World War I at a moment when Americans could have been celebrating victory and their rising power in the world but instead went looking for new enemies. As we learned in Chapter 5, the war and climate extremes caused food and other commodity prices to skyrocket worldwide and generated widespread popular unrest. This fueled the success of the Bolshevik Revolution and produced unprecedented interest in technocratic governance.

The revival of Malthusian ideas in the United States during the late 1910s owes much to a timely doctoral dissertation. Warren Thompson (1887–1973) was born in rural Nebraska not far from the birthplace of the Arbor Day movement but eventually made his way east to complete a Ph.D. in sociology at Columbia University. He worked closely with Franklin Giddings, a sociologist intent on applying probability theory to the investigation of ethnic assimilation, and with Henry Seager, an economist obsessed with consumption and other measures of human welfare. Thompson embraced their Progressive enthusiasm for applying rigorous statistical techniques to the solution of social problems but was far less impressed by the urban lifestyles he encountered in the world's largest city, both among rich and poor.[5] Thompson's interest in Malthus grew out of his attempts to measure worldwide patterns of population growth and correlate them with regional increases in food prices. In Japan, for example, prices for rice, barley, legumes, and sake had more than doubled since 1890. His comparative statistical investigations seemed to confirm Malthus's belief that population will invariably increase beyond the means of subsistence whenever checks on growth are removed. Thompson emphatically warned: "The United States is rapidly approaching the point where it will not be a self-supporting nation" and produced evidence suggesting that the pace of technological improvements in food production had reached a point of "diminishing returns." Starvation was not an immediate threat for the world's "most civilized" peoples, however. They instead faced numerical displacement by societies with higher birth rates and a lower "standard of living," such as that experienced by Germans living among Poles in eastern Prussia. In contrast to most of his peers, Thompson remained unconvinced by the eugenic argument that America's "better stocks" were dying out and arrived at the unpopular conclusion that lack of "pride of family and of achievement" and self-destructive love of luxury were largely to blame for low fertility among America's urbane "upper classes." For Thompson, this inevitably meant that some classes of humanity would have to "simplify"

---

[5] Dorothy Ross, *The Origins of American Social Science* (Cambridge and New York, 1992), 227–29; Guide to the Henry Seager Research Notes and Monographs, Cornell University Library, http://rmc.library.cornell.edu/ead/htmldocs/KCL05249.html.

their standard of living, while the whole world sought to reduce its rate of population increase. In the final analysis, he viewed differential living standards as the fundamental barrier to achieving "a truly progressive civilization."[6]

Columbia published Thompson's dissertation at a moment when the world's wartime food supply had become an issue of paramount public interest. In April 1917, President Wilson established the U.S. Food Administration under Herbert Hoover to take command of the situation. This institution served as a nursery both for Malthusian thinking and the technocratic ideal in the United States. Hoover immediately commissioned a crash study of American eating patterns from Raymond Pearl (1879–1940), an expert on animal diseases based at the Maine Agricultural Experiment Station. Statisticians under his command produced the country's first rigorous estimates of per capita food consumption. On the bright side, these numbers suggested that Hoover's Food Administration had been mildly successful in convincing Americans to increase production and reduce consumption of meat and grain to help the Allied cause. More ominously, these statistics confirmed Thompson's finding that the nation's per capita living standard was falling, and had been for some time. As an extension of this work, Pearl coauthored a controversial 1920 paper proposing "a first approximation to a true law of population growth" using the logistic curve. The asymptote of this curve placed an upper limit on the U.S. population of 197 million – *if* American farmers and importers could figure out a way to coax 260 trillion calories of food energy from the earth and seas every year. This was four times the amount of food U.S. farmers had proven capable of producing in an average year during the 1910s.[7]

Another scientist with close ties to the Food Administration, Harvard plant geneticist Edward East (1879–1938), was even more pessimistic about the future. His mentor Cyril Hopkins had loudly proclaimed the nation's agricultural scientists as "the rightful guardians of American soils" and long since warned that the country's phosphate reserves were rapidly being "drained for the benefit of the worn-out farm lands of foreign countries."[8] East helped organize a groundbreaking research program to investigate

[6] Thompson, "Population: A Study in Malthusianism" (Ph.D. diss., Columbia University, 1915), 115, 130, 143–44, 159, 164–65, 217; idem, "Race Suicide in the United States," *Scientific Monthly* 5 (1917): 263, 268–69.

[7] Pearl, *The Nation's Food* (Philadelphia, 1920), 9, 17–18, 25, 222, 232, 244; Pearl and Lowell Reed, "On the Rate of Growth of the Population of the United States since 1790 and Its Mathematical Representation," *Proceedings of the National Academy of Sciences* 6 (1920): 286, 288 n. 12; Nash, *Life of Herbert Hoover*, 3:41–44, 152–60, 227–55; Edmund Ramsden, "Carving Up Population Science: Eugenics, Demography, and the Controversy over the 'Biological Law' of Population Growth," *Social Studies of Science* 32 (2002): 857–99.

[8] Hopkins, *Soil Fertility and Permanent Agriculture* (Boston, 1910), v, xviii–xix, 595–99.

how inbreeding and crossbreeding affected the productivity of maize. These experiments established a Mendelian basis for the development of high-yielding maize hybrids – the bedrock of farm productivity in today's United States. Reading Thompson's dissertation led East to read Malthus for himself – and to the sober conclusion that optimists had grossly exaggerated the ability of science and technology to produce marked gains in food production. In a widely cited 1920 address, East echoed Thompson's conclusion that an "era of diminishing returns" was upon the United States – and threatened its political dominance by the "North European, Northern Aryan, Nordic" race.[9]

Competition for resources, racial chauvinism, and Malthusian fears of this sort helped turn the Pacific Basin into a hotspot for geopolitical struggle in the aftermath of the Great War. In 1917, Japan made a secret agreement with Britain and France to retain control of Germany's former island colonies in the western Pacific north of the equator, as well as the treaty port, railways, and coal mines of China's Shandong province. This agreement included Angaur and several other phosphate-rich atolls but conceded Australian-occupied Nauru to the British Empire. Japanese diplomats were prepared to walk out of the Paris Peace Conference if the other victorious powers had refused to concede to some of its ambitions in the western Pacific. Japan did not have to fight for recognition of its mandate over German Micronesia. Australia, New Zealand, and South Africa were also eager to establish themselves as imperial powers and obtained formal rights to the fertilizer resources of Nauru, Banaba, and Namibia for their efforts. The peace talks came close to collapse in April 1919, however, over the right of Shandong to national self-determination. The northern Shandong plain had reemerged as China's preeminent cotton-producing regions after the disastrous relocation of the mouth of the Yellow River between 1855 and 1897. Its soils fed Japanese textile mills with the help of an immensely productive, locally based system of compost fertilization that mixed hog, draft animal, and human feces with earth and vegetable waste. The neo-European powers at the Paris Conference eventually conceded Japanese control over Shandong but steadfastly refused Japan's demand for a global declaration of racial equality by the League of Nations.[10]

[9] East, "Population," *Scientific Monthly* 10 (1920): 603–24; Donald Jones, "Edward Murray East" *Biographical Memoirs of the National Academy of Sciences* 23 (1944): 217–42; East and Jones, *Inbreeding and Outbreeding: Their Genetic and Sociological Significance* (Philadelphia, 1919), ch. 9–10; Perkins, *Geopolitics and the Green Revolution*, 123, 293 n. 14–18.

[10] Noriko Kawamura, "Wilsonian Idealism and Japanese Claims at the Paris Peace Conference," *Pacific Historical Review* 66 (1997): 509, 511, 514; Williams and Macdonald, *The Phosphateers*, 135–50; Philip Huang, *The Peasant Economy and Social Change in North China* (Stanford, CA, 1985), 125–30, 143–54.

Western strategists of this era were aware of the significance of coal, cotton, and phosphate from these regions to Japan's aspirations but were generally ignorant of the broader importance of fertilizer resources to Japan's rise to prominence as an imperial and industrial power. For generations, the most intensively farmed regions of Japan relied on an elaborate system of fertilization based on composted vegetable matter, human feces, fish offal, and local mud, much of it recycled from urban areas. Nitrogen-fixing cyanobacteria in wet-paddy rice cultivation also contributed mightily to the productivity of traditional Japanese agriculture. Long before the Meiji Restoration of 1868, productivity-minded farmers began importing soybean and fishmeal fertilizers from much greater distances – a form of neo-ecological imperialism. During the eighteenth century, an elaborate fertilizer industry developed on the newly colonized island of Hokkaido that used indigenous Ainu laborers and local wood resources to process herring meal and sardines for long-distance trade. During the late nineteenth century, the Japanese state annulled all customary fishing rights on Hokkaido to encourage the full industrialization of the herring fishery but increased production to such an extent that the fishery collapsed catastrophically during the late 1920s and 1930s.[11]

Fertilizer also played a significant role in Japan's rapid industrialization after 1890 and the widening search for energy and raw materials to feed Japanese farms and factories. During the late nineteenth century, Japanese farmers became increasingly dependent on soybean cake from northeastern China. The Sino-Japanese War of 1894–95 abruptly disrupted these supplies and convinced a consortium of engineers, agronomists, and government officials to begin seeking industrial solutions to the problem of fertilizer supply. Japan's superphosphate industry took off during the late 1890s, creating a dependence on imports of raw phosphate rock mined primarily on Christmas Island. From 1906 through 1908, Noguchi Shitagau (1873–1944) developed a cutting-edge industrial facility at Minamata to produce nitrolim (calcium cyanimide). This triumph of government-sponsored technology transfer from Europe used an energy-intensive electrochemical process to extract reactive nitrogen from the atmosphere, adapted to consume hydropower from the scenic Sogi waterfall, "the Niagara of the Orient." It liberated Japan from dependence on Chilean nitrates for explosives manufacture during the First World War. Between the wars, Noguchi systematically expanded his chemical empire. He developed an electrochemical plastics plant at Minamata during the 1920s that made use of mercury catalysts.

---

[11] Penelope Francks, *Technological and Agricultural Development in Pre-War Japan* (New Haven, 1984), 30–31, 51, 59, 109–10, 123; Howell, *Capitalism from Within*, xi, 2, 5, 38–39, 50, 56, 98–99, 106–10, 117–19; Brian Whitton, "Soils and Rice Fields," in *The Ecology of Cyanobacteria* (Dordrecht, Netherlands, 2000); Brett Walker, *The Conquest of Ainu Lands*.

Waste mercury from this factory gradually accumulated within local marine organisms and eventually resulted in the outbreak of Minamata disease, a degenerative nervous condition among seafood consumers that sparked the Japanese environmental movement. Noguchi also participated enthusiastically in the colonization of Korea and Manchuria by Japan during the 1930s. In northern Korea, his projects converted the fishing village of Hŭngnam into the world's third-largest industrial complex and buried long sections of the forested Yalu and Changjin river valleys under hydroelectric reservoirs. Japan continued mining the soil and sea for nitrogen and other valuable compounds. Noguchi's companies became engaged in large-scale sardine fishing to produce glycerine for dynamite and munitions manufacture. Meanwhile, the Japanese-controlled South Manchurian Railway profited enormously from the export of soybeans for use as fertilizer, feedcake, and vegetable fat, and, by the end of the 1920s, controlled over half the world's soybean supply.[12]

The residents of Pacific North America, Australia, and New Zealand expressed far greater concern about Japan's demographic expansion. These regions achieved their ethnic status as neo-Europes not only because of the rapid growth of populations derived from western Eurasia but also because of the racist exclusion of ethnic groups from the eastern two-thirds of the continent. In 1913, California passed antialien legislation that forbid ownership and long-term leasehold of agricultural land by Asian immigrants. Washington, Arizona, British Columbia, and several Australian states all passed similar legislation about this time. In 1916, the Hearst media conglomerate released the silent film *Patria* portraying a fictional, Japanese-organized invasion of the southwestern United States from Mexico. Propaganda of this sort blurred the line between anti-Asian and anti-Hispanic chauvinism, alerting the American public to the dangers of uncontrolled immigration across the U.S.-Mexico border. Historians have given undue attention to hot-blooded diatribes against this era's "rising tide of color." Xenophobic arguments with the appearance of scientific objectivity occupied a far more important place in immigration discourse. In June 1920, California's State Board of Control issued a report claiming to evaluate the "Oriental question" in a "cold statistical way." It identified 185,368 hectares of land in the state that were owned, leased, or otherwise managed by people of Japanese descent – an area constituting more than a tenth of the state's irrigated acreage. Like latter-day population alarmists, this report emphasized recent *rates of growth* to make its findings more striking: Since 1910, California's Japanese population had more than doubled to 87,279; amount of land farmed had increased by 413 percent, and the annual value of crops produced on Japanese-controlled lands had increased by ten times

---

[12] Molony, *Technology and Investment*, 5–6, 10–12, 15, 24–37, 51–57, 70–73, 98–99, 151–69, 209–26, 242; Tsuru, *Political Economy of the Environment*, 79–96; Young, *Japan's Total Empire*, 32.

(ignoring wartime inflation). The state's booming fishing industry reflected similar trends.[13]

A sympathetic observer could have viewed these as valuable accomplishments in a world starving for food. In an open letter to President Wilson, the Japanese Association of America cited similar statistics with great pride, and made special note of the San Joaquin and Sacramento River deltas, where "a water-submerged swamp" of reeds, willow, saltgrass, and mosquitoes had been converted by Japanese ingenuity into irrigated fields of rice. California farmers from other ethnicities quickly adopted Japanese varietals and techniques for rice growing, which were soon transferred back across the Pacific for use on irrigated farmsteads distributed to white war veterans on the Murrumbidgee Project in Australia. Wataribune rice (*Oryza sativa* var. *japonica*), a short-grain variety brought by Japanese immigrants to California, provided the parent genetic stock for most of the medium-grain varietals grown in these regions today.[14] Japanese immigrants also played a leading role in establishing industrial-scale tuna fishing off Southern California during the 1910s. In 1908, Kondo Masaharu, an agronomist with ties to the Imperial Fisheries Institute in Kobe, went into partnership with a Mexican entrepreneur living in Los Angeles to fish the waters off Baja California. They introduced the Japanese practice of chumming the ocean with small fish to cause a feeding frenzy among schools of predatory tuna, which could then be caught with live bait using a bamboo pole, hook, and short line. The booming fishery for albacore (*Thunnus alalunga*) of the 1910s came to an abrupt end in 1917–18 when cool La Niña conditions abruptly gave way to El Niño. This crisis led several borderland companies to switch to tropical tunas, mainly using Japanese captains and crews. Kondo's company introduced the first fully refrigerated boats to the region from Japan in 1924 so it could engage in long-distance tuna fishing to the south, and his company was one of the first to use cannery waste to produce fishmeal on a large scale for agricultural use. Other Southern California companies kept careful watch on technological innovations introduced by Kondo and his partners but otherwise viewed these activities with alarm.[15]

[13] State Board of Control, *California and the Oriental* (Sacramento, 1920), 7–8, 11–12, 26, 45–50, 56, 65–68, 87–96; Roger Daniels, *The Politics of Prejudice: The Anti-Japanese Movement in California and the Struggle for Japanese Exclusion* (Berkeley and Los Angeles, 1977), 65–78; Matthew Connelly, "Seeing beyond the State: The Population Control Movement and the Problem of Sovereignty," *Past & Present* 193 (2006): 204–5.

[14] Quoted in State Board of Control, *California and the Oriental*, 227; Pearl, *The Nation's Food*, 241–42; Wayne Smith and Robert Daldy, eds., *Rice: Evolution, History, Production, and Technology* (Hoboken, NJ, 2002), 17–19, 80, 95; A. B. Blackeney et al., "Rice Cultivation and Quality in Australia," *Cahiers Options Méditerranénnes* 24 (1997): 89–94.

[15] Don Estes, "Kondo Masaharu and the Best of All Fishermen," *Journal of San Diego History* 23 (1977), http://www.sandiegohistory.org/journal/77summer/kondo.htm; McEvoy, *The Fishermen's Problem*, 130–37, 152, 168.

In an official letter to the U.S. secretary of state, California Governor William Stevens twisted these achievements into something to be feared. He thought the "virile, progressive, and aggressive" nature of the Japanese race had made them "crushing competitors to our white rural populations" and threatened to displace this "outpost on the western edge of Occidental civilization." He begged the California legislature and federal government to enforce more rigorous exclusions, including a registration program that would require all people of suspected Japanese descent to definitively prove they were legal residents or face immediate deportation. Meanwhile, hygienists spread the belief that Japanese vegetable growers' use of night soil as a fertilizer put white consumers at risk of typhoid, dysentery, and other diseases – foreshadowing later concerns about pesticide residues.[16]

"Must We Fight Japan?"

California's challenge elicited a vigorous response from population scientists. Their insertion into the debate over Asian immigration played an important role in the institutionalization of demography as a policy-oriented science. This controversy generated some key concepts that continue to influence demographic theory and environmental discourse on population, even today. These include (1) a preoccupation with standard of living as a determinant of patterns of population growth among particular social groups, (2) the connection of population growth to natural resource depletion and the disappearance of scenic and wilderness areas, (3) the application of the ecological concept of living space (*Lebensraum*) to political conflicts, (4) an ethical emphasis on the welfare of future generations, and (5) a recognition of the global nature of population problems. Geopolitical conflict within the Pacific World was central to these developments.

San Diego provided the locale for a long-forgotten but deeply influential two-week conference on "Orientals and Occidentals in the Pacific Coast Area" – an event that may qualify as the birthplace of the scientific population control movement in the United States. The site of this August 1920 meeting was itself significant. San Diego boosters were intent on building their small, borderland city into the metropole of a Pacific empire. The Panama-California Exposition of 1915, which celebrated the opening of the Panama Canal, centered on a resplendent Spanish colonial town and Japanese tea garden in Balboa Park and played a critical role in convincing the U.S. Navy to turn this port into a major naval base. The setting of this 1920 meeting communicated similar geopolitical messages. Each evening a single speaker presented a popular lecture at the Unitarian Church of San

---

[16] Quoted in State Board of Control, *California and the Oriental*, 9–10, 12; Ralph Burnight, "The Japanese in Rural Los Angeles County," *Studies in Sociology* 4, no. 4 (1920): 8–9; Walter Pitkin, *Must We Fight Japan?* (New York, 1921), 256–58.

Diego, another exemplar of Spanish Revival architecture. The following day, the conference reconvened for "discussions of a technical nature" at Scripps Biological Station in La Jolla; its picture-frame windows made the Pacific Ocean an important feature of the proceedings.[17]

Ohio-born newspaper magnate E. W. Scripps (1868–1926) sponsored this 1920 conference – his first major act as a patron of population science. He illustrates the ideological complexity of the early population control movement in the United States. Scripps founded the country's first national newspaper chain, which highlighted issues of interest to its working-class readership, such as the price of food. In this vein, Scripps closely followed Hoover's activities as food administrator and tried to convince him to run for president in 1920 on the premise that "the only way to make democracy safe is to make it more scientific." Populist attitudes also influenced Scripps's patronage of science. In 1919–20, he organized the Science News Service to accelerate the pace that the general public learned about scientific innovations, and he began looking for an opportunity to create "a really scientific sociological laboratory" to supplement his support for the La Jolla station. Scripps was a man of intense racial prejudice and contradiction. Even though he made his millions on urban newspapers sales, Scripps hated crowds, cities, and public attention, but he was no lover of wilderness, either. He was disgusted with the "dead-weight drag" that "short-sighted sentimentalists" such as U.S. Forest Service founder Gifford Pinchot had placed on modern society with their dedication to "monstrous Mother Nature." By this date, Scripps had become convinced that world population growth had locked "the white race . . . in a life and death struggle, with all the other races," which would eventually force them into a great war "to supply sustenance and room" for themselves. His newspapers had long served as rabble-rousers against Asian immigration and growing Japanese power in the Pacific even though Scripps, for a time, would only employ Japanese servants at his ranch north of San Diego.[18]

The 1920 conference reflected these concerns. Columbia School of Journalism professor Walter Pitkin started it off with "a general statement of

---

[17] "Biological Station Notes," Aug. 1920, History in the News, 1919–36, SIO Archives; Richard Amero, "The Making of the Panama-California Exposition, 1909–1915," *Journal of San Diego History* 36, no. 1 (1990). http://www.sandiegohistory.org/journal/90winter/expo.htm; Roger Lotchin, *Fortress California, 1910–1961: From Warfare to Welfare* (New York, 1992), 33.

[18] Scripps to Hoover, 20 June 1917; Hoover to Ujiro Oyama, 24 Mar. 1917, Ohio University Libraries, E. W. Scripps papers; Oliver Knight, ed., *I Protest: Selected Disquisitions of E. W. Scripps* (Madison, WI, 1966), 410–13, 433–35, 616–21; Negley Cochran, *E.W. Scripps* (New York, 1933), 103–15; Vance Trimble, *The Astonishing Mr. Scripps: The Turbulent Life of America's Penny Press Lord* (Ames, IO, 1992), 372, 413, 416, 423–25, 445–48; Gerald Baldasty, *E.W. Scripps and the Business of Newspapers* (Urbana, IL, 1999), 102, 115–18, 152–53.

troubles and local problems due to Oriental migration." Warren Thompson spent two days discussing the "growth of world population, past and future" and "problems of cheap labor, race prejudice, and standards of living," followed by Edward East's consideration of the "adequacy of basic supplies for probable world population." The chairman of the California Land Settlement Board, Elwood Mead, brought a rhetorical flair to the conference: "*Our country stands at the parting of ways,*" he declared, deploying a metaphor that was soon picked up by East and later by William Vogt. "It must protect its white civilization by excluding the brown, or it must be prepared for continued rural conflict." He praised farmers living on "the eastern frontier of the white man's world" in Australia, where he had worked for years as an irrigation technocrat. "In order to protect the opportunities and rights of the unborn," white Australians had "chosen slower material progress with a higher human standard" rather than employ cheap Asian labor. "'A house divided against itself cannot stand.'... East is East and West is West," Mead concluded. The following day, a University of California scientist ominously held up the genocidal extermination of the Canaanites by the children of Israel as a model "biological victory." In 1923, Mead took these ideas to British-ruled Palestine, where he provided a major boost to the efforts of Zionist colonists to take control of water resource development before ending his career as the powerful head of the U.S. Bureau of Reclamation and builder of Hoover Dam.[19]

Much of this discussion made it into the key publication to emerge from this conference: Pitkin's best-selling book *Must We Fight Japan?* Pitkin is most often remembered for self-help books such as *Life Begins at Forty* (1932), in which he sought to redirect "the consumer" away from an obsession with material acquisition toward personal cultivation and fulfillment. Standard of living was also the central theme of this earlier book. After traveling 5,000 kilometers around California and Northern Mexico, Pitkin concluded that "the Japanese crisis" was but "one minor phase of a world problem" which had its roots "in the elemental struggle for existence.... The world is short of food and clothes.... Too many babies are being born in the wrong places, and too few in the right places. The rich lands of the earth have all been occupied, and the poorer acres are now being pressed into service." Meanwhile, the good "land is wearing out;... larger yields mean costly fertilizer and unpleasant labor;... food prices are bound to be higher than ever. All of which is the price we must pay for the recklessness of our grandfathers and fathers, who... used to laugh at Malthus and his

---

[19] Emphasis added; "Biological Station Notes"; Mead, "New Agrarian Policies in Australia and California," in Pitkin, *Must We Fight Japan?*, 474–77; S. J. Holmes, "Shall East Wed West? Racial Intermarriage," in ibid., 487–490, 500–1; Worster, *Rivers of Empire*, 182–88; Robert Rook, "An American in Palestine: Elwood Mead and Zionist Water Resource Planning, 1923–36," *Arab Studies Quarterly* 22 (2000): 71–90.

gloomy prognostications of an overcrowded world and universe." Another world war was the most likely outcome. Pitkin laid out a list of similarities between Germany in 1910 and Japan in 1920. Item number six was "over-population": Japan could not feed itself, and was frantically importing rice from Siam and French Indochina. But Pitkin was even more concerned by the "disquieting surplus of highly trained professional and technical men" and "astonishing concentration of scientists and all other technical experts in service of the state." This underpaid "intellectual proletariat" and ambi-tious "aristocracy of brains" constituted a dangerous mix, which he thought was destined to "blow up within a decade or two" as the country struggled to maintain its standard of living. Pitkin did not think war with Japan was inevitable, however. "Concerted international action" to allow Japan to dominate Soviet-ruled Siberia might stave off conflict over land and natural resources in the short term, but a lasting solution would only come about if all sides checked their "fatal increase of population" by "putting a stop to immigration," by promoting "scientific birth control," and most signifi-cantly, by "forcing up the standard of living of the lower economic classes," thereby decreasing their fertility. Here we can see an essential doctrine of demographic transition theory already at work.[20]

Warren Thompson statistical work heavily influenced these conclusions. E. W. Scripps responded by making him director of the new Scripps Foun-dation for Research in Population Problems at Miami University, close to Scripps's first home in rural Ohio. To cement their association, Scripps invited Thompson along on a six-month circum-Pacific voyage in 1923 that turned into a fact-finding mission regarding the dangers of a Pacific war with Japan. In 1924, agricultural economist Pascal Whelpton (1893–1964) joined Thompson at the Scripps Foundation where they developed a groundbreaking technique for projecting population growth using age cohort analysis. Scripps also sponsored a lengthy trip by Whelpton so he could investigate population problems in South America. These actions, for a time, turned Miami University into the hemisphere's premier demographic research center.[21]

Elsewhere, interest in population problems began to pick up at an acceler-ating pace. In 1923, Edward East published his own best-selling jeremiad on the situation, *Mankind at the Crossroads*. "Man stands to-day at the parting of ways," East declared, "with the choice of controlling his own destiny or

---

[20] Pitkin, *Must We Fight Japan?*, v–x, 72, 77, 117, 226, 298–300, 307–8, 367, 379, 391; Sue Currell, "Depression and Recovery: Self-Help and America in the 1930s," in *Historicizing Lifestyles* (Burlington, VT, 2006); Simon Szreter, "The Idea of Demographic Transition and the Study of Fertility Change: A Critical Intellectual History," *Population and Development Review* 19 (1993): 659–701.

[21] Cochrane, *E. W. Scripps*, 117–18, 213–18; John Durand, "Pascal Kidder Whelpton," *Population Index* 30 (1964): 323–28; Ramsden, "Carving Up Population Science," 871; Szreter, "Idea of Demographic Transition," 663.

of being tossed about until the end of time by the blind forces of the environment.... All wars, all poverty, and much of the general misery prevalent in the world are laid at the door of overpopulation." Citing Thompson and Pitkin, East placed Japan's standard of living at the heart of his analysis: yes, East Asian agriculture was more productive than almost anywhere else, but not enough to include "the steaks, roasts, and chops, so dear to American hearts." For East, "China and Japan are contemporary examples of what the world as a whole is coming to in a very short time.... If we do not grasp the wisdom of aiding agricultural reconstruction to-day, may God pity those who follow."[22] This book appeared the same month that one of history's most destructive earthquakes and urban fires struck the Yokohama-Tokyo region. This quake caused a widely publicized crisis of homelessness and unemployment in Japan, which provided an excuse for the brutal murder of left-wing activists and as many as 6,000 Korean immigrants – events that combined to undermine Japan's liberal government and empower right-wing militarists.[23] In 1924, the Johnson-Reed Immigration Act put a decisive end to the possibility that the United States might provide haven to the world's tempest-tossed masses. It abolished legal immigration from Asia, established strict national quotas from Europe, but placed no restrictions on population movements from Latin America as a concession to California agribusiness and Pan Americanists. Japan retaliated by placing a 100 percent tariff on U.S. imports, while Japanese investment firms and emigrants like Alberto Fujimori's parents looked to Brazil and Peru for opportunities.[24]

Overpopulation concerns were by no means restricted to the United States. In 1922, feminist birth-control activist Margaret Sanger journeyed to Japan "to discuss population control" at the invitation of feminist activist Ishimoto Shidzue and the liberal magazine *Kaizō* (Reconstruction). Sanger also played a major role in organizing the 1927 World Population Conference held in Geneva. According to historian Alison Bashford, this "precociously global" delegation almost universally accepted the idea that the world was entering an era of limits, when geopolitical competition for virgin soil and wilderness would become a zero-sum game, as rapidly developing states like Japan and Italy searched for the *Lebensraum* they needed to grow. These themes were all clearly present at the 1920 San Diego meeting.

[22] East, *Mankind at the Crossroads* (New York, 1923), viiii, 10–11, 72–75, 92–93, 196.
[23] Joshua Hammer, *Yokohama Burning: The Deadly 1923 Earthquake and Fire That Helped Forge the Path to World War II* (New York, 2006); Sonia Ryang, "The Great Kanto Earthquake and the Massacre of Koreans in 1923," *Anthropological Quarterly* 76 (2003): 731–48.
[24] Mae Ngai, *Impossible Subjects: Illegal Aliens and the Making of Modern America* (Princeton, NJ, 2004), ch. 1; Jeffrey Lesser, *Negotiating National Identity: Immigrants, Minorities, and the Struggle for Ethnicity in Brazil* (Durham, NC, 1999), 97–102, 120; Luis Jochamowitz, *Ciudadano Fujimori: La construcción de un político* (Lima, 1993), 37–48.

Likewise, the Geneva Conference inspired a growing list of international institutions and meetings dedicated to population studies.[25]

Warren Thompson, meanwhile, became frustrated by the biological determinism and class prejudice expressed by fellow population control advocates, and joined a number of Geneva delegates in criticizing immigration restrictions by the world's neo-European nations. Thompson had already called on America's wealthy to "simplify their mode of life" and spoken out against intelligence testing and eugenic ideas, which he saw as "merely another method of glorifying the dominant class in society" with "no scientific basis."[26] In 1929, Thompson published a statistical paper comparing historical trends in birth rates, death rates, and natural increase that empirically identified three categories of population growth potential among the world's nations. Japan, India, and Soviet Russia showed very high birth and death rates and exhibited corresponding susceptibility to the Malthusian checks of war, famine, and disease. Italy and the Slavic peoples of Eastern Europe had declining birth rates but death rates that were falling even faster. Both categories possessed prodigious potential for population increase. The countries of northern and western Europe and their settler colonies, on the other hand, were "rapidly approaching a stationary or decreasing population," particularly in regions most affected by industrialization and urbanization.[27] In a separate piece, Thompson proposed that declining fertility came about as a *natural* result of improvements in economic efficiency, sanitation, hygiene, and "cultural development" that took place among peoples trying to attain a higher standard of living. In stark contrast to most of his peers, Thompson thought these tendencies applied to all races of humanity.[28] These benchmark papers provided statistical evidence and social explanations for Raymond Pearl's mathematical "law of population growth" based on the logistic curve. They also represent fully formed statements of what came to be known as the demographic transition and even divided the earth into First, Second, and Third Worlds.

Thompson expanded these ideas into a Malthusian theory of global conflict titled *Danger Spots in World Population*. In this controversial book, he set forth the thesis that "differential pressure of peoples on their resources" and their "unjust" division among the world's imperial powers was the fundamental cause of warfare in the modern world. By Thompson's

---

[25] Helen Hopper, *A New Woman of Japan: A Political Biography of Katō Shidzue* (Boulder, CO, 1995), ch. 2; Bashford, "Nation, Empire, Globe"; Perkins, *Geopolitics and the Green Revolution*, 123.

[26] Thompson, "Standards of Living as the Effect of Growth of Competing Population Groups," *Scientific Monthly* 17 (1923): 57–65; Thompson, "Eugenics and the Social Good," *Journal of Social Forces* 3 (1925): 414–19.

[27] Thompson, "Population," *American Journal of Sociology* 34 (1929): 959–75.

[28] Thompson, "Standards of Living as the Effect of Growth of Competing Population Groups," *Scientific Monthly* 17 (1923): 57–65.

calculations, the western Pacific was by far the most significant danger spot on earth. The European-derived nations that governed most territory in this region were done "swarming" as peoples and possessed abundant territory. The Japanese, Chinese, and Italians, on the other hand, were now "swarming" in search of resources and colonies to feed their rapidly growing populations. What if Japan, Italy, or Germany were to create a "Malthusian alliance," Thompson asked, and demand a larger "place in the sun" from the world's imperial powers? To Thompson, these demographic findings suggested a technocratic strategy for averting another great war. The colonized lands and wilderness areas of the world should be redistributed in a planned manner to "take account of the vital needs of those who are still 'swarming.'" For Japan, this might involve taking control of the American-ruled Philippines or Australian-ruled New Guinea. This transfer would enable the Japanese to experience a higher standard of living, which would encourage lower rates of population increase and eliminate their danger to the world's other civilized peoples. (Thompson gave little consideration to the impact of colonialism on indigenous peoples, and he tended to dismiss the effectiveness of birth control programs until basic socioeconomic changes were accomplished.) These ideas gained wider currency in Thompson's *Population Problems* (1930), which for three decades served as the standard college textbook for the new field of demography.[29]

Few statesmen found Thompson's proposal to reengineer the world's colonial order at all attractive, but this does not mean that Malthusian thinking failed to influence international politics. In the wake of the Great Crash of 1929, population technocrats obtained unprecedented influence over the relocation of peoples, usually as a strategy to obtain ethnic control over land and resources. The ideas and actions of these ethnocrats must bear heavy blame for the outbreak of hostilities and the worst atrocities of the Second World War.

The belief that overpopulation threatened Japan's future profoundly influenced its pursuit of "total empire" in the western Pacific during the interwar period. A 1930 study of Japanese population policy concluded that "since the financial crisis of 1920 and the earthquake of 1923 the Government has sought to encourage emigration in every possible way, on the assumption that the national economic depression is due to the pressure of over-population." Japan's Commission on Food and Population even briefly promoted the distribution of contraceptives.[30] During the 1930s, right-wing militarists reoriented national population policy toward extending

---

[29] Thompson, *Danger Spots in World Population* (New York, 1930), v, 13, 16, 42–45, 81, 88, 93–94, 119, 126, 132, 226, 253, 329–31.

[30] Seishi Idei, "Japan's Migration Problem," *International Labour Review* 22 (1930): 773–89; Deborah Oakley, "American-Japanese Interaction in the Development of Population Policy in Japan, 1945–52," *Population and Development Review* 4 (1978): 621.

imperial control over the Asian mainland. In 1936, the government announced a grandiose plan to resettle one million farming households – a fifth of Japan's agricultural population – to Manchuria by 1956. Brazil and Peru had just shut themselves off as havens for Japanese immigration, but climate extremes also played a role in this decision. In 1931 and 1934–35, anomalously cool and damp Baiu weather conditions greatly restricted summer growth in the northern rice-growing region of Tōkohu. This caused a significant drop in national rice production, inspired the massive export of girls from this region to work in prostitution, and resulted in famine in some areas – all confirming the worst fears of Japanese Malthusians. A fifth of the 300,000 Japanese colonists who resettled in Manchuria by 1945 came from this cold-stricken zone. Catastrophic floods also struck China's Yellow River delta in 1931 and 1935 – especially western Shandong, a key supplier of cotton to Japan. Despite concerted attempts by Chinese population experts to manage this humanitarian crisis, these floods fueled an epidemic of famine diseases and female infanticide. This disruption also played into Japanese plans to erode Nationalist governmental control over northeastern China, a policy that devolved into open war in 1937.[31]

In the fall of 1938, the Italian government sent its first shipment of 16,000 agricultural colonists to settle in coastal Libya. Italy hoped to send an eventual 100,000 settlers to convert this Arab-dominated "sandbox" into the country's Fourth Shore. Corrado Gini, the head of fascist Italy's Central Statistical Institute and most influential anti-Malthusian population scientist of this era, had long argued that population increase would provide the Italian nation with the energy it needed for rapid industrial growth, agrarian renewal, and territorial conquests. However, the Libyan colonization scheme could not hide the embarrassing fact that a decade of pro-natalist policies, marsh draining, and technocratic controls over internal migration had failed to increase the birth rate, decrease child mortality, or improve living standards in fascist Italy.[32]

The success of Nazi Germany's pro-natalist policies, on the other hand, have caused many to overlook the fact that National Socialist ideologues accepted many basic tenets of Malthusian geopolitical thinking. In *Mein Kampf*, Adolf Hitler famously declared that "the acquisition of new soil

---

[31] Louise Young, *Japan's Total Empire: Manchuria and the Culture of Wartime Imperialism* (Berkeley and Los Angeles, 1998), ch. 7–8; Lesser, *Negotiating National Identity* 112–35; Junsei Kondo, "Volcanic Eruptions, Cool Summers, and Famines in the Northeastern Part of Japan," *Journal of Climate* 1 (1998): 775–88; Lillian Li, "Life and Death in a Chinese Famine: Infanticide as a Demographic Consequence of the 1935 Yellow River Flood," *Comparative Studies in Society and History* 33 (1991): 466–510.

[32] Roberta Pergher, "A Tale of Two Borders: Settlement and National Transformation in Libya and South Tyrol under Facism" (Ph.D. diss., University of Michigan, 2007), xii, 92–109, 394–398, 532; Ramsden, "Carving Up Population Science," 874–80; Maria Sophia Quine, *Population Politics in Twentieth-Century Europe* (London and New York, 1996), ch. 1.

for the settlement of excess population possesses an infinite number of advantages, particularly if we turn from the present to the future," and he disturbed many German conservationists with his call to leave "no square meter of German soil...uncultivated" to increase national food production.[33] Germany invaded Poland in September 1939 primarily to obtain "living space" for 200,000 ethnic Germans from South Tyrol, Hungary, and other foreign-ruled lands that had been slated for resettlement. This plan was intended to bring about the rapid consolidation of Germany as a territorial nation-state. However, Nazi ethnocrats got bogged down with the effort of resettling hundreds of thousands of displaced Poles – long a source of ethnic resentment because of their association with cheap labor, high fecundity, low standards of living, and unfair economic competition in East Prussia. Many Germans projected for resettlement instead spent long periods in concentration camps of their own. The General Plan East, a landmark in the history of environmental planning, reveals the sheer audacity of this quest to create *Lebensraum* for the German people. This technocratic project proposed deporting two-thirds of the Slavic population from eastern Europe to western Siberia by 1970 and replanting the vacated region in accord with the latest principles of natural resource conservation and landscape design – complete with nature reserves. At one point, this plan included an intermediate phase to drain the vast Pripyat Marshes using resettled Jews, until it was nixed by Hitler because of the fear that wetland destruction would cause regional climate change and unleash massive dust storms. The daunting logistical difficulties of managing so many people who were not growing food – German, Slav, or Jew – soon caused this ethnocratic apparatus to break down under its own Malthusian weight and led to the official abandonment of mass resettlement programs in favor of mass murder.[34]

These tendencies were not restricted to the Axis Powers. Stalinist agents in the Soviet Union forcibly resettled millions of people belonging to ethnic minorities to thinly settled lands in Siberia and Central Asia, starting with 172,000 Koreans accused of helping Japanese infiltration of the Soviet Far East.[35] In the United States, Herbert Hoover and Franklin Roosevelt's governments made increasing use of population experts, especially from the Scripps Foundation. In 1938, the National Resources Committee issued a

---

[33] Quoted in Frank Uekoetter, *The Green and the Brown: A History of Conservation in Nazi Germany* (Cambridge and New York, 2006), 30, 155.

[34] Götz Aly, *"Final Solution": Nazi Population Policy and the Murder of the European Jews* (London, 1999), 18, 24, 175–76; Philip Rutherford, *Prelude to the Final Solution: The Nazi Program for Deporting Ethnic Poles, 1939–1941* (Lawrence, KS, 2007); David Blackbourn, *The Conquest of Nature: Water, Landscape, and the Making of Modern Germany* (New York, 2006), ch. 5; Uekoetter, *The Green and the Brown*, 155–60; Quine, *Population Politics*, ch. 3.

[35] Otto Pohl, *Ethnic Cleansing in the USSR, 1937–1949* (Westport, CT, 1999).

massive study of population and resources in the country. It concluded that reducing the country's rate of population growth was necessary but censored any mention of birth control.[36] A few contributors therefore issued dissenting statements of their own. Pascal Whelpton was of the opinion that "the United States is *now* overpopulated from the standpoint of per capita economic welfare, but fortunately not as seriously overpopulated as most nations." He advocated reducing the U.S. population to an optimum level of 100 million while encouraging the reproduction of "the more able, intelligent and farsighted portion of the population." Such attitudes help to explain why U.S. officials were so reluctant to open the country's doors to wartime refugees – no matter how desperate.[37]

In the Desert Southwest, Malthusian ideas produced a holocaust of a different kind. From 1933 through 1946, rangeland technocrats forced Navajo pastoralists to kill half a million livestock, based on the argument that rapid increases in the population of the Navajo and their sheep had overgrazed the region, causing massive soil erosion and threatening the long-term existence of the Navajo Nation and the gigantic reservoir named after Elwood Mead that stood behind Hoover Dam. Most of these animals were shot en masse and left to rot in remote canyons and corrals. Interethnic competition for land and resources was the real cause for these actions.[38] In October 1937, Dominican dictator Rafael Trujillo ordered the mass killing of Haitians living along his country's poorly defined border. Fifteen to twenty thousand were hacked to death or hanged during this brutal campaign; tens of thousands more fled west to save their skins. The United States nevertheless remained a staunch supporter of Trujillo for another quarter century. This genocidal episode was a fundamental cause for the abrupt contrast in forest cover visible on either side of the Haitian-Dominican border today.[39] After the outbreak of World War II, several Latin American countries systematically rounded up Japanese, German, and Italian residents for internment, following the lead of the United States. Okada Nikumatsu had emigrated from Japan to Peru to work on a coastal sugar plantation. After completing his indenture, he became a cotton sharecropper and worked his way up to

---

[36] *Recent Social Trends in the United States* (New York, 1933), preface, ch. 1; Ramsden, "Carving up Population Science," 879; Oakley, "American-Japanese Interaction," 621.

[37] Whelpton's emphasis; Whelpton, "Population Policy for the United States," 403, 406; Richard Breitman and Alan Kraut, *American Refugee Policy and European Jewry, 1933–1945* (Bloomington, IN, 1987).

[38] Richard White, *The Roots of Dependency: Subsistence, Environment, and Social Change among the Choctaws, Pawnees, and Navajos,* (Lincoln, NE, 1983), 226–35, 271–76, 311–13.

[39] Richard Turits, "A World Destroyed, A Nation Imposed: The 1937 Haitian Massacre in the Dominican Republic," *Hispanic American Historical Review* 82 (2002): 590–635; contra Jared Diamond, *Collapse: How Societies Choose to Fail or Succeed* (New York, 2005), ch. 11.

water manager. In 1923, he began restoring a derelict estate in the Chancay valley. With the help of Tangüis cotton and 2,500 tons of guano, he made it big as an agribusinessman – only to lose everything when Peru deported him to the United States after Pearl Harbor, where he lived out the war locked up in an internment camp – all for the crime of belonging to the wrong ethnicity.[40]

Population Bomb in the Central Pacific

The catastrophic events of World War I and its aftermath also inspired reconsideration of Malthus's ideas within the British Empire. These ideas profoundly influenced humanity's relationship with the guano and phosphate islands of the Central Pacific.

Alexander Morris Carr-Saunders (1886–1966) exercised a broad influence over this discourse. He offered a far more optimistic evaluation of humanity's capacity for self-control than most Malthusians. On the basis of a heavily documented survey of world ethnographic literature, Carr-Saunders concluded that even societies living close to a "state of nature" were capable of using abortion, infanticide, abstinence, and other controls to adapt their population to an "optimum number" that offered "the highest average return per head." This optimum number might rise or fall over time, depending on the varying "nature of the environment" and technological improvements. His economic approach to population numbers profoundly influenced the science of animal ecology through his disciple Charles Elton and inspired Oxford reproductive zoologist John Baker to develop Volpar paste, a mercury-based spermicide, to provide a "eugenically perfect contraceptive" for attacking the world's population problems. Similar to Thompson, Carr-Saunders was hopeful circa 1930 that a global board of ethnocrats could figure out a way to "adjust population to supplies."[41]

Anglo scientists and officials living in the southwestern Pacific also expressed concern about Japanese expansion but placed greater emphasis than most on the subject of indigenous depopulation. Australian-born historian Stephen Henry Roberts, for example, presented a paper on this theme to the Institute of Pacific Relations in Honolulu in 1925 – a conference remarkable for its optimism regarding the harmonious coexistence of civilizations in the Pacific World. This article grew into the monumental

---

[40] Jochamowitz, *Ciudadano Fujimori*, 30–31; Max Friedman, *Nazis and Good Neighbors: The United States Campaign against the Germans of Latin America in World War II* (Cambridge and New York, 2003).

[41] Carr-Saunders, *The Population Problem: A Study in Human Evolution* (Oxford, 1922), 5–6, 475–82, app. 1; Anker, *Imperial Ecology* 86–107, 114–15; Ramsden, "Carving up Population Science," 869–70; Richard Soloway, "The 'Perfect Contraceptive': Eugenics and Birth Control Research in Britain and America in the Interwar Years," *Journal of Contemporary History* 30 (1995): 654.

book *Population Problems in the Pacific,* which focused on the environmental determinants of white settlement patterns and indigenous depopulation, especially disease. Roberts noted with satisfaction that most indigenous populations in the region had begun to stabilize and in some cases were growing rapidly under hygiene-obsessed colonial rule. The Empire Census of 1931 confirmed that native numbers had indeed "turned the corner" after years of steady decline. Niue's population, for example, had begun to rebound after sending 150 men to fight in World War I with the Third Maori Regiment and the depredations of the 1918–20 influenza pandemic (table 3.1). By this date, the Rapanui had also grown to 450 – but still had to share Easter Island with 70,000 sheep.[42]

This meant that colonial administrators would have to make room for growing populations in their future plans. In 1931, Arthur Grimble, the resident commissioner of the Gilbert and Ellice Islands Colony (G&EIC), appointed Henry Evans Maude to make the first island-by-island census of this territory since 1911. Maude was born in 1906 in Patna, India, which had fallen into decline from its days as the world's greatest nitrate producer. As the son of a colonial officer, he had plenty of opportunity to hear talk of overpopulation as a youth, particularly in 1918 when the monsoon failed and famine and flu struck down millions on the subcontinent, including Maude. He read voraciously on the subject of political economy, including Carr-Saunders book and was one of the first to complete a formal degree in anthropology at Cambridge University. As we saw in Chapter 4, Grimble encouraged Maude to apply his anthropological expertise to colonial administration. In 1932, he gave Maude the delicate task of adjudicating indigenous land disputes on the highly contested island of Banaba. This experience made Maude intensely aware of the difficulties posed by renewed population growth. Colonial rule had made a mess of indigenous property regimes and mostly destroyed "the old controls" natives had used to live within natural limits on these barren atolls. Maude thought the British possessed "a definite moral obligation" to provide the Gilbertese with "room for expansion for the youth." As a solution, he recommended the colonization of uninhabited guano islands in the Central Pacific.[43]

---

[42] Roberts, *Population Problems in the Pacific* (London, 1927), esp. 126–28, 387–88; H. L. Wilkinson, *The World's Population Problems and a White Australia* (London, 1930), 4, 312–16; "Population Problems in the Pacific," *Nature* 8 Apr. 1933: 519–20; Tomoko Akami, *Internationalizing the Pacific: The United States, Japan and the Institute of Pacific Relations in War and Peace, 1919–45* (London and New York, 2002), 87–95, 102–4; Margaret Pointer and Kalasi Folau, *My Heart Is Crying a Little: Niue Island Involvement in the Great War, 1914–1918* (Suva, Fiji, 2000); Fischer, *Island at the End of the World,* 188.

[43] Maude, "Report on the Colonization of the Phoenix Islands by the Surplus Population of the Gilbert and Ellice Islands" (1938), NAUK-BFO 371–21515; Maude, "The Colonization of the Phoenix Islands," in *Of Islands and Men* (Melbourne, 1968), 317–21; Susan Woodburn,

An accelerating ecological catastrophe turned Maude into an all-out evangelist for this line of thought. On Banaba, the systematic destruction of coconut groves by phosphate mining had begun to take its toll. Thirteen adults and sixteen children died of beriberi in 1934 among 157 officially reported cases. Such deaths were unheard of among islanders who consumed plenty of coconut toddy and other traditional foods. This disease of the world's new ecological regime, caused by vitamin B_1 deficiency from eating too much processed food, remained a problem for the rest of the decade. Maude tried to start a movement to require indigenous workers within the colony to consume local produce, but medical staff vetoed this proposal on the grounds that it would reduce consumption of muscle-building canned beef. With Maude's encouragement, 750 drought-stricken Beru islanders signed an unsuccessful petition to allow resettlement among the coconut plantations of Washington Island, which had been abandoned due to the Great Depression and 1933–34 La Niña drought. He was helped in these endeavors by his wife Honor (1905–2001). She dedicated herself to improving the nutrition, health, and economic status of indigenous women and children, like the wives of Arthur Grimble and Albert Ellis before her – when they did not have their hands full with the dirty task of nursing white men with amebic dysentery. The Maudes eventually brought about the repeal of Grimble's repressive Uniform Code with the help of anthropologist Camilla Wedgwood, an outspoken critic of indigenous women's marginalization under colonial rule. In 1935, Maude had to accept reassignment to Zanzibar, ostensibly so he could recover from "dietary deficiency" caused by too much defecation and the consumption of too little fresh milk, butter, and meat. After they left, a classic virgin soil epidemic struck the Gilbert Islands from Fiji that seemingly confirmed Maude's views regarding the dangers of overcrowding. Measles officially infected 14,282 within the colony, over half the population. To the surprise of many, only 100 died.[44]

In a colony as frugal and conservative as the Gilbert and Ellice Islands, Maude's colonization scheme might never have gotten off the ground if not for intense geopolitical contention over the guano islands of the Central Pacific. By the mid 1930s, Pan American Airways was eager to expand its aviation empire deep into the Southern Hemisphere. Pan Am had already

Where Our Hearts Still Lie: Harry and Honor Maude in the Pacific Islands (Adelaide, 2003), 7, 26–30, 46–48, 64–70.

[44] CEI; Woodburn, *Where Our Hearts Still Lie*, 33, 47, 50, 78, 86, 88–89, 98–99, 111, 125, 137–40; Maude, "Colonization of the Phoenix Islands," 321; Simmons et al., *Global Epidemiology*, 1:264–66; Marie-Hélèn Sachet, "Climate and Meteorology of the Gilbert Islands," *Atoll Research Bulletin* no. 60 (1957), table E; Sigrah and King, *Te Rii ni Banaba*, 183; Roberts, *Population Problems in the Pacific*, 78; Kenneth Carpenter, *Beriberi, White Rice, and Vitamin B: A Disease, a Cause, and a Cure* (Berkeley and Los Angeles, 2000); Nancy Lutkehaus, "'She Was "Very" Cambridge': Camilla Wedgwood and the History of Women in British Social Anthropology," *American Ethnologist* 13 (1986): 776–98.

pushed aside or swallowed a host of rival companies in Latin America and the North Atlantic with the help of lucrative subsidies from the U.S. government, and was engaged in a fierce rivalry with German-equipped airlines in southern South America.[45] To help Pan American Airways fly across the Pacific to the Antipodes, the United States formally annexed Baker, Howland, and Jarvis Islands in 1936 based on claims under the Guano Islands Act of 1856. The British Empire responded by annexing eight of the Phoenix Islands to the G&EIC in March 1937. Japan also got in on the action by trying to purchase Easter Island from Chile as a stepping-stone to South America. On 3 March 1938, the United States made a counter-claim to Canton and Enderbury Islands, which possessed lagoons suitable for landing seaplanes, based on their supposed "first discovery" by New England whalers. Three days later, following an occupation strategy similar to territorial claimants in Antarctica,[46] Pan American Airways landed a scientific expedition on Canton Island that set up a meteorological observatory and radio station, which was followed by a team of solar astronomers sent by the National Geographic Society in June. Maude's scheme suddenly received support at the highest levels as a means to solidify British territorial claims, and brought about his abrupt reassignment back to the Pacific.[47]

In September 1937, Maude and a team of native Gilbertese officials embarked on an expedition to survey the eight Phoenix Islands. They stopped first at Gardner Island, one of the last islands of its kind in the Pacific Basin. It was thickly cloaked by an old-growth forest of *buka* trees inhabited by thousands of huge coconut crabs and tiny white terns (*Gygis alba*). Expedition members gorged themselves on masked boobies (*Sula dactylatra*), which were so tame they could walk up and wring their necks. Five small groves of overgrown coconut trees provided the only obvious sign of John Arundel's former presence. None of them had ever seen an atoll with such a wealth of natural resources. In stark contrast, their second stop Canton Island was "barren and unprepossessing" and covered with so many nests that they could barely walk without breaking eggs. On the bright side, it had a vast lagoon teeming with fish. Only ten coconut trees remained from Arundel's experiments, but Maude was still optimistic that

[45] Cushman, "Struggle over Airways."

[46] Adrian Howkins, "Political Meteorology: Weather, Climate and the Contest for Antarctic Sovereignty, 1939–1959," *History of Meteorology* 4 (2008): 27–40.

[47] Maude "Report on Colonization," 28–32; A. Richards to Foreign Office, 14 Feb. 1938; R. Lindsey to Foreign Office, 8 Mar. 1938; A. Acheson to A. Henderson, 9 Mar. 1938; Colonial Office to U.K. Department of State, 12 Mar. 1938; A. Bevir to T. Balfour, 25 Mar. 1938; High Commissioner of the Western Pacific to Secretary of State for the Colonies, 26 Apr. 1938; Colonial Office memorandum to Foreign Office, 13 May 1938; Balfour to G. Mounsey, 13 May 1938; Washington Chancery to American Department of Foreign Office, 19 May 1938; all in NAUK-FO 371/21514–21516. Woodburn, *Where Our Hearts Still Lie*, 128, 133; Fischer, *Island at the End of the World*, 192–93.

massive tree planting would "keep the ground moist and cool" and "result in increased rainfall." He encouraged his associates to bestow their own names to these islands as ceremonies of possession; they renamed the former island Nikumaroro for the mythic land of the first *buka* tree, and the latter Aba Riringa, "land of sunshine."[48]

Both of these islands would require environmental transformation before they could support large numbers of colonists. Hull and Sydney Islands, on the other hand, had flourishing coconut plantations and numerous feral pigs. More ominously, their coconut trees showed signs of experiencing severe droughts in the past; freshwater was scarce; and their reefs had many poisonous fish. Maude reassured his superiors that "It would not be long before the natives became experts in knowing the species of fish that should be avoided." The remaining four islands in the Phoenix group were much more arid, showed abundant signs of former guano extraction, and absolutely teemed with marine birds. Maude strongly recommended protecting them as bird sanctuaries. On 27 October 1937, Maude's company raised the Union Jack over McKean Island in the name of His Britannic Majesty George V. As it turned out, this "favourite breeding place of the frigate bird" was the very last territory to become an official part of the British Empire. The British government promptly declared Birnie, Phoenix, and McKean Islands as bird sanctuaries, and directed Maude to look further into colonizing the coconut plantations of Washington, Fanning, and Kiritimati (Christmas) as "the ultimate solution of the Gilbertese population problem."[49]

From London's point of view, birds and settlers were little more than pawns in a geopolitical gambit to secure lines of communication between North America and the southwestern Pacific. The United States and Great Britain eventually agreed to joint occupation of Canton and Enderbury Islands and paved over Canton Island's bird colonies and demolished its coral reefs to make way for the aviation age. The native inhabitants of the seven southernmost Gilbert Islands had their own reasons for participating in this colonization program. They expressed enormous enthusiasm "mixed...with certain incredulity" that they would be offered outright ownership of additional atolls. Thanks to the advent of another La Niña drought in 1938, Maude received 4,611 applications for resettlement – even though colonists had to give up lands on their home islands as a part of the bargain.[50] In December of that year, sixty-one Gilbertese pioneers set

[48] Maude "Report on Colonization," 5–9, 15–16, 18; Maude, "Colonization of the Phoenix Islands," 328; P. B. Laxton, "Nikumaroro," *Journal of the Polynesian Society* 60 (1951): 136.

[49] Maude "Report on Colonization," 10–13, 28–32; Maude, "Colonization of the Phoenix Islands," 339; Richards to Foreign Office, 14 Feb. 1938; Woodburn, *Where Our Hearts Still Lie*, 149–57.

[50] CEI; Maude "Report on Colonization," 13–14, 20–21; Otto Degener and Edwin Gillaspy, "Canton Island, South Pacific," *Atoll Research Bulletin* no. 41 (1955): 8; Woodburn, *Where Our Hearts Still Lie*, 143, 154 n. 32; Sachet, "Climate and Meteorology," table E.

off with Maude for the Phoenix Islands. The expedition again feasted on
boobies and coconut crabs when ten men disembarked on Gardener Island
to begin cutting down forest for coconut planting. A U.S. warship was
anchored off Hull Island, but Maude did not hesitate to plant a new settlement right in the midst of land marked out for an American aerodrome.
The bulk of the group landed on Sydney Island, which they rechristened
as Manra. To prevent disease, Maude closely supervised the positioning of
latrines, while Honor personally oversaw the scrubbing of children from
head to foot before embarkation. In this way, the Maudes brought the age
of soap and water to these guano islands.[51]

In their rush to settle the Phoenix Islands while they enjoyed favorable
political winds, Harry Maude and his associates neglected to account for
weather and war. Coconut trees stopped bearing fruit and toddy because of
the severe 1938 La Niña. Settlers on Gardner could not find any freshwater.
Maude moved forward, anyway, bringing 729 colonists, 546 of them to
Sydney Island. The drought forced colonists to place heavy reliance on eating
guano birds and other wild foods. Almost the entire Sydney Island settlement
got sick with fish poisoning; some died despite taking traditional herbal
emetics. Practically all of the plant cuttings the colonists brought with them
wilted before an extended El Niño event broke the drought late in 1939.
This caused its own problems: heavy rains filled Sydney Island's hypersaline
central lagoon and flooded croplands with saltwater. Strong westerly gales
damaged coconut trees and made deep-sea fishing even more dangerous.
Malnutrition, flu, and chicken pox also swept the islands. Even the project's
Anglo resident supervisor was affected; he died on Gardner Island from
a confluence of intestinal ailments and malnutrition at age twenty-nine.
Cloth deteriorated rapidly in the humidity, forcing colonists to return to
traditional grass skirts. Colonists at first turned up their noses at consuming
boi or yellow purslane (*Portulaca lutea*), a salt-tolerant succulent native to
the region that was rich in vitamin C. This traditional famine food soon
became an indispensable staple and enabled colonists to survive years of
neglect during World War II.[52]

As we saw in Chapter 4, Albert Ellis and other propagandists for the
British Phosphate Commission had also come to rely on overpopulation
discourse to defend their despoliation of Banaba and Nauru. A horrific subsistence crisis struck these remote Pacific Islands during the war. In February
1942, the BPC and colonial officials abruptly abandoned Banaba, Nauru,
and the Gilbert Islands after suffering repeated losses from German and

---

[51] Maude, "Colonization of the Phoenix Islands," 333–36; Knudson, *Titiana*, 50; Laxton,
"Nikumaroro," 147; Woodburn, *Where Our Hearts Still Lie*, 143, 146.

[52] CEI; Maude, "Colonization of the Phoenix Islands," 324, 336–37, 341; Woodburn, *Where
Our Hearts Still Lie*, 148; Kenneth Knudson, *Titiana: A Gilbertese Community in the
Solomon Islands* (Eugene, OR, 1965), 50, 52, 57, 157, 160–62; Laxton, "Nikumaroro,"
139–40; I. G. Turbot, "Portulaca: A Specialty in the Diet of the Gilbertese in the Phoenix
Islands, Central Pacific," *Journal of the Polynesian Society* 63 (1954): 77–85.

Japanese bombardment. Neither party made any attempt to repatriate 713 Gilbert and Ellice Islanders working on Banaba, and left them to fend for themselves for the duration of the war along with 800 family members and indigenous Banabans. During the late 1930s, resource-hungry Japan imported up to one million tons of phosphate a year, so few were surprised when the Japanese military occupied Christmas Island, Nauru, and Banaba later that year and heavily fortified them. This forced farmers in Australia and New Zealand to make do with strictly rationed phosphate supplies from Makatea and Australian bird islands.[53]

Historians have sometimes wondered why Banaba, of all the islands on the southeastern edge of the zone of Japanese control, was the only one to suffer atrocities comparable to a Nazi concentration camp. This question may have a Malthusian answer. The BPC had already destroyed much of the island's capacity to feed its residents – even during years of relative abundance. Unfortunately, 1942 was a dry La Niña year, and the island's paltry food stockpiles were long gone by the time the Japanese invaded Banaba in August 1942 with a force of 500 soldiers and 50 Okinawan and Korean laborers. Baiu weather conditions again struck northern Japanese rice-growing areas in 1941 and 1945, and these newcomers were understandably reluctant to share their own meager rations with their new colonial subjects when their own families were hungry back home. They made matters much worse by forcing locals to hand over most of their daily catch. Banaba's ticking population bomb exploded in violence and suffering. Of the 462 individuals abandoned on Banaba who are known to have died during the war, at least 97 succumbed to starvation or related sickness. Locals did not take this situation lying down but met with vicious reprisals when they showed even a hint of disobedience. Japanese soldiers publicly beheaded at least twenty-five, usually for the crime of pilfering food. They shot twenty lepers, rather than following British practice and sending them off for a lifetime of incarceration at a leper asylum. In an attempt to diffuse this situation, the Japanese shipped a few dozen men to the Caroline Islands to harvest coconuts, but the food they sent back arrived in spoiled condition. Like the colonists of the Phoenix Islands, Banabans were reduced to eating *boi*. In July 1943, the Japanese deported the surviving population of indigenous Banabans and all other women and children to Nauru, Kusaie, and the northern Gilberts – a decision that probably saved many of them from starvation. The U.S. military liberated the Gilbert Islands soon after but left Banaba, Nauru, Kusaie, and many other islands to "wither on the vine" until the bitter end. U.S. air patrols successfully cut off these islands from

---

[53] Ellis to Sydney Arundel Aris, 21 Aug. 1941, 3 July 1942, 12 Nov. 1943, PMB 497; Maude, *Memorandum on Post-War Reorganization and Administrative Policy* (Auckland, 1945), 32, 36; Kathleen Barnes, "Pacific Islands Double Phosphate Output," *Far Eastern Survey* 22 May 1940: 132; Ellis, *Mid-Pacific Outposts* (Aukland, 1946), 264–65; Sigrah and King, *Te Rii ni Banaba*, 243–46; Williams and Macdonald, *The Phosphateers*, 324.

Japanese lines of supply with the goal of starving them into submission; any Pacific Islanders who starved to death were considered collateral damage. Japanese garrisons on Nauru and Banaba adopted an ingenious strategy to prevent Malthusian catastrophe, however. They required everyone to collect their excrement and other organic refuse in petrol drums, bury them partway in the ground, and use them to plant crops. These guano gardens produced a bumper crop of pumpkins, as well as maize, sweet potatoes, and a little tobacco, and kept a population of more than 5,500 alive and in relatively good health until an Australian relief expedition arrived in September 1945.[54]

Albert Ellis served as an official representative of New Zealand at the surrender of Nauru and Banaba in 1945. He was "shocked by the devastation" he encountered in the region. Much of Tarawa in the Gilbert Islands had been converted into "huge airstrips, bare and hot." The Allies had bombed Tarawa and Nauru heavily. "Hundreds if not thousands" of "horrid sewerage tins" lay scattered about on Nauru, surrounded by clouds of blowflies. The Australian hygiene squad poured gasoline onto every one of Nauru and Banaba's guano gardens and set them ablaze, then sprayed the islands liberally with DDT and disinfectant. Banaba, by comparison, escaped almost unscathed. Lilian Point had been heavily fortified using forced labor; the BPC's opulent residency lay in ruins; and Ellis searched in vain for his first wife's gravestone. Banaba escaped heavy bombardment, however, and the rest of the island's facilities were in quite good condition, even if they smelled like rotting pumpkins. Two things were conspicuously absent from the landscape, however: there were "no natives" or their dwellings anywhere to be seen. Ellis found out why one day after his arrival: The island's Japanese commander, Suzuki Naacomi, confessed to ordering the shooting of the last 140 Gilbert and Ellice Islanders left on Banaba, two days after Japan announced its official surrender. According to Ellis, Suzuki feared they might use dynamite given to them for fishing to exact their revenge. A frightened survivor emerged two months later from a water cave to tell a harrowing tale of how he escaped his botched execution by pretending to die in the ocean. An Australian military court in New Guinea later hanged Suzuki for war crimes based on this survivor's testimony. The Japanese systematically destroyed all but one native "hut" on Banaba, probably to use them as building materials.[55]

---

[54] Ellis journal, 15 Sept. 1945; Ellis to Aris, 9 Jan. 1946, PMB 497. Ellis, *Mid-Pacific Outposts*, 81–85, 117, 131, 136, 138, 295; Sigrah and King, *Te Rii ni Banaba*, 242–57, app. 10; Williams and Macdonald, *Phosphateers*, ch. 35–36; Macdonald, *Cinderellas of Empire*, 147–49; Kondo, "Famines in the Northeastern Part of Japan"; Jane Buckingham, "The Pacific Leprosy Foundation Archive and Oral Histories of Leprosy in the South Pacific," *Journal of Pacific History* 41 (2006): 81–86.

[55] Ellis to Aris, 9 Jan., 8 Mar. 1946; Ellis, *Mid-Pacific Outposts*, 81–85, 105–6, 244–50; Sigrah and King, *Te Rii ni Banaba*, 255; "World War II on Banaba" (2004), http://www.janeresture.com/banaba/ww2.htm.

Many soldiers under Suzuki's command were themselves victims of war crimes. The Australian relief expedition to Banaba and Nauru transferred the entire Japanese contingent to what Ellis gleefully referred to as a "huge concentration camp... in the blazing sun" near Torokina in the Solomon Islands. "Carrying their bundles, they had to march 12 miles to the concentration area, the officers faring similarly to the others. Some were knocked up *en route*." Of this group, "three out of the 2,500 died on the march, a relatively small number, but I was informed that several more died during the next few days." Those suspected of war crimes, including soldiers once stationed on Banaba, reputedly had their rations cut by 40 percent, had to do extra forced labor and marches, and were withheld medical care in a camp overrun with malaria and other diseases as payback for the Sandakan death marches and other Japanese atrocities. More than 1,000 of the 4,500 surrendered soldiers interned at Torokina died from this sort of mistreatment by Australian soldiers, thus multiplying Banaba's wartime tragedy.[56]

The Road to Underdevelopment

The Second World War provided an ideal environment for Malthusian ideas to flourish regarding the territoriality of ethnic groups, which enabled population technocrats to acquire more influence than ever. This time around, their actions left the world hungering for something new: development.[57]

Once again, Japan was on the leading edge of these trends. Warren Thompson looked like a prophet when the country invaded the Philippines and New Guinea two months after bombing Pearl Harbor. In 1942, he became a key member of President Roosevelt's M Project to study how population problems had contributed to hostilities and to secretly recommend policies for resettling wartime refugees in places like Amazonia and Iraq. Thompson's works were required reading for the flood of population experts who traveled to Japan during the U.S. Occupation (1945–52). Allied ethnocrats forcibly resettled 4.9 million ethnic Japanese from around the globe to the home islands during the two years following the war (including Okada Nikumatsu), even though Japan was suffering a severe shortage of consumables. This situation emboldened IUD-inventor Ōta Tenrei and remarried activist Katō Shidzue to resume promoting the legalization of birth control and abortion. They gained conservative support from physicians eager to establish professional control over pregnancy and birth. Thompson's ideas

---

56 Ellis's emphasis, *Mid-Pacific Outposts*, 102, 194; Toshiyuki Tanaka et al., *Hidden Horrors: Japanese War Crimes in World War II* (Boulder, CO, 1996), 75; Karl James, "The Final Campaigns: Bougainville 1944–45" (Ph.D. thesis, University of Wollongong, 2005), 343–44.

57 Arturo Escobar, *Encountering Development: The Making and Unmaking of the Third World* (Princeton, NJ, 1995).

exercised particular influence over the Supreme Command's 1947 decision to restore Japan's standard of living to prewar levels via rapid reindustrialization. Field research in Japan by two of the architects of demographic transition theory, Irene Taeuber and Frank Notestein, had seemed to show that "decline in fertility is a necessary reaction to the conditions of living in a modernizing economy, whether the culture be Western or Eastern." In 1949, General Douglas MacArthur brought in Thompson and Whelpton for direct advice on these issues. Their presence corresponded with the Japanese prime minister's abrupt decision to back passage of the Eugenic Protection Law, which decriminalized abortion. These events stirred up so much controversy that population control activist William Vogt had to cancel a planned tour of Japan to advocate conservation.[58] Japanese anxieties about population and resources evolved from there into a national obsession with economic growth. This pushed environmental concerns to the sidelines until the Minamata controversy broke out a decade later.[59]

Further to the south, Harry Maude used the opportunities presented by war to accelerate his own attack on "the serious over-population situation" in the Gilbert and Ellice Islands Colony. He obtained new islands for indigenous resettlement whenever he got the chance. In 1941, he tried to purchase leaseholds on three more uninhabited guano islands: Caroline, Flint, and Vostok. In 1943, he set up native settlements on Fanning and Kiritimati for striking copra workers who could not be repatriated to Japanese-occupied lands. After the war, he made aborted arrangements to buy Washington and Fanning Islands outright for A£103,000. In 1944 and 1946, he purchased Niulakita and Kioa Islands on behalf of the natives of Vaitupu. These actions had a decisive impact on the lands controversy on Banaba. In 1940, when approached by the BPC to lease additional property for phosphate mining, Banaban landowners broached the possibility of purchasing Wakaya Island, a forested atoll near Fiji's capital city, to serve as "a second home." The Western Pacific High Commissioner rejected this proposal on the grounds that its soil and water resources were too poor to support a large, growing population – even though the island was far better endowed than any of

---

[58] Rudolf Janssens, *"What Future for Japan?": UK Wartime Planning for the Postwar Era* (Amsterdam, 1995), 53–54, 113–14; David Price, *Anthropological Intelligence: The Deployment and Neglect of American Anthropology in the Second World War* (Durham, NC, 2008), 122–36; Taeuber and Notestein, "The Changing Fertility of the Japanese," *Population Studies* 1 (1947): 28; Szreter, "Idea of Demographic Transition," 666–67; Oakley, "American-Japanese Interaction"; Tiana Norgren, "Abortion before Birth Control: The Interest Group Politics behind Postwar Japanese Reproduction Policy," *Journal of Japanese Studies* 24 (1998): 59–94.

[59] Eric Dinmore, "A Small Island Nation Poor in Resources: Natural and Human Resource Anxieties in Trans-World War II Japan" (Ph.D. diss., Princeton University, 2006); Scott O'Bryan, *The Growth Idea: Purpose and Prosperity in Postwar Japan* (Honolulu, 2009); Shigeto Tsuru, *The Political Economy of the Environment: The Case of Japan* (Vancouver, 2000).

the Phoenix Islands. (Today, Wakaya is an ultra-exclusive resort that has hosted the honeymoons of Celine Dion and Bill Gates, illustrative of far greater inequalities that now divide humanity.) As an alternative, the Banabans were offered Rabi Island: a much larger, more expensive, and remote island on the northern edge of the Fiji archipelago. They rejected this proposal on a number of grounds. Maude bought Rabi Island, anyway, in March 1942 – mere days after the colonial government abruptly abandoned Banaba to its wartime fate and he received an administrative promotion. He paid A£25,000, three-fifths of the Banaban Provident Fund, to Lever's Pacific Plantations. This divested the vast Unilever Corporation of the last speck of Pacific land bought from John Arundel back in 1901.[60]

Once Maude purchased Rabi Island, Banaba's colonizers became more eager than ever to bring about William Lever's "final solution." Maude effusively praised Rabi Island's "flourishing" coconut plantations, its "broad and sandy beaches," its high, well-watered peak, and deep volcanic soils – environmental features that were all completely foreign to the Banaban experience. At seventy square kilometers, he hoped Rabi would provide abundant room "for the younger generation...to preserve their racial identity and culture" away from the "Europeanized...atmosphere" of tiny Banaba "in the shadow of a great commercial machine." Maude wholeheartedly believed that resettlement here was "so very much in their true interests that every endeavor should be made to persuade them to take the step." For all his anthropological expertise, he still failed to grasp that the Banabans' relationship to *the land itself* constituted the backbone (*rii*) of their culture.[61]

Maude shamefully avoided divulging the environmental factor that enabled him to purchase two of these islands in the first place. On 27 April 1941, a hurricane struck Rabi and Kioa directly from the north-northwest. This storm was "said to have been more intense, over a very limited area, than the major February storm" that slammed Fiji's capital earlier that year, "one of the worst to strike Fiji in its recorded history." Even moderate storms cause major damage to fruiting trees – particularly old, tall coconut trees like those on Rabi. A second hurricane struck these two islands on New Year's Day 1943, bringing down "coconut trees in their thousands" in the wider archipelago. "It was expected that it would take three years for many of the plantations to recover," and then, only with systematic replanting.[62]

---

[60] Equal to US$4 million and US$1 million in 2007, respectively. Maude, *Memorandum on Post-War Reorganization*, 22–23; Maude, *Memorandum on the Future of the Banaban Population of Ocean Island; with Special Relation to Their Land and Funds* (Auckland, NZ, 1946), 7, 9, 11–12; Woodburn, *Where Our Hearts Still Lie*, 177–78, 185–86, 190, 193–94, 199, 213 n. 17.

[61] Maude, *Memorandum on the Banaban Population*, 11, 17.

[62] I. S. Kerr, *Tropical Storms and Hurricanes in the Southwest Pacific* (Wellington, 1976), pp. 72, 74–75, charts 1.1, 1.2, 1.5; R. F. McLean, "The Hurricane Hazard in the Eastern

Top-level officials decided "the time was opportune for taking" the Banabans "direct to their new home" on Rabi as soon as the Japanese surrendered and worked out the final logistics at BPC headquarters in Melbourne. On 30 November 1945, Maude arrived at the mustering point on Tarawa in the Gilbert Islands to address 1,788 Banaban residents and workers newly gathered from wartime internment. For all the talk of Japanese "cruelty and terrorism," Banaban numbers had actually grown by 15 percent during the war. Maude presented them with an offer they could not refuse: he painted an exaggerated picture of conditions on their home island, claiming the colonial government did not have the resources "to import sufficient food reserves" or "for the provision of temporary shelters." Therefore, they could try out life at a prepared settlement on Rabi for two years in the company of their loved ones, or wait indefinitely on Tarawa until the government decided what to do with them. After much discussion, 185 adult men, 200 adult women, and 318 children of Banaban descent, plus 300 Gilbertese spouses, relations, and friends agreed to participate in Maude's "Rabi Settlement Scheme." On 15 December 1945, the whole group disembarked on the dry northwestern corner of Rabi Island, 2,100 kilometers to the south, and took up residence in a beach camp of 150 army surplus tents and 12 prefab houses supplied with a paltry one month's rations. This population transfer was a drop in the bucket compared to the massive displacement of peoples elsewhere in the world demanded by ethnocrats after the war. Ethnicity continued to play a determinative role in decisions governing these population movements.[63]

The Banaban case exemplifies the sort of difficulties that faced uprooted peoples – and the new hunger for development that emerged from this experience. Maude expected the Banabans to take up the humble life of subsistence farmers and copra cutters on Rabi, but this was an unwelcome proposition for a group used to living close to Banaba's phosphate mines as small-time landlords, wage workers, and market fishermen. Food was scarce on Rabi from the start: store-bought food was almost nonexistent; the fishing was terrible compared with Banaba's upwelling ecosystem; and no one knew how to hunt the island's unfamiliar wildlife. A conflict immediately sprang up over how to manage the island's feral cows and pigs. Many hungry Banabans thought they possessed the right to kill and eat them, but the island's Welfare Officer mandated that all livestock be reserved as community property under his control to be included in various development

---

Islands of Fiji: An Historical Analysis," in *The Hurricane Hazard: Natural Disaster and Small Populations* (Canberra, 1977), 20–21.

[63] Ellis, *Mid-Pacific Outposts*, 237–43, 294–95; Maude, *Memorandum on Post-War Reorganization*, 32–33, 36; Maude, *Memorandum on the Banaban Population*, 12–14; Woodburn, *Where Our Hearts Still Lie*, 194–95, 198, 201, 214 n. 21; Sigrah and King, *Te Rii ni Banaba*, 261, 263; Williams and Macdonald, *The Phosphateers*, 341.

projects. He opened a "somewhat primitive hospital" and required the set-tlement to build a long line of beach latrines out over the surf, but sickness swept the island anyway, including dysentery, measles, and a host of "pul-monary troubles" blamed on Rabi's unfamiliar climate. Twenty-seven died during the settlement's first eight months, including a number of respected elders who had survived everything the Japanese dished out.[64]

"Many, if not most, of the community" turned against the colonization project. Rotan Tito encouraged them to openly flaunt the authority of the officer in charge of them by killing cows, riding horses without permission, and refusing to work on official projects. Maude made an emergency visit to Rabi in 1946 to try to put a lid on unrest. He blamed their discontent on years of living "for the next 'dole' payment" on Banaba and on their experience of seeing "the European beaten, if only for a time, by a brown-skinned race such as themselves."[65]

This was hardly an isolated occurrence. Islanders throughout the cen-tral and western Pacific were intensely dissatisfied by their treatment by both sides during the war. On occasion, brief prosperity rained down from the skies. An airplane fell to earth on Sydney Island, presenting a valuable source of sheet aluminum. American warplanes dropped Hershey chocolate bars, Wrigley's gum, bars of soap, and cigarettes over the Phoenix Island settlements. Colonists were mostly indifferent to North American consumer goods, although they greatly valued the opportunity to work at the bustling new airport on Canton Island and to supply its souvenir shops with hand-icrafts. On their home islands, many Gilbertese protested against the reim-position of British rule after the departure of the Americans at the end of the war, especially when they dumped vast numbers of vehicles and other mili-tary "surplus" out at sea, based on the supposition that the Gilbert Islanders were not ready for the machine age. In 1948, 1,000 Gilbertese workers went on strike and forced phosphate mining to stop for three months on Banaba Island in fury over the reinstitution of prewar, race-based wage scales and store pricing. The BPC tried to use interethnic rivalries between workers to break the strike but eventually conceded to most of their demands.[66]

Farther to the west, these feelings often manifested themselves in potent religious movements referred to derisively as cargo cults. On the northern coast of New Guinea, a former hotel waiter and policeman named Yali (ca. 1912–75) returned from dangerous wartime service against the Japanese to find his home district being overtaken by these new cults. As a youth,

[64] Maude, *Memorandum on the Banaban Population*, 14–15, 23; Ellis, *Mid-Pacific Outposts*, 242, photos; Sigrah and King, *Te Rii ni Banaba*, 63–64; Silverman, *Disconcerting Issue*, 173.

[65] Maude, *Memorandum on the Banaban Population*, 12, 15–16.

[66] Knudson, *Titiana*, 53, 57, 167–71, table 2; Williams and Macdonald, *The Phosphateers*, 375–81, 470; Macdonald, *Cinderellas of Empire*, 156–59.

Yali had experienced the forced concentration of his people into a handful of villages by the new Australian administration. During World War II, he joined the Allied Intelligence Corps and received training that took him on tours of an Australian sugarmill, a brewery, the Queensland Museum, and Brisbane Zoo. Yali vividly remembered a white officer telling native recruits: "In the past, you natives have been kept backward. But now if you help us win the war and get rid of the Japanese from New Guinea, we Europeans will help you. We will help you get houses with galvanized iron roofs, plank walls and floors, electric light, and motor vehicles, boats, good clothes, and good food. Life will be very different for you after the war." Yali helped disseminate this apparent promise by speaking on army-sponsored native-language radio broadcasts. After the war, he exhorted his countrymen to resettle in carefully ordered and landscaped villages, to build pig sties and latrines, to wash themselves often with soap, and to live a life more generally that was pleasing to the Australian Administration, so it would honor this pledge. Yali's Rehabilitation Scheme caught on locally and soon gained official support. In 1947, Yali headed a native delegation to the colonial capital, Port Moresby, and learned some eye-opening truths about his place in the world: cargo received greater priority for aircraft transport than the highest prestige black man. Australian officials told him development spending would be small, piecemeal, and take years to have an impact, rather than arriving in a flood (as it did in Japan). Yali even learned about evolution, which was supposed to provide scientific backing for these inequalities.

Suddenly, everything Yali had witnessed in the civilized world took on a new meaning: "I realized now that the talk of the officers in Brisbane was bullshit – that was done with now – we just wouldn't get anything – the white men had lied to us and didn't want to help us." He gained a new reverence for the Old Ways and began openly denouncing Christianity. At a meeting in his home village, he dramatically ripped off his carefully ironed European clothing and appeared in a tree bark girdle: "If this is all the white men want," he declared, "then we shall be *kanakas* [native work-men] in earnest!" All this was rather mild when compared to anticolonial uprisings in other lands during these years. Yet few readers of Jared Diamond's best-seller *Guns, Germs, and Steel* are probably aware of any of this, much less that Yali spent five years in prison for trying to undermine Anglo dominance in his homeland. Yali's imprisonment crushed his political aspirations but failed to stop his uprising's metamorphosis into one of the most widespread religious movements of the era. If Jared Diamond had been more willing to listen, Yali would have been pleased to provide his own answer to "Yali's Question" about the historical origin of global inequalities: Banaban tree huggers, Gilbertese migrant workers, New Guinea cargo cultists, South Asian salt marchers, returned African American veterans, and Peruvian Apristas of this era all understood that racial exploitation explained much about how whites had come to possess so much more "cargo" than blacks.[67]

In response to Banaban unrest on Rabi, Harry Maude removed the offending Welfare Officer, so as not to jeopardize the forthcoming vote on Banaban relocation. He also held out the prospect that development would happen more quickly on Rabi than Banaba, enabling them to "have their children well-educated and capable of obtaining senior positions in the professions, trades, and civil service in Fiji." After another year disseminating "patient explanation and propaganda," Maude personally chaired three days of discussion leading up to the long-promised plebiscite – ready to use "bull-headed" threats if necessary. To his relief, Banaban landowners agreed to a new "covenant" with the BPC to mine remaining high-grade deposits and voted 270 to 48 to stay on Rabi permanently. As payback, Maude made it possible for them to return to Banaba en masse to pace out their lands and visit sacred places. "The Banabans have certainly done very well for themselves," Albert Ellis concluded. "So a long standing problem has been solved."[68]

Things might have played out differently if all this had happened eighteen months later. On 7 December 1948, another hurricane swept across Rabi Island and the eastern half of the Fiji archipelago. This unfamiliar hazard completely destroyed the Banabans' main beach settlement, along with all their possessions. During an unprecedented all-clan meeting after the storm, they decided to form four inland settlements and divide up most of the island according to the old village and genealogical system on Banaba. Some devoted themselves to growing traditional crops, others to cutting copra; a few bought motorboats to help with fishing. Many rededicated themselves toward preserving the Old Ways; a few embraced divisive new religions like Seventh-day Adventism; but nearly everyone resented their fate.[69]

Maude's other resettlement schemes also experienced a storm of criticism and eventually collapsed under their own ecological and administrative weight. The G&EIC's new lands commissioner, B. C. Cartland, had a different vision of "progressive development" based on the egalitarian redistribution of indigenous lands and their intensified cultivation under expert

---

[67] Yali quoted in Peter Lawrence, *Road Belong Cargo: A Study of the Cargo Movement in the Southern Madang District, New Guinea* (Manchester, England, 1964), 117–18, 123–24, 129, 132, 142–44, 169–71, 174, 187, 219–21, 274; contra Diamond, *Guns, Germs, and Steel: The Fates of Human Societies* (New York, 1997).

[68] Ellis to Aris, 25 Sept. 1947, 3 Sept. 1948, PMB 497; Maude, *Memorandum on Post-War Reorganization*, 2–3; Maude, *Memorandum on the Banaban Population*, 22–24; Woodburn, *Where Our Hearts Still Lie*, 201–2, 206–7; Silverman, *Disconcerting Issue*, 167–71; Williams and Macdonald, *The Phosphateers*, 365–67.

[69] Kerr, *Tropical Storms and Hurricanes*, p. 90, chart 1.1; McLean, "Hurricane Hazard," 49–50; Sigrah and King, *Te Rii ni Banaba*, 64; Silverman, *Disconcerting Issue*, 193; Macdonald, *Cinderellas of Empire*, ch. 14.

supervision. He lambasted Maude's "blind faith" in "ancient land custom" and threatened to resign if forced to tackle his duties "on purely anthropological lines.... I should like to treat the islander more as an ordinary human being with every right to have a say in his own affairs, than as an anthropological museum piece, to be preserved in statu[s] quo under a glass case." Maude's campaign to purchase additional islands for native resettlement and to supply colony medical dispensaries with Volpar spermicidal paste died under this assault and convinced Maude to leave the colonial service altogether.[70] "A howling drought" fueled by La Niña struck the region in 1950, killing all of the new coconut and pandanus trees planted on Sydney Island since the war. This generated an intense debate among the Phoenix Island colonists: what good was a life in which the natural elements destroyed their every attempt at improvement and reduced them to eating *boi*? The events of 1954–56 decided the issue. The Pacific Basin experienced the most severe La Niña event since 1916–17. Intense drought caused copra production, the region's main source of external income, to collapse throughout the G&EIC. In response, the colonial government abruptly revived its population resettlement program but redirected it to the densely forested British Solomon Islands, far to the west of the drought zone.[71]

A scouting expedition from Sydney Island liked what it saw at Titiana Point on Gizo Island in the Solomons, which had superficial similarities to the atoll environment they were familiar with. They began full-scale colonization in August 1955. Like the Banabans on Rabi, the Titiana colonists soon learned that life in this new environment had unfamiliar difficulties and dangers. They had to familiarize themselves with new garden crops, which jungle vegetation quickly choked out without constant weeding. They also had to learn the laborious task of felling large trees to clear new lands to stay ahead of the rapid pace of soil exhaustion. Many did not have the volition and tried to subsist largely on manioc, which put them at risk for nutritional deficiencies. Fishing was much more difficult at Titiana, and settlers rapidly exhausted local shellfish beds. To make matters worse, *vivax* and deadly *falciparum* malaria affected virtually everyone, even though colonists received stomach-turning antimalarial drugs and plenty of DDT free of charge. Gizo's existing inhabitants were also less than welcoming and blamed these newcomers for starting a dysentery epidemic. By March 1957, most Gilbertese settlers were eager to leave, but the G&EIC government convinced them to stay by purchasing two nearby islands from Lever's Pacific Plantations so they could harvest copra. In 1963, the G&EIC required all remaining settlers

---

[70] Quoted in Woodburn, *Where Our Hearts Still Lie*, 208–11; Macdonald, *Cinderellas of Empire*, 165.

[71] CEI; Laxton, "Nikumaroro," 141–42, 145, Ellis to Aris, 25 Apr. 1950, PMB 497; Knudson, *Titiana*, 56–57; Macdonald, *Cinderellas of Empire*, 167.

to abandon Sydney, Hull, and Gardner Islands for the western Solomons, whether they wanted to or not, because these isolated outposts had grown too expensive to administer. Other colonists from the southern Gilberts followed them west to obtain "improvement through relocation." Many found good-paying jobs working for Lever's Pacific Timbers, at first in selective cutting of *Calophyllum* trees for export to Japan, but later in wholesale clear-cutting that converted vast stretches of lowland rain forest in the western Solomons into an expanse of invasive *Meremia* vines. In 2007, the 366 Gilbertese residents of Titiana learned one final lesson in the hazards of resettlement: thirteen died when a four-meter tsunami inundated the village after a massive earthquake. None need have perished if they had possessed indigenous familiarity with this environment and ran to high ground at the first sign that the sea was pulling back from the shore. As usual, the Unilever Corporation benefited more than anyone from these arrangements. Thus, Maude's Malthusian obsession with resettlement contributed to large-scale environmental alterations across a broad swath of the equatorial Pacific.[72]

On the basis of these examples, the indigenous inhabitants of Nauru also began to consider resettlement during the early 1960s, but they could not reach a consensus on where to go. Hammer DeRoburt, a Nauruan boy scout turned high school teacher turned head chief, pursued the idea of resettling on Australia's sandy Fraser Island (now a World Heritage Site) but nixed moving to Curtis Island (now a national park) when white Queensland racists threatened to punch "on the nose the first nigger who comes ashore." Through a brilliant act of statesmanship that took advantage of Cold War rivalries within the United Nations, he eventually secured an infinitely more desirable alternative: Nauru's conversion from a UN Trust Territory to a tiny independent republic with full indigenous control over the island's phosphate reserves. DeRoburt and the Nauruans became heroes of the global decolonization movement when they celebrated their independence on 31 January 1968 and rapidly achieved incomes and lifestyles comparable to the First World. They did so, however, at the cost of becoming highly susceptible to obesity, diabetes, cardiovascular problems, and other diseases of prosperity, and by the end of the century, they had completely converted Nauru's "topside" into a barren wasteland of limestone pinnacles, weedy plants, and cadmium-laced soils. Australia and New Zealand have long refused to concede the Nauruans' demand to rehabilitate mined-out lands but are now paying their own price for their environmental sins: vast expanses of land in

[72] Knudson, *Titiana*, 61–62, 75–76, 78, 87, 136–39, 191–92; Knudson, "Sydney Island, Titiana, and Kamaleai: Southern Gilbertese in the Phoenix and Solomon Islands," in *Exiles and Migrants in Oceania* (Honolulu, 1977); Mueller-Dombois and Fosberg. *Vegetation of the Tropical Pacific Islands*, 72–74, 79; Judith Bennett, *Pacific Forest: A History of Resource Control and Contest in the Solomon Islands, c. 1800–1997* (Cambridge, 2000); B. C. McAdoo, "Near-Field Population Response during the 2 April 2007 Solomon Islands Tsunami," *Eos: Fall Meeting Supplement* 88, no. 52 (2007): S13A–1051.

Australia and New Zealand are dangerously contaminated with cadmium and other heavy metals that arrived with island phosphate – an unwanted gift of the marine processes that created these ancient deposits. Nauruans now face a dilemma affecting many peoples living in blighted postindustrial environments: are their lifestyles and investments worth enough to make up for destroying their homeland's ability to produce? The fact that the last decent part of Nauru is highly vulnerable to rising sea levels makes this question all the more pressing.[73]

Many Banabans wish they shared Nauru's problems. By the early 1960s, they were already jealous regarding the paltry amount of development spending they received compared with other ethnic groups in the region, and in April 1965, several hundred marched on the Rabi Public Hall to demand changes. Inspired by Nauru's accomplishments, Rotan Tito briefly sought independence for the Banaban Nation and eventually filed suit against the BPC for its failure to replant Banaba in accord with the 1913 land agreement. In 1977, the Banabans won the longest civil case in British legal history (since surpassed by the "McLibel" suit against London Greenpeace). The judge refused to require the BPC to do any environmental rehabilitation, however, and instead offered the Banabans A$14,000 in recompense for lost tree-fruit production. This decision saddled the Banabans with enormous legal bills and an even larger sense of injustice – compensated for, ever so slightly, by the fact that the judge experienced a severe case of diarrhea during his tour of Rabi, an environmental danger they faced on a daily basis. Banabans eventually negotiated a far more lucrative settlement, but with high-grade deposits on Banaba mined out, living in a country where they experience ethnic discrimination from Fiji nationalists, they now face a difficult path forward as citizens of the underdeveloped world.[74]

Some Banabans wish they had the option to move somewhere else like the indigenous citizens of Niue. Its resident population surpassed 5,000 in the early 1960s – returning to the level it had a century before, when the guano industry came looking for workers. Unlike these other Pacific peoples, Niueans obtained New Zealand citizenship and the right to free migration during the transition to self-rule in the early 1970s – and immediately began

[73] Williams and Macdonald, *The Phosphateers*, 25, 262, 279, 404, 432–33, 464–65, 471, 486–500; Harley Manner et al., "Phosphate Mining Induced Vegetation Change on Nauru Island," *Ecology* 65 (1984): 1454–65; A. H. Roberts et al., "Cadmium Status of Soils, Plants, and Grazing Animals in New Zealand," *New Zealand Journal of Agricultural Research* 37 (1994): 119–29; M. J. McLaughlin et al., "Review: The Behaviour and Environmental Impact of Contaminants in Fertilizers," *Australian Journal of Soil Research* 34 (1996): 1–54; Carl McDaniel and John Gowdy, *Paradise for Sale: A Parable of Nature* (Berkeley and Los Angeles, 2000).
[74] Silverman, *Disconcerting Issue*, 195–97; Williams and Macdonald, *The Phosphateers*, 451–52, 505–23; "McLibel: Longest Case in English History," *BBC News* 15 Feb. 2005, http://news.bbc.co.uk/go/pr/fr/-/1/hi/uk/4266741.stm.

emigrating in great numbers. In 2006, two years after a category five cyclone obliterated the island's capital Alofi, 22,230 people of Niuean descent lived in New Zealand, but only 1,538 still considered Niue to be their permanent home. In this way, Niue has mirrored the fate of hundreds of dying small towns around the world left vacant by emigrants hoping to improve their standard of living by moving to the city or to the First World. In places like Niue, underdevelopment has accomplished what Malthusian forces and colonialist exploitation never did.[75]

In this chapter, we have seen widespread instances in which Malthusian fears of growing population, land hunger, and diminishing natural resources profoundly influenced global geopolitics during the mid-twentieth century. From the desert sands of Southern California and coastal Libya, to the frigid plains of Manchuria and Poland, to the equatorial lowlands of New Guinea and guano islands of the Central Pacific, imperialist competition for land and resources inspired tragic campaigns to reconfigure the distribution of the world's peoples. Warren Thompson, Harry Maude, Heinrich Himmler, and other population technocrats of this era all shared a common belief that obtaining scientific mastery over human numbers was essential to improving the quality of human life. Rotan Tito, Yali, and Katō Shidzue, on the other hand, forcefully argued that this mastery possessed little value if it entailed their subjugation to others. To an extent that historians have failed to recognize, some of the twentieth century's farthest-reaching political movements and military conflicts were inspired by these concerns – including the biggest event of them all, World War II.

From the perspective of environmental history, one factor has been conspicuously absent from this discussion: concern about the environmental transformations that these massive movements of peoples would accomplish. As we see in the next chapter, a small cadre of conservation technocrats based in the Western Hemisphere came to recognize a linkage between population growth and environmental degradation while participating in these events. They contributed an overtly ecological perspective to the issue of human population growth, standard of living, and industrialization, and in the process, gave birth to the modern environmental movement. To see this, we must head for the wilderness of northern Mexico and back again to the guano islands of coastal Peru.

[75] See table 3.1; Howe et al., *Tides of History*, 196, 198–99, 205–6.

8

The Road to Survival

The plants and animals grown in one region are now consumed and returned to the soil in another. Transportation taps the energy stored in rocks, and in the air, and uses it elsewhere; thus we fertilize the garden with nitrogen gleaned from guano birds from the fishes of the seas on the other side of the Equator. Thus the formerly localized and self-contained circuits are pooled on a wide scale....

These releases of biotic capital tend to becloud or postpone the penalties of violence.... Violence, in turn, varies with human population density; a dense population requires a more violent conversion.... This deduction runs counter to our current philosophy, which assumes that because a small increase in density enriched human life, that an indefinite increase will enrich it indefinitely. Ecology knows of no density relationship that holds for indefinitely wide limits. All gains from density are subject to a law of diminishing returns.

– Aldo Leopold, "The Land Ethic" (1949)

On 1 September 1936, wildlife ecologist Aldo Leopold embarked from his home in Wisconsin for a seventeen-day hunting trip to the highland wilderness of Chihuahua, Mexico. That summer had been one of the driest in the history of the Upper Midwest and caused his first attempt at starting a tree plantation at his Sand County shack to fail miserably. He went south with the hope of experiencing a glimpse of what life had been like back in the Pleistocene, before humans became addicted to the axe, plow, and rifle.[1] Exactly one year before, he had gone across the Atlantic to examine the latest techniques of forest and wildlife management in Germany. But the need for artificial deer feeding and protective fences around saplings in reserves troubled him; the lack of "woodcraft" practiced by aristocratic hunters annoyed him; and he was deeply disturbed by Europe's poverty of

---

[1] Hunting journal for 1936, 1–17 Sept., UWDC-ALA; Curt Meine, *Aldo Leopold: His Life and Work* (Madison, WI, 1988), 365–66, 376.

wilderness, the "land-hunger of its teeming millions," and growing tendency toward militarism.[2]

Leopold was also unfavorably impressed by the gullied landscape he rode through on his way up to Colonia Pacheco, a Sierra Madre community established by Mormons during the 1880s to escape U.S. polygamy laws. In the old days, Mormons logged and "often cut hay on these mesas." Now, it was a state-sponsored agricultural settlement, where "you can hardly keep a goat alive." Locals ascribed "this merely to dry years, but I incline to think the sod is gone. Some pretty active erosion is extending up the watercourses." Nearby Laguna Guzmán, once part of a vast inland sea, had dried up completely.[3]

Two miles west of the Colonia on the hike up to the Continental Divide, a noisy troop of *guacamaja* or thick-billed parrots (*Rhynchopsitta pachyrhyncha*) awoke something in Leopold. He knew that these birds were virtually gone from their old haunts in the U.S. Southwest, and that no native member of the parrot family had been seen east of the Rockies since the last Carolina parakeet died in 1918. He never tired of watching these bright green birds "wheeling high in the air – again reminding me of cranes," which for him represented the "imponderable essence" of wildness.[4] Leopold had every reason to expect a parched landscape heavily browsed by hungry deer when he arrived at the oak-pine woodlands of the Río Gavilán. But the deer were fat, "abundant but not excessive," and tree saplings grew unguarded, despite the persistent drought. Compared with everything he had seen up north for many a year, the Río Gavilán was "near to being the cream of creation" and provided him with a life-changing opportunity to see the difference between a sick and healthy natural landscape.[5]

A year later, Leopold went back to hunt with his brother Carl and son Starker during Christmas break. There were no parrots this time, but they saw even more deer, the hidden corpse of a colt killed by a mountain lion, fifty-two species of bird, and "fresh wolf tracks on the trail down the river." Only ghosts of the grizzly bear and imperial woodpecker (*Campephilus imperialis*) still inhabited these mountains, however. The last grizzlies had been shot only a few years before, and Leopold could not suppress the fear that the absence of these great cousins of the ivory-billed woodpecker might bode poorly for the guacamaja if they were needed to excavate nesting holes in old growth trees. The ancient remnants of masonry waterworks left by the ancestral Pueblo also hinted that these lands might have been densely

---

[2] Leopold quoted in Meine, *Aldo Leopold*, 351–60; Flader, *Thinking Like a Mountain*, 139–44.

[3] Hunting journal for 1936, 4–5, 13–14 Sept., UWDC-ALA.

[4] Hunting journal for 1936, 5–6, 12 Sept., UWDC-ALA; Leopold, *A Sand County Almanac and Sketches Here and There* (New York, 1949), 95–97, 137–40.

[5] Hunting journal for 1936, 11 Sept, UWDC-ALA; Leopold, *A Sand County Almanac*, 149–54; quoted in Meine, *Aldo Leopold*, 367.

settled and profoundly changed in centuries past. This realization fixated Leopold on the idea of preserving this wilderness as a natural laboratory for studying ecological change.[6]

Aldo Leopold's biographers are unanimous in their opinion that these trips south profoundly altered his ecological understanding of the world. According to an oft-cited passage of an unpublished autobiographical essay, it was in the mountains of Mexico where "I first realized that land is an organism, that all my life I had seen only sick land, whereas here was a biota still in perfect aboriginal health. The term 'unspoiled wilderness' took on a new meaning." From this date forward, Leopold also came to see humanity's relationship to the earth as one of sickness or health, and he is often remembered as "the Prophet of the Age of Ecology" for these discoveries.[7]

Leopold did not arrive at these conclusions by himself. He was just one of a host of scientists who migrated north and south within the Western Hemisphere during the late 1930s and 1940s in search of solutions to the puzzle of environmental variability and degradation. Some did so as part of a concerted geopolitical strategy by the United States to build alliances, root out enemies, secure resources, and increase understanding of natural and social dynamics in the region.[8] Others, like Leopold and William Vogt, came south to experience and study the abundance of wild nature that their homelands had lost. Many Latin Americans made similar pilgrimages north in search of new ideas and techniques, professional opportunities, and international legitimation for their own programs. In the process, this technocratic elite built a small international movement dedicated to environmental conservation in the hemisphere.

These scientists also built intellectual and institutional foundations for something far more influential and lasting – the beginnings of a global environmental movement. As this chapter shows, the Compañía Administradora del Guano's hiring of Vogt in 1939 proved critical to these developments. It led to his recruitment as head of a new Conservation Section of the Pan American Union, which provided Vogt with unprecedented opportunities

---

[6] Hunting journal for 1936, 5 Sept.; Hunting journal for 1937–38, 27 Dec. 1937, 3, 6 Jan. 1938; "Bird List" and assorted photographs, 25 Dec. 1937 to 9 Jan. 1938, UWDC-ALA. Leopold, *A Sand County Almanac*, 140–41, 149–54; Juan-Pablo Gallo-Reynoso et al., "Probable Occurrence of a Brown Bear (*Ursus arctos*) in Sonora, Mexico, in 1976," *The Southwestern Naturalist* 53 (2008): 256–60; Martjan Lammertink, "The Lost Empire of the Imperial Woodpecker," *World Birdwatch* 18, no. 2 (1996): 8–11.

[7] "Forward," 31 July 1947, unpublished ms no. 112, UWDC-ALA; Roderick Nash, *Wilderness and the American Mind* (New Haven, 1982), 192; Flader, *Thinking Like a Mountain*, 153–56; Meine, *Aldo Leopold*, 367–68, 379–80; Worster, *Nature's Economy*, 271–74, 284–90; Max Oelschlager, *The Idea of Wilderness: From Prehistory to the Age of Ecology* (New Haven, 1991), ch. 7; Newton, *Aldo Leopold's Odyssey* 3–16, 223–29.

[8] Cushman, "Struggle over Airways."

to travel internationally, to interact with high-level officials, to study environmental degradation, and to organize conservation programs – including the first nongovernmental organization in Peru exclusively dedicated to conservation advocacy. Vogt never forgot his experience with the guano birds and El Niño and passionately held up the Peruvian guano industry as an exemplar of environmental management in accord with the technocratic ideal.

In tight collaboration with Leopold and Fairfield Osborn, Vogt also developed a new perspective on human population growth that unified many of the concerns of the interwar population debate with anxieties about environmental degradation, the disappearance of wilderness, and the future of industrialism. Vogt's controversial 1948 book on these topics, *Road to Survival*, acquired the largest international readership of any book on conservation issues before Rachel Carson's *Silent Spring* (1962) and inspired vigorous opposition from a range of development technocrats, most notably Brazilian physician Josué de Castro. Leopold incorporated some of Vogt's ideas into his celebrated essay "The Land Ethic" (1949) – arguably the most significant contribution to environmental philosophy in any language published during the twentieth century. These perspectives also acquired an institutional existence within the Conservation Foundation (est. 1947), population control movements of the 1950s, and as we see in Chapter 9, in Latin America's engagement with the Green and Blue Revolutions. In these ways and more, the guanays of Peru and guacamajas of the Gavilán played a role in the formulation of modern ecological ideas that was just as significant as that played by the mockingbirds, finches, and tortoises of the Galápagos in the development of modern evolutionary thought.[9]

Peru and the Pan American Conservation Movement

Leopold and Vogt were just two of a growing number of scientists and activists who became interested in the international protection of wildlife and their habitats within the Western Hemisphere during the late 1930s. Natural scientists from the United States took the lead in organizing the Pan American Conservation Movement of 1938–48. However, their campaign to establish a hemispheric legal framework for accomplishing these goals would have accomplished little, if not for the presence of small but robust conservation movements in several Latin American republics.

Three tendencies drove these movements. One was a continuing trend by national states to assert centralized, technocratic control over natural resources. This tendency was best represented by Brazil where the new constitution of 1934 required state and national governments to protect

[9] Cf. Jonathan Weiner, *The Beak of the Finch: A Story of Evolution in Our Time* (New York, 1995).

monuments of natural, historical, and artistic value. Brazil's new Forest and Water Codes of 1934 placed strict limitations on the rights of private landowners to cut trees and use water on their property to protect rare species and to mitigate against soil erosion, floods, and water shortages affecting citizens living downstream. Latin American conservationists of this era placed much greater emphasis on habitat and landscape preservation than they had in earlier decades. This second tendency was exemplified by the establishment of Argentine and Brazilian units of Iguazú National Park in 1934 and 1939. This reserve not only protected one of the world's most beautiful waterfalls from hydroelectric development – unlike the fate that befell North America's Niagara, Italy's Marmore, Japan's Sogi, and Brazil's Sete Quedas – but also realized a longstanding dream of Argentine ornithologist Hugo Salomon by preserving 237,720 hectares of prime forest habitat for resident and migratory wildlife.[10]

Few are aware of a third, overtly ecofeminist tendency among Latin American conservationists of this era. In 1931, future Nobel Laureate Gabriela Mistral issued a call in an influential Costa Rican literary magazine for Latin American women to join the battle to protect the land and keep it out of the hands of neo-imperialists. She had been writing poetry on these themes for years and explicitly appealed to women to embrace their ancient connection with the feminine earth. As literary scholar Erin Finzer has discovered, Latin American women profoundly influenced the theory and practice of conservationism in Latin America from the late 1920s to 1940s: as classroom teachers who formed the region's Arbor Day movement, as feminist critics of the technocratic tendencies of male-dominated conservation, and as celebrants of a spiritual link to the earth deriving from indigenous blood flowing through their veins.[11]

Two U.S. scientists took the initial lead in organizing the Pan American Conservation Movement of 1938–48. Harold Coolidge, Jr. (1904–85) was an avid hunter, photographer, and specimen collector with long ties to European movements to preserve big-game animals in colonized regions.

---

[10] Warren Dean, *With Broadax and Firebrand: The Destruction of the Brazilian Atlantic Forest* (Berkeley and Los Angeles, 1995), 260–63, 295, 338–39; Keri Lewis, "Negotiating for Nature: Conservation Diplomacy and the Convention on Nature Protection and Wildlife Preservation in the Western Hemisphere, 1919–1976" (Ph.D. diss., University of New Hampshire, 2008), 80–90; David Sheinin, "'Its Most Destructive Agents': Pan American Environmentalism in the Early Twentieth Century," in *Beyond the Ideal: Pan Americanism in Inter-American Affairs* (Westport, CT, 2000), 115–16, 118–24. On parallel trends in Mexico, see Simonian, *Defending the Land of the Jaguar*, ch. 4–5.

[11] Mistral, "Conversando sobre la tierra," *Repertorio Americano* (San José, Costa Rica) 23, no. 11 (1931): 172–73; Finzer, "Grafting the Maya World Tree: Cosmic Conservationism in Romelia Alarcón de Folgar's *Llamaradas* (Guatemala, 1938)," unpublished ms.; Niall Binn, "Landscapes of Hope and Destruction: Ecological Poetry in Spanish America," in *The ISLE Reader: Ecocriticism, 1993–2003* (Athens, GA, 2003).

During the 1930s, he shifted these organizing activities to East Asia, then to Latin America with the explicit goal of addressing Japanese and German expansionism in these regions. He teamed up with ornithologist Alexander Wetmore (1886–1978), the long-time assistant secretary of the Smithsonian Institution. Wetmore had gotten his start in Latin American bird conservation in 1912 when he surveyed Desecheo Island off the western coast of Puerto Rico and convinced President Taft to declare this important breeding site for brown and red-footed boobies (*Sula leucogaster* and *S. sula*) as a wildlife refuge. (Unfortunately, U.S. military scientists later used this island as a laboratory for studying environmental adaptation among rhesus macaques, which destroyed the island's guano bird population.) Wetmore also campaigned against the use of lead shot because it unintentionally poisoned birds like the California condor that consumed it, and he journeyed south to the Argentine Pampas to investigate the status of rare North American migrants, such as the upland sandpiper (*Bartramia longicauda*) and now extinct Eskimo curlew (*Numenius borealis*). Coolidge unveiled a proposal for drafting a Convention on Nature Protection and Wildlife Preservation in the Western Hemisphere at the Eighth Conference of the Pan American Union held in Lima, Peru, in December 1938. The Conference agreed to organize an Inter-American Committee of Experts under Wetmore's leadership to draft a treaty to be presented for approval at the 1940 Pan American Scientific Conference in Washington, DC.[12]

As historian Keri Lewis has shown, the international network of technocrats involved in crafting the convention became divided among idealists who wanted to establish a strict preservationist framework focused on habitat protection and among pragmatists preoccupied with creating an enforceable treaty with broad-based support. Peru's main contributor to these proceedings, Germán Morales Macedo, was one of many who sought to exclude marine fauna from the convention to head off objections that the treaty would get in the way of fishery development. Gilbert Pearson introduced restrictions on the use of agricultural pesticides into the convention to prevent the poisoning of migratory birds – a key concern of the modern environmental movement. Pan American diplomats later removed this language based on the Malthusian objection that this treaty would reduce food production and slow down the development of industrial agriculture. The most significant part of the convention established a five-tier classification of protected areas. National monuments recognized the cultural attributes of certain landscapes – such as the ancient statues found on Easter Island. The most rigorously protected category provided for "rigid exclusion of the

---

[12] Lewis, "Negotiating for Nature," ch. 2; Mark Barrow, *Nature's Ghosts: Confronting Extinction from the Age of Jefferson to the Age of Ecology* (Chicago, 2010), ch. 6; Wetmore, "The Birds of Desecheo Island, Porto Rico," *Auk* 35 (1918): 333–40; M. A. Evans, "Ecology and Removal of Introduced Rhesus Monkeys: Desecheo Island National Wildlife Refuge, Puerto Rico," *Puerto Rico Health Sciences Journal* 8 (1989): 139–56.

public" from "strict wilderness reserves." This classification displayed the tangible influence of wilderness advocates like Leopold on conservation law in the Americas a quarter century before passage of the U.S. Wilderness Act. Intermediate categorizations explicitly linked the preservation of individual species to protection of their natural habitat. The final convention thus integrated both conservationist and preservationist goals. On 12 October 1940, representatives from eight countries, including Peru, signed the finished document at Pan American Union headquarters in Washington. Nine more countries signed on by May 1941, and the convention went into force seven months later when Haiti became the fifth republic to formally ratify the treaty.[13]

These international proceedings were accompanied by a flurry of organizing activity elsewhere in the Americas and Pacific World. Just a few years removed from decreeing the systematic erosion of Banaba, Arthur Grimble became the colonial administrator of St. Vincent, the birthplace of the twentieth-century soil conservation movement in the British West Indies. Later, as governor of the Windward Islands, he signed off on a series of 1940s ordinances intended to save the archipelago's forests, soils, water, and birds from destruction.[14] In Hawaii, a direct descendant of two founders of the Pacific guano industry, forester Charles Judd, waged an aggressive campaign to restore native forest, protect watersheds from erosion, and eliminate non-native animals.[15] In Peru, William Vogt and CAG orchestrated a meeting between Gilbert Pearson and a distinguished group of Peruvian scientists and professionals at the swank Hotel Bolívar in downtown Lima in April 1940. Pearson had been a major figure within the National Association of Audubon Societies since 1905. In 1939, he began traveling around South America distributing conservation literature and campaigning for the Hemispheric Convention. At the end of this meeting, twenty-five Peruvian notables founded their country's first NGO dedicated to conservation advocacy. The Comité Nacional de Protección a la Naturaleza set out to protect "animals, plant species, and beautiful scenery" in Peru and to promote the "culture, science, and economy of our country today, and even more for generations to come." Its members vowed to fight the destruction of "our biological patrimony" and to "instill in youth a love for Nature, exalting its aesthetic, scientific, and industrial values."[16]

[13] Lewis, "Negotiating for Nature," 127–32, 152–54, 157–60, 178–79, 187, 192–93; Sheinen, "Its Most Destructive Agents," 117–18.

[14] Macdonald, "Grimble of the Gilbert Islands," 228; Lawrence Grossman, "Soil Conservation, Political Ecology, and Technological Change on Saint Vincent," *Geographical Review* 87 (1997): 353–74; World Conservation Monitoring Centre, *Protected Areas of the World* (Gland, Switzerland, 1992), 4:417–40.

[15] Thomas Cox, "The Birth of Hawaiian Forestry: The Web of Influences," *Pacific Historical Review* 61 (1992): 169–92.

[16] BCNPN 1, no. 1 (1944): 1–2, 5–6, 8–9; "Comments by T. Gilbert Pearson" [1942], DPL-VP 3/3; Graham, *Audubon Ark*, 46–47, 117.

Pearson's tour of nine South American republics was a big success. Paraguay, Chile, Bolivia, and Colombia founded similar societies within six months of Peru, all of which were tied in with the International Committee for the Conservation of Birds. Mexico and Argentina had already done so, followed by Brazil in 1942. The list of directors of these associations reads like a who's who list of important scientists in the region – yet another indication of the connection between conservation and technocracy during this era. The membership of Peru's Comité Nacional was no exception. Five founding members had direct ties to the guano industry and agribusiness. These included Francisco Ballén (1875–1949), an international businessman with close ties to Leguía who served as CAG's general manager almost continuously from 1909–45 and was a major architect of its success. Other scientists of international prominence who later joined included physician Carlos Monge, a founder of the science of altitudinal physiology, and German-immigrant entomologist Johannes Wille, an outspoken critic of the overuse of agricultural insecticides. Only one woman associated with the Comité Nacional over the years. Luz Jarrín de Peñaloza was a major force in women's political causes known best for founding a legal aide service for the poor. Like female conservationists elsewhere in the region, she was particularly active in tree-planting campaigns but was never granted official membership in this males-only conservation club.[17]

Carlos Barreda (b. 1890) presided over the Comité Nacional for thirty years. He was a native of the highland city of Puno and an enthusiastic agent of agricultural modernization in the Sierra. After earning an agronomy degree in 1919, Barreda returned to the highlands to teach and to manage various livestock haciendas and a model farm. He was elected senator for the Department of Puno during Peru's redemocratization in 1939. As senator, he authored laws that established the Ministry of Agriculture and a national center for domestication of the vicuña. Barreda also published an influential 1940 pamphlet on national parks and was an outspoken advocate for soil conservation in Peru. He epitomized the importance of agricultural concerns within the Peruvian conservation movement – a key legacy of the guano industry.[18]

Barreda is best known for his promotion of Law no. 4197, often referred to as the Barreda Law, which banned the hunting and export of three Andean fur-bearing mammals: the vicuña (*Vicugna vicugna*), guanaco (*Lama guanicoe*), and short-tailed chinchilla (*Chinchilla chinchilla*). This bill was directly

[17] BCNPN 1, no. 1 (1944): 1, 2, 176–90; 7 (1950): 2–3; 11, no. 1 (1954): 2; 20 (1965–70): 65–69, 118; "Comments by T. Gilbert Pearson"; *Diccionario biográfico de peruanos contemporáneos*, s.v. "Ballén, Francisco."

[18] BCNPN 1, no. 1 (1944): 31, 112–36; 5 (1948): 90–148; 7 (1951): ?–148; 20 (1965–70): 26, 44–48, 68; *Diccionario biográfico del Perú contemporáneo: Siglo XX* (Lima, 2004), s.v. "Barreda y Ramos, Carlos A."

inspired by Pan American organizing activity and was signed into law by President Prado in June 1940, but it provided no effective means for enforcement – much less for dealing with the socioeconomic conditions that motivated relentless hunting of these rare animals. Their fate sheds light on why CAG was so successful as an animal conservation project and why the Comité Nacional's legalist approach to conservation failed to accomplish much in practice. The chinchilla was almost certainly extinct in the wild in Peru years before this law was passed. It was eventually reintroduced to Peru as a semidomesticated object of commerce, thanks to captive breeding in the United States. Today, a few scattered wild populations survive in the remote borderland region of Chile and Bolivia, high above the Atacama Desert, and the species is classified as critically endangered. The vicuña, meanwhile, continued to decline in numbers until the late 1960s. Its spectacular recovery owed little to the Comité Nacional but had everything to do with the engagement of local interests by wildlife technocrats. A wealthy Peruvian diplomat, Felipe Benavides Barreda (1917–91), used personal connections with Prince Philip and other members of the British upper class (by far the largest consumers of luxury wool fabric produced from poached skins) to do something about the vicuña's plight. The British government funded a two-year field investigation by zoologist Ian Grimwood, and he developed a plan that placed management of wild herds and shearing of captured animals in the hands of indigenous peasants. In 1966, Peru established the 6,000-hectare Pampa Galeras National Reserve to protect 6,500 animals. Premised on local involvement and strict international protections, it was a remarkable success. The Pampas Galeras population now numbers more than 65,000. Similar programs elsewhere in the Andes have brought official vicuña numbers to 347,273 – making this one of the most successful wildlife conservation programs in world history. Unfortunately, the same cannot be said for Peru's guanaco populations, which have little economic value and compete directly with sheep for pasture. They now number under 3,500.[19]

The Comité Nacional produced more tangible results in the realm of nature tourism. Albert Giesecke (1883–1968) served as its secretary for a quarter century. His career again illustrates the influence that U.S. experts have exercised over Peruvian affairs of state. After completing a Ph.D. at Cornell supervised by Leo Rowe, future president of the Pan American Union, Giesecke accepted the Leguía government's offer to come to Peru to create a business faculty at the central state secondary school in Lima. From there, he served variously as rector of the university in Cuzco, then as the city's mayor for twelve years, followed by three decades as an

[19] BCNPN 20 (1965–70): 30–32; Wilfredo Pérez Ruiz, *La saga de la vicuña* (Lima, 1994); William Franklin, "High, Wild World of the Vicuña," *National Geographic Magazine* Jan. 1973: 77–91; *Diccionario histórico y biográfico*, s.v. "Benavides Barreda, Felipe"; 2008 *IUCN Red List*.

official advisor to the U.S. ambassador. He married into a prominent *cuzqueña* family and raised his children as Peruvians but maintained his American identity by eating a bowl of Kellogg's Corn Flakes every morning. Giesecke was responsible for uniting the cause of environmental conservation with cultural preservation and mass tourism in Peru. As Cuzco's *alcalde*, he organized logistics for the Yale expedition that discovered Machu Picchu in 1912 and built a paved road to the megalithic Inca ruin Sacsayhuaman. Giesecke was an enthusiastic promoter of automobile tourism and the formation of professional tourism schools. To this end, he led the restoration of the ruins of Pachacamac for the 1938 Pan American Conference – the first of a string of tourist-friendly parks he hoped to establish along the new Pan American Highway through Peru. His idea to plant a forest of native trees around these ruins and turn it into the country's first national park never panned out. But Giesecke campaigned tirelessly for tree planting and landscape protection along Peru's highway system, and presided over an event of great symbolic significance, the opening of the tourist road to Machu Picchu in 1948.[20] Although anathema to wilderness advocates like Aldo Leopold, such advocacy reflects the once widespread belief that highway construction and mass tourism would help the conservationist cause, and it serves as a reminder that cultural preservation has long been integral to the national parks movement in the United States.[21]

Most of the Comité Nacional's attempts to protect Peruvian nature accomplished little. Its experience with the Santa Lucía forest in the Ica valley was typical. In 1945, the Beneficiencia de Ica requested permission to sell off a sixty-eight-hectare plot of riparian forest to support its public welfare programs. This grove represented one of the last old-growth stands of *algarrobo* trees (*Prosopis* spp.) along the central Peruvian coast. As we saw in Chapter 2, the Atacama nitrate industry consumed vast numbers of these deep-rooted trees. The rapid growth of coastal cities had greatly increased demand for charcoal, the country's main source of cooking fuel. Circa 1945, the metropolis of Lima by itself consumed one million bags a year (50,000 metric tons), most of which came from North Coast woodlands. Old trees produced the best charcoal. Saving the Santa Lucía forest would have accomplished a long list of goals of the Comité Nacional. From Giesecke's perspective, the forest would have made an ideal tourist park because it was adjacent to the Pan American Highway and close to the city of Ica. From Barreda's point of view, it was vital to discourage

---

[20] *BCNPN* 1, no. 1 (1944): 21, 23, 34; 6 (1949): 43; 7 (1951): 69–71; 9 (1952): 20 (1965–70): 58–64, 128–30; *Diccionario histórico y biográfico*, s.v. "Giesecke, Alberto"; Albert Giesecke III, personal communication.

[21] Cushman, "Environmental Therapy for Soil and Social Erosion: Landscape Architecture and Depression-Era Highway Construction in Texas," in *Environmentalism in Landscape Architecture* (Washington, DC, 2001); Hal Rothman, *America's National Monuments: The Politics of Preservation* (Lawrence, KS, 1994).

unsustainable use of Peru's forests and promote the development of alternative energy sources, such as the vast coal and hydroelectricity project underway in the Santa Valley. Saving the Santa Lucía forest also appealed to German botanist August Weberbauer (1871–1948) and biogeographer Javier Pulgar Vidal (1911–2003). These members believed that Peru's system of natural preserves should seek to protect examples of every one of the country's major plant assemblages, starting with the rarest. To these ends, the Comité Nacional offered to purchase the plot and made a well-publicized visitation to promote its protection as a national park, but their pocketbooks were too small and their dreams too grand. As an accommodation, the Peruvian executive required the Beneficiencia to submit a scientific plan for managing the forest on a sustainable basis. This merely delayed its total conversion to charcoal for urban resale.[22]

Members of the Comité Nacional achieved more tangible success in convincing the Peruvian state to create technocratic agencies charged with managing the country's forest, wildlife, and fishing resources. Within the Forestry Department, agronomist Ernesto Noriega Calmet organized a national campaign to encourage the nation's reforestation. President Prado banned the cutting of high-altitude forests of *queñua* (*Polylepis rasemosa*), and the Ministry of Education directed the country's normal schools to establish tree plantations and lead rural tree planting campaigns each Arbor Day. This gave women an official role in national conservation programs. However, these campaigns mainly planted Australian eucalyptus and casuarina trees, which increased the country's wood supply but at the cost of sopping up scarce water. The Hunting Department, meanwhile, did little more than gather statistics tracking the holocaust of ocelots, jaguars, caimans, sea otters, and other animals for the international fur and leather trades.[23]

Like their colleagues in Mexico, the leaders of the Comité Nacional had visions of a popular conservation movement, led by Peruvian youth, but their project could hardly have been less populist in organization and style. As a "committee," this organization was elitist by definition, with a membership limited to twenty-five notables living in Lima. Over the years, the Comité Nacional sent missions to organize regional chapters in Iquitos, Cuzco, Trujillo, Arequipa, Puno, and Puerto Maldonado, typically in collaboration with the local Rotary Club.[24] Committee leaders figured their professional and social prestige would gain them influence over national conservation policy and sometimes hesitated to admit new members who

[22] Barreda to Vogt, 12 Oct. 1946, DPL-VP 1/1; *BCNPN* 1, no. 1 (1944): 89–92; 2, no. 1 (1945): 218, 231–46; 5, no. 1 (1948): 37–44; 20 (1965–70): 29–30.
[23] *BCNPN* 1, no. 1 (1944): 29, 92–96, 100–4, 166; 2, no. 1 (1945): 68–80, 215–21; *Pesca y caza* 8 (1958): 44–48, 9 (1959): 112–37; Doughty, *The Eucalyptus*, 102, 154–56, 187, 189.
[24] *BCNPN* 1, no. 1 (1944): 9, 29, 74–87, 89–90, 186–88; 2 (1945): 164–67, 219–21; 7 (1951): 55–68; 10, no. 1 (1953): 57–59.

did not fit their social mold. Marine scientist Enrique Ávila expressed an interest in joining after returning from studies with Aldo Leopold at the University of Wisconsin. Giesecke rejected his overture with the reply that membership was "severely restricted." Ávila got the message: it was reserved for "certain Peruvian Big-shots" who had not been born with brown skin on a highland farmstead. Ávila eventually obtained admission, but continued to despise the Committee's tendency to "enthusiastic talk" with little action. He openly criticized these elitist tendencies in a 1954 essay that introduced Leopold's land ethic to Peru: "There will be no true *Conservation* while this discipline is the patrimony of distinguished professors, outstanding academic circles, cultivated social nuclei, calloused institutions. In order to be effective, Conservation has to become the ABC of the man on the street."[25]

Barreda, for his part, loved to blame the failures of the Comité Nacional on the failings of common Peruvians. They lacked his "high civic concept" and "education that generalizes the love of nature and affectionate respect for animal life." The popular threat to wild nature, therefore, needed "police vigilance and control." Barreda's view of proper recreation betrayed a disdain for plebeian culture that cynically ignored the everyday demands of survival for most Peruvians. For Barreda, sport hunting, rural tourism, and "contemplation of living nature" provided "spiritual satisfaction to the modern man who tires of the daily burdens of urban life" and desires a "return to the simple, primitive life." He thought "true national parks" should be playgrounds for the leisure class with "comfortable hotels and restaurants for the rest and lodging of tourists ... guided ... by expert forest guards." In his zeal for the greening of rainless Lima, Barreda despised the use of open public space for fairs and *fútbol* and favored their conversion to closed forests and contemplative gardens. On this last count, the Comité Nacional deserves credit for real action. Led by beautification advocate Francisco Ruiz Alarco, the Committee achieved its most tangible success through their promotion of zoos, museums, gardens, and municipal parks in Lima.[26] However, most green spaces in Lima have been designed to protect their thirsty lawns and exotic plants from trampling by the urban horde – not for popular access. For example, the central object of Barreda's scorn, the Campo de Marte, is no longer a site for plebeian recreation. Instead, it is one of the largest green expanses in central Lima today, fenced off from adjacent neighborhoods except for a small gate on the Avenida de Peruanidad, a paved parade ground where Peru's modern, mechanized military displays its might each

---

[25] Ávila's emphasis; "Ética en marcha," originally published in *BCAG* 30 (May 1954): 22–23; republished in *BCNPN* 12 (1959): 69–70; Ávila to Vogt, 17 Sept. 1945, 19 Dec. 1946, Vogt to Ávila, 25 Nov. 1946, Barreda to Vogt, 12 Oct. 1946, DPL-VP 1/1.

[26] *BCNPN* 2, no. 1 (1945): 172–75; 6 (1949): 43; 8 (1952): 31–38; 20 (1965–70): 26, 30, 35–38, 63.

July during Peru's independence celebration. Many other green spaces are walled off in a different way: they are surrounded by dangerous urban thoroughfares or located in guarded affluent neighborhoods. In this way, Lima mirrors the elitism of its first society of conservation advocates.

Latin America and the Land Ethic

When Peru's guano industry reluctantly terminated William Vogt's contract in December 1941, they opened up a hemisphere of possibilities for him as a conservation organizer. Under different circumstances, Vogt probably would have gone on to complete a Ph.D. under Aldo Leopold focused on the ecology of Peru's guano birds, but Vogt felt a patriotic duty to contribute to the war effort. After spending two months investigating the climatology of the Chilean coast (and spying on German-Chileans for the U.S. Army), Vogt accepted a position as associate director of the Division of Science and Education at the Office of the Coordinator of Inter-American Affairs in Washington, D.C. From this post, Vogt made arrangements for Leopold to do his part for the wartime alliance by going to Latin America to address "the almost complete absence of ecological understanding in the countries to the south of us," until his boss Nelson Rockefeller abruptly cancelled most of the Division's efforts to "promote hemispheric science." Fortunately for Vogt, at Harold Coolidge's behest, the U.S. State Department funded the creation of a Conservation Section within the Pan American Union in April 1943 to act as an advocate for the Convention on Nature Protection. They were looking for a scientifically trained "National Park man" to serve as its director, and hired Vogt as its head after Wetmore turned down the job. In this position, Vogt visited every one of the independent nations of the hemisphere over the next five years promoting the cause of environmental conservation.[27]

As he had in Peru, Vogt collaborated closely with local scientists in these efforts. In Mexico, where he spent the greatest amount of time, he teamed up with Enrique Beltrán (1903–94) on a series of projects. Beltrán again illustrates the technocratic tendencies of the conservation movement in Latin America – but with a populist tinge. During the first phase of his career, Beltrán worked as a scientific researcher and administrator. After completing a degree in marine biology at the national university, he led two government expeditions to survey the Gulf of Mexico. In 1931, he accepted a Guggenheim scholarship to study protozoan biology at Columbia

---

[27] Vogt to Leopold, 15 Dec. 1940, 26 Mar., 28 Apr., 16 May, 8 Aug. 1942, 5 July 1943; Leopold to Vogt, 12 Aug., 9 Sept. 1942, 8 July 1943; Leopold to E.B. Fred, 27 Jan. 1943, UWDC-ALA; Lewis, "Negotiating for Nature," 194–98; Maureen McCormick, "Of Birds, Guano, and Men: William Vogt's *Road to Survival*," Ph.D. diss. (University of Oklahoma, 2005), 93–94, 102–3.

University. This resulted in his expulsion from the Mexican Communist Party but allowed him to become the first Mexican to complete a doctoral degree in biology. On his return, President Lázaro Cárdenas appointed him director of a short-lived national agency charged with making sure all governmental investigations related to natural resource management served the utilitarian "necessities of the collective." Later in life, as the longtime director of the Instituto Mexicano de Recursos Naturales Renovables (IMERNAR), Beltrán campaigned tirelessly in support of population control and organized an annual public roundtable of experts to discuss environmental issues. Vogt and Beltrán worked together most closely in developing educational materials – another major emphasis of the Cárdenas era. They collaborated on a series of radio broadcasts presenting "brief essays on the ecology of conservation" that then formed the basis for a mass-produced booklet aimed at Mexico's rural populace, a curriculum for teacher training at the Escuela Normal Superior, and a secondary school textbook. Vogt later adapted this booklet, *El hombre y la tierra* (1944), for republication by the Amigos de la Tierra in El Salvador. Leopold was not impressed by these efforts at popularization and opposed Vogt's idea of adapting them for use in U.S. schools. He appreciated Vogt and Beltrán's call to arms against "the sickness of the land" but disapproved of the simplistic hatred toward insects and birds that sometime came through: "The only thing to hate is too many, too few, or [organisms] in the wrong place. Hate should never attach to species or classes." Meanwhile, Vogt worked to develop advanced ecological understanding in Mexico by arranging for the translation of key texts, such as Elton's *Animal Ecology*, by handing out copies of Leopold's *Game Management*, and by orchestrating a multiyear survey of Mexican wildlife headed by Leopold's son Starker.[28]

Vogt also completed conservation surveys of Chile, Guatemala, Venezuela, El Salvador, and Costa Rica. His bilingual reports all emphasized the threat of overpopulation, the deterioration of agricultural and forested land, and the "progressively lower living standards" that would inevitably result. He beseeched Venezuelans to stop their parasitism of the soil and to begin the "costly, distasteful, and difficult" process of curing "the sickness of the land." Vogt's visit to El Salvador, the most densely populated country in the Americas, convinced him that the rapid growth of human numbers doomed much of Latin America to future poverty. Costa Rica, on the other hand, still had extensive areas that merited protection as

[28] Vogt to Leopold, 5 July, 4 Nov. 1943, 1, 23 Mar. 1944, 18 Nov. 1945; Leopold to Vogt, 8 July 1943; Jay Darling to Leopold, 29 Sept. 1944; Leopold to Darling, 31 Oct. 1944, UWDC-ALA; Vogt, *Progress Report* (1946), DPL-VP 3/3; Vogt, *El hombre y la tierra* (San Salvador, 1958), 117–20; Juan José Saldaña, "El sector externo y la ciencia nacional: El conservacionismo en México," in *Nacionalismo e internacionalismo en las ciencias y la tecnología en América Latina* (Cali, 1997); Simonian, *Defending the Land of the Jaguar*, 81, 133–40, 248 n. 51; McCormick, "Of Birds, Guano, and Men," 103–11.

wilderness areas for scientific study or national parks, which "might well become a tourist attraction that would bring thousands of people and millions of dollars to the country." In this vein, his visit to Chile resulted in the establishment of Cape Horn National Park, which protected 2,000 square kilometers at the far southern tip of South America. In all of these countries, Vogt recommended placing "land-use management" in the hands of "adequately trained scientists" belonging to a "non-political" Natural Resources Board.[29]

Vogt's repeated use of the phrase "land sickness" in these reports revealed his deep intellectual debt to Aldo Leopold. Environmental historians and philosophers have long credited Leopold with originating the idea of *land health* – the key concept in his seminal essay on "The Land Ethic." It is more accurate to say that they developed this and other ideas in tandem, with Vogt playing the role of Plato to Leopold as Socrates, in one of the most important collaborations in the history of environmental thought. They became close friends in the mid-1930s while Vogt edited *Bird-Lore* and Leopold served on the national board of the Audubon Societies. Leopold invited Vogt to the University of Wisconsin to lead a seminar in spring 1937, and they spent a memorable time birding together at Faville Grove, where they observed the mating displays of the rare upland sandpiper just returned from the South American Pampas. This happened halfway between Leopold's two trips to the Río Gavilán when he was beginning to think intensively about "land pathology" and becoming obsessed with deer overpopulation. They were already in conversation about the cyclic crash of bird populations before Vogt went to Peru, from where he sent back numerous letters reporting on the effects of El Niño on the guano birds. Their shared interest in the "irruption sequence" among wild populations cemented their intellectual relationship.[30]

Leopold's interest in human population growth and its ramifications for environmental degradation likewise owed much to Vogt. This concern grew directly from their shared preoccupation with the threat that the automobile poses toward wilderness. From his years at Jones Beach on Long Island, Vogt had learned to despise "the mechanization and urbanization of the outdoors, advocated by my old chief, Robert Moses," who had since grown into the

---

[29] Vogt, *The Population of Venezuela and Its Natural Resources* (Washington, DC, 1946), 1, 10, 28, 30, 35; Vogt, *The Population of El Salvador and Its Natural Resources* (Washington, DC, 1946), 19–23; Vogt, *The Population of Costa Rica and Its Natural Resources* (Washington, DC, 1946), 2, 9, 17, 20, 24–25; Vogt, *Progress Report*, DPL-VP 3/3; "Se realizan estudios para formar una Comisión de Protección a la Naturaleza," *El Mercurio* (Santiago de Chile) 4 Mar. 1945, DPL-VP, clippings from Latin American newspapers.

[30] John Baker to Leopold, 7 Nov. 1936, 24 May 1938; Leopold to Vogt, 16 June [1937?]; Vogt to Leopold, 13 Oct. 1938; Robert Cushman Murphy to Leopold, 22 May 1939; Leopold, "Land Pathology" (1935), unpublished ms. no. 94, UWDC-ALA; Meine, *Aldo Leopold*, 312–13, 368–70, 405; Flader, *Thinking Like a Mountain*, 242–43, 268–70.

most powerful "bulldozer-subdivider" in the history of New York City.[31] In
a 1938 essay commissioned by Vogt for *Bird-Lore*, Leopold railed against
the "ant-like swarms" of humans that had descended on the planet's natural
areas in search of recreation, causing "a direct dilution of the opportunity
for solitude."[32] Vogt made his own pilgrimage to the Kaibab Plateau of
Arizona – the textbook case of a deer irruption – as part of an autumn 1943
tour of western national parks. He was not as concerned by deer overpopulation as by signs of human overuse on the North Rim of Grand Canyon.
"The emphasis on [the] quantitative rather than the qualitative aspect of
the Parks was a shock to me. Juke boxes, dance halls, swimming pools
and cheap-jack stores.... Here again it seems to me the conservationists
have fallen down on their job by letting the Philistines take over." Leopold
agreed with Vogt about this undesirable "toleration of Coney Island" but
admitted: "I shy off all parks – haven't seen one for 20 years." Vogt wrote
an essay for the *Bulletin of the Pan American Union* praising the natural
beauty that could be accessed from the new Pan American Highway, including "one of the world's greatest natural wonders,... the winged multitudes"
of Peru's guano islands. Vogt was hopeful that this work of modern engineering would provide inspiration for the establishment of a "necklace"
of protected sanctuaries "to include *all* plant and animal associations typical of each country." But he boldly warned in this article and his survey
reports that this highway would more likely accelerate the exploitation of
the natural world. Vogt, thus, interjected a cornerstone concern of the U.S.
wilderness movement into Latin American conservation discourse.[33]

Planning for an Inter-American Conservation Congress provided the two
of them with an opportunity to hash out some basic issues together in 1946.
Vogt submitted his draft prospectus to Leopold for careful review. This
document clearly revealed Vogt's debt to Warren Thompson and interwar
population discourse. For Vogt, the world's environmental crisis came down
to the carrying capacity of the earth, which was close to reaching its limits
because of rapid population growth, the dangers of which had been obscured
by humanity's "ability to draw on natural resources in distant parts of the
world or by developing techniques that make it possible to temporarily
raise the crop of natural resources." Vogt organized the conference into
sections focused on human population pressure, living standards, unequal
exploitation of resources, and the threat to world peace posed by these

[31] "Some Notes on WV," n.d., DPL-VP 5/1; Vogt to Morris Cooke, 24 Feb. 1948, UWDC-
ALA; Robert Caro, *The Power Broker: Robert Moses and the Fall of New York* (New York,
1974).

[32] Leopold, "Conservation Esthetic," *Bird-Lore* Mar.–Apr. 1938: 102, 106.

[33] Vogt's emphasis; Vogt to Leopold, 16 Sept. 1943, Leopold to Vogt, 27 Sept. 1943, UWDC-
ALA; Vogt, "Road to Beauty," *Bulletin of the Pan American Union* 77 (1943): 666, 670;
Paul Sutter, *Driven Wild: How the Fight against Automobiles Launched the Modern Wilder-
ness Movement* (Seattle, 2002).

phenomena. He even included a section on "renewable resources and history" that brought environmental history into the conversation. His comments on the "qualitative use of land" versus "quantitative use of recreational resources" came straight from his correspondence with Leopold, and by sleight-of-hand, reoriented discussion of "quality" away from eugenic emphasis on race and inheritance toward aesthetics and culture. As he had in his Peruvian work, Vogt insisted on "the unity of the environment, and the integration of all its components" when discussing issues such as climate variability, population dynamics, conservation education, and "Hemispheric planning" by environmental technocrats.[34] Leopold thought Vogt's proposal omitted discussion of basic philosophical issues:

The only thing you have left out is whether the philosophy of industrial culture is not, in its ultimate development, irreconcilable with ecological conservation. I think it so.... Industrialism might theoretically be conservative if there were an ethic limiting its application to what does not impair (a) permanence and stability of the land (b) beauty of the land. But there is no such ethic, nor likely to be.... Bill, your outline is excellent. That the situation is hopeless should not prevent us from doing our best.

Vogt responded: "You are, of course, correct in what you say about industrialism. I don't know how you would define ethic, but I am hopeful that horse sense may some day ... preserve the permanence and stability of the land, even though there seems to be little hope of saving its beauty." Leopold and Vogt spent a couple of weeks together in March 1946 in New York and Wisconsin, during which they worked out a list of prospective presenters. They met again a year later at meetings that resulted in the creation of the Conservation Foundation, during which "Bill and I found ourselves giving identical views, even tho we had hardly seen each other for years." Leopold was so affected by these interactions that he began lobbying for Vogt's hire as "professor of ecological economics" so University of Wisconsin graduates would leave with an understanding of the "worldwide conflict between economics and conservation."[35]

After three years of diplomatic wrangling, the Inter-American Conference on Conservation of Renewable Natural Resources finally came together in Denver, Colorado, in 1948, with Vogt serving as general secretary. It involved 111 presenters from twenty American states and a "large proportion of the conservation leaders of the hemisphere," including Carlos Barreda and CAG's general manager Carlos Llosa. Participants traveled a thousand kilometers across the Great Plains and Mountain West to see U.S. government conservation projects in action. At one point, 25,000 people

34 Vogt, "Preliminary Statement" [Jan. 1946]; Leopold to Vogt, 27 Sept. 1943; Vogt to Leopold, 21 Jan. 1946, UWDC-ALA.
35 Vogt to Leopold, 28 Jan. 1946; Leopold to Vogt, 25 Jan., 8 Feb. 1946, 16 Apr. 1948; Leopold to Noble Clark, 14 Jan. 1948, UWDC-ALA; Meine, *Aldo Leopold*, 477–79, 495.

convened on a family farm near Denver to observe soil conservation techniques. President Truman gave the closing address. Mexico's contingent, in response, organized its own series of regional conservation conferences south of the border. To a remarkable extent, this landmark meeting fulfilled Vogt's original vision and marked the high point of his organizing efforts with the Pan American Union.[36]

This relationship with Vogt, Leopold's most important correspondent during the last years of his life,[37] played a critical role in the final development and publication of Leopold's crowning work, *A Sand County Almanac* (1949). Vogt's mark is particularly apparent in Leopold's final essay, "The Land Ethic." Leopold had also been paying attention to interwar Malthusian rhetoric. In a 1933 precursor to this essay, Leopold noted the existence of "wars and rumors of wars which foretold the saturation of the world's best soils and climates." He also posited that increasing population density would require the human species to evolve an ethics-based alternative to "salvation by machinery" like that promised by the technocracy movement and other state-centered "isms" of the era.[38] "Man cannot live by bread, or Fords, alone."[39] As other historians have noted, Leopold became increasingly preoccupied with the "violence" of humanity's treatment of the land as World War II unfolded.[40] By 1944, he had come to define "land-health" as

the capacity for self-renewal in the soils, waters, plants, and animals that collectively comprise the land.... This leads to the 'rule of thumb' which is the basic premise of ecological conservation: the land should retain as much of its original membership as is compatible with human land use. The land must of course be modified, but... as gently and as little as possible.[41]

In August 1947, Leopold finished the final version of "The Land Ethic." He parroted Vogt's opinion that "accelerating wastage" due to "exploitative agriculture" had led many parts of the world to exceed "their sustained carrying capacity. Most of South America is overpopulated in this sense." Leopold directly related the level of human violence toward the land to population density, and used "the guano birds... of the Antarctic seas"

---

[36] *Proceedings of the Inter-American Conference on the Conservation of Renewable Natural Resources, Denver, Colorado, September 7–20, 1948* (Washington, DC, 1949); Vogt, "New Farms for Old," *Américas* Mar. 1949: 30–32, 40; Ávila to Vogt, 19 Dec. 1946, DPL-VP; MCAG 40 (1949): xc.

[37] Meine, *Aldo Leopold*, 477.

[38] Leopold, "Conservation Ethic," *Journal of Forestry* 31 (1933): 634–35, 639.

[39] Leopold, *Game Management*, vii.

[40] Meine, *Aldo Leopold*, 413–15.

[41] Leopold, "Conservation: In Whole or in Part?" (Nov. 1944), unpublished ms. no. 128, UWDC-ALA.

to exemplify the human species' ability to glean nutrients "on a world-wide scale" and thus "becloud and postpone the penalties of violence." The most important statement of the entire essay, however, derives closely from Leopold's 1946 correspondence with Vogt regarding the Inter-American Conference:

The case for a land ethic would appear hopeless but for the minority which is in obvious revolt against these "modern" trends. The "key-log" which must be moved to release the evolutionary process for an ethic is simply this: quit thinking about decent land-use as solely an economic problem. Examine each question in terms of what is ethically and esthetically right, as well as what is economically expedient. A thing is right when it tends to preserve the integrity, stability, and beauty of the biotic community. It is wrong when it tends otherwise.[42]

Leopold died of a heart attack while fighting a range fire at his shack in April 1948. His health had been troubling him for some months, and he had come to rely on Vogt to "speak for me" at national meetings. Vogt worked diligently with Leopold's son Luna to guide *A Sand County Almanac* to posthumous publication – and is responsible for the small correction to Leopold's statement on Peru's guano birds. Vogt was disappointed that these essays "so rich in wisdom" attracted little public notice when they first appeared, but he did help diffuse these writings behind the scenes. Vogt was responsible for providing activist Bernard DeVoto with drafts of Leopold's essays, which DeVoto applied to the budding controversy over dam construction in national parks and monuments – one of the foundational moments of the U.S. environmental movement. *A Sand County Almanac* eventually became a mass-market best-seller in the late 1960s, by which time Vogt and his own transformational book on environmental issues had faded from popular memory.[43]

The Environmentalist Manifesto

While Vogt was spreading the conservation gospel in Latin America, he also began to map out his own solution to the globe's environmental problems. Like Leopold, who viewed his trip to Chihuahua as beginning his fascination with land health, Vogt knew exactly when he became attuned to the "the rising tidal wave" of human numbers.

[42] Leopold, "The Land Ethic," 25 Aug. 1947, pp. 133–36, 140, Sand County Almanac ms., UWDC-ALA. Cf. Leopold, *A Sand County Almanac*, 217–20, 224–25; Meine, *Aldo Leopold*, 500–5.

[43] Vogt annotations to "Great Possessions," p. 134; Leopold to Vogt, 13 Oct. 1947, 16 Mar. 1948; Leopold to A. W. Smith, 28 Feb. 1948; Vogt to Joe Hickey, 27 Apr., 25 May, 7 June 1948; "Nomination for Discussion Leaders," 17 Feb. 1948, UWDC-ALA; Nash, *Wilderness and the American Mind*, 214; Meine, *Aldo Leopold*, 524.

In 1940, while I was doing research on the guano bird colonies... off the coast of Peru, one of the recurrent famines hit. The islands were covered with young birds, each nearly as tall as a year-old child, and to the unprofessional eye, resembling black-fronted penguins.

As the food supply shrank and the adults had to range farther and farther afield in search of fish, the young became thinner and more vocal. Like human babies, these cried from hunger and... I could roughly gauge the success of the adults' fishing by the cries from the two million young.... I would go out on the *pampa* in the morning and be almost knocked down by the horde of downy babies. They would flap their unfledged wings, while they gave their hunger call, at the feet of this strange, uncormorant-like creature.

There was not a thing one could do for them. Day by day there were fewer begging, more staggering about and listlessly drooping. And then more – hundreds of thousands more – of the pitiful, collapsed, downy clumps that were the dead.... Finally, perhaps because they were themselves dying, the parent birds simply did not return to the island.

What had been an animated nursery turned into a wide desolation with no sound but the sea and the gulls, and no movement but the scavenging gulls and condors.

Human beings die more stoically. But here was mass death in unforgettable shape and sound. Somehow, ever since, it has been possible to understand more fully the famines of China and India.[44]

In May 1945, Vogt published an article in the hugely popular *Saturday Evening Post* titled "Hunger at the Peace Table." Just like at the end of the First World War, food was extremely scarce in many parts of the world, resulting in Herbert Hoover's appointment, for the umpteenth time, to an international commission tasked with famine control. Vogt's article attracted a "whopping big advance" from a New York publisher to write a global survey "in human terms" of "the natural resource-population problem." He turned in the finished manuscript, titled "No Loaves, No Fishes" in December 1947, and his publisher spent the next several months organizing publicity for what promised to be a blockbuster. This included the appearance of an excerpt on Latin America in *Harper's Magazine* and the book's selection by the 800,000-member Book-of-the-Month Club. (The latter required Vogt to change the title to the more optimistic *Road to Survival*, the central metaphor of Edward East's 1923 best-seller *Mankind at the Crossroads*.) Twenty-six U.S. colleges and universities adopted the book as an assigned text in fall 1948 – many more in subsequent years. In January 1949, *Reader's Digest* brought out a condensed version of the book that reached a large segment of its 15 million subscribers worldwide, including

---

[44] Vogt, *People! Challenge to Survival* (New York, 1960), 124–25.

a huge Spanish-language readership.[45] The full text eventually appeared in at least eleven foreign editions, including a 1981 translation issued to bolster China's one-child policy. This made Vogt's 1948 jeremiad on human overpopulation the world's most widely read book on environmental issues before Rachel Carson's *Silent Spring* (1962). It therefore deserves close textual analysis.[46]

Road to Survival was a manifesto "to regain ecological freedom for our civilization." It was based on three premises. First, "we live in one world in an ecological-environmental sense," Vogt reasoned, expressing the globalist ideology that had recently given birth to the United Nations and his own Pan American experience. Second, the combination of human numbers and "environmental resistance" put a "practical ceiling" on all human endeavors, Vogt argued, applying the principle of carrying capacity that had guided his study of the guano birds. Third, Vogt idealized a world in "ecological equilibrium" with a democratic government based on "checks and balances." From this background, Vogt proceeded to paint a grim picture of a world out of balance that explicitly sought to refute technological optimism and to vindicate Malthus.[47]

Vogt's first target was "that sacred cow, free enterprise." Echoing Leopold, Vogt had little but scorn for free-market capitalism, although he hesitated to take clear sides in the emerging Cold War. "The good of the individual, and even of groups, must be sacrificed for the general good," Vogt pleaded. Western cattlemen typified America's "ecological Fifth Column" and were at the top of Vogt's blacklist: "The freebooting, rugged individualist . . . we must now recognize, where his activities destroy resources, as the Enemy of the People he has become." But in contrast to Leopold, Vogt believed that government intervention, perhaps even government ownership, was necessary to increase democratic access to natural resources. This position reflected Vogt's positive opinion of the Peruvian guano industry, but he was no fan of the Soviet "police state" (nor of Latin American military states), which he viewed as deceived by the same sin of progressivism that had given rise to modern capitalism.[48]

The recent war haunted Vogt, and he desperately wanted to avoid the "atomic or bacterial" holocaust of a Third World War. Echoing Warren

---

45 *Saturday Evening Post*, 12 May 1945: 109; Vogt to Leopold, 5 Aug. 1946; A. W. Smith to Leopold, 27 Feb., 12 Mar. 1947, UWDC-ALA; Vogt, "A Continent Slides to Ruin," *Harper's Magazine* June 1948: 481–89; McCormick, "Of Birds, Guano, and Men," 121, 126–27, 213; Perkins, *Geopolitics and the Green Revolution* 127–30.

46 Foreign editions include Stockholm 1948, London 1949, Milan 1949, Amsterdam 1950, Frankfurt 1950, Paris 1950, São Paulo 1951, Buenos Aires 1952, Taipei 1954, Tokyo 195[?], Beijing 1981. As a condensed book, it appeared in three additional languages: Danish, Finnish, and Norwegian.

47 Vogt, *Road to Survival* (New York, 1948), 14–15, 22, 63, 68, 72, 86, 88–89, 284.

48 Ibid., 15, 136, 143–44, 228–34, 285.

Thompson, he faulted the *Lebensraum* idea as the proximate cause for recent hostilities, but Vogt laid ultimate blame for World War II at the feet of the industrial West, which he thought had egregiously encouraged international competition for resources in the decades leading up to the war. Countries with limited natural resources were not the only villains:

The culpability of Japan in seeking this way out of her Malthusian dilemma is a culpability shared by most of the nations that have been self-righteously preaching democracy. We grabbed enormous territories from Mexico, and under Theodore Roosevelt we unblushingly did to Colombia [by establishing the Panama Canal Zone] what Russia would now like to do to Turkey [in the Bosporus Strait]. The chief justification for our present attitude seems to be that we did our grabbing several decades ago. We did not have the very eminent excuse of such population pressure as confronted Japan.

Echoing the rhetoric of Justus von Liebig a century before, Vogt believed the "contented parasite" Great Britain had done the greatest harm. While feeding off the rest of the world to drive its industrial growth, imperial Britain had removed the checks of "disease, famine, and fighting" on the Indian subcontinent and allowed its people, for whom "sex play is the national sport," to go on "breeding with the irresponsibility of codfish." Similar policies elsewhere had put pressure on the United States and other relatively unsettled lands to open their doors to immigration "to reduce the pressure caused by untrammeled copulation." As a consequence, the United States stood to see its own living standard fall in order "to raise that of the backward billion of Asia."[49]

Vogt's main innovation was to give an overt ecological dimension to this overpopulation discourse. At the core of this book was a historical comparison between the United States and Latin America. This was the empirical foundation of his analysis, acquired by long experience as a conservation organizer, and critical to his observation that "without the New World on which to draw, the Industrial Revolution would have been a stunted dwarf." North America's tremendous fortune was built on spoilage. "Our forefathers... were one of the most destructive groups of human beings that have ever raped the earth." Citing early environmental historian Avery Craven, Vogt concluded that this fortune was built on soil mining for the production of plantation crops, followed by parasitic industrial development. To make matters worse, the Americas had enabled Europe's own population problem to fester by exporting cultivars such as the potato and then importing vast numbers of European castoffs. Quoting Pascal Whelpton's 1939 article in the *Journal of Heredity*, Vogt concluded, "The United States is *now* overpopulated from the standpoint of per capita economic welfare" and

---

[49] Ibid., 216–17, 223–25. On these points, Vogt cited Thompson, *Population and Peace in the Pacific* (Chicago, 1946) and Guy Burch and Irving Pendell, *Population Roads to Peace and War* (Washington, DC, 1945).

needed to reduce its population to 100 million if it hoped to sustain "The American Standard of Living." Vogt had similar things to say about Australia's orgy of sodbusting and overgrazing. This southern land had "reached one of the world's highest living standards by the well-known methods of the drunken sailor: it is throwing its patrimony to the winds – literally – and having a wonderful time."[50] Vogt scrupulously avoided any mention of Whelpton's desire to produce a "better population" by encouraging the reproduction of "native white women" and "the more able, intelligent and farsighted portion of the population."[51] However, Vogt's close association with eugenicists over the years, including service on the council of the American Genetic Association, indicate that he shared some white-supremacist views regarding the racial "quality" of the human population, even though he was the definitive environmental determinist.[52]

In comparison, Latin America was in the condition of a tubercular patient. "All Latin American countries except three or four are overpopulated.... Biological bankruptcy hangs over their heads like a shaking avalanche." Vogt diagnosed Latin America's regional illness as traceable to four basic causes: first, Vogt concluded that this so-called Land of Opportunity was already heavily degraded and did not possess sufficient soil fertility to continue producing wealth without further depleting the region's "ecological capital." Second, Vogt declared that a "cultural lag" inherited from imperial Spain and nineteenth-century France held back Latin America's political development. This historical legacy was most visible in the region's domination by large landowners and corrupt "spoils system" that ruled its centralized governments. Third, Vogt thought the region's "primitive New World folkways" produced even deeper problems. Vogt did not think this was due to "lack of intelligence or ability," even among the poorest *indios*, as his interaction with Enrique Ávila had shown him. Rather, it was due to a fundamental lack of economic resources related to causes one and two. Fourth, and worst of all, "the 'American standard of living' ... has sent all classes awhoring after strange gods." In Vogt's prognosis, industrialization was simply impossible in most Latin American countries. Most lacked abundant energy resources (because Vogt dogmatically rejected big hydroelectric dams), had small internal markets (impoverished by the scarcity of arable land), and depended on high protectionist tariffs (which enriched a handful of industrialists while drastically raising the cost of living for the masses.)

---

[50] Vogt's emphasis; Vogt, *Road to Survival*, xiv, 59–66, 114–16, 146, 235–36; cf. Craven, *Soil Exhaustion.*

[51] Whelpton, "Population Policy for the United States," 402, 405–6.

[52] Vogt journal, Sept. 1940; Frederick Osborn to Vogt, 30 Nov. 1948; C. E. Leighty to Vogt, 13 Aug. 1949, DPL-VP 1/2, 3/1. "Nominations for Discussion Leaders," 17 Feb. 1948, UWDC-ALA; Vogt, *Road to Survival*, xvi; McCormick, "Of Birds, Guano, and Men," 156–58, 197; Daniel Kevles, *In the Name of Eugenics: Genetics and the Uses of Human Heredity* (Berkeley and Los Angeles, 1985), 60, 85–95, 170–75, 251–52, 258–59.

Only Argentina, Brazil, and perhaps the Dominican Republic, which had "protected itself against the Haitian hordes," seemed to be in a position to escape from this vicious cycle, Vogt concluded. Interestingly, a negative evaluation of Roman Catholicism and its opposition to birth control did not yet figure into this formulation, but he did placed heavy blame on the United States' "dollar diplomacy" for this situation. Five years before Fidel Castro initiated the 26th of July Movement in Cuba, Vogt called on his compatriots to

control American vandals abroad. We have spent millions of dollars trying to prove that we mean what we say about the Good Neighbor Policy – and at the same time we permit, even encourage, American business men to destroy the very means of subsistence of millions of people. This.... can scarcely fail to have violent repercussions when the people of Latin America awake to what is being done to them. The fact that Latin Americans themselves are selling out their countries will be forgotten; the dead cats will be heaved at the Colossus of the North.

Peru was not so bad off in Vogt's evaluation. "Were it not for guano, Peru would indeed be in a sorry state," but "with guano they have few equals." CAG

set an example not only for the Americas but for the entire world. Were natural resources generally managed as intelligently as the Peruvians have – in this century – managed their guano, the future of the human race could be regarded with considerably more optimism.

Vogt also praised the use of night soil by South Chinese farmers and admonished the sanitized world to "close the circle" and stop flushing away valuable manure out of fear of disease. Vogt used Peru's guano island ecology as an object lesson in other ways. He noted with approval that *lagartija* lizard eat their own young and that competition for nesting space among guano birds led breeding colonies to break up when food is scarce – powerful forms of natural birth control.[53]

It is remarkable how many shibboleths of latter-day environmentalists and environmental historians that Vogt expressed in this 1948 book: nature as pristine before humans became "civilized," the "goat-god" and ax as destroyers of ancient Mediterranean civilization, sheep as the "devourers of men," erosion as "the cancer of the land," predators and endangered species as integral to the "balance of nature," the dams of the Tennessee Valley Authority (TVA) as "cross-purpose" rather than "multi-purpose," "good roads" as the highways to environmental destruction, China as the land of starvation, Africa as a "dying land" condemned by desertification. Echoing Leopold, Vogt argued that a true "revolution" in humanity's relationship

[53] Vogt, *Road to Survival*, 75, 92, 110, 152–53, 161–62, 164–66, 168, 183–86, 191, 221, 226.

with the earth would only occur after "a profound change of fundamental ideas" led us to discard "our elementalistic Aristotelean heritage."[54]

Road to Survival also made a fundamental innovation in ecological philosophy. Vogt's repeated comments on "the inestimable advantage of a high death rate" and the ecological "importance of dying" repulsed many readers. Far more emphatically than Leopold, Vogt asserted the ethical position that humanity's one-sided defense of life was at the root of the planet's ecological crisis. Without human death, there can be no life – particularly for rare creatures. Vogt actually played a far more important role than Leopold, early on, in popularizing what has come to be known as deep ecology or ecocentric philosophy demanding that humans act in ways that are compatible with *all* life on earth.[55]

The *Road to Survival* did not inevitably lead human society down the toilet, however. Vogt's intense pessimism about population growth was balanced against an abundant technocratic optimism and ethical sensibility. He envisioned the establishment of an "international WPA" funded by the richer countries to promote "ecological health" in the rest of the world – not unlike the "global Marshall Plan" later promoted by Albert Gore. Human salvation required keeping two commandments: (1) renewable resources shall be managed to produce as much wealth as possible on a sustained-yield basis – the conservationist's old "gospel of efficiency." (2) Humans shall adjust their consumption to this limited supply, either by lowering their living standard or by maintaining fewer people – a means to fulfill Leopold's land ethic and accomplish what we now call "sustainability." Vogt thought reducing the human population was the only reasonable choice if modern civilization was to survive.[56]

Environmental scientists would be the lords of Vogt's New Ecological Order. The first task in regions with a "scientific vacuum" like Latin America would be to begin "ecological bookkeeping" by conducting biological surveys and collecting other "elementary data." Vogt despised the "dangerously misleading conclusions... so-called scientific work done in some of the poor countries" had produced, and therefore called for the adjudication of all this work by boards of "scientific bureaucrats," who would advise politicians and directly administer some programs. This implied that enormous power would fall into the hands of ecocrats from the North, at least until cooperative research, translation centers, and other programs created adequate scientific capacity in other regions. Vogt thought Vannevar Bush's plan for a National Science Foundation in the United States was a step in

---

54 Ibid., 19, 38–39, 94, 99, 120, 131, 142–43, 204, 219, 240.
55 Ibid., 93–95. Cf. Kohák, *The Green Halo*, 87–93, 108–18; Baird Calicott, *In Defense of the Land Ethic: Essays in Environmental Philosophy* (Albany, NY, 1988).
56 Vogt, *Road to Survival*, 265; Gore, *Earth in the Balance: Ecology and the Human Spirit* (Boston, 1992), ch. 15.

the right direction, as long as funding went to the study of land health and not to military and medical nostrums.[57]

Yet Vogt did not have blind faith in technocracy. He possessed a profound distrust for engineers and purely technical knowledge. While in Mexico, Vogt had engaged in a heated debate with Irrigation Commissioner Adolfo Orive Alba over the value of large dams. Vogt and Leopold privately despised the growing number of "power and flood control enthusiasts [who] have begun to steal a ride on the conservation band wagon" in the United States.[58] In *Road to Survival*, Vogt strongly criticized the U.S. Army Corps of Engineers, which had drowned so much fertile farmland behind dams in the name of conservation, and expressed grave doubts about the wisdom of creating "a world dotted with TVAs." Vogt hoped that room could somehow be found for popular democracy in this new order. He approved of the ongoing process of decolonization for countries like Indonesia and India but strongly disapproved of the populist consumerism represented by these movements. Like any good liberal, Vogt believed proper education provided an escape from this dilemma, even for "so-called backward people," and hoped to generalize the strategy he and Beltrán had begun to develop for the Mexican state. Vogt called on the governments of the world to implement a holistic system of scientific and humanitarian education for all classes of society based on the principle of ecological health. Teachers were critical to this proposal. They would require proper training – preferably obtained on the land and among the people they would teach, so that they could adapt their learning to the world's profound local diversity of environmental and cultural conditions. Vogt offered the Inter-American Institute of Agricultural Sciences at Turrialba, Costa Rica, as a possible model. Vogt envisioned the use of mass media campaigns to sell better approaches to land management: "Advertising and publicity techniques that have girdled the globe with American tooth paste should sell sound land-use and ecological awareness; instead of promoting an American standard of living, they should promote a rational, national standard." Vogt had great faith in the possibilities of educational programs: after all, he had observed Peruvian guano workers "many of them unable to read or write" who learned to "faithfully brush their teeth twice daily."[59]

Vogt still believed technology had an important role to play in this struggle. Having witnessed the sprouting of the Green Revolution at research labs in Mexico, Vogt had great hopes for genetically improved cultivars whose productivity would, he hoped, allow farmers to take marginal lands out of cultivation. The linchpin of his plans, however, involved "outwitting

[57] Vogt, *Road to Survival*, 141, 143, 159, 265, 268–72.
[58] Simonian, *Defending the Land of the Jaguar*, 120–21; Leopold to Vogt, 1 Mar. 1948; Vogt to Morris Cooke, 24 Feb. 1948, UWDC-ALA.
[59] Vogt, *Road to Survival*, 127, 138–39, 268–77, 282.

the libido." This required "a completely new approach to contraception" that went beyond condoms. Above all, women needed a contraceptive technology of their own that was cheap and dependable. "If the United States had spent two billion dollars developing such a contraceptive, instead of the atom bomb, it would have contributed far more to our national security, while, at the same time, it promoted a rising living standard for the entire world." No matter what their cultural or educational background, Vogt thought families would choose to control their fertility when shown its practicality and necessity, out of love for their children and a desire to make the world better for future generations. "Freedom of contraception" became Vogt's most influential and controversial maxim.[60]

"The handwriting on the wall of five continents" told Vogt that "the Day of Judgment is at hand." There would be no miracles in the offing to provide the world with loaves and fishes, but Vogt, like Malthus, does not fully deserve his reputation for apocalyptic gloom. In *Road to Survival*, he presented a coherent, expert-led program for reform without wallowing in objections to his proposals. Vogt made it appear that the road to survival for the human species was broad, once humanity recognized the one, true ecological gospel.[61]

Exploding the Population Bomb

"Vogt's ecological Doomsday Book" was widely reviewed in the popular and scholarly press, worldwide, and served as a key point of discussion at the National Conference of Editorial Writers held in late November 1948.[62] As so often happens with works of great popular interest, a caricature of his argument came to dominate mass media coverage. These distortions continue to be perpetuated uncritically by historians.

Many critics took aim at Vogt's scientific credentials, oblivious to his time among the guano birds and the international prestige he enjoyed among ornithologists, ecologists, and ethologists. From the left, a geographer writing for *The Nation* condemned Vogt for his "hysterical efforts" against "the spawning millions of backward countries, who must now have fewer children and conserve their dwindling resources – so that *we* may maintain our standard of living." This writer thought nobody could "foresee the end of technological advances." For example, "the sea has a virtually limitless sustenance capacity which can be developed through scientific research." Vogt's failure to ask "the Chinese, Puerto Ricans, Indians, or Africans what they

---

[60] Ibid., 265, 277–83.
[61] Ibid., 280–81.
[62] "This Starving Planet," *Newsweek* 9 Aug. 1948: 69–70; George Patterson, "Soil Conservationists Refuse to Be Optimistic," *Courier-Journal* (Louisville, KY) 26 Nov. 1948; McCormick, "Of Birds, Guano, and Men," 139–40.

think," on the other hand, represented "the extent of science's bankruptcy in the face of modern problems."[63] Near the political center, an unsigned column in *Time* magazine claimed that for "real agricultural scientists, close to the soil and its sciences, such pessimism sounds silly or worse." Through the use of hybrids, agricultural chemicals, and scientific understanding, *Time* argued, "Man is master not only of the soil, but of the plants that grow in it, molding them plastically to suit human purposes." For example, the U.S. South was supposedly in the midst of "a real agricultural rebirth" in which

on thousands of once sterile slopes, the miraculous vine, kudzu, clambers like Jack's beanstalk. It chokes devouring gullies with entangled soil. It buries fences, leaps into trees. Its big leaves, which stay green until Christmas, are as nourishing to cattle as excellent alfalfa. When plowed under, kudzu enriches the soil.

Elsewhere, "enormous areas, especially in the tropics, will almost certainly yield, sooner or later, to scientific agriculture."[64]

The condensed version published in *Reader's Digest* systematically omitted Vogt's criticism of the United States and European colonialism. In this account butchered to fit right-wing sensibilities, "the Japs who came to dinner" and poor "men and women in overpopulated countries who produce excessive numbers of children" became the real threat to the "American standard of living" and world peace. Vogt's recommendation that "colonial lands...be placed under an ecological trusteeship" and that international organizations offer poor people "a sterilization bonus" took on a perverted meaning in this context. To complete the debasement of Vogt's arguments, DeWitt Wallace, the powerful right-wing ideologue who edited the magazine, published a "critique of *Road to Survival*" condensed from *Nation's Business* that told Americans to get ready for unprecedented prosperity by the end of the 1950s.[65]

Vogt's notoriety caused trouble for him as a Pan American diplomat. A July 1949 article in the *Saturday Evening Post* brought his situation to a head. Vogt harshly criticized the "Santa Claus complex" that inspired President Truman's Point Four Program promising technical assistance and economic aid to counter "hunger, misery, and despair" among the world's "undeveloped areas and backward peoples." Vogt feared that this well-meaning program would exacerbate economic and social inequalities, while doing nothing of substance to address the population problem or other underlying causes of poverty. Vogt chose to resign as head of the Conservation Section rather than give in to State Department pressure to put down his pen. He was briefly replaced by biologist Annette Flugger, but the

[63] Earl Hanson, "Mankind Need Not Starve," *The Nation* 12 Nov. 1949: 464–67.
[64] "Eat Hearty," *Time* 8 Nov. 1948: 27–31.
[65] "*Road to Survival*: A Condensation from the Book by William Vogt," *Reader's Digest* Jan. 1949: 141–42, 151–53, 156; Vergil Reed, "Jackpot for 1960," *Reader's Digest* Feb. 1949: 88–90.

State Department did not renew its funding, and the organization became extinct.[66]

Treatment of this sort infuriated friends close to Vogt and Leopold, including ornithologist Joe Hickey.[67] In response, they waged a counter-campaign that laid important foundations for the modern environmental movement. In *Scientific Monthly*, Yale ecologist George Evelyn Hutchinson admonished that "anyone with any technical knowledge understands that the dangers described" in Vogt's book "are real enough, and perhaps more real and more dangerous than the threat of an atomic war." Leopold, before he died, expressed similar sentiments in an extended blurb for the cover of *Road to Survival*. Hutchinson was in the process of researching a massive tome on the world's guano resources inspired by Vogt, and beseeched his readers to pay greater attention to the cycling of phosphorus necessary for food production. Hutchinson was concerned that American overconsumption of the world's resources was making "a considerable section of our population to be definitely overweight" and held out the hope that "we can substitute the delights of ballet and Mozartian opera, which are geochemically very cheap, for part of those provided by hot dogs or apple pie and ice cream."[68] Bernard DeVoto plugged the book whenever he could as a part of his wilderness advocacy: "I am more steamed up about it than I can remember having been about any book for years." Robert Cushman Murphy's wife Grace Barstow Murphy, who later headed the Long Island Citizens Against Mass Poisoning, wrote Vogt: "Your book is the new Bible. I've already written... a clergyman you know to found a new religion on it." Hugh Moore, the wealthy founder of the Dixie Cup Corporation and outspoken promoter of the cleanliness movement, claimed to have received "a religious revelation" from reading *Road to Survival* in 1948. These individuals integrated pieces of Vogt's argument into three pivotal controversies of the next quarter century: the 1950–55 battle against the construction of a dam in Dinosaur National Monument (DeVoto), lawsuits against the spraying of DDT beginning on Long Island in 1958 (Murphy and Hickey), and the debate over the need for legalized birth control, abortion, and government-coerced population control (Moore).[69]

---

[66] Vogt, "Let's Examine Our Santa Claus Complex," *Saturday Evening Post* 23 July 1949: 17–19, 76, 78; "Vogt's Stand Costs Job," *Science News Letter* 31 Dec. 1949: 424; Lewis, "Negotiating for Nature," 198–200; McCormick, "Of Birds, Guano, and Men," 183–85.

[67] Vogt to Joseph Hickey, 7 June 1948; Hickey to William Sarles, 23 Nov. 1948; Doug Wade to Hickey, 2 Dec. 1948, UWDC-ALA.

[68] Hutchinson, "On Living in the Biosphere," *Scientific Monthly* 67 (1948): 393–97; Leopold to E. P. Swenson, 2, 9 Mar. 1948, UWDC-ALA.

[69] DeVoto quoted in Stephen Fox, *The American Conservation Movement: John Muir and His Legacy* (Madison, WI, 1981), 308; Grace Murphy to Vogt, n.d., DPL-VP 1/2; Thomas Dunlap, *DDT: Scientists, Citizens, and Public Policy* (Princeton, NJ, 1981), 82–86, 94–95, 131–39, 152–53, 168–69, 222; Lear, *Rachel Carson*, 333, 557 n. 65; Donald Crichtlow,

A sophomore at the University of Pennsylvania named Paul Ehrlich was also deeply affected by reading Vogt's book. In 1949, he befriended a group of veterans who protected him from abuse by upperclassmen for refusing to wear the freshman beanie. Rather than joining a fraternity, Ehrlich decided to rent a house with them, which they named the Autonomous People's Republic of Chestnut Street. They passed around important books of the day, including a copy of Road to Survival. Eighteen years later, after distinguishing himself as an ecologist, Ehrlich published a mass-market paperback on the relationship between population, resources, and environment, to which his publisher gave the title The Population Bomb after a 1954 pamphlet distributed in the millions by Hugh Moore. This book proved so popular that many people have come to believe that Ehrlich and the Club of Rome originated this foundational concern of modern environmentalism.[70]

A book remarkably similar to Road to Survival also appeared in 1948. Our Plundered Planet covered much the same ground but was more impressionistic and less programmatic than Road to Survival. Its author Fairfield Osborn (1887–1969) had quite a pedigree as a scientist and conservationist: he was the long-time director of the New York Zoological Society, son of famed paleontologist Henry Fairfield Osborn, and cousin to prominent eugenicist Frederick Osborn. During World War II, he became fixated on environmental destruction in the Pacific while serving as editor of a series of informational books on The Pacific World.[71] Osborn often asked Leopold and Vogt for examples of their unpublished work and openly admitted that this pair – alone among his network of advisors – had provided him with "a philosophical approach to the problem." The Latin American section of Our Plundered Planet came straight from Vogt's reports; many other ideas in the book are strikingly similar. The destructiveness of World Wars I and II inspired Osborn to write about another "silent war . . . man's conflict with nature," which promised to destroy "world society" unless humanity chose to take the "slow road to reclamation." In his view, the predictions of Malthus for industrialized Europe had been merely forestalled by the extension of environmental exploitation to the Americas, Africa, and Australia and the invention of chemical fertilizers and pesticides. Like Vogt, Osborn condemned the unending quest of European colonizers for "cash returns through export," their inattention to "basic subsistence," and their use of "government taxation" as a "thin veneer to cover forced labor or economic slavery" among the colonized – all for the false cause of "higher

Intended Consequences: Birth Control, Abortion, and the Federal Government in Modern America (New York, 1999), 30–31.

[70] Paul Ehrlich, personal communication, 27 Mar. 2009; contra Mauricio Shoijet, "Limits to Growth and the Rise of Catastrophism," Environmental History 4 (1999): 515–30.

[71] Robertson, "The Population Bomb," 34–44.

civilization." Unlike Vogt, Osborn had a high opinion of "ably adminis-
tered" big development projects like the TVA. But in the end, he saw only
one real solution to the world's "oncoming crisis":

Man must recognize the necessity of cooperating with nature. He must temper his
demands and use and conserve the natural living resources of the earth in a manner
that alone can provide for the continuation of his civilization. The final answer is to
be found only through comprehension of the enduring processes of nature. The time
for defiance is at an end.

These books are so similar that they were often lumped together in the minds
of contemporaries and in historical memory.[72]

Osborn and Vogt's collaboration extended far beyond the realm of ideas.
In March 1947, Osborn organized a meeting in New York City at the Zoological Society involving Vogt, Leopold, and a handful of others to discuss
the formation of a "Conservation Institute" of "world-wide" scope dedicated to research and education "at the grassroots." This meeting led to the
formal incorporation of the Conservation Foundation eight months later.
The initial program of this important environmental NGO bore the marks
of Vogt and Leopold's influence at almost every turn. It operated from the
premise that "the well-being and even the survival... of civilization as a
whole... is, in the final analysis, dependent upon the preservation and intelligent use of the life-supporting resources of this and other countries." It
placed "population growth and population pressure... at the core of the
conservation problem" and repeatedly identified a connection between "the
health of the earth" and "human health." Leopold was adamant that the
Conservation Foundation should not serve as "a development program,"
but he strongly approved of its technocratic orientation. Its original board
of directors included a familiar cast of characters: Osborn (as president),
Vogt, Leopold, Hutchinson, Elton, Wetmore, and Coolidge (as executive
secretary).[73] During its first decade under Osborn, the Conservation Foundation gave its support to a variety of data-gathering projects, educational
films, and publications but tried to stay above the political fray. Many of
these focused on North America, but the organization also supported studies of population growth in Jamaica, a geographical survey of soil erosion
in Latin America, and a worldwide examination of marine resources that
could be used as human food. In accord with the technocratic ideal, it also
organized a program for training environmental experts for careers in business, industry, and government. Most significantly, it sponsored a series of

[72] Osborn to Leopold, 20 Mar. 1947, UWDC-ALA; Osborn, *Our Plundered Planet* (Boston,
1948), vii, 33, 38, 67–74, 102–3, 116–17, 139–42, 166–75, 191, 192–93, 201, 204–5.
[73] Osborn to Leopold, 18 Feb., 21 Nov. 1947; George Brewer to Leopold, 8 Feb., 1 Mar., 5
Apr. 1947; Leopold to Brewer, 16 Apr. 1947; "The Conservation Foundation-Prospectus,"
(Nov. 1947): 4, 7, 19–21, UWDC-ALA; Osborn to Vogt, 4 Nov. 1948, DPL-VP 1/2.

reports on the impact of pesticides on wildlife that served as a key resource for Rachel Carson in writing *Silent Spring*.[74]

From 1961 until his death in 1968, Vogt wrapped up his career as the Conservation Foundation's executive secretary. By this time, the organization had acquired a stellar reputation as a clearinghouse for environmental information, and under Vogt's watch, organized a groundbreaking 1963 conference, which warned for the first time that a doubling of CO_2 in the atmosphere could cause the whole earth to warm by an average of 3.8 degrees Celsius and result in "immense" coastal flooding.[75] Research grants that Vogt doled out jump-started a number of important careers, including that of one of Hutchinson's students, Amazonian conservation biologist Tom Lovejoy, who is widely credited with popularizing the biodiversity concept and inventing the debt-for-nature swap in the 1980s.[76] Environmental historian Samuel Hays detected a shift in the Conservation Foundation's emphasis during the 1970s away from the anti-developmental bias of its founders, as a new generation of leaders searched for common ground between business and the environment. Hays considered the Conservation Foundation representative of a broader tendency for "technical professionals" to neutralize the more radical demands of grassroots environmental activists during the 1970s and 1980s. This interpretation mistakenly discounts the powerful technocratic tendency that always drove the Conservation Foundation's activities, and the importance of scientific expertise to the postwar environmental movement more generally.[77]

Vogt and Osborn's initiatives inspired a vigorous response from scientists interested in the population problem. In 1949, Fairfield Osborn was invited to present his views on "the problem of world production" at the Mid-Century Convocation on the Social Implications of Scientific Progress at MIT. This was a setup. After Osborn had his say, a high-powered panel of scientists and engineers including two of the masterminds behind the atomic bomb, Vannevar Bush and Britain's Henry Tizard, ruthlessly attacked neo-Malthusianism. "Science also increases exponentially; in the same way that men lead to more men and machines make more machines, so ideas create more ideas," Bush retorted, repeating the theme of his own bestseller *Science: The Endless Frontier* (1945). "The point I think is this, that science gets there

---

[74] *Soil Erosion Survey of Latin America* (New York, 1955); G. W. Roberts, *The Population of Jamaica* (Cambridge, 1957); Lionel Walford, *Living Resources of the Sea* (New York, 1957); *Resource Training for Business, Industry, Government* (New York, 1958); Lear, *Rachel Carson*, 317, 320–21, 329–33, 345, 461, 566 n. 18.

[75] *Implications of Rising Carbon Dioxide Content of the Atmosphere* (New York, 1963); Spencer Weart, *The Discovery of Global Warming* (Cambridge, MA, 2003), 43–44.

[76] Lovejoy, personal communication, 11 May 2009.

[77] Hays, *Beauty, Health, and Permanence: Environmental Politics in the United States, 1955–1985* (Cambridge and New York, 1987), ch. 12.

first."[78] Marston Bates, a biologist well known for his popular writings on ecology and population, could remember the exact date and time in 1948 when the director of the Rockefeller Foundation's International Health Division suggested that he change the focus of his South American research from the relationship between mosquitoes, yellow fever virus, and primates to human ecology. He

> went on to explain. We were living in a time when some people were beginning to question the philosophy and value of public health work as now carried out. He and other public health men were increasingly subject to jibes about public health being a "bad thing," ... [that] by forestalling death through disease, might be ... changing the disease problem into a population problem.[79]

Just two months before, after reading Vogt's book, the new president of the Rockefeller Foundation had caused a quite a stir by asking his underlings to reconsider the wisdom of the organization's programs to improve agricultural production and public health if they were exacerbating overpopulation. In a 1954 address, the long-time head of the Rockefeller Foundation's Medical Sciences Division explicitly compared the earth's human population to a cancerous growth and called the colonization of the Western Hemisphere the "metastasis of the white race." The Rockefeller Foundation never gave explicit support to population control efforts, however, leading John Rockefeller III to establish the Population Council in 1952.[80]

Vogt also did his part to advance these efforts. In May 1951, the Planned Parenthood Federation of America (PPFA) named Vogt its national director. Planned Parenthood was the keystone organization of a movement that aggressively promoted the use of scientific understanding and contraceptive technologies for family planning. His appointment symbolized the convergence of the birth and population control movements during the 1950s. With financial assistance from Hugh Moore, he turned Planned Parenthood into a leading voice for global population control. But Vogt often fought over turf and program priorities with Margaret Sanger, the founder of the PPFA and new International Planned Parenthood Federation. He infuriated philanthropist Katherine Dexter McCormick when he tried to divert PPFA funds away from basic research into the use of hormones to control ovulation in mammals toward widening the distribution of birth control information. He thought birth control research should be left to Rockefeller's far better funded Population Council. These conflicts have led some historians to unjustly portray Vogt as an enemy of the development of the Pill – even

---

[78] *Mid-Century: The Social Implications of Scientific Progress* (Cambridge, MA, 1950), ch. 3.
[79] Bates, *The Prevalence of People* (New York, 1955), 1–2.
[80] Alan Gregg, "A Medical Aspect of the Population Problem," *Science* 13 May 1955: 681–82; Perkins, *Geopolitics and the Green Revolution* 137–38; Connelly, *Fatal Misconception*, 159–63.

to suggest that his struggle with polio and interest in bird-watching handicapped his personality and made him "more of an artist than a dynamic leader." In 1954, with McCormick's support, the Searle pharmaceutical company initiated tests of hormonal contraceptives in colonial Puerto Rico using female medical students and poor women involved in a slum clearance program as guinea pigs. These field trials were a resounding success, and by the time Vogt was pushed out as PPFA director in 1961, his dream of a mass-market oral contraceptive enabling women to control their own fertility had finally come true.[81]

U.S. population scientists produced the most influential response to Vogt and Osborn. The ideas and policies they advocated continue to affect the ways we think and act toward the global South to this day. In 1951, Northwestern University organized another high-powered conference involving the chair of the Atomic Energy Commission, the recent head of the International Emergency Food Council, and several of the country's leading population experts. Warren Thompson presented a schema for dividing the planet into three worlds based on demographic characteristics and level of industrialization, similar to the one in his 1946 book *Population and Peace in the Pacific* (fig. 8.1). This schema provided an organizing framework for the whole conference. Joseph Spengler examined first-class countries, which he referred to as "areas of advanced industrialization." Irene Taeuber outlined the characteristics of second-class countries, or "transitional areas" on their way to first-class status. Kingsley Davis itemized the challenges facing third-class countries, or "underdeveloped areas." These experts explicitly agreed with Vogt and Osborn on some points. Davis conceded that the industrialization of the "underdeveloped three-fourths of the world" was unlikely and probably undesirable because of the pressure it would place on the world's resources. Frank Notestein and ecologist Paul Sears both reiterated the necessity of birth control programs. Nonetheless, nearly everyone at the conference expressed faith in the ability of agricultural improvements and increased exploitation of oceanic resources to keep up with world population growth. Broad-based development programs leading to per capita increases in living standards and the demographic transition provided their solution to the world's population problem.[82] Population scientists in the United

[81] McCormick, "Of Birds, Guano, and Men," 187–202; James Reed, *From Private Vice to Public Virtue: The Birth Control Movement and American Society since 1830* (New York, 1978), 281–93, 334–45, 341–42 [quote], 411 n. 1, 434 n. 32; Linda Gordon, *Woman's Body, Woman's Right: A Social History of Birth Control in America* (New York, 1977), 341–90, 396–97; Elizabeth Siegel Watkins, *On the Pill: A Social History of Oral Contraceptives* (Baltimore, 1998), 13–28; Crichtlow, *Intended Consequences*, 13–19, 30–31; Annette Ramírez de Arellano and Conrad Seipp, *Colonialism, Catholicism, and Contraception: A History of Birth Control in Puerto Rico* (Chapel Hill, NC, 1983), ch. 9.

[82] Paul Hatt, ed., *World Population and Future Resources* (New York, 1952), xviii, 3–5, 13–16, 22, 25, 39, 43, 67, 71, 78, 88, 109, 122–23, 127–30, 132.

States were already dividing the nations of the world into three parts based on their developmental status well before a French demographer coined the term "Third World" in 1952 to refer to the exploited, potentially revolutionary countries of Africa, Asia, Latin America, and Oceania, as an analogy to the Third Estate of revolutionary France. The 1955 Bandung Conference then appropriated this term to refer to countries belonging to the nonaligned movement. These innovations pushed environmental concerns even farther to the wayside of this discussion.[83]

The impact of Vogt and *Road to Survival* extended far beyond the United States. He and British zoologist Julian Huxley, the first director-general of UNESCO, worked together closely in creating the International Union for the Protection of Nature in 1947 (now International Union for the Conservation of Nature, or IUCN). Huxley was a lifetime bird enthusiast and had long been an advocate for human population control. In fact, Aldous Huxley wrote the dystopian novel *Brave New World* (1932) to parody his brother's technocratic approach to human ecology and reproduction. Huxley almost succeeded in his plan to have Vogt appointed as the IUCN's first president. Vogt also greatly influenced Swedish food scientist Georg Borgström, who became a forceful international spokesman for the cause of population control and powerfully influenced the development of an environmental movement in Scandinavia.[84]

Vogt's most influential international criticism came from an expert on the environmental conditions of the poor in Brazil. Josué de Castro (1908–73) grew up in the northeastern metropolis of Recife, where his father had fled from the region's parched backlands during the Great El Niño Drought of 1877–78. In 1925, he completed a medical degree at a Bahian school known for its tradition of environmental medicine but only became preoccupied with the issue of hunger after completing a study of 500 families of factory workers in his hometown in 1933. To his shock, he discovered that the average adult only consumed 1,645 calories a day, mostly in the form of starch. This experience led Castro to become an evangelist for the view that nutrition was far more important than race or climate in determining the "quality" of Brazil's population, as well as a fervent advocate for government programs to improve the lives of the poor. After moving to Rio de Janeiro in 1935 to take a position at the Federal University, Castro involved himself in a flurry of organizing activity, both in Brazil and abroad, focused on the scientific study and improvement of human nutrition. On the eve of

---

[83] Contra Leslie Wolf-Phillips, "Why 'Third World'?: Origin, Definition and Usage," *Third World Quarterly* 9 (1987): 1311–27; Mark Berger, "After the Third World? History, Destiny and the Fate of Third Worldism," *Third World Quarterly* 25 (2004): 9–39; Connelly, *Fatal Misconception*, 143–44, 153–54.

[84] Anker, *Imperial Ecology*, 26, 97, 109, 114–15, 198, 202–8; Linnér, *The Return of Malthus*, 10, 36–39, 76–77, 158–59; McCormick, "Of Birds, Guano, and Men," 168–83, 188.

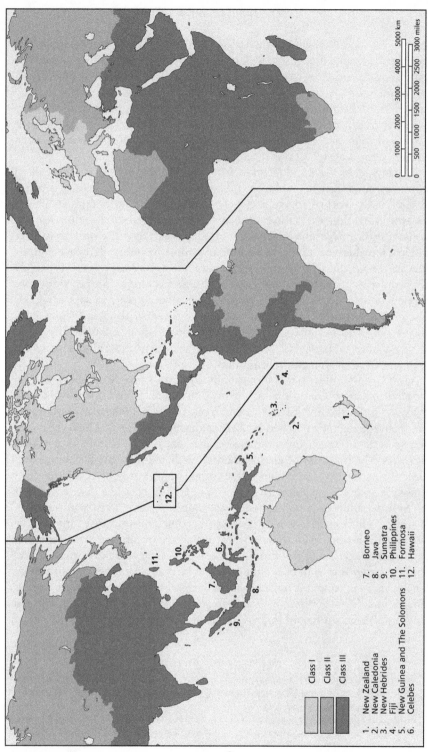

Class I
Class II
Class III

1. New Zealand
2. New Caledonia
3. New Hebrides
4. Fiji
5. New Guinea and The Solomons
6. Celebes

7. Borneo
8. Java
9. Sumatra
10. Philippines
11. Formosa
12. Hawaii

the war, he spent several months in Italy, where he came under the influence of Corrado Gini and the belief that rapid population growth can provide a source of national vitality. After World War II, Castro took part in early nutritional programs at the United Nations Food and Agriculture Organization (FAO), and in November 1951, was elected to a four-year term as chairman of its governing council. From 1955 to 1963, he served as a federal deputy for his home state of Pernambuco, and then for a few months as Brazil's ambassador to the UN programs in Geneva, before having his political rights taken away by the right-wing military coup of 1964.[85]

These positions provided Castro with a very visible platform for promoting alternatives to Vogt's views. In 1952, at the request of Osborn's publisher Little, Brown & Co., Castro produced *The Geography of Hunger*, an English-language edition of a book he had published in Brazil on the geopolitics of famine and malnutrition. Its central purpose was "to study the terrible erosion that hunger is causing in the human race and its civilization, an erosion that threatens to blot from the earth all the gigantic works of man." He unfairly attacked Vogt as the "standard-bearer of...those who go in for neo-Malthusian theories while they defend and benefit from an imperialist economy." Castro instead promulgated the thesis that

[85] Rosana Magalhães, *Fome: Uma (re)leitura de Josué de Castro* (Rio de Janeiro, 1997), 25–48, 58; Armando Sales, *Josué de Castro: O homem e o sonho* (Recife, 1996), 39–40, 50–54, 67, 89; Julyan Peard, *Race, Place, and Medicine: The Idea of the Tropics in Nineteenth-Century Brazil* (Durham, NC, 2000).

FIGURE 8.1. The invention of the Third World: Warren Thompson's three-world system. In this classification of national states and colonized regions by their demographic characteristics, circa 1940, Class I "stationary" countries such as the United States, Germany, and Australia had low birth and death rates and high levels of urbanization and industrialization; Class II "expanding" countries such as the Soviet Union, Japan, Algeria, and Brazil were beginning to feel the effects of industrialization and had declining death rates but exploding population growth; Class III "preindustrial" countries, including most of Africa, Asia, Latin America, and tropical Oceania, had high birth and death rates, and the overwhelming majority of their populations lived off the land. Thompson originated this analysis around 1930 to help identify hotspots of geopolitical conflict. This schema provided direct inspiration for the three-world geopolitical system of the Cold War, consisting of a capitalist, industrialized First World; a communist, developing Second World; and an unaligned, underdeveloped Third World. The stark colors of the original map also communicated a racial message regarding the world's neo-Europes and Dark Continents. In the book, Thompson also made brief reference to a fourth class of countries experiencing rapid population decline; use of the moniker Fourth World to refer to the planet's indigenous, stateless, and marginalized peoples became common beginning in the 1970s. *Source*: Thompson, *Population and Peace in the Pacific* (Chicago, 1946); reproduced courtesy of Bruce D. Thompson.

overpopulation was the *result* of widespread starvation, rather than the other way around, arguing from a Freudian perspective that the chronic inability of individuals to satisfy their biological drive for food hyperactivated their drive for sex, and from a nutritional perspective that high animal protein consumption as seen in the industrialized world inhibited fertility. Like many of Vogt's critics, Castro had abundant faith in the ability of technological progress and industrialization to raise the living standards of the world's poorest countries. Their food had to come from somewhere, however, and he called for the breakup of the world's mono-crop plantation system and colonization of new lands in the Amazon Basin and Siberia to increase food production for the poor. At the height of the Cold War, this runaway best-seller was showered with prizes in both the capitalist West and communist East and eventually translated into thirty languages.[86]

Castro had more in common with Vogt than he realized. Castro, too, was suspicious of the "partial truths" and amorality of purely technical knowledge, and thought that the world's problems largely derived from the fact that "human groups were always in conflict and almost never in harmony with the natural scene." They both despised basic features of the world's imperialist economy and thought that the state possessed a responsibility to discipline private interests for the collective good. They differed fundamentally, however, on their approach to ecology and environmental justice. Vogt emphasized the relationships between whole communities of organisms and stood in defense of rare species threatened with extinction, whereas Castro emphasized the physiological ecology of hunger and the fundamental right of all humans to adequate nutrition. Castro despised wasted human life, whereas Vogt welcomed death as a necessity enabling others to live.[87]

Castro expressed his differences with Vogt most vividly in his delineation of the "crab cycle" that dictated life for some of Brazil's poorest – a bitter parody of the guano cycle described in Vogt's book. Castro had grown up close to a deeply impoverished, flood-prone barrio of stilt houses, mangroves, mosquitoes, and mud on Recife's main estuary. Famished human residents relentlessly hunted the ubiquitous crabs of this environment. They lived to crush these animals and lick out their shells, to the point that Castro believed they took on aspects of the crabs' animal existence – existing merely for the next opportunity to eat, to procreate, and to create the excrement that fed a new generation of crabs.[88] Sentiments of this sort played a powerful role in opening up an ideological gulf between advocates of environmental conservation and environmental justice, between white and brown, rich and

[86] Castro, *The Geopolitics of Hunger* (1952; New York, 1977), 19–21, 64–68, 71, 77, 123–34, 466–84; Magalhães, *Fome*, 47, 55.

[87] Quoted in Magalhães, *Fome*, 50, 52, 71–74; Castro, *The Geopolitics of Hunger*, 60; Sales, *Josué de Castro*, 81.

[88] Castro, "O ciclo de caranguejo" (1937), later published as part of a 1966 novel with the same title, in Magalhães, *Fome*, 63.

poor, North and South that continues to fracture the environmental movement around the globe. These sentiments turned Latin American leftists, in particular, against Vogt's vision of environmentalism.[89]

Environmental historians have sometimes referred to the years between the bombing of Hiroshima and the publication of *Silent Spring* (1945–62) as an "age of ecological innocence" in which governments and civil society around the world charged blindly toward an ecological precipice, heedless of the dangers of human population growth, resource depletion, and uncontrolled development.[90] In this chapter, we have seen how the North-South dialogue between Aldo Leopold, William Vogt, Enrique Beltrán, Carlos Barreda, Josué de Castro, and other scientists and politicians powerfully influenced the development of ecological thought and the organization of conservation programs during the 1940s and early 1950s. One of the most important strands of this movement owes a tremendous amount to the success of Peru's guano bird management program and to the upsets of El Niño and La Niña.

It has long been the habit of historians to portray these figures as voices crying in the wilderness whose true influence had to await the mobilization of a mass environmental movement during the 1960s and 1970s. To be sure, the elitist, technocratic, and sometimes racist tendencies of these figures inhibited the attraction of a popular following – particularly among the poor – with lasting repercussions for environmentalism today. But to claim, as some have, that these thinkers failed to influence public policy and produce substantive historical change in the short term is to ignore the basic direction of population and resource politics during this era. Vogt and Castro's books generated so much interest and controversy *because* so many people had already accepted the notion that the world was facing an immediate crisis, in which poverty, hunger, and war were destined to spread explosively, unless the world did something revolutionary to keep up with the exploding growth of the world's human population. The idea of a three-world system dividing the world between haves and have-nots derived directly from this overpopulation discourse.

As we see in the next chapter, world leaders North and South from both sides of the Cold War political spectrum began waging an all-out campaign to increase fertilizer production and extraction of food from the sea *because* so many feared the truth of Vogt's predictions. We know these campaigns as the Green and Blue Revolutions. Tragically, environmental technocrats gave up the world's guano birds as acceptable casualties in this global war against poverty, hunger, and overpopulation in the hope that they could create a better environment for the world's human inhabitants.

[89] Rafael José Cortés, *Replica a William Vogt: ¿Camino de supervivencia?* (Caracas, 1960).
[90] Guha, *Environmentalism: A Global History.*

9

Guano and the Blue Revolution

Your prophecies on Mexican agriculture at the end of the next 100 years have produced quite a national commotion. "Guano," my dear Doctor, "guano" is the word.
— Carlos Benítez to William Vogt (1946)

Perhaps we should "lose" guano.
— Milner "Benny" Schaefer (1966)

Guano and the Green Revolution

A politically explosive food crisis struck Mexico in 1943. Food prices were already spiraling upward because of World War II. Official policy exacerbated this situation by encouraging the planting of cotton and oilseed instead of grain at the behest of the United States to help the hemispheric alliance against the Axis. A strong La Niña event lasting from July 1942 to mid-1943 brought widespread drought and sharply reduced crop yields in regions such as Sonora dependent on winter and spring rains. This followed directly on the heels of an extreme El Niño event, which contributed to poor summer rainfall in south-central Mexico. This conjuncture of factors placed enormous stress on the Mexican food supply. Many millers had to shut down for lack of grain. Bread and tortilla lines became commonplace. Yucatan, which experienced one of its worst droughts of the past 500 years, suffered a near-famine. Food riots broke out in Mexico City in May 1943. Women's groups and the state labor union threatened much larger demonstrations if President Manuel Ávila Camacho's government did not act forcefully to reduce the cost of living. In response, the State Food Agency dramatically increased the marketing of subsidized food to urban consumers, and tried to arrange for massive grain imports from the United States and Argentina. Wartime disruptions to transportation limited these efforts, however. A good harvest in 1944 alleviated the situation somewhat, but La Niña and drought conditions returned in 1945, sending food prices even higher. The U.S. ambassador to Mexico begged his superiors to send more grain or risk "revolution and the red flag" taking over the country.[1] Mexican officials had good reason to be fearful. In northeastern India, damp conditions during the 1942 dry season provided ideal conditions for the spread of brown spot fungus (*Cochliobous miyabeanus*), which devastated the year's main rice crop and fueled a famine that killed over three million people. Similar disasters in northern Vietnam and north-central China helped communist insurgents lay down roots. All of these subsistence crises – including the Banaba famine described in Chapter 7 – were connected together by large-scale anomalies in the Indo-Pacific climate system and Asian monsoon, not just the winds of war.[2]

William Vogt stepped directly into the middle of this situation in May 1943. He spent several days in Mexico on his way back from an organizing tour in South America, and was profoundly affected by the unrest he witnessed. Both Mexican and U.S. Embassy officials listened carefully to his descriptions of the revival of Peru's guano industry. In response, Ávila Camacho issued a decree on 10 July 1943 "taking into account the experience of the Republic of Peru" that created Guanos y Fertilizantes de México (Guanomex). This parastatal company received full control over all bird islands and guano extraction on the Pacific coast from the U.S. border to Acapulco.[3]

The history of Mexico's relationship with guano is almost as old as Peru's. During the colonial era, indigenous farmers in the vicinity of cities eagerly sought urban night soil and animal manures to produce *tlalauiac* – soil enriched with dung. Those from Xochimilco added bat guano from the caves of Ixtapalapa to their *chinampas*. Ancient farmers probably did, as well. During the nineteenth century, Mexico had a modest guano export industry. In 1854, the famous caudillo Antonio López de Santa Anna issued decrees that prohibited the export of guano by foreigners, banned the hunting of guano birds with firearms, and commissioned a series of expeditions

---

[1] CEI; quoted in Enrique Ochoa, *Feeding Mexico: The Political Uses of Food since 1910* (Wilmington, DE, 2000), ch. 4; Perkins, *Geopolitics and the Green Revolution*, 125–30; Richard Seager et al., "Mexican Drought: An Observational Modeling and Tree Ring Study of Variability and Climate Change," *Atmósfera* 22 (2009): 1–31; Blanca Mendoza, "Frequency and Duration of Historical Droughts from the 16th to the 19th Centuries in the Mexican Maya Lands, Yucatan Peninsula," *Climatic Change* 83 (2007): 151–68.

[2] Mark Tauger, "Entitlement, Shortage and the 1943 Bengal Famine: Another Look," *Journal of Peasant Studies* 31 (2003): 45–72; Bin Wang et al., "Interannual Variability of the Asian Summer Monsoon: Contrasts between the Indian and the Western North Pacific-East Asian Monsoons," *Journal of Climate* 14 (2001): 4073–90; contra Sugata Bose, "Starvation amidst Plenty: The Making of Famine in Bengal, Honan and Tonkin, 1942–45," *Modern Asian Studies* 24 (1990): 699–727.

[3] Decree quoted in Jesús Gracia Fadrique, ed., *Estado y Fertilizantes, 1760–1985* (Mexico City, 1988), 174–77; Vogt to Leopold, 5 July 1943, UWDC-ALA.

to determine the extent of Mexico's guano deposits. This marked the beginning of a sixty-year battle to prevent interlopers from stealing this valuable fertilizer without paying the Mexican state for the privilege. Most of this conflict centered on bird islands off the Yucatan coast such as Isla Cancún, which in those days was known for its colonies of pelicans and magnifiscent frigatebirds (*Fregata magnificens*) instead of flocks of sunburned tourists. Guano mining off the coast of Baja California began soon after, following on the heels of hunters who devastated the region's nursery for gray whales (*Eschrichtius robustus*). Extraction in this region centered on Rasa Island, a low basaltic platform that harbored enormous colonies of elegant terns (*Sterna elegans*) and Heermann's gulls (*Larus heermanni*); its landscape is now littered with thousands of stone cairns left behind by guano workers. Indigenous Seri from the region often accepted temporary employment as guano miners in return for trade goods, but a large number of Yaqui worked forcibly on the islands as punishment for resisting white colonization of their lands. Most guano from the Gulf of California ended up in Germany or the new agricultural empires of California. Modest quantities of Mexican and Peruvian guano, Chilean nitrates, and locally produced bone and blood meal made it into Mexican soils during the early twentieth century. Circa 1940, however, Mexican farmers applied concentrated fertilizers to only 3 percent of the country's ten million cultivated hectares, at a rate of less than 45,000 tons per year, half of which was imported.[4]

In 1944, Guanomex began extracting guano in the Gulf of California from colonies of brown and blue-footed boobies, and along the Pacific coast of Baja California from colonies of brown pelican and Brandt's cormorant (*Phalacrocorax penicillatus*). Guanomex ignored the colony on Isla Rasa, which had been nearly destroyed by decades of egg collecting to serve the Sonora mining industry. These efforts only produced a paltry thousand tons of nitrogenous guano a year. In response, the director general of Guanomex, Dr. Carlos Benítez, began promoting the idea that Mexican guano production could be increased by more than 200 times by transplanting Peruvian guano birds to the arid Baja coast. Geographers had long contended that the California and Peru Current environments are mirror images of one another, and Benítez hoped that the gregarious guanay and piquero would

4 Charles Gibson, *The Aztecs under Spanish Rule: A History of the Indians of the Valley of Mexico, 1519–1810* (Stanford, CA, 1976), 300, 306–7, 558 n. 121; Felipe Buenrostro, *Historia del Segundo Congreso Constitucional de la República Méxicana* (Mexico City, 1875), 2:430–35; *Cayo Arenas y otras islas guaneras de los mares de Campeche y Yucatán* (Mexico City, 1895), 20–28; Gabriel Aarón Macías Zapata, "El ombligo de los hatos: Payo Obispo y su *hinterland* forestal," in *El vacío imaginario: Geopolítica de la ocupación territorial en el Caribe oriental mexicano* (Mexico City, 2004), 125–28; Thomas Bowen, *Unknown Island: Seri Indians, Europeans, and San Estéban Island in the Gulf of California* (Albuquerque, NM, 2000), 122–38; Gracia, ed., *Estado y fertilizantes*, 24, 32–42, 115–20, 124–25, 147–48.

"know better what to do" with offshore shoals of California sardine and anchovy.[5] This fit with conservation orthodoxy of the time, which advocated the transplant of alien organisms such as kudzu, eucalyptus, cane toads, and Nile perch as an environmental improvement strategy – often with catastrophic consequences.[6]

Peruvian experts soon got involved. In 1944, Compañía Administradora del Guano agronomist Luis Gamarra traveled to Mexico to examine the situation and became an enthusiastic promoter of Benítez's scheme, but CAG's general manager Francisco Ballén refused to give a single egg to Mexico at a time when Peru's guano bird population was at a two-decade low. Benítez dismissed him as "un loco de la casa" and asked Vogt to approach Chilean authorities to arrange the import of guanays. Ballén's retirement in July 1945 gave the transplantation project a new lease on life. Under pressure from top governmental officials in both countries, CAG and Guanomex drew up a contract to airlift 200,000 eggs and 50,000 live birds a year for twenty-nine years to Mexico. The eggs would be used to trick Mexican birds to raise changelings. Vogt and Gamarra both returned to Baja California late in 1945 to evaluate this new plan with biologist Bibiano Osorio Tafall (1902–90), a prominent political exile from fascist Spain who had been hired by Guanomex to do basic marine research. Osorio Tafall's studies of marine productivity firmly convinced him that the project to increase guano production was doomed to failure – even if the transplantation succeeded – because upwelling in the region turned out to be much weaker and far more dispersed than off the Peruvian coast. Osorio Tafall kept these views under wraps, however, because he did not want to endanger his job, and instead depended on Vogt and Robert Cushman Murphy to communicate these opinions to his superiors. Vogt offered to wager Benítez "a hundred to one odds that any attempts to establish the guanay on the west coast of Mexico will be a failure."[7]

These behaviors reveal a major shortcoming of the technocratic ideal. The livelihoods of many experts depend on producing recommendations that advance the narrow political and ideological goals of their employers.

[5] Gracia, ed., *Estado y fertilizantes*, 177–78; Hutchinson, "Biogeochemistry of Vertebrate Excretion," 122–32; Johnsgard, *Cormorants, Darters, and Pelicans*, 172–79, 201–8, 387–97; Steve Howell and Sophie Webb, *A Guide to the Birds of Mexico and Northern Central America* (New York, 1995), 123–24, 128–29, 292–93, 305–6.

[6] Doughty, *The Eucalyptus*; *Cane Toads: An Unnatural History*, dir. Mark Lewis (1987); Tijs Goldschmidt, *Darwin's Dreampond: Drama in Lake Victoria* (Cambridge, MA, 1996).

[7] Benítez to Vogt, 20 Mar. 1944, 4 July 1945, 12 Jan. 1946; Vogt to Benítez, 4 Apr. 1944, 18 Feb. 1946; Vogt to José Colom, 28 Mar. 1945; Osorio to Vogt, 26 May 1945; Ávila to Vogt, 12 Dec. 1945, 2 Apr. 1946, 6 June 1946, 2 July 1946; Vogt to Ávila, 28 Dec. 1945, 26 Sept. 1947, DPL-VP 1/1–3; MCAG 36 (1945): 47–48; MCAG 36 (1946): xi; Rómulo Lanatta, *Informe sobre la Compañía Administradora del Guano* (Lima, 1948), 37–39; Mary Carmel Finley, "The Tragedy of Enclosure: Fish, Fisheries Science, and U.S. Foreign Policy, 1920–1960," (Ph.D. diss., University of California, San Diego, 2007), 159–62.

To have an effect, forceful criticism often has to come from outside an organization or country. As a consequence, boosters of the Mexican trans-plantation scheme found it easy to use nationalist posturing to undermine the opinion of foreign scientists. José Carlos Arenas traveled all the way to Peru to promote his extravagant plan to buy US$600,000 worth of boats, tractors, and bulldozers to collect the wealth of excrement that Peru's guano birds would eventually provide to Mexico.[8] He boldly dismissed Vogt as "a sentimentalist nature lover who wants to confuse Latin American con-servationists for the sole purpose of saving" the sagging California sardine industry. CAG eventually decided to err on the side of caution and close down the project. Osorio Tafall lost his job at Guanomex as a consequence but, with Vogt's assistance, soon acquired a far more prominent position as head of the United Nations Food and Agriculture Organization's (FAO) Latin American office in Santiago de Chile and later served as director of the UN's program of technical assistance to developing countries, where he was an outspoken proponent of fishery development to increase the food supply of the Third World.[9]

To survive, Guanomex had to adopt a dramatically different approach to increasing Mexico's food supply. Ávila Camacho's handpicked successor, Miguel Alemán, made the increase of agricultural production a centerpiece of his 1946 presidential campaign. After his election, he raised the Irriga-tion Department to cabinet-level status, and initiated a major program to build dams, canals, and farm-to-market roads – to the enormous benefit of Mexico's state-run concrete and petroleum industries. Fertilizer manufacture also occupied a major place in this industrialization program. In 1947, with the aid of a Boston engineering firm, Guanomex opened a fertilizer plant in San Luis Potosí capable of producing seventy-five tons of superphosphate a day using rock imported by railroad from Florida. Guanomex also opened a small bone meal plant in Mexico City and commissioned designs for the country's first ammonia synthesis plant. The U.S.-based engineering firm Chemico won the bid with its innovative design to synthesize ammonium sulfate using high-sulfur natural gas brought to the Valley of Mexico by a new pipeline from Poza Rica, Veracruz. As an added bonus, this process also produced sulfuric acid that could be used for superphosphate production. This industrial facility at Cuautitlán instantaneously increased Mexico's nitrogen-producing capacity by seven times when it opened in 1951. This was the first ammonia-producing plant of any kind in Latin America and

[8] Equal to US$6 million in 2007.
[9] Ávila to Vogt, 12 Dec. 1945, 30 Apr. 1946; Vogt to Ávila, 28 Dec. 1945; Vogt to Osorio, 14 Jan. 1946, DPL-VP 1/1, 3–4; *MCAG* 38 (1947): xv; Ávila to Mary Sears, [1958], WHOI-SP; Osorio, "El destino marítimo de México," *Revista de economía* (Mexico City) 10 (Aug. 1947); Finley, "Tragedy of Enclosure," 426; Francisco Giral, *Ciencia española en el exilio (1939–1989)* (Barcelona, 1994), 162–65.

TABLE 9.1. *Fertilizer Consumption and Crop Productivity in Mexico,*
1950–82

	1950	1967	1982	% change 1950–82
Cultivated area (million Ha)	10.9	15.3	22.5	207
Fertilized area (million Ha)	0.5	4.0	12.9	2,554
Total area fertilized (%)	4.6	26.2	57.2	–
Nitrogen consumed (thousand mt)	8.5	295.0	1,160.0	13,691
Phosphate consumed (thousand mt)	3.4	101.5	473.4	14,056
Potassium consumed (thousand mt)	0	16.6	118.2	–
Total NPK consumed (thousand mt)	11.8	413.1	1,751.9	14,792
Application rate (kg/Ha)	23.5	103.1	136.0	579
Maize productivity (kg/Ha)	721	1,130	1,779	247
Wheat productivity (kg/Ha)	911	2,727	4,409	484
Bean productivity (kg/Ha)	259	508	638	246
Cotton productivity (kg/Ha)	342	747	895	262
Sugar cane productivity (kg/Ha)	51,300	65,600	67,700	132

mt, metric tons.
Source: Gracia, ed., *Estado y fertilizantes,* 47–66.

provided an influential model for transferring the technology of nitrogen production to Colombia, Peru, and other Third World countries.[10]

Fueled by Mexico's rich hydrocarbon resources, large international development loans, and government investments in agricultural education and extension services, Mexican fertilizer production increased by leaps and bounds over the next three decades. By the late 1970s, when Guanomex belatedly changed its name to Fertilizantes Mexicanos (Fertimex), this mammoth state-owned corporation had bought out virtually all of its Mexican competitors, employed close to 10,000 workers, and begun construction of a vast chemical complex in Michoacán capable of producing 1.7 million tons of fertilizer a year. Mexican fertilizer consumption also increased spectacularly (table 9.1). As in Peru, large, highly capitalized cotton, wheat, and sugar cane growers led the way in embracing manufactured fertilizers, but more than half of maize growers and a quarter of bean growers also adopted input-intensive forms of cultivation by the late 1970s. All of these crops experienced major increases in yields. This was especially true of new

[10] Gracia, ed., *Estado y fertilizantes,* 179–83, 262; Hewitt, *Modernización de la agricultura,* 83–88; U.K. Agency for International Development, Mission to Colombia, *Report on Examination of Assistance for Development of the Fertilizer Industry in Colombia* (1967).

varieties of wheat developed by Rockefeller Foundation plant breeders in Mexico, which were then exported to India, Colombia, and other hungry nations around the world. These high-yielding varieties would have been useless without massive nutrient inputs. Such levels of crop productivity made it possible for Mexico to transform itself from a grain importer to one of the world's major food exporters. Agronomists played a foundational role as architects of these transformations, which came to be known as "the Mexican Miracle" – one of the great success stories of the Green Revolution in global crop production after World War II. Vogt's prediction of Malthusian disaster for Mexico, it would seem, turned out to be wrong.[11]

Before shortcomings of these policies began to emerge, developmentalists all over the world came to view the growth of industries that served agricultural development as indispensable to handling the world's rapidly growing and urbanizing human population in the Third World. The world's policy makers did not ignore the Malthusian warnings of Vogt and Fairfield Osborn. As Mexico's case illustrates, they actually took to heart their apocalyptic predictions – and did their utmost to pave a different road to survival using industrial technologies. It is critical to recognize that *human-centered ecological concerns* relating overpopulation, resource degradation, poverty and hunger, political instability, communist insurgency, and war profoundly influenced the formation of public policy on food, fertilizer, meat, and fish production during the three decades that followed World War II. This was not an "age of ecological innocence" as some environmental historians have claimed.[12] A form of ecological thinking inspired some of the signature international programs of the era. Moreover, the ideological consensus advocating industrialization and development as the answer to the Third World's woes transcended the political dividing lines of the Cold War.

Chapters 7 and 8 explained why population growth, living standards, soil fertility, and food production became so central to these concerns and showed how technocrats acquired so much influence over these activities. This chapter examines how these same issues drove the spectacular growth of fertilizer manufacture, industrial fishing, and meat production in Mexico, Peru, and beyond after 1940. During this period, Mexico exemplified the cornucopian possibilities of the Green Revolution, and inspired Peruvian

---

[11] Gracia, ed., *Estado y fertilizantes*, 42–78, 209, 277–78; Perkins, *Geopolitics and the Green Revolution*, ch. 5; Ochoa, *Feeding Mexico*, 125–26, 138; Hewitt, *Modernización de la agricultura*, pt. 1; Joseph Cotter, *Troubled Harvest: Agronomy and Revolution in Mexico, 1880–2002* (Westport, CT, 2003), ch. 4–5.

[12] Guha, *Environmentalism: A Global History*, pt. 3; Perkins, *Geopolitics and the Green Revolution*, 119–24, 130.

officials to use similar means to increase fertilizer production. In similar fashion, Peru came to exemplify the possibilities and pitfalls of a Blue Revolution in marine fish production and aquaculture. Even though the term is used infrequently, the Blue Revolution was just as important as the Green Revolution in transforming humanity's extraction of nutrition from land and sea during the late twentieth century.[13] Like Mexico's Green Revolution, Peru's Blue Revolution grew directly out of the guano industry and its dedication to the technocratic ideal. By some measures, Peru's Blue Revolution was an even more spectacular success. In two decades, industrialized fish production grew from nothing to a point where Peru became the largest fish-producing nation on earth. Dozens of countries tried to follow this oceanic path toward development. Once again, the Pacific World was the epicenter of these innovations.

The Geopolitics of the Blue Revolution

The Blue Revolution had its beginning in two circumstances: (1) the Peruvian guano industry's drive to extend its technocratic authority over Peru's marine ecosystem and (2) the international, interethnic competition for Pacific resources that sparked World War II. As we learned in Chapters 5 and 6, the Peruvian state had long sought expert assistance in developing a mechanized fishing industry. In 1928, in the wake of a destructive El Niño, President Leguía authorized CAG to hire a foreign scientist to investigate "the most rational and scientific form of exploitation" of fish along the Peruvian coast. It hired Erwin Hirsch-Schweigger (1888–1965), who from 1923 to 1937 was Fishereidirektor for Altona, the most important port of entry for fish into Greater Hamburg and points inland. This sort of exchange was quite common during the 1920s, when a number of German institutions reached out to Latin America, "the last free continent" open to Germany under the strictures of the Versailles Treaty. The Fischereidirektor for Hamburg made similar investigations for Chile and the Bank of Egypt.[14] Schweigger spent seven months in Peru in 1929–30 touring the Pacific coast and Lake Titicaca. He strongly recommended the creation of a government fishing company similar to CAG that would direct scientific research, diffuse

---

[13] Connor Bailey, "The Blue Revolution: The Impact of Technological Innovation on Third-World Fisheries," *Rural Sociologist* 5 (1985): 259–66; James Coull, "Will a Blue Revolution Follow the Green Revolution?: The Modern Upsurge of Aquaculture," *Area* 25 (1993): 350–57.

[14] *BCAG* 5 (July 1929): 366–67; *Der Fischerbote* 15 (1923): 18; 20 (1928): 195–96, 345–47, 363–65; 22 (1930): 119–22, 377–83; 29 (1937): 367–72; *Diccionario histórico y biográfico*, s.v. "Schweigger, Erwin"; Stefan Rinke, *"Die letzte freie Kontinent": Deutsche Lateinamerikapolitik im Zeichen transnationaler Beziehungen, 1918–1933* (Stuttgart, 1996).

new fishing techniques, market refrigerated fish, and perhaps manufacture fishmeal for use as fertilizer or livestock feed, but the Great Crash prevented Peru from acting on his suggestions. Gildemeister & Co.'s parallel attempt to establish a motorized fishing fleet to producing cheap food for its agroindustrial labor force met a more violent end. Native Peruvian fishermen from Puerto Chicama torched Gildemeister's Italian-operated fleet to eliminate this threat to their livelihoods, as part of a wave of xenophobic violence against immigrant fishermen along the Peruvian coast.[15] Schweigger was of Jewish descent and convinced CAG to give him a permanent job to help him escape from Nazi Germany in 1937. Like Mexico with Osorio Tafall, Peru was thus able to take advantage of the global diaspora of technical experts away from countries under authoritarian rule during this era.[16]

The worsening crisis in Peruvian guano production caused by the Tangüis cotton boom and 1939–41 El Niño led CAG officials to consider a new way to harvest nutrients from the sea. Schweigger had long been a proponent of creating a German fishmeal industry, and at his suggestion, CAG hatched a plan to directly exploit the guano birds' main food source, the anchoveta. In 1940, CAG sent agronomist Luis Gamarra on an expedition to the United States to study the harvest and processing of menhaden and sardines for use as livestock feed. Gamarra's enthusiastic report described how CAG could quickly set up a manufacturing complex capable of producing 50,000 metric tons of fishmeal per year. This new industry promised to satisfy "rising demand for nitrogen fertilizer by the nation's agriculture" while producing "a product with excellent market openings" for export abroad. CAG's conservation technocrats are the ones who gave birth to the original plan to replace Peru's guano birds with a fishmeal industry, based on the ecological argument that Peru could dramatically increase its production from the sea by directly exploiting a lower level of the Humboldt Current food chain.[17]

Enthusiasm for Gamarra's plan quickly spread. In 1940, Manuel Prado's government issued Law 9140 for the Promotion of Industry, a landmark in the history of Peru's industrialization. This decree included a clause that established an expert commission charged with mapping out the future of the fishing industry in Peru. In parallel, Prado asked the U.S. government to send a mission of fishing experts to the country. In January 1941, three members of the U.S. Fish and Wildlife Service arrived in Peru, two with experience

[15] *MCAG* 22 (1931): 268–80; 15 (Aug. 1939): 315–16; *Pesca* Jan.–Feb. 1962: 13–14; Baltazar Caravedo Molinari, *Estado, pesca y burguesía: Teoría y realidad* (Lima, 1979), 20–21.

[16] Ávila to Sears, 12 Mar. 1952, 30 Apr. 1952, 12 Aug. 1953, 19 Mar. 1955, 14 June 1957, 14 July 1959; Betulfo Vaca to Sears, 19 May 1952, WHOI-SP; *BCONAFER* 3 (Aug. 1965): 3–4; Giral, *Ciencia española en el exilio*; Mitchell Ash and Alfons Sollner, eds., *Forced Migration and Scientific Change: Emigré German-Speaking Scientists and Scholars after 1933* (Cambridge and New York, 1996).

[17] *Der Fischerbote* 26 (1934): 194–95; 27 (1935): 52–56; *BCAG* 16 (Nov. 1940): 340–79.

developing the fishing industries of U.S. colonies in the Caribbean. This mission, like many of this era, was intended to advance the United States' Good Neighbor Policy and strengthen international ties with a potential wartime ally.[18]

These experts came to reverse a paradoxical situation. In 1940, Peru produced a total catch of 11,863 metric tons worth S/.2,373,000, but exported a paltry 208 tons of fish products. Even though Peru had one of the richest marine ecosystems in the world, it imported around a thousand tons of fish products a year, mostly canned fish from Japan. Like many developmental experts of this era, the North American Fishery Mission framed this situation as a technological problem to be solved by the introduction of new craft and techniques. To this end, its staff sailed to Peru in the *Pacific Queen*, an eighty-foot purse-seine trawler (*bolichera*) newly built in Tacoma, Washington, and used it to train Peruvians in the use of fishing gear and the taking of scientific measurements.[19] At the conclusion of the mission, CAG borrowed S/.650,000 from the Banco Industrial del Perú to purchase the *Pacific Queen*, a full purse-seine net outfit, a complete terrestrial fishmeal plant with lighter fleet, and a mechanized storage and transport facility from California. To help ensure the success of this venture, Prado gave CAG the sole right to "anchoveta fishing on a grand scale" in Peru's territorial waters, but the wartime interruption of regular shipping, rapid inflation, and problems raising capital prevented CAG from completing this fishmeal complex, even after spending three times the amount of the original loan. CAG eventually sold this unfinished plant to Italian-Peruvian entrepreneur Marcos Ghio in 1955 at a steep discount and turned over the *Pacific Queen* to its own scientists for use in oceanographic research. CAG never produced a gram of fishmeal.[20]

The North American Fishery Mission to Peru was a tremendous success in other respects, however. Industrialized fishing for bonito (*Sarda chilensis*) took off in the wake of its visit as suppliers of vitamin-rich fish livers and life-giving protein to a war-torn world. Hostilities cut off the international supply of preserved fish and fish liver oils from two of the world's largest

---

[18] *MCAG* 30 (1939): 61–62; *MCAG* 33 (1942): ix, 67–68; Norman Jarvis, *The Fisheries of Puerto Rico*, Bureau of Fisheries Investigational Report [BFIR] no. 13 (1932); Reginald Fiedler and Jarvis, *Fisheries of the Virgin Islands of the United States*, BFIR no. 14 (1932); Thorp and Bertram, *Peru, 1890–1977*, 186–87, 190–95, 205–6; David Green, *The Containment of Latin America: A History of the Myths and Realities of the Good Neighbor Policy* (Chicago, 1971), vii–x, 294–95.

[19] Equal to US$4.5 million in 2007. Fiedler, Jarvis, and Milton Lobell, *The Fisheries and the Fishery Industries of Peru with Recommendations for Their Expansion and Development* (Washington, DC, 1942), 2–3, 8–9, 14, 16, 36, 191–23, 333–38, 351; Caravedo, *Estado, pesca y burguesía*, 25–26.

[20] Equal to US$1.1 million in 2007. *MCAG* 33 (1942): ix, 69–72; 37 (1946): ix; 42 (1951): vii; 46 (1955): 16; Lanatta, *Informe*, 90–91.

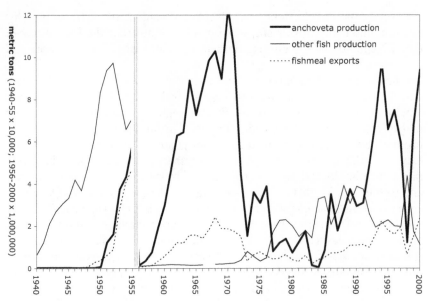

FIGURE 9.1. Fish and fishmeal production in Peru, 1940–2000. *Source:* Cushman, "Lords of Guano," table 7, app. 9.

producers, Japan and Norway. In 1942, Peruvian entrepreneurs exported 320 tons of fish livers cut from bonito and sharks. At first, they wastefully discarded everything else, but the U.S. War Foods Administration soon began buying barrel-salted fish and canned bonito produced by three plants financed by the Prado family bank. Prado's government helped out by negotiating the removal of all duties and tariffs on U.S. imports and by creating an official agency to provide technical assistance. By the end of the war, there were twelve companies operating twenty-three canneries in Peru with installed equipment valued at S/.15 million, despite logistical difficulties importing gear.[21] In 1946, the peak of wartime production, Peruvian companies extracted 41,722 metric tons of fish from the Pacific, 10,560 tons of which were exported (fig. 9.1). Wilbur-Ellis Peruana, a subsidiary of the San Francisco fishing company, played a crucial role in these developments as a provider of technical expertise, canning equipment and supplies, and served as the main distributor of Peruvian bonito on the U.S. market.[22] Meanwhile, the North American Fishery Mission to Peru served as a model for technical missions sent elsewhere to increase the supply of fish to Allied forces.

[21] Equal to US$22 million in 2007.
[22] Cushman, "The Guano Lords," table 7; Harold Cary, "Report #7," 11 Sept 1953, SIO-AC40, 28/1, p. 4; *Pesca* Mar. 1961: 11–13; Sept. 1962: 58; Caravedo, *Estado, pesca y burguesía*, 23–27; Thorp and Bertram, *Peru, 1890–1977*, 180–81; Belaúnde, *La legislación pesquera*, 229.

Two participants headed straight from Peru to the West Indies, "to further economic and social cooperation among the nations of the Western Hemisphere," then to the South Pacific, Iceland, England, and Chile. The success of these missions helped convince ideologues in many parts of the world to view the ocean as the next frontier for industrial-scale food production.[23]

Peru's Blue Revolution came into being thanks to the combined efforts of government officials, local entrepreneurs, and foreign experts working in fortuitous historical circumstances. Like many Third World development programs, this new industry almost went belly up when these conditions turned unfavorable. Peru's market for salted fish and fish livers dried up almost overnight when Japan, Norway, and other war-torn countries resumed fish production with the help of economic aid and trading preferences provided by the United States. Many Peruvians felt deeply betrayed that Japan was able to regain its status as the world's largest fish-producing nation in this way. Peru also had new competitors to deal with. Fiji, American Samoa, Tahiti, and Australia developed tuna canning industries of their own during the 1940s, whereas the U.S. tuna industry received a massive transfer of decommissioned military craft, most of which were sent to fishing grounds off Latin America. Spending by the Marshall Plan and Point Four programs explicitly supported the expansion of industrial fishing in China, West Germany, and South Africa to increase the world's supply of high-protein food. In 1949, under pressure from the California tuna industry, the U.S. Food and Drug Administration made Peru's situation even more difficult by banning the sale of bonito as "tuna" based on the harmless but off-putting tendency for the flesh of Peruvian fish that season to turn green when canned and the dubious scientific claim that bonito belonged to an entirely different classification of fish. The Peruvian fishing industry figured out how to remedy the former problem, but these taxonomic regulations remained in force, leading Peruvians to accuse the United States of practicing fish "racism" against the darker-toned flesh of the bonito. Wilbur-Ellis saved the day, temporarily, with discount supermarket pricing and an expensive advertising campaign favoring Peruvian bonito. By 1953, however, thanks to overproduction by competitors in the northern and central Pacific, almost all of Peru's 50 canneries and 630 motorized fishing craft were operating far below capacity. Many were completely inactive. The collapse of U.S. tuna prices in 1954 and increased protective tariffs in 1956 made the situation even worse. Meanwhile, Peru's fleet of vessels for

---

[23] Fiedler, Lobell, and Clarence Lucas, *The Fisheries and Fishery Resources of the Caribbean* (Washington, DC, 1947); *American Men of Science* (New York, 1949), s.v. "Fiedler, R(eginald) H(obson)"; Milner Schaefer, "Confidential: Report on Assistance to the Government of Chile," draft manuscript, n.d. [1961], SIO-MC2, 3/212; Osorio Tafall, "El destino marítimo de México," *Revista de economía* (Mexico City) 10 (Aug. 1947); W. H. Chapman, "The Wealth of the Oceans," *Scientific Monthly* 65 (1947): 192–97.

producing frozen yellowfin tuna (*Neothunnus macropterus*) and swordfish (*Xiphias gladius*) was barely utilized, thanks to an abrupt but lasting change in their geographic distribution far away from the Peruvian coast during the El Niño of 1953. These problems caused social dislocations. Since the war, competition from mechanized boats and the prospect of well-paid work in the fishing industry had convinced thousands of male artisanal fishermen to leave their traditional craft and become industrial proletarians. Thousands of women had also taken jobs in canning factories, which followed the California industry's practice of only hiring female shop-floor workers. Both groups now faced massive unemployment. The Peruvian government tried to mitigate these problems and diversify the industry by building modern market terminals in Callao and Lima and by waging publicity campaigns to encourage domestic fish consumption. These efforts failed to create a robust Peruvian market for marine fish. These woes – underutilization of equipment capacity, dependence on imported technology and expertise, flaccid local markets, and underemployment – typified those that have faced industrialization programs in the Third World, and they have continued to dog the Peruvian fishing industry for the rest of its history.[24]

Peruvians had other reasons to feel anxious about the future of fishing off their coast. The end of the war enabled long-distance fishing fleets to again set their sights on this productive region. As early as 1936, Van Camp Sea Food of California had approached the Peruvian government for permission to enter Peru's three-mile territorial sea so its tuna clippers could catch anchoveta for use as bait. Peru was not the only country that feared foreign depredation of its offshore resources. During the late 1930s, Japanese interest in pelagic salmon off the coast of Alaska greatly increased geopolitical tensions with the United States in the far northern Pacific. Meanwhile, the use of offshore factory ships to process fishmeal severely undermined attempts by the State of California to regulate sardine production, to the point that this lucrative fishery was on the verge of collapse. In 1945, under intense pressure from U.S. oil and fishing companies, President Harry Truman unilaterally issued two proclamations claiming the "natural resources of the subsoil and sea bed of the continental shelf beneath the high seas but contiguous to the coasts as appertaining to the United States" and the right to establish fishery "conservation zones... subject to the regulation and control of the United States" beyond the traditional territorial sea. In places, these proclamations extended the country's territorial claims hundreds of miles offshore. The United States was not the first country to do

---

[24] Cushman, "The Guano Lords," table 7; interview with Aurora Chirinos de Vildoso, 11 June 2001; *Pesca y caza* 2 (1951): 3–16; Antonio Tarnawiecki, "A Survey of the Development of Oceanic Fisheries in Peru," *Peruvian Yearbook & Northern Peru Supplement of the Peruvian Times* Jan. 1955: 129–30, 135; *Pesca* Feb. 1961: 14–16; Mar. 1961: 12–15; Mar. 1967: 15–21; Finley, "The Tragedy of Enclosure," 236, 257–67, 278–85, 355–60, 417–18, 422–23, 426–27, 434, 535, 540.

this. In 1942, the United Kingdom and Venezuela signed a treaty asserting Venezuela's territorial rights to undersea petroleum resources several miles off its coast. Argentina and Mexico followed with similar proclamations in 1944 and 1945. However, such claims made little sense for the narrow continental shelf lining the Pacific coast of South America, which did not encompass the region's rich upwelling zones. In 1947, Peru followed Chile in declaring an Exclusive Economic Zone (EEZ) extending 200 nautical miles (370.4 kilometers) from its coast. In 1948–49, Iceland, Costa Rica, and several Arab states claimed similar territorial rights to petroleum and fishery resources far off their shorelines. In 1952, Ecuador declared its own 200-mile EEZ and joined Peru and Chile in signing the Santiago Declaration on the Maritime Zone. This agreement stated that "the geological and biological factors that condition the existence, conservation, and development of . . . maritime flora and fauna" had made "the ancient extension of the territorial sea . . . insufficient for the conservation, development, and exploitation of these riches to which adjacent coastal countries have a right." This codified what became known in international law as the "biome" or ecosystem defense of the 200-mile EEZ, a neologism introduced to these debates by CAG scientist Enrique Ávila at the First Latin American Congress on Marine Biology held in Chile in 1949, based on his work with William Vogt and Aldo Leopold. These competing declarations threw the international Law of the Sea governing territorial rights to the ocean into utter chaos. The Truman administration eventually withdrew its Fisheries Proclamation but could not close this Pandora's box.[25]

What started as a battle of words focused on the marine resources of the Pacific Basin soon degenerated into a battle of blows. In 1947, the Peruvian navy seized its first U.S. tuna clipper for violating Peru's EEZ in search for anchoveta to bait its hooks. In 1954, Aristotle Onassis sent out a whaling fleet from Hamburg explicitly to challenge Peru's 200-mile limit. After a lengthy game of cat and mouse, the Peruvian navy triumphantly seized five ships, the remains of 3,000 whales, and forced Onassis to pay a US$3 million fine.[26] Buoyed by this defeat of a Goliath of international shipping, the Peruvian navy began to seize and fine U.S. tuna trawlers for violating the zone. Active hostilities came to a halt in 1956 when the American Tunaboat Association negotiated a licensing agreement with Peru that reinvested the

[25] Quoted in Eduardo Ferrero Costa, "Evolución del derecho del mar," *Revista del Instituto de Estudios Histórico-Marítimos del Perú* (Lima) 3 (1980): 79; Ávila, "Necesidad de afianzar el respecto de las declaraciones de los estados sobre sus respectivos mares territoriales," *Revista de Biología Marina* (Valparaiso) 6 (1955): 200–7; Sergio Teitelboim Volosky, *Chile y la soberanía en el mar* (Santiago de Chile, 1965), 55–61, 66–72; David Loring, "The Fisheries Dispute," in *U.S. Foreign Policy and Peru* (Austin, TX, 1972), 62–67, 72, 86–87, 115–18; S. N. Nandan, "The Exclusive Economic Zone: A Historical Perspective," in *The Law and the Sea* (Rome, 1987); McEvoy, *The Fisherman's Problem*, 148–49, 192; Finley, "The Tragedy of Enclosure," 167–183, 200–8, 412, 495–96.

[26] Equal to US$19 million in 2007.

resulting income in scientific research. This agreement eventually collapsed, however, when tuna fishermen switched from bait fishing to drift nets in the early 1960s. From 1947 to 1974, the Pacific Tuna War, as this confrontation came to be known, resulted in the seizure of more than 250 U.S. ships and the payment of over US$6 million in fines to six Latin America states.[27]

Global opinion eventually turned in favor of Peru's position toward the territorial sea. In 1982, after years of negotiations, 150 countries signed a 320-article convention enabling any coastal state to declare jurisdiction over ocean resources up to 200 miles off its coast. This massive allocation of property rights – the largest in the history of the planet – profoundly affected the small island nations of the Pacific. Long before it was signed, this agreement began generating licensing income from long-distance tuna fishermen and gave renewed energy to the independence movement in the Gilbert & Ellice Islands Colony, which split into the nations of Tuvalu and Kiribati in 1978–79. Some held out the hope that this would result in the creation of a locally based fishing industry that would serve indigenous consumers. At twenty-six square kilometers, Tuvalu trails just behind Nauru as the fourth smallest independent state on earth, but Kiribati, Tuvalu, and Nauru together possess exclusive economic rights to 4.6 million square kilometers of the Pacific Ocean, about a third of the size of claims by the world's largest maritime empire, the United States.[28] Thanks to the efforts of Peru and its neighbors to defend the right of small states to a share of the sea, the guano islands of the Central Pacific now possess new importance as territorial placeholders determining who can exploit the ocean. Once again, the history of the Pacific World was profoundly shaped by events emanating from the coast of South America.

"To Fish or Not to Fish?"

Garrett Hardin's "tragedy of the commons" posits that a natural resource left open to competitive harvesting will tend to be exploited until it is degraded or destroyed, unless some from of "mutual coercion mutually agreed upon" forces the parties involved to utilize the resource in a sustainable way. Economists call this "the fisherman's problem" and have recognized the difficulties of producing a sustainable yield from the ocean since the 1950s. Of course, this is the basic premise that inspired the formation of CAG's monopoly over guano extraction and a host of other state-led conservation programs around the world during the twentieth century. The

[27] MCAG 47 (1956): xviii; Loring, "The Fisheries Dispute," 70–73; Thomas Wolff, *In Pursuit of Tuna: The Expansion of a Fishing Industry and Its International Ramifications* (Tempe, AZ, 1980), 53–54, 96–102, 118.

[28] Macdonald, *Cinderellas of Empire*, 177–82, 272–73; Flanders Maritime Institute, VLIZ Maritime Boundaries Database, http://www.vliz.be/vmdcdata/marbound/index.php.

belief that government jurisdiction is required to prevent the destructive overexploitation of the ocean's fisheries also played an important part in the rhetoric defending extension of the territorial sea. In fact, many advocates of the 1982 Law of the Sea Convention hoped these innovations would place a far greater portion of the ocean under technocratic control.[29]

The fear that uncontrolled exploitation would eventually destroy Peru's marine resources also pervaded three decades of debate regarding the development of industrialized fishing for anchoveta. In 1936 when Van Camp Sea Food asked for permission to fish for bait, Francisco Ballén enunciated what eventually became the guano industry's party line:

In Peru, the exercise of fishing is intimately tied to the guano industry and the abundance of certain fish, especially the anchoveta.... Every method of fishing on a grand scale along the coast would thus be plainly inadvisable, all the more so taking into consideration that it will be impossible to exercise effective control over the fishing methods put into practice. It is also worth taking into consideration... that the fish obtained will be exported. The meager duties this firm offers will not compensate in the least for this waste.[30]

Luis Gamarra used a form of ecological reasoning to try to counter these concerns. As part of his advocacy for the creation of a fishmeal industry, Gamarra performed an incompetent experiment involving cage-fed guanays to determine the biological efficiency of guano production. He concluded that each guano bird consumed 32 kilograms of fish for every kilogram of guano it produced. This compared quite unfavorably to the 4:1 efficiency he claimed for the fishmeal industry. William Vogt pointed out fatal flaws in Gamarra's work and pleaded for caution, citing problems facing the California sardine fishery. "Exploitation of natural resources by man is *almost always a dangerous proceeding*, unless it is done with care and skill," Vogt admonished, "especially since guano is a resource that will exist in perpetuity." Gamarra responded by comparing guano birds to "wild animals and insects that attack crops" and accused Vogt of trying to take money out of the pockets of future Peruvians.[31] Later feeding experiments showed that guano bird chicks are capable of converting anchoveta to guano at an efficiency as high as 4.46:1, but fishing industry partisans conveniently ignored these findings and continued to cite Gamarra's junk science decades after the fact.[32] The ceremonial display of quantitative findings with little

[29] Hardin, "Tragedy of the Commons"; McEvoy, *The Fisherman's* Problem, ch. 1; *Our Common Future: Report of the World Commission on Environment and Development* (Oxford, 1987), 272–74, 287 n. 17.

[30] *MCAG* 28 (1937): 183–84.

[31] Vogt's emphasis; *BCAG* 17 (Mar. 1941): 103–15; 18 (Mar. 1942): 60–64, 109; Gamarra, "Memorandum," 9 May 1941; Vogt to Ballén, 16 May 1941, DPL-VP 1/4, 3/2.

[32] *BCCAG* 1, no. 2 (1954): 21–49; *BCAG* 35 (Apr. 1959): 10–22; SNP, *La anchoveta y la harina de pescado* (Lima, 1954), 52–53; *Pesca* Oct. 1960: 13–16; July 1970: 28–29.

substance is disturbingly common when science is used to produce public policy. It is the Achilles heel of technocratic forms of governance.[33]

The defenders of the guano birds won the initial debate: CAG received exclusive control over the direct production of fishmeal from anchoveta, but nothing prohibited the manufacture of fishmeal from other sources. In 1945, Peruvian canners began producing fishmeal on a significant scale from spoiled bonito; two years later, they started exporting it. They found a ready market because of an ongoing ecological disaster in the northern Pacific. Overfishing and climate variability caused the fishery for sardines (*Sardinops sagax*) to collapse abruptly in the Pacific Northwest during the late 1940s. The Southern California fishery followed suit in the mid-1950s. Despite multiple interventions by science and government, total production of sardines along the Pacific Coast of North America fell progressively from 614,045 metric tons in 1944–45 to a low of 14,873 in 1953–54, and it never recovered. The huge Japanese fishery for herring off Hokkaido also collapsed in close parallel. Firms like Wilbur-Ellis suddenly had a mountain of surplus industrial machinery on their hands and offered it to enterprising Peruvians at bargain prices. By the end of 1953, at least nine Peruvian canners had installed fishmeal reduction equipment, led by companies with ties to Wilbur-Ellis, but their ability to manufacture fishmeal was strictly limited by levels of canned fish production, which had declining prospects. To bolster the industry's sagging fortunes, the right-wing military government of Manuel Odría (president 1948–56) abolished CAG's monopoly on fishmeal from anchoveta soon after taking power. In 1950 in Chimbote, a Peruvian entrepreneur with close ties to Wilbur-Ellis, Manuel Elguera McParlin, opened Peru's first factory devoted solely to the reduction of fishmeal from anchoveta. He also organized a political advocacy group, the Sociedad Nacional de Pesquería (SNP), to defend the right to freely exploit the ocean's resources. A severe drop in the abundance of bonito and tuna off the Peruvian coast during the moderate El Niño of 1953 led a number of Peruvian canners to abruptly refocus their efforts toward fishmeal production. By the end of that year, there were ten fishmeal plants in Peru devoted solely to the exploitation of anchoveta.[34]

---

[33] Markoff and Montecinos, "The Ubiquitous Rise of Economists"; Guillermo O'Donnell, *Modernization and Bureaucratic-Authoritarianism in South American Politics* (Berkeley and Los Angeles, 1979), 79–82, 99, 102–5; Naomi Oreskes and Erik Conway, *Merchants of Doubt: How a Handful of Scientists Obscured the Truth on Issues from Tobacco Smoke to Global Warming* (New York, 2010).

[34] Mary Sears to Columbus Iselin, 2 Sept. 1953, WHOI-MC9; MCAG 44 (1953), 8–9; Tarnawiecki, "Development of Oceanic Fisheries," 129–31, 135; Roemer, *Fishing for Growth*, 61, 80–83; Caravedo, *Estado, pesca y burguesía*, 35–37; McEvoy, *The Fisherman's Problem*, 146–47; Edward Ueber and Alec MacCall, "The Rise and Fall of the California Sardine Empire," in *Climate Variability, Climate Change, and Fisheries* (Cambridge and New York, 1992); Tokimassa Kobayashi et al., "Long-Term Fluctuation of the Catch of Pacific Herring in Northern Japan," *PICES Scientific Report* no. 15 (2000): 103–6.

These actions inspired another round of intense debate regarding the wisdom of creating a fishing industry that would compete directly with the guano birds. In 1952, Erwin Schweigger and Enrique Ávila submitted a seven-point proposal to the Ministry of Agriculture recommending the prohibition of daytime fishing for anchoveta (to protect the birds) and limitation of the annual catch to 25,000 metric tons (later increased to 100,000 tons). The SNP rejected these arbitrary limits on principle, noting that they lacked any explicit scientific justification. In response, CAG advocated for the creation of an independent board of experts to develop fishing standards that would not threaten the "unstable equilibrium" of Peru's marine ecosystem. CAG explicitly pointed to the ongoing collapse of the California sardine fishery in support of strict fishing quotas. Scientists from the government's Dirección de Pesquería y Caza, on the other hand, argued that the guano and anchoveta industries could develop safely in parallel. As a compromise, high-level officials placed limits on the number of construction permits granted to fishmeal plants but refused to set production quotas.[35]

In an attempt to break this impasse, CAG invited two conservation scientists of "worldwide fame" to study Peru's marine environment with "disinterest" and "affection for pure science." CAG explicitly hoped that the opinions of these outsiders would "reach the higher spheres of our Government more forcefully." Frances Clark (1894–1987) was one of the world's preeminent authorities on the California sardine and northern anchovy (*Engraulis mordax*). She served as director of the California State Fisheries Laboratory at Terminal Island from 1941–57, which made her the only U.S. woman scientist with a significant policy-making position during this period.[36] In 1939, she publicly predicted the immanent collapse of California sardine stocks and recommended strict limits on their harvest at a level not greater than 250,000 metric tons – half the catch at the time. She eventually led a faction of scientists who blamed human harvesting for the dramatic decline of the sardine against those who blamed natural environmental fluctuations. She worked closely with CAG's scientific team during three survey cruises, which allowed Clark to have a level of access to shipboard research she was totally unused to as a woman in the sexist United States. She drafted a detailed plan for anchoveta research, but to CAG's chagrin, she cautiously refused to offer explicit recommendations for the regulation of the anchoveta fishery.[37]

---

[35] Ávila to Sears, 14 Nov. 1952, WHOI-MC9; *MCAG* 44 (1953): 4–12, 49–51; *MCAG* 45 (1954): 5–6, 7–9, 11; *BCNPN* 11, no. 1 (1954): 11–13; Cary, "Report #7," 11 Sept. 1953, SIO-AC40, 28/1, pp. 8–9; Caravedo, *Estado, pesca, y burguesía*, 35.

[36] Carlos Llosa to Clark, 21 July 1953, WHOI-MC9; *MCAG* 45 (1954): viii; Patricia Stocking Brown, "Early Women Ichthyologists," *Environmental Biology of Fishes* 41 (1994): 23–24, 28; Rossiter, *Women Scientists in America*, 301.

[37] Clark, "Can the Supply of Sardines Be Maintained in California Waters?" *California Fish and Game* 2 (1939): 172–76; Clark, "Biology of the Anchoveta," 25 June 1954; Clark,

This might have been fatal to CAG's position, if not for adamant support for strict regulation by U.S. ornithologist Robert Cushman Murphy. After a whirlwind survey of the Peruvian and Chilean coasts, Murphy made his report at a widely publicized conference at the University of San Marcos in January 1954. He unambiguously warned against killing "the hen that lays the golden egg" by allowing a large industrialized fishery oriented toward export to threaten the guano birds. He thought guano and fish production were both "equally subject to ecological depressions of irregular incidence," thanks to El Niño, and reasoned that "stable production or populations probably do not exist" in the Peru Current ecosystem. "Wisdom" therefore mandated that Peru place strict limits on industrial fishing until "much more has been learned about the life cycle of anchoveta." Otherwise, "a new 'Saturnalia'" akin to Peru's Guano Age might result, and perhaps lead the Peruvian anchoveta fishery to the same "calamitous" fate as the California sardine, Chesapeake oyster, or extinct passenger pigeon.[38]

In response, Lima's most prestigious daily newspaper, *El Comercio*, restated its strong support for strict fishing regulations. Peruvian fishing industry executives, on the other hand, quickly rounded up their own "scientific circle" to refute Murphy. Following a strategy similar to the campaign waged by U.S. chemical companies against Murphy and other critics of pesticide use, the SNP boldly sought to discredit Murphy's expertise and objectivity. Because he was an ornithologist, Murphy supposedly "cannot be considered capable to carry out studies and arrive at solutions for problems related to marine fauna and biology." "No serious investigator" would dare present such "incongruous ecological examples." By their calculus, the guano birds were the ones that threatened the ecological "equilibrium" of the ocean: their "indiscriminate multiplication" would inevitably lead to their "overpopulation" and collapse – all the while, snatching anchoveta away from the fishing industry and stealing needed animal protein from the world's exploding population.[39] On two separate occasions, an SNP spokesman used the front page of the archconservative Lima daily *La Prensa* to present "the exploitation of guano birds" as "an index of the industrial backwardness of the nation," because it supposedly stood in the way of the development of home-grown chemical fertilizer and fishing industries. Modern Peruvians needed "neither guano birds, nor fishmeal as fertilizer, only the extended and planned protection of the national fishing industry as a productive source of excellent cheap food."[40]

"Program for Anchoveta Investigations," 26 Apr. 1954, SIO-AC6 17/25; McEvoy, *The Fisherman's Problem*, 158–66.

[38] Murphy, *El guano y la pesca de anchoveta* (Lima, 1954), 9–10, 14–18, 29–31, 36–39.

[39] BCNPN 11, no. 1 (1954): 15–17, 20–21; SNP, *La anchoveta y la harina de pescado*, 1–5, 54–56.

[40] Pedro Cortázar, "¿Comen más de lo que producen?" *La Prensa* 29 Jan. 1954; Cortázar, "Ni guano, ni harina, sino protección a la pesca," *La Prensa* 21 Mar. 1954.

This increasingly hostile debate had direct political repercussions. CAG's general manager Carlos Llosa was hardly surprised when Odría's government fired him as a scapegoat for the impasse, but this act could not obscure the fact that popular opinion and public officials remained divided on the issue of strict regulation. All parties concerned decided to put the question to a new set of outside experts – powerful testimony to the strength of the technocratic ideal in Peru. CAG already had a foreign consultant in mind that was sure to be acceptable to the fishing industry: fishery biologist Milner "Benny" Schaefer (1912–70). He had collegial relationships with a broad range of marine scientists, government officials, and fish producers within the Pacific Basin, thanks to his efforts at developing a scientific system for managing international tuna fishing under the auspices of the Inter-American Tropical Tuna Commission. Schaefer convened a roundtable meeting that brought together representatives from the various sides in August 1954. His intervention resulted in the formation of a Consejo de Investigaciones Hidrobiológicos to "coordinate and support marine biological studies with a view to the greater utilization and control of natural resources." This action had an immediate impact by convincing the American Tunaboat Association to begin purchasing licenses so it could work within Peru's Exclusive Economic Zone, on the condition that payments went straight to the Consejo. This brought an end to the Tuna War for the time being, but political red tape within the Consejo hamstrung its scientific work and caused it to produce little of value for shaping policy.[41]

While Peruvian marine science got itself organized, CAG's "take it slow" approach governed public policy toward the ocean. Manuel Prado's second government adopted a loose fiscal policy when it took power in 1956 to encourage industrial development and consumer purchases. This had the unintentional result of sparking an abrupt construction boom that rapidly doubled the anchoveta fishery's capacity to more than 100,000 tons. Prado responded by suspending the licensing of new plant construction and plant expansion in December to avoid threatening "the equilibrium of the biological chain" of the Peru Current ecosystem. However, the speculative sale of existing licenses and government corruption severely undermined this attempt to limit the growth of the fishmeal industry.[42]

---

[41] Ávila to Sears, 20 Aug. 1953, 19 July, 15 Oct. 1954, WHOI-MC9; Schaefer to Ávila, 2 Aug. 1954, SIO-MC2 17/54; U.S. Fishery Mission to Peru, "Proposal for a Fisheries Research Contract in Peru," 30 Oct. 1954, SIO-AC6 17/25; "Memorándum," [1954]; ATA to Guillermo Tirado, 15 Nov. 1954; "Agreement on the Granting of Permits for Exploitation of the Resources of the South Pacific," TC No. 13424-A, T-36/52/R-V, SIO-AC40, box 60; Warren Wooster, Peru journal, 1957–58; Wooster to Presidente del Consejo, 2 May 1958, Wooster papers; interview with Wooster, 9 Jan. 2005.

[42] *MCAG* 48 (1957): 25–26; Belaúnde, *La legislación pesquera en el Perú*, 141; Caravedo, *Estado, pesca, y burguesía*, 47–48, 142–43; Thorp and Bertram, *Peru, 1890–1977*, 245–46.

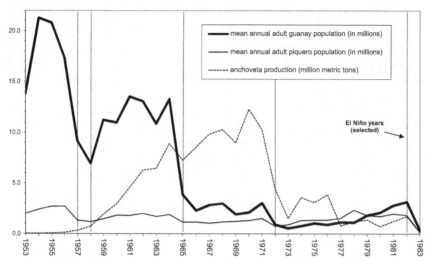

FIGURE 9.2. Anchoveta production and guano bird numbers in Peru, 1953–83. *Source:* Tovar, Guillén, and Nakama, "Monthly Population Size of Three Guano Bird Species."

Then came the "ecological depression" everyone had dreaded. In 1957–58, a strong El Niño event struck the Pacific Basin. As we learned in Chapter 6, Peru's guano birds had increased dramatically over the preceding decade, thanks to years of La Niña conditions, strong upwelling, and CAG's policy of creating new breeding locales. As SNP officials predicted, bird numbers and guano production crashed catastrophically (fig. 9.2). In response, CAG beseeched Prado's government to deploy "more energetic methods" to slow down the "frenetic" development of the fishmeal industry. To pacify CAG, the Ministry of Agriculture held a roundtable meeting of experts in September 1957, but little came of it. In the meantime, the construction boom continued, causing Peruvian anchoveta production to almost triple in 1957, then double again in 1958. Two years of declining guano production finally convinced the government to act. In December 1958, Prado issued regulations restricting the time, season, location, and net size of anchoveta fishing, particularly in the vicinity of the guano islands, and prohibited the transfer of fishmeal production licenses from old to new plants. These laws were to remain in place until "biological studies... determine the maximum yield possible that will protect the national economy."[43]

The fact that the Prado administration acted in this way is testimony to the political importance that the guano industry and conservation principles still possessed, but his government had far more pressing problems to

[43] See fig. 9.1; *MCAG* 49 (1958): vi-vii, 7, 10, 12–14, 18, 21; *MCAG* 50 (1959): v, 14–17; Belaúnde, *La legislación pesquera en el Perú*, 372–75; Caravedo, *Estado, pesca y burguesía*, 47–48.

deal with. A prolonged drought in the Sierra caused a dangerous shortfall in food production that required Peru to use precious foreign exchange to import food. Sugar cane and cotton growers also experienced poor yields because of a dearth of fertilizer and irrigation water and a self-induced plague of pesticide-resistant insects; what they did produce sold for low prices because of a sharp downturn in the world economy. The Prado administration's loose credit policies also resulted in unexpectedly heavy purchases of imported goods. As a consequence, Peru experienced its worst trade deficit since before the turn of the century. Late in 1957, Prado called out to the International Monetary Fund (IMF) for help. The IMF gave Peru's central bank a substantial line of credit with the understanding that it would impose austerity measures. Prado and his allies balked at these suggestions. If he put the squeeze on wages, salaries, and consumption, he risked losing his political base among Peru's popular classes and stirring up massive urban unrest. If he imposed direct currency exchange controls to stop the outflow of capital, he risked harming the export sector and cutting off foreign investment. Prado's government instead tried to weather the crisis through increased deficit spending, but this only worsened Peru's balance-of-payments situation and plunged the country into deeper recession. In 1959, the Peruvian Congress gave a vote of no-confidence that almost caused Prado's fragile democratic coalition to collapse entirely.[44]

In July 1959, Prado appointed a new breed of technocrat to clean up this mess. Pedro Beltrán (1894–1979) was a product of Peru's new guano age. He was born into one of the most influential families of the Aristocratic Republic and earned an economics degree at the London School of Economics in 1918 but decided to take up cotton growing just as the Tangüis cotton boom was getting underway. Beltrán embraced the role of the progressive farmer: he hired a team of agronomists to manage his Cañete valley plantation, mechanized its cultivation, and was reputedly the first Peruvian to apply arsenical insecticides to his crops using airplanes. Under his tenure, Montalván estate quickly rose among the ranks of CAG's top guano consumers. While engaged in these endeavors, Beltrán emerged as a major spokesman for agroexporters on Peru's far right wing. He was fiercely dedicated to classical free-market principles and an outspoken supporter of the military takeover of 1948. As director of the Banco Central de Reserva under General Odría, he engineered a marked shift toward a monetarist economic policy that brought enormous wealth to Peru's agroexporters. He turned into a vocal critic of Odría's regime, however, when his superiors reversed course and adopted Keynesian prescriptions promoted by the IMF. Beltrán countered by inviting Austrian economist Ludwig von Mises, one of the founding ideologues of neoliberalism, to stand by his side when he

[44] Thorp and Bertram, *Peru, 1890–1977*, 278–79; Bertram, "Peru, 1930–60," in *The Cambridge History of Latin America* (Cambridge and New York, 1991), 8:442–47; Portocarrero et al., *Compendio estadístico del Perú*, 40, 42, 168, 170.

stepped down as central banker in 1950. Beltrán continued broadcasting his doctrinaire opinions from his newspaper *La Prensa* – including tireless support for Peru's fishmeal industrialists – and ended up in prison in 1956 for criticizing Odría's authoritarian regime. Beltrán was a true forerunner of the neoliberal technocrats of the late twentieth century.[45]

Prado gave Beltrán free reign over Peru's economic policy. Beltrán proceeded to devalue the sol markedly, raise fuel prices, and establish a series of special tax exemptions for business. He also revoked most of the laws limiting the growth of the fishmeal industry to "stimulate the commercial development of the country on the basis of free enterprise." These actions brought a sudden end to the debate "to fish or not to fish." The international economy cooperated with Beltrán's designs: the recession passed. Planting and production of cotton and sugar cane went up sharply, notwithstanding problems with pests and the fertilizer supply. Anchoveta production and fishmeal export income mushroomed from 737,019 metric tons worth US$17.9 million in 1958, to 6.2 million tons worth US$119.8 million in 1962.[46] In that year, Peru passed Japan as the number one producer of fish by tonnage in the world and immediately became the poster child for the Blue Revolution. This export boom turned into a general economic boom. To some, Beltrán looked like a genius, even though his policies mainly benefited the rich and did nothing to address the rural crisis that fed the growth of vast, unplanned shantytowns in coastal cities. At the end of Prado's term in 1962, Beltrán tried to use these achievements to springboard to the presidency, but he failed to recognize that much of Peru's populace had grown to hate his unending rhetoric against land reform, "wage inflation," and workers that "consume more than they produce." Beltrán quickly dropped out of the race and political life but left a legacy that doomed Peru's marine environment to ecological catastrophe.[47]

Chicken from the Sea

The spectacular growth of Peru's fishmeal industry has often been portrayed as inevitable, once California's sardine fishery collapsed and the sentimental defenders of the guano birds got out of the way. As fishing industry boosters

[45] Arturo Salazar Larraín, ed., *Pedro G. Beltrán: Pensamiento y acción* (Lima, 1994), 7–21; Dennis Gilbert, *The Oligarchy and the Old Regime in Peru* (Ithaca, NY, 1977), 342, 352–58; César Hildebrandt, *Cambio de palabras: 26 entrevistas* (Lima, 1981), 96–98; *Diccionario histórico y biográfico*, s.v. "Beltrán Espantoso, Pedro"; *Enciclopedia ilustrada del Perú*, s.v. "Beltrán, Pedro."

[46] Equal to US$105 million and US$797 million in 2007, respectively.

[47] Cushman, "The Lords of Guano," app. 6, 9; *Pesca y caza* 9 (1959): 130–31; MCAG 51 (1960): 25–27; MCAG 54 (1963): 21–24; *Pesca* May-June 1962: 66; Belaúnde, *La legislación pesquera en el Perú*, 144–45; Edmonds, "Reasons Underlying Development of the Peruvian Fishing Industry," 81–86; Bertram, "Peru, 1930–60," 8:420–22, 436–47; Pike, *The Modern History of Peru*, 273–74, 296–99; Salazar, ed., *Beltrán*, passim.

loved to point out, the world's exploding population was too hungry for protein to let this enormous resource go to waste. These explanations underestimate the continuing influence of conservation principles in Peru, however; they fail to explain how Peru's industry grew to be twenty times larger than the North American industry it replaced; and they simply ignore the final destination of these fish.

A global ecological perspective on history reveals that the Peruvian fishmeal boom was a key constituent of an ongoing revolution in the world's eating patterns. Like the nineteenth-century guano boom, this sudden opening of the Pacific Ocean to outside exploitation did little to increase the world's total food supply. Instead, it enabled an affluent minority of the planet's population to eat higher on the food chain. Peru's Blue Revolution represents an extreme form of neo-ecological imperialism that had the further effect of teaching the world to think that development would allow everyone to eat large quantities of meat and fish.

As we learned in Chapters 7 and 8, one of the main preoccupations of commentators on human population growth focused on the ability of Japan and other nations to attain the steady diet of meat associated with the "American standard of living." William Vogt, for example, privately blamed Peruvians' high death rate, alleged "lack of vigor," inability to concentrate, and "national mournfulness" on a diet too low in protein.[48] Beliefs of this sort drove agricultural researchers after World War II to give almost as much attention to the development of heavier, faster-growing livestock as they did to high-yielding crops. The growth of the U.S. beef industry and its environmental impacts has received substantial attention from historians, but hog- and chicken-raising actually achieved far more spectacular gains in scale and productivity (table 9.2). The average weight of "young meat-type" broiler chickens in the United States, for example, increased from 1,360 grams in 1945, to 1,720 grams in 1975, to 2,130 grams in 1995. Feed-to-meat conversion efficiencies rose from 26 to 48 to 53 percent and time-to-market maturity dropped from 95 to 56 to 47 days over this same period. In Western Europe and the Soviet Bloc, research instead focused on fast-growing pigs. There are biological reasons why chickens and pigs achieved such spectacular gains: they are capable of converting feed to body tissue with far greater efficiency than cows, sheep, and other ungulates, which evolved to subsist mainly on plant cellulose. Similar to the "miracle crops" of the Green Revolution, these advances in animal production resulted from a package of developments in breeding, nutrition, disease management, enclosure air conditioning, and other forms of environmental control. By many measures, these programs were an amazing success. Since 1961 when comprehensive FAO statistics begin, global meat production has tripled, per capita consumption has nearly doubled, and the international meat trade has grown by more than seven times. In 2007, chickens accounted for 51.1 billion of

---

[48] Vogt journal, Sept. 1940, DPL-VP 3/1.

TABLE 9.2. *Global Meat and Fish Production and Consumption, 1961–2000*

	1961	1971	1981	1991	2000
World slaughtered animals (millions of head)					
Beef cattle	173	204	237	258	278
Chickens	6,585	11,405	19,334	28,080	41,377
Pigs	376	595	749	936	1,151
Sheep	331	372	401	473	487
Andean camelids	0.8	0.5	0.4	0.4	0.5
Total (all types[a])	8,365	13,808	22,426	32,350	47,691
World slaughtered animal production (thousands of metric tons)					
Beef cattle	27,685	38,074	45,940	53,896	56,517
Chickens	7,553	13,643	24,321	37,269	58,187
Pigs	24,743	39,414	52,986	70,908	89,584
Sheep	4,930	5,626	5,860	7,121	7,624
Andean camelids	27	18	15	14	14
Total (all types[a])	71,177	104,575	139,055	183,836	232,965
Per capita meat consumption (kilocalories/day)					
World	110	136	155	181	210
United States	335	378	389	411	445
European Union[b]	266	346	397	417	427
USSR	189	249	303	362	185[c]
China	29	87	132	240	402
Japan	26	75	116	149	165
Latin America and Caribbean[d]	177	167	213	216	281
Brazil	112	126	168	235	358
Mexico	148	137	242	199	265
Peru	78	78	71	75	74
Sub-Saharan Africa[e]	67	67	68	65	65
Australia and New Zealand	510	495	461	480	461
Kiribati	149	156	151	107	151
Marine fish production (thousands of metric tons)					
World	28,051	46,425	48,604	66,767	71,103
United States	1,817	1,672	2,039	3,534	3,303
European Union[b]	4,906	6,316	6,093	5,471	5,334
USSR	2,287	6,050	8,049	7,807	3,978[c]
China	1,560	1,830	2,257	4,719	8,787
Japan	4,848	7,845	8,905	7,202	3,639
Indonesia	473	744	1,199	2,170	3,279
Sri Lanka	57	65	172	188	283
Latin America and Caribbean[d]	6,163	13,258	9,403	15,886	18,122
Chile	70	389	1,389	3,291	5,787
Cuba	18	106	132	128	51
Ecuador	32	92	512	312	591
Mexico	97	260	1,354	1,082	966
Peru	5,209	10,489	2,675	6,807	10,507

	1961	1971	1981	1991	2000
Marine fish production (thousands of metric tons)					
Sub-Saharan Africa[e]	1,555	2,277	1,916	2,048	3,175
Angola	241	318	123	109	228
Ghana	35	190	195	293	371
Australia and New Zealand	69	94	221	479	629
Other Oceania[f]	31	67	126	183	303
Per capita seafood consumption (kilocalories/day)					
World	17	21	23	24	28
United States	20	22	29	30	31
European Union[b]	29	32	32	40	50
USSR	33	47	56	49	27[c]
China	8	9	8	17	35
Japan	113	159	182	194	178
Indonesia	17	20	25	31	44
Sri Lanka	28	22	30	38	53
Latin America and Caribbean[d]	8	12	16	14	15
Chile	12	15	31	33	22
Cuba	12	27	33	25	24
Ecuador	11	13	24	12	9
Mexico	4	7	24	21	20
Peru	25	21	28	25	37
Sub-Saharan Africa[e]	10	14	17	14	14
Angola	12	19	23	22	22
Ghana	37	74	44	50	64
Australia and New Zealand	19	20	25	29	32
Kiribati	75	93	99	136	132

[a] Includes asses, beef cattle, buffalo, camels, other camelids (alpaca, llama, guanaco, vicuña), chickens, ducks, goats, geese, horses, mules, pigeons and other birds, pigs, rabbits and other rodents, sheep, and turkeys. Production by weight also includes game meat, snails, and other miscellanea.

[b] Includes member states as of 2000.

[c] Russian Federation and former Soviet Republics.

[d] No data for Anguilla, Aruba, British Virgin Islands, Cayman Is., Falkland Is., French Guiana, Guadeloupe, Martinique, Monserrat, Puerto Rico, St. Pierre and Miquelon, Turks and Caicos Islands, U.S. Virgin Islands.

[e] No data for Equatorial Guinea, Réunion, St. Helena, Somalia.

[f] Includes American Samoa, Cook Island, Fiji, French Polynesia, Guam, Kiribati, Marshall Islands, Micronesia, Nauru, New Caldeonia, Niue, Norfolk Island, Northern Mariana Island, Palau, Papua New Guinea, Pitcairn Island, Samoa, Solomon Islands, Tokelau, Tonga, Tuvalu, Vanuatu, Wallis and Fortuna Islands. FAO data for Oceania is too incomplete to estimate consumption levels.

Source: FAO Statistical Databases.

the 58.6 billion animals killed for meat, and 28.2 percent of the 269 million tons of meat produced worldwide. The pork industry did even better, producing 99 million tons of meat from the slaughter of 1.3 billion pigs. When we look at the globe as a whole, chicken and pork, not beef, are the true modern meats.[49]

As table 9.2 shows, consumers in the First World and Soviet Bloc were the first to benefit from these trends. Consumers in other regions eventually benefited as well – China more than anyone. Since the "Three Bad Years" of 1959–61 when starvation killed an estimated 30 million people, meat consumption by the world's most populous nation has increased by a power of ten. In terms of food calories, the Chinese now consumes almost as much meat as the First World and twice that of fish-eating Japan. Thanks to such dense sources of energy, the average citizen in these high-consuming countries now takes in more than 2,900 kilocalories per day – making these the fattest human societies in the history of the earth. These national accounts also reveal some troubling regional inequalities. Peruvians, sub-Saharan Africans, and the I-Kiribati, per capita, consume nearly the same amounts of meat as they did a half-century ago – and it is no coincidence that poor citizens of these regions have replaced the Chinese as mass-media icons of hunger and misery.[50]

The widespread use of concentrated fertilizers and nutritionally balanced, high-protein feeds was fundamental to these developments. As we learned in Chapter 4, massive imports of island phosphate used to fertilize pasture made it possible for Australia and New Zealand to consume meat in great quantities. Meat production today in many other parts of the world is based on a throughput system formed from an ecological triumvirate of nitrogen fertilizer manufacture, maize and soybean cultivation, and pen-raising of livestock. All three steps require enormous amounts of fossil fuel energy and provide a nasty, brutish, and short existence for most of the animals involved. In a stark reversal of the guano age, pen-raising of livestock now produces concentrations of excrement so great that animal manure has become an environmental hazard in many locales, rather than a boon to soil fertility.[51]

---

[49] FAO statistical databases; William Boyd, "Making Meat: Science, Technology, and the Industrialization of American Poultry Production," *Technology and Culture* 42 (2001): 631–64; János Kovács, *Egyetemes és Magyar agrárfejlődés* (Budapest, 2005), ch. 5, §14–17; Ted Steinberg, *Down to Earth: Nature's Role in American History* (New York, 2008), ch. 12; Orville Schell, *Modern Meat* (New York, 1984).

[50] B. M. Popkin, "The Nutrition Transition and Obesity in the Developing World," *Journal of Nutrition* 131 (2001): 871S–73S; Greg Critser, *Fat Land: How Americans Became the Fattest People in the World* (New York, 2003).

[51] Smil, *Enriching the Earth*, ch. 7–10; David Kirby, *Animal Factory: The Looming Threat of Industrial Pig, Dairy, and Poultry Farms to Humans and the Environment* (New York, 2010).

This modern meat-focused agroecosystem did not spring into existence fully formed. The industrial production of fishmeal from Peru's coastal waters for use as high-protein feed gave an important boost to its creation. From 1948 to 1958, the global fishmeal industry doubled in size, and the market for imported fishmeal multiplied by over six times, from 111,000 metric tons worth US$15.3 million to 693,000 metric tons worth US$103.4 million.[52] From there, the Peruvian boom almost single-handedly caused global production of fishmeal to jump to two million tons a year in 1960. This new supply temporarily glutted the international market for high-protein feeds and caused prices to fall to the point where far more livestock farmers could afford them. On the consumption side, West German swine farmers and U.S. chicken raisers bought the largest quantities of Peruvian fishmeal, followed by the United Kingdom and Netherlands. During the 1960s, U.S. purchasers of supermarket broilers and buckets of fast-food fried chicken were literally consuming chicken from the sea.[53]

These economic changes had geopolitical repercussions. Fishmeal-based chicken production proved so profitable for U.S. farmers that they were able to undersell their counterparts in Western Europe. This sparked the so-called Chicken War over meat exports to the European Economic Community, which convinced its member nations to aggressively promote industrial animal production and to close ranks around the idea of forming a federal union. Meanwhile, the Soviet Union tried to keep up with the West by deploying a fleet of massive factory ships to harvest seafood and fishmeal, which proved to be frighteningly efficient at vacuuming up everything in reach of their nets, hooks, and harpoons on the high seas – often just beyond the reach of the territorial sea of Western nations. As table 9.2 shows, per capita meat consumption in the USSR and what became the EU both increased by more than 30 percent during the 1960s, and Soviet marine fish production almost tripled as a result of these policies.[54]

Fishmeal production on this scale required fundamental changes to humanity's relationship with the marine environment, especially off the coast of Peru. Industrial anchoveta fishing began with the purse-seine trawler, a technology that was transferred directly from U.S. salmon and sardine fisheries by the North American Fishery Mission. At first, Peruvian anchoveta fishermen simply motored along the coast close to port and searched for surface schools by sight. They depended heavily on watching guano birds to locate schools of fish – just like the ancient kin of Don Pedro Guaneque.

[52] Equal to US$112 million and US$604 million in 2007, respectively.

[53] FAO statistical databases; *Pesca* June 1961: 15, 23–35; Edmonds, "Reasons Underlying Development," 111–12, 116–17, 120, 123–25, 131, 138–40, 142–43.

[54] Ross Talbot, *The Chicken War: An International Trade Conflict between the United States and the European Economic Community, 1961–64* (Ames, IO, 1978); C. P. Idyll, *The Sea against Hunger: Harvesting the Ocean to Feed a Hungry World* (New York, 1970), 42–45, 114–21.

Fish were easiest to find between October and February, when the breeding of guano birds also reached its peak. A secondary fishing season
lasted from April to June when the year's new crop of fry (*peladilla*)
became large enough to catch, even though they had not yet reached sexual
maturity.[55]

The widespread adoption of several new technologies by the Peruvian
anchoveta fishery utterly transformed the industry's capacity to locate and
capture fish. In 1954, directional echo-locaters (SONAR) originally developed by northern militaries to hunt submarines went on sale in Peru. But
these imported, high-tech instruments were expensive and required substantial technical skill and experience to operate. Their growing popularity in
the mid-1960s dramatically increased the depth and distance at which fishing boats could locate subsurface schools of fish and eventually made the
guano birds superfluous to the search. As a result, birds came to be considered pests, rather than friends, of the fisherman.[56] In 1955, nylon nets first
became available in Peru. The development of this revolutionary synthetic
fiber by the Du Pont Corporation was itself a derivative of large-scale production of nitrogen compounds using the Haber-Bosch process. Engineers
in several countries adapted it for use in fishing nets after World War II.
The most successful of these was the Momoi Fishing Net Manufacturing
Co. of Ako, Japan, which eventually conquered the Peruvian market. Synthetic nets were technically superior to Peruvian-produced cotton nets in
almost every way. By 1959, the use of cotton nets in Peru had virtually
disappeared – to the direct detriment of Peruvian cotton growers. Nylon
nets were also amenable for use with high-powered cranks, which made it
possible to manipulate enormous drift nets that reached much deeper than
the guano birds could effectively dive. Besides sweeping the sea of fish, these
nets also snared and drowned vast numbers of guanays, which swim under-
water to catch their prey.[57] This only begins to account for the dazzling
array of goods that the Peruvian fishing industry imported from around the
world and that local industries sprang up to produce. These included water-
proof clothing from Norway, manila fiber rope from the Philippines, foam
floats and rubber hose from the United States, steel cable and metal sheeting
from the United Kingdom, and entire fishmeal plants from Denmark. Boat
construction factories sprouted up by the dozens in Callao during the height
of the fishmeal boom and, at their peak, built 1,200 new craft in a single

[55] *Bol.Inst.Mar* 1, no. 2 (1965): 89–90, 98–102; *Inf.Inst.Mar* 6 (1965): 8–16, 25.

[56] *Bol.Inst.Mar* 1, no. 2 (1965): 97; *Pesca* Apr.-May 1961: 16–19, Aug. 1961: 8–9, June 1963:
     45, 64; Jan. 1966: 28–29.

[57] *Pesca* Oct. 1961: 44–50, Sept. 1964: 23–25, July 1965: 27, Apr. 1966: 37, Apr. 1968:
     30, Jan. 1968: 8–12, Apr. 1968: 30; David Hounshell, "Du Pont and the Management of
     Large-Scale Development," in *Big Science: The Growth of Large-Scale Research* (Stanford,
     CA, 1992).

year. One enterprising Peruvian developed a jute sack factory using new fiber supplies from the Peruvian Amazon.[58]

Finding and catching anchoveta was only half the story. The conversion of wet, perishable fish into dry, inert fishmeal also required the direct transfer of reduction plant technology from the United States and Scandinavia. At the peak of the industry, these plants produced 1 ton of fishmeal for every 5.4 tons of anchoveta unloaded at the plant – far below the efficiencies Gamarra claimed. Unlike guano production, these plants were not environmentally benign. They required large amounts of energy produced by smoke-belching, on-site diesel generators or Peru's overstressed electrical network. Fishing boats also used diesel engines, usually Caterpillar-brand, and the industry as a whole used prodigious quantities of fuel oil. From 1960 to 1964, the industry burned 217 million liters costing S/.628 million to do something the guano birds did for free. This fuel was mainly produced from Peruvian wells by the International Petroleum Company, a subsidiary of Standard Oil operating in far northern Peru.[59]

Most of Peru's early fishmeal factories sprouted up either in Callao or Chimbote, although dozens of other coastal settlements eventually came to possess their own smelly plants. Chimbote was situated to become the world's largest fish-producing city thanks to massive environmental alterations accomplished by a government development project started during World War II. This program drained 225 square kilometers of coastal wetland in the vicinity, connected the town to the Pan-American Highway and Huaraz railway, constructed a high dam and 50-Mw hydroelectric facility on the Santa River, and built a state-owned steel mill. Immigrants from rural areas poured into Chimbote looking for work, causing it to grow from a malaria-ridden 4,000 in 1940 to more than 60,000 in 1960.[60]

The rapid pace of the fishmeal industry's development eventually inspired an environmentalist backlash in Peru's largest city. Fishmeal plants were notorious for emitting vile fumes. The Lima-Callao area, like much of the Peruvian coast, is also subject to temperature inversions, when a cap of warm upper air sits on top of a cool marine layer and prevents the dispersal of pollutants. When the region's prevailing southeastern winds failed to blow, the smell of rotten fish could permeate everything – including districts populated by the country's elite. In 1960–61, municipal health inspectors in the Lima-Callao area began organizing a grassroots movement against fishmeal odor, based on the specious claim that plant emissions were responsible for epidemic rates of allergies, skin and eye problems, and asthma. High concentrations of noxious gases produced by fishmeal plant equipment and

[58] *Pesca* Nov. 1960: 28, 30; Nov. 1961: 57; Apr. 1963: 27–32; Jan. 1967: 22.
[59] Equal to US$127 million in 2007; *Pesca* Jan.–Feb. 1962: 7; Apr. 1964: 15; June 1965: 48.
[60] *Pesca* June 1961: 87–97; *Peru: Obra de gobierno del Presidente de la República Dr. Manuel Prado, 1939–1945* (Buenos Aires, 1945), 43–48.

decomposing fish were indeed responsible for causing worker injuries and occasional deaths, but defenders of the fishing industry rightfully pointed out that the rapid proliferation of buses, trucks, private automobiles, and other smokestack industries during the 1950s was a far more likely cause for these urban health problems. Peoples' noses told them differently, however, and the fishing industry soon found itself on the run. Municipal officials in Callao acted first to mandate the installation of deodorizing equipment. Peru's central government followed suit in March 1961 but dragged its feet about enforcement while a commission sought assistance from experts who had installed similar equipment at fishmeal factories in smog-prone Los Angeles. Unfortunately, the least costly abatement option required abundant fresh water. The main concentration of factories along Avenida Argentina in Callao would have to use expensive gas incineration, which required burning an additional 100 to 200 liters of fuel oil for every ton of fishmeal produced. The inspector of hygiene in Callao brought this controversy to a head during the austral spring of 1961 when he made a series of surprise visits to fishmeal plants and handed out hefty fines for various workplace violations. President Prado responded by issuing a decree in August 1961 giving Callao producers four months to install deodorizers. To prevent escalating the controversy and causing it to spread to other cities, the SNP gave in and promised to discipline noncompliant companies, as long as the government helped out with short-term loans. This caused the air pollution issue to die-down, but provided a strong motivation for producers to build factories elsewhere, thereby exporting the problem to less-regulated locales along the coast.[61]

The fishing industry also generated gigantic quantities of water pollution, but no comparable movement emerged to clean up Peru's coastal waters. Every time a fishing boat unloaded its catch, it dumped hundreds of liters of bilge water into the sea containing 10 percent anchoveta blood and other biological matter. Scandinavian engineers who had been compelled by environmental laws to clean up the North Sea fishmeal industry determined that Peru lost a quarter of its potential production by dumping unprocessed wastewater into the sea. The "gospel of efficiency" mandated action, but importing the stainless-steel equipment needed to process stickwater was prohibitively expensive. This machinery also required new recirculating driers, additional energy expenditures, and abundant supplies of freshwater. In 1968, the Peruvian Congress extended tax breaks to importers of stickwater processors, but only a third of fishmeal factories took advantage. Even with these improvements, an estimated 4,200 tons of untreated stickwater entered the ocean *every hour* during peak season in 1970. The Bays of Chimbote,

[61] *Pesca* Dec. 1960: 18–19; Feb. 1961: 22; Mar. 1961: 8–9; Apr.–May 1961: 24–25; June 1961: 108; July 1961: 48; Sept. 1961: 47; Nov. 1961: 15–27; Mar.–Apr. 1962: 15–23; July–Aug. 1962: 71–72; Feb. 1968: 10–14; Apr. 1970: 16–21.

Supe, and Tambo de Mora were the worst affected and became eutrophied dead zones. The Bay of Callao was also negatively affected – and had the additional challenge of dealing with industrial effluent and untreated sewage from a city of three million people. Artisanal fishermen living in these polluted ports had to travel far away to locate fish; many simply abandoned the trade entirely. Peru's guano birds, of course, produced none of these problems.[62]

At this stage, however, most observers tended to overlook these signs of trouble and emphasize the industry's spectacular growth. A few lucky investors acquired enormous fortunes. Luis Banchero (1929–72) was the golden boy of the fishmeal boom. He began his working life in a small liquor store run by his Italian-Peruvian parents in the southern city of Tacna. In 1955, he bought a down-and-out bonito cannery in Chimbote and used assistance from Wilbur-Ellis to purchase a purse-seine outfit and convert the factory to fishmeal production. From there, he rode the fishmeal boom to the very top. By age thirty-one, he was one of the richest men in South America and the second largest fishmeal producer in the world, after the U.S. Gulf Coast's "king of menhaden" Harvey Smith.[63] This industry also proved attractive to a number of agroexporters, including Gildemeister & Co., W. R. Grace & Co., and the Pardo, Lavalle, Klinge, and Graña families – a circumstance that further undermined support for the guano industry. In 1961, Rafael Graña sold his cotton plantation to buy into the fishing business. Within two years, he owned the second largest fishmeal company in Peru and soon expanded into ship construction. He went bankrupt one year later when the fishmeal industry experienced its first major downturn causing Chancay, a fishing city he helped build overnight, to become the first coastal boomtown to go bust when the anchoveta mysteriously disappeared from its vicinity. As time passed, more and more large multinational corporations such as Ralston-Purina, Heinz, Cargill, General Mills, and Gold Kist became noticeable in the upper echelons of the Peruvian fishmeal industry.[64]

Dozens of other Third World countries set out to imitate these accomplishments. Benny Schaefer was one of the most vocal proponents of the idea that the world could dramatically increase its supply of high-protein

[62] *Pesca* Jan. 1961: 19–27; Jan.–Feb. 1962: 13–25; Jan.–Feb. 1963: 71; Oct. 1963: 64–67; Jan. 1967: 28–30; June 1968: 28; Mar. 1971: 22; Apr. 1971: 10–16; Luis Arriaga, "Contaminación en el Océano Pacífico Suroriental (Ecuador-Perú-Chile)," *Revista de la Comisión Permanente del Pacífico Sur* 5 (1976): 3–62.

[63] *Pesca* Oct. 1960: 22–26; Mar. 1963: 33–34; June 1966: 57; Edmonds, "Reasons Underlying Development of the Peruvian Fishing Industry," 62; *Diccionario histórico y biográfico*, s.v. "Banchero Rossi, Luis."

[64] *Pesca* Sept. 1961: 39; May–June 1962: 66; Sept. 1963: 15–22; Mar. 1963: 44; Apr. 1963: 51; Sept. 1964: 32; July 1965: 12–17; Jan. 1966: 24; Feb. 1966: 12–16; Apr. 1966: 35; May 1967: 20–25, 36; July 1967: 36, 38; Aug. 1967: 27–28; May 1969: 27; Feb. 1970: 20–21; Jan. 1971: 29.

food if it followed Peru's example. He believed it would be easy to double, and perhaps quadruple, production from the seas to 200 million tons of fish a year if the rest of the world followed Peru's example and focused on lower levels of the marine food chain. This estimate was widely cited during the debate surrounding Paul Ehrlich's *Population Bomb* (1968).[65] The FAO and UN Development Programme provided one major source of support for these endeavors. They were the initial builders of Ecuador's fishing industry, for example. The United States, Scandinavia, and Japan also funded fishery missions to the Third World, both to extend the influence of their experts and to stimulate exports of industrial equipment. Cold War geopolitics provided the main motivation for Soviet sponsorship of fishery industrialization programs in Ghana and Cuba. Third World governments also provided their own impetus to these programs. The Chilean Development Corporation (Corfo) nationalized fishmeal the industry just south of the Peruvian border after disruptions caused by the El Niño of 1965–66 and later used Soviet help to begin developing a trawling fleet; the industry grew even faster after Augusto Pinochet's technocrats turned it over to private investors in the late 1970s. Lucrative funding from the Mexican state during the 1970s built thousands of artisanal vessels and a long-distance tuna fleet almost as large as the United States. These craft have littered the shores of the Gulf of California with discarded shark remains, however, and harvest most of the small fish that once fed Mexico's guano birds. In recent years, China has rapidly emerged as one of the earth's great fish-producing powers. In 2007, it produced an incredible 41.1 million metric tons of fish and other aquatic organisms from aquaculture, marine, and inland sources, 33.8 million of which were consumed directly by the Chinese – almost a third of world totals. At least there, the Blue Revolution seems to have accomplished everything it promised.[66]

The results of these programs elsewhere have been quite mixed. As fig. 9.2 shows, marine fish production and per capita seafood consumption quickly multiplied in Ghana, Cuba, and Mexico with these forms of aid but later stagnated or collapsed when the support went away. Portuguese-ruled Angola was one of the world's first major exporters of fishmeal after the Second World War, but the Angolan industry almost closed down when bacteriologists discovered that air-dried Angolan fishmeal harbored an astounding

---

[65] Schaefer, "The Potential Harvest from the Sea," *Transactions of the American Fisheries Society* 94 (1965): 123–28; D. L. Alverson et al., "How Much Food from the Sea?" *Science* 24 Apr. 1970: 503–5; Idyll, *The Sea against Hunger*, 20–23.

[66] FAO statistical databases; Hiroshi Kasahara, "Confidential Report on National Fisheries Institute, Ecuador," 6 Nov. 1963, SIO-AC3, 4/210; *Pesca* Aug. 1961: 26–27; Dec. 1961: 49–50; May–June 1962: 21–29, 37–39, 70; July–Aug. 1962: 23–28; June 1966: 74; Mar. 1967: 36; Aug. 1968: 10–21; Nov. 1971: 30–33; Apr. 1972: 20–29; Alonso Aguilar Ibarra et al., "The Political Economy of Marine Fisheries Development in Peru, Chile and Mexico," *JLAS* 32 (2000): 514–16, 519–25.

diversity of *Salmonella* strains. This raised fears that contaminated animal feeds were responsible for bacterial infection in pigs and poultry and for food poisoning in human consumers. Meanwhile, little of this fish made it to the stomachs of Angolan nationals, and the industry later collapsed for reasons similar to Peru.[67] For many years, Sri Lanka was considered one of the great success stories of small-scale fishery industrialization. Unlike most countries, its postcolonial government decided it could not afford to follow expert advice and import large boats and canning plants. In 1959, the FAO sent Finnish boat construction expert Erik Estlander to Sri Lanka to build a fleet of small motorized trawlers. By 1962, there were 600 boats of his design operating in this island nation; by 1977, there were 2,500. These efforts resulted in immediate increases in Sri Lanka's national catch from 36,000 tons in 1956 to 57,000 tons in 1961. By the mid-1970s, the country was a major exporter of tuna and shark fin. For most coastal peasants living on the southern half of the island, however, Sri Lanka's Blue Revolution can only be described as "dismal": it benefited a tiny segment of the population and focused overwhelmingly on high-value fish that were consumed by distant city dwellers and foreigners. Per capita fish consumption barely improved over the course of this program.[68] Ethnic Chinese entrepreneurs introduced motorized fishing trawlers to Indonesia in 1966. These boats dramatically increased the country's marine fish production but were used indiscriminately to sweep the sea for one species after another – much of which ended up as fishmeal. These changes caused so much social and ecological disruption that major riots broke out in the late 1970s and early 1980s. Under intense political pressure, President Suharto banned the use of trawlers within Indonesia's territorial waters in 1983. In 1971, the Gilbert & Ellice Islands Colony signed a lucrative agreement with Van Camp Sea Food to develop a locally based fishing industry, but Hurricane Bebe in 1972 destroyed the entire fleet, and the program along with it. Similar problems also beset fishery industrialization programs in Panama, French Polynesia, Malaysia, and the Philippines during 1960s and 1970s.[69] Even the outspoken promoters of these programs at the FAO expressed concern that the

[67] *Pesca* June 1961: 32–33; July 1961: 36; Nov. 1967: 16–20; P. R. Edwards, "Salmonellosis: Observations on Incidence and Control," *Annals of the New York Academy of Sciences* 70 (1958): 598–613; K. W. Newell et al., "Salmonellosis in Northern Ireland, with Special Reference to Pigs and Salmonella-Contaminated Pig Meal," *Journal of Hygiene* 57 (1959): 92–105.

[68] *Pesca* Dec. 1962: 57–58; Paul Alexander, "The Modernization of Peasant Fisheries in Sri Lanka," in *Marine Policy and the Coastal Community* (London, 1976); Alexander, "Lessons from Pacific Technology Transfer and Fishing Communities: The Sri Lankan Experience," in *Development and Social Change in the Pacific Islands* (London and New York, 1989).

[69] *Pesca* May 1965: 30–34; Nov. 1966: 38–40; Bailey, "The Blue Revolution"; Bailey, "The Political Economy of Marine Fisheries Development in Indonesia," *Indonesia* 46 (1988): 25–38; Macdonald, *Cinderellas of Empire*, 180–81.

overwhelming majority of the increase in global fish production went "to expand consumption of pig and poultry products in high income countries and... *made little impact on dietary deficiencies in the developing world.*"[70]

Peru's fishing executives were quite sensitive to the criticism that 99 percent of Peru's fish production ended up in the First World. To try to make amends, the Clínica Anglo-Norteamericana in Lima initiated a program funded by the SNP and U.S. National Institute of Health in 1961 to test the nutritional attributes of fishmeal for direct human consumption. Medical outposts in Lima's impoverished shantytowns provided malnourished children to be used as guinea pigs. They were fed soup, bread, and pasta fortified with fishmeal produced by an experimental South African refinery. One dangerously underweight infant, "Isabelita," was fattened up on fishmeal and turned into a propaganda tool by the Peruvian fishing industry (fig. 9.3). Entrepreneurs also built pilot plants for producing "fish protein concentrate" in the United States, Sweden, Morocco, Peru, and Chile, often with international funding from organizations such as UNICEF. Advocates usually neglected to mention, however, that large quantities of isopropyl alcohol or hexane solvent were needed to remove the rancid fish odor from fishmeal, which destroyed much of its nutritional value. In January 1962, the U.S. Food and Drug Administration determined fish protein concentrate to be unfit for human consumption, leading Peruvian fishmeal producers to drop their support for this project. This revealed their cynical intention: to gain a foothold in the U.S. processed-food industry.[71] Other programs to increase Peruvian fish consumption also accomplished little of substance, with the marked exception of a network of government hatcheries that introduced rainbow trout (*Oncorhynchus mykiss*) and lake trout (*Salvelinus namaycush*) to highland lakes and rivers. They did so, however, at the cost of driving to extinction a fish species endemic to Lake Titicaca (*Orestias cuvieri*). Per capita consumption of fish in Peru actually declined during the 1960s while the country was the world's largest fish producer – an astounding case of ecological injustice for the nation's poor.[72]

[70] Their emphasis; *The Prospects for World Fishery Development in 1975 and 1985*, FAO Fisheries Circular no. 118 (Rome, 1969), 1.

[71] *Pesca* Oct. 1960: 5–8; Aug. 1961: 13–21; Sept. 1961: 16–37, 45; Mar.–Apr. 1962: 43; July–Aug. 1962: 23–28; Nov. 1962: 67–69; Jan.–Feb. 1963: 41–48; June 1963: 57–63; Sept. 1963: 14–20, 52–54; Sept. 1964: 14–20; Apr. 1972: 28–32.

[72] *Pesca* Nov. 1960: 37; Oct. 1962: 22–23, 57–59; Nov. 1962: 67–69; Jan. 1964: 15–27, 35–45; Feb. 1964: 11–22; Dec. 1964: 11; Apr. 1965: 22–24; Jan. 1966: 11, 30; June 1967: 22–24; Sept. 1967: 20–22; Oct. 1967: 16–18, 24–25, 28; Nov. 1968: 8–10; Nov. 1969: 12–15; Hernán Ortega and Max Hidalgo, "Freshwater Fishes and Aquatic Habitats in Peru: Current Knowledge and Conservation," *Aquatic Ecosystem Health & Management* 11 (2008): 257–71; Joan Martínez-Alier, "Ecology and the Poor: A Neglected Dimension of Latin American History," *JLAS* 23 (1991): 629–30.

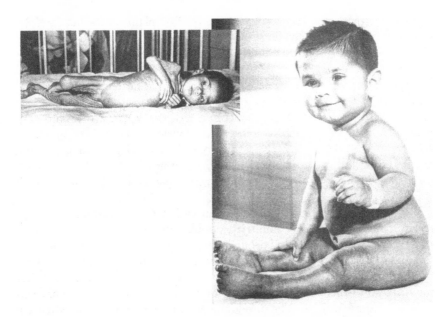

FIGURE 9.3. "Isabelita," the Peruvian fishing industry's poster child for the end of world hunger. With a diet of pasta fortified with fishmeal, physicians at the Clínica Anglo-Norteamericana raised the weight of this dangerously malnourished infant from 3.5 kg at 8 months of age to 9 kg at 12 months. These images were reproduced in a number of Peruvian periodicals, including the front page of the archconservative daily *La Prensa*. Similar images often appeared in international publications touting the production of food from the sea. *Source: Pesca*, Aug. 1961, reproduced with permission.

Replacing the Guano Birds

The ecological injustice and destructiveness of Peru's Blue Revolution looks even worse when we consider the problems it caused for Peru's attempts to participate in the Green Revolution. During the late 1950s and 1960s, an alphabet soup of international organizations gave concerted attention to increasing the production and consumption of fertilizers in the Third World. Malthusian fears of overpopulation also provided enormous impetus to these programs. Indonesia, India, and several other postcolonial states built highly successful input-substituting fertilizer industries with foreign aid and expertise, but similar attempts by the People's Republic of China (PRC) started out disastrously. With the help of the Soviet Union and Czechoslovakia, China brought a half-dozen coal-powered fertilizer plants on line just in time for the Great Leap Forward of 1958–59, but the country discovered the hard way that industrialized agriculture remains vulnerable to climatic and logistical disruptions. Thirty million people died during the "Three

Bad Years" that followed. The response of PRC planners to this carefully hidden catastrophe vividly illustrates the centrality of fertilizer to Green Revolution programs to increase the world's food supply. China immediately commissioned Western European engineers to build a natural gas-powered urea plant and aggressively developed homegrown designs for large- and small-scale plants. These efforts soon turned China into the world's largest producer and consumer of manufactured fertilizer in the world and contributed tangibly to the improvement of crop yields, food security, and meat consumption in the country. They did so at the cost of producing air, soil, and water pollution on a scale that has caused nearly all of China's major lakes and estuaries to become choked with algae and the whole earth to warm up.[73]

Development planners gave similar attention to the fertilizer situation in Latin America. In most countries, population growth considerably outpaced increases in agricultural production during the 1950s. Urban areas and food consumption grew even more explosively, with clamor for rural land reform and social revolution intensifying in close parallel, especially after the triumph of the Cuban Revolution of 1959. These trends were particularly worrisome in Peru. The development of import-substituting chemical industries to produce concentrated fertilizers provided a popular strategy for easing these burdens. From the agronomist's perspective, Peru's concentrated fertilizer usage actually compared quite favorably to the rest of the world. In 1963, Peru consumed 45 kilograms of nitrogen, phosphorus, and potassium (NPK) fertilizer per hectare cultivated. This slightly surpassed the United States and Canada (at 44 kg/ha) and came close to the average for all developed countries in the First World and Communist Bloc (50 kg/ha). It greatly surpassed levels in Latin America (12 kg/ha) and the world as a whole (27 kg/ha). These amounts actually represented a significant decrease from the mid-1950s, when Peru used nearly 100 million kilograms of concentrated NPK fertilizer a year at rates of consumption that ranked ahead of most First World nations. Eighty-five percent of this came directly from Peru's guano birds. Chile looked even better than Peru in these national accounts, thanks to its nitrate industry and heavy importation of phosphate and potassium. Peru's situation looked very different from the point of view of population technocrats, however. In 1963, it only consumed 9.2 kilograms of NPK fertilizer per person, compared to 46 kg in North America, 33 kg in developed countries, and 15 kg for the world population as a whole. Developmental economists projected that Peru would need to bring a whopping one million hectares of new land into more intensive

[73] Jung-Chao Liu, *China's Fertilizer Economy* (Chicago, 1970); Justin Yifu Lin and Dennis Tao Yang, "Food Availability, Entitlements and the Chinese Famine of 1959–61," *Economic Journal* 110 (2000): 136–58; Ma et al., "Nitrogen Flow and Use Efficiency"; Smil, *Enriching the Earth*, 116–17, 124–25, 167–70.

cultivation over the coming decade just to keep up with the country's expanding population.[74] It is important to realize that these statistics did not include traditional manures. For example, they fail to account for Chilean wheat farmers' long reliance on nitrogen-fixing clover and alfalfa, the grazing of cattle, and inputs of Andean silt to maintain the productivity of their crops.[75] By emphasizing manufactured fertilizers, developmental economists of this era greatly exaggerated the problems facing Third World farmers, in the same way that their calculations of gross national product automatically exaggerated the economic production of cold versus tropical countries by crediting the consumption of energy to produce winter heat.

Building a new industry to replace the guano birds proved more challenging than expected. Peru's first superphosphate plant opened in 1957, but it depended on imported phosphate rock and quickly went bankrupt once the country's guano birds bounced back from the 1957–58 El Niño. Three years later, Fertilizantes Sintéticos S.A. (Fertisa) opened an ammonium nitrate plant at the mouth of the Rímac River in Callao modeled after similar plants in Colombia and Mexico. It burned heavy fuel oil produced in northern Peru and was a notorious emitter of sulfur oxides and particulates. Thanks to tariff protections, Fertisa at least made a profit but still barely made a dent in fertilizer imports.[76]

Political change gave a notable boost to these endeavors. The presidential election of 1962 ended in a virtual three-way tie, and a reformist group of military officers took command of the Peruvian state for a year to break the impasse. Presaging the events of 1968, these officers embraced a closely controlled approach to economic development similar to other bureaucratic-authoritarian governments of the era. They immediately took measures to reign in the fishmeal industry's free-for-all and created an Institute of National Planning to supervise a series of technocratic commissions charged with laying out a new course for Peruvian society.[77]

To this end, CAG was reorganized as the Corporación Nacional de Fertilizantes (CONAFER) in 1963 and directed to take part in a five-year National Fertilizer Plan aimed at increasing Peru's production of synthetic fertilizers. CONAFER did not think small. The cheapest project it considered would

[74] Organización de Estados Americanos, *Analisis del mercado de fertilizantes de Argentina-Bolivia-Chile-Paraguay-Uruguay* (Washington, DC, 1961), iii, 172–73; CEPAL, *El uso de fertilizantes en América Latina*, Doc. E/CN.12/760 (1966), 1–6, 8, 11–12; CEPAL, *La oferta de fertilizantes en América Latina*, Doc. E/CN.12/761 (1966), v, 102–5.

[75] Claudio Robles-Ortiz, "Agrarian Capitalism in an Export Economy: Chilean Agriculture in the Nitrate Era, 1880–1930" (Ph.D. diss., University of California, Davis, 2002).

[76] Thyrele Robertson, *The Peruvian Fertilizer Industry: Present Situation and Future Prospects* (Lima, 1968), 58; CEPAL, *El uso de fertilizantes*, 43–45, 90–95; CEPAL, *La oferta de fertilizantes*, 106–7.

[77] *Pesca* July–Aug. 1962: 52–53; Sept. 1962: 22–24, 62; Klarén, *Peru*, 320–22; O'Donnell, *Modernization and Bureaucratic-Authoritarianism*.

have spent US$20.9 million to build a natural gas-powered plant outside Paita capable of producing 200 tons of ammonia and 340 tons of urea each day.[78] Peru's military government instead gave the go-ahead to another state-owned enterprise. The Development and Reconstruction Corporation of Cuzco wanted to build a 120-Mw hydroelectric plant on the Urubamba River within sight of Machu Picchu but needed a large electricity consumer to justify the "need" for such a large project in this thinly settled area. An energy-intensive ammonia plant fit the bill nicely. National security concerns also drove this decision. The province just to the east was the site of a bloody confrontation over land reform and supported a small guerrilla army of communist insurgents. The military government hoped to head off these threats by breaking up twenty-three haciendas and distributing their land to 14,000 colonists who would be taught the latest techniques of scientific agriculture. This electrolytic fertilizer plant thus became central to the military's strategy for agrarian reform. The junta's successor, University of Texas–trained architect Fernando Belaúnde (president 1963–68, 1980–85), hoped to expand the use of settlement programs of this sort to relieve population pressure in the country, and planned to build a 1,500-kilometer highway through the jungle wilderness along the eastern edge of the Andes to connect these endeavors.[79]

The result was a fiasco. A German contractor completed this highland plant for the enormous sum of S/.648 million.[80] When it opened in 1965, it had a productive capacity *ten times* greater than existing demand for purchased nitrogen fertilizer in all of southern Peru. The plant quickly filled its warehouse and had to shut down in May 1967. Plant managers made a deal to distribute their wares on the coast far away, but when they reopened, they could not meet their production goals – or even cover the interest on their operating loans. This boondoggle had grown too big to be allowed to fail, however, so the government kept it in operation, despite chronic unprofitability. Today, travelers to Machu Picchu can still see this monument to state developmentalism. The Cachimayo plant is the only industrial complex of any significance on the railway from Cuzco, where it is still surrounded by fields cultivated with the ancient Andean digging stick (*taki chaclla*). A huge landslide caused by the 1997–98 El Niño buried the Machu Picchu hydroelectric plant under 28 million cubic meters of rock, water, and mud. Against expert advice, the Peruvian state rebuilt the plant at a cost of US$53 million. It reopened to great fanfare in 2001, proving that Peru could recover

---

[78] Equal to US$108 million in 2007; *BCONAFER* 1 (July 1963): 3–4; 4 (Jan.–Apr. 1966): 13–23; *MCONAFER* 2 (1965): 9–14; Robertson, *The Peruvian Fertilizer Industry*, 14–17, 32, 55.

[79] Klarén, *Peru*, 321, 327–32; Julio Cotler, *Clases, estado y nación en el Perú* (Lima, 1978), 345–47.

[80] Equal to US$129 million in 2007.

from natural disaster but dug the financial hole needed to replace the guano birds ever deeper.[81]

To compound this disaster, Peruvian officials allowed the guano industry to pass into oblivion in a doomed attempt to make room for other industrialization programs to succeed. Environmental conditions in the Pacific switched rapidly from La Niña to El Niño during the first months of 1965 and continued this way until the middle of 1966. Nesting data produced by CONAFER's island guardians showed that the breeding guano bird population crashed from a post-1957 high of 28.2 million in May 1964, to 12.3 million in March 1965, to three or four million birds the next year. People living in Lima and other coastal cities did not need experts to tell them something terrible was going on. Tens of thousands of starving birds descended on urban markets in search of food during the crisis. Millions more wandered listlessly along the coast waiting for death. Peru's world-famous guano industry died in full public view.[82]

This event caused enormous uproar, both in Peru and abroad. Many scientists and journalists faulted the fishmeal industry for this situation. Luis Gamarra upbraided them for destroying the "climax state" of Peru's marine environment and demanded that the industry concede to strict measures to protect the birds. The minister of agriculture, agronomist Rafael Cubas, used the opportunity to scare Peru's fishing magnates into funding a program to produce marine fish for direct human consumption. William Vogt made a brief visit on behalf of the Conservation Foundation to put in his two cents, and the Smithsonian Institution and Comité Nacional de Protección a la Naturaleza tried to drum up interest in an international conference focused on the guano birds' plight. News of this disaster even reached the United Kingdom's Prince Philip, a longtime friend of Peruvian conservationists, who "call[ed] for emergency action . . . to safeguard this unique Peruvian asset." An editorial in *El Comercio* went even further: "It would not be surprising if the extinction of the guano birds were closely followed by the extinction of the anchoveta."[83]

Representatives of the fishing industry preferred to blame El Niño for the birds' demise. Citing fish population expert Benny Schaefer, they argued that

[81] Robertson, *The Peruvian Fertilizer Industry*, 18–19, 22–25; MCONAFER 4 (1967): 14; Bernabé Calderón, "Machu Picchu vuelve a dar luz," *El Comercio* 25 May 2001: A11.

[82] CEI; *Inf.Inst.Mar* 10 (1966); Trygve Sparre to Wib Chapman, 2 Apr. 1964, p. 9; Rómulo Jordán to John Kask, 27 Jan. 1966; Alfredo Freyre to Milner Schaefer, 3 Feb. 1966, SIO-AC3 3/174, 4/178; Tovar et al., "Monthly Population Size of Three Guano Bird Species."

[83] MCONAFER 2 (1965): 13, 33–37; 4 (Jan.–Apr. 1966): 57–60, 67–69, 94–108; *Pesca* May 1966: 37–40; Sept. 1966: 21–23; *Mem.Inst.Mar* (1966): 36–38; William Warner, "Preliminary Proposal for a Conference on Peruvian Marine Research," 2 June 1966; Carlos Barreda to Milner Schaefer, 26 May 1967, 30 June 1967; Schaefer to Barreda, 6 June 1967, SIO-AC3 4/184, 4/187; Prince Philip to Felipe Benavides, 5 Apr. 1966, Biblioteca Municipal, Pueblo Libre, Peru, special exhibition, Apr. 2001.

fish were far more resilient to climatic variation than their predators: "Self-renewable resources, like anchoveta, have to maintain a certain dynamic balance. If for some reason the population decreases, the rate of renewal increases, so that the population recovers its balance." From their point of view, there was only one rational path forward: full replacement of the "inconsistent, obsolete, anti-economic guano industry" with a chemical fertilizer industry capable of expanding "at a rate compatible with population increase and just expectations of the elevation of food needs."[84]

The fishmeal industry could not hide the fact that it was facing grave problems of its own. however. Unbridled expansion had allowed producers to glut the international fishmeal market during the early 1960s, which made it difficult for small, less efficient producers to make a profit. To stay afloat, many companies acquired exorbitant debts. According to the journal *Pesca*, total industry indebtedness in Peru reached S/.5.4 billion in 1965. Companies also tried to slash their payrolls, which resulted in labor unrest. Even Pedro Beltrán's newspaper began calling for government intervention to help the industry.[85] Marine scientists also expressed worry about the ecological impact of the industry. Planktonologists working for Peru's new oceanographic research institution, the Instituto del Mar del Perú (IMARPE), detected a "notable poverty" of anchoveta eggs during the 1965 El Niño. In April 1965, IMARPE and the UN Special Fund brought in an international team of experts from the FAO to analyze the mountain of fishing statistics that Peru had accumulated over the years. They came to the troubling conclusion that the fishing industry had caused a dramatic decrease in the average weight of anchoveta caught and significantly surpassed their estimates of the fishery's maximum sustainable yield. They strongly recommended reducing the size of the fishing fleet and plant capacity to prevent the industry from destroying itself.[86]

These findings inspired President Belaúnde's government to issue a series of new regulations intended to limit the capacity of the fishmeal industry and save the guano birds. It again stopped issuing licenses for fishmeal plant expansion, created no-fishing reserves around the guano islands, and empowered CONAFER to issue fines to trespassing boats. Most importantly, it mandated a strict quota on anchoveta production during the 1965–66 fishing season of seven million metric tons and mandated the industry's complete closure from June through August (when fishing activity was at a minimum, anyway). IMARPE recommended even more stringent regulations for 1966–67, including a six-week closed season (*veda*) during the summer

[84] *Informe singular de la Sociedad Nacional de Pesquería* (Lima, 1966); SNP, *Memoria, 1964–1965* (Lima, 1965), 27–30, 43–44; SNP, *Memoria, 1965–1966* (Lima, 1966), 25–28.
[85] Equal to US$1.1 billion in 2007; *Pesca* June 1963: 15–23; July–Aug. 1963: 15–22, 52; Apr. 1964: 23; Aug. 1964: 17–23; Jan. 1965: 11–14; July 1965: 12–17; Nov. 1966, 14–20.
[86] *Mem.Inst.Mar* (1965): 23–26, 74–76; *Bol.Inst.Mar* 1, no. 4 (1967): 133–86.

to protect the new year-class of anchoveta fry (*peladilla*) and a five-day workweek for the entire industry.[87]

The SNP cooperated with most of these mandates but employed its own expert to check IMARPE's math. In April 1966, Benny Schaefer traveled to Lima at the fishing industry's expense to do a reanalysis of Peru's 1964–65 fishing data. As we have seen, Schaefer had long served as an advisor to Peru, and he was considered by many to be the Pacific's *experto número uno* when it came to marine fish populations. Schaefer was also one of the world's leading proponents of the use of the concept of maximum sustainable yield (MSY) as a tool of fishery management. During the mid-1950s, he developed a technique based on Raymond Pearl's logistic curve to quantify the reproductive dynamics of an exploited fish population using total catch statistics. The Schaefer Model, as it became known, provided a convenient management tool because it provided an objective measure of overfishing focused on fishing effort.[88]

Schaefer's intervention abruptly changed the way officials viewed the guano versus fishmeal controversy. His initial calculations showed that production in 1964–65 had indeed come close to surpassing the "long-term" MSY of the anchoveta fishery and required aggressive regulatory action. Schaefer then took the innovative step of including estimates of guano bird predation in his model of anchoveta population dynamics. This allowed him to raise his long-term estimate of MSY for the entire anchoveta fishery to a total of ten million tons per year. From this perspective, the 1965–66 El Niño had provided a windfall for the fishing industry. The abrupt decline in the guano bird population meant that humans could now safely harvest up to 9.5 million metric tons of anchoveta per year. Schaefer left it to Peru to decide whether they wanted to maximize fishmeal production or give some fish to the guano birds. "Such a choice cannot be avoided, the only question is whether it will be made on the basis of objective analysis or through... emotional arguments," Schaefer told Peruvian officials – though privately he was not planning to shed any tears if "we should 'lose' guano."[89]

[87] *Inf.Inst.Mar* 1 (1965); 7 (Oct. 1965); 14 (Dec. 1966); BCONAFER 4 (Jan.–Apr. 1966): 77–82; *Pesca* May 1965: 11.
[88] *Pesca* Nov. 1960: 32–33; Dec. 1964: 36; Tim Smith, *Scaling Fisheries: The Science of Measuring the Effects of Fishing, 1855–1955* (Cambridge and New York, 1994), 249–66; Finley, "The Tragedy of Enclosure," 99–101, 188–90, 317–18, 465–73.
[89] Carlos Otero to Schaefer, 20 Apr., 9, 10 Nov. 1965; Schaefer to Otero, 20 May, 15 Nov. 1965; Schaefer to Garth Murphy, 18 May 1966; Schaefer to Alfonso Elejalde, 19 May 1966; L. K. Boerema to Schaefer, 20 May 1966; Schaefer to Boerema, 2, 29 June 1966; Schaefer, "Progress Report Concerning Analysis of the Dynamics of the *Anchoveta* Fishery," 30 June 1966; Alfredo Freyre to Schaefer, 26 Aug. 1966; Schaefer to Freyre, 6 Oct. 1966; marginalia by Schaefer in Warner, "Preliminary Proposal for a Conference on Peruvian Marine Research," 2 June 1966, SIO-AC3, 4/178–79, 4/181, 4/187.

While Schaefer crunched these numbers, a nasty confrontation was brewing. Anchoveta fishermen were rapidly approaching the seven million ton quota set by IMARPE for 1965–66, and the minister of agriculture, who was no friend of the fishmeal industry, was prepared to shut down the fishery the moment it surpassed it. Plant owners as a group were almost evenly divided about the merits of government efforts to protect anchoveta stocks. Labor unions and independent boat owners, however, were staunchly opposed to catch quotas and a closed season. A handful of small plant owners and southern producers wanted exemptions from the national quota to help them compete against the industry's "big boys" and to prevent Chilean boats from taking the fish they left behind. Schaefer's findings enabled government officials in good conscience to allow fishing to continue well beyond the original quota until the scheduled 1 June closure date, for a total of 222 days worked during the 1965–66 season. Schaefer's calculations made it politically palatable to implement the first closed season in the history of the Peruvian fishing industry.[90]

In subsequent years, Schaefer and other population biologists helped IMARPE refine its methods for estimating the maximum sustainable yield each season and convinced fishmeal manufacturers to embrace the quota system. In many ways, these efforts constituted one of the most rigorous technocratic procedures for managing a marine fishery the world had ever seen. However, the quotas at the core of this system did little to control fishing intensity – a problem that Belaúnde's government exacerbated by providing tax breaks to companies that replaced old, wasteful factories and boats with high efficiency equipment. This meant progressively shorter fishing seasons and smaller paychecks for the industry's shrinking workforce: from 166 days in 1966–67 down to 116 days in 1971–72.[91]

The fishing industry's embrace of conservationist principles and the technocratic ideal cut out the legs from under the defenders of the guano industry. The guanay and piquero populations failed to recover from the 1965–66 El Niño, and the crisis soon began to affect other marine birds. In 1967, large flocks of hungry pelicans again showed up at markets in Lima, and scientists began noticing increased numbers of dead blue-footed boobies, terns, and other species. Some tried to blame this on chemical pesticides such as DDT, which Peruvian farmers were consuming at the rate of several thousand tons a year, but the long-term stability of the Peruvian pelican population argues strongly against this. It only declined slightly from an average of 270,000 breeding adults during the period 1957–64 to 240,000 in 1965–71, whereas in North America, brown pelican populations dropped so severely from pesticide exposure that they came to be classified as an endangered species.

[90] *Pesca* Apr. 1966: 36; May 1966: 9; Sept. 1966: 14–18; Dec. 1966: 15–18.
[91] *Mem.Inst.Mar* (1967): 18–19, 34–36; *Pesca* Jan. 1967: 12–20; Jan. 1968: 8–12; Feb. 1968: 22; June 1967: 24–26, July 1967: 29–31; Sept. 1968: 9–13; Apr. 1968: 24–27, 30; Caravedo, *Estado, pesca y burguesía*, 63, 123–24.

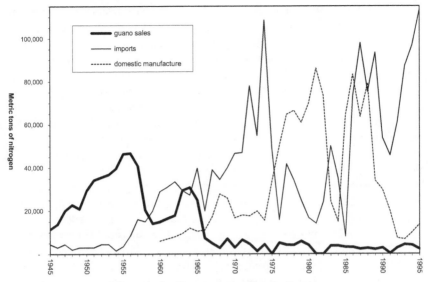

FIGURE 9.4. Nitrogen fertilizer consumption in Peru, 1945–1995.

The Peruvian Congress held one last high-level meeting to discuss the guano birds' fate in June 1967. CONAFER officials faced a chorus of opposition when they demanded even greater limitations on the anchoveta fishery and made the grave tactical error of insinuating that IMARPE scientists were stooges for the fishing industry. This poor performance sealed the fate of the guano birds.[92]

Meanwhile, Peruvian farmers struggled mightily to find a replacement for the cheap fertilizer they once enjoyed. As fig. 9.4 shows, total fertilizer consumption in Peru plummeted in 1966 as Belaúnde's government tried to reign in imports to jump-start fertilizer manufacturing. Fertilizer imports soon rebounded, but protective tariffs made them prohibitively expensive for most farmers. This situation contributed tangibly to the malaise that affected producers of food and export crops during the late 1960s and ratcheted-up pressure on the central government to do something decisive to fix this rural crisis.[93]

In October 1968, after months of secret planning, the Revolutionary Government of the Armed Forces overthrew Belaúnde's financially belea-guered, gridlocked, and scandal-ridden administration. Taking over where the previous military regime had left off, General Juan Velasco Alvarado

[92] *Mem.Inst.Mar* (1967): 21–22, 30, 65; *Bol.Inst.Mar* 1, no. 10 (1968): 523–46; 2, no. 7 (1972): 451–53; Tovar et al., "Monthly Population Size of Three Guano Bird Species"; Arriaga, "Contaminación Pacífico Suroriental," 35; Johnsgard, *Cormorants, Darters, and Pelicans*, 131, 139–40.

[93] Hopkins, *Desarrollo desigual y crisis en la agricultura*, 103–8, 185; Elena Álvarez, *Política económica y agricultura en el Perú, 1969–1979* (Lima, 1983), 155–56.

and his associates installed a bureaucratic-authoritarian state dominated by technical experts – many with training at Peru's Centro de Altos Estudios Militares. This reformist, center-left government gradually took control of the means of production in Peru, starting with unpopular foreign-owned companies such as the Peruvian Corporation of London and the International Petroleum Company. In 1969, it launched a massive agrarian reform meant to remedy a situation in which less than 1 percent of landowners owned a whopping four-fifths of all agricultural land in Peru. It eventually distributed 8.5 million hectares representing 60 percent of Peru's farm income to 375,000 families. This land reform actually went much farther than the Mexican Revolution.[94]

The Revolutionary Government of the Armed Forces also dedicated itself to bringing the full benefits of the Blue Revolution to Peru. At least at first, it allowed the fishmeal industry to operate much as before and concentrated instead on exploiting other species of marine fish. In 1969, the Revolutionary Government invited a team of experts from the Japanese Fishery Agency to develop a comprehensive plan for developing food fish production, which started off by authorizing a Japanese firm to reopen whaling operations from Paita to produce whale sausage for Peru. In 1970, it formed an agreement with the UN Development Programme and FAO to create a state-owned company charged with producing and marketing fish for direct human consumption. In 1971, the U.S.S.R. offered a credit of US$30 million to construct a massive processing facility in far northern Peru capable of producing 200,000 tons of fish per year. On the consumption side, the military government took the radical step in 1972 of prohibiting beef sales in Lima for fifteen days each month to encourage fish and chicken purchases. Thanks to these programs, marine fish consumption in Peru increased abruptly from 133,663 metric tons in 1968 to 342,455 in 1973 to 466,780 in 1980, and has never dropped below 200,000 metric tons a year, even during severe El Niño events. On average, each Peruvian today consumes a modest 40 kcal of seafood per day: about twice what they did in 1968.[95]

Increasing the supply of artificial fertilizer was also an important part of the Revolutionary Government's economic strategy. It abolished import taxes on fertilizer soon after taking power and eventually developed an elaborate program of price controls and subsidies to encourage their use. In 1975, Petroperú opened a urea plant as part of its much-anticipated Gran Complejo Industrial Petroquímico del Norte. Within two years, this factory more than tripled the supply of nitrogen fertilizer produced in Peru and took a huge bite out of fertilizer imports, freeing up precious foreign exchange. Much of this fertilizer was used to produce feed for poultry farms, which

[94] Klarén, *Peru*, 336–49; Alfred Stepan, *The State and Society: Peru in Comparative Perspective* (Princeton, NJ, 1978), pt. 2.
[95] FAO statistical databases; *Pesca* Dec. 1968: 27; Oct. 1969: 20–25; Apr. 1970: 11–14; Sept. 1970: 8–15; Mar. 1971: 8–10; July 1971: 18–21; Apr. 1972: 5.

enabled Peruvian poultry consumption to increase from 45,630 metric tons in 1968 to 140,059 in 1977. By burning up the country's petroleum reserves, Peruvian agriculture briefly escaped the ecological limitations inherent to extracting nutrients from Peru's marine environment. From 1975–91, the Peruvian fertilizer industry produced 918,225 metric tons of nitrogen fertilizer – an amount almost identical to that produced by Peru's guano birds from 1909–66. It did so, however, at unsustainable ecological and economic cost. Chicken production fell back to earth first, and per capita meat consumption in Peru actually declined from 1961 to 1991, before poultry producers began to use Peruvian fishmeal in large quantities. The removal of state protections and renewed foreign competition eventually left Peruvian fertilizer production about where it had been at the end of the War of the Pacific. In 2000, with the exception of 15,661 metric tons of guano supplied to organic farms and other traditional manures, Peru produced *zero* nitrogenous fertilizer. For the first time in its 2,500-year history, input-intensive agriculture in Peru has become almost totally dependent on foreign fertilizer supplies. Import-substituting industrialization turned out to be far more volatile as a strategy of economic development than depending on the guano birds.[96]

The Green Revolution in Mexico has received similar criticism. The growth of fertilizer production also proved impossible to sustain in Mexico during the long-lived economic crisis of the 1980s and privatization mania of the 1990s, when fiscal strictures forced the Mexican state to reduce its heavy subsidization of the industry. In November 1985, Mexico's Secretariat of Urban Development and Ecology (SEDUE) forcibly closed the fertilizer plant at Cuautitlán, throwing more than 1,000 state employees out of work, because the plant violated the 1982 Law for the Protection of the Environment requiring smokestack industries to use pollution control devices. By this date, Mexico City had become infamous for its horrific air pollution and other environmental problems caused by uncontrolled growth. This was the first time that this law had been used for this purpose and marked the symbolic beginning of a concerted governmental campaign to improve Mexico City's air quality. Even in its demise, this revolutionary fertilizer plant played an important role in Mexico's environmental history.[97] On the consumption side, input-intensive agriculture has been harshly criticized for creating enormous social inequalities. These continue to drive emigration from the countryside in central and southern Mexico to agricultural districts in northern Mexico and the United States, and to cities in both countries. In

[96] FAO statistical databases; Empresa Nacional de Comercialización de Insumos, *ENCI y la comercialización de fertilizantes,* 6, 12–14; Álvarez, *Política económica y agricultura,* 39–42, 156–61.
[97] Gracia, ed., *Estado y fertilizantes,* 80–88, 184, 209, 277–78; Otto Friedrich, "A Proud Capital's Distress," *Time* 6 Aug. 1984; Simonian, *Defending the Land of the Jaguar,* 183–84, 212.

parallel with its fertilizer advocacy, Guanomex also led a massive governmental campaign to expand the use of DDT and other organo-insecticides,
which proved to be highly toxic to birds, particularly when these chemicals
enter the marine food chain. The eventual replacement of these destructive
chemicals with less persistent, but more acutely toxic pesticides has had the
harsh side effect of increasing the hazards experienced by agricultural workers. Perhaps Mexicans can take satisfaction in the fact that they are now
eating three times more meat per capita than Peruvians.[98]

Like the guano and nitrate booms of the nineteenth century, the Green
and Blue Revolutions involved fundamental changes in humanity's relationship to nitrogen, phosphorus, and the Pacific Ocean. In the case of the
Green Revolution, the adoption of new, high-yielding varieties of grain was
premised on the availability of large quantities of concentrated fertilizer.
From Mexico, to China, to Peru, the quest to increase agricultural productivity inspired the creation of energy-intensive industries to put these
elements in usable form. In the case of the Blue Revolution, the development
of high-yielding chickens and pigs was premised on the availability of high
protein feeds. For many years, a major share of this protein came from the
Pacific coast of Peru. In both cases, these revolutions started out with the
intention of improving the living standards of Third World peoples so that
they would experience the demographic transition and avert Malthusian crisis and Marxist revolution. In the end, these programs became so entwined
with developmental politics that they transcended the ideological divisions
of the Cold War and resulted in fundamental changes to the Law of the
Sea. Both revolutions dramatically increased the world's food supply but
preferentially went to the production of meat, which enabled a portion of
the world's population to become fatter but left billions thin or thinner than
they have ever been.

The case studies in this chapter have revealed some of the environmental
costs of these programs. The Green and Blue Revolutions both had roots
in the guano industries of Mexico and Peru – further testimony of the
importance of guano to modern history. As a further legacy, environmental
scientists attained unprecedented authority over Peru's marine fisheries during the late 1960s. In both cases, however, government officials sacrificed
the guano birds on the altar of developmentalism once it became clear they
could not fulfill their aspirations for growth. As we will see in the concluding chapter, technocratic decisions of this sort ended up making the Pacific
World a much deadlier place for birds, fish, and humans.

---

[98] Angus Wright, *The Death of Ramón González: The Modern Agricultural Dilemma* (Austin,
TX, 1990); Hewitt, *Modernización de la agricultura*, 83–88; Cotter, *Troubled Harvest*,
ch. 6.

10

Conclusion

Who has made the decision that sets in motion... this ever-widening wave of death?... Who has decided – who has the right to decide – for the countless legions of people who were not consulted that the supreme value is... a sterile world ungraced by the curving wing of a bird in flight?
— Rachel Carson, *Silent Spring* (1962)

"How'd You Like to Spend Christmas on Christmas Island?"

Colin Grant[1] spent the holiday season of 1956 swimming, boating, and acquainting himself with the tropical marine life on Kiritimati (Christmas Island) – the world's largest atoll. He might have enjoyed himself, if not for a severe sunburn, a near drowning in a rip current, "a bad stomach attack," torrential rains, and clouds of flies – all made worse by the fact that he and 4,000 other British servicemen were there, not by choice, to detonate the United Kingdom's first hydrogen bomb.[2]

This locale was not the British government's first choice to test these huge weapons either. Australia prohibited nuclear tests larger than 50 kilotons in its territory. New Zealand refused to allow testing of any kind on its outlying islands. British officials briefly considered using McKean Island, an uninhabited equatorial atoll that had been brought into the British Empire as a bird sanctuary in the late 1930s but then settled on Malden and Christmas Islands in the Gilbert & Ellice Islands Colony. British and global opinion had turned strongly against atomic testing after radioactive fallout from a gigantic H-bomb exploded on Bikini Atoll had sickened and killed a number of Japanese fishermen aboard the ill-fated tuna boat the *Lucky Dragon* in

---

[1] A pseudonym.
[2] "Diary of a 'Grapple,'" 8–9, 16, 27–28 Dec. 1956; J. Hagges, *Christmas Island: The Wrong Place at the Wrong Time* (London, 1997), 17, 40, 48; Lorna Arnold, *Britain and the H-Bomb* (Basingstoke, England, 2001), 106, 142.

1954. A series of scientific reports had since shown that these tests were spreading strontium-90 and other dangerous isotopes across the face of the globe. British officials nonetheless decided to pursue the 1957–58 Grapple series of nuclear tests on the remote guano islands of the Central Pacific to demonstrate that "clean," affordable tests producing small amounts of radioactive fallout were possible, and to prove that Great Britain was still one of the Great Powers of the nuclear age.[3]

During the late months of 1956, a massive invasion force turned a sleepy coconut plantation on Christmas Island into a small nuclear city. British forces landed hundreds of vehicles and thousands of tons of equipment, laid down 35 miles of all-weather road, and built two concrete airstrips and a tank farm holding one million gallons of fuel. A rock crushing facility capable of processing 3,000 tons of material per week dug huge pits in the landscape and covered much of the island in dust. The British had no intention of staying long term and cut corners wherever they could. Almost everyone lived in cloth tents, and there was no sewage service. Regular servicemen had to defecate in the open air over long rows of metal drums filled with chemicals. Many elected to shit in the woods rather than suffer these disgusting "thunderboxes." Dysentery soon reached epidemic proportions and killed several conscripts. This epidemic was made worse by strong El Niño rains, which flooded the camps, rotted the tents, encouraged the proliferation of mosquitoes and flies, and delayed a couple of nuclear shots. Fliers repeatedly sprayed the island with DDT, but the insects soon returned.[4]

Malden, for the moment, was an island of peace. Colin Grant greatly enjoyed his one-month tour as a radio operator on this small bird island overrun by Polynesian rats. Servicemen frequently ate fresh fish caught in its lagoons and roasted feral pigs left by guano workers decades before. In his spare time, he explored the old guano workings, ancient Polynesian ruins, and visited the graves of Andrew McCulloch and his wife, two individuals who gave their lives to the guano age.[5]

A blinding flash abruptly interrupted this tranquility on Malden at 10:38 AM local time on 15 May 1957. The blast was nothing more than a "dull thump" to Grant and other soldiers stationed on Kiritimati, 750 kilometers to the north, but it set off huge fires on Malden, even though it was detonated at a "safe" distance 2,341 meters above the ground. A second, much larger blast two weeks later caused far more damage. Major General Denis Moore was one of the select few taken on a tour of ground zero soon after the Malden shots. "He was greatly moved by the sight of live birds entirely denuded of feathers wandering on this desolate surface,"

[3] Arnold, *Britain and the H-Bomb*, xi–xii, 35, 44–45, 63, 95–98, 111–16, 121, 124–27.
[4] CEI; "Diary of a Grapple," 6–7, 14, 30–31 Jan., 14 Feb., 3 Mar. 1957; Hagges, *Christmas Island*, 41, 51; Arnold, *Britain and the H-Bomb*, 103–6, 225.
[5] "Diary of a Grapple," 1, 4–5 Apr. 1957.

his wife recalled. "The sight made a vivid impression on him and he could not forget it. On a later airborne survey of the site all traces of wildlife had gone." Ernest Cox, a radiation technician sent to measure gamma radiation at ground zero, had a similar response: "We noticed no flies, no movement of lizards and no booby birds. We found several burnt and dead birds and...heard one of the three [remaining] wild pigs but we didn't dare approach too close to it. It was badly burnt and was going around in circles, blind." He was issued no protective clothing, and ten days later developed suspicious blisters that left permanent scars. The health physics crew determined that he had received 3.9 rem units of radiation during his brief stay on the island – considered well within safety limits. According to population studies done since then, this amount of radiation exposure increases a person's probability of dying from cancer by 0.3 percent; 5 rem per year is the legal exposure limit for workers in the United States.[6]

Subsequent tests left a far more striking impact on the human and avian inhabitants of Kiritimati. After producing evidence that atmospheric tests of this sort were "safe," military brass moved testing to the southern tip of Christmas Island in order to speed up logistics. Test planners nonetheless implemented elaborate safety measures, including the temporary evacuation of most of the island's Gilbertese population, who watched Disney cartoons below deck on ships during the tests. They gave little notice to the island's enormous seabird colonies, except to assign crews to clean up their destruction. The second series of British nuclear tests took place in November 1957 during peak breeding season for the blue-grey noddy (*Procelesterna cerulea*) and white-throated storm petrel (*Neofregata albigularis*). The third series took place in April 1958 during peak breeding for three species of booby, two species of frigatebird, the lesser noddy (*Anous ternuirostris*), grey-backed tern (*Sterna lunata*), and white fairy tern (*Gygis alba*). Jim Hagges and Ken McGinley both witnessed the detonation of a 3.0-megaton H-bomb on 28 April 1958. They were carefully instructed to shield their eyes and faces from the blinding blast. To Hagges, who was positioned on the northern end of the island, the detonation was like watching "an awesome, second setting sun" followed by "the momentary heat of an open furnace door." McGinley was much closer, and a colleague standing next to him "shat himself" when the shockwave hit, but everyone was too frightened to laugh. He then headed off to his bulldozer to shovel up dead and wounded birds, many of which he buried alive "with their eyes burned out of their pointed heads." The

[6] "Diary of a Grapple," 15 May 1957; Ken McGinley and Eamon O'Neil, *No Risk Involved: The Ken McGinley Story: Survivor of a Nuclear Experiment* (Edinburgh, 1991), 187–88; Arnold, *Britain and the H-Bomb*, 143; "About Christmas Island and Bomb Tests," http://www.janeresture.com/christmas-bombs/index.htm; National Academy of Sciences, *The Effects on Populations of Exposure to Low Levels of Ionizing Radiation* (Washington, DC, 1990).

fourth series of British tests in August–September 1958, and a frightening 23 nuclear detonations by the United States' Operation Dominic in April–July 1962 ensured that the world's largest nesting colony of sooty terns, numbering over 10 million, was exposed repeatedly to nuclear Armageddon. Great Britian and the United States exploded the equivalent of 31.3 million tons of nitrogen high explosive over Malden and Kiritimati, including the 7.65-megaton "Bighorn" shot detonated 30 miles to the south of Christmas Island. All told, this amounted to more than 1,000 times the destructive power of the atomic bombs that destroyed Hiroshima and Nagasaki.[7]

Diplomatic pressure from Japan, Indonesia, and Vietnam; appeals from British women's groups; and hard questioning from parliamentary MPs about the safety of residents in the Gilbert and Phoenix Islands all failed to stop the tests, but they did lead the United Kingdom and United States to give careful study to the spread of radiation contamination.[8] Radiation biologists detected small but "ubiquitous" quantities of radioactive isotopes in food, soil, water, plant, and animal tissue in the surrounding region produced by fallout from these tests. This included more than 200 picocuries of radioactivity per gram in *Scaevola* leaves from nearby Washington Island (which would have set off alarms in the Tokyo fish market) and detectable quantities in tuna fished from waters more than 4,000 kilometers to the west. These amounts were small, however, compared with the environmental mess left by nuclear detonations on Bikini and Eniwetok atolls.[9]

These studies failed to account adequately for long-term harm caused by extended exposure to low levels of radiation among the 13,950 people who officially served in the vicinity of the Christmas and Malden Island tests. General Moore went to the grave as a result of multiple myeloma, a cancer of the white blood cells, without revealing his misgivings about Malden's guano birds to anyone but his wife. Etiological studies have since demonstrated a strong association between the incidence of myeloma and occupational exposure to radiation at an advanced age. As early as 1958, various branches of the U.K. government began investigating the incidence of cancer among test veterans. A research article published in *The Lancet* in 1983 reported

---

[7] McGinley and O'Neil, *No Risk Involved*, 57–59; Hagges, *Christmas Island*, 71; Wilfrid Oulton, *Christmas Island Cracker: An Account of the Planning and Execution of the British Thermo-Nuclear Bomb Tests, 1957* (London, 1987), 275, 287 ff.; Arnold, *Britain and the H-Bomb*, 157, 161; Schreiber and Ashmole, "Sea-bird Breeding Seasons." For a comprehensive list of tests, see "Atomic Forum: An Illustrated History of Nuclear Weapons" (2006), http://www.atomicforum.org.

[8] See NAUK-FO 371/129259–129281.

[9] Ralph Palumbo, *Radionucleotide Content of Food Stuffs Collected at Christmas Island and at Other Islands of the Central Pacific during Operation Dominic, 1962* (Seattle, 1963); Palumbo et al., "Radionuclides in Foods from the Central Pacific, 1962" *Nature* 19 Mar. 1966: 1190–92; cf. Susan Shultz and Vincent Shultz. "Bikini and Enewetak Marshallese: Their Atolls and Nuclear Weapons Testing," *Critical Reviews in Environmental Science and Technology* 24 (1994): 33–118.

higher rates of leukemia and other blood cancers among test veterans. This inspired a heated political controversy within the United Kingdom, which still has not been resolved. In 1984, members of the Nuclear Test Veterans Association installed a monument on Christmas Island "dedicated to the millions of people whose lives were sacrificed on the altar of the Atomic Age." Much has also been written about indigenous Pacific Islanders who were forced to leave their homelands by these tests, but no one has yet made an accounting of the tens of millions of guano birds that these tests blinded and silenced – much less raised a monument to their memory. These intentional disasters were all premised on the belief that the world's inhabitants had to make great sacrifices to avert far greater catastrophe.[10]

Silent Spring on Isla Don Martín

The nuclear age also imposed itself irreparably on the life of Peruvian guano bird expert Enrique Ávila (1917–72). As we learned in Chapter 6, this native of the Lake Titicaca region used his relationship with William Vogt and Aldo Leopold to obtain work as Peru's first native-born professional ornithologist. Ávila repeatedly suffered ethnic and political discrimination that at one point resulted in his banishment to a tiny bird research station on Isla Don Martín. He made the best of this opportunity to live among millions of breeding birds and served as an outspoken advocate for them in the guano versus fishmeal controversy, but he eventually realized that this was a career dead end and migrated to California to obtain advanced training in the population biology of marine fish.[11] In its general features, Ávila's biography is representative of millions of aspiring professionals worldwide who have sought to use education and technical accomplishment to escape from disadvantaged backgrounds and improve the world. Men and women like him gave tremendous social impetus to the rise of scientists and technicians to political influence around the world during the past two centuries. This book has been as much their story as it has been about guano.

Ávila still had a tragic role to play in this history's climax. He eventually landed at the Puerto Rico Nuclear Center, where he took a position in the

---

[10] Inquest on Sapper William Brian Morris (1958), NAUK-TS 50/81; Inquest on death of Staff Sergeant B. E. Power (1963–70), NAUK-TS 50/140; Case of an appellant who died of leukemia (1959–62), NAUK-PIN 59/161; Incidences of leukemia among members of armed forces (1965), NAUK-PREM 13/587; Incidences of deaths from leukemia among servicemen (1965–66), NAUK-DEFE 69/415; McGinley and O'Neil, *No Risk Involved*, 61, 67, 94, 120, 150–59; Arnold, *Britain and the H-Bomb*, 240–43; E. G. Knox et al., "Cancer Following Nuclear Weapons Tests," *The Lancet* 8 Oct 1983: 856–57; Peter Wierneck et al., *Neoplastic Diseases of the Blood* (Cambridge and New York, 2003), 169, 438; Schultz and Schultz, "Bikini and Eniwetok Mashellese."

[11] Summarized from interview with Basilia Díaz, 13 June 2001; Ávila to Vogt correspondence, UW-ALA; Ávila to Sears correspondence, WHOI-MC9.

laboratory of Frank Lowman, a scientist who had gotten his start in radiation biology studying the ability of Polynesian rat populations to survive the intense radiation of H-bomb tests on Enewetak Atoll. Ávila used a variety of radiobiological techniques to study the productivity of the Peru Current using samples provided by IMARPE. He also examined levels of radioactive contamination of plankton, fishmeal, and guano from the Peruvian coast and discovered that they had indeed been affected at very low levels by nuclear tests in the Central Pacific. After working for two years with these materials, Ávila's health took a turn for the worse. He lost twenty kilograms in the course of eighteen months and had to quit his job and return to Peru. He blamed his condition on "the tropical climate," but his close friend Mary Sears immediately suspected cancer.[12]

By this time, fishery management in Peru had begun to catch up to Ávila's view of scientific conservation. As a direct legacy of the guano industry, environmental scientists attained unprecedented authority over Peru's marine ecosystem during the late 1960s. In January 1970, with UN assistance, the Revolutionary Government of the Armed Forces brought in a panel of leading foreign scientists to review the regulatory regime that governed Peru's gigantic fishmeal industry. At this point, even Benny Schaefer agreed that the government had to rein in the industry or risk irreparable damage to this valuable resource. Peru's fleet of 1,500 purse seiners had become so efficient that it only took ten days of fishing for the industry to overshoot the panel's recommended catch by a million tons. The military government promptly shut down the bigger companies but caved in to a petition by smaller producers for an extension, who proceeded to catch an additional 300,000 metric tons. All told, the industry officially landed an all-time record catch of 10.8 million metric tons during the 1969–70 season – more than 10 trillion individual fish – in just 151 days of fishing.[13]

This outcome caused great consternation among the experts involved. Major fishmeal industries were collapsing all over the world. The sardine fishery off South Africa and Namibia, the Atlantic menhaden fishery, and the North Sea and Atlanto-Scandian herring fisheries off Norway all experienced rapid decline during the late 1960s. Fisheries for the Far Eastern

---

[12] Solicitud de beca, 1960; Ávila to Sears, 13 Aug. 1960, 9 Apr. 1962, 26 Nov. 1964, 1 Mar., 18 June 1965, 8 Mar. 1968, 20 Feb. 1969; Ávila to Trygve Sparre, 9 Sept. 1963; Sears to Ernst Foyn, 20 Feb. 1969, WHOI-MC9; Ávila, *First Report on the Time and Spatial Distribution of Some of the Properties of the Peru Current* (Mayagüez, 1963); Ávila, "Radioisotopes and Stable Elements in Plankton, Fish Meal, and Guano from Perú," Report to the Atomic Energy Commission (1965); Ávila, "Nivel de radioactividad y tenores de radioisotopes en muestras de harina de anchoveta del Perú," *Revista de la Facultad de Ciencias de la Universidad Nacional de San Agustín, Arequipa* (1969).

[13] *Pesca* Feb. 1970: 10–14; Nov. 1970: 25–28; July 1971: 14; *Inf.Inst.Mar* 31 (1970): 34 (1970); Gerald Paulik, "Anchovies, Birds and Fishermen in the Peru Current," in *Environment: Resources, Pollution and Society* (Stamford, CT, 1971), 156–58, 172–76, 181–82.

sardine, California sardine, Hokkaido-Sakhalin herring, and herring catches off Iceland, in the English Channel, and southern North Sea had long since become economically extinct.[14]

A Second Panel of Experts, convened in March 1971, brought together an amazing array of international talent to discuss the limitations inherent to the scientific management of Peru's fishing industry. The heart of their discussion focused on their ability to model the population dynamics of marine fish, but it revealed a much larger conundrum facing the world's environmental managers. Benny Schaefer's logistic model suggested that an exploited population of marine fish would experience a "gentle descent into overfishing" that would be easy to detect. Other mathematical models suggested a very different reality in which at some indeterminate point, the anchoveta population could drop to near zero within a matter of months if environmental conditions changed slightly or if the stock experienced a poor year or two of new recruitment – exactly as had been observed with the California sardine. In the end, the Panel of Experts could not come to a consensus about these matters but warned emphatically: "it is of the utmost importance to set up an accurate and timely monitoring system to detect any evidence of population distress such as recruitment failure. This must then be used to reduce fishing quickly to a value that will allow the population to recover."[15]

Ávila had a keener sense of the stakes involved than most. In November 1970, he revisited Isla Don Martín for the first time in 15 years. Spring breeding should have been nearing its peak after a year of record fish recruitment, but the island was "almost totally devoid of guano birds. The warden told me that it is 4 years now that Don Martín is in that sad state. The same holds true for most of the other islands, yes including the beautiful Chinchas! Small wonder though, because the guano bird population has shrunken to a paltry 4 million individuals – thanks to the greedy exploitation of the fish-meal industry." When Ávila lived there, this single island had been capable of hosting that many birds. Spring was deadly silent on Isla Don Martín.[16]

He did not have to look far for the reason why. The smokestack plumes of at least a dozen fishmeal factories were clearly visible from the island, and if the wind was right, their stench was overpowering. A constant stream of fishing boats chugged in and out of the adjacent port of Végueta and stopped within a stone's throw of the island if they were lucky enough to encounter any fish. Ávila felt a keen sense of injustice about the way "man's craving for wealth" was allowing so much of Peru's marine resources to

---

[14] Glantz, ed., *Climate Variability, Climate Change and Fisheries*, 130–31, 214–16, 237–42, 326–29; Kobayashi et al., "Long-Term Fluctuation of the Catch of Pacific Herring"; Best, Crawford, and Elst, "Top Predators in Southern Africa's Marine Ecosystems."

[15] *Bol.Inst.Mar* 2, no. 7 (1972): esp. pp. 442–43, 445–47.

[16] Ávila to Sears, 1 Jan. 1971, WHOI-MC9.

leave the country, while "the great majority of the Peruvian population is still protein-starved to an appalling degree." The residents of Végueta had clearly forgotten the ancient origin myth of their town, in which the god Vichama turned its founder into stone – into this very island – to punish him for allowing the murder of the bird woman who gave the first Peruvians the means to grow crops for their sustenance.[17]

Under these dire circumstances, Ávila's expertise and impeccable reputation as a conservationist made him the ideal man to take command of scientific efforts to keep track of the anchoveta's status. IMARPE promptly hired him to take over as head of the Department of Anchoveta after the Second Panel of Experts concluded its work – the sort of job he had been working all of his life to attain.[18] Ávila was not a doctrinaire opponent of large-scale fishing. While living in Puerto Rico he had written the following: "The first axiom of the Conservation of Renewable Natural Resources is not 'to preserve without exploiting,' but to the complete contrary, 'to exploit *rationally* for the benefit of man.' . . . '*Rational exploitation*' implicitly mandates that the object of exploitation should be studied exhaustively, so its wise and efficient administration can be instituted, not only contemplating the interests of present society, but also *those of generations to come.*"[19]

Ávila's new position gave him an opportunity to put these views into practice, but even he did not expect such a sudden and complete collapse of the anchoveta fishery when El Niño returned. His department set a preliminary quota of 9.5 million metric tons when the 1971–72 fishing season opened in September. Meanwhile, the military government stepped up implementing a complicated program begun the previous season to reduce fleet and factory capacity while protecting small-scale producers. Early catch rates were high and the fishery closed down, as scheduled, in January–February 1972 to allow new spawn to mature. This is when the first unambiguous signs of trouble began to appear. Water much warmer than normal made an appearance several hundred kilometers off the Peruvian coast, but temperatures remained near normal close to shore from December through February. Recruitment of new young fish was nonetheless poor. Fast, decisive action to close down the fishery at this point might have averted disaster, but the Peruvian government had never taken such a radical step. It was hamstrung by the fact that fishmeal sales represented a third of the country's

[17] Ávila to Sears, 8 Mar. 1968, WHOI-MC9; Rostworowski, *Señoríos indíginas de Lima y Canta*, 144–46.

[18] Ávila to Sears,7, 29 July 1971, WHOI-MC9.

[19] Ávila's emphasis; "Investigaciones científicas conducidas por el autor en los laboratorios de biología marina de la Compañía Administradora del Guano" (Bachiller thesis, University of Arequipa, 1961), 59.

export income and a vital source of funds to pay for the government's ambitious reform program. The minister of fisheries allowed anchoveta fishing to reopen on schedule in March 1972 just when a full-blown El Niño made its appearance. Catch rates remained high for about a month, but then the anchoveta suddenly disappeared. Ávila's office recommended immediate closure of the fishery in April, once these problems became clear, but the government elected to allow fishing to continue until the scheduled end of the season in a foolhardy attempt to prevent the whole country from plunging into economic crisis. By June, exploratory craft could not find any schools of anchoveta in the whole region.[20]

Exactly why the anchoveta population crashed remains a controversial question. From studies of marine sediments and archaeological evidence, we now know that populations of anchoveta, sardine, and herring sometimes experience abrupt, lasting changes in abundance from purely natural causes. Blaming El Niño for this tragedy will, thus, always be popular.[21] We cannot give much credence to the belief that Garrett Hardin's "tragedy of the commons" is responsible for this situation, however. Peru's anchoveta fishery was among the most carefully supervised and rigorously regulated the world had ever seen when it suddenly collapsed under Ávila's attentive gaze. When we consider that First World consumers ate up practically all of this resource in the form of chicken and pork, it was a bit ridiculous for Hardin – a close follower of the crisis facing the world's fisheries – to blame Third World overpopulation and immigration for threatening the future of civilization in his follow-up essay about modern society's inability to provide for the poor.[22] Our overinflated faith in the ability of science and government to sustainably manage production from a volatile environment deserves far more blame than these other factors for bringing a silent spring to the coast of Peru. This realization should give us pause when evaluating the historical accomplishments of Peru's guano industry and when considering the merits of handing over management of the earth to a new generation of ecocrats or geoengineers.[23]

---

[20] *Bol.Inst.Mar* 2, no. 9 (1973): 562, 575, 576–87, 593–94.

[21] Francisco Chávez et al., "From Anchovies to Sardines and Back: Multidecadal Change in the Pacific Ocean," *Science* 10 Jan. 2003: 217–21; Daniel Sandweiss et al., "Geoarchaeological Evidence for Multidedadal Natural Climatic Variability and Ancient Peruvian Fisheries," *Quaternary Research* 61 (2004): 330–34; C. P. Idyll, "The Anchovy Crisis," *Scientific American* June 1973: 22–29.

[22] Contra Hardin, "The Tragedy of the Commons," 1245; Hardin, "Lifeboat Ethics: The Case against Helping the Poor," *Psychology Today* Sept. 1974: 38–43, 123–26.

[23] "Managing Planet Earth," special issue of *Scientific American* Sept. 1989; Wolfgang Sachs, "Environment and Development: The Story of a Dangerous Liaison," *The Ecologist* 21, no. 6 (1991): 252–57; James Fleming, *Fixing the Sky: The Checkered History of Weather and Climate Control* (New York, 2010).

Waking Up from a Silent Spring

The meeting of a Third Panel of Experts in July 1972 gave Enrique Ávila's department high marks for the service it provided in this difficult situation, but this was small recompense for a man who had devoted his life to the prevention of such occurrences. Ávila died of cancer later that year – probably contracted in the course of his work in Puerto Rico – without knowing whether the world's largest marine fishery would ever recover. Like most of the figures we have met in this book whose lives have intersected with guano, guano islands, and the marine organisms of the Pacific World, Ávila envisioned something much better for his life than presiding over an ever-widening wave of death and environmental destruction.

This disaster extended far beyond Peru. It contributed to a historic crisis in the world's resource supplies, culminating in the Arab Oil Embargo of 1973–74, which fueled the perception that environmental mismanagement and uneven patterns of economic development threatened the long-term prosperity of the human species. A young counterculture of "technocracy's children" sprang up around the world to question "The Quest for Truth, The Conquest of Nature, The Abundant Society," and other values that had given rise to these problems, but it did little to erode the power that technocrats had already acquired.[24] In fact, these crises probably strengthened their hand. In its best-selling 1972 book on the *Limits to Growth*, the Club of Rome pointed to the increasing scarcity of marine fish as a major threat to the world's food supply. To this group of experts, the world's fisheries provided clear proof that "pressures... not of human choosing" were destined to bring all forms of growth based on finite resources to a grinding halt – but they left the impression that people like them were best suited to saving the world. The 1972 UN Conference on the Human Environment held in Stockholm overtly insisted that expert-led development was the best way to remedy hunger and "the environmental problems of the Third World," and few UN technocrats expressed strong criticism of Blue Revolution programs over the next decade. Norman Borlaug, who won the 1970 Nobel Peace Prize as an architect of the Green Revolution, expressed great alarm regarding the anchoveta collapse and the world's falling reserves of wheat and rice. He nonetheless remained confident that science and government would prevent the crisis from expanding too far.[25]

---

[24] Theodore Roszak, *The Making of a Counter Culture: Reflections on the Technocratic Society and Its Youthful Opposition* (Garden City, NY, 1969), xiv; Eric Zolov, *Refried Elvis: The Rise of the Mexican Counterculture* (Berkeley and Los Angeles, 1999).

[25] Donella Meadows et al., *The Limits to Growth: A Report for the Club of Rome's Project on the Predicament of Mankind* (New York, 1972), 151–54; Wade Rowland, *The Plot to Save the World: The Life and Times of the Stockholm Conference on the Human Environment* (Toronto, 1973); George Kent, *Fish, Food, and Hunger: The Potential of Fisheries for*

The anchoveta crisis and climate extremes of the early 1970s did inspire aggressive action aimed at protecting the world's food supply, although much of this effort focused on maintaining levels of meat production. In 1972, U.S. poultry raisers killed more than a million birds because they could not afford the price of high-protein feed. Some militant homemakers organized a meat boycott in protest against high prices, and others called for government price controls. The California fishing industry dramatically increased its production of fishmeal from the northern anchovy but gave scientists unprecedented power to limit their efforts – to the point that they left enough fish for the endangered brown pelican. President Richard Nixon responded by empowering a former FAO technocrat, agricultural economist Earl Butz, to discourage fishmeal use by livestock raisers while encouraging "fencerow to fencerow" planting of maize and soybeans to make up for the feed shortfall. Butz became notorious for his advice to family farmers "to get big or get out." These policy changes had enormous repercussions for U.S. farming, food consumption, and public health over the next quarter century.[26] The Soviet Union experienced far deeper trouble on these fronts. After the failure of Kruschchev's "virgin lands campaign" during the early 1960s, agricultural policy within the Eastern Bloc shifted decisively toward the intensification of agrochemical use and the industrialization of meat production. Notable gains in these areas proved impossible to sustain, however, when "the two largest droughts in the history of the U.S.S.R." struck in short succession from 1972–75. The Soviet Union was already importing large quantities of frozen meat and grain from the world's neo-Europes (including the United States) but had to increase these imports markedly and divert large quantities of grain to farm animals to prevent the collapse of meat production. Critics would be wrong, however, to suggest that Soviet failure to keep up with Western consumption in these areas contributed to the end of the Cold War. As table 9.2 shows, per capita meat consumption kept climbing until the end of the Soviet Union, despite these problems. The collapse of communism was the real tragedy for meat and fish consumers in this huge region – albeit, a blessing for the natural world.[27]

These problems paled before the catastrophe that beset the African Sahel during the early 1970s. Meat had a major role to play here as well. Development projects and decolonization encouraged the northward displacement of cattle to the edge of the Sahara Desert during the 1950s and 1960s. Growing demand for meat in prosperous sectors of Nigeria and other West

---

Alleviating Malnutrition (Boulder, CO, 1987); Borlaug, "Civilization's Future: A Call for International Granaries," *Science and Public Affairs* Sept. 1973: 7–15.

[26] McEvoy, *The Fisherman's Problem*, 229–36; Carolyn Dimitri et al., *The 20th-Century Transformation of U.S. Agriculture and Farm Policy* (Washington, DC, 2005).

[27] Dronin and Ballinger, *Climate Dependence and Food Problems in Russia*, 219–66, 307–30; Barbara Jancar-Webster, *Environmental Action in Eastern Europe: Responses to Crisis* (Armonk, NY, 1993), esp. ch. 7.

African countries, in turn, encouraged high stocking rates. This resulted in an abrupt collapse of the cattle population when monsoon rains failed during the early 1970s. More than 100,000 died from famine in 1972–73, and two million ended up in refugee camps – in part because Soviet grain purchases created a bottleneck in international shipping and delayed the arrival of relief supplies. This situation again drew attention to the fact that most West Africans consumed pitiful amounts of meat and fish while exporting huge amounts of fishmeal to the First World. It also created the perception that humans were causing irreversible desertification in some parts of the globe.[28]

As in all ecological catastrophes, someone benefited from these misfortunes. The skyrocketing price for high-protein feeds inspired farmers around the world to increase the area planted in soybeans by a quarter from 1971–74. Almost half of this increase was in Brazil, where the military government provided subsidized fertilizers and other benefits to encourage soybean planting. The Great Frost of 1975, which destroyed hundreds of millions of coffee trees, provided an additional stimulus. Since then, Brazilian agribusiness has converted vast stretches of interior savanna into input-intensive soybean plantations and gained control of a huge portion of the international soybean trade. Brazil also built its own network of animal factories and became one of the world's largest chicken producers. As a consequence, per capita meat consumption in Brazil has increased by almost three times since 1972. The total area planted in soybeans around the world is now on the verge of passing one million square kilometers – an area greater than the U.S. states of California, Nevada, and Oregon combined.[29]

In an attempt to take advantage of high feed prices, the military government in Peru went against expert advice and reopened anchoveta fishing on a limited scale in 1972–73. Much of the fish caught that season was sardines – a species changeover that contributed to the replacement of the guanay by the piquero as the most numerous bird species in the region. In May 1973, the military government took even more radical action to fix this troubled industry by nationalizing the country's eighty-four remaining fishmeal companies, which involved taking on the industry's S/.10 billion of debt and paying owners an indemnity of S/.4 billion for their good stewardship of the ocean. In 1975, the government handed over the remains of the guano and

[28] Richard Franke and Barbara Chasin, *Seeds of Famine: Ecological Destruction and the Development Dilemma in the West African Sahel* (Totowa, NJ, 1980), 98–106, 158–59; Michael Glantz, ed., *The Politics of Natural Disaster: The Case of the Sahel Drought* (New York, 1976), ch. 2, 8, 11–12; Reid Bryson and Thomas Murray, *Climates of Hunger: Mankind and the World's Changing Weather* (Madison, WI, 1979).

[29] FAO statistical databases; Philip Warnken, *The Development and Growth of the Soybean Industry in Brazil* (Ames, IO, 1999), ch. 2, 5; Maxine Margolis, "Green Gold and Ice: The Impact of Frosts on the Coffee Growing Region of Northern Paraná, Brazil," *Mass Emergencies* 4 (1979): 135–44.

fishmeal industries to a state-run company, Pesca-Perú, which was given the mission to unify the management of Peru's marine environment under one entity – much like CAG had once envisioned. This gigantic enterprise greatly diversified Peru's fishing industry but failed miserably in its efforts to return fishmeal production to its glory days. Historians have greatly underestimated the significance of the anchoveta crisis in causing the developmental plans of the Revolutionary Government of the Armed Forces to run aground during the late 1970s.[30] Peru's anchoveta fishery eventually recovered from this mishandling after a hiatus lasting two decades, but its guano birds have never come close to regaining their former glory. They have joined the great whales, sea turtles, fur seals, extinct Steller's sea cow and great auk, and dozens of species of fish on an ever-growing list of valuable marine species destroyed by humanity's ecological greed.[31]

This book about the place of guano and the Pacific World in modern history started from the premise that humans have willfully ignored the history of our relationship with excrement and often failed to recognize that our relationship with the ocean and atmosphere does not function by the same rules that govern terrestrial existence. This book set out to follow these entities and the people who cared about them wherever they went – even when they moved far beyond the geographic borders and disciplinary boundaries that traditionally constrain our understanding of the past. In the process, it endeavored to uncover the existence of historical forces acting on a scale invisible to histories developed under more traditional constraints, and to demonstrate the relevance of remote territories, obscure peoples, and little-known organisms to some of the most important trends of the modern age. In the end, it has revealed some basic lessons about our moral relationship to the natural world and the rest of the human species that may be unexpected, or even unwelcome.

This book has discovered a number of these forces and trends acting on large scales over the past two centuries. First, it has demonstrated the importance of nitrogen, phosphorus, and excrement to the life of the soil in all agricultural societies, and the difficulties that can result when these humble substances are ignored. Second, this book has delineated the influence of extreme phases of the El Niño-Southern Oscillation on the timing and synchronization of historical events – often across great distances – while revealing the complexity and uniqueness of individual events at the local scale. Third, it has connected increased fertilizer and meat consumption to the emergence of a number of large-scale inequalities: from the unprecedented prosperity of neo-European societies in Australia, New Zealand, and

---

[30] Equal to US$1.0 billion and US$385 million in 2007, respectively; *Pesca* Nov. 1972: 20–22; *Bol.Inst.Mar* 3, no. 2 (1974): 46–47; Pesca-Perú, *Qué ha hecho y adonde va* (Lima, 1982); Caravedo, *Estado, pesca y burguesía*, 79–85.

[31] Callum Roberts, *The Unnatural History of the Sea* (Washington, DC, 2007).

the United States, to the near destruction of indigenous societies on Banaba and Easter Island, to the oscillating accomplishments of the citizens of Peru. Fourth, this book has established the significance of scientific conservation and the technocratic ideal to world history, their international nature, and their broad attraction to privileged social groups as well as to disadvantaged peoples, from Alexander von Humboldt to Enrique Ávila. Fifth, it has unearthed the transnational roots of modern environmental ideas and movements and revealed the centrality of fears of overpopulation to geopolitical conflict and developmental politics from World War I to the end of the Cold War. Sixth, this book has drawn attention to the existence of a Blue Revolution meant to increase the world supply of ocean fish after World War II.

The discovery of the phosphate deposits of Banaba and Nauru and the development of the Peruvian guano and fishmeal industries represent signature accomplishments of these movements, while exemplifying the environmental injustice and ecological destructiveness they often spawned. On the bright side, these accomplishments enabled a vast segment of the human species to enjoy unprecedented prosperity. These incidents taught new truths to a few observant men and women about the ecological functioning of the planet. However, these deeds also generated enormous jealousies and conflicts, and these gains took place at the cost of destroying hard-won truths about how the earth works, which were once cherished by peoples who saw themselves as the sons and daughters of the Pacific's guano birds.

These perspectives force us to qualify our understanding of some large-scale forces of world history. (1) Modern societies have tended to treat environmental degradation as a cumulative process that gnaws away at the ability of soils, forests, and animal populations to rebound from abuse; that gradually poisons our air, water, and bodies. However, small environmental alterations and tiny exposures to harm can also have abrupt consequences and large downstream effects. Environment and society are susceptible to "tipping points" and "the butterfly effect," with results that are difficult to foresee. (2) Ecological imperialism, unlike the way it has been portrayed by Alfred Crosby and Jared Diamond, required concerted colonialism and conscious exploitation of distant peoples and environments to create neo-European societies and modern inequalities. Nature did not predetermine these outcomes. Yali understood this well. (3) The development of new ways to manipulate the soil's fertility and increase food production were just as important – if not more so – than improvements in health and hygiene in bringing an end to the "biological old regime" that once limited human numbers. In some ways, the guano age gave birth to the age of soap and water. (4) The conquest and colonization of the Pacific Ocean was far more central to the development of industrial capitalism, geopolitical conflict, and international law than historians typically recognize, from whaling to the Law of the Sea. To an extent comparable to African slavery in the early modern Atlantic World, the extraction of guano, phosphates, and fish brought together a Pacific World that spanned the world's largest ocean basin. (5) Both indigenous and postcolonial societies exercised significant agency in creating the ecological order of the modern world. Even the Rapanui had reasons for voyaging to guano age Peru. We can gain great insight about how to survive in limited environments by the tribulations and resilience of peoples who learned to prosper on tiny Pacific islands. (6) Above all, this book demonstrates that large-scale perspectives are possible without overreliance on theoretical abstractions that write the agency of individuals out of history.

An ecological perspective on history has brought this book to some startling – some might say radical – conclusions. Who could have imagined that the relocation of nitrates, phosphates, and bird shit from the Pacific World would have such far-reaching repercussions for the Industrial Revolution and humanity's power to mine and graze the earth, geoengineer its surface, and wage war? Who might have guessed that a global climate anomaly centered in the equatorial Pacific during the late 1910s could bring the workers of the world to the cusp of revolution, trigger the realignment of empires, and throw open the way for the most deadly pandemic of the industrial age? How will we come to grips with the realization that ecological thinking and our faith in expertise played such important roles in cursing humanity with a Second World War and saddling us with a global economy premised on growth? These empirical discoveries seem less of a surprise, however, when we recognize how little attention has been given to the Pacific Ocean's place in world history. From an ecological point of view, we should expect the abrupt opening of the world's largest environmental realm to have gigantic consequences. This book has not argued that ecological factors were the main driving force behind all these events, merely that they were essential contributors to a conjuncture of causes responsible for these great transformations.

As amazing as these conclusions may still seem, they may understate the long-term impact of these trends in the grand scheme of earth history. Scientists concerned with the changes we are foisting on the environment have begun referring to our current epoch as the Anthropocene, the "human era." Some have proposed that this era began at the end of the eighteenth century with the invention of the steam engine and progressive changeover from solar-derived forms of energy to the combustion of fossil fuels. Carbon compounds have been steadily accumulating in the atmosphere and ocean with global warming and ocean acidification as inevitable results.[32] Others point out that the intensification of agriculture and expansion of pastoralism on a global scale between 2,500 and 8,000 years ago also brought about

[32] Paul Cruzten, "Geology of Mankind," *Nature* 31 Jan. 2002: 23; Crutzen and Will Steffen, "How Long Have We Been in the Anthropocene Era?" *Climatic Change* 61 (2003): 251–57.

significant planetary alterations. In fact, these changes may have initiated
a process, now long underway, that has uncoupled the evolution of earth
systems from celestial cycles affecting the amount of energy that reaches
us from the sun.[33] We are accumulating evidence that human pandemics
and alteration of forest cover have affected regional climate, atmospheric
chemistry, and perhaps contributed to global climate oscillations, such as
the Little Ice Age.[34] Meanwhile, conservation biologists are increasingly
alarmed by the homogenization of biodiversity and high rate of extinction
our activities are bringing about.[35] (These trends are most obvious among
birds and other endemic life on tropical islands.)[36] Environmental historian
John McNeill played a significant role in the initiation of this discussion by
demonstrating how the cumulative impact of human activities since 1900
has created a situation qualitatively different from the rest of our history as
a species. Humans have become "the dominant animal" on earth.[37] These
assertions are not entirely new. More than two centuries ago, the Comte de
Buffon and Alexander von Humboldt made similar observations regarding
environmental change during what they called the "Epoch of Man" – well
before George Perkins Marsh and Antonio Stoppani.[38]

Which of these changes is destined to leave a detectable impact on the
earth's lithosphere millions of years after our species has gone extinct? How
might an extraterrestrial geologist or newly evolved race of scientists identify
the Anthropocene? The international body that decides how scientists divvy
up deep time into eons, eras, and epochs must identify such a criterion to
officially declare the Anthropocene as a unique age of earth's history. It is
not yet clear whether the ongoing "sixth mass extinction" will be readily
apparent in the paleontological record millions of years from now in a
way that can be readily distinguished from the rest of the era since the
last ice age. The same is true for contributions by preindustrial agriculture.

[33] William Ruddiman, "The Anthropogenic Greenhouse Ear Began Thousands of Years Ago," *Climatic Change* 61 (2003): 261–93; "The Early Anthropocene," special issue of *The Holocene* 21, no. 5 (2011).

[34] Gordon Bonan, "Frost Followed the Plow: Impacts of Deforestation on the Climate of the United States," *Ecological Applications* 9 (1999): 1305–15; Richard Nevle and Dennis Bird, "Effects of Syn-Pandemic Fire Reduction and Reforestation in the Tropical Americas on Atmospheric CO_2 during European Conquest," *Palaeogeography, Palaeoclimatology, Palaeoecology* 264 (2008): 25–38.

[35] Michael Samways, "Editorial: Translocating Fauna to Foreign Lands: Here Comes the Homogenocene," *Journal of Insect Conservation* 3 (1999): 65–66; Samuel Turvey, ed., *Holocene Extinctions* (Oxford, 2009).

[36] Steadman, "Prehistoric Extinctions of Pacific Island Birds"; Anthony Cheke and Julian Hume, *Lost Land of the Dodo: An Ecological History of Mauritius, Réunion and Rodrigues* (New Haven, 2008).

[37] John McNeill, *Something New Under the Sun: An Environmental History of the Twentieth-Century World* (New York, 2001); Paul Ehrlich and Anne Ehrlich, *The Dominant Animal: Human Evolution and the Environment* (Washington, DC, 2008).

[38] Glacken, *Traces on the Rhodian Shore*, ch. 14; Cushman, "Humboldtian Science."

Radioisotopes left at Kiritimati, Eniwetok, and other locales scarred by the nuclear age will turn out to be ephemeral, thanks to the relentless process of radioactive decay. New soils created by humans (known as anthrosols) also have poor potential for long-term preservation.[39]

A prime candidate for such a criterion is eminently tied to the historical developments described in this book. Enormous deposits of eroded sediment are accumulating at the end of the world's rivers. This has been true since the first river flowed into the ocean. Now, so-called dead zones are forming at the mouths of the Mississippi, Yangtze, Danube, and other rivers that flow through heavily populated and cultivated regions. These zones are not really dead; they are choked by the over-proliferation of microscopic life fed by unprecedented inputs of reactive nitrogen and phosphorus compounds flowing from farm and sewer to the sea. Unlike most aquatic creatures we value, these organisms can thrive in environments lacking oxygen. The torrent of dead organic matter, nutrients, silt, heavy metals, and synthetics reaching the seafloor in these eutrophic locales is certainly unique in the planet's history, and these new forms of "made ground" are accumulating in quantities so large and dispersed across the face of the earth that they are increasingly likely to survive somewhere even after eons of geological change. The same process is affecting lakebed sediments on a smaller scale.[40] Ongoing research suggests that abrupt alterations in the nitrogen cycle also accompanied mass extinction at the Permian–Triassic boundary, the worst such event in earth history.[41]

From this point of view, we already have good reason to declare 1830 as year one of the Anthropocene. In that year, seaborne merchants finally realized Mariano de Rivero's dream by exporting the first shipments of Atacama nitrates to England. A decade later, they followed suit with Peruvian guano.

[39] Paul Voosen, "Science: Geologists Drive Golden Spike toward Anthropocene's Base," *Greenwire* 17 Sept. 2012, http://eenews.net/public/Greenwire/2012/09/17/1; Jan Zlasiewicz et al., "Are We Now Living in the Anthropocene?" *GSA Today* 18, no. 2 (2008): 4–8; "The Anthropocene: A New Epoch of Geological Time?" special issue of *Philosophical Transactions of the Royal Society A* 369 no. 1938 (2011); Whitney Autin and John Holbrook, "Is the Anthropocene an Issue of Stratigraphy or Pop Culture?" *GSA Today* 22, no. 7 (2012): 60–66; S. J. Gale and P. G. Hoare, "The Stratigraphic Status of the Anthropocene," *The Holocene*, published online 6 July 2012, http://hol.sagepub.com/content/early/2012/07/06/0959683612449764.abstract.
[40] Galloway and Cowling, "Reactive Nitrogen and the World"; Fred Mackenzie et al., "Century-Scale Nitrogen and Phosphorus Controls of the Carbon Cycle," *Chemical Geology* 190 (2002): 13–32; Howard Dalton and Richard Brand-Hardy, "Nitrogen: The Essential Public Enemy," *Journal of Applied Ecology* 40 (2003): 771–81; James Elser, "A World Awash with Nitrogen," *Science* 16 Dec. 2011: 1504–5.
[41] Genming Luo et al., "Enhanced Nitrogen Fixation in the Immediate Aftermath of the Latest Permian Marine Mass Extinction," *Geology* 39 (2011): 647–50; Shane Schoepfer et al., "Increasing Nitrogen Limitation at the P-Tr Boundary: A Pan-Oceanic Phenomenon?" Geological Society of America *Abstracts with Programs* 43, no. 5 (2011): 506; C. Jia et al., "Microbial Response to Limited Nutrients in Shallow Water Immediately after the End-Permian Mass Extinction," *Geobiology* 10 (2012): 60–71.

These substances broke open the bottleneck in the nitrogen cycle that had limited northern production of workhorse chemicals, explosives, food and fodder, which in turn have been used to feed and fatten unprecedented numbers of people, manufacture synthetic chemicals and materials never before seen, and heave out mountains of coal, copper, silver, and gold. The Haber-Bosch process accelerated a trend already long underway and detectable in lake sediments.[42] Nitrogen compounds have turned the Andean legend of El Dorado into a reality, down to nitrogen-based cyanide now used to leach gold from its ore. Unfortunately, they are also choking our lungs, poisoning our forests, warming the planet, and making the ocean, lakes, and soil inhospitable to many forms of life. Reactive nitrogen – not carbon dioxide, DDT, or plutonium – is the world's most dangerous chemical, at least for now. Its growing abundance will soon create a global phosphate bottleneck, which will make the world's finite phosphate reserves all the more precious and magnify the ecological impact of phosphate runoff.[43] Our waste nitrogen and phosphate is likely to leave a mark that will last until our planet dies in the red blazing fire of our aging sun.

Who, then, was responsible for the "ever-widening wave of death" that has left so much of the world "ungraced by the curving wing of a bird in flight"? Rachel Carson knew the answer. She also had many connections to the people and places in this history. Like Enrique Ávila, she aspired to become a marine scientist, but social discrimination stood in the way of this pursuit, and she received enormous help from Robert Cushman Murphy and William Vogt in pursuing an alternative career as an environmental writer. The Murphys went on to play a foundational role in the movement against indiscriminate spraying of DDT and other persistent pesticides, and for a time, held up Peru's guano industry as a better way for society to treat its birds.[44] Both Murphy and Vogt attended the official party celebrating the publication of *Silent Spring*. All of these prophets of the age of ecology faced a phalanx of opposition from experts convinced that they understood better the workings of nature. Murphy even carried Carson's casket up the aisle of Washington Cathedral when she passed on prematurely from cancer, at an age only two years older than Ávila when he died.[45] Carson would have concluded that the poisoned, paved over wetlands of Long Island, the charred surface of Christmas Island, and the silent spring on Isla Don Martín were all the result of decisions made by "the authoritarian temporarily

[42] Gordon Holtgrieve et al., "A Coherent Signature of Anthropogenic Nitrogen Deposition to Remote Watersheds of the Northern Hemisphere," *Science* 26 Dec. 2011: 1545–48.

[43] Josep Peñuelas et al., "The Human-Induced Imbalance between C, N and P in Earth's Life System," *Global Change Biology* 18 (2012): 3–6.

[44] Murphy, "Peru Profits from Sea Fowl," *National Geographic Magazine* Mar. 1959: 395–413.

[45] Linda Lear, *Rachel Carson: Witness for Nature* (New York, 1997), 154–55, 180–82, 276, 305–7, 319, 422, 481, 555 n. 65.

entrusted with power... during a moment of inattention by millions to whom beauty and the ordered world of nature still have a meaning that is deep and imperative."[46]

The most disturbing finding of this book was the discovery that conscious-ness of nature's limitations has often provided authoritarians and experts with a pretext for increasing their power. In the drive to feed and protect their own people, all too often, they used their authority to attack, dis-place, and destroy entire species and ethnicities – from guano birds and anchovies to Banabans, Japanese, and Jews. This explains much about *how* experts attained such authority over matters of life and death. Capitalists, fascists, and communists were not the only perpetrators of these sins. The widespread conviction that one ethnicity, nation, or species deserves to exist at the expense of another explains much about *why* our species intention-ally committed these actions. Our carnivorous craving for meat and other emblems of high living standards only intensified these beastly tendencies.

Such harsh realizations risk paralyzing us with pessimism. Therefore, it is vital to end this book with some glimmer of hope. The main beneficiaries of the opening of the Pacific World have sometimes been forced to pay for their environmental sins. In 2001, 134 years after Bryce, Grace, & Co. was founded to outfit guano ships off the coast of Peru and started its climb to become one of the world's foremost capitalist institutions, W. R. Grace & Co. filed for bankruptcy. It did so because of enormous liability for deadly asbestos contamination in Libby, Montana – this after surviving dispossession by Peru's Revolutionary Government of the Armed Forces and another massive lawsuit involving cancer-causing chemical pollution in Massachusetts, as portrayed in A Civil Action, the bestselling book and feature film starring John Travolta. Grace & Co. might have faced discipline sooner if the Environmental Protection Agency had not ignored a 1982 report that clearly linked high cancer risks to Libby's vermiculite processing facility, a decision that suspiciously coincided with the involvement of J. Peter Grace on a Reagan administration commission to dismantle the federal government's regulatory apparatus.[47]

The guano islands of the Central Pacific are now on their way to ecologi-cal recovery from the guano age. During the 1960s, conservation biologists began eradicating rats, cats, and pigs introduced by guano miners to the region. On Jarvis Island, they used feline panleukopenia virus to complete the job. This has worked wonders for the marine bird populations of Baker, Howland, and Jarvis Islands, which are now protected as U.S. National Wildlife Refuges. Despite years of thermonuclear testing, small islets in Kiritimati's vast central lagoon continued to provide sanctuary for

---

[46] Carson, *Silent Spring*, 127.
[47] Living on Earth, "Libby's Asbestos Legacy," broadcast 29 June 2001; "EPA Investigates Itself," broadcast 28 July 2000, http://www.loe.org/shows.

burrowing petrels and shearwaters. They are now repopulating other bird islands where these introduced predators have been extirpated. This huge atoll once again hosts the world's largest colony of sooty terns, and the citizens of Kiribati hope these birds will become popular with ecotourists. Even heavily disturbed habitats can play a role in conservation. John Arundel and Mouga's abandoned coconut plantations on Flint and Caroline Islands now serve as an important refuge for the rare coconut crab (*Birgus latro*). Nature has proven remarkably resilient on the remote guano islands of the Central Pacific.[48]

The same cannot be said for Banaba, Nauru, and other phosphate islands. Miners have systematically removed forest, fruit trees, and topsoil to get at high-grade deposits below. In the case of Nauru, mining has directly disturbed nine-tenths of the island's total surface area and left behind a karst limestone landscape so rugged that it is impossible to walk across. The process of primary succession and soil formation on Nauru has been excruciatingly slow. Native *Calophyllum* and *Ficus* trees have begun to reclaim older mined areas, but many undisturbed forest remnants has been overtaken by invasive guava (*Psidium guajava*) and *Lantana*. (Easter Island is undergoing a similar takeover by these same plant species and a plague of horses.) Groves of fruit-bearing coconut and pandanus on Nauru are gone for good. Meanwhile, the habitable outer rim of the island is extremely vulnerable to rising sea level. On the Indian Ocean's largest phosphate island, systematic deforestation, surface removal, and dust production have almost doomed to extinction Abbott's booby (*Parasula abbotti*) and the Christmas Island frigatebird (*Fregata andrewsii*), even though this Australian-ruled territory is now a national park. Like St. Helena and Mauritius for a previous age, these tropical island edens have become international symbols for the unsustainability of industrial civilization.[49]

In Peru, the anchoveta fishery recovered spectacularly during the late 1980s. This inspired substantial reinvestment in the fishing industry during the privatization binge of the 1990s, leading to fears that the industry would repeat the errors of the past. During the powerful El Niño of 1997–98, the authoritarian government of Alberto Fujimori (president 1990–2000) rigorously enforced IMARPE's recommendation to close the fishery completely, and it quickly recovered. From 1989 to 2008, Peru produced an annual average of 8.1 million metric tons of marine fish from its territorial waters, much of it destined for export. Some fishmeal, however, now goes to feed chickens raised in industrial enclosures lining Peru's desert coast, which

---

[48] Manuel Nogales et al., "A Review of Feral Cat Eradication on Islands," *Conservation Biology* 18 (2004): 310–19; *2008 IUCN Red List*.

[49] Harley Manner et al., "Phosphate Mining Induced Vegetation Change on Nauru Island," *Ecology* 65 (1984): 1454–65; *2008 IUCN Red List*; Carl McDaniel and John Gowdy, *Paradise for Sale: A Parable of Nature* (Berkeley and Los Angeles, 2000).

supply the country's ubiquitous fast-food restaurants serving *pollo a la brasa*.[50]

With this renewed competition, Peru's guano birds have failed to regain anything resembling their former numbers. The main species are stable, but the Humboldt penguin and potoyunco are in immanent danger of extinction. Nevertheless, a new generation of conservationists is trying to make use of their guano. In 1997, the Fujimori administration created the Proyecto Especial de Promoción del Aprovechamiento de Abonos Provenientes de Aves Marinas (PROABONOS), a parastatal company modeled after CAG. It now supplies fertilizer to certified organic farms in Peru and a few hundred tons each year to farms in the industrial North. Someday soon, the organic quinoa and Peruvian asparagus imported by your local supermarket may contain nitrogen that passed through the gut of a guano bird. From 1986 to 2007, PROABONOS and its predecessor harvested 342,637 metric tons of guano – the same quantity that Peru's guano birds were once capable of producing in a single year.[51]

Enrique Ávila's family faced hard times when its only breadwinner died from cancer. For a time, Basilia Díaz ended up living in a shantytown on Lima's outskirts, and she lost most of her possessions, including most of Enrique's archive of professional papers, when a torrential rainstorm flooded her house during the El Niño of 1982. The Ávila family's small highland ranch near Lake Titicaca with its beautiful waterfall also no longer exists. It was destroyed to make way for a massive concrete plant that has covered the region with dust. Nevertheless, Enrique's dogged attempt to improve his family's status through education eventually paid off. They taught their son Yuri English and math skills that he used to obtain an engineering degree and employment in the United States. He now lives in New Jersey and supports his mother and sister from income derived from his engineering practice.[52]

Peruvians have also found new uses for old relics of the guano and fishmeal industries. The concrete tower that once housed the Ministry of Fisheries is now home to Peru's Museo de la Nación. The hollowed-out palace built for CAG's managers in the 1920s is now a sweatshop producing cutrate clothing for Lima's working class. Paracas National Park and Marine Reserve was originally established in the 1960s as an automobile park to protect remnants of the Paracas culture but now protects the Bahía de

---

[50] FAO statistical databases; *Pesca* Mar.–Apr. 1994: 5, Sept.–Oct. 1996: 3, Nov.–Dec. 1996: 9–11; Antonio Zapata and Juan Carlos Sueiro, *Naturaleza y política: El gobierno y el Fenómeno del Niño en el Perú, 1997–1998* (Lima, 1999).

[51] PROABONOS, *Memoria anual 1997*, 5, 7; PROABONOS, *Memoria anual 1998*, 14–16, 19; PROABONOS, *Memoria anual 1999*, 10–12; Armando Rivera Calle, personal communication, June 2001; PROABONOS, "Presentación," (2008), available at http://www.agrorural.net/agrorural.

[52] Díaz interview.

Independencia and several guano islands.[53] On Isla Don Martín, the old marine biology station that Enrique Ávila built still stands almost how he left it, but outside things could not be more different. The island is now mostly barren, with a few vultures perched ready to take advantage of another animal's demise. In its glory days under CAG, the entire island was one continuous squawking colony. Looking east toward the coast, one can see giant *bolicheras* chugging in and out of port and the unmistakable plumes of several fishmeal plants. That pungent "smell of money" comes from fishmeal, not from guano like it used to. The island is silent, except for the sound of the surrounding sea. Spring will always be silent on Isla Don Martín as long as we continue to hunger for chicken from the sea.

But the possibility of another guano age still exists. Surging prices for petroleum, synthetic fertilizer, and organic food are beginning to influence the relationship between guano and fishmeal.[54] Guano could suddenly become quite valuable under a carbon-trading scheme to avert global warming. If the course of civilization does not change soon, however, the Pacific Ocean's other guano islands are doomed. Even modest amounts of sea-level rise will drown these low-lying atolls. Banaba and Nauru may soon be the only remaining specks of land left in the vast expanse of equatorial ocean between the Galápagos and Solomon Islands – and the final refuge for marine birds that populate this region. The dead guano birds on Christmas and Malden Islands told nuclear test participants that they were putting their own lives at great risk. Perhaps this book will make us realize our own connection to these remote places before it is too late to save them – and ourselves. We can start by recalling the ways of Don Pedro Guaneque, recognizing the guano birds as our ancient kin, and using their excrement to make the land and sea healthy once again.

[53] Marcia Bonta, "A Peruvian Safari." *Americas* Mar.–Apr. 1986: 16–23.
[54] Simón Romero, "Peru Guards Its Guano as Demand Soars," *New York Times* 30 May 2008.

Select Bibliography

Manuscript, Picture, and Photograph Collections

The Advertising Archive, United Kingdom. http://www.advertisingarchives.co.uk

Auckland City Libraries, Special Collections, New Zealand. John Webster Papers.

Berlin-Brandenburgische Akademie der Wissenschaften, Humboldt Forschungsstelle, Berlin, Germany.

Biblioteca Nacional del Perú, Oficina de Investigaciones, Lima, Peru.

Denver Public Library, Western History/Genealogy Department, Denver, Colorado. CONS76, William Vogt Papers.

"Diary of a 'Grapple,'" 1956–1957. "Christmas Island Remembered" (2004). http://www.christmas-island.org/diary/galleries/read-off-page.htm.

Ministerio de Agricultura, Proyecto Especial de Promoción del Aprovechamiento de Abonos Provenientes de Aves Marinas (PROABONOS), Archivos de la Compañía Administradora del Guano/Corporación Nacional de Fertilizantes, Callao, Peru.

Archivo de Admón, Zona Norte.

Archivo de Fotos.

Archivo de la Estación de Biología Marina, Isla Don Martín, near Huacho, Peru.

Ministerio de Transporte, Comunicación, Vivienda y Construcción, Centro de Documentación e Información, Archivo del Ministerio de Fomento y Obras Públicas, Lima, Peru.

National Archives, Kew, United Kingdom.

CO, British Colonial Office Records.

FO, British Foreign Office Records.

Ohio University Libraries, Manuscripts and Special Collections, Athens, Ohio. Edward Willis Scripps Papers. http://www.library.ohiou.edu/archives/mss/mss-117.html.

Pacific Manuscripts Bureau, Australian National University, Canberra, Australia.

PMB 14, Diary of H. I. N. Moouga, 1889–1891 (microfilm).

PMB 494, John T. Arundel, "Sundry Data of My Life," 1865–1892 (microfilm).

PMB 497, Albert F. Ellis, Miscellaneous Papers and Correspondence, 1900–1951 (microfilm).

PMB 1139, Joseph Meek Papers Relating to Lever Pacific Plantations Ltd., 1894–1928 (microfilm).
PMB 1227, Arundel Family Papers, 1803–1935 (microfilm).
Royal Geographical Society, London, United Kingdom. WSR, William Scoresby Routledge and Katherine Routledge Collection of Easter Island materials.
Scripps Institution of Oceanography Archives, University of California, San Diego, La Jolla, California.
  AC3, University of California, Institute of Marine Resources, Records of the Office of the Director.
  AC5, Scripps Institution of Oceanography, Biographical Files.
  AC6, Scripps Institution of Oceanography, Subject Files Records.
  AC40, American Tunaboat Association, Records.
  "History in the News," 1919–1933.
  MC2, Milner Bailey Schaefer Papers.
Smithsonian Institution Archives, Institutional History Division, Washington, DC. Joseph Henry Papers.
State Library of New South Wales, Sydney, Australia. Joseph Banks Papers. http://www.sl.nsw.gov.au.
University of Wisconsin Digital Collections, Madison, Wisconsin. Aldo Leopold Archives. http://digital.library.wisc.edu/1711.dl/AldoLeopold.
University of Washington, School of Marine Affairs, Seattle, Washington. Warren S. Wooster Papers (private collection).
Woods Hole Oceanographic Institution, Data Library and Archives, Woods Hole, MA. MC9, Mary Sears Papers.

Oral Interviews

Aurora Chirinos de Vildoso, Callao, Peru, 11 June 2001.
Basilia Díaz viuda de Ávila, Lima, Peru, 13 June 2001.
Rómulo Jordán Sotelo, Lima, Peru, 16 June 2001.
Abelardo Vildoso, Callao, Peru, 11 June 2001.
Warren Wooster, Seattle, Washington, 9 Jan. 2005.

Periodicals

Boletín científico de la Compañía Administradora del Guano (Lima) 1–2 (1953–1955).
Boletín de la Compañía Administradora del Guano (Lima) 1–38 (1925–1962).
Boletín de la Corporación Nacional de Fertilizantes (Lima) 1–5 (1963–1967).
Boletín del Comité Nacional de Protección a la Naturaleza (Lima) 1–20 (1944–1970).
Boletín del Cuerpo de Ingenieros de Minas (Lima) no. 1–108 (1902–1926).
Boletín del Instituto de Investigación de los Recursos Marinos (Callao) 1, no. 1–5 (1963–1964).
Boletín del Instituto del Mar del Perú (Callao) 1–2 (1964–1974).
Boletín del Ministerio de Fomento (Lima) 1–9 (1903–1911).
Der Fischerbote (Cuxhaven, Germany) 1–29 (1906–1937).
Food and Agriculture Organization of the United Nations. *Fertilizer Yearbook* 12–53 (1962–2003).

Informe del Instituto de Investigaciones de los Recursos Marinos (Callao) 1–28 (1962–1964).
Informe del Instituto del Mar del Perú (Callao) 1–20 (1964–1970).
IUCN Red List of Threatened Species (2008). http://www.iucnredlist.org
Memoria anual del Instituto del Mar del Perú (Callao) 1964–1967, 1969, 1972.
Memoria anual del Proyecto Especial de Promoción del Aprovechamiento de Abonos Provenientes de Aves Marinas (Callao) 1997–1999.
Memoria del Directorio de la Compañía Administradora del Guano (Lima) 3–54 (1912–1963).
Memoria de la Corporación Nacional de Fertilizantes (Lima) 1–2, 4 (1964–1965, 1967).
Memoria del Ministerio de Fomento (Lima) 1, 10–13 (1896, 1906–1909).
Memorial de ciencias naturales y de industria nacional y extranjera (Lima) 1–3 (1827–1829).
New York Times 1857-present. ProQuest Historical Newspapers.
Pesca (Lima) 1–27 (1960–1973).
Pesca y caza (Lima) 1–9 (1950–1959).
La Prensa (Lima) 1909–1910, 1953–1954.
United States. Department of Commerce. National Oceanic and Atmospheric Administration. *Monthly Climatic Data for the World.* 17–60 (1964–2007).

Books, Articles, and Dissertations

"Address by Sir William Crookes, President." In *Report of the Sixty-eighth Meeting of the British Association for the Advancement of Science.* London, 1899.
Anderson, Warwick. "Excremental Colonialism: Public Health and the Poetics of Pollution." *Critical Inquiry* 21 (1995): 640–69.
Anker, Peder. *Imperial Ecology: Environmental Order in the British Empire, 1895–1945.* Cambridge, MA, 2001.
Arriaga, Pablo Joseph de. *The Extirpation of Idolatry in Peru.* 1621; Lexington, KY, 1968.
Belaúnde Guinassi, César. *La legislación pesquera en el Perú.* Lima, 1963.
Bermúdez, Oscar. *Historia del salitre desde sus orígenes hasta la Guerra del Pacífico.* Santiago de Chile, 1963.
Bonilla, Heraclio. *Guano y burguesía en el Perú.* Lima, 1974.
Boserup, Ester. *The Conditions of Agricultural Growth: The Economics of Agrarian Change under Population Pressure.* Chicago, 1965.
Busch, Briton. *The War against the Seals: A History of the North American Seal Fishery.* Toronto, 1985.
Bustíos Romaní, Carlos. *Cuatrocientos años de la salud pública en el Perú, 1533–1933.* Lima, 2004.
Carson, Rachel. *Silent Spring.* New York, 1962.
Chalhoub, Sidney. *Cidade febril: Cortiços e epidemias na corte imperial.* São Paulo, 1996.
Cohen, Benjamin. *Notes from the Ground: Science, Soil and Agricultural Improvement in the American Countryside.* New Haven, 2009.
Comisión Económica para América Latina. *El uso de fertilizantes en América Latina.* Doc. E/CN.12/760 (10 Oct. 1966).

Connelly, Matthew. *Fatal Misconception: The Struggle to Control World Population.* Cambridge, MA, 2008.

Corbin, Alain. *The Foul and the Fragrant: Odor and the French Social Imagination.* Cambridge, MA, 1986.

Craven, Avery. *Soil Exhaustion as a Factor in the Agricultural History of Virginia and Maryland, 1606–1860.* Urbana, IL, 1925.

Creighton, Charles. *A History of Epidemics in Britain.* Cambridge, 1894.

Crosby, Alfred. *Ecological Imperialism: The Biological Expansion of Europe, 900–1900.* Cambridge and New York, 1986.

Cueto, Marcos. *The Return of the Epidemics in 20th-Century Peru.* Brookfield, VT, 2001.

Cueto, Marcos, and Jorge Lossio. *Inovación en la agricultura: Fermín Tangüis y el algodón en el Perú.* Lima, 1999.

Cushman, Gregory T. "The Lords of Guano: Science and the Management of Peru's Marine Environment, 1800–1973." Ph.D. dissertation, University of Texas at Austin, 2003. http://www.lib.utexas.edu/etd/d/2003/cushmangto32/cushmangto32.pdf.

"The Struggle over Airways in the Americas, 1919–1945: Atmospheric Science, Aviation Technology, and Neocolonialism." In *Intimate Universality: Local and Global Themes in the History of Weather and Climate.* Sagamore Beach, MA, 2006.

"Humboldtian Science, Creole Meteorology, and the Discovery of Human-Caused Climate Change in Northern South America." *Osiris* 26 (2011): 19–44.

Davis, Mike. *Late Victorian Holocausts: El Niño Famines and the Making of the Third World.* London and New York, 2001.

Diccionario biográfico de peruanos contemporáneos. Lima, 1917, 1921.

Diccionario histórico y biográfico del Perú. Lima, 1986.

Doughty, Robin. *The Eucalyptus: A Natural and Commercial History of the Gum Tree.* Baltimore, 2000.

Drayton, Richard. *Nature's Government: Science, British Imperialism, and the "Improvement of the World."* New Haven, 2000.

Dronin, Nikolai, and Edward Bellinger. *Climate Dependence and Food Problems in Russia, 1900–1990.* Budapest, 2005.

Ellis, Albert. *Ocean Island and Nauru.* Sydney, 1936.

Mid-Pacific Outposts. Aukland, 1946.

Enciclopedia ilustrada del Perú. Edited by Alberto Tauro. Lima, 1987.

Fischer, Steven. *Island at the End of the World: The Turbulent History of Easter Island.* London, 2005.

Fischer-Kowalski, Marina, and Helmut Haberl, eds. *Socioecological Transitions and Global Change: Trajectories of Social Metabolism and Land Use.* Cheltenham, England, 2007.

Fitzgerald, Deborah. *Every Farm a Factory: The Industrial Ideal in American Agriculture.* New Haven, 2003.

Flader, Susan. *Thinking Like a Mountain: Aldo Leopold and the Evolution of an Ecological Attitude toward Deer, Wolves, and Forests.* Columbia, MO, 1974.

Galloway, J., and E. Cowling, "Reactive Nitrogen and the World: 200 Years of Change." *Ambio* 31 (2002): 64–71.

Garden, Don. *Droughts, Floods & Cyclones: El Niños That Shaped Our Colonial Past.* Melbourne, 2009.

Gergis, Joëlle, and Anthony Fowler. "Classification of Synchronous Oceanic and Atmospheric El Niño-Southern Oscillation (ENSO) Events for Paleoclimate Reconstruction." *International Journal of Climatology* 25 (2005): 1541–65.

"A History of ENSO Events since A.D. 1525: Implications for Future Climate Change." *Climatic Change* 92 (2009): 343–87.

Glacken, Clarence. *Traces on the Rhodian Shore: Nature and Culture in Western Thought from Ancient Times to the End of the Eighteenth Century.* Berkeley and Los Angeles, 1967.

Goetzmann, William. *Exploration and Empire: The Explorer and Scientist in the Winning of the American West.* New York, 1966.

Gonzales, Michael. *Plantation Agriculture and Social Control in Northern Peru, 1875–1933.* Austin, TX, 1985.

"The Rise of Cotton Tenant Farming in Peru, 1890–1920: The Condor Valley." *Agricultural History* 65 (1991): 51–71.

Gracia Fadrique, Jesús, ed. *Estado y Fertilizantes, 1760–1985.* Mexico City, 1988.

Graham, Frank, Jr. *The Audubon Ark: A History of the National Audubon Society.* New York, 1990.

Grove, Richard. *Green Imperialism: Colonial Expansion, Tropical Island Edens and the Origins of Environmentalism, 1600–1860.* Cambridge and New York, 1995.

Guha, Ramachandra. *Environmentalism: A Global History.* New York, 2000.

The Unquiet Woods: Ecological Change and Peasant Resistance in the Himalaya. Berkeley and Los Angeles, 2000.

Hardin, Garrett. "The Tragedy of the Commons." *Science* 13 Dec. 1968: 1243–48.

Herweijer, Celine, et al. "North American Droughts of the Mid to Late Nineteenth Century: A History, Simulation and Implication for Medieval Drought." *The Holocene* 16 (2006): 159–71.

Hopkins, Raúl. *Desarrollo desigual y crisis en la agricultura peruana, 1944–1969.* Lima, 1981.

Howe, Kerry Ross, et al., eds. *Tides of History: The Pacific Islands in the Twentieth Century.* Honolulu, 1994.

Howell, David. *Capitalism from Within: Economy, Society, and the State in a Japanese Fishery.* Berkeley and Los Angeles, 1995.

The Huarochirí Manuscript: A Testament of Ancient and Colonial Andean Religion. Trans. Frank Salomon and George Urioste. Austin, TX, 1991.

Hunt, Shane. "Price and Quantum Estimates of Peruvian Exports, 1830–1862." Discussion paper no. 33, Research Program in Economic Development, Woodrow Wilson School of Public and International Affairs, Princeton University, 1973.

"Growth and Guano in Nineteenth-Century Peru." In *The Latin American Economies: Growth and the Export Sector, 1830–1930.* New York, 1985.

Hutchinson, George Evelyn. "Survey of Existing Knowledge of Biogeochemistry: 3. The Biogeochemistry of Vertebrate Excretion." *Bulletin of the American Museum of Natural History* 96 (1950): 1–554.

Jacoby, Karl. *Crimes against Nature: Squatters, Poachers, Thieves, and the Hidden History of American Conservation.* Berkeley and Los Angeles, 2001.

Johnsgard, Paul. *Cormorants, Darters, and Pelicans of the World.* Washington, DC, 1993.

Julien, Catherine. "Guano and Resource Control in Sixteenth-Century Arequipa." In *Andean Ecology and Civilization.* Tokyo, 1985.

Klarén, Peter. *Modernization, Dislocation and Aprismo: Origins of the Peruvian Aprista Party, 1870–1932.* Austin, TX, 1973.

——. *Peru: Society and Nationhood in the Andes.* New York, 2000.

Koháк, Erazim. *The Green Halo: A Bird's-Eye View of Ecological Ethics.* Chicago, 2000.

Krausmann, Fridolin. "Milk, Manure, and Muscular Power: Livestock and the Industrialization of Agriculture." *Human Ecology* 32 (2004): 735–73.

Laporte, Dominique. *History of Shit.* 1978; Cambridge, MA, 2002.

Lear, Linda. *Rachel Carson: Witness for Nature.* New York, 1997.

Leopold, Aldo. *Game Management.* New York, 1933.

——. *A Sand County Almanac and Sketches Here and There.* New York, 1949.

Linnér, Björn-Ola. *The Return of Malthus: Environmentalism and Post-war Population-Resource Crises.* Strond, England, 2003.

Ma, Wenqi, et al. "Nitrogen Flows and Nitrogen Use Efficiency in Chinese Production and Consumption of Wheat, Rice and Maize." *Agricultural Systems* 99 (2009): 53–63.

Macdonald, Barrie. *Cinderellas of Empire: Toward a History of Kiribati and Tuvalu.* Canberra, 1982.

——. "Grimble of the Gilbert Islands: Myth and Man." In *More Pacific Island Portraits.* Canberra, 1982.

Macera, Pablo. "El guano y la agricultura peruana de exportación, 1909–1945." In *Trabajos de historia.* Vol. 4. Lima, 1977.

Markoff, John, and Verónica Montecinos. "The Ubiquitous Rise of Economists." *Journal of Public Policy* 13 (1993): 37–68.

Marks, Robert. *Tigers, Rice, Silk, and Silt: Environment and Economy in Late Imperial South China.* Cambridge and New York, 1988.

Mathew, W. M. *The House of Gibbs and the Peruvian Guano Monopoly.* London, 1981.

Maude, H. E. *Of Islands and Men.* Melbourne, 1968.

McCook, Stuart. *States of Nature: Science, Agriculture, and Environment in the Spanish Caribbean, 1760–1940.* Austin, TX, 2002.

Mc Evoy, Carmen. *La utopía republicana: Ideales y realidades en la formación de la cultura política peruana (1871–1919).* Lima, 1997.

McEvoy, Arthur. *The Fisherman's Problem: Ecology and Law in the California Fisheries, 1850–1980.* Cambridge and New York, 1986.

Melosi, Martin. *The Sanitary City: Urban Infrastructure in America from Colonial Times to the Present.* Baltimore, 2000.

Mohr, James. *Plague and Fire: Battling Black Death and the 1900 Burning of Honolulu's Chinatown.* New York, 2004.

Mueller-Dombois, Dieter, and Raymond Fosberg. *Vegetation of the Tropical Pacific Islands.* New York, 1998.

Murphy, Robert Cushman. *Bird Islands of Peru: The Record of a Sojourn on the West Coast.* New York, 1925.

Oceanic Birds of South America. 2 vols. New York, 1936.

Nash, George. *The Life of Herbert Hoover*. 3 vols. New York, 1983–96.

Newton, Julianne Lutz. *Aldo Leopold's Odyssey*. Washington, DC, 2006.

Nunn, Patrick. *Environmental Change in the Pacific Basin*. Chichester, England, 1999.

Núñez, Estuardo, and Georg Petersen, eds. *Alexander von Humboldt en el Perú: Diario de viaje y otros escritos*. Lima, 2002.

Oxford Dictionary of National Biography. Online edition. Oxford University Press, 2007–8. http://www.oxforddnb.com.

Oxford English Dictionary. Online edition. Oxford University Press, 2007. http://dictionary.oed.com.

Perkins, John. *Geopolitics and the Green Revolution: Wheat, Genes, and the Cold War*. New York, 1997.

Pike, Frederick. *The Modern History of Peru*. New York, 1967.

Portocarrero, Felipe, et al. *Compendio estadístico del Perú, 1900–1990*. Lima, 1992.

Post, John. *The Last Great Subsistence Crisis in the Western World*. Baltimore, 1977.

Quinn, W. H., and V. T. Neal. "The Historical Record of El Niño Events." In *Climate Since A.D. 1500*. London and New York, 1995.

Rivero y Ustáriz, Mariano Eduardo de. *Colección de memorias científicas, agrícolas é industriales*. Brussels, 1857.

Roberts, Stephen. *Population Problems in the Pacific*. London, 1927.

Robertson, Thomas. "The Population Bomb: Population Growth, Globalization, and American Environmentalism, 1945–1980." Ph.D. dissertation, University of Wisconsin–Madison, 2005.

Rossiter, Margaret. *Women Scientists in America: Before Affirmative Action, 1940–1972*. Baltimore, 1995.

Rostworowski de Diez Canseco, María. *Recursos naturales renovables y pesca, siglos XVI y XVII*. Lima, 1981.

Señoríos indígenas de Lima y Canta. Lima, 1981.

"Las islas del litoral peruano: Mitos y recursos naturales." In *Ensayos de historia andina II*. Lima, 1998.

Sachs, Aaron. *The Humboldt Current: Nineteenth-Century Exploration and the Roots of American Environmentalism*. New York, 2006.

Safford, Frank. *The Ideal of the Practical: Colombia's Struggle to Form a Technical Elite*. Austin, TX, 1976.

Schlomowitz, Ralph. "Epidemiology and the Pacific Labor Trade." *Journal of Interdisciplinary History* 19 (1989): 585–610.

Schreiber, Ralph, and Philip Ashmole. "Sea-bird Breeding Seasons on Christmas Island, Pacific Ocean." *Ibis* 112 (1970): 363–94.

Scobie, James *Revolution on the Pampas: A Social History of Argentine Wheat, 1860–1910*. Austin, TX, 1964.

Buenos Aires: Plaza to Suburb, 1870–1910. New York, 1974.

Sigrah, Raobeia, and Stacey King. *Te Rii ni Banaba*. Suva, Fiji, 2001.

Silverman, Martin. *Disconcerting Issue: Meaning and Struggle in a Resettled Pacific Community*. Chicago, 1971.

Simmons, James, et al. *Global Epidemiology: A Geography of Disease and Sanitation*. Philadelphia, 1944.

Simonian, Lane. *Defending the Land of the Jaguar: A History of Conservation in Mexico.* Austin, TX, 1995.

Skaggs, Jimmy. *The Great Guano Rush: Entrepreneurs and American Overseas Expansion.* New York, 1994.

Smil, Vaclav. *Enriching the Earth: Fritz Haber, Carl Bosch, and the Transformation of World Food Production.* Cambridge, MA, 2001.

Soluri, John. *Banana Cultures: Agriculture, Consumption, and Environmental Change in Honduras and the United States.* Austin, TX, 2006.

Steadman, David. "Prehistoric Extinctions of Pacific Island Birds." *Science* 24 Feb. 1995: 1123–31.

Stewart, Watt. *Chinese Bondage in Peru: A History of the Chinese Coolie, 1849–1874.* Durham, NC, 1951.

Thorp, Rosemary, and Geoffrey Bertram. *Peru 1890–1977: Growth and Policy in an Open Economy.* London, 1978.

Tovar, Humberto, et al. "Monthly Population Size of Three Guano Bird Species off Peru, 1953 to 1982." In *The Peruvian Anchoveta and Its Upwelling Ecosystem.* Callao, 1987.

Walker, Brett. *The Conquest of Ainu Lands: Ecology and Culture in Japanese Expansion, 1590–1800.* Berkeley and Los Angeles, 2001.

Weinerskirch, Henri, et al. "Foraging Strategies of a Top Predator in Tropical Waters: Great Frigatebirds in the Mozambique Channel." *Marine Ecology Progress Series* 275 (2004): 297–308.

Whelpton, P. K. "Population Policy for the United States." *Journal of Heredity* 30 (1939): 401–6.

Williams, Maslyn, and Barrie Macdonald. *The Phosphateers: A History of the British Phosphate Commissioners and the Christmas Island Phosphate Commission.* Carlton, Australia, 1985.

Wines, Richard. *Fertilizer in America: From Waste Recycling to Resource Exploitation.* Philadelphia, 1985.

Worster, Donald. *Nature's Economy: A History of Ecological Ideas.* Cambridge and New York, 1994.

Index

Haber, Fritz, 155
Haber-Bosch process. *See under* ammonia
  and ammonia industry
Haenke, Tadeáš, 64
Hague, James D., 83
Haiti, 81–2, 164, 223, 249, 266. *See also*
  Navassa Island
Hamburg, 44, 68, 107, 289, 295
Hanson, Henry, 163
Hardin, Garrett, 22, 296, 337
Hawaii, 71, 82–3, 90, 95, 100, 116, 163,
  224, 249
Haya de la Torre, Raúl, 165
heath hen (*Tympanuchus cupido cupido*),
  190
Henry, Joseph, 83
herring (*Clupea* spp.), 211, 298, 334, 337
Hickey, Joe, 271
highway construction, 54, 142, 162, 183,
  252, 320. *See also* Pan American
  Highway
Hitler, Adolf, 221
Hokkaido, 12, 211, 298
Honduras, 137
honeybee (*Apis mellifera*), 129–30
Hoover, Herbert, 158, 164, 199, 209, 215,
  262
Hopkins, Cyril, 209
horses, 28, 48, 58, 67, 91, 144, 236,
  348
Howland Island, 92, 99, 117, 227, 347
Humboldt Current. *See* Peru Current
Humboldt, Alexander von, 66
  discovery of Anthropocene by, 344
  discovery of guano by, 25–30, 50
  explorations in Peru, 18–19, 23–5
  political influence of, 32, 38, 73
  scientific disciples of, 27, 32–6, 65, 67,
    84
Hungary, 29, 100, 157, 160, 222
hurricanes. *See* disasters, tropical cyclones
Hutchinson, G. Evelyn, 271, 273–4
Huxley, Julian, 278

Ica valley, 145, 162, 186, 252
Iceland, 293, 295, 335
I-Kiribati. *See* indigenous peoples, of Gilbert
  Islands
imperialism, 20, 72
  Australian, 17, 19, 78, 82, 93, 110, 128,
    133, 210, 220, 237, 348
  Belgian, 85, 107

British, 224
  in Africa, 85
  in Ireland, 48, 102
  in Middle East, 81, 157, 216
  in Pacific Islands, 19, 82, 93, 98, 104,
    107, 118–19, 121, 128, 151, 210,
    227–8, 236, 239
  in South America, 54
  in South Asia, 30, 32, 64–6, 102, 178,
    207, 264
Chilean
  in Atacama Desert, 19, 72–3
  in Pacific Islands, 19, 78, 82, 89–91,
    227
Dutch, 63–4, 66, 152
Ecuadorian, 19, 82
European, 30, 38, 270
French, 32, 54, 56, 81–2, 85, 90,
  157
German
  in Europe, 135, 220
  in Latin America, 248, 289
  in Pacific Islands, 82, 121, 128, 151,
    210
  on Nauru, 118, 124
Hawaiian, 82
Inca, 4, 8, 24
Italian, 220–1
Japanese, 21, 135, 207, 210–11, 215, 220,
  224, 264
  in China and Manchuria, 21, 206,
    210–12, 221
  in Hokkaido, 12, 211
  in Korea, 212
  in Latin America, 248
  in Pacific Islands, 82, 128, 210, 227,
    230
Mexican, 82
New Zealand, 17, 19, 78, 93, 104, 128,
  133, 210
Peruvian, 19, 78
Portuguese, 32, 314
South African, 210
Soviet, 157
Spanish, 29
  after 1807, 53, 56–7, 72
  before 1807, 3–4, 24–5, 265
U.S., 42, 82, 270
  in Latin America, 54, 81–2, 264,
    266
  in open ocean, 296
  in Pacific Islands, 19, 78, 227

wheat (*Triticum* spp.) (*cont.*)
  in Australia and New Zealand, 71, 110,
    130, 135
  in California, 71
  in Chile, 70, 319
  in Green Revolution, 288
  in Mexico, 287
  in Peru, 200, 203
  wheat problem before and during World
    War I, 106, 156, 158
Whelpton, Pascal, 217, 223, 233, 264
Wilbur-Ellis Co., 292–3, 298, 313
wilderness areas, 9, 80, 123, 170, 190, 207,
  214–15, 218, 220, 243, 249, 320. *See
  also under* conservation movement;
  Leopold, Aldo; Vogt, William
Wilkes, Charles, 42, 83
Wille, Johannes, 203, 250
willet, eastern (*Catoptrophorus
  semipalmatus*), 191
Wisconsin, 80, 197, 243, 254, 257, 259
women. *See also* birth control and abortion
  as birth and population control activists,
    218, 232, 275
  as scientists, 139, 151, 192, 195, 197,
    233, 270, 276, 299
  as targets of advertising, 102
  as traditional caretakers of environment,
    113, 247
  environmental activism of, 125, 133, 139,
    151, 237, 247, 250, 253, 271, 299,
    346
  gender division of labor and resources, 95,
    113–14, 116, 125
  in fishing industry, 294
  political activism of, 126–7, 132, 226,
    250, 282, 332, 339
woodpecker, imperial (*Campephilus
  imperialis*), 244
Wooster, Warren, 203
workers and working class, 117. *See also*
  labor trade; sex and sex trade; slavery
  and slave trade; *and under* fishing and
  fishmeal industries; guano and guano
  industry; Peru; phosphates and
  phosphate industry
  consumption patterns of, 304
  exposure to environmental hazards, 55,
    121, 179, 312, 328–9, 331, 334

  in agriculture and herding, 85–6, 160–2,
    223, 290, 328
  in Brazil, 279
  in copra production, 78, 85, 96–8, 107,
    122, 233
  in domestic work, 96–7, 102
  in lumber industry, 240
  in Mexican fertilizer industry, 287, 327
  in nitrate industry, 73
  in Peruvian clothing industry, 349
  in traditional societies, 39, 63
  in transportation, 88, 236
  leisure activities of, 215
  living conditions of, 103, 106
  political activism of, 153, 160–2, 180,
    190, 236, 282, 290, 322, 324
World Population Conference of 1927, 218
World War I, 141, 154. *See also under*
  individual countries and regions
  climate and subsistence crises during,
    156–7
  impact on agricultural commodities, 138,
    155, 157–8, 160, 164, 186, 209
  impact on nitrate and ammonia industries,
    154–5, 164
  impact on phosphate industry, 128
  in Pacific Islands, 82, 128, 225
  influence on Malthusian thought, 20,
    207–10, 224
  influence on technocratic governance,
    158–9, 165
World War II, 198, 220. *See also under*
  individual countries and regions
  causes of, 156, 220–2, 242, 264, 289
  climate and subsistence crises during,
    229–30, 234, 262, 282–3, 290
  impact on agricultural commodities, 199,
    282
  impact on fishing industry, 291
  impact on phosphate industry, 131, 230
  in Pacific Islands, 229–32, 237
  influence on environmental thought, 260,
    263, 272
  influence on Malthusian thought, 232,
    262
  resettlement programs during, 21, 207,
    222–3, 230, 232–3

Yali, 236–7, 342